ISSUES IN CONTEMPORARY MICROECONOMICS AND WELFARE

The purpose of this and the companion volume, *Issues in Contemporary Macroeconomics and Distribution*, is to capture and convey the spirit, fundamental issues, underlying tensions, rich variety, accomplishments and failures in contemporary economics. The chapters reflect a wide gamut of alternative approaches in many cases presented and interpreted by those who participated in shaping and advancing the ideas. Many of the contributors are of architectonic stature. Some of them have shaped economics in the last thirty years or more; others are bright new lights.

ISSUES IN CONTEMPORARY MICROECONOMICS AND WELFARE

Edited by

George R. Feiwel

MACMILLAN

First published 1985 by
THE MACMILLAN PRESS LTD
London and Basingstoke
Companies and representatives
throughout the world

Typeset in Great Britain by
STYLESET LIMITED
Salisbury, Wiltshire

Printed in Hong Kong

British Library Cataloguing in Publication Data
Issues in contemporary microeconomics and welfare.
1. Microeconomics
I. Feiwel, George R.
338.5   HB172
ISBN 0–333–35482–6

Contents

Notes on the Contributors

Kenneth J. Arrow is Joan Kenney Professor of Economics and Professor of Operations Research, Stanford University. He was formerly James Bryant Conant University Professor of Economics, Harvard University. He has been President of the Econometric Society, the American Economic Association, the Institute of Management Sciences, and the Western Economic Association, and is currently President of the International Society for Inventory Research. He has received the John Bates Clark medal of the American Economic Association and the Nobel Memorial Prize in Economic Science. He is a Member of the National Academy of Sciences and a Corresponding Member of the British Academy. His many contributions include *Social Choice and Individual Values* (1951, 1963), *Essays in the Theory of Risk Bearing* (1971), *Limits to Organization* (1974), and *General Competitive Analysis* (with F. H. Hahn, 1971).

Robert J. Aumann is Professor of Mathematics, Hebrew University of Jerusalem. He was a Fellow of the Institute for Advanced Studies, Hebrew University of Jerusalem and Visiting Professor Cowles Foundation and Department of Statistics, Yale University; Center for Operations Research and Econometrics, Université Catholique de Louvain; Department of Economics, Stanford University; and Ford Visiting Research Professor of Economics, University of California (Berkeley). He is a Foreign Honorary Member of the American Academy of Arts and Sciences and was awarded the Harvey Prize in Science and Technology. He is a major and prolific contributor to the theory of games and the author of *Values of Non-Atomic Games* (with L. S. Shapley, 1974).

William J. Baumol is Joseph Douglas Green Professor of Economics, Princeton University and Professor of Economics, New York University. He is a Member of the American Academy of Arts and Sciences and a former President of the American Economic Association, the Association of Environmental and Resource Economists, and the Eastern Economic

Association. He has contributed extensively in the areas of microeconomic theory, industrial organization theory, environmental economics, and other fields. He is the author of more than twelve books, including *Economic Dynamics* (1951), *Welfare Economics and the Theory of the State* (1952), *Business Behavior, Value and Growth* (1959), *Economic Theory and Operations Analysis* (1960), and *Contestable Markets and the Theory of Industry Structure* (with J. D. Panzar, and R. D. Willig, 1982).

George R. Feiwel is Alumni Distinguished Service Professor and Professor of Economics, University of Tennessee. He has been Visiting Professor, University of Stockholm, Harvard University, University of California (Berkeley and Davis) and on several occasions has been Senior Faculty Visitor, Cambridge University. He is the author of more than ten books, including *The Economics of a Socialist Enterprise* (1965), *The Soviet Quest for Economic Efficiency* (1967, 1972), *Industrialization Policy and Planning under Polish Socialism*, 2 vols (1971), *The Intellectual Capital of Michal Kalecki* (1975), and *Growth and Reforms in Centrally Planned Economies* (1977). He is also a contributor to and editor of *Samuelson and Neoclassical Economics* (1982).

Victor P. Goldberg is Professor of Law, Northwestern University. He was formerly Professor of Economics at the University of California (Davis). He was Visiting Professor of Law and Economics, University of California (Berkeley) and Visiting Professor, University of Virginia School of Law. In 1978–9 he was a Member of the Institute for Advanced Study, Princeton. He has published numerous articles on regulation, anti-trust, and law and economics.

Peter Hammond is Professor of Economics, Stanford University. He was formerly at the University of Essex and was Joint Managing Editor of the *Review of Economic Studies*. In 1983 he was a Fellow of the Institute for Advanced Studies, Hebrew University of Jerusalem and Schumpeter Professor at the University of Graz. He is the author of many articles on welfare economics and social choice theory and is currently working on a book on welfare economic theory.

Milton Harris, formerly on the faculty of the University of Chicago and Carnegie-Mellon University, is Professor of Economics, Departments of Finance and Managerial Economics and Decision Sciences, Kellogg Graduate School of Management, Northwestern University. He is the author of a number of articles in mathematical economics and industrial organization.

Leonid Hurwicz is Regents' Professor of Economics, University of Minnesota. He is a Distinguished Fellow of the American Economic Association, a Member of the National Academy of Sciences, and past president of the Econometric Society. He was Visiting Professor, the Cowles Commission (University of Chicago), Stanford University, Harvard University (where he was also Frank W. Taussig Visiting Research Professor), University of California (Berkeley), and Tokyo University. He has contributed extensively to mathematical economics, design of mechanisms for resource allocation, and general economic theory and statistics. Among his numerous publications is *Studies in Resource Allocation Processes* (with K. J. Arrow, 1977).

Murray Kemp is Research Professor of Economics, University of New South Wales. He has been Visiting Professor at the Universities of Paris, Mannheim, Essex, and Minnesota, and at Columbia University and MIT. He has contributed widely to the theory of international trade, resource economics, and welfare economics. His many publications include *The Pure Theory of International Trade and Investment* (1964, 1969), *Three Topics in the Theory of International Trade: Distribution, Welfare, and Uncertainty* (1976), and *Variational Methods in Economics* (with G. Hadley, 1971).

Shoichi Kojima is Economist of the United Nations Conference on Trade and Development (UNCTAD). He was formerly Deputy Director of the International Economic Co-operations Division of the Economic Planning Agency, Japanese Government and has extensive experience in international economic and aid policy-making. He is the author of *Neoclassical Theory of a New International Economic Order* (1982).

David M. Kreps is Professor of Economics, Harvard University. He was formerly Professor of Decision Sciences, the Graduate School of Business, Stanford University. He has conducted research and written on the theory of multi-period economies and the economics of uncertainty, especially in the areas of choice theory, finance, and non-co-operative game theory.

Robert E. Kuenne is Professor of Economics and Director of the General Economic Systems Project, Princeton University. He has published numerous articles in the field of oligopoly theory and is the author of *The Theory of General Economic Equilibrium* (1963) and *The Microeconomic Theory of the Market Mechanism* (1968) among other books, and the editor of *Monopolistic Competition Theory: Studies in Impact* (1967).

Mordecai Kurz is Professor of Economics, and Director of Economics, at the Institute for Mathematical Studies in the Social Sciences, Stanford University. He was a Fellow of the Institute for Advanced Studies, Hebrew University of Jerusalem. He is the author of numerous articles in mathematical economics, econometrics, and social policy, and of *Components of Economic Growth of National Output* (1967) and *Public Investment, the Rate of Return, and Optimal Fiscal Policy* (with K. J. Arrow, 1970).

Lawrence J. Lau is Professor of Economics, Stanford University. He was Visiting Professor at Harvard University and in 1982—83 he was a Fellow of the Center for Advanced Study in the Behavioral Sciences. He is the author of *Farmer Education and Farm Efficiency* (with D. T. Jamison) and of numerous articles in economic theory, economic development, and econmetrics.

Leonard J. Mirman is Professor of Economics, University of Illinois. He is the author or many articles in mathematical economics and growth theory and the editor of *Essays in the Economy of Renewable Resources* (with D. Spulber, 1982).

Yew-Kwang Ng is Reader in Economics, Monash University (Australia). He was a Visiting Fellow at Nuffield College and Visiting Professor at Virginia Polytechnic Institute. He is the author or a number of articles on welfare economics and on macroeconomics under imperfect competition, as well as of *Welfare Economics: Introduction and Development of Basic Concepts* (1979, 1983).

A. Michael Spence is Professor of Economics and Business Administration and Chairman of the Economics Department, and in July, 1984 will be Dean, Faculty of Arts and Sciences, Harvard University. In 1981 he was awarded the John Bates Clark medal of the American Economic Association. He has written numerous articles in the field of industrial organization; on subjects including the informational structure of markets, product differentiation, entry barriers, and dynamic aspects of competition. He is also the author of *Market Signalling, Competition in the Open Economy*, and *Competitive Structure in Investment Banking*.

Yair Tauman, a former student of Robert J. Aumann, is Xerox Professor at the Kellogg Graduate School of Management, Northwestern University. He was Visiting Professor of Economics, Stanford University, and has been associated with the Institute for Advanced Studies, Hebrew University of

Jerusalem, and the Center for Operations Research and Econometrics, Université Catholique de Louvain. He has published a number of articles in mathematical economics and specializes in game theory.

Robert M. Townsend is Professor of Economics at Carnegie-Mellon University. He is the author of many articles in information economics, the theory of contracts and long-term economic relationships, the theory of organizational design, and decision-making, with information incentive problems.

Robert B. Wilson is Atholl McBean Professor of Decision Sciences, Graduate School of Business, and Assistant Director of the Center for Research on Organizational Efficiency, Stanford University. He was Visiting Professor, Université Catholique de Louvain and Fellow of the Center for Advanced Study in the Behavioral Sciences. He is a Member of the American Academy of Arts and Sciences. He has published papers on game theory and its applications to economics. His research studies the role of information in markets and organizations, particularly its effect on strategic behaviour, and the design of efficient institutions.

Israel Zang is Senior Lecturer, Faculty of Management, Tel Aviv University. He was Visiting Professor, Center for Operations Research and Econometrics, Université Catholique de Louvain, and Visiting Associate Professor, Faculty of Commerce and Business Administration, at the University of British Columbia. His research interests and publications centre on mathematical (non-linear) programming and its applications to economics. Aside from a number of articles, he is also the author of the forthcoming *Generalized Concavity* (with M. Avriel, W. E. Diewert, and S. Schaible).

Preface

These two volumes are modest attempts to capture and convey the spirit, essence, controversies, richness, variety, achievements and failures of some major advances in contemporary economics. They make no pretence at being comprehensive surveys of contemporary economics, nor at an encyclopaedic exposition of selected issues. They strive to shed some light on the fundamental issues, underlying tensions, and perennial challenges in contemporary economics. They present the reader with a sampling of the recent and ongoing quest to provide solid, 'hard', scientific foundations for the dismal, yet fascinating subject of economics. This modern quest seeks to define more precisely the limits of economic knowledge and the conditions under which certain theorems hold, to exploit opportunities, and wherever possible to transgress previous limits with an enriched conceptual apparatus and more sophisticated techniques of analysis and measurement.

Modern economists often ask smaller questions than did their predecessors. But whether large or small, old questions are being reiterated not only because of their intrinsic vitality and the fact that the available equipment is more sophisticated and thus may yield different and more precisely formulated answers, but also because the questions are framed somewhat differently, possibly affecting some of the answers. They also focus on new questions that have been attacked more or less (un)successfully with the aid of existing techniques. At the same time these techniques are being refined and amended or new ones invented and tried. In scholarly analysis, as in real life, it is the dynamics of the process that matter.

The state of the art and science of economics depends vitally on its practitioners' ability to identify real problems, to devise means for overcoming apparently insurmountable difficulties, and to take advantage of unexploited opportunities for doing useful and exciting work. Modern economics is characterized by sharp disagreements about some of the fundamentals and large gaping lacunae in our knowledge and understanding. If it is true that a science lives and flourishes on its unsolved problems, economics is one of the most vital, exciting, and promising sciences.

Economic theory is often criticized for its elegant articulation of states that never did and never will exist, for producing models that abstract from the most essential features of reality, and for evolving theory for the sake of theory that is further and further removed from the real world. Ultimately, however, the best of economic theory, no matter how abstract, is concerned with the understanding and improvement of the human condition in the ordinary business of life and with explaining and influencing the forces that govern the dynamics of production, organization, exchange, and distribution of the complex, interdependent, and evolving world around us.

Among the multiplicity of factors that foster or constrain an economy's dynamism, structure, and welfare of its actors, the quality of economic theory and policy really matters. From the perspective of accretion of economic knowledge, the continuing clashes of competing perceptions of economic processes tend to advance, refine, and spread economic knowledge, no matter how futile and retrogressive particular debates seem to be or how little we sometimes appear to have learned from the history of our subject or policy experience.

With a science whose several branches are as interdependent as those of economics, the compartmentalization of subjects is not without its pitfalls. This is particularly true of the conventional and artificial separation into micro and macro, which was undertaken for pragmatic purposes. The problem is further complicated by the fact that a vocal challenge to mainstream pragmatic macroeconomics is in some sense nothing but a microeconomic analysis of macroeconomic phenomena.

In eliciting the contributions to these volumes no effort was spared to offer the reader (within the obvious feasibility constraints) the widest possible gamut of alternative approaches, presented and interpreted often by those who participated in shaping or advancing the ideas. My aim was to have an eclectic and open-minded approach and to learn all that is constructive in different streams of thought. By and large the response to the invitations was gratifying, but understandably and regretably certain important gaps remained. Thus, with some compunction, I undertook the task of expanding the two introductory chapters to these volumes beyond the scope of background material and overview originally envisaged. Recognizing the limits of my own objectivity, I endeavoured to remain in the background in these introductions. It would be wrong and presumptuous of me to steer the reader in the 'right' direction: I point to alternatives; the choice is the reader's.

INTRODUCTION TO TWO VOLUMES

Issues in Contemporary Microeconomics and Welfare

Chapter 1 of this volume offers a perspective for the eloquent analysis in the chapters that follow. The account is perforce selective and an attempt is made to provide a perception of the alternative approaches, achievements, controversies and issues together with the underlying tensions and their sources.

Part I concentrates on resource allocation processes. There is no more fitting way to begin than with a subject that is one of the pivots of economics, sets the stage for the analyses and controversies in both volumes, and is a continuous and increasing source of tensions; that is, the potentials and limits of the market. It is our good fortune to have this analysed by Arrow in Chapter 2. He observes that at this juncture pure economic theory enjoys prestige status, yet there remain widespread doubts about the descriptive power and normative utility of general competitive equilibrium. Indeed, neoclassical microeconomic equilibrium theory, with fully flexible prices, represents a beautiful picture of mutual articulations of a complex structure, with full employment as one of its major elements. But, Arrow asks, what is its relationship to the real world? He calls attention to three major unsolved problems of general competitive equilibrium: (i) the failure to provide a microfoundation for Keynesian macroeconomics, (ii) the failure to take seriously, capture the essence of, and integrate imperfect competition into the system, and (iii) the failure to account for costs of transaction and of obtaining information, thus of running the market resources allocation process itself. He adds that demand and supply for money has not been fully integrated with general competitive equilibrium. Moreover, other objections to neoclassical theory revolve about its neglect of 'non-economic' arguments in the utility function such as power, status, social approval, etc. that also motivate economic actors, and of such constraints as capacity for calculation and social controls. More specifically, in Chapter 2, Arrow examines the relations between competitive equilibrium and Pareto efficiency. He then takes time and uncertainty into account and provides an extension of general equilibrium under uncertainty. A discussion of externalities, market failures, and transaction costs follows. He concludes that though the price system is valuable in many respects, it suffers from serious defects and cannot be left to itself to guide social life. In many situations the market should be supplemented by social decision-making – a subject he explores in Chapter 3 of the companion volume, *Issues in Contemporary Macroeconomics and Distribution.*

In Chapter 3 Hurwicz penetratingly illuminates the designer's point of view – the position of the economist designing the organizational structure. He makes the important, and yet subjective, distinction between what the designer considers as given (the environment) and what he can redesign (the machanism). Specifically, this chapter deals with some major problems in designing efficient resource allocation systems when there is dispersal of information among the economic agents. It focuses on the minimum of communication that such a system requires, giving consideration to the incentives that condition the agent's behaviour. The channel capacity needed for communication can be measured by the dimension of the message space of the process. Hurwicz warns that the systems thus far obtained by the procedures for simplified situations that he outlines in his Chapter should only be considered illustrative: 'We are still a long way off from designing systems for real economies.'

In a somewhat similar vein, Wilson (Chapter 4) points to the organization of trading when the participants have market power and private information (itself a source of market power). The problem is one of designing trading rules that promote efficient transactions while taking into account the effects of strategic behaviour. The purpose is to elaborate precisely how the trading rules and each participant's strategic behaviour (using his private information) combine to determine terms of trade that substantially mirror the dispersed information. Specifically, Wilson concentrates on incomplete information and on multilateral trade in a static environment, which is in addition 'severely restricted' by the absence of a number of other important features. The methods used are relatively new in theoretical economic literature. They serve to illuminate the role of institutionalized trading rules (represented here by the double auction) in promoting gains from trade. Wilson concludes: 'One can rejoice as well that a single trading rule suffices to attain incentive efficiency *uniformly* over a fairly wide class of economic environments: the usefulness of market processes to allocate resources and their persistence as institutionalized forms depend ultimately on their robustness in coping with a variety of circumstances.'

The game theory methodology, into which Aumann offers us valuable insights in Chapter 5, has had a love–hate relationship with economics for many years. Whatever its instrinsic merits, it is of special significance in these volumes because so many of our authors apply (or in some cases specifically reject) it in attempting to solve the problems they pose. Aumann's exposition of the theory of repeated games goes to the heart of the process of co-operation that emerges from repetition. To this extent the theory of repeated games provides a paradigm for bargaining. The fundamental result is the 'Folk Theorem' which suggests that the set of outcomes of repeated play may be very large; restrictions in various directions (e.g. on the information available to agents) yield sharper, more specific results.

Using the repeated game as a basis for co-operation, in the opening chapter (6) of Part II, concerned with duopoly and oligopoly, Kurz develops a theory of oligopolistic behaviour in non-contestable markets and where optimal firm size is not negligible. He suggests that such markets will develop a systematic and stable co-operative behaviour. This will take the form of an implicit contract among firms with respect to the procedures they use to change their output in equilibrium. The chapter focuses on the characterization of this procedure and on the resulting equilibrium. Kurz points out that the co-operative theory that he proposes for a duopoly can be extended to any oligopolistic industry. And his analysis suggests a rather novel connection between co-operation in oligopoly and social allocation of public goods. He shows that the allocation suggested by a 'Lindahl Equilibrium' may have a counterpart in co-operative oligopoly situations giving rise to 'Lindahl Agreements'.

In Chapter 7 Kuenne provides a contrasting view of oligopoly but one that, like Kurz, seeks to capture the often neglected co-operative aspects of oligopoly. He stresses the concept of 'power structure' in mature industries that contains an amalgam of the competitive and co-operative specific to each industry and that reflects a 'rivalrous consonance of interests' among the firms in the process of decision-making. He suggests that methods and frameworks have to be tailored to the specifics of various industries at various times. Thus the 'institutional' dominates the general as the power structure gains in importance in defining the firms' objectives and conditioning their actions. Kuenne concludes that the concepts of rivalrous consonance and crippled optimization are promising flexible tools for operational analysis of oligopolistic pricing, and uses them in this chapter to analyse target-rate-of-return strategies.

Part III, which presents the new developments in the theory of industry structure, opens with Baumol's analysis of contestable markets. He suggests that the theory of contestable markets, defined roughly as markets without barriers to entry or exit, constitutes a significant new departure in the analysis of firm and industry structure and provides a standard for public policy that is far broader and more widely applicable than the traditional ideal of perfect competition. Essentially it challanges some previously held notions about entry barriers; it rejects the notion that economies of scale are an entry barrier, defined as an invariable source of welfare losses and considers the presence of sunk costs as the prime form of entry barrier. The main features of a perfectly contestable market are no excessive profits for anyone; absence of any sort of inefficiency in production; no cross subsidy for any product; and the sufficiency of even two firms to ensure that equilibrium prices will satisfy the necessary conditions for Pareto optimality. Thus in a perfectly contestable market the structure that emerges in any particular industry in the long run is the one that produces the output as cheaply as possible. On the theoretical side, contestability theory provides an extensive set of tools for the analysis of multiproduct firms and industries and, albeit for a polar case yields a unique working model of oligopoly behaviour. In addition because in such markets their prices must be parametric, the theory promises to permit incorporation of imperfectly competitive and oligopolistic firms into general equilibrium models. On a policy plane, by stressing that market structure is ultimately shaped by market forces, contestability theory points to the difficulties, sometime failures, and relative undesirability of government's attempts to alter this structure. The implication is that public policy should aim at obtaining industry performance that approximates as much as possible a contestable market, rather than the unattainable goal of perfect competition.

In Chapter 9 Mirman, Tauman, and Zang take up the issue of perfectly contestable markets. In particular, they study the properties of equilibrium in such markets. Their questions revolve about the conditions (taking into account potential entry) that in perfectly contestable markets would result in only one firm producing the entire vector of outputs and operating under sustainable prices. They show that when technology is expressed by a joint subadditive cost function, the notion of a sustainable monopoly can be derived as a result of a Bertrand–Nash equilibrium of an economy consisting of many potential multiproduct firms.

In Chapter 10 Kreps and Spence provide an insightful survey of some interesting recent developments in the area of new industrial organization pertaining to the role of history in industrial competition. Their main theme is that the behaviour and performance of a mature industry are significantly conditioned by that industry's history. They contend that if the basic trichotomy (structure, conduct, performance) were to be extended by variables that are encompassed by the category of history, the power of prediction in mature industries would be considerably enhanced, a position that is also supported by Kuenne's analysis. The role of history can be properly understood by studying the process of industry dynamics. They concentrate on two basic approaches: (i) the rational actors approach which maintains that firms are able to anticipate the future consequences of their current actions, and (ii) the Simon-like approach that denies 'super' rationality, that relies on custom and routine, adaptation to unanticipated events, and evolution of decision-making procedures. In the latter case they focus on the Nelson and Winter framwork (which is also outlined in Chapter 1.

This is followed by a chapter (11) by Harris and Townsend who propose a novel approach for the prediction of both the allocation of resources and the resource allocation mechanism in specific environments where before trading the agents are asymmetrically informed. The thrust of their approach is to define the concept of an optimal resource allocation mechanism and to characterize such optimal mechanisms and their associated optimal allocations for given economic environments. Their approach uses the 'Revelation Principle', that is, any equilibrium allocation of any mechanism can be achieved by a truthful, direct machanism. By using this principle, they can find an optimal mechanism (and its associated equilibrium allocation) by choosing an allocation rule that maximizes some social welfare function, subject to technological feasibility and incentive—compatibility conditions. They argue that to analyse the resource allocation in certain types of environments with asymmetric information, the process of achieving allocations must first be considered. They present a methodology for such analyses and apply this approach to a specific, abstract environment characterized by asymmetry of information between two agents.

In Chapter 12, Goldberg focuses on the New Institutionalism, in particular on two concepts: namely, the production function and transaction costs. He warns about the need for greater care in the use of the former and is strongly critical of the latter. (A contrasting review of the transaction-cost approach can be found in Chapter 1.)

Part IV of this volume deals with welfare economics, social choice (which is also dealt with in Part I of this volume and in Chapter 3 of the companion volume), and consumption. It opens with a far-ranging and insightful survey by Hammond of the contemporary sweeping changes in welfare economics. After a lull of about a decade, the abundant crop of contributions to welfare economics in the 1970s has effectively broken away from both the 'old' and 'new' welfare economics. This modern breakthrough, still very much in progress, consists of three main parts: (i) the development of optimal tax theory, (ii) the elaboration of the theory of incentives (also dealt with in Chapter 3) and (iii) the emergence of a coherent theory of social choice with interpersonal comparisons. The latter at last permits us to address the classic issues of public finance such as how to redistribute income for economic justice (an issue also dealt with in Chapter 3 of the companion volume) and how to raise taxes equitably for the financing of public goods. Hammond concludes that the major progress is that it allows us to discuss the classic issues of public finance on a sounder basis of theoretical welfare economics than was possible even in the late 1970s.

Taking up some fundamental issues in social welfare, in Chapter 14 Ng defends welfarism and the Pareto principle. He argues that even when non-welfarist principles are accepted and the Pareto principle correspondingly extended, ordinalism is still an insufficient foundation for social welfare judgements and interpersonal comparable cardinal utilities are still essential. He argues that the belief in the sufficiency of ordinalism is inconsistent with the Bergson–Samuelson tradition of individualistic social-welfare functions. He defends some methods of measuring cardinal utilities (such as the Neumann–Morgenstern index, some voting and market mechanisms and the use of just noticeable differences). Though the methods are imperfect, he considers that they can contribute to more informative social welfare judgements.

In Chapter 15 Kemp and Kojima examine the paradox (in contrast to received doctrine that foreign aid is frequently more harmful than beneficial to the recipient country and is advantageous for exporters in the donor country. Their aim is to rework the economics of foreign aid under relaxed assumptions. In particular, they make allowance that for the possibility that aid is either wholly or partly tied in the donor or the recipient. They verify that the donor may gain and the recipient lose and that these outcomes may be compatible with market stability. The formal analysis of the major part of their paper culminates in a set of necessary and sufficient conditions for perverse outcomes in stable economies.

In the final chapter of this volume (Chapter 16), Lau offers a formal analysis of the common assertion that 'two can live as cheaply as one' which is often backed by casual empiricism. He proposes a novel way of modelling the technology of joint consumption within a household, to allow for potential empirical identification of the nature of economies of scale, if such indeed exist. The crucial idea is one of distinguishing between the quantity of a consumer good bought and the quantities of 'services' that this good renders to each household member. The latter are assumed as produced in accordance with a production function, using the purchased good as an input. The production function must satisfy certain plausible restrictions. Lau characterizes the class of production functions that in fact meet these restrictions. Given the individual utility functions of the members of the household and the rules of allocation and distribution within the household, the production functions can be used to analyse the demand patterns of two-individual households relative to single-individual households.

Issues in Contemporary Macroeconomics and Distribution

Chapter 1 sets the stage by highlighting the alternative approaches to macroeconomics, allowing the various protagonists to speak for themselves, and by pointing to the issues and tensions. In the opening chapter (2) of Part I (concerned with some alternative perspectives on macroeconomics and distribution issues) the lively and sometimes bitter controversies surrounding such a strongly and directly policy-oriented subject as macroeconomics are reviewed by a major and creative veteran of the clashes. Tobin concentrates on the theoretical issues among the contestants – revolutionary and counter-revolutionary alike. Of major interest here is not only his perception of the counter-revolutions, but also of the *General Theory* as elaborated, applied and modified in the postwar period. He uses general equilibrium as a central frame of reference and points to the vulnerability of Keynesian economics to come to terms with this powerful tradition and to the contemporary attempts to reformulate Keynesian economics in order to overcome this failure – if such it is.

Looking at the economy from the normative perspective, in Chapter 3 Arrow makes a powerful case for distributive justice. Though he disagrees on many other points with Rawls. Arrow agrees with the basic thrust: justice values both liberty and equality. Arrow denies that there is any contradiction between these two ideals and asserts the opposite: one is not realizable without the other. He reviews the issues of trade-off between efficiency and equity – the market and distributive justice. He then proceeds to illuminate the role of social choice in guiding income distribution. In making his case for redistribution, Arrow poses the fundamental questions as to whether equality is really the meaning of distributive justice; the essence of the meaning of just or equal distribution of income, power, and other economic goods; the possibility of conflict between other legitimate social goals and justice and how to evaluate the trade-offs; the just intergenerational allocation of goods; and the extent to which the nature, ideology, functioning, and institutional arrangements of capitalism promote or hamper the achievement of justice. Even under assumptions most favourable to decentralization, there is an irreducible need for social choice on distribution. Indeed, there are a number of solutions where replacement of the market by collective action is desirable.

Chapter 4 provides some insights into Joan Robinson's perspective. She starts out with a brief critique of pre-Keynesian economics and proceeds to a challenge of the Keynesian neoclassical synthesis and the unfortunate compartmentalization of economics into micro and macro. She sees this as an attempt to save equilibrium theory from Keynes which has landed it in a number of contradictions. On the analytical plane there is the problem of time: 'Equilibrium, it seems lies in the future. Why has it not been established already? Jam tomorrow but never jam today.' She also castigates the inequalities stemming from the free play of market forces. She then takes to task capital theory and points to Sraffa's inspiration.

As these volumes were going to press it was with much sadness that we have learned of Joan Robinson's death. In many respects she has made a real difference to the economics of our age. Both those that agree and those that disagree with her will probably miss her challenges. This is not the place to pay tribute to the truly great economist she was, but to record how privileged I am to share with the reader her last contribution. It is presented here in the draft form Joan originally sent me. Because of her prolonged and incapacitating illness she was not able to revise it. Naturally I consider it inappropriate to tamper with her writing. In Chapter 1 of this volume I have attempted to provide some background on the development of her thought.

Part II is concerned with finding an appropriate microeconomic underpinning for Keynesian macroeconomics. It opens with a chapter (4) by Negishi who develops a non-Walrasian microeconomic theory as a basis for the Keynesian fixprice model. His inspiration stems from Menger who pointed out that the price is not the sole important factor in the theory of exchange and stressed the asymmetry between demand and supply. Negishi argues the case for microfoundations based on the theory of kinked demand curves not perceived by oligopolistic but by more competitive firms. He concludes by pointing to the essential differences between Walrasian and non-Walrasian economics.

In a similar vein, in Chapter 6 Benassy presents a two-market model that diverges from the 'standard' fixprice non-Walrasian macro-models in the sense that (i) there is upward but not downward price flexibility. (ii) wages are related to the price level, with allowance for situations ranging from no indexation to full indexation. The model is an application of more general concepts of non-Walrasian equilibrium. The study concentrates on the relative efficiency of combating unemployment via Keynesian demand management policies versus 'classical' incomes policies, aimed at reducing the wage level. The model is studied under three different regimes. (Regime A – excess supply of labour and goods; regime B – excess supply of labour with goods market cleared; and regime C – excess demand for labour, with goods market cleared.) While regime A displays standard Keynesian features, it appears in regime B that indexation can reduce considerably the effectiveness of demand management even though involuntary unemployment exists. In the corresponding case, however, incomes policies are effective in reducing unemployment. Benassy concludes that analysis of macroeconomic problems by means of non-Walrasian equilibrium concepts appears to be effective both to predict the policy consequences of various price formation mechanisms and to synthesize hitherto antogonistic models.

Also in the non-Walrasian approach, Sondermann shows in the next chapter that for a three-commodity model there exist equilibrium states with involuntary unemployment. Unemployment equilibria may occur whenever prices (and wages) adjust slower than quantities. The characteristics of the equilibria arrived at in his model include: the inequality of demand and supply (non-Walrasian); stability in the sense that neither producers nor consumers find it advantageous to upset the *status quo*; a non-tâtonnement generation process for both quantities and prices; involuntary unemployment; prices that are neither fixed nor set by an auctioneer, but by producers with normal price expectations; wages that are neither fixed, arbitrary, nor inflexible, but depend on the economy's history; and finally the possible inefficiency of the equilibrium at which the economy may arrive, providing room for the types of government intervention suggested by Keynes.

In the final Chapter (8) in Part II, Ng outlines a micro—macro method to study the effects of industry-wide and economy-wide changes in demand, costs, expectations, etc. on the average price and aggregate output. He uses the concept of the representative firm but, in contrast to the Marshallian tradition, the response of the representative firm is used to approximate that of a typically non-perfectly competitive industry or the whole economy, with interesting non-traditional results. Ng uses the analysis to show the possibility of real expansion and contraction without affecting the price level in a monopolistically competitive economy (not possible in a perfectly competitive one since no lags, no misinformation or other frictions are assumed). He shows that an increase in nominal aggregate demand may lift the real-wage demand-for-labour function, leading to a real expansion and that the practical possibility of this non-traditional result is increased if some firms are revenue maximizers. In the last section of his chapter, Ng summarizes some further results (on entry/exit of firms, oligopoly, and some applications of his analysis) that he elaborates in a forthcoming book.

The arguments of the new classical macroeconomics (also known as rational expectations or equilibrium business-cycle theory) are expounded in Chapter 1 of this volume. Part III deals with theoretical and policy conceptions and evaluations of this approach. It opens with a chapter (9) by Wan who disputes the claims of the new classical macroeconomics from a game-theoretic perspective. He contends that: (i) any policy evaluation reminds all agents that policies once made can also be remade and unmade later. Rational agents do not confuse the incumbent's present intent with policy rules of the future. Future rules are predicted only in the light of what is said and done by the current government. To influence agents, words and deeds of the current regime play the same roles as those of its predecessors. 'How influential?' is on econometric record. Thus Keynesian econometrics is not fatally flawed. (ii) Any time-inconsistent policy is not 'sub-game perfect' and hence tempts future regimes to renege. Thus, any policy that is credible to rational agents must be time-consistent. (iii) In any world where agents are heterogeneous policy almost surely is effective.

In Chapter 10 Burmeister shows that both rational expectations and perfect foresight models feature a similar indeterminacy problem. This is an important economic problem which if it remains unresolved (as it has thus far) hampers empirical and policy evaluation work. Since most existing rational expectation models postulate convergence convergent expectations are a crucial assumption that is basic to both the theoretical analysis and empirical estimation of these models. Burmeister conjectures that we would be in a better position to understand the business cycle if we built models that were capable of dynamic instability and/or non-stochastic oscillations instead of ruling them out by assumption as is frequently the case when standard procedures for 'solving' rational expectations models are used.

Benjamin Friedman's chapter (11) concludes this part with further insights into trends in macroeconomics and into the macro problems. He offers the thesis that the experience of the early 1980s — the anticipated, non-surprise disinflationary policy and its aftermath — directly contradicts the central policy conclusions of new classical macroeconomics. It represents at least as powerful a refutation as that which earlier led to disillusionment with the existing macroeconomic orthodoxy. Friedman makes a point for a symbiosis of old and new developments in macroeconomics, to derive policy conclusions in conformity with the perceived functioning of the economy; that is, that money is not neutral, that trade-offs do exist, and that policy influences real economic outcomes.

Part IV on inflation and disinflation opens with Chapter 12 by Klein who defends mainstream macroeconometric models against the charge that they did not anticipate the inflationary surge of the 1970s. He shows that the variances between forecasts and actual outcomes were not as significant as some critics claimed and reveals how the models were gradually extended to give increasing cognizance to the energy and food sector. He acknowledges the need for constant model improvement, but rejects radical model reform or abandonment.

In Chapter 13 Eckstein analyses the disinflation process of the early 1980s. He asks the pertinent questions whther the severity of the 1982 recession finally reduced core inflation, whether inflationary expectations have come down as much as actual prices; whether the economy's structure has altered sufficiently to reduce the inflationary bias built-in in the last three decades; whether inflation will return quickly in the recovery; and finally what can be done to ensure that the recovery does not suffer from its predecessors' ills. He attempts to answer these questions by quantitative analysis on the basis of a cohesive theoretical structure.

In Chapter 14 Beguelin and Schiltknecht discuss monetarism and monetary policy from the standpoint of central bankers. They point out, *inter alia*, that central bankers cannot be assumed to have more information than the rest of the world and that they more or less frequently make wrong decisions that destabilize the economy. They contend that the only means of bridging the credibility gap is to control the trend of money supply in the long run. They believe that central banks should lean towards medium-term control of the money supply through a succession of annual rather than quarterly targets, and conclude that, though it is not an ideal solution for all problems, the monetarist approach to monetary policy is the optimal solution.

Part V, concerned with distribution, growth, and policy alternatives, opens with Chapter 15 by Tinbergen who surveys the factors that condition income distribution in developed countries. He illuminates a wide variety of economically relevant factors, including the morphology of markets, production functions, innate or learned abilities, sociological factors such as power and discrimination, and non-productive sources such as households and institutional units (e.g. the military) as well as income transfers primarily from a social security system.

In Chapter 16 Bronfenbrenner presents a modern, temperate defence of marginal productivity as a theory of input demand rather than of wages and takes up some aspects of the capital controversy with Joan Robinson.

In the following chapter (17) Don Harris points to the discord between the historical picture of uneven growth as a persistent phenomenon and growth theory that essentially negates this phenomenon. He presents an overview of some of the theoretical issues involved and proposes the analyses of uneven growth where one of the central analytical problems is understanding the mechanism of mutual interaction and interdependence among the development of various sectors.

The concern with the economy's productive capacity has a long and respectable ancestry. In Chapter 18 Feiwel discusses the driving forces of and constraints to economic growth. He then contrasts basically two approaches to stimulate growth: one that concentrates, exclusively on supply and the other that integrates supply and demand, or from a somewhat different vantage point, one that uses a microeconomic approach to macroeconomic problems and the other that integrates both macro and micro approaches. Fundamentally the approaches differ in their perceptions of the dynamics and *modus operandi* of a modern economy, the range and effectiveness of policy options, and the elasticity of response of agents to economic stimuli. Economic models of the first approach essentially distort reality if they do not perceive the economy as subject to trend, fluctuations, stochastic disturbances, and major market failures, in contrast to the second approach which does make an attempt to incorporate those factors in its models.

In Chapter 19 Summers summarizes his recent research on the development of an asset price approach for analysing capital income taxation. He discusses a number of reasons for focusing on the role of asset prices in analysing public finance problems, including the role of asset prices in determining investment decisions and the role of changes in asset prices as indicators of the horizontal and vertical equity effects of tax reforms. He also reviews recent empirical research that studies asset price information in order to measure the effects of tax reforms on economic behaviour and to distinguish between alternative models of the effects of capital income taxation.

Many of the most important modelling and policy issues in both macroeconomics and income distribution revolve around the emphasis placed the length of the time horizon, the role of expectations, and the responsiveness of behaviour to incentives. In the final chapter (20) of this volume. Boskin examines these issues by developing several examples. The potential role of fiscal policy in stabilizing the economy is discussed in terms to various perceptions of the role of government debt and the relative importance of short- and long-run perceptions about income in determining spending behaviour. The incidence of various alternative tax policies is also pursued from the perspectives of annual and lifetime income; *ex ante* and *ex post* realizations of income; and presumed time horizons governing consumption and saving behaviour. Boskin demonstrates that the answers to many frequently posed policy questions depend on the modeller's assumptions concerning the above-mentioned three factors and conjectures about them on the basis of available statistical studies. He concludes that introduction of a longer term focus in macro-economics and income distribution debates has been one of the most important developments in economics in the last fifteen years, but that problems such as incomplete markets lead to models that combine emphasis on shorter-run current income and longer-term expected values.

ACKNOWLEDGEMENTS

I am beholden and deeply grateful to all the contributors. They and their selfless co-operation, often in the face of considerable difficulties, have made the real difference. One of the great rewards in seeing this project through the processes of design, gestation, and fruition has been in experiencing the spirit of professionalism and dedication revealed by the contributors. Many of them are of architectonic stature in their fields; some of them have shaped economics in the last thrity years or more, others are bright new lights. As editor I have sought to weave their contributions into designs that reflect the major developments in micro- and macroeconomics of the last two decades or so and to anticipate those of the next, filling in the inevitable gaps in the fabric with my own efforts. All inadequacies are the editor's; all praise goes to the contributors.

I am a bankrupt when it comes to thanking those contributors who unsparingly gave of their time to discuss the various aspects of the project, offered wise counsel, and/or graciously commented on my introductory chapters. Special gratitude is owed to: Arrow, Aumann, Baumol, Benassy, Boskin, Bronfenbrenner, Eckstein, Ben Friedman, Hammond, Milt Harris, Hurwicz, Kemp, Klein, Kreps, Kuenne, Kurz, Lau, Negishi, Tauman, Tinbergen, Tobin, Townsend, Wan, and Wilson.

A large number of people made an imprint on these volumes. I fear that this acknowledgement can hardly do justice to the debt I owe them for their influence, time, patience and good advice. I will spare the reader the major names in the history of economic thought and reluctantly will abstain from enumerating my teachers, colleagues, and students. But I should be remiss not to mention G. Debreu, F. Hahn, D. Jorgenson, E. Kalai, A. Roth, L. Shapley, E. Sheshinsky, and O. Williamson. Thanks are also due for interesting discussions with M. Abramovitz, G. Ackley, I. Adelman, A. Blinder, J. Chipman, P. David, D. Dillard, S. Fischer, F. Fisher, C. Garison, N. Georgescu-Roegen, E. Glustoff, J. Green, R. Hall, H. Jensen, D. Kaserman, J. Kendrick, D. Laidler, H. Leibenstein, J. Letiche, A. Lindbeck, R. Looney, B. McCallum, B. Holmstrom, A. Mas-Colell, E.

Maskin, T. Mayer, P. Milgrom, J. R. Moore, M. Morishima, M. Nerlove, N. Rosenberg, T. W. Schultz, J. Stiglitz, and J. Tirole.

My research burden was lightened, and hopefully the coverage broadened, by the kind co-operation of numerous authors who have sent me their writings (often in unpublished form). My thanks to K. Brunner, M. Friedman, R. Gordon, S. Grossman, G. Harcourt, Sir John Hicks, L. Johansen, Lord Kahn, Lord Kaldor, I. Kirzner, R. E. Lucas Jr. J. E. Meade, A. Meltzer, F. Modigliani, J. Muth, R. Nelson, W. Nordhaus, R. Radner, John Roberts, T. Sargent, A. Sen, C. Sims, G. Stigler, and J. E. Taylor.

Once again I am happy to acknowledge a special debt of gratitude to Robert Bassett (and his assistant Warner Granade) of the reference department of the University of Tennessee library for imagination, initiative, and exertions beyond the call of duty. Thanks are also due to to the Greene Library at Stanford, the University of California (Berkeley) libraries and numerous colleagues who graciously lent me their books and materials.

The customary disclaimer applies to all the above mentioned – *mea culpa* all the way, except for my wife, Ida, who shares much greater culpability than she allows me to mention.

Whatever is wrong with economics (and, indeed, there is much), one cannot but feel proud to belong to a profession that numbers among its members someone like Jan Tinbergen – who, as H. C. Bos records in the *International Encyclopedia of the Social Sciences*, would have been as worthy a condidate for the Nobel peace prize as for the one he was awarded in economics. Ida and I feel privileged to respectfully and affectionately dedicate these two volumes to Jan who is 80 years young this year.

G. R. Feiwel

1 Some Perceptions and Tensions in Microeconomics: A Background

G. R. FEIWEL

In this introductory chapter we attempt to provide a partial background to the analysis that our contributors articulate so eloquently. Inevitably, in a volume of this nature many gaps remain and while we make no pretence at filling them, we hope that in the pages that follow, these gaps will be somewhat reduced and that the ensuing chapters will be placed in perspective. An attempt is made to provide a perception of the alternative approaches, achievements, controversies and issues, and underlying tensions and their sources. The account is perforce selective and an attempt is made to be as impartial as humanly possible (i.e. to let the various protagonists speak for themselves), though I am fully aware that my own preferences and prejudices inevitably creep in.

The opening section briefly reviews the essence of modern general equilibrium theory (GE). We than proceed with activity analysis (also known as linear programming), its development and usefulness in market-type and planned economies, and the closely related subjects of input–output analysis and game theory. Proceeding in this vein, we examine the normative approach to economics, the impulses that motivate system designers, and their use of some of the tools previously outlined, including a cursory survey of team theory and information.

In quite a different tradition in the Chicago school's approach to the theory of the firm (its methodology is scrutinzed in the last part of this chapter and its macro and monetary theory are explored in Chapter 1 of the companion volume). We also attempt here to provide a glimpse of the Chicago school's economic imperialism – its invasion of political science, jurisprudence, and especially sociology and psychology.

In the next section we concentrate on some external attacks on GE that often probe the weak spots that the GE theorists themselves have been

1

prompt to point to and have attempted more or less successfully to remedy in at least the last two decades. Some of the weaknesses, indeed, seem unsurmountable.

In the past a very influential stream of thought, at least in the USA, has been institutionalism. In contemporary economic thought it has lost its lustre and appears in several disparate varieties, ranging from the broad and colourful social criticism of Galbraith and Myrdal to the more restrained and specific critics of the traditional theory of the firm. The latter (including Simon, Leibenstein, Marris, Williamson, Nelson, and Winter, and many other), who disagree among themselves on a number of issues and whose ideas are analysed here separately, generally concentrate their attacks on the super-rationality of economic agents and argue, *inter alia*, for an analysis of the firm based on bounded rationality, satisficing, routine, and evolutionary economic change.

Finally we tackle the thorny issues of social, ideological, and political underpinnings of economics – crucial issues fully recognized by many leading economists (usually of the older generation) and often blatantly disregarded by others. Some attempt is made to differentiate the natural from the social sciences, and to raise the questions of verification (or refutation) in the latter. This is related to the dismal (or what Dennis Robertson called the distasteful) subject of methodology in economics, the pertinent question of whether 'tools (e.g. mathematics) are used to solve real problems or problems are 'invented' to suit the available tools, and to the state and future of the science and the art.

MODERN GENERAL EQUILIBRIUM THEORY

The neoclassical GE,[1] elucidated in Chapter 2 by no less an authority than Kenneth J. Arrow, clarifies, *inter alia*, the extent to which a social disposition of resources can be attained in a highly decentralized economy by a multiplicity of independent decisions (each agent pursuing only private values) co-ordinated and rendered mutually consistent through the market process. As Arrow and Hahn (1971, p. 1) point out in their standard treatise, whatever the origin of the concept of equilibrium, 'the notion that a social system moved by independent actions in pursuit of different values is consistent with a final coherent state of balance, and one in which the, outcomes may be quite different from those intended by the agents, is surely the most important intellectual contribution that economic thought has made to the general understanding of social processes'.

And, it may be added, that no matter what its shortcomings, it is a major analytical feat in rigorously modelling the interaction of economic agents. It is, indeed, difficult to disagree with Hahn (1982a, p. 4) that:

> one must be far gone in philistine turpitude not to appreciate the quite surprising nature of this result, or to be unmoved by the elegant means by which it is proved. It establishes the astonishing claim that it is logically possible to describe an economy in which millions of agents, looking no further than their own interests and responding to the sparse information system of prices only, can nonetheless attain a coherent economic disposition of resources.

The claim is really astonishing for intuitively one would expect that the multiplicity of uncoordinated self-seeking actions would lead to chaos.

It was a major contribution of Arrow, Debreu, McKenzie, and others not only to demonstate that a coherent and orderly economic allocation can be theoretically achieved and to specify precisely what conditions must be satisfied to reach this result, but also to show that the outcome has the added property of being Pareto efficient. This is, indeed, a very weak property. As Sen (1983, p. 6) stresses, and as is also discussed in both of Arrow's chapters in these volumes:

> all that Pareto optimality implies is that there is no other feasible alternative that is better for everyone without exception, or better for some and no worse for anyone. A state in which some people are starving and suffering from acute deprivation while others are tasting the good life can still be Pareto optimal if the poor cannot be made better off without cutting into the pleasures of the rich — no matter by how small in amount. Pareto optimality is faint praise indeed (see also Sen, 1982; Schumpeter, 1950; Dobb, 1973).

The close relations between Pareto efficiency and competitive equilibrium is the central result both on theoretical and policy planes. The equivalence of the two concepts is known as two fundamental theorems of welfare economics: (i) every competitive equilibrium is Pareto efficient, (ii) for every Pareto efficient allocation there is a redistribution of endowments such that the given Pareto efficient allocation is a competitive equilibrium for the new endowment distribution. The first theorem does not imply that such a state is a social optimum and ethically just, for there is nothing in the process that assures distributive justice. On the other hand, the second implies that the questions of distributional judgements can be separated from efficiency considerations. If a decentralized market solution is adopted and alteration of existing distribution is desired, the analysis implies that the modification proceed by varying the initial distribution of endowments, then allowing the market to function unhampered.

Naturally, the two theorems are valid only if certain crucial and highly exacting hypotheses are met — such as completeness of all intertemporal and contingent relevant markets (including those for externalities) and absence of significant economies of scale in production. In the real world these hypotheses are frequently invalidated. In addition, two other essential warnings should be sounded:

(1) While the second theorem 'is a tribute to the market mechanism, it is not a tribute to the invisible hand, i.e. to the market unassisted by political intervention. The initial distribution of resources has to be got right, and this of course does involve a political process, indeed — quite possibly — a totally revolutionary one requiring a thorough redistribution of the ownership of means of production, depending on the particular Pareto optimal outcome that is identified as socially best.'

(2) One also needs to go 'beyond the market mechanism to get the information that would be needed to decide how best to distribute the resources initially. Under the market mechanism, given the right initial distribution and right prices, people may have the incentive to take the right decisions about production, consumption, etc. But they don't have a similar incentive to reveal information about themselves that makes decisions regarding the initial distribution of resources possible. Disclosures about productive abilities, tastes, etc. can go against one's own interests in the determination of the initial distribution of resources, e.g. confession of higher ability or lower needs may have the effect of one's getting a lower share of non-labour resources in the initial split up' (Sen, 1983, p. 5).

The issue in point, however, is that by elucidating the required set of conditions, the theory not only shows us what the world would have to be like for the results to be achieved, but it also allows us to focus on the absence of these conditions in the real world and to attempt to take remedial steps.[2] The theory exemplifies the potentials and limits of economic analysis.

In summation, elucidation of the pure logic of relative scarcity and prices has been the *tour de force* of neoclassical economics. As such this is a pre-institutional mode of analysis: in principle, the GE solution to the allocaton problem could be fruitfully employed by a central planner or, under some specific conditions, it could be found in competitive markets. For many years now some of the most sophisticated economists have been drawn by the logic, clarity, and aesthetic qualities of the concept. They have been and continue to be preoccupied with explaining, elucidating, refining, and extending it. And, the best and brightest among them are supremely aware of the concept's limitations (a telling example is Chapter 2 of this volume).

INPUT–OUTPUT AND ACTIVITY ANALYSIS

Three strands of analysis of fairly recent vintage, which originated separately and only gradually came to be compared to each other – input–output analysis, linear activity analysis (or linear programming), and game theory – can be placed in the same family and furthermore have a strong affinity to GE. As Koopmans (1957, p. 40), one of the architects of activity analysis, points out, of the two models of GE and linear activity analysis

> that of competitive equilibrium is *in a mathematical sense* the more general one. In fact, we shall be able to derive the main results of activity analysis by a specialization of the model of competitive equilibrium (and a slight sharpening of the separation theorem used in it) . . . *In an economic sense*, however, one may claim in one important aspect a higher degree of generality for the model of activity analysis. It constructs a theory of valuation of resources that assumes nothing more, on the consumption side of the market, than a state of non-saturation with respect to each commodity classified as desired for consumption.

All three are subtly intertwinted in their dependence on stress of the linear features of economic problems, for example, the notion of limited resources and the different purposes to which they may be allocated in various ways, resulting in different consequences (see Wood and Dantzig, 1951, pp. 15–16). Besides being a question of welfare economics and production theory, this is also 'a problem in *linear* economics, the word "linear" being introduced to call attention to the fact that the basic restrictions in the problem take the form of the simplest of all mathematical functions. In this case the restrictions state that the total amount of any factor devoted to all tasks must not exceed the total amount available; this mathematically each restriction is a simple sum (Dorfman, Samuelson, and Solow, 1958, p. 1). Input–output analysis is conceptually akin to activity analysis (linear programming). The relationship to game theory is less substantive; it revolves only around the use of the same mathematical tools – the properties of systems of linear inequalities or of the convex sets defined by such inequalities (see Koopmans, 1970, p. 249).

While its roots go back to Quesnay's *Tableau Économique*, in its modern version, input—output analysis is largely the brainchild of Wassily Leontief (1936, 1941). Input—output analysis has at least four major features: (i) it provides a far-reaching simplification of GE; (ii) it provides a more comprehensive breakdown of the macroeconomic aggregates and monetary flows; (iii) it may be viewed as an especially simple form of activity analysis: 'in the simplest Leontief system, in which no substitutions of inputs are technologically feasible, the optimizing solution is the one and only efficient solution possible; but in more general models, in which substitution is possible, the system can be made determinate only by solving an appropriately formulated linear-programming problem (or by requiring the solution to satisfy some restrictive outside conditions)' (Dorfman, Samuelson and Solow, 1958, p. 204); and (iv) besides being a useful tool for studying the quantitative interdependence among inter-related economic activities, input—output analysis is a valuable device for prediction and is particularly suited to national economic planning.

Originally elaborated to analyse and measure the flows among the different producing and consuming sectors of a national economy, input—output has been successfully used in studying more compact economic systems such as regions or very large enterprises. It was later extended to the analysis of international economic relations and in its most ambitious form to the structure of the world economy. Essentially, input—output concentrates on the interdependence of the various sectors of a system described by a set of linear equations. The numerical magnitude of these equations' coefficients defines the particular structural features of the system. The coefficients have to be empirically determined; that is, they are usually deduced from a statistical input—output table that can be more or less aggregated and that depicts the intersectoral flows within a national economy over a period of a year. Although in principle these flows can be depicted in physical terms, in practice they are measured in value terms (with the usual intricate problems involved in such measurement). Such an input—output table in value terms can be interpreted as a system of national accounts.

Leontief's original construct raised basic questions of economic interpretation. It was questioned on the grounds of its strong technological assumptions, the quality of the available data base, the fixed coefficients of production, the ruling out of joint products, the narrowness of the focus on the technical aspects of production and relative neglect of demand theory, and the like. Indeed, the general tenor of the questions was whether the bold and crude simplifications initially made were not an excessive price to pay for making GE implementable. It is noteworthy that the debate around the Leontief system inspired Samuelson's far-reaching non-substitutability theorem of modern input—output, which ensures that even though technological substitutions of input proportions are possible, they need, in fact, never be made in a single-primary-input economy where technology exhibits constant returns to scale and joint products are ruled out (Samuelson, 1966, pp. 515–35).

Leontief has attempted to remedy some of these shortcomings in successive refinements of the theoretical construct and various empirical variants of his model. He developed a dynamic input—output theory that takes into account intersectoral dependences that involve lags (rates of change of variables over time). The thoretical basis for the input—output approach to empirical analysis of the accumulation process and of development planning comprises the structural relations between stocks and flows of goods. The innovative effort met with a mixed reception and reservations. Thus, for instance, Dorfman, Samuelson and Solow (1958, p. 283) write:

> The dynamic input—output system is a straightforward generalization of the static model . . . Its distinguishing characteristics are the same . . . As in the static model, it then appears that no quantitative problems of optimization could arise.

Whatever else needs to be said about Leontief's pioneering effort, it was a major *tour de force* in posing the problems of mutual compatibility and accommodation between theoretical formulation and observational capability (development of the empirical data base) and the difficulties in analysing and describing in concrete numerical magnitudes the specific operational features of the modern economy characterized by super complexity of the intersectoral links.

Essentially, 'activity analysis is concerned with the study of efficient allocation in production systems by models capable of numerical application. It was developed for these purposes prior to the modern version of the theory of Pareto optima' (Koopmans, 1970, p. 336).

In the USA, where linear programming was initially outlined by Koopmans (1970, pp. 77–86) in 1942 in an unpublished memorandum to the Combined Shipping Adjustment Board and independently developed by Dantzig (1951) in 1947 as a planning technique for the Air Force, there appears to have been some disinterest in this mode of analysis on the part of the economics profession as a whole (with, as usual, some notable exceptions) and compensating and spreading interest in the then new fields of operations research and management science. The problems these fields tackle, Koopmans (1977b) feels, were a natural outgrowth of economics, but not all of his fellow economists agree. This may appear surprising since linear programming has borrowed its problems from traditional economic theory and provided answers to some of the economists' questions. It has also supplied the economist 'with fairly rigorous proofs for some of his theorems . . . No one who understands both economic theory and programming theory is likely to deny that the latter's fundamental duality theorems have added to his understanding of the pricing mechanism and its limitations' (Samuelson, 1966, p. 497). For the economist, programming is 'a useful theoretical tool, a convenient way of idealizing the production and profit-maximizing side of a model designed for answering abstract economic questions' (Dorfman, Samuelson, and Solow, 1958, p. 346). Koopmans (1977b) attributes the economists' disinterest partly to differences in tools of analysis (linear inequalities rather than calculus), partly to an excessively narrow definition of economics as a discipline, and partly to a misconception of the principles of best utilization which can not only be applied within a plant or firm, but also on the scale of the national or even world economy.

In this vein, in tracing the development of linear activity analysis, Koopmans (1977a, p. 264) points out that 'it was already foreshadowed in the work of Lange and Lerner that hypothetical perfect competition and hypothetical perfect planning both imply efficient allocation of resources although neither occurs in reality.'[3]

To recall, Lange's and Lerner's contributions were in response to a challenge of Ludwig von Mises (1951, pp. 385–6) in the 1920s. He maintained that a condition for the existence of rational prices is a genuine market. The latter can only exist where means of production are privately owned. With the collectivization of the means of production, the market and market valuations for producer and consumer goods disappear. Hence, there can be no rational price system and no rational economic calculation essential for efficient organization of production. The socialist economy would 'grope in the dark' producing 'senseless output' by an 'absurd apparatus'. Without market valuations indicating what and how to produce, there would be no intrinsic basis for the rationality of decisions which would become purely arbitrary.

Lange's (1938) reply was that, in any society that faces choice between alternatives, to solve the allocative problem three sets of data are required: (i) a preference function to guide choice, (ii) choice indicators, or 'the knowledge of the terms on which alternatives are offered' and (iii) production function. If the data under (i) (which may reflect consumers' or planners' preferences) and (iii) are known, (ii) can be determined. Hence, it is not a condition that an actual market must determine the scarcity price. The socialist economy can operate with rational prices established on a simulated market. Lange assumes consumers' and wage-earners' sovereignty, a genuine market for consumer goods and labour, but only a simulated market for producer goods.

Lange demonstrated that prices of producer goods do not have to be determined as a result of actual market transactions. Rational prices (representing the terms at which alternatives are offered) derived as equilibrium values, can be determined by the condition that demand for each commodity is to be equal to its supply and 'as Walras has so brilliantly shown, this is done by a series of successive trials (tatonnements)'. Lange's Central Planning Board can set initially any price at random (Walras's *prix criés par hasard*), but as a rule the starting point for the successive trials would be 'historically given' prices. Should there be excess demand or supply the planners will adjust the price through increase or decrease respectively in order to equilibrate demand and supply. And, if this is not achieved, the price will be altered again and again until equilibrium is finally reached.

The solution of the series of successive trials is based on the parametric function of prices, that is every participant in the simulated market process is separately a price-taker and regards the price set by the planner as a datum beyond his power to change, adjusting his behaviour (quantity adjuster) to take advantage of the market situation confronting him and which he cannot control. Apart from performing the function of the market by setting the prices, the planner establishes and imposes on the managers of production the observance of rules of conduct for combining productive factors so as to minimize average production costs and for fixing the scale of the plant's output so that marginal cost equals the price of the product. The managers of decreasing-cost industries would increase production, irrespective of the average cost, until marginal cost equals price. The aggregate investment volume is not dictated by market considerations, but is established by the planner to eliminate fluctuations and foster growth. Allocation of capital among enterprises relies on the interest rate that balances availability and demand for capital.

Koopmans (1977a, p. 264) confirms that he found it useful to turn the Lange problem around:

and just postulate allocative efficiency as a model for abstract, pre-institutional study. Thereafter, one can go on to explore alternative institutional arrangements for approximating the model. I believe that the linear model offers a good foothold for this purpose. First, it makes a rigorous discussion easier. Secondly, the most challenging *non*linearity

– that connected with increasing returns to scale – in fact undermines competition. It also greatly escalates the mathematical and computational requirements for good planning. The linear model, therefore, makes a natural first chapter in the theory of best allocation of resources.

Thus far we have been using the terms linear programming and activity analysis interchangeably. At this stage a subtle distinction should be made – the first seems to best describe the contributions of the mathematicians, whereas the second applies rather to those of economists:[4]

> Thus the emphasis in linear programming was from the beginning on the computation of explicit solutions to complicated practical allocation problems for which numerical data are available. However, the connection between these methods and the much older idea of pricing, implicit or market, of scarce resources soon became apparent to the economists who took part in the development. At the same time, they considered more general cases involving the simultaneous maximization of several linear functions in analogy to Pareto's idea of the simultaneous maximization of all consumers' satisfactions. The terms (*linear*) *activity analysis* came to be associated with this generalization (Koopmans, 1957, pp. 67–8).

Essentially, 'activity analysis is concerned with the construction of conceptual models to study and appraise criteria, rules, and practices for the allocation of resources' (Koopmans, 1970, p. 222). It can be distinguished from traditional theory of production and prices in three ways: (i) It does not start from a production function; rather it views the various production methods as decision variables. Thus it starts from a model of production possibilities. (ii) It is pre-institutional in nature, in that it is free of institutional arrangements and leaves much scope for choosing and evaluating different organizational forms. (iii) 'The main service it renders is to show that value theory – that is, the theory of prices as guides to allocation of resources and of the relations between these prices and the technology – is of such a fundamental character that it can be constructed without reference to institutional postulates regarding the existence and the behaviour of firms and of consumers' (Koopmans, 1957, p. 148). 'It provides us with methods of computation indicating what program will best serve a given objective and how to translate given valuations of final commodities into valuations of intermediate and primary commodities' (Koopmans, 1970, pp. 222–3).

It is in the latter context that Koopmans (1977a, p. 263) sees its greatest significance for economic theory; that is, 'the analysis of the *role or*

use of prices toward best allocation of resources, either through the operation of competitive markets, or as an instrument of national palnning'.
He sees activity analysis as having confirmed by rigorous mathematical
analysis and only for a relatively restricted model of production the
economist's traditional belief in competitive markets as a means for
efficient allocation of resources (Koopmans, 1970, pp. 223 and 246–7).

The characteristics of this admittedly narrow model, whose assumptions
often significantly diverge from reality, are: numerous production processes
each with determined input–output ratios; no indivisibilities; full predic-
tability of outcomes; fixed limits to availability of basic resources; and
additiveness of production processes. Using this model and the concept of
Pareto efficiency:

> it is a matter of straightforward mathematical proof . . . to arrive at a
> theorem which, in honor of Adam Smith, I shall call the Invisible Hand
> Theorem. For the validity of this theorem, it does not matter whether
> an efficient use of resources has been achieved by sheer luck, by hard
> calculation, or through the action of a market with a price system. The
> theorem merely says that if efficiency has somehow been achieved,
> then there must exist a set of prices on all goods and services such that
> all production processes in use break even; and such that if anyone
> were to engage in a production process that does not fit in with an
> efficient use of resources, he would sustain a loss. By 'existence' of
> these prices I do not necessarily mean that these are quoted in some
> markets or even that anyone should have a knowledge of any of these
> prices. I mean 'existence' in the mathematical sense. If a man from
> Mars with unlimited powers of observation and calculation would study
> the efficient economy in question he would be able to calculate a set
> of prices and satisfy himself that it endows the various processes of
> production with the profitability features indicated. In application to a
> competitive market economy, of course, the main significance of the
> theorem is that it gives us some confidence in market prices as a guide
> to decisions (Koopmans, 1970, p. 248).

Bearing in mind the divergencies between this model and reality, Koopmans
(1970, p. 249) wisely cautions that:

> any inferences from this model to our actual economy must be regarded
> as extrapolations. When uncertainty actually enters, or when indivis-
> ibilities are important, we just do not know at present whether or to
> what extent the price system or a competitive market economy is a
> reliable guide to the allocation of rosources. This must be regarded as

an open question, which at some future time may be resolved through somebody's ingenuity in constructing more realistic models accessible to mathematical analysis. While some progress has been made recently toward the recognition of uncertainty . . . in models, the incorporation of indivisibilities has proved extremely difficult except in a few very simple cases.

And, reflecting on the merits of this type of analysis on the occasion of the award to him and Kantorovich of the Nobel Prize for this feat, Koopmans (1977a, pp. 264–5) mused on the principal merits of activity analysis developments:

One is their initially pre-institutional character. Technology and human needs are universal. To start with just these elements has facilitated and intensified professional contacts and interactions between economists from market and socialist countries. The other merit is the combination and merging of economic theory, mathematical modeling, data collection, and computational methods and algorithms made possible by the modern computer.

In the USSR the most promising approach to the problem of pricing and resource allocation is that of the rising mathematical school, whose pioneering propagators include the economist Novozhilov and the mathematician Kantorovich.[5]

Novozhilov reached his conclusions while pursuing the analysis of investment efficiency. He recognized that the latter is only a special case and its solution hinges on a more general theory of valuation and resource allocation, extended to the entire sphere of co-operating factors. Novozhilov questioned the rationale of the underlying price structure. He perceived the interdependence of the economic system and the need for simultaneous determination of prices for all non-labour inputs as opportunity cost and scarcity, derived from the plan, taken as datum. Whereas Kantorovich was more concerned with techniques, Novozhilov emphasized the general theory of value and resource allocation in a socialist economy. And, in that respect, he was closer to Koopmans.

Novozhilov solved the problem by techniques akin to GE. His analytical approach differed from that school mainly in so far as he formulated the extremal problem as a minimization of current labour inputs for a predetermined output, rather than maximization of output utility from a given endowment of factors subject to constraints.

Kantorovich's chief achievement lies in originating the basic proposition of linear programming and applying those techniques to finding extremal solution in planning. He sees the aim of planning not as merely construction of a feasible plan, but as a selection of an optimal one from a number of conceivable ones. An optimal plan is one that maximizes (or minimizes), subject to constraints. The optimal plan must ensure that: (i) the planned employment of each production factor does not exceed its availability, (ii) the products are produced in required proportions, and (iii) specified assortments are produced in the largest possible quantities. From the optimal plan, Kantorovich derives valuations for all scarce factors of production and for the goods to whose production they constribute, forming a consistent system corresponding to and satisfying the conditions of the plan.

How can one ascertain that a plan is the optimal one? The very effective answer is by means of resolving multipliers associated with the plan. These were later evolved as 'objectively determined valuations' (odv) to integrate value and allocative aspects. They are scarcity measures, having essentially the same significance for the solution of the problem as opportunity cost, scarcity prices. They are imputed values of essentially Lagrangian multipliers, corresponding to an efficient programme constructed on the minimax theorem.

Kantorovich insists that the odv's for all scarce factors — labour, capital, land, and goods produced with their assistance — representing demand and supply equilibrium shadow prices are not chosen arbitrarily, as actual Soviet prices are, but are objective, concrete, and realistic, for they are entirely determined by the totality of plan conditions and vary only with them. The ratio of odv's is realistic for it mirrors the genuine marginal rate of transformation and this property is helpful for it clearly indicates the kind of alterations that can be made in the plan. The odv's should be used essentially not for deciding what but how to produce. Kantorovich envisages the odv's not only as informational devices summarizing factor scarcities derived from the plan, economic verifiers of technological alternatives, choice coefficients, but also as operational indexes for implementing the plan.

In the USSR Kantorovich's approach was accused of being static in nature and essentially unfit for a dynamic economy — a deficiency of which he was not unaware. In 1964 he stressed that the study of optimal planning requires special mathematical methods of linear, non-linear, and dynamic programming; and that in his previous work he concentrated on a static model, whereas the dynamic model is of primary importance. The critics grant that linear programming may be advantageous in its applications to some special problems, but they disclaim its general applicability to pricing and national economic planning. Those who are willing to grant general applicability in some remote future, propose initial application to planning of enterprises, regions, branches, and special problems, finally graduating to the macro level, culminating in the planning of the national economy. Opinions differ about the feasibility of constructing an optimal national economic plan and deriving prices from it in the near future.

In his Nobel address to the Federation of Swedish Industries, Kantorovich (Kantorovich and Koopmans, 1975, p. 33) voiced his own doubts:

> I want to say that I do not take the utilization of optimum model methods in the planning of the economy as a whole as hopeless. Not as hopeless, but I cannot take it as resolved either. There is much research in the Soviet Union concerning the problem. The main task of this research is to construct a system of models of many levels of hierarchy ... I think that this problem will be solved in the near future, but the estimates are not very refined for the moment.

The limiting assumptions of constant returns to scale circumscribe the application of linear programming essentially to those activities where, over the relevant range, the effects are independent of the scale of operations, but are in direct proportion to the means applied. The rising Soviet mathematical school is exerting its efforts beyond the pioneering groundbreaking toils of its initiators. Attempts are made at breaking with the restricting assumptions of linearity (similarly as in the West). Initial attempts are being made to formalize the objective function for the Soviet economy. Only time will tell whether the storming of the citadel attempted by the mathematical school will result in victory.

Since we started with Lange, perhaps it would be of some interest to note what he perceived to be the problem of efficient allocation of resources in a socialist economy nearly thirty years later. In fact, in his last published work before his untimely death in 1965 (1966, pp. 448–54), Lange states that should he attack the problem now his task would be much simpler: his answer would be to programme the system of simultaneous equations on a computer. The solution would be obtained in less than a second. To him the market process, with its sluggish method of trial and error, seems to be outdated and may be considered a calculatory device of the pre-electronic age. The market mechanism and the *à tâtonnements* method of his prewar essay actually perform the function of calculatory devices for the solution of the system of simultaneous equations. The solution is achieved through the iterative process, where a displacement is followed by a corrective movement restoring equilibrium (assuming convergence). The equilibrating process acts as a servo-mechanism.

Similarly, the process may be accomplished with the aid of a computer that imitates the iterative process of the market mechanism. But, Lange argues, this statement may be reversed: the market imitates the computer. The market may be conceived as a *sui generis* computer, solving a system of simultaneous equations, a servo-mechanism operating on the feedback principle. The market may be thought of as historically one of the oldest methods for solving simultaneous equations. Its specific feature is that this 'solution mechanism' acts as a social and not as a physical process. At present the central planner may choose between two tools of economic calculation: the computer and the market. The computer is undoubtedly faster, whereas the market is a cumbersome and slowly operating servo-mechanism. Its iterative processes are considerably delayed, oscillate, and finally may not converge (cobweb cycles). The computer is unquestionably superior for it performs with unusual rapidity, it does not provoke fluctuations, and the convergence of iterations is assured by its very construction. Another shortcoming of the market is that the iterative processes have income effects. Each price change has income-distribution effects that may cause social and political unrest. However, the market is not devoid of relative merits.

Even the most powerful computers have a limited capacity. There are such complex economic processes, in so far as the number of products and types of interdependencies that exist, that either no computer can cope with them, or the construction of one that could would be too costly. In such cases, Lange argues, there is no other alternative but to revert to the old-fashioned market mechanism. Furthermore, the market is an institutional arrangement that is already in place. It would be pointless to replace it by another calculatory device. The computer may be used for planning, but the plans must be verified by the market.

The essential limitations of the market are that the calculations are static by nature; there are no sufficient bases for solving the problems of growth and development planning. For example, current prices cannot be used for investment decisions. However, the theory and practice of linear and non-linear programming permit the adoption of rational economic calculation. Having determined the objective function and the state of constraints, it is possible to arrive at future shadow prices that could be used as choice coefficients for development planning. Computers are essential for long-term optimal planning. In this instance the computer is not a substitute for the market, for it performs functions that the market cannot discharge.

GAME THEORY

Economic problems often revolve around partly congruous and partly conflicting situations. Indeed, the issue of congruence often has a deep-rooted conflict situation because congruent pursuits can be achieved in many ways and with considerably divergent distribution of joint benefits. This in itself entails a bargaining problem. The market mechanism plays a co-ordinating role geared to the congruence exercise; it does not address the problem of conflict which is left at the mercy of relative powers, formalized in the notion of core in the theory of games (see Sen, 1983, pp. 4–5).

The theory of games (pursued so eloquently in Chapter 5 by Aumann and applied by Kurz and a number of others in this and the companion volume) has been called the mathematics of competition and co-operation (see Shapley, 1979). It is concerned with the behaviour of independent agents 'whose fortunes are linked in an interplay of collusion, conflict, and compromise'. It provides a mathematical approach for studying human interactions from the viewpoint of strategic potentialities of individuals and groups (Shubik, 1982, pp. 3 and 7).

First formulated in 1928, von Neumann's game theory only made a considerable and controversial impact on economics in the 1940s with the publication of *The Theory of Games and Economic Behavior* (in collaboration with Morgenstern). (For a brief summary, see Morgenstern, 1958, pp. 172–3.) Indeed, Morgenstern (1955, pp. 172–3) advanced very strong claims for the potentials of the theory in revolutionizing economics:

> Should game theory prevail, the break with conventional economics would go much deeper than the one that occurred in the 1870s with the arrival of the marginalistic schools. The latter were a fairly continuous development within the framework of the concepts that had originated in the eighteenth century. This is similar to the . . . situation produced in physics by quantum mechanics. The comparison should, of course, not be taken literally: it was von Neumann's firm conviction that the state of economic theory now is comparable to that of physics before Newton.

Since then, economists have intermittently questioned whether game theory has really and profoundly enriched our approach and mode of analysis; what the scope and significance of its application to economics has been and will be; and what, if anything, essentially new has been learned. Shubik (1982, pp. 368–85) provides a useful survey of impressive achievements, including the important application of game theory to the formulation of various models of oligopolistic markets (such as duopoly, non-co-operative and quasi-co-operative oligopoly, bilateral monopoly and bargaining, experimental gaming, and auctions and bidding); the contro- versial analysis of the GE models of the economy; and such other applic- tions to economics as public goods, externalities, welfare economics, money and financial institutions, and some macroeconomic problems.

Granted that game-theoretic investigations and application of game theory to economics fascinate some mathematically inclined economists, the question is 'what does the theory of games add beyond being a math- ematical tidying-up device that translates the insights of others into a more heavily symbolic language?' (Shubik, 1982, p. 372). A partial answer, Shubik (1982, p. 372) suggests, is that 'the discipline required for speci- fying in detail the strategic options of individual actors leads to the dis- covery of gaps in the logic of less formally defined models. Many models of competition are "quasidynamic" in description. They describe com- petition in terms that gloss over the details of process and information conditions'.

But Shubik, the maverick, warns in the same breath that 'no amount of mathematical rigor can make up for lack of economic insight and understanding in the creation of the model to be analyzed' (1982, p. 372). For instance, the development of an adequate theory of oligopolistic markets requires the skills of the institutionally inclined economist who would capture the operations and activities of economic institutions and select the strategic variables and relationships; one who would also be endowed with the approach and techniques of the model-builder in formu- lating the mathematical structure that portrays essential economic dimen- sions and would have the training of the analyst for deducing the properties of the mathematical construct.

Shubik (1982), then asks the pertinent question whether the develop- ment of usable theory depends more heavily on literary or verbal descrip- tion or on formal modelling. He offers the example of Chamberlin's investi- gation of oligopolistic markets which may be considered as a significant advance over the early architects of the theory of oligopoly, Cournot and Bertrand, when viewed from the standpoint of greater relevance and reality, but may have been a retrogression from the vantage point of a rigorous mathematical apparatus (see also Maskin and Tirole, 1982; J. Friedman, 1977; Roberts and Sonnenschein, 1977; and Kurz, 1983).

In a perceptive review of Shubik (1982), Kurz (1983) contrasts Shubik's claims against the expectations of the architects. Kurz contends that, however substantive, the contemporary achievements are exaggerated. For example, 'an economist's criticism of cooperative game theory would insist that very few of the ideas in this theory were developed from economic reality in an organic way' (Kurz, 1983, p. 571). But the non-co-operative solutions of games have gained wide acceptance among economists as a mode of analysis:

> However, we need to keep in mind the fact that the concept of 'Nash Equilibrium' simply formalizes equilibrium concepts that were used by economists since Cournot and Bertrand. It is true that in a Cournot–Nash equilibrium every player takes the *Strategy* of the others as given while in a general competitive equilibrium every agent takes the *prices* as given. However, the existence of both equilibria is proved utilizing the same mathematical tools and on a deeper level they are close concepts; recent research has concentrated on the question of how good an approximation to a competitive equilibrium is provided by a Cournot–Nash equilibrium. We conclude that contrary to early anticipations the theory of non-co-operative games has developed very much in tandem with the theory of General Competitive Equilibrium (Kurz, 1983 p. 571.

The more complicated question is the impact of game theory on imperfect competition whose progress, according to Kurz (1983, p. 572), has not been impressive:

> If one contrasts this lack of progress with the dramatic advancements in mathematical tools and in the conceptualization of conflict situations one must be puzzled. It is difficult to escape the conclusion that the problem must not be one of lacking mathematical tools or an 'ideological' opposition to game theory on the part of economists. Rather, one is inclined to believe that our failure to make progress on this front must reflect the fact that our formulation of the underlying economic model is not adequate. This lack of understanding of how oligopolistic markets really function leads us to work with a paradigm within which it is difficult to make significant progress.

SYSTEM DISIGN AND INCENTIVES

The theory of economic systems can be studied either from a positive or normative point of view. The former approach aims to provide a useful, even if partial, analytical construct for studying observed phenomena. The latter, on the other hand, aims to present models of mechanisms for study rather than for implementation purposes, yet with an underlying normative objective (see Hurwiza, 1972, 1977, pp. 425–6).

Mainstream economic theory tended to view the economic system as a given, whereas modern system designers (represented in Chapter 3 of this volume by one of their leading lights, Leonid Hurwicz) treat the economic system as an unknown (to make the problem meaningful some domain of variation for this unknown is defined) in the problem of finding a system that in some specific sense is superior to the existing one. The designer's point of view widens the field of vision of economics. Even when the new mechanisms are unusable in practice, their study sharpens the designers' grasp of the potentials, intricacies, and limits of their science and art (see Hurwicz, 1973, p. 27).

Our contemporary system designers descend, however, from an old and distinguished tradition of 'activists' redesigners and critics of social and economic systems; going at least as far back as Plato, through Utopians, Utopian Socialists, J. S. Mill, Pareto, Boehm-Bawerk, and von Wieser. More directly their roots are in the famous interwar debate on the feasibility and merit of a socialist economy. As mentioned Mises's famous challenge gave impetus to an interesting stream of thought on rational resource allocation under socialism. (Lange's pioneering system-design work was a strong influence on Hurwicz.) Concurrently, groundwork was also laid by Hotelling's contribution to the theory of marginal cost pricing and the 'new welfare economics' of Allais (1943), Barone (1908), Bergson (1938), Hicks (1939a), Hotelling (1938), Kaldor (1939), Lange (1938 and 1942), and Lerner (1944).[6] Another closely related stream of thought was the developments in, and refinement of, propositions and criteria of welfare economics (particularly of Pareto optimality or some social welfare functions) and the mathematization of 'classical' welfare economics in the 1940s and 1950s (see Arrow and Hahn, 1971; Debreu, 1959; Chipman, 1982). (For a comprehensive review of both streams in welfare economics, see Chapter 13 by Hammond in this volume.)

In the normative spirit, the modern system designers repudiate the essentially passive approach to the system. They search for means of intervening with the system that would draw it as near to optimality as possible, while attempting to eschew Utopianism by recognizing that intervention and its results are subject to constraints (Hurwicz, 1979a, p. 23). System designers build models that are not only oriented to aggregative or national economic systems, but are also highly relevant to modern large corporations or administrative agencies (especially the team theory model developed by Marschak, Radner, Groves and others). Their investigations are also closely related to information theory and issues in administrative organization. As Hurwicz (1973, p. 3) remarked, the contemporary system designers have achieved two categories of results: 'On the one hand, quite a few specific allocation mechanisms have been invented and their properties, such as feasibility, optimality, and convergence, rigorously established. On the other hand, there are also some more general results, dealing with the possibility or impossibility of various types of decentralized mechanisms, depending on the environments with which they must cope.'

Informational and incentive feasibility is a touchstone of a mechanism's study-worthiness. With regard to information the issue is the extent to which the mechanism permits dispersion of information and the extent to which the various units are capable of processing it (capacity limitations). With regard to incentives the issue is the extent to which the mechanism's rules are compatible with personal or group incentives. Assuming a mechanism is feasible, the question is whether it is efficient. Alternative mechanisms may be more or less costly (or expensive to operate) in terms of resources absorbed in the processing of information. Also, achievement of incentive-compatibility may be more or less resource-absorbing. Hence a computation of the 'net' welfare that a mechanism produces (with the environment as a given) has to take account of the costs of information processing and incentive-inducing activities (Hurwicz, 1972, p. 426).

Much valuable partial work is being done by the contemporary system designers. (Chapter 3 in this volume is a case in point.) As Hurwicz (1972, p. 431) points out, one of the issues is 'to see to what extent, with satisfactoriness as the welfare criterion, it is possible to overcome the limitations of the competitive process'. One of the limitations is:

> the lack of Pareto-satisfactoriness of the competitive process in non-classical environments. The question then arises as to whether one could design alternative informationally decentralized mechanisms that would be satisfactory even in non-classical environments . . . Briefly, it appears that it is possible to design such mechanisms for broad classes of environments including those characterized by indivisibilities and nonconvexities, provided externalities are absent. On the other hand, examples are given to show that there may fail to exist informationally decentralized mechanisms guaranteeing satisfactoriness in the presence of externalities (Hurwicz, 1972, pp. 431–2).[7]

The other limitations that Hurwicz refers to is the problem of incentive-compatibility. Incentive theory comes into play when the centre's objectives and those of the agents (periphery) do not coincide. In this sense incentive theory is distinct from team theory (where coincidence of objectives is postulated) though the two share many other features. In a similar vein incentive theory is distinct from social-choice theory, for the former postulates that the centre (a kind of surrogate for society) has a specific set of objectives, whereas the latter attempts to derive social objectives from individual preferences. Furthermore, this lack of coincidence of objectives is not sufficient. The centre's objective function must also be dependent on the agents' information and/or behaviour (see Laffont and Maskin, 1982).

With respect to incentive-compatibility, the system designers' problems are further complicated when they pose the following question: Assuming that a process that exhibits the suitable properties can be designed, could one suppose that the participants would adhere to the rules, given the possibilities of individual or colluded non-adherence? Results of research so far have shown that the difficulties are not so much the result of a lack of ingenuity, as of an obdurate conflict among such mechanism attributes as optimality of equilibria, incentive-compatibility of rules, and requirements of informational decentralization. At least one of these attributes has to be relaxed. Furthermore, there is need for an investigation of the interplay of authority, incentive, information, and performance issues (Hurwicz, 1973, pp. 23–6).

Owing to the complexity of the problem, thus far the attempts to design behaviour rules to which the agents would adhere (even without control), and which would result in optimal allocation of resources, have been limited to only very special, simple examples. 'Certain problems of system design can already be studied in the context of non-manipulative equilibria of the type that arise in "one-move" games' where 'optimality can be obtained. However, it turns out that there are severe limitations on the implementability of other objectives a social planner might have in mind' (Hurwicz, 1981, p. 94). For example, Hurwicz (1979b) has shown that if the requirement is that the welfare level of no participant be diminished and that the end result be optimal, only a very restricted class of performance functions (or correspondences) can be achieved. These results are important because 'not all seemingly reasonable social criteria can be implemented by a "one-move" Nash–non-co-operative-game mechanism. In particular, one cannot, in general, reconcile the following three criteria: Pareto optimality, fairness (in the sense of being envy-free), and individual rationality' (Hurwicz, 1979c, pp. 212–13). The 'one-move' game framework is also unsatisfactory because decision situations repeat themselves and the actors' future behaviour is bound to be influenced by their past experiences. Moreover, the actors will only approach the correct move by the *à tâtonnement* method which implies many repetitions (see Hurwicz, 1979c, pp. 213–15).

In the final analysis, while much significant progress has been made, 'the proper integration of the information and incentive aspects of resource allocation models is perhaps the major unsolved problem in the theory of mechanism deisgn' (Hurwicz, 1973, p. 27).

TEAM THEORY AND INFORMATION

The theory of teams was put forth by Marschak (1955) in order to explicitly introduce information costs into the allocation process.[8] The thrust of the theory centres on 'economic, that is, optimal, efficient ways of providing information and of allocating it among the decision-makers who constitute a team: optimal, that is, with respect to common interests and beliefs' (Marschak and Radner, 1972, p. ix).[9] Team theory is a simplification of game theory in the sense that it abstracts from variety and conflict of interests.[10] In Marschak's and Radner's (1972, p. 4) perception:

> In the theory of games . . . two or more persons follow generally different desirability criteria ('interests', 'preferences'), and are constrained by different feasibility conditions ('rules of the game') or at least attach to them different probabilities; but each player is efficient in a well-defined sense. The problem is to find which arrangements exist (if any) that would be supported by each player's self-interest as he sees it, because no change that he might be able to enforce would better him. Such arrangements, if attained, would be maintained. They are called viable. In this sense, viability can be regarded as a generalization of the optimality requirement, extended from decision-making by a single person to the case of several persons. Corresponding to the choice of the best information it provides, the viable arrangement between players of a game is implemented by allocating to each certain activities, possibly including the tasks of gathering or communicating specified kinds of information. Viewed in this way, the problem of viable arrangements in games can be conveniently called a theory of efficient organizations. The problem of the optimal information instrument and the optimal decision for a single person can then be regarded as a special (though by no means trivial) case.

Traditionally, discussions of alternative mechanisms of resource allocation (whether economy-wide or within a large organization) tended to equivocate about the relative facility of the process of transmission of information. Whereas the desirability of decentralization presupposes that the transmission process is costly (were it not, all information about availability of resources and production technology could be transferred to one locus where the optimum allocation of resources could be instantly computed), the literature on the subject has been seeking algorithms that would reduce the amount of information to be transmitted but that would result in the fully optimal allocation of resources. If there were any real trade-off between information costs and other resource costs, an optimal allocation of resources that reckons with information costs would differ from one that does not. The traditional position can be reasoned only on the assumption that information costs are very small but not nil. Thus they should be reduced as much as possible without bearing upon the overall allocation (Arrow 1982b, pp. 1–2).

Team theory is a synthesis of statistical decision theory, the economics of decision-making under uncertainty, and the theory of organization. Broadly, it represents a novel and refined interpretation of the economic co-ordination problem (Arrow, 1981, p. 337; and 1979, p. 505). More specifically, it assumes a constant amount of communication in constant channels, while the costs of communication are modelled by scarcity. It puts to greater use previous information about the economy than does the standard approach.

Team theory presupposes that some or all the fundamental parameters of resources or technology are unknown. But probable values of the parameters can be estimated on the basis of previous information. Hence decentralized decisions can profit from this knowledge and counteract as much as possible erroneous decisions. Morever, team theory envisages that various members of the team possess irreducible differences in information, and this also distinguishes it from the standard approach. In the latter, the individual members are only information sources, while the decisions are all ultimately made at the centre. *Par contre*, in team theory there is genuine decentralization for the allocations ultimately result from a multiplicity of individual decisions. In this sense, team theory is also closer to reality (see Arrow, 1982b, pp. 2–3).

A team is an organization composed of a number of members or agents. Initially each agent has some specific, if restricted, information that other agents do not have. The entire organization's (or economy's) information may well be restricted. All agents are decision-makers and choose various actions on the basis of their different information: The end result for the organization (or economy) as a whole depends on the decisions made and on some facts about the world. A central point of team theory is that it abstracts from the possibility of a variety of (possibly conflicting) interests of agents and assumes that all of them have the same preferences. Marschak and Radner (1972, p. ix) conceive of this as an 'intermediate case . . . useful as a step toward a fuller and more complex economic theory of organization'. The problem then is to choose an optimal set of decision rules that would prescribe for each agent what decisions he is to make on the basis of the information at his disposal.

As Radner (1972, p. 189) put it, 'in the theory of teams, as in statistical decision problems in general, two basic questions are: (a) for a given structure of information, what is the optimal decision function? (b) what are the relative values of alternative structures of information?' These problems can also be cast in the guise of questions facing an organizer: 'How should the tasks of inquiring, communicating, and deciding be allocated among the members of an organization so as to achieve results that would be best from the point of view of their common interests and beliefs, or of those of the organizer?' (Marschak and Radner, 1972, p. ix). This framework throws into sharper focus the essence of the concept of informational decentralization. Radner (1972, p. 188), for example, speaks of 'decentralization as a special case of division of labor, where the 'labor in question is that of making decisions. The organizer can regard the members of the organization as "machines", receiving messages as inputs, and producing messages and actions as outputs, according to predictable (although possibly stochastic) modes of behavior'. He then points out that:

> an organization is *information-decentralized* to the extent that different members have different information, and *authority decentralized* to the extent that individual members are expected (by the organizer) to choose strategies and/or modify the rules of the game. With these concepts of decentralization, all but the simplest organizations are decentralized to some extent in both senses. This serves to emphasize that the crucial question usually is not 'how much decentralization', but rather 'how to decentralize!'

The system is amplified by communication (i.e. agents transmit their specific information to one another). The essence of this approach is that transmission of information is scarce and costly. Thus the rules must be so formulated as to prescribe the cost of or the restrictions on the amount of communication (see Marschak and Radner, 1972, pp. 267–324). This has resulted in a number of auxiliary studies, the foremost of which is the search for a better understanding of the economics of information.[11]

Simon (1982b, p. 454) suggests that though team theory recognizes the bounds of human rationality, it aims to encompass bounded rationality by rational calculus. While the theory is concerned with the possible improvement of a team's decisions through exchange of information among agents, it also attempts to compute the content, conditions, and costs of exchanges. Not only the total amount of information, but the content of communications is relevent. The agents' bounds on rationality are external to the problem and are encompassed by the costs of communication; thus, they, together with costs and benefits of outcomes, are included in the economic calculus.

THE CHICAGO SCHOOL

What has come to be identified in the postwar period as the Chicago school makes very strong assumptions about the market mechanism: about its workability, adaptability, speed, and power of adjustment. In broad contours it stresses that the competitive market economy excels in allocative and productive efficiency, that it is an inherently stable, self-equilibrating mechanism capable of eliminating excess supply or demand, and that it is a source of economic freedom and a means of achieving political freedom. Characteristically, the Chicago school tends to minimize 'market imperfections'. and the dynamics and costs of 'transitional' processes.

The Chicago position — or what Reder (1982) calls tight prior equilibrium — is a strong version of the neoclassical model and features the following criteria: competitive markets clear, decision-makers optimize, and there is no money illusion. [12] There is a particularly tenuous relationship between this position and GE. According to Hahn (1980, p. 126), Chicago-type economists 'have taken the theory in practical applications a good deal more seriously than at present there is any justification for doing. Paradoxically they are rather hostile to its abstract foundations, yet are happy to put a great deal of weight on them'.

The tensions between the model that the Chicago school uses and the quandaries thrown up by the real world tend to be resolved by minimizing the importance of the latter. Thus the 'good approximation assumption' is an essential feature of the Chicago school. Essentially, it means that as there is no other sufficiently strong refuting evidence (and presumably, for example, observed price and wage stickiness is not such evidence), current prices and quantities can be viewed as close to what they would be in the long-run competitive equilibrium. Hence it is possible to discount such market imperfections as monopolies on the grounds that they seldom appear and that they have only a limited impact on resource misallocation and underutilization.[13] This goes hand in hand with the view that market failures of all sorts (or the economic actor's inability to achieve the optimum) are the exceptions, rather than the rule. They should be investigated separately and in no way imply a rethinking of the competitive model (see Stigler, 1974). It follows that the Chicago school has strong and irreconcilable aversions to all sorts of institutional explanations of economic phenomena and to any kind of satisficing or behaviouralist theory (see Reder, 1982, pp. 12, 14–17).[14]

As the long-time observer of Chicago (both as student and as outside and inside faculty member), Melvin Reder (1982, p. 13) attests, 'Chicago economists tend strongly to appraise their own research and that of others by a standard which requires (*inter alia*) that the findings of empirical research be consistent with the implication of standard price theory.' If there is inconsistency between theory and the empirical findings, the investigator can resort to (i) verification of data, (ii) redefinition of variables, (iii) alterations of the theoretical assumptions to take into account divergent behaviour, and (iv) conclusion that the finding is an anomaly. Reder (1982, p. 13) observed that the Chicago economist tends to zero in on (i) and (ii) and if the anomaly persists, he moves on to (iv), but avoids (iii). Moreover, 'resistance to paradigm-distrubing evidence is paralleled by reluctance to accept disruptive theoretical innovations. A theoretical innovator must squeeze between the rock: 'if an innovation is consistent with what is known, it serves no useful purpose' and the hard place: "if inconsistent with what was previously believed, it must be wrong"' (Reder, 1982, p. 21).

An interesting development of the Chicago school is its unabashed attempt to invade other social or 'soft' sciences – what has come to be called economic imperialism. Perhaps the most striking examples are Stigler (19745) on political behaviour, Posner (1973) on the legal system, and Becker (1976 and 1981) on a wide spectrum of sociological and psychological phenomena.[15]

Becker (1976, p. 5) boldly states that he considers the economic approach as sufficiently general to embrace all human behaviour. To him the 'heart of the economic approach' consists of the 'combined assumptions of maximizing behavior, market equilibrium and stable preferences, used relentlessly and unflinchingly.'[16] Of particular interest is his eschewing of the problems of differences in tastes among people and over time. This permits him to bypass the need to deal with the entire psychological make-up of human beings, emptying their actions of emotional content and of the myriad of differences that go into their make-up.[17] He continues along these lines in his later work (1981, p. ix) where he 'uses the assumptions of maximizing behavior, stable preferences, and equilibrium in implicit or explicit markets to provide a systematic analysis of the family'. And he (1981, p. 3) sets himself a very broad task: 'to present a comprehensive analysis that is applicable, at least in part, in the past as well as the present, in primitive as well as modern societies, and in Eastern as well as Western cultures'.

In a nutshell, Becker (1981)[18] assumes that in entering the marriage institution individuals maximize their utility and joint income (defined to include extra market activities). Each individual is further assumed to have a *known* fixed shadow price. The contributions of each partner can supposedly be detected to some extent. All this allegedly allows individuals to reconnoitre the marriage market and compute their 'potential incomes' with various partners. Becker describes altruism as the dependence of one individual's utility on another's, and the family's utility as reflecting the altruists' preferences which all members of the family (whether they be selfish or altruistic) are interested in maximizing. He treats fertility decisions in the context of a general comsumption model, stressing the quantity versus quality of children trade-offs. All this assumes perfect information. Becker relaxes this assumption in treating divorce. He (1981, p.218) admits that 'participants in marriage markets hardly know their own interests and capabilities, let alone the dependability, sexual compatibility, and other traits of potential spouses'. Thus he contends that divorce is caused by information gaps before marriage and their accelerated filling after marriage, resulting in a relatively higher share of divorces in the first few years of marriage.

In conclusion, Becker (who faithfully disregards institutional mechanisms) claims that the economic approach he uses provides sufficient explanations of the large-scale institutional changes that we have witnessed in the evolution of the family. In his (1981, p. 256) words:

> The economic approach provides a powerful framework for analyzing both the dramatic changes in the family during the last half-century and the much slower, yet even larger changes extending over hundreds of years during the evolution from traditional to modern societies. Although the economic approach does not encompass all facets of human behavior, it does appear to focus attention on those aspects primarily responsible for changing the family over time.

CRITIQUES OF GENERAL EQUILIBRIUM

In their assault on mainstream economic theory, the critics raise many interesting questions, even though some of the accusations are based on misunderstandings. In many instances GE is criticized for the sins of the textbook writers who fail to give adequate weight to its limitations or to incorporate the findings of GE theorists working on the frontiers of the subject. The critics often fail to distinguish among the current streams of neoclassical theory and wrongly cast a plague on all their houses.

There are at least three principal weaknesses of GE that are not clearly spelled out either by the textbook writers or the instructors:

(1) The very restricted definition of individually owned goods – an assumption whose generality or lack of it is precisely stated by the original theorists, but which becomes watered down in the transmission belt.

(2) The existence of markets – a concept that is often taught by switching assumptions midstream. GE is frequently taught by making it independent of the number of consumers or producers, starting out with two traders and then switching to *n* traders. In this process of switching many assumptions about communication, information, trade, etc. are made and not spelled out.

(3) A closely related assumption is that all traders act as price-takers and are bereft of economic power (see Shubik, 1970, pp. 426–7):

> General equilibrium economics is undoubtedly a splendid intellectual achievement. But it is not by any means on the level of Newtonian mechanics. In a world with large complicated corporations, selling thousands of goods and services (and often selling whole systems), the way we stick to our simple models (which at best cover one simple limiting case) is ludicrous. I am reminded of the story of the drunk who had lost his keys at night and spent his time searching for them under a streetlamp fifty yards from where he had lost them because that was the only place where he could see anything (Shubik, 1970, p. 415).

To stress the practical significance of theorizing is not always a reputable task in economics. Many economists treat sophisticated model-building as an end in itself. The challenge of irrelevance, incongruity, esoteric nature, and ephemeral substance of certain theories in explaining and improving economic processes is of long standing. Some critics tend to stress the logical flaws in the 'accepted' body of knowledge, with or without laying foundations for new theory in its stead, while others tend to focus attention on the essential discordance between theory and reality. Not only is the logic of the arguments advanced of considerable importance, but also the source from which they emanate. This is not only because the ideological (or prejudicial) components are weighty (as we shall see in the postcript to this chapter), but the applicability of the apparatus to new situations brings into focus novel features.

In a treatise under the telling title *Anti-equilibrium*,[19] Janos Kornai (1971) impugned GE and its postulates:[20]

(1) GE is of static or stationary character.

(2) The set of organizations remains constant over time.

(3) The world of Walras is a strictly single-level economic system, which consists exclusively of two types of actors: producers and consumers. There is no other component (e.g. government) that affects the outcome and there is no room for macroeconomic planning. All organizations have equal status, with no vertical subordination. Internal conflicts are ignored and only the final compromise is described. This approach makes the study of multi-level control phenomenon impossible.

(4) The system produces a finite number of products; their number and set is constant over time.

(5) The activities of firms can be described by a vector where the positive components give the inputs and the negative components the outputs. *Ex ante* and *ex post* production and sales are equal (no inventories). On the factor side, *ex ante* employment equals *ex post*; and buying plans are fully implemented. Household activities can be described by a vector of identical dimensions where the positive component is consumption. Supply is identified with production. Time lags or qualitative differences between *ex ante* and *ex post* buying and selling, and production and consumption, are ignored. Selling intentions mature gradually and original aspriations are revised as new informaton is acquired.

(6) The set of feasible production is convex and constant over time (absence of indivisible inputs and outputs; the input—output relationships can be described by continuous and differentiable functions; there are no increasing returns to scale).

(7) The firms maximize profit.

(8) Consumers maximize utility. The set of preference ordering of organizations is constant over time. But many fundamental economic decisions are of a non-repetitive nature, owing to shifts in the exogenous factors affecting choice, change in the relative position of the decision-maker, etc. Technical progress affects not only the shifts of the set of technically possible and implementable alternatives over time, but also preference ordering.

(9) Concentration is on the operation of the market and on behaviour governed by prices. No direct or indirect flows of information other than of the price-type exists among the units of economy and prices are the signals by which information about scarcities is transmitted at no cost to the agents. But prices do not provide sufficient information for effective decision-making. Behaviour is in part governed by non-price variables such

as quantity signals, movements of inventories, input limits, output tasks, etc. Observation of changes in inventories play an important role as signals for decisions about production, procurement, and employment. Furthermore, GE tends to exaggerate the importance of price (income) effects in the explanation of consumers' demand. There are also other important explantory variables such as imitation, fashion, keeping up with the Joneses, new products, etc. One cannot tell a *a priori* how strong the price changes must be in order to elicit appropriate response and time lags tend to be protracted.

(10) Market relations are anonymous. Each economic actor has no consequential market power. In fact, information flows are not anonymous; there is specification of senders and recipients and contractual parties display distinct preferences about their patterns and do exercise their market power.

(11) There is no uncertainty. Each economic actor knows his own set of possibilities and his preference ordering over it.

(12) 'The GE school gives the impression that the rules of the behavior of microeconomics are completely independent of the state of the macroeconomic situation' (Kornai, 1971, p. 331).

Kornai recognizes that some of the assumptions of GE were weakened in later elaborations and recent refinements (e.g. the theory of contingent markets). The major difference between him and GE is not on the interpretation of the equilibrium concept. By choosing their subject of investigation economists reveal their normative views. It is at least implied that GE views equilibrium as desirable. Kornai (1971, p. 309) 'is profoundly opposed to the viewpoint that equilibrium is good'.

In a thoughtful reply to Kornai, Koopmans (1974, p. 325) agrees with him that the GE model ignores numerous aspects of reality, emphasizing in particular the crucial aspects of the control system in all types of economies, the role of information about quantities, and the importance of increasing returns to scale. He points out, however, that he differs from Kornai on the agenda for research. 'Kornai's "revolutionary" proposals is now to start afresh with entirely new approaches embodying other aspects of reality, which he enumerates with care and perception. The "reformist" alternative, which Kornai rejects, is to amend and extend the given special case by grafting other important aspects on to it. I think *both* should be attempted' (Koopmans, 1974, p. 325).

A similar theme is picked up by Hahn (1973b). He grants that, unlike many other critics of GE, Kornai is knowledgeable and technically competent, but, according to Hahn, he is only partially successful and on many important issues beside the point. Hahn perceives Kornai as viewing the economic system as an engineer, through cybernetics and systems theory. Accordingly Hahn sees Kornai as attempting a minimally realistic description of organizations and the flows among them; pointing to the organization as a complicated system of authority relations reflected in the decision process; and, in an approach reminiscent of Simon, stressing the meaninglessness of optimization. Kornai underlines the sequential movement through time of development, information, and decision-making, without the organizations ever achieving 'that state of tranquility which we call an equilibrium in GE' (Hahn, 1973b, p. 326). Hahn (1973b, p. 327) agrees with Kornai that 'GE is strong on equilibrium and very weak on how it comes about. It is a fair generalization to say that the theory has proved so far less helpful in studying processes whether of decisions or of information or of organization.' But he (1973b, p. 329) castigates Kornai for writing as if GE had ever entertained the 'lunatic claim' that it is a true and complete theory of a decentralized economy, with nothing else to be learned since all relevant events have been explained. Hahn (1973b, pp. 328–9) is definitely not persuaded by Kornai's call for an 'anti-GE synthesis'. He contends that the relevant gaps can be filled — an ongoing process.

One should also point out that Kornai's critique of GE is somewhat handicapped by his lack of attention to the literature on the subject that has a long tradition; nor does he take notice of the recent writings of the representatives of the Cambridge school.

From a different vantage point, Kaldor (1972, p. 1237) challenged GE on the grounds that it 'is barren and irrelevant as an apparatus of thought to deal with the manner of operation of economic forces, or as an instrument for non-trivial predictions concerning the effects of economic change'. Furthermore, 'the powerful attraction of the habits of thought engendered by "equilibrium economics" has become a major obstacle to the development of economics as a *science*', that is, 'a body of theorems based on assumptions that are *empirically* derived (from observations) and which embody hypotheses that are capable of verification both in regard to the assumptions and the predictions'. In even stronger terms than Kornai, Kaldor (1972, p. 1240) calls for 'a major act of demolition' for 'without destroying the basic conceptual framework . . . it is impossible to make any real progress'.

Kaldor's (1975, p. 347) objections are not directed at the abstraction of GE, but rather at its very essence; that is, that 'it gives a misleading impression of the nature and the manner of operation of economic forces'. Essentially he sees economic theory taking a wrong turn when the focus shifted to the theory of value and thus to resource allocation by the market, to the detriment of the creative functions of the market (i.e. as a mechanism for transmitting impulses to economic change) — not unlike Nelson and Winter (1982) more about whom later. Thus he argues that the spotlight fell on subsidiary rather than major aspects of the forces in operation. In this vein, Kaldor claims, the law of variable proportions is erroneously singled out as a basis for explaining both the price and production systems, implying that in the real world elasticities of substitution are significant, and ignoring essential complementarities between inputs and activities. It is the focus on substitution that 'makes "pure" equilibrium theory so lifeless and motionless: it purports to "explain" a system of market-clearing prices that are the resultant of various interactions: it cannot therefore deal with the problem of prices as signals or incentives to change' (Kaldor, 1975, p. 348).

Kaldor (1972, p. 1241) traces the major source of error to the middle of the fourth chapter of *The Wealth of Nations* where Smith focuses on the distinction between money and real prices and exchange values and gets embroiled in the question of how relative prices are determined. From then on, 'one can trace a more or less continuous development of price theory from the subsequent chapters of Smith through Ricardo, Walras, Marshall, right up to Debreu and the most sophisticated present-day Americans'.

In Smith and Ricardo the basic assumption of this theory (i.e. constant costs, or constant returns to scale) was implied in the notion of the natural price. In the rigorous formulations of modern neoclassical theory, Kaldor (1972, pp. 1241–2) claims 'it was explicit in the assumption of homogeneous and linear production functions which is one of the required "axioms" necessary to make the assumptions of perfect competition and profit-maximisation consistent with one another'. He goes on to say that 'the general equilibrium school (as distinct from Marshall) has always fully recognised the *absence* of increasing returns as one of the basic "axioms" of the system. As a result, the existence of increasing returns and its consequences for the whole framework of economic theory have been completely neglected.'

In answer to Kaldor's challenge, Koopmans (1974, pp. 325–6) suggests that the important problem of increasing returns to scale 'can be met at least half-way, by introducing further assumptions that bear on the way time and space enter into the problem'. He then goes on to say that he expects 'that an efficient stringing together of a sequence of such processes are now the more challenging objects of research' and enumerates the reasons for this expectation.

Kaldor's gauntlet was picked up be Hahn (1973a, p. 8) in his Inaugural

Lecture at Cambridge:

> Professor Kaldor's theory of what it is that Debreu's book ... might be about is thus incorrect, as a perusal of its ninety-odd pages will quickly show. I do not here refer to his remarkable belief ... that Debreu or for that matter any of the general equilibrium theorists postulate 'linear homogeneous and continuously differentiable production functions', nor to the even more surprising claim that the inventors of the beautiful theory of contingent markets postulate 'perfect foresight'. Nor again do I want to blame him for not reading the large literature on the 'removal of scaffolding', not even for not knowing that Arrow ... has provided a rigorous general equilibrium model with increasing returns and imperfect competition. What I want to note here is the incorrectness of the claim that Debreu was looking for the 'minimum basic assumptions for establishing the existence of an equilibrium set of prices which is (a) unique (b) stable'. Debreu did not concern himself with either (a) or (b). Here is one of those perennial misunderstandings.

While Hahn (1973a, pp. 12–14) agrees with Kaldor that increasing returns pose a significant problem for the GE notion, he (1973a, p. 31) cannot see how Kaldor can for this reason dismiss the entire notion as irrelevant or sterile:

> It is simply a muddle to go from the difficulties increasing returns pose to perfect competitive decentralisation to the view that allocation does not matter. Indeed the truth is orthogonal to this view. For the more important increasing returns are, especially the dynamic variety, the greater the potential losses from misallocation.

And defender turned critic Hahn (1973a, p. 32) points out:

> that not only do Professor Kaldor's critical thrusts go astray, but they are also far too mild. For at no stage does he notice that important increasing returns, not only in production but also in information in the widest sense, will in due course have profound consequences for the institutional arrangements of an economy. Indeed one answer is that it is precisely the difficulty of efficient decentralised acts, if you like the growing realisation of their potential wastefulness and irrationality, which will generate just these forces which may bring the whole system down. In addition of course there are the classical Marxian forces of increased concentration and formation of coalitions. It is at this point ... when a large historical vision is at issue, that equilibrium economics, whether my kind or Professor Kaldor's, is inadequate to the task.

The modern world is characterized by pervasive market power of all kinds which is in striking variance with the GE concept of decentralized competitive economy and poses serious conceptual problems for theoretical analysis.[21] Countless economists have criticized mainstream neoclassical economics for neither perceiving nor treating economic power as a central issue of the contemporary world, but perhaps none of them in the inimitable prose of John Kenneth Galbraith. Excerpts of his Presidential Address to the American Economic Association (1973a, pp. 2–3) may well be worth reproducing:

> The most commonplace features of neoclassical . . . economics are the assumptions by which power, and therewith political content, is removed from the subject . . . If the business firm is subordinate to the market – if that is its master – then it does not have power to deploy in the economy save as this is in the service of the market and the consumer. And the winning of action to influence or rig the behavior of markets apart, it cannot bring power to bear on the state for there the citizen is in charge.
>
> The decisive weakness in neoclassical . . . economics is . . . in eliding power – in making economics a nonpolitical subject – neoclassical theory, by the same process, destroys its relation with the real world . . .
>
> It is now the considered sense of the community, even of economists when unhampered by professional doctrine, that the most prominent areas of market oligopoly . . . are areas not of low but of high development, not of inadequate but of excessive resource use . . .
>
> In further contradiction of the established microeconomic conclusions, we have an increasing reaction by the community to deficient resource use in industries that, at least in the scale and structure of the firm, approach the market model. Housing, health services, and local transportation are among the leading cases . . .
>
> In fact the neoclassical model has no explanation of the most important microeconomic problem of our time. The problem is why we have a highly unequal development as between industries of great market power and industries of slight market power, with the development, in defiance of all doctrine, greatly favoring the first.

Kaldor's and others' well-taken point about the dominance of significant economies of scale places 'the whole theory . . . at risk'. 'This risk is not only due' to the fact that this is associated with large firms that are not price-takers (monopoly power) – which GE excludes by assuming the parametric function of prices – but also to 'the fact that, even if firms continued to act as price-takers, there may exist no equilibrium prices' (Hahn, 1982a, p. 5).

In the presence of market power the problems of mutual interdependence (reaction and counter-reaction) engage the economic actors in a game where they have to choose strategies. Here as we have seen, the theory of games developed by von Neumann and Morgenstern has been applied with some success. The game-theoretic approach meets, however, with mixed reception from economists. GE has serious difficulties in coping

> with economies in which agents have market power. If such an economy attains some coherent state to be called equilibrium all market information will not be summarised by prices. The signals to which agents respond will be much richer and the kind of things they would like to know, in order to arrive at decisions, much more varied. One can, however, assert that the outcome will, in general, not be Pareto-efficient (Hahn, 1982a, p. 6).

The vexed question of how equilibrium prices come to be established has not been satisfactorily resolved: 'the proposition that, in certain circumstances, there is a set of prices which ensures equality between demand and supply in all markets tells us nothing of whether these prices will indeed be established by a market economy. On this central question neither economic theory nor evidence is at all satisfactory' (Hahn, 1982a, p. 13; see Radner, 1982, p. 924). Indeed, the entire question of stability is subject to cyclical appeal and fashion (see Fisher, 1976; Arrow and Hurwicz, 1977, p. 199).[22] The issue and the state of our knowledge have been clearly analysed by Hahn (1982b). He (p. 747) concludes that:

> a great deal of skilled and sophisticated work has gone into the study of processes by which an economy could attain an equilibrium. Some of the (mainly) technical work will surely remain valuable in the future. But the whole subject has a distressing ad hoc aspect. There is at present no satisfactory axiomatic foundation on which to build a theory of learning, of adjusting to errors and of delay times in each of these. It may be that in some intrinsic sense such a theory is impossible. But without it this branch of the subject can aspire to no more than the study of a series of suggestive examples.

Following Joan Robinson's (1977, p. 1321) charge that neoclassical micro theory emphasizes exchange and neglects production, accumulation, and growth, Walsh and Gram (1980) sharply contrast classical and neoclassical themes where the former is concerned with production, extraction, accumulation and distribution of the surplus, and the latter with the allocation of given resources among alternative uses. Hahn (1975, p. 361) retorts that neoclassical theory is relevant to understanding growth, in particular to understanding the investment – consumption choice. He contends that those who, like Kornai, conceive of equilibrium as stationary or even quasi-stationary are in error: 'Neoclassical theory has understood the formal identity between intertemporal and a-temporal allocation. It is open to the objection that its inter-temporal treatment is too abstract and unrealistic. But that has nothing to do with its chosen emphasis.'[23]

Many of the critics of GE (like Joan Robinson, Kaldor, and others) search for a theory that affords an explanation of the Ricaridan question of income distribution among social classes (more about this point in the companion volume). GE does not lend itself to a formulation of a theory of distribution where class conflict and economic power are crucial variables. Hahn (1980, p. 128) asks the more subtle question whether GE directly conflicts with such a distribution theory or whether it can be of some use. Such distribution theory cannot, after all, ignore the fundamental notion of self-interest of economic actors.

That GE is vastly incomplete is not a controversial issue. What is debatable is whether in future economics will develop through recasting and refinements of the received apparatus or through a revolutionary change of paradigm. The question posed by Hahn (1980, pp. 128–9) is whether there are credible alternative theories that explain the particular questions with which GE is concerned. That these questions may be too narrow and that their range should be extended is also not disputable, as attested by the ongoing extensions of the analysis. However, as Arrow himself recognizes (in Chapter 2 in this volume) there are many questions that should be asked but cannot be answered within the GE framework.

Nevertheless Hahn (1975, p. 360) claims that there are no credible alternative theories.[24] In particular, he contends that the neo-Ricardians, Joan Robinson, Kaldor, and their followers 'address themselves to the wrong issues' and use 'wrong arguments'. Hahn, (1975, p. 362; and 1980, p. 129) denies that the Sraffa revival (elucidated in Chapter 4 by Joan Robinson in the companion volume) either challenges or presents an alternative to GE for the Sraffian analysis contains no 'logically coherent propositions' that are also not contained in GE. The Sraffian analysis also formally abstracts from power and conflict and historical time, though its proponents often stress these factors. Harcourt (1975, p. 369) retorts that as Sraffa's subtitle indicates, his book is not 'the whole or even the major part of the whole foundation for an alternative approach'.

After almost conquering mainstream theory and accomplishing many feats, the 'mature' GE is in a state of disarray. Even its protagonists admit that the results are far less illuminating than the aspirations. Even the questions posed are too restrictive and often lack relevance to the real world. One of the problems is that the modern economies are far more centralized than the model envisages. Furthermore, the model neglects economic power, historical setting, institutional specificities, and social class as an explanatory variable. 'This lack of contact between the economic theory and sociological reality may well be the most damaging criticism of the neo-classical construction' (Hahn, 1972, p. 2).

Partly as a result of 'self-criticism', GE theorists have attempted to fill the gaps and to refine the theory. For, as Samuelson (1977, p. 858) has noted, 'the most useful criticism of a subject must often bore from within'. Instead of heeding the 'outside' critics who propose novel approaches that pursue other aspects of reality, the GE theorists have chosen a reformist path. Hahn (1973b. p. 329; 1973a, pp. 16 and 40) — a worthy critic from within — contends that the reformist approach will probably be productive. Considerable research is being conducted on extending GE, *inter alia*, to conceptually serious problems of sequence economies (to take account of real time, uncertainty, and market expectations), stochastic equilibria, equilibria relative to information structures, and transactions and transaction costs.[25] On the whole, Hahn (1980, p. 137) is optimistic, for:

> while we are still in the tunnel there are also chinks of light. If we successfully reach the end, I believe it will be found that the route has been straighter and cleaner than it would have been had we not started from General Equilibrium Theory. The theory itself, however, is likely to recede and be superseded. There seems absolutely no reason to believe that the new theory will have been anticipated by some defunct 19th century economist or that it will be in the form of linear identities.

On the other hand, Morishima (n.d., p. 7) has a gloomier outlook. He strongly criticizes what he calls the 'highly sophisticated mock-ups' that the improvers on GE have produced. He attributes 'the continuous frustration which has beset the development of economic theory over the last thirty years or more' to 'the failure of economic theorists to carry out sweeping, systematic research into the actual mechanisms of the economy and economic organisations, despite being aware that their own models are inappropriate to analysis of the actual economy'. Most damaging is the fact that 'the institutional foundation of these so-called high brow economic theories is an extremely shaky one' (Morishima, n.d., p. 8). GE is still 'remarkably backward in examining how a system works under given institutions'. Thus there is a proliferation of 'new models and new theories based on ideas which assume crude institutional arrangements conceived from highly superficial observations' (Morishima, n.d., pp. 13–14). Morishima (p. 16) is in favour of a 'pursuit of mathematization in accordance with fact', for which purpose he claims 'we must know a great deal more about such things as history, sociology, and institutions'.

One of the perennial issues and sources of tension has been whether and to what extent our theories are shaped by ideology – a subject treated at greater length in the postscript to this chapter and pointed to by Joan Robinson in Chapter 4 in the companion volume. Among others, Dobb (1975, p. 357; see 1973, ch. 1) has posed the question of:

> the extent to which the shaping of any theoretical model, or set of abstract propositions, in a subject such as economics is inevitably influenced . . . by what may be termed a larger conceptual framework of ideas about the nature of existing society and its history . . . that is current at any given time or place; this in turn being largely dependent on an individual's or school's "place in history" or place in society.

Hahn (1975, p. 364) calls it a 'non-issue'. He (1973a, p. 4) points to many misunderstandings, even such basic ones as the claims that GE theorists believe that a competitive equilibrium gives the unique social optimum – an obvious misinterpretation of one of the most important clarifications of contemporary GE.

As Samuelson (1966, p. 1592) so aptly put it, 'despite Mussolini's decorating of Pareto, the old canard that "a reactionary is a man who believes in equilibrium" is not sustained by the history of mathematical economists'. At this point of time, the fraternity of mathematical economists is, indeed, a mixed bag. But its most illustrious members certainly include some of the most enlightened liberals in the modern American sense.[26]

INSTITUTIONALISM

The genealogy of a number of motley dissenters on the contemporary scene can be traced to institutionalism – a characteristically US movement that flourished at the close of the nineteenth and during the first three decades of the twentieth centuries. This movement itself consisted of a miscellany of rebels of which the most distinguished were Veblen, Commons, and Mitchell. What united them was their common antipathy to and criticism of pure theory (especially the theory of comparative statics, the utility analysis of consumer behaviour, and the marginal productivity theory of distribution). It was a reaction against the abstract deductive reasoning in economics. Their dissent from the mainstream was not of uniform strength and they lacked a clearly defined common methodology (see Blaug, 1980, pp. 126–7). They were influenced by Darwin's biological theory of evolution (but *not* by social Darwinism) and by the American philosophy of pragmatism. They considered that the social sciences were supposed to explain how the human agent adapts and survives in a world of continuously evolving social, economic, and political conditions. They inclined towards the verification of ideas by testing them in the real world. And they repulsed apriorism and espoused empiricism.

In all this they differed in vision, style, and emphasis, as, indeed, do their contemporary descendants. Besides being a corrosive social critic, Veblen mercilessly ridiculed the neoclassical assumption of the economic actor's perfect rationality and suggested that not enough attention is paid to habit and custom. To him 'the world is indeed full of injustices, and the writings of economists full of attempts to disguise them; but these propositions are causes for laughter and scorn, not for agitation' (Arrow, 1975, p. 2). He painted large vistas of evolutionary cultural, social, and economic change. Commons approached the economic system through the legal foundations. He was deeply concerned with the history of labour and found common cause with the economic reform movement. Mitchell studied the evolution of the economy in terms of business cycles and to that end ammassed vast quantities of statistical and empirical material. He was a founding father and for many years the moving spirit of the National Bureau of Economic Research. In that role he influenced many distinguished spiritual descendants (such as Kuznets and Abramovitz) who have little in common with institutionalism but much with sober and painstaking empirical research.[27]

The contemporary descendants of institutionalists are a no less heterogeneous amalgam of dissenters than their predecessors. For our purposes we shall distinguish two groups: (i) the highly articulate social critics and visionaries (Myrdal and Galbraith) direct descendants of Veblen, and (ii) the more restrained critics of mainstream microeconomics (such as Simon, Winter, Nelson, Leibenstein, Marris, Williamson, and many others) whose style is closer to Commons and Mitchell, whose ideas are influenced by Veblen, whose work has gained far more recognition and respectability within the economic fraternity and who are not even identified as institutionalists *per se*.[28] In this section we shall briefly pause on (i) and then proceed in subsequent ones to (ii).

There are many similarities between Myrdal, the Swede, and Galbraith, the Canadian–American. Both are irreverent, irrepressible iconoclasts.

Both are fundamentally moralists and social reformers. Both use bright colours and large canvasses to present us with views of society where economics is subtly interwoven with politics, sociology, and psychology. And both are sometimes thorns in the flesh of what Myrdal calls their establishment colleagues, but more often than not both are quite simply ignored by these colleagues. At a luncheon, honouring him and his wife Alva at the 1971 meeting of the American Economic Association (organized by none other than the then President-Elect of the Association, Galbraith) Myrdal (1972, p.. 14—15) did not mince words:

> I am well aware that I am often considered almost not a part of the profession of establishment economists, though sometimes given credit for what I did during the first decade of my working life. I am even referred to as a sociologist. And by that, economists usually do not mean anything flattering. Another in some respects, like-minded rebel, Galbraith, who in addition writes a beautiful and forcible English, is often handled even more rudely by sometimes being classified by his colleagues as a journalist. But we insist on remaining economists.

Solow (1967, pp. 100—1) suggests that one of the reasons for this cold shoulder is that economists who, by the very essence of their profession, are what he calls 'little-thinkers' do not find these large vistas either enlightening or useful. Galbraith (1967a, pp 409—12), on the other hand, puts much of the blame on professional conservatism and vested interests. He considers (1967b, p. 118) that his work 'is a threat to those whose prestige and academic position is profoundly associated with the existing structure'. In rejoinder, Solow (1967, p. 119) adroitly manages to appear to agree and still brands Galbraith a sociologist.

Myrdal (1982, p. 314) is highly critical of the abstractions of mainstream or conventional economics, which he blames for obstructing vision so that the whole complex social system is left in limbo. Moreover, those who build the impressive mathematical models, by restricting the variables to only a few, do not clearly state what they leave out and, what is worse, they often do not even consciously perceive it. He (1982, pp. 312—14) spells out the institutionalist credo:

> The most fundamental thought that holds institutional economists together, however different they otherwise are, is our recognition that even if we focus attention on specific economic problems, our study must take account of the entire social system, including everything else of importance for what happens in the economic field: foremost, among other things, distribution of power in society, and, generally,

economic, social, and political stratification, and indeed all institutions and attitudes. To this we have to add, as an exogenous set of factors, induced policy measures applied with the purpose of changing one or several of these endogenous factors . . .

So the whole system will be moving in one direction or another, and it may even be turning around its axis. There is no one basic factor, but everything causes everything else. This implies *interdependence* within the whole social process. And there is generally no equilibrium in sight . . .

As the system is moving, partly under the influence of policy measures, the *coefficients of interrelations* among the various conditions in circular causation are ordinarily not known with quantitative precision. Elements of inertia, time lags, and, in extreme cases, the total non-responsiveness of one or several conditions to changes in some set of other conditions raise problems about which precise knowledge is seldom available . . .

The institutional economists will so regularly stretch out their analyses into fields where, for reasons already hinted at, quantitative precision is not yet possible. This easily leads to a facile characterization of much of our research as qualitative instead of quantitative. But we are equally, or more, intent on reaching quantitative knowledge as soon and as widely as possible. We are in fundamental agreement with Jevons's old dictum that more perfect knowledge is attainable only when we can measure conditions and changes of conditions.

Galbraith's acerbic criticisms of the economists' 'conventional wisdom' reach a wide audience assured him by his lucid and felicitous prose. He has long given up writing only for economists perhaps partly because they do not heed him and partly because his opportunities lie elsewhere. One of the rare occasions when he addressed economists directly was in his Presidential Address to the American Economic Association (1973a, pp. 5 and 11):

Neoclassical economics is not without an instinct for survival. It rightly sees the unmanaged sovereignty of the consumer, the ultimate sovereignty of the citizen and the maximization of profits and resulting subordination of the firm to the market as the three legs of a tripod on which it stands. These are what exclude the role of power in the system. All three propositions tax the capacity for belief . . . It tells the young and susceptible and the old and vulnerable that economic life has no content of power and politics because the firm is safely subordinate to the market and to the state and for this reason it is safely at the command of the consumer and citizen. Such an economics is not neutral. It is the influential and invaluable ally of those whose exercise of power depends on an acquiescent public.

His neoclassical friends retort that 'by now the running battle with neoclassical foes is pretty tiresome' (Tobin, 1982, p. 667):

There is goodness knows, plenty of blindness, obtuseness, irrelevance, and parochial scholasticism in the discipline of economics. It is just not true, however, that the profession insists on analyzing the American economy as if it were an ideal type described by Adam Smith. Modern economics does not contend that competitive markets without public intervention do or could achieve maximum satisfaction of the wants of 'sovereign' consumers (Tobin, 1982, p. 668).

Galbraith's vision of modern industrial society has evolved over the years (see 1976 (original edn 1958), 1967a, and 1973b). Its salient arguments may be briefly summarized as follows:

(1) There are two systems in the US economy. About half the economy, consisting of the 2000 largest corporations, is planned. The other half, the market system, consists of small enterprises serving such basic needs as housing construction, health services, local transportation, and the like. Contrary to the 'conventional wisdom' the former are high-technology and high-resource-use areas, whereas the latter are not resource-intensive. The former set their own terms of trade (in conjunction with trade unions), whereas the latter cannot easily pass costs on to consumers. The two systems feature built-in inequalities of income along with inequalities of power.

(2) Power is the key work in the Galbraithian vision. The industrial giants' power to manipulate prices and costs is only the tip of the iceberg. It extends to shaping social values through brainwashing the consumer by advertising, to organizing its own or controlling the sources of supply, to controlling its sources of capital, and to influencing domestic and foreign government policies. The corporation wields power over the state in demanding what it needs: that is, more research and development, increased technical training, a better infrastructure, emergency financial aid, enlarged military procurement, and the like.

(3) The power is exercised by the technostructure: 'The men who guide the modern corporation, including the financial, legal, technical, advertising, and other sacerdotal authorities in corporate function, are the most respectable, affluent, and prestigious members of the national com-

munity. They are the Establishment' (Galbraith, 1973a, p. 5). There is a 'symbiotic relationship', and *entente cordiale*, between this private and the public bureaucracies. More than that, their members often play musical chairs.

(4) Like in the Marris conception (to be discussed later), the corporation's technostructure pursues profit as a source of further growth and for its attributes of prestige and influence. But it does not maximize profits. Rather it more forcefully pursues growth as a goal —a goal that allows it to wield greater power in the future and that carries strong personal rewards of a pecuniary, advancement, and prestige nature.

(5) Galbraith, the moralist, objects to the resultant debasement of tastes and more importantly of social and moral values. He objects even more vehemently to the danger of the giant corporations' interests becoming the public interest. He (1973a, p. 7) calls for a common defence of the public purpose:

> That the present system should lead to an excessive output of automobiles, an improbable effort to cover the economically developed sections of the planet with asphalt, a lunar preoccupation with moon exploration, a fantastically expensive and potentially suicidal investment in missiles, submarines, bombers, and aircraft carriers, is as one would expect. These are the industries with power to command resources for growth. And central to public purpose — to sound resource utilization — will be a cutback in such industries, as all instinct now suggests.

He sees permanent wage and price controls as a means of curbing the power of the corporations and the unions and of correcting distributional inequalities. He calls for more extensive regulation to cope with ecological problems and to protect the consumer from multifarious abuses. But 'is emancipation of the state from the control of the planning system possible? No one knows. And in the absence of knowledge no one certainly will suggest that it will be easy.' (Galbraith, 1973a, p. 10).

The mainstream has not always been silent. Some of its most distinguished practitioners have painstakingly answered Galbraith's accusations. It is often pointed out that Galbraith vastly exaggerates the size of the planned sector (see Solow, 1967, pp. 103–4; Tobin, 1982, pp. 671–2). In Solow's (1967, p. 104) words, 'Galbraith's story that the industrial firm has "planned" itself into complete insulation from the vagaries of the market is an exaggeration, so much an exaggeration that it smacks of the put-on'. 'Galbraith is accused by Friedman (1977a, pp. 30–4) of elitism, of wanting to impose his own preferences over those of the public, while

Friedman defends the public's manipulation by advertising on the grounds of freedom of speech. Galbraith's critics often accuse him of offering 'little evidence for the propositions he does assert. By contrast a conventional economist tries to state testable, refutable hypotheses. He is generally impressed with the difficulty of empirical verification, and he goes to great pains to tease information from recalcitrant and ambiguous data' (Tobin, 1982, p. 670; see Solow, 1967; Friedman, 1977a, p. 13). Fundamentally, the difference between Galbraith and the mainstream economist is also one of approach. As Tobin (1982, p. 670) points out, Galbraith's distinction between the planned and market systems in the economy is:

> important and illuminating. But the observation is only a beginning. Any recent Ph.D. from M.I.T. would embed it in a model which takes account of trade and mobility between the two sectors. Solved or simulated, the model would suggest some observable effects on employment, wages, prices, inflation . . . With luck the credibility of the model could be statistically checked; it might turn out to be an accurate reflection of reality. No one says Galbraith has to play this game, though one hopes he might have students who would. But does he have to denigrate the serious scientific economists who do engage in this kind of work? The answer is no. It is unbecoming, unwarranted, and unnecessary.

BOUNDED RATIONALITY

Rationality of the economic actor has been a concept central to mainstream economics and refined over successive generations. From the very beginning it has been strongly criticized for being empirically unsubstantiated. Among others, Veblen ridiculed those of his colleagues (*nota bene* John Bates Clark) who imputed exceptional computational power and proficiency to the average economic actor (see Arrow, 1982a, pp. 1–2; 1975, p. 4). On the contemporary scene, Simon and others – descendants of the institutionalist tradition (Simon, 1982b, pp. 447 and 480) – have been stressing that neither do individual actors possess the computational abilities demanded of them for rational choices nor do we pay sufficient attention to custom or convention as factors in decision-making. This position (which runs along grooves similar to cognitive psychology) placed their investigations in the 1950s and early 1960s somewhat outside the pale of economics (at least as conceived by a relatively large group of economists).[29] In fact, Simon (1982b, p. xv) sees organisation theory, the economic (behaviouralist) theory of the firm, and cognitive psychology as theories of human decision-making and problem-solving processes that have followed relatively separate paths of development and that he has sought to integrate.

In this section we focus on the approach to microeconomics of what may be loosely termed the Carnegie school (see for example, Simon, 1982a and 1982b; Cyert and March, 1963), whose essential characteristics can be summarized as follows: bounded rationality, satisficing, miltifariousness of sub-goals that are attended to sequentially, feedback, standardized procedures, observance of custom and unwillingness towards change, conflict resolution via factions entrenched by organizational slack, and, or course, keeping the firm viable (see Day, 1964).

In explaining the concept of bounded rationality, Simon (1982b, pp. 402, 405–7, 424–43) distinguishes the psychological or the simpler dictionary meaning of the term rationality ('agreeable to reason; not absurd, preposterous . . . etc.; intelligent; sensible') — what he has come to call procedural rationality — from its meaning in economics — what he has come to call substantive retionality; that is, 'the rationality of the utility maximizer, and a pretty smart one at that . . . As is well known, the rational man of economics is a maximizer, who will settle for nothing less than the best. Even his expectations, as we have learned in the past few years, are rational . . . And his rationality extends as far as the bedroom . . . as Gary Becker tells us' (Simon, 1982b, p. 445).

This may be contrasted with the notions of bounded rationality that Simon (1982b, p. 491) considers to be 'the need to search for decision alternatives, the replacement of optimization by targets and satisficing goals, and mechanisms of learning and adaptation'. He (1982b, p. 483; see also pp. 408–23) sees rationality as bounded 'when it falls short of omniscience. And the failures of omniscience are largely failures of knowing all the alternatives, uncertainty about relevant exogenous events, and inability to calculate consequences.'

Thus Simon (1982b, p. 477) contrasts the essence of the classical or neoclassical marginalist theory of the firm and the behaviouralist one as follows:

> The classical theory of omniscient rationality is strikingly simple and beautiful. Moreover, it allows us to predict (correctly or not) human behavior without stirring out of our armchairs to observe what such behavior is like. All the predictive power comes from characterizing the shape of the environment in which the behavior takes place. The en-

vironment, combined with the assumptions of perfect rationality, fully determines the behavior. Behavioral theories of rational choice — theories of bounded rationality — do not have this kind of simplicity. But, by way of compensation, their assumptions about human capabilities are far weaker than those of the classical theory. Thus, they make modest and realistic demands on the knowledge and computational abilities of the human agents, but they also fail to predict that those agents will equate costs and returns at the margin.

The thrust of Simon's (1982b, p. 481) criticism is directed at the omniscience of the economic actor assumed by neoclassical theory. He views this theory as calling for:

> knowledge of all the alternatives that are open to choice. It calls for complete knowledge of, or ability to compute, the consequences that will follow on each of the alternatives. It calls for certainty in the decision maker's present and future evaluation of these consequences. It calls for the ability to compare consequences, no matter how diverse and heterogeneous, in terms of some consistent measure of utility.

In a similar vein, Radner (1972, pp. 16–17) calls attention to the fact that 'the very *complexity* of a real-world decision problem will typically prevent the decision maker from satisfying the criteria of rational choice' and to 'the limited capacities of an individual decision maker for imagination and computation. The existence of these limitations raises serious problems for the concept of rational choice . . . in terms of *optimizing behavior*. A mode of behavior that is not even *feasible* can hardly qualify as *rational!*' And he points to the importance of the 'concept of *Satisficing behavior* as an alternative to optimizing'.

Another GE protagonist, Hahn, speculates that in economics the term rational has been much abused and invested with too much meaning when, he thinks, that all that was meant was correct calculations and an orderly personality. Advocating a somewhat similar version to Simon's bounded rationality, Hahn and Hollis (1979, p. 11) suggest that 'a notion of "bounded" or restricted, but still objective, rationality is the best way to face up to' the lack of realism about the universal assumption of the relation among the elements of the economic actor's preferences. And, although 'pure economic theory has found it hard to make the change', they contend that 'welfare economics would have to judge social states on the basis not just of preferences but also of varying perceptions and computational skills, with great loss of persuasiveness'.

Simon (1982b, p. 478) sees one of the major failures of the neoclassical theory of the firm in the lack of confirmation by empirical observation.[30] He grants that the theory may be sufficiently 'patched up' to tackle situations that do not involve uncertainty and outguessing (i.e. relatively stable economies not too far from competitive equilibrium). But he denies such possibilities in situations involving uncertainty and imperfect competition. He admits that 'statistical decision theory employing the idea of subjective expected utility, on the one hand, and game theory, on the other, have contributed enormous conceptual clarification to these kinds of situations'. However, empirical testing has shown that the behaviour or economic actors was usually at variance with the concept of expected utility (Simon, 1982b, pp. 452–3, 478–9, and 486–8). In this respect, his views somewhat converge with Arrow's.

It is interesting to note that, according to Arrow (1982a, p.1), in application to the static world of certainty the concept of rationality 'has turned out to be a weak hypothesis, not easily refuted and therefore not very useful as an explanation, though not literally a tautology'. For many years now stronger versions of this concept have been elaborated with reference to a dynamic world of uncertainty. It brought to light, *inter alia*, the criteria for consistency in intertemporal allocation, the hypothesis of expected utility (or subjective expected utility) behaviour under uncertainty, and the Baysian hypothesis for learning. 'These hypotheses have been used widely in offering explanations of empirically observed behavior, though, as not infrequently in economics, the theoretical development has gone much further than the empirical implementation.' Arrow (1982a, p. 8) concludes that 'an important class of interemporal markets shows systematic deviations from individual rational behavior and that these deviations are consonant with evidence from very different sources collected by psychologists'.

The notion of scarcity of information (not unlike that expounded by Marschak and others too numerous to mention) is an integral part of Simon's (see 1982a, pp. 236–7) work. The two concepts of search and satisficing are central to the formal characterization of the choice mechanisms under bounded rationality.[31]

Search is undertaken when the actor does not initially possess the information that would enable him to make a choice. This search is expensive and becomes increasingly so the longer it lasts. In the mid-1950s Simon (1982b, pp. 239–68) and somewhat later Stigler (1961) made the point respectively with reference to the purchase of a home and a car. They have derived, however, different conclusions about the extent of the search. Whereas the latter claims that the search is terminated when the marginal cost of search is equated with the expected marginal improvement in the alternatives found, the former stipulates that the search is interrupted when the best alternative exceeds expectations, with the aspiration level adjusting gradually to the value of alternatives found. Information processing theories that envisage selectivity based on heuristics and that interrupt search after satisfactory solutions have been found are also within the framework of bounded rationality (see Simon, 1982a, pp. 386–9; 1982b, pp. 146–70, 186–201, and 488).

The notion that economic actors are incapable of taking into account all the alternatives runs through Simon's work. He (1982b, p. 456; see also pp. 171–85) sees information as 'almost always a positive good', where there is a relative shortage of it and where there are not many complicated decision problems. But 'in a world where attention is a major scarce resource, information may be an expensive luxury, for it may turn our attention from what is important to what is unimportant. We cannot afford to attend to information simply because it is there. I am not aware that there has been any systematic development of a theory of information and communication that treats attention rather than information as the scarce resource.'

The stringent conditions imposed by the need for practical computability have given impetus to two types of models: (i) those that simplify the world sufficiently to be able to compute the optimum (and Simon sees team theory in this category), and (ii) those that attempt to arrive at sufficiently satisfactory (satisficing) solutions at relatively low costs of computation (bounded rationality approach). Or, in Simon's (1982b, p. 479) words, 'decision makers can satisfice either by finding optimum solutions for a simplified world, or by finding satisfactory solutions for a more realistic world'.

Satisficing is only one of the generally applicable and widely used procedures for cutting the Gordian knot of decision quandries. Another, according to Simon (1982b, p. 482), is to zero in on realistic sub-goals that can be empirically detected and measured, rather than on indefinite all-encompassing goals. Yet another is to apportion decision-making functions among a number of specialists whose work is co-ordinated through organized communication channels and authority relations. 'All of these, and others, fit the general rubric of "bounded rationality", and it is now clear that the elaborate organizations that human beings have constructed in the modern world to carry out the work of production and government can only be understood as machinery for coping with the limits of man's abilities to comprehend and compute in the face of complexity and uncertainty.'

In his early work, Simon (1947), following in the footsteps of his chief inspirer Barnard (1938), pointed out that a firm's survival depends on 'the balance between the inducements that were provided by organizations to their participants, and the contributions those participants made to the organizations' resources' (Simon, 1982b, p. 483) – what he called a motivational theory. His (1982b, pp. 24–42) formalization of this theory does not drastically depart from the neoclassical theory of the firm.[32] The difference lies in the latter's assumption that the firm's owners are the sole profit recipients and Simon's allowance for bargaining for a share of profit among the participants, under conditions of monopoly or oligopoly. The survival conditions for the firm that he (1982b, p. 483) postulates – 'positive profits rather than maximum profits – also permit a departure from the assumption of perfect rationality'.[33]

ALTERNATIVE THEORIES OF THE FIRM

Despite the fairly general adherence of textbooks and courses in micro-economics to the standard, mainstream, neoclassical view, modern economics is replete with alternative theories of the firm – at least with various building blocks. Most classifications are hazardous. For our purposes we could view these building blocks as filling into at least two categories: (i) the behaviouralist, with close affinity to the bounded rationality concept (the latter Williamson, Leibenstein, and Nelson and Winter), and (ii) the managerialist, using maximizing models of managerial utility, rather than profit (Baumol, 1959; Williamson, 1964; and Marris). Since the concepts of the second group are somewhat closer to standard microeconomics, we shall proceed with it first.

The second group deviates from the concept of the firm as a profit maximizer, replacing it with the maximization of some other goal of management, usually under the constraint of achieving a certain level of profit. Thus, Baumol (1959) suggests sales as the maximand. Williamson (1964) claims that management diverts a share of profit before it is reported (by increasing operating costs) for its own benefits (e.g. high salaries, expense accounts, luxurious offices, etc.). Hence reported profits are lower than they would have been had management maximized profits.[34] In a somewhat similar vein, Marris (1963, 1964) uses the minimum stock price as a constraint and suggests the firm's growth as the maximand.

Marris (1963, 1964, 1968) sees the real world behaviour as quite at variance with that implied by neoclassical theory (i.e. that corporations would choose to grow less rapidly and distribute higher dividends among stockholders). Two major problems face the growing corporation: how to enhance demand for its products and how to finance expansion. The corporation may attempt to realize maximum profits from existing markets, but the expansion of markets is costly (research and development, marketing, potential failures, etc.). Thus an acceleration of growth is bound to depress the average rate of return.

Marris (1963, 1964) specifies that in pursuit of growth, management is constrained by the threat of takeover:

> If stock-market value falls sufficiently so that a takeover raid becomes likely, . . . management job security is threatened. Thus, in the managerial utility function: growth rate is proxy for income, power, prestige, and accompanying managerial gains from growth; . . . and stock-market value is proxy for job security (Marris and Mueller, 1980, pp. 41–2).

In a sense, the managerial growth theories involve a trade-off between growth rate and stock market value; that is, a trade-off between current and future dividends. For a number of reasons (including management's technical and professional competence and relative independence from external financing), management can depress the safe minimum level of stock price and enhance the safe maximum growth rate respectively below and above the values that would have obtained were management actually concerned only with stockholders' benefits (see Marris, 1968). The more weight management attaches to current profit rather than growth, the closer is its behaviour to the mainstream model. Solow (1968, 1971) claims that, since the managerial growth and neoclassical theories differ only in how the short-run maximized profits of the firm are apportioned between management's goal of growth and the stockholders' goal of profits, this difference is not overly important. Marris and Mueller (1980, p. 44) respond that 'such an inference is naive; we can show that managerial motivation is a crucial influence on the adaptive efficiency of the economic system and thence on economic welfare'.

Within the context of managerial growth theories, the theme of conflict between management and stockholders was further developed by Mueller (1972) in the firm's life-cycle hypothesis – a subject also treated in Chapter 17 of the companion volume. He sees a considerable convergence of management and stockholders' interests in maximum possible growth when the firm is 'young' (i.e. when due to some technological or commercial breakthrough it takes off into a rapid and accelerating growth with high rates of return). It is as the firm 'ages' (i.e. as the exceptional circumstances attenuate) that conflict emerges, with the most acute management–stockholders conflict likely to arise in firms that virtually stagnate and where profitability is very low. In such extreme cases, the stockholders might benefit from winding up operations and selling off assets, whereas management obviously does not. This is also a convenient way of explaining mergers — as an attempt to counteract growth deceleration brought about by the ageing process.

With regard to the ongoing process of concentration, Marris and Mueller (1980, p. 50) conclude that:

> the legal and institutional permissions of capitalism imply a self-organizing process leading to persistently increasing concentration in the absence of special legal restrictions on conglomerate growth or in the absence of specific fiscal handicaps imposed on larger firms ... To the extent that the evolution of the size distribution of firms is the outcome of stochastic growth in a Gibration world, this evolution is without normative implications. To the extent that the process of increasing concentration is enhanced by managerial pursuit of growth through internal expansion, macroeconomic growth may be increased, and with it social welfare. But, if managerial pursuit of growth is by socially unproductive investments (e.g. in merger activity), increasing aggregate concentration may imply declining social welfare.

Odagiri (1980) applies the managerial growth theory to macroanalysis of growth. Using a two-sector (one essentially corporate, the other neoclassical) model of the economy and extending Pasinetti (1962), he indicates the dominance of the corporate sector over the growth equation. The growth rate is faster when management has the strongest stakes in corporate growth and, hence, promotes acceleration of technical progress. These stakes are reinforced under conditions where managerial prestige is enhanced by sales volume, where managerial mobility is restricted, and where the costs of takeovers are high. He then ingeniously applies these deductions in analysing the better growth rate performance of Japan (where the above factors are present) in comparison to the USA (where the factors are much weaker).

What are the implications of the managerial growth theory for society? Marris (1968, p. 45) suggests that it is subversive of the existing order.[35] Marris and Mueller (1980, p. 59) point out that in the USA industrial policy faces the following alternatives:

> (1) preservation of the present form of managerial capitalism with its heavy emphasis on growth through merger and nonprice competition among the few; (2) further movement along the road to democratic socialism or a government-business partnership as predicted by Schumpeter, Galbraith, and Baran and Sweezy; (3) a reverse shift ... through

the breakup of large corporations and possible restrictions on mergers and on some forms of nonprice competition such as advertising.

The choice among them cannot be left up to the evolutionary process with the hope that the one evolved would be best simply because it was the one chosen. They believe 'that a system of some hundreds of competing planned economies (i.e. giant corporations) operating in close partnership with government will be both more X-efficient and offer more personal liberty than a system that had literally converged into a Soviet-type system'.

We shall now return to the behaviouralist group. In a series of publications, Williamson (1970, 1975, 1979, 1981) who has been particularly concerned with developing refutable implications, stresses that, aside from such other important factors as search for monopoly profits and technological imperatives,[36] 'the modern corporation is mainly to be understood as the product of a series of organizational innovations that have had the purpose and effect of economizing on transaction costs' (1981, p. 1537). According to him (1981, p. 1564), 'the strongest argument favoring transaction cost economizing . . . is that this is the only hypothesis that is able to provide a discriminating rationale for the succession of organizational innovations that have occurred over the past 150 years and out of which the modern corporation has emerged'.

The two behavioural assumptions on which Williamson (1981, p. 1545) bases his transaction-cost analysis are: bounded rationality and opportunism (which he also calls 'human nature as we know it'). The latter, though similar in concept to Knight's 'moral hazard', is more general and extends the concept of the economic agent's self-interest to include forms of deceit and cunning. Thus some agents' tendency to behave opportunistically undermines their reliability. These two behavioural assumptions threaten the validity of contractual obligations. Thus, Williamson (1981, p. 1546) suggests that in a nutshell the problem of economic organization is to 'assess alternative governance structures in terms of their capacities to economize on bounded rationality while simultaneously safeguarding transactions against opportunism. This is not inconsistent with the imperative "maximize profits!" but it focusses attention somewhat differently.'

Williamson (1981, p. 1547–51) deals with three principles of organizational design: (i) asset specificity, (ii) externality (forward integration), and (iii) hierarchical decomposition (internal organization). (i) Pertains to advantages of internal organization over market contracting for transactions based on highly specific assets, as such contracting is costly and often unreliable. (ii) Refers principally to distribution stages and pertains to unintended lowering of quality which is easier to control internally. (iii) Is a reflection of (i) and (ii). Without bounded rationality and opportunism, (i) and (ii) would pose no problem. Thus arises the recognition of the need for separating problems into manageable units and of preventing agents from engaging in dysfunctional pursuits.

Williamson (1981, p. 1564) differentiates the transaction-cost approach from neoclassical analysis and from the 'inhospitality' tradition of anti-trust law. Unlike the first, this approach gives much weight to internal organization and unlike the second, it assumes that structural differences arise mainly to enhance savings of transactions costs:

> The application of these ideas to the study of transactions in general and of the modern corporation in particular requires that (1) the transaction be made the principal unit of analysis, (2) an elementary appreciation for 'human nature as we know it' supplant the fiction of economic man, (3) transactions be dimensionalized, (4) rudimentary principles of market and hierarchcal organization be recognized, and (5) a guiding principle of comparative institutional study be the hypothesis that transactions are assigned to and organized within governance structures in a discriminating (transaction-cost economizing) way.

To Williamson (1981, p. 1565) the transaction-cost approach is valuable for studying the modern corporation for it:

> permits a wide variety of significant organizational events to be interpreted in a coherent way . . . It links up comfortably with the type of business history studies that have been pioneered by Chandler. It has ramifications for the study of regulation . . . and for antitrust enforcement. Applications to aspects of labor economics and comparative systems have been made, and others would appear to be fruitful. More generally, while there is room for the need for refinement, a comparative approach to the study of economic institutions in which the economy of transaction costs is the focus of analysis, appears to have considerable promise.

Leibenstein (1976, p. 266) summarizes the fundamental differences between his theory and conventional microeconomics. According to him, his theory:

> differs in the following: (1) its psychological underpinnings; (2) it is based primarily on individual behavior rather than on firms and households; (3) it is applicable to the behavior of agents as well as of principals; (4) under it, effort is a fundamental economic variable; (5) in the fact that it takes into account a new type of inefficiency ignored

by conventional economics that I have called X-inefficiency; and (6) the theory implies that typically firms neither minimize costs nor maximize profits.

Leibenstein (1976, p. viii) acknowledges that there is a 'family resemblance' between his owrk and Simon's and explains at length (pp. 71–94) his concept of selective rationality which is close to bounded rationality. Perhaps the main area of difference is Leibenstein's express focus on what, for want of a better term, could be called micro-micro theory; that is, the individual, rather than the firm.

A pivotal theme in this theory is effort and the effort decision:

> The basic hypothesis upon which the X-efficiency theory rests is that there is always a degree to which effort, in its broadest sense, is a variable . . . I will argue that effort is a variable in all instances. This flows in part from the assumption that employment contracts are incomplete and open. Not every aspect of the job is specified in advance (Leibenstein, 1976, p. 98).

Effort and motivation are closely interwoven.

> Neither individuals nor firms work as hard or search for information as effectively as they could. The importance of motivation and its association with degree of effort and search arises because the relation between inputs and outputs is *not* a determinate one. There are four reasons why given inputs cannot be transformed into predetermined outputs: contracts for labor are incomplete; not all factors of production are marketed; the production function is not completely specified or known; and interdependence and uncertainty lead competing firms to cooperate tacitly with each other in some respects, and to imitate each other with respect to technique to some degree (Leibenstein, 1976, pp. 44–5).

Leibenstein (1978, p. 95) asserts that 'X-inefficiency exists almost everywhere and that its magnitude is significant. The existence of X-inefficiency implies that except in extreme cases firms do not minimize costs, maximize profits, or optimize the rate of technological change'. He (1976, p. 96) outlines the assumptions on which the theory is based:

> (1) The firm is the organization in which, for the most part, the inducements are generated that determine effort choices. (2) Labor contracts are incomplete. (3) Not all inputs are purchasable in terms of the units in which they are used in production. (4) There is no fixed trade-off between the units on the basis of which inputs are purchased (for

example, time) and those of which they are used (for example, effort).
(5) Beyond some point there is diminishing utility to effort, and beyond some other point negative marginal utility. (6) Not all inputs are traded. (7) The objective function of the firm is not completely determined and specified externally to the firm. The obectives of the firm depend on the preferences for a variety of things of those in the interrelated groups which make up the organization which we call the firm.

He (1976, pp. 111–15) considers the concept of inert areas (a more or less large grey area within which one can improve a given position, but where the pay-off is not worth the effort) as a critical element in his theory. 'Opportunities for change which do not lead to a gain in utility (or an evident loss of utility) greater than the cost of the shift in utility will not be entertained seriously' (1976, p. 112). Leibenstein (1976, pp. 162ff.) claims that the X-efficiency theory is particularly applicable to the modern corporation where agents have largely replaced principals:

> If an organization using agents . . . operates well, it extends the capacity of the principal far beyond what a principal could do on his own. On the other hand, there is the possibility that the agents operate with X-inefficiency. In examining the world of the firm we are examining a structure made up largely of agents in which there exists innumerable possibilities of nonprofitable transactions and missed opportunities carried out by agents (1976, p. 163).

Thus he (1976, p. 200) arrives at a theory of the firm that is characterized by (i) individuals choosing effort positions that do not interfere with those of their colleagues and do not transgress the inert areas, (ii) the existence of such inert areas that do not warrant a shift of effort, (iii) the firm's employees are influenced by all sorts of material and moral incentives that prompt them to either transgress or shy away from the inert areas, and (iv) an incentive system that can be either internal or external with respect to the firm.

Finally, Leibeinstein (1976, pp. 269–70) claims that his theory can explain inflation, whereas 'conventional microtheory says almost nothing about inflation'. For example, controlling prices by means of a 'normal' profit rate presumes that firms minimize costs. If they are X-inefficient, the controlled prices would sanction any cost level and the firms' degree of inefficiency would be borne by the consumer (as, indeed, is the case of firms in Soviet-type economies). Thus:

> since firms neither minimize costs nor maximize profits, there is a clear-

cut area in the decision process under which firms play a distinct role in generating inflationary pressure . . . Inert area theory also suggests strong reasons why firms would in fact under various circumstances raise prices. Since the inert areas also apply to consumers there are some price increases to which consumers will not react.

Another area of investigation where X-efficiency theory can be useful, according to Leibenstein (1976, pp. 270–1), is the analysis of productivity in various countries. He (1976, p. 270) suggests that 'the main differences can be explained by the motivations of firms' members during their work, by the motivational atmosphere they find on the job, and on the type of interactions and influences toward work and production that people have on each other as well as the attitudes they bring to the work context'.

As we have seen, it has often been argued that the allocative function of the market is vastly exaggerated. Rather, it excels in opportunities for entrepreneurship, inventiveness, ingenuity, and dynamism resulting in expansion and increased welfare. This was the classical view of competition. In its modern (early 1900s) revival, it is Schumpeter's (1934) focus, rather than that of GE, that grasped the propelling force of the capitalist engine.[37] However, one should note that towards the end of his life, Schumpeter (1950) has perceived new configurations of forces at work. His entrepreneur–innovator was no longer the dominant force – a subject also treated in Chapter 18 of the companion volume. His role was taken over by the large corporation and this, in turn, could be performed by government without loss of dynamic efficiency. Marris and Mueller (1980, p. 58) draw an interesting parallel between this latter-day Schumpeter and Galbraith (1967a) where they perceive a similar evolutionary view of capitalism, with the distinction that Galbraith envisions a partnership between the corporate sector and government rather than absorption of the former by the latter.[38] Be that as it may, it is the inspiration by Schumpeter (1934) that interests us here.

A major challenge to mainstream neoclassical economics has been the development of an 'evolutionary theory of economic change' (in a series of publications spanning more than a decade and culminating in the 1982 publication of a book under that title) by Nelson and Winter who relate it to biological evolutionary theory (see also Chapter 10 in this volume). Basically their theory is neo-Schumpeterian and neo-Simonian.[39] Their aim is to characterize and explain significant unforeseen economic change (as examples of the latter they offer the oil price shocks of the 1970s and the computer revolution).

Nelson and Winter (1982, pp. 12–13, 21, 28, 399–400) argue that orthodox microeconomic theory is a 'flagrant distortion of reality', which obscures the 'essential features of the processes of economic change'. Because this theory rests on the twin pillars of firms' maximizing behaviour and industry equilibrium, models built on this basis, according to them either disregard or mishandle the fundamental features of economic change such as the 'exogenousness' of change, uncertainty, the trial and error process, the duration of the time span for implementation of change, the transient gains and losses, and the heterogeneity of firms' characteristics and stretegies.

Nelson and Winter claim that, its positive achievements notwithstanding, neoclassical growth theory is not a satisfactory instrument for analysing technical change. They are not alone in this (see, for example, Nordhaus and Tobin, 1972, p. 2; see also Rosenberg, 1982). This growth theory 'represses the uncertainty associated with attempts to innovate, the publicness of knowledge associated with the outcomes of these attempts, and the diversity of firm behavior and fortune that is inherent in a world in which innovation is important. Thus, it is unable to come to grips with what is known about technological advance at the level of the individual firm or individual invention, where virtually all studies have shown these aspects to be central' (Nelson and Winter, 1982, p. 202). Thus, 'the orthodox formulation offers no possibility of reconciling analyses of growth undertaken at the level of the economy or the sector with what is known about the processes of technical change at the microeconomic level' (Nelson and Winter, 1982, p. 206). Nelson and Winter (p. 203) argue that 'the role of competition seems better characterized in the Schumpeterian terms of competitive advantage gained through innovation or through early adoption of a new product or process than in the equilibrium language of neoclassical theory'.

Considerable tension has developed between the historical and micro studies of the process of technical change and the analytical apparatus involved in modelling technical progress at the sectoral or macro levels. 'The differences among firms and the disequlibrium in the system appear to be an essential feature of growth driven by technical change. Neoclassical modeling cannot avail itself of this insight' (Nelson and Winter, 1982, p. 203).

Neoclassical theory stresses that at any given time firms face a broad gamut of technological opportunities (including those that have not yet been chosen by any of them). But Nelson and Winter (1982, p. 201) claim that it is unrealistic to suppose that there exists a clearly described set of technical knowledge about production possibilities and input combinations outside the realms of actual experience. Hence, 'the idea of movements along the production function into previously unexperienced regions – the conceptual core of the neoclassical explanation of growth – must be rejected as a theoretical concept'.

Nelson and Winter (1982, p. 18) emphatically stress that 'the core concern of evolutionary theory is with the dynamic process by which firm behavior patterns and market outcomes are jointly determined over time'. They claim (1982, p. 22) that an evolutionary growth theory is particularly more suitable for combining the micro and macro dimensions of technical change than is orthodox theory.

Evolutionary theory treats firms as behavioural entities that are endowed with certain capabilities, procedures, and decision rules that prescribe their actions under certain exogenous conditions, and that take part in search for information that would permit them to judge possible alterations in their activity. 'Firms whose decision rules are profitable, given the market environment, expand; those firms that are unprofitable contract. The market environment surrounding individual firms may be in part endogenous to the behavioral system taken as a whole' (Nelson and Winter, 1982, p. 207). However, it is important to note that this theory (1982, pp. 9–10) also sees firms as better suited to the *status quo* than to major change and better suited to a kind of dynamics of perpetuation than to more innovative change.

This evolutionary theory rests on three basic concepts:

(1) Organizational routine that Nelson and Winter (1982, p. 14) use as a 'general term for all regular and predictable behavioral patterns of firms'. This includes a firm's characteristics from production techniques through, administrative, sales, and advertising procedures, to investment, research and development, and strategic policies. 'In our evolutionary theory, these routines play the role that genes play in biological evolutionary theory.'

(2) Nelson and Winter (1982, p. 400) use 'the term "search" to denote all those organizational activities which are associated with the evaluation of current routines and which may lead to their modification, to more drastic change, or to their replacement'. Although the search activities are in themslves predictable and routinized, they are also of a stochastic nature. Their concept of search parallels that of mutation in biological evolutionary theory (see Nelson and Winter, 1982, p. 18).

(3) The firm's 'selection environment' is the configaration of factors that determines its dynamics. This is partly conditioned by factors exogenous to the firm, but relating to the specific industry and partly by the behaviour and characteristics of the other firms in the industry.

'The selection mechanism here clearly is analogous to the natural selection of genotypes with differential net reproduction rates in biological evolutionary theory' (Nelson and Winter, 1982, p. 17).

Nelson and Winter explore three topics with the aid of the evolutionary model: (1) the firms' and industry responses to altered market conditions, (2) long-run growth, propelled by technological progress, and (3) Schumpeterian-type competition:

(1) Here they (1982, ch. 7) attempt to account for the effects of a price shock, stressing the divergent approaches of the orthodox and evolutionary theories. In the former the firm's decision rule is considered as the best of all possible ones. In the latter, in addition to that decision rule, a change occurs in the light of research and development and operations research, with finally selection effects affecting share weights in the final rule. This decomposition is apparently analytically useful because of the different speeds at which the three effects occur. Thus the analysis rejects the orthodox view of how decision rules are formed and stresses the expected effects of change in time. The analysis suggests that a firm's or industry's substitution and supply responsiveness would depend on the quantity and quality of the search and innovation effort induced by higher prices. On a policy plane, the orthodox approach suggests that the market will take care of the problems, whereas the evolutionary theory approach, which does not take elasticities of supply and substitution as given, suggests that the government may evolve policies to influence and support research and development.

(2) Nelson and Winter (1982, chs 8–11) point out that not only is orthodox micro-theory devoid of serious concern with long-run change, but it is inconsistent with accumulated knowledge about such change. They attempt to fill this gap by using a model with fixed coefficients, all profits plowed back into investment, both internal and external searches, and on a macro scale no deficiency of demand.[40] Basically their results (rising wage rates owing to more rapid growth of capital than labour supply, increasingly capital-intensive techniques becoming more profitable, innovation directed towards labour-saving devices, and rising capital–labour ratios and output per worker) are similar to the ones of the orthodox model, But they are able to derive them without assuming either maximization or equilibrium, replacing these concepts with 'profit-oriented' behaviour and competitive selection pressure. Moreover, the results are apparently more consistent on the micro level.

(3) Orthodox theory with its assumptions of maximization and equilibrium is at loggerheads with Schumpeterian competition which centres on competition in research and development the gains to society from continuing innovaton as against the benefits associated with competitive pricing, and a high degree of monopoly power as the price for technological advance (i.e. the trade-off between dynamic and static efficiency). Applying evolutionary theory to Schumpeterian competition, Nelson and Winter (1982, chs 12—14) show the two-way causal connection between technical change and market structure. Innovation may not necessarily be the forte of large corporations, but those who excel in innovation grow. Here it is possible for competition to self-destruct and for a successful innovator to diminate the industry. However, if innovation is expensive and imitation relatively simple, in order to survive the innovators must be large. The model used here differs from the one under (2) in the following: there are no differences among techniques in the capital—labour ratio, only in total efficiency (defined as output per unit of capital); research and development policies are assumed to relate total research and development to firm size (the larger the research and development budget, the better are the chances of successful finds); the firm's investment is related to its market share; and the model is a sectorial one with a downward-sloping curve. At least three factors help the model to examine the conditions under which competition might or might not self-destruct: the magnitude of the efficiency edge that the innovator gets over his competitors; the relative simplicity of imitation in terms of research and development resources needed before one firm's innovation can be imitated by another; and the extent to which profitable large firms perpetuate their advantage through further gowth.

With reference to these three topics, Nelson and Winter (1982, pp. 401—2) draw the following conclusions:

(1) Models based on their theory not only perform well on the home grounds of orthodox theory, but 'evolutionary models provide insight about adjustment mechanisms that orthodox theory's *ad hoc* treatment of disequilibrium adjustment processes does not'.

(2) As regards processes of long-term economic change propelled by innovation, their models 'have been shown capable of the same kind of qualitative consistency with the aggregative data as are orthodox models. But ours also are consistent with at least the broad features of the processes of technological advance, and can generate predictions that are qualitatively consistent with such microeconomic phenomena as the size distribution of business firms and the qualitative shape of "diffusion curves" — topics on which orthodox models are mute.'

(3) Moreover, orthodox theory, even if considerably bent, cannot accommodate a serious dynamic disequilibrium analysis essential for a fully Schumpeterian model. However, 'our models contain such a dynamic analysis. And they point clearly to some key determinants of industry structure and performance under Schumpeterian competition: ease of imitation, the degree to which large firms restrain investment, the character of the technological change regime.'

In final analysis it is not so much the details of particular models in their evolutionary theory that matter, but the fact that Nelson and Winter propose a different approach to theorizing about economic change.

Nelson and Winter (1982, p. 402) also assert that their perspective can provide normative insights into the economic system. The concept of social optimum does not enter their analysis:

Occupying a central place are the notions that society ought to be engaging in experimentation and that the information and feedback from experimentation are of central concern in guiding the evolution of the economic system ... More important, when one views normative economic questions from an evolutionary perspective one begins to get a better appreciation not only of why our current economic system is so mixed in institutional form, but why it is appropriate that this is so.

Samuelson (1966, p. 1568) once said that 'it takes a theory to kill a theory; facts can only dent the theorist's hide'. In this vein, the authors reviewed in this section and many others claim that there is an alternative theory to the neoclassical theory of the firm. Simon (1982b, p. 484) suggests that by the mid-1950s:

a theory of bounded rationality had been proposed as an alternative to classical omniscient rationality, a significant number of empirical studies had been carried out that showed actual business decision making to conform reasonably well with the assumptions of bounded rationality but not with the assumptions of perfect rationality, and key components of the theory – the nature of the authority and employment relations, organizational equilibrium, and the mechanism of search and satisficing – had been elucidated formally.

In fact, contemporary economics abounds with a number of theories of the firm based on managerial and behavioural assumptions and deviating in some way or other from the assumptions of neoclassical theory. 'If anything there is an embarrassing richness of alternatives ... A number of theories have been constructed ... and while these theories certainly do not yet constitute a single coherent whole, there is much in common among them' (Simon, 1982b, p. 491). And herein perhaps lies a kernel of truth. There is an *embarras de richesses*. Is there is plethora of incomplete and unintegrated theories? Are there many valuable ingredients, but no coherent whole?[41] An affirmative answer would be ungenerous and would detract from the major innovative intellectual efforts outlined above. Yet there appears to be a consensus that a fully integrated and developed alternative theory of the firm is still to be worked out.

Why has the neoclassical theory of the firm proved to be such a hardy plant?[42] Part of the answer may well be in habit – an unwillingness to discard received doctrine and part in Friedman-type methodological arguments (about which presently). Simon (1982b, p. 485), however, attributes the brunt of the answer to the development of mathematical economics. This, according to his rather harsh statement, allowed the neoclassical theory of the firm (revivified in combination with statistical decision theory and game theory) to sore to new heights of refinement and elegance and to spread its wings over certain aspects of uncertainty and information lacunae, though in extremely simplified form:

> The flowering of mathematical economics and econometrics has provided two generations of economic theorists with a vast garden of formal and technical problems that have absorbed their energies and postponed encounters with the inelegancies of the real world . . .
>
> In none of these theories – any more than in statistical decision theory or the theory of games – is the assumption of perfect maximization abandoned. Limits and costs of information are introduced, not as psychological characteristics of the decision maker, but as part of his technological environment. Hence, the new theories do nothing to alleviate the computational complexities facing the decision maker – do not see him coping with them by heroic approximation, simplifying and satisficing, but simply magnify and multiply them . . . Hence, to some extent, the impression that these new theories deal with the hitherto ignored phenomena of uncertainty and information transmission is illusory. For many economists, however, the illusion has been persuasive.

A POSTSCRIPT ON UNDERLYING TENSIONS AMONG ECONOMISTS

Economic theories never really die. Like good soldiers they often fade away. But unlike the soldiers, they are frequently resurrected in modified form. They are tenacious and persistent. In his inaugural lecture at Lund University in 1904, Knut Wicksell spoke about the failure of economics to reach a consensus, just 'like theology and for approximately the same reasons' (quoted after Myrdal, 1972, p. 151). Scientific progress, he pointed out, is achieved through controversy and, in the luckier natural sciences, the clashes result in refutations and obsolescence of inadequate theories that give way to the more advanced ones. Not so in economics. On the other hand, Milton Friedman (1977b, pp. 451–3), who believes that positive economics can be a value-free science, rejects the concept that the natural sciences are luckier. According to him (1977b, p. 452) in both social and natural sciences:

> there is no 'certain' substantive knowledge; only tentative hypotheses that can never be 'proved' but can only fail to be rejected, hypotheses in which we may have more or less confidence, depending on such features as the breadth of experience they encompass relative to their own complexity and relative to alternative hypotheses, and the number of occasions on which they have escaped possible rejection. In both social and natural sciences, the body of positive knowledge grows by the failure of a tentative hypothesis to predict phenomena that the hypothesis professes to explain; by the patching up of that hypothesis until someone suggests a new hypothesis that more elegantly and simply embodies the troublesome phenomena, and so ad infinitum. In both, experiment is sometimes possible, sometimes not (witness meteorology). In both, no experiment is ever completely controlled, and experience often offers evidence that is the equivalent of controlled experiment. In both, there is no way to have a self-contained closed system or to avoid interaction between the observer and the observed.[43]

Paradoxically, controversies in economics are both deeper and more superficial. They at times go to the very root of our beliefs and at others are only a demonstration of a general vogue. Samuelson (1966, p. 1518) suggested that 'fashion always plays an important role in economic science; new concepts become the mode and then are passé. A cynic might even be tempted to speculate as to whether academic discussion is itself equilibrating: whether assertion, reply, and rejoinder do not represent an oscillating divergent series, in which .., "bad talk drives out good".' Even more bluntly, Shubik (1970, pp. 405–6) points out that the main difference between academia and the garment industry is that the latter is aware of the role of fashion, whereas the former often deludes itself about the objectivity with which truth is pursued. 'The pressures of the problems of society are real; but it takes both moral and intellectual stature to be able to distinguish between today's fashions and the basic problems that an economist might help to solve' (Shubik, 1970, p. 406).

The closest to Wicksell's reference to the similarities between economics and theology is Joan Ribinson's (1962, pp. 2 and 3) implication that ideology is like metaphysics; that is, 'if an ideological proposition is treated in a logical manner, it either dissolves into a completely meaningless noise or turns out to be a circular argument . . . Yet metaphysical statements are not without content. They express a point of view and formulate feelings which are a guide to conduct.' And, in a vein similar to Schumpeter (1954) and Lange (1945–6), she (1962, p. 3) sees ideology as a necessary component of science: 'Metaphysical prepositons also provide a quarry from which hypotheses can be drawn. They do not belong to the realm of science and yet they are necessary to it.' However, she (1962, p. 14) is closer to Myrdal (1972, pp. 148–9) in perceiving economics as pervasively value impregnated. Its very terminology is coloured: 'Bigger is close to better; equal to equitable; goods sound good; disequilibrium sounds uncomfortable; exploitation, wicked; and sub-normal profits, rather sad.' Even in attempting to describe the technical features of an economic system objectively, we cannot escape from making moral judgements:

> For to look at a system from the outside implies that it is not the only possible system; in describing it we compare it (openly or tacitly) with other actual or imagined systems. Differences imply choices, and choices imply judgment. We cannot escape from making judgments and the judgments that we make arise from the ethical preconceptions that have soaked into our view of life and are somehow printed in our brains (Joan Robinson, 1962, p. 14).

Schumpeter (1954, pp. 34–5) views ideological bias as part of the process of rationalization: 'This habit consists in comforting ourselves and impressing others by drawing a picture of ourselves, our motives, our friends, our enemies, our vocation, our church, our country, which may have more to do with what we like them to be than with what they are.' Thus, he (1949, p. 349) stresses that, like Marx, most economists are apt to recognize the presence of ideological bias, but 'they find it only in others and never in themselves'.

Schumpeter's (1954, p. 37) amended version of Marx's concept of ideological bias fully accepts 'the doctrine of the ubiquity of ideological bias and therefore cannot see anything else in the belief of some groups in their freedom from it but a particularly vicious part of their own system of delusions'. Schumpeter (1949, pp. 347–8) also makes the important distinction between ideology and value judgement. He (1954, p. 37) considers that 'an economist's value judgments often *reveal* his ideology but they *are not* his ideology: it is possible to pass value judgments upon irreproachably established facts and the relations between them, and it is possible to refrain from passing any value judgments upon facts that are seen in an ideologically deflected light'. $_c$

Schumpeter (1954, pp. 41–2) locates the ideological element in the 'preanalytic cognitive act' that he calls Vision.[44] He very convincingly illustrates it with the example of the Keynesian vision that was already formulated, but still analytically unarmed, in *The Economic Consequences of the Peace*. In our own day and age, an eloquent example is the notorious and often recondite Cambridge–Cambridge controversy that transcends the theory of capital and involves the whole corpus of economic theory and underlying ideologies. On both sides of the fence there are those who confirm (Samuelson, 1977, pp. 113 and 141; Harcourt, 1972) and those who deny (Solow, 1975, p. 277; Stiglitz, 1974, pp. 901–2) the ideological underpinnings.

Schumpeter (1954, p. 42) claims that 'analytic work begins with material provided by our vision of things, and this vision is ideological almost by definition'. But Schumpeter (1949, p. 359) does not see this as a misfortune, for:

that prescientific cognitive act which is the source of our ideologies is also the prerequisite of our scientific work. No new departure in any science is possible without it. Through it we acquire new material for our scientific endeavors and something to formulate, to defend, to attack. Our stock of facts and tools grows and rejuvenates itself in the process. And so – though we proceed slowly because of our ideologies, we might not proceed at all without them (see also Lange, 1945–6, pp. 10–11).

Perhaps somewhat optimistically, Schumpeter (1954, pp. 43–4) feels that in the process of working out the analytical armature, ideology is bound to wither away. He also speaks of the ideological neutrality of many of our theoretical and statistical tools (a cogent example of which might be, as we have seen, linear programming, a pre-institutional analysis). Thus he (1949, p. 359) claims that fact finding and analysis 'tend to destroy whatever will not stand their tests'. Hence, 'no economic ideology could survive indefinitely even in a stationary social world. As time wears on and these tests are being perfected, they do their work more quickly and more effectively. But this still leaves us with the result that some ideology will always be with us and so, I feel convinced, it will'.

Ideology also enters economic investigations through less lofty motives than Vision. Besides being like other human beings, members of society living under given institutions and products of a civilization, economists depend professionally on such institutions as universities, research institutes, foundations, publishers, press, government agencies, and business firms. That most of these institutions have objectives other than the untramelled pursuit of truth is indisputable. As T. W. Schultz (1981, p. 90) put it:

> Patrons of economic research are not renowned for their neutrality. Politicized economic research has become the order of the day. A new breed of economic research institutions is in the ascendancy supported by private patrons, by foundations, and by federal funds. I am mainly concerned about the adverse effects of this development on the research and educational fuctions of academic economists (see Lange, 1945–6, p. 9; Galbraith, 1973a, p. 1; Myrdal, 1972, pp. 1–3).

Multifarious rewards flow from orthodoxy both within and outside of academia. This, as Schultz (1981, pp. 92–3) points out, gives rise to accommodation and complacency and stifles the necessary criticism:

> It is my contention that many academic economists are complacent about their freedom of inquiry, about safeguarding their university functions, and about the conditions under which research funds are made available to them by institutions other than the university. This complacency about the special and specific usefulness of inquiry that is free of outside intrusion is exemplified in their failure to challenge publicly private patrons, foundations and governmental agencies on their allocation of funds for economic research. But to do this competently requires firm knowledge of utility of economic thought and research appropriate to the functions of the university. It also requires courage because it entails the risk of alienating the patrons and causing them to reduce further their support of university research. This risk is neatly avoided by the art of accommodation, by quietly and gracefully submitting proposals for research grants that seem to fit the demands of the patrons ...
>
> The thrust of my argument is that one of the primary functions of academic economists is to question society's institutions. Economists are all too complacent about their freedom of inquiry. They are not sufficiently vigilant in safeguarding their function as educators. They should give a high priority to scholarly criticism of the economics of society's institutions. The distortions of economic research will not fade away by accommodating the patrons of research funds.

One of the subjects on which most economists agree (yet not always, as indicated in the opening paragraph of this section) is the difference between their subject and the natural sciences. As Keynes (1973, p. 297) suggests, 'economics is essentially a moral science and not a natural science. That is to say, it employs introspection and judgements of value.' The primary difference is the lack in economics of an accepted standard for the verification or disproof of a hypothesis. Because no controlled experiment can be conducted, interpretation of such evidence as is thrown up by the real world necessarily involves judgement and that, as we have seen, can be coloured by values. While both the natural and social scientists exhibit the human failings of chauvinism for what they have produced, the latter are subject to far greater ideological influences and because they lack controlled experiments are always left with loopholes (see Koopmans, 1957, p. 140; Joan Robinson, 1962, pp. 22–3).

Lord Robbins (1979, p. 999) traces the differences between economics and the natural sciences to 'the need for the so-called "hard core" of the assumptions of economic analysis to be buttressed by so many auxiliary assumptions, explicit or implicit'. In addition he acknowledges that 'the possibilities of testing are so hedged about with both practical and intellectual difficulties as to constitute almost a difference in kind'. Friedman (1953, pp. 10–11) agrees that empirical evidence is often incomplete and indirect and difficult to interpret. Moreover, 'its interpretation generally requires subtle analysis and involved chains of reasoning, which seldom carry real conviction'. Thus there is considerable difficulty in 'achieving a reasonably prompt and wide consensus on the conclusions justified by the available evidence. It renders the weeding-out of unsuccessful hypotheses slow and difficult. They are seldom downed for good and are always cropping up again.' Nevertheless Friedman (1953, p. 10) contends that 'the inability to conduct so-called "controlled experiments" does not . . . reflect a basic difference between the social and physical sciences . . . because the distinction between a controlled experiment and uncontrolled experience is at best one of degree . . . Evidence cast up by experience is abundant and frequently as conclusive as that from contrived experiments.'

The lack of controlled experiments aside, unlike natural scientists, economists 'study a system that is not only exceedingly complex but is also in a state of constant flux' (Leontief, 1971, p. 3). In this sense, the natural scientists deal with less complex problems to which definitive universal and timeless solutions can be found, whereas economists deal with complicated, fluid, and shifting phenomena which, in addition, vary among different places and groups (see Hicks, 1976, p. 207; Myrdal, 1972, p. 139).

One of the most astute observations about the differences between economics and the natural sciences comes to us from Jacob Marschak, via Koopmans (1979, p. 6):

> Jacob Marschak used to say that economists carry the combined burdens of meteorologists and engineers. Like the meteorologists, they are expected to predict the future course of important variables in their field of study. Just as engineers design more and more efficient machines, economists are also expected to improve the design of society where it affects good use of resources. But, like the meteorologist, the economist has traditionally been confined to drawing inferences from passive observations, records of data generated by the turbulence of the atmosphere or the fluctuations and trends of economic life. Finally — a very important difference — meteorologists and engineers have all the laws and measurements established by physics and chemistry available to them, fully documented by experimental tests and results.
>
> Traditionally, economists have not searched for similar inputs from experimental or observational research of a psychological or sociological nature.

All this should lead economists to be somewhat cautious about the claims they make for their science. Two economists, of quite divergent theoretical and policy viewpoints, warn us that the economist's 'claims should be limited, especially in the field of quantitative prediction' (Robbins, 1979, p. 1000). And because 'economists are not strictly enough compelled to reduce metaphysical concepts to falsifiable terms and cannot compel each other to agree as to what has been falsified . . . economics limps along with one foot in untested hypotheses and the other in untestable slogans' (Joan Robinson, 1962, p.25).

Before proceeding to one of the burning issues of controversy among economists — the tension between theory and reality — let us pose and examine the contemporary economists' differing views of positive and normative economics; that is, the difference between 'what is' and 'what ought to be'.

Koopmans (1957, p. 134) equates positive with descriptive or explanatory analysis and normative with prescriptive analysis. He perceives the difference between these two modes of analysis as revolving basically around the motivations of the research and the use made of the conclusions. In the conclusions or predictions of explanatory (positive) analysis he looks for 'the possibility of testing, that is, of verification or refutation by observation . . . Verification, or absence of refutation, lends support to the set of postulates taken as a whole. Refutation indicates that at least one of the postulates is inadequate for the purpose of "explaining" the phenomena to which the conclusions refer.' And Koopmans, who is more in his element with normative economics (see Malinvaud, 1972, p. 802), sees its purposes as unconstrained by the need for empirical testing. Here the purpose is to recommend a course of action that may be expected to be of better service for given objectives:

If the recommendation is implemented, this may provide an opportunity for testing the postulates on which it is based. However, it may also happen that, because of the continual impact of factors disregarded in the anlysis, or because of the all-pervasive effect of the action implemented, no opportunity remains for observing the effect of not taking the recommended action or of taking some alternative action. In such cases, the recommendation is as good as the postulates from which it is correctly derived, but the analysis need not be less worthwhile for that reason (Koopmans, 1957, p. 134).

In Friedman's (1953, pp. 4–5) view:

Positive economics is in principle independent of any particular ethical position or normative judgments . . . Its task is to provide a system of generalizations that can be used to make correct predictions about the consequences of any change in circumstances. Its performance is to be judged by the precision, scope, and conformity with experience of the predictions it yields. In short, positive economics is, or can be, an 'objective' science, in precisely the same sense as any of the physical sciences . . .

Normative economics and the art of economics, on the other hand, cannot be independent of positive economics. Any policy conclusion necessarily rests on a prediction about the consequences of doing one thing rather than another, a prediction that must be based – implicitly or explicitly – on positive economics.

At the centre of these two conflicting ı   of positive and normative economics seems to be Koopman's conc ı   positive economics' power to explain and Friedman's of the pow ı   predict.[45] Robbins (1979, p. 1003) makes the distinction quite clea

In my judgment current appreciation oı the real value of economic science has been too much influenced by excessive focus on its power to *predict* to the neglect of its wider power to *explain*. This emphasis runs two dangers. From the point of view of the lay philistine, the record is not good – the claims have been much too extensive and have often been just wrong. From the professional point of view, all generalizations that have not predictive power tend to be regarded as worthless, although some of the most profound insights into the nature of the economic system – the Walrasian analysis for instance – most probably do not possess this power.

Among others, Georgescu-Roegen (1971, p. 37) has pointed out that not prediction but 'knowledge for its own sake' is the purpose of science. But he concedes that prediction is none the less 'the touchstone of scientific knowledge'. Few economists will deny the need for theory, though many are disillusioned with its accomplishments.[46] As Shackle (1967, pp. 288–9) pointed out:

> Theory serves deep needs of the human spirit: it subordinates nature to man, imposes a beautiful simplicity on the unbearable multiplicity of fact, gives comfort in face of the unknown and unexperienced, stops the teasing of mystery and doubt which, though salutary and life-preserving, is uncomfortable, so that we seek by theory to sort out the justified from the unjustified fear. Theories by their nature and purpose, their role of administering to a 'good state of mind', are things to be held and cherished. Theories are altered or discarded only when they fail us.

Hicks (1976, p. 208) calls theories blinkers that help us focus on essentials. 'But it is obvious that a theory which is to perform this function satisfactorily must be well chosen; otherwise it will illumine the wrong things.' And he also warns us that since economics studies a changing world, 'a theory which illumines the right things now may illumine the wrong things another time'. Thus:

> there is, there can be, no economic theory which will do for us everything we want all the time. Accordingly, while we are right to allow ourselves to become wrapped up in those theories which are useful now, we are unwise if we allow ourselves to forget that the time may come when we shall need something different. We may then be right to reject our present theories, not because they are wrong, but because they have become inappropriate.

For Samuelson (1972, p. 261), a beautiful problem in science may reflect logical beauty:

> Proof that the set of prime numbers cannot be finite – since the product of any set of finite numbers plus one gives a new prime number – is

as aesthetically neat in our times as it was in Euclid's. But a problem
takes on extra luster, if in addition to its logical elegance, it provides
useful knowledge. That the shortest distance between two points on a
sphere is the arc of a great circle is an agreeable curiosity; that ships on
earth actually follow such paths enhances its interest.

Hicks (1976, p. 218) is in agreement about the need for useful theories.
But, he adds:

> That means that they must be selective. But all selection is dangerous.
> So there is plenty of room for criticism, and for the filling in of gaps,
> building some sort of bridge between one selective theory and another.
> There is plenty of room for academic work, doing that sort of a job.
> Much of it, I am well aware, works in its own 'blinkers', seeing the mote
> that is in one's brother's eye but not the beam that is in one's own.
> That, I am afraid, is the nature of the case. Still, one could learn a little
> humility.

And what of the early Hicks (1939b)? How does his theoretical work of
yesterday stand up to his views of theory today? To a large extent, it does
not. Shubik (1970, p. 413) criticizes Hicks (1939b) for a 'pervading sense
of sterility' and an 'overpowering aura of specious generality'.[47] Hicks
(1939b) set himself the task of analysing the pure logic of capitalism
which, indeed, would have been a feat had it been accomplished. The
result, however, was a study of a system composed of an indefinite number
of perfectly informed utility maximizers who trade only in individually
owned commodities in frictionless instantaneous markets that operate in
an environment where there are no individibilities, no externalities, no
government, no taxation, and no money. As Shubik (1970, p. 413) points
out, such a study, even at its most abstract level, is 'something less than a
pure logical analysis of capitalism':

> Economics is, at its best, an applied science (if it can be considered a
> science at all). The quality of the model or abstraction must be ques-
> tioned as well as the quality and elegance of the analysis. The very
> power and elegance of Hicks' analysis may have set the subject back as
> far as it set it forward. I am not sure that it did happen, but it may
> have happened because the power of the analysis – combined with the
> pontifical style – made it appear that Hicks' abstraction was somehow
> central, universal, and of broad application. Men of lesser intellect, but
> more common sense, were served warning in his introduction that they
> could muck about with other models if they wanted to be economic

historians, but if it was *reine Wissenschaft* that they were after, this was it (Shubik, 1970, pp. 413–14).

Most economists agree that some degree of abstraction is necessary in theory and model building. The tension, however, resides in the degree of abstraction – the thorny issue why some economists choose assumptions that they not only believe are erroneous in some aspects but also fundamentally wrong (see Sen, 1976–7, pp. 317–18). Others, however, favour theories whose assumptions are sufficiently approximated by the conditions of the real world and reject hypotheses whose approximations to reality transgress the threshold of their tolerance (see Simon, 1982b, pp. 370–1; Solow, 1980, pp. 7–8).

Economic models are the embodiment of theory which can be viewed in this sense as an architectural plan for building an analogue system that would mimic in *some* restrictive sense the real world (see Lucas, 1981, p. 272). For our purposes it would be useful to follow the important distinction that Klein (1964, pp. 188–9) makes between pedagogical and econometric models. The former concentrates on questions of principle: on the formal, logical, mathematical construct of a self-contained system that elucidates economic dynamics by zeroing in on specific aspects of behaviour. 'From very few main principles of behaviour, systems that are not wholly realistic or practical are built to exhibit movement like that of the actual dynamic economy . . . This exercise belongs largely to *mathematical economics.*' The latter deals with considerably larger, detailed, and less neat models constructed on the bases of actual data. Its purpose is to detect intertemporal movements of variables. These models 'are pieced together by combining several *a priori* hypotheses from the pedagogical models of mathematical economics and adding equations to bring out the institutional nature of the economy being studied – its tax laws, banking practices, degree of market imperfection, dependence on external trading relationships, exchange controls, etc'.

At this juncture it is the mathematical model that is of interest to us. Here too, besides the tensions between abstraction and reality that underlie economic theory, there is the additional and, in the light of contemporary developments, not so minor tension between the art of choosing relevant models and the fascination with rapidly developing more sophisticated techniques. Here too there crops up the additional tension infused by a new generation of economists who sometimes have the tendency to evaluate progress in economics by the degree of sophistication of the apparatus.

To illustrate this, let us contrast two diametrically different theorists:

Keynes and Lucas. In 1938, in a letter to Roy Harrod, Keynes (1973, pp. 296–7) describes economics as 'a science of thinking in terms of models joined to the art of choosing models which are relevant to the contemporary world'. Thus, according to him, 'progress in economics consists almost entirely in a progressive improvement in the choice of models'. But such a choice is not a simple matter. 'Good economists are scarce because the gift for using "vigilant observation" to choose good models, although it does not require a highly specialised intellectual technique, appears to be a very rare one.'

Lucas, (1981, pp. 271–72), on the other hand, believes that 'any model that is well enough articulated to give clear answers to the questions we put to it will necessarily be artificial, abstract, patently "unreal".' Furthermore, 'the more dimensions on which the model mimics the answers actual economies give to simple questions, the more we trust its answers to harder questions. This is the sense in which more "realism" in a model is clearly preferred to less . . . A "good" model . . . will not be exactly more "real" than a poor one, but will provide better imitations.' But he (1981, p. 272) attributes extraordinary importance to refinements of techniques and much less to the quandaries of a changing world:

> Marshall's world was enough like ours and Marshall was an astute enough observer of his world that it is difficult to make general observations about our economy which do not have close precedent in some Marshallian observation about his. Our ability to construct analogue economies is, however, much greater, so that we have the capacity to study in detail market interactions about which Marshall could only conjecture.

Essentially a most deep-rooted subject of dissent among economists is the extent to which theory should approximate the real world, the essence of abstraction in theory, and whether a theory stands or falls on the assumption made. As Hicks (1939b, p. 23) remarked, 'pure economics has a remarkable way of producing rabbits out of a hat – apparently *a priori* propositions which apparently refer to reality'.

Mises's (1979, p. 62) and the Austrians' 'radical apriorism', which survives to this day among their followers (see, *interalia*, Spadaro, 1978, pp. 40–56; Kirzner, 1982), claims that 'what we know about the fundamental categories of action . . . is not derived from experience. We conceive all this from within, just as we conceive logical and mathematical truths, *a priori*, without reference to any experience. Nor could experience ever lead anyone to the knowledge of these things if he did not comprehend them from within himself.' Mises continues that 'it would be possible to construct, by the use of the axiomatic method, a universal praxeology so general that its system would embrace not only all the patterns of action in the world that we actually encounter, but also patterns of action in worlds whose conditions are purely imaginary and do not correspond to any experience'.

In a somewhat similar vein, but with a far milder apriorism, Robbins (1935, pp. 78–9) maintains that:

> The propositions of economic theory, like all scientific theory, are abviously deductions from a series of postulates. And the chief of these postulates are all assumptions involving in some way simple and indisputable facts of experience relating to the way in which the scarcity of goods which is the subject-matter of our science actually shows itself in the world of reality . . . We do not need controlled experiments to establish their validity: they are so much the stuff of our everyday experience that they have only to be stated to be recognised as obvious.

Robbins (1935, p. 94) rationalizes the tension between reality and unrealistic assumptions such as perfect rationality and perfect foresight by claiming that their purpose 'is not to foster the belief that the world of reality corresponds to the constructions in which they figure, but rather to enable us to study, in isolation, tendencies which, in the world of reality, operate only in conjunction with many others, and then, by contrast as much as by comparison, to turn back to apply the knowledge thus gained to the explanations of more complicated situations'.

As Koopmans (1957, pp. 136–7) notes (illustrating his argument by an analysis of the postulate of complete preference ordering of all consumers), when one tries to unravel in detail the basic postulates of economic theory, one soon comes to grief over the fact that they are far from obvious. Samuelson (1966, p. 1757) points out that 'it is clear that no a priori empirical truths can exist in any field. If a thing has a priori irrefutable truth, it must be empty of empirical content. It must be regarded as a meaningless proposition in the technical sense of modern philosophy.' And, in a well-turned parallel, Samuelson (1972, p. 761) scathingly criticizes Menger, Robbins, Mises, and the disciples of Knight:

> In connection with slavery, Thomas Jefferson said that, when he considered that there is a just God in Heaven, he trembled for his country. Well in connection with the exaggerated claims that used to be made in economics for the power of deduction and a priori reasoning . . . I tremble for the reputation of my subject.

Contrary to Robbins, Friedman is not concerned with whether or not the assumptions are realistic, only with the theory's predictive power, as we have previously alluded. Friedman (1953, p. 14) rejects the supposition that:

> hypotheses have not only 'implications' but also 'assumptions' and that the conformity of these 'assumptions' to 'reality' is a test of the validity of the hypothesis *different from* or *additional to* the test by implications. This widely held view is fundamentally wrong and productive of much mischief. Far from providing an easier means for sifting valid from invalid hypotheses, it only confuses the issue, promotes misunderstanding about the significance of empirical evidence for economic theory, produces a misdirection of much intellectual effort devoted to the development of positive economics, and impedes the attainment of consensus on tentative hypotheses in positive economics.

In the milder version of his positon,[48] Friedman (1953, p. 15) claims that:

> the relevant question to ask about the 'assumptions' of a theory is not whether they are descriptively 'realistic', for they never are, but whether they are sufficiently good approximations for the purpose in hand. And this question can be answered only by seeing whether the theory works, which means whether it yields sufficiently accurate predictions. The two supposedly independent tests thus reduce to one test.

Obviously, the key words here, on which some of modern economics has built, are *good approximation*.

Friedman (1953, pp. 19–23) then goes on to explain, in a spirit similar to Alchian (1950), that whether or not the assumed behaviour of economic actors is close to reality does not matter as long as the observed result of that behaviour is what could have been predicted, had the actors actually behaved as was assumed. He uses very effectively examples from biology, physics, and other fields to illustrate and drive home the point that though 'businessmen do not actually and literally solve the system of simultaneous equations', they behave *as if* they did. Thus:

> individual firms behave *as if* they were seeking rationally to maximize their expected returns . . . and had full knowledge of the data needed to succeed in this attempt; *as if* that is, they knew the relevant cost and demand functions, calculated marginal cost and marginal revenue from all actions open to them, and pushed each line of action to the point at which the relevant marginal cost and marginal revenue were equal (Friedman, 1953, pp. 21–2).

In addition, Friedman (1953, p. 10) stresses that a number of different hypotheses can be verified by the same evidence, but that the significant attributes of the 'correct' hypothesis are its simplicity and fruitfulness:

> The choice among alternative hypotheses equally consistent with the available evidence must to some extent be arbitrary, though there is general agreement that relevant considerations are suggested by the criteria 'simplicity' and 'fruitfulness', themselves notions that defy completely objective specification. A theory is 'simpler' the less the initial knowledge needed to make a prediction within a given field of phenomena; it is more 'fruitful' the more precise the resulting prediction, the wider the area within which the theory yields predictions, and the more additional lines for further research it suggests.

Friedman's position gave rise to a heated controversy that continues to exercise many economists to this day.[49] His most faithful and consistent critic, Samuelson (1966, p. 1774), has dubbed Friedman's position the 'F-twist', which he understands to mean that 'a theory is vindicable if (some of) its consequences are empirically valid to a useful degree of approximation; the (empirical) unrealism of the theory "itself", or of its "assumptions", is quite irrelevant to its validity and worth". The F-twist, Samuelson continues, 'is fundamentally wrong in thinking that unrealism in the sense of factual inaccuracy even to a tolerable degree of approximation is anything but a demerit for a theory or hypothesis'. In this sense, the whole force of Samuelson's (1972, p. 761) attack on the F-twist centres on the contention that 'the doughnut of empirical correctness in a theory constitutes its worth, while its hole of untruth constitutes its weakness. I regard it as a monstrous perversion of science to claim that a theory is *all the better for its shortcomings*; and I notice that in the luckier exact sciences, no one dreams of making such a claim'.

In a similar vein, Simon (1928b, p. 369) refers to the F-twist as 'Friedman's principle of unreality', which leads Friedman to presume that 'he already knows what an economist will find when he looks into a business firm, and that even if he finds something quite different it does not matter for economics' (1953, p. 58). And again, like Samuelson, Simon (1982b, p. 371) concludes that 'unreality of premises is not a virtue in scientific theory; it is a necessary evil — a concession to the finite computing capacity of the scientist that is made tolerable by the principle of continuity of approximation'.

A Chicago 'insider', Harry Johnson (1971a, pp. 9 and 13), suggests that Friedman's methodology has been instrumental in allowing individual scholars (independent of large-scale research teams and expensive computer programmes) to make sweeping predictions from restrictive assumptions – thus its appeal. Surprising results can be reported without necessarily having to explain how they were achieved simply by relying on the *as if* approach. Johnson (1971a, p. 13) contends that this methodology is 'in conflict with long run trends in the development of the subject'.

While Johnson (1971a) only implies it, Samuelson (1966, p. 1774) explicitly accuses Friedman of having 'a strong effective demand which a valid F-Twist brand of positivism could supply'. The motivation is:

> to help the case for (1) the perfectly competitive laissez-faire model of economics, which has been under continuous attack from outside the profession for a century and from within since the monopolistic competition revolution of thirty years past; and (2) but of lesser moment, the 'maximization-of-profit' hypothesis, that mixture of triusm, truth untruth.[50]

Somewhat admittedly unfairly and rather surrealistically, Samuelson (1966, p. 1775) hoists Friedman on his own petard, while paradoxically denying the existence of such a petard. Samuelson concludes that the F-twist could be interpreted as saying that its origin and purpose 'may be "unrealistic" (a euphemism for "empirically dead wrong"), but what of that?' It is of no consequence as long as the 'theory agrees with the fact that Chicagoans use the methodology to explain away objections to their assertions'.[51]

Samuelson again calls into play the tension between the concepts of perfect and imperfect competition in criticizing Friedman's preference for a simple theory (see also Simon, 1982b, p. 476). Samuelson (1966, p. 1777) recalls that at Chicago he was taught to reject 'monopolistic competition on the ground that it is not a "nice, simple, unified" theory like that of perfect competition' which is 'simpler and more manageable. If perfect competition is the best simple theory in town, that is no excuse for saying we should regard it as a good theory if it is not a good theory. To use the F-Twist to minimize its imperfections or irrelevancies is . . . simply wrong.' He (1972, pp. 21–2) buttresses this argument by concluding, in another context, that:

> Perfect competition provides an empirically inadequate model of the real world. This forces us to work with some versions of monopolistic or imperfect competition. Chicago economists can continue to shout until they are blue in the face that there is no elegant alternative to the theory of perfect competion . . . If not, the proper moral is, 'So much

the worse for elegance' rather than, 'Economists of the world unite in proclaiming that the Emperor has almost no clothes, and in pretending that the model of perfect competition does a good enough job in fitting the real world.'

From another angle, Koopmans (1957, p. 139) objects to Friedman's concept of theory construction on the grounds that in order to obtain a refutable theory the postulates have to be supplemented with 'a clear description of the class of implications by which the theory stands or falls'. Friedman meets this objection by requiring that the type of phenomena the hypothesis is supposed to explain be specified. Yet Koopmans (1957, p. 139) sees that a 'second objection arises out of this answer to the first. To state a set of postulates, and then to exempt a subclass of their implications from verification is a curiously roundabout way of specifying the content of a theory that is regarded as open to empirical refutation.'

Koopmans (1957, pp. 139–40) feels 'uneasy' in the face of Friedman's ingenuity:

> Truth, like peace, is indivisible. It cannot be compartmentalized. Before we can accept the view that obvious discrepancies between behavior postulates and directly observed behavior do not affect the predictive power of specified implications of the postulates, we need to understand the reasons why these discrepancies do not matter. This is all the more important in a field such as economics where . . . the opportunities for verification of the predictions and implications derived from the postulates are scarce and the outcome of such verification often remains somewhat uncertain . . . If, in comparison with some other sciences, economics is handicapped by severe and possibly unsurmountable obstacles of meaningful experimentation, the opportunities for direct introspection by and direct observation of, individual decision makers are a much needed source of evidence which in some degree offsets the handicap. We cannot really feel confident in acting upon our economic knowledge until its deductions reconcile directly observed patterns of individual behavior with such implications for the economy as a whole as we find ourselves able to subject ot test.

Koopmans's own approach to economics is very much in line with this significant passage from Wald (1951, p. 369):

> It must be admitted that in many areas of mathematical economics very substantial abstractions are being used, so that one can hardly speak of a good approximation to reality. But it should be remembered

that, on the one hand, mathematical economics is a very young science and, on the other, that economic phenomena are of such a complicated, involved nature that far-reaching abstractions must be used at the start merely to be able to survey the problem, and that the transition to more realistic assumptions must be carried out step by step.

Koopmans (1957, p. 143) posits that verification of a theory does not admit of intentional disregard of 'obviously important aspects of reality'. And verification 'is indispensable for the gradual unfolding of a body of logically valid implications of economically relevant (but not necessarily by themselves valid) postulates'. By adopting this concept one may relax the apparent tension between rigour and realism. The latter will always precede the former in the progress of the science, 'but unless rigor follows along to consolidate the gains in realism, we shall not know which conclusions or recommendations depend on which postulates, and which postulates depend for their validity on which verifications of their implications by accumulated experience'. Koopmans (1957, p. 147) suggests that if the approach he advocates 'of economic theory as a sequence of models is more widely accepted, however, dissatisfaction with the relevance of available models will provide the necessary stimulas for cumulative refinement of models to take into account more and more relevant aspects of reality'. He (1957, p. 143) admits that this is neither a novel nor controversial approach. 'It is in the practice of our professional activities that we do not live up to it.'[52]

Koopmans (1957, pp. 146–7) warns of the danger of overestimating the conclusions of economic theory. As an example he offers 'the overextended belief of the liberalist school of economic thought in the efficiency of competitive markets as a means of allocating resources in a world full of uncertainty'. And, as a safeguard against such overestimation, 'is a careful spelling out of the premises on which . . . [the propositions] rest. Precision and rigor in the statement of premises and proofs can be expected to have a sobering effect on our beliefs about the reach of the propositions we have developed'.

Unlike many other economists, Koopmans is a prime example of a man who follows his own advice. As Malinvaud (1972, pp. 799–801) attests, Koopmans's writings closely follow the precepts of modern science: respect for rigour and objectivity. Most economists cannot resist the temptation to judge social organizations and to make recommendations. Not so Koopmans. He 'aims at complete rigor in his argumentation. He avoids conjectures and digressions, or rather he limits them to what is directly pertinent for his subject' (Malinvaud, 1972, p. 800).

Koopman's style has lent itself particularly well to the pre-institutional type of analysis to which he has devoted much effort. While much of earlier discussion about efficient allocation of resources in production (emanating from the famous interwar debate on the economic merit of socialism) centred on the evaluation of alternative institutional or working arrangements, Koopmans and others shifted attention to 'the formal conditions for the efficient use of resources' (Koopmans, 1970, p. 213). That is, to 'what may be called a *pre*-institutional theory of allocation of resources' and the 'underlying pre-institutional optimizing theory' (Koopmans, 1977a, p. 264). In a similar vein, Koopmans (1970, p. 549) describes the development in the theory of optimal economic growth. These studies 'are not tied to any particular form of economic organization. Their postulates concern (a) production possibilities, and (b) intertemporal preferences regarding consumption. Technology is, indeed, universal.' While he (1970, p. 549) recognizes the importance of institutional differences in arriving at and implementing intertemporal preferences, the pre-institutional type of analysis merely assumes 'that such preferences are given, without inquiring how they are determined and given effect to'. It may be noted that Koopmans (1970, p. 565) perceives the simplest interpretation of the theory of optimal economic growth 'in terms of an economy in which growth rates are centrally planned in a manner capable of implementation. It is hoped that the analysis can also serve as background for the discussion of growth policies in an individual or corporate enterprise society, or under conditions of less perfect and dependable planning.'

And what of the economist's role in this kind of approach?

The economist as such does not advocate criteria of optimality. He may invent them. He will discuss their pros and cons, sometimes before but preferably after trying out their implications. He may also draw attention to situations where all-over objectives, such as productive efficiency, can be served in a decentralized manner by particularized criteria, such as profit maximization. But the ultimate choice is made, usually only implicitly and not always consistently by the procedures of decision making inherent in the institutions, laws and customs of society. A wide range of professional competences enters into the preparation and deliberation of these decisions. To the extent that the economist takes part in this decisive phase, he does so in a double role, as economist, and as a citizen of his polity: local polity, national polity, or world polity (Koopmans, 1977a, p. 272).

Whereas classical economics was concerned with grand historical themes, mainstream contemporary economics is in the main preoccupied with small questions.[53] In looking at the development of the subject, one is tempted to distinguish political economy from economic analysis.[54] The political economists of yore (Smith, Ricardo, J. S. Mill, Marx, and, to some extent, Marshall) gained by concentrating their attention on such fundamentals as accumulation, production, and distribution (and, in the case of Marx, also the enthralling vision of the complex capitalist system in motion, emphasizing conflicting class interests, and treating the institutional arrangements and social relations as key determinants of a system's dynamics and as 'variables' in the problem of utilization of resources).

In a perceptive, revealing, and instructive passage, Schumpeter (1950, p. 43) evaluates Marx as an economic theorist and, more importantly, Marx's legacy for modern economic analysis. He argues that in the court that sits on theoretical techniques, the verdict on Marx would be rather adverse:

> But a court of appeal — even though still confined to theoretical matters — might feel inclined to reverse this verdict altogether. For there is one truly great achievement to be set against Marx's theoretical misdemeanors. Through all that is faulty or even unscientific in his analysis runs a fundamental idea that is neither — the idea of a theory, not merely of an indefinite number of disjointed individual patterns or of the logic of economic quantities in general, but of the actual sequence of those patterns or of the economic process as it goes on, under its own steam, in historic time, producing at every instant that state which will of itself determine the next one. Thus, the author of so many misconceptions was also the first to visualize what even at the present time is still the economic theory of the future for which we are slowly and laboriously accumulating stone and mortar, statistical facts and functional equations.

Looking at the development of classical theory, Hicks (1976, p. 211) speculates that the transitions from one stage to another (Hicks calls them revolutions) 'did not come about, in the scientific manner, because of the need to take account of new facts, revealed by experiment or observation, facts which however had been *there* all the time. It did come about as a result of the need to accommodate new facts, but they were genuinely new facts, facts which had come into existence in the course of history — new *events*.' *Par contre*, the development of neoclassical economics — the rise of the marginalist school that Hicks (1976, pp. 212–14) calls catallactics — centred on exchange. It was not closely related to real-world events; it 'had always been a possibility. The novelty in the work of the great catallactists is just that they achieved it. The appeal of catallactics lay in its intellectual quality' (Hicks, 1976, p. 214). In this sense it conquered mainstream economics and the way we look at economics past and present. An excellent example is Schumpeter's (1954) masterful and insightful look at the development of the science. He evaluates economists by their scientific contributions, giving high credit to Walras, Jevons, Menger, and others; as against political economists, treating Smith, Ricardo, and Marshall somewhat condescendingly (see Hicks, 1976, pp. 214—15).

For contemporary economists the appeal of the stream of thought that Hicks has labelled catallactics lies also in the fact that its fathers were thinking in mathematical terms: 'and the mathematics that is implied in their theories has proved to be capable of enormous development' (Hicks, 1976 p. 214). One may also agree that the modern theorists' more timid approach is due not so much to their being less daring and imaginative than the classics, but simply more wary of oversimplifications (see Baumol, 1970, p. 13). Samuelson (1966, p. 422) points out that the classical economists 'declared so many things to be necessarily so that we today recognize as not having to be so. This is, in a sense, a step backward.' The modern theorist is 'more humble' and, at the expense of being dull, he 'must face the facts of life — the infinite multiplicity of patterns that can emerge in actuality. Good, advanced theory must be the antidote for overly-simple, intuitive theory.' Yet Samuelson himself is an odd mixture of classic and neoclassic, for beyond Samuelson the superb technician lurks Samuelson the political economist. He speaks of economic theory as 'a mistress of even too tempting grace . . . When man sets himself the challenge to theorize and *yet stay within the constraint of explaining reality*, the task is much the harder — but how much more satisfying the hunt. At night by the fireside let them who will display their easy tiger skins; for man the greatest quarry of all is the study of man. For what do they know of economics, who political economy do not know?' (Samuelson, 1966, pp. 1680—1).

There is more than a grain of truth in the observation that tools do have a life of their own and may strongly influence various schools of thought or even entire periods (see Lucas, 1981, pp. 272—3). At times certain important problems remain unsolved because the required tools are not formulated and at others the availability of some tools may influence concentration on certain less important problems. As Koopmans (1957, p. 170) suggests, 'the present phase in the development of economics provides vivid examples of the manifold interactions between tools and problems'. Problems are derived from the conditions and requirements of the world around us, whereas the tools and training in their use are our own intellectual capital. As we have seen, we have a hard time to be objective about the world we live in. 'But it is even harder to be objective about what are promising tools for unsolved problems: the usefulness of our own individual minds and of the investments of personal effort sunk in our training and direction of interest are involved.'

The modern economist's predilection for tools is somewhat influenced by his training. Unlike economists of yore who were sometimes businessmen (like Ricardo), but more often trained as historians, philosophers, mathematicians, or lawyers, their modern counterparts specialize very early in economic analysis and lack a broader perspective and interdisciplinary perception of society. Nowadays also the graduate students who have not started their training in economics are more likely to come from mathematics or the natural sciences. All this makes them somewhat narrow and less perturbed by the apparent irrelevance of their own and their colleagues' models to the real world. It also makes them more prone to believe that of all social sciences economics is closest to the natural sciences and reinforces their emulation of the latter's methods (see Myrdal, 1972, pp. 61–2 and 141–4).

Mathematics has gained pre-eminence in the economist's toolbox.[55] Following Willard Gibbs, Samuelson (1966, p. 1751) affirms that ' "mathematics *is* language". Now I mean this entirely literally. In principle, mathematics cannot be worse than prose in economic theory; in principle, it certainly cannot be better than prose. For in deepest logic – and leaving out all tactical and pedagogical questions – the two media are strictly identical.'[56] But Koopmans (1957, pp. 178–9) distinguishes between literary and mathematical language. He considers that 'at the present stage of our knowledge' the former 'can only be so perceptive and so rich in distinctions because words are cheap . . . One enters a different, and in many ways poorer and more rigid, world when one examines the mathematically expressed literature.' The older statemen in our profession – many of whom have been in the avant-garde of the present mathematical trend, but who have either a broader training or are more concerned with social issues and their own social responsibility than their younger colleagues – have repeatedly and perhaps with an element of introspection expressed their disquietude about the state of the science. As Leontief (1971, p. 1) put it, 'an uneasy feeling about the present state of our discipline has been growing in some of us who have watched its unprecedented development over the last three decades. This concern seems to be shared even by those who are themselves contributing successfully to the present boom. They play the game with professional skill but have serious doubts about its rules.' Samuelson (1972, pp. 42–3) admitted that the mathematization of economic theory in which he himself participated has been subject to sharply decreasing returns. 'In-equalities, convex sets, and the theories of cones have made modern formulations more elegant and easier.' In deploring this state of affairs, he pointed to such modern treatises as Dorfman, Samuelson, and Solow (1958) and Debreu (1959) which often 'score easy victories and represent a retrogression where realism in dealing with market imperfections is concerned'.

Leontief (1971, p. 1) is adamant that there is in fact a 'fundamental imbalance in the present state of our discipline. The weak and all too slowly growing empirical foundation clearly cannot support the prolif-erating superstructure of pure, or should I say, speculative economic theory.' He (1982, p. 104) points out that nowadays economists escape 'the harsh discipline of systematic fact-finding', and have thus 'developed a nearly irresistible predilection for deductive reasoning . . . Page after page of professional economic journals are filled with mathematical formulas leading the reader from sets of more or less plausible but entirely arbitrary assumptions to precisely stated but irrelevant theoretical conclusions.'

> The mathematical model-building industry has grown into one of the most prestigious, possibly the most prestigious branch of economics . . .
>
> In the presentation of a new model, attention nowadays is usually centered on a step-by-step derivation of its formal properties. But . . . such mathematical manipulations, however long and intricate, can even without further checking be accepted as correct. Nevertheless, they are usually spelled out at great length. By the time it comes to interpretation of the substantive *conclusions*, the assumptions on which the model has been based are easily forgotten. But it is precisely the empirical validity of these *assumptions* on which the usefulness of the entire exercise depends (Leontief, 1971, p. 2).

Georgescu-Roegen (1970, p. 1) also reminds us that 'in our haste to mathe-matize economics we have often been carried away by mathematical formalism to the point of disregarding a basic requirement of science; namely, to have as clear an idea as possible about what corresponds in actuality to every piece of our symbolism'. In a similar vein, Joan Robin-son (1980, p. xi) points out that:

> Contrary to the hopes of its practitioners, the apparent precision of methematics has generated vagueness. Mathematical operations are performed upon entities that cannot be defined; calculations are made in terms of units that cannot be measured; accounting identities are

mistaken for functional relationships; correlations are confused with causal laws; differences are identified as changes; and one-way movements in time are treated like movements to and fro in space. The complexity of models is elaborated merely for display, far and away beyond the possibility of application to reality.

Yet the majority of modern model-builders display a deep-rooted aversion to being contaminated by data. This is apparent in 'the methodological devices that they employ to avoid or cut short the use of concrete factual information. Instead of constructing theoretical models capable of preserving the identity of hundreds, even thousands, of variables needed for the concrete description and analysis of a modern economy, they first of all resort to "aggregation" ' (Leontief, 1982, p. 104). The seldom neat and always arduous task of empirical verification does not often capture the model-builders' interests. When their assumptions are questioned, they are usually not willing to verify them; rather, they would be more prone to change them and, hey presto, create a new theory (see Leontief, 1971, p. 2).

Morishima's (n.d., p. 14) appraisal of the situation runs along similar grooves. He believes that the curcial factor responsible for the 'present remarkably "anaemic" ' condition of mathematical economics is due to the fact that it has failed to establish a good, co-operative relationship with empirical, institutional studies. He deplores the almost total absence (or severe underdevelopment) of institutional—analytical economics (that would abstract from actual empirical descriptions of actual institutions), yet would 'conceive ideal-typical institutions and analyse their working in a rational, mathematical fashion'. And he (p. 15) warns that 'however beautiful or however elegant the whole system may be, those who devote themselves to a learning which is useless are inevitably just playing at a pastime, and it is likely that before long its learning will come to a standstill'.

All this is indeed somewhat unpalatable and disquieting. Undoubtedly 'the achievements of economic theory in the last two decades are both impressive and in many ways beautiful. But it cannot be denied that there is something scandalous in the spectacle of so many people refining the analysis of economic states which they give no reason to suppose will ever, or have ever, come about' (Hahn, 1970, p. 1) .

Morishima (n.d., p. 18), who now rejects mainstream mathematical economics, considers that contemporary economics has lapsed into a 'wretched state of affairs'. He attributes it to the deep and extensive mathematization of economics since 1940 so that economics:

has lost all sense of balance, becoming divorced from knowledge of economic systems and economic history. There is only one medicine which will cure this malaise, and that is for theorists to make a serious effort in the direction of institutionalization of economics, in the sense of slowing the speed of all development towards mathematization and developing economic theory in accordance with knowledge of economic organizations, industrial structure and economic history.

What Hahn (1970, p. 2) terms this 'unsatisfactory and slightly dishonest state of affairs', has resulted in theorists, even those 'quite removed from Cook country' retrogressing 'in the last quarter of a century, taking the coward's way of avoiding the important questions thrown up by the real economic world and fobbing off in their place nice answers to less interesting easy questions' (Samuelson, 1972, p. 22).

NOTES

1. For a historical background of the various strands in GE theory, especially the interwar literature such as the contributions of Abraham Wald and others, see Arrow, 1974, pp. 260–3. See also Debreu, 1982; Weintraub, 1983; and Arrow and Intriligator, 1982 *passim*.
2. For example, 'when it is claimed that foreign aid is unnecessary *because* only investment profitable to private investors can be beneficial, we know at once that the speaker or writer does not know the findings of GE. Anyone who has this knowledge will have no difficulty in pointing to those features of the actual situation which are at variance with what would have to be true if such a claim were to be true. Or take the discussions on floating exchange rates and concentrate only on the claim that the rate will tend to the equilibrium level. Quite apart from all the dynamic problems, the student of GE would note at once not only that there may be no equilibrium level, but also that if there is one such level there may be very many. It may for instance be to the advantage of a country to support an otherwise unstable equilibrium' (Hahn, 1973b, p. 324).
3. The similarity of thought is obvious in the following statement by Lange (1945–6, p. 7), written before publication of linear programming analysis, at least in English: 'The social objectives being given, rules of use of scarce resources can be found which are most conducive to the attainment of these objectives. The use of resources which follows these rules is referred to as the "ideal" use.'
4. With all due scholarly integrity, in his Nobel Lecture, Koopmans (1977a, p. 263) traces the independent initial contributions to this area as follows: 'Kantorovich's work of 1939 did not become known

in the West until the late 1950s or early 1960s. Meanwhile the transportation model was redeveloped in the West without knowledge of the work on this topic by Kantorovich (1942, reprinted 1958) and Kantorovich and Gavurin (1940, 1949). The Western contributions were made by Hitchcock (1941), the author (memo dated 1942, published 1970; articles of 1949 and 1951 (with Reiter)), Dantzig (ch. 23 in Koopmans, ed. 1951).'

5. For an account of the development of this school, see Feiwel, 1972, ch. 4, and references therein.

6. For a succinct exposition and retrospective insight into what Hicks has come to call the Second Welfare Economics, see Hicks, 1975, pp. 308–10.

7. Pareto-satisfactoriness refers to a property of a mechanism while optimality is a property of an allocation. A classical environment is one where there are no externalities, no indivisibilities, and the technology and preferences are convex. On the other hand, a non-classical environment is one characterized by indivisibilities, increasing returns, externalities, and public goods (see Hurwicz, 1972, pp. 426 and 431; 1973, pp. 15–16.)

8. This may be contrasted with Hayek's (1935 and 1940) praise for the swiftness and efficiency of information communicated through market prices to those directly involved in the transactions, without apparent heed to the costs of gathering and processing this information.

9. Simon (1982b, pp. 450 and 485) claims, however, that because of computational difficulties, team theory is essentially illustrative and restricted to very simple situations in miniature organizations.

10. For the relation of the team problem to those of elaborate conflict-ridden organizations and especially to the problem of a non-zero sum game, see Marschak and Radner, 1972, pp. 327–33.

11. Noteworthy is Marschak's exploration of the relations between entropy-kind of measures of information and those clearly related to such economic criteria as cost, scarcity, and benefit (see Marschak and Miyasawa, 1968; Marschak, 1971; and Marschak, 1975).

12. In addition, the following further assumptions are made: (i) parametric function of prices, (ii) current transaction prices clear the market and conform to optimization by all participants, (iii) information is handled like any other commodity, and (iv) government or monopolies have no significant impact on relative prices or quantities. It is recognized that tastes, techniques, resources, and information are affected by random disturbances, but presumably they can be handled through a stochastic analogue of the non-stochastic general competitive model (see Reder, 1982, pp. 11–12 and 19).

13. For example, Milton Friedman (1953, p. 38) claims that 'the theory of imperfect or monopolistic competition . . . possesses none of the

attributes that would make it a truly useful general theory. Its contribution has been limited largely to improving the exposition of the economics of the individual firm and thereby the derivation of implications of the Marshallian model, refining Marshall's monopoly analysis, and enriching the vocabulary available for describing industrial experience.' However, though the Chicago school adamantly opposes the imperfect competition view of the world, Chicago economists have not refrained from analysing the phenomenon of imperfect markets. See, for example, Stigler, 1968 and 1982. Similarly, they have attempted to harmonize observed price stickiness with the assumption of continuous optimization (see Stigler, 1961 and 1962; Becker, 1964 and 1965).

14. In a telling passage, Friedman (1953, p. 31) asserts that, 'answers given by businessmen to questions about the factors affecting their decisions' amount to 'a procedure for testing economic theories that is about on a par with testing theories of longevity by asking octogenarians how they account for their long life – or from descriptive studies of the decision-making activities of individual firms'.

15. Samuelson (1978, p. 182) claims that his 'analysis seems to emerge with a debunking indictment of the claims for maximizing and teleological constructs in biology, evolution, sociobiology, and imperialist-economics (which threatens to absorb sociology, law, and biology, by its pretentious applying to them the jargon of economists).'

16. This may be contrasted with attempts at a behaviourial theory of households such as, for example, that of Mack and Leigland (1982) where 'rational behaviour' is combined with behavioural analysis and selective gleanings from psychology, sociology, and antropology to arrive at what they call 'intendedly rational', quasi-optimizing, or even 'optificing' decision-making.

17. Blaug (1980, p. 242) notes that Becker's reasons are methodological; that is, 'to produce unambiguously falsifiable predictions about behavior and to avoid, whenever possible, ad hoc explanations based on changes of tastes, differences in tastes, ignorance, and impulsive or neurotic behavior. It would appear, therefore, that the Chicago research program is firmly committed, as are few other research programs in modern economics, to the methodological norms laid down by Karl Popper.'

18. For comprehensive and on the whole favourable reviews of Becker's treatise, see Ben-Porath, 1982; and Hannan, 1982. For critiques of Becker's earlier fertility studies, see Samuelson, 1976; and Leibenstein, 1974 and 1975. For an evaluation from a methodological perspective, see Blaug, 1980, pp. 240–9.

19. To place Kornai's work in proper focus, one should note that some of the blueprints for the relatively radical Hungarian reform were inspired

by the notions of GE. Kornai (1971, p. 329) notes that 'illusions have developed that partial' changes in *modus operandi* 'would be sufficient to secure economic efficiency'. It was his exasperation with the disparity between the analytical structure of Walrasian GE (as manifested in the most prominent representatives – the Arrow–Debreu models) and the *realities* of the economic system it attempts to analyse that have inspired his sharp attack.

20. Kornai admits that GE does not use all of the basic assumptions in the proof of each of its theorems.

21. This paramount issue will be dealt with in greater detail in Chapters 1 and 5–8 of the companion volume.

22. Clearly the issue of stability in GE needs to be distinguished from the paramount question of stability of the capitalist economy as Fisher (1976, p. 4) points out: 'an extremely prominent economist long ago remarked to me in passing that the study of stability is unimportant because it is obvious that the economy is stable and, if it isn't we are all wasting our time'.

23. Hahn (1980, p. 127) questions why the critics make such an issue of exogenously given endowments. After all, no sensible theory would start from prehistoric times. We have to take endowments and distribution as historical givens at a particular point of time. From this point on there are numerous futures which, *inter alia*, depend on technology and the rate of increase of durable inputs. While GE considers only a narrow subset of these futures, this restriction, according to Hahn, is not the issue. These futures are characterized by accumulation and distribution of wealth is a resultant and not a datum.

24. Speaking of the critics, Vernon Smith (1974, p. 320) suggests that 'they are good at expounding alleged faults, but bad, on the whole, at correcting them; good at suggesting new directions, but bad at charting them. If there is a new economics in the future (and I predict that there is) it will not be born of sloppy new theory, any more than it will be born of old textbook theory.'

25. For a valuable account of the state of GE and specific developments to date, see Arrow and Intriligator, 1982.

26. Incidentally, at the conclusion of his Nobel Lecture, Samuelson (1972, p. 16) quoted H. J. Davenport, who once said: 'There is no reason why theoretical economics should be a monopoly of the reactionaries.' Samuelson added: 'All my life I have tried to take this warning to heart, and I dare call it to your favorable attention.'

27. Lucas (1981) also acknowledges his indebtedness to Mitchell's work on business cycles. In a different vein, Friedman (1977b, p. 453) claims that Mitchell impressed on him the significance of pursuing a value-free science.

28. This group would also include the breed of mathematical economists

who see game theory as a tool for reintroducing the role of institutions into economic theory. For example, Shubik (1970, p. 428, the Yale University Professor of Mathematical and Institutional economics) believes that 'there is no such thing as institution-free economics. Explicitly or implicitly we slip in assumptions concerning the nature and role of property, political, legal, and social organization. This act does not mean that it is not possible to theorize at levels of great generality. It does mean however that between any two economies there may be subtle differences caused by law or custom which may influence our theorizing.' He (1970, p. 429) concludes that 'new mathematical methods, additional data-gathering, and added computational capability combined yield greater support than ever before for the development of an understanding of microeconomic phenomena. This step taken, our greater wisdom will provide us with the opportunity to be able to put detail and institutions back into microeconomic theorizing.'

29. For Simon's still bitter recollections of the criticism of his work by Edward Mason and Fritz Machlup and his polemic with Milton Friedman about what Samuelson has called the 'F-twist', see Simon, 1982a, p.xix; 1982b, pp. 205–6, 369–71, and 475–6. Simon (1982b, pp. 401–2) recalls that in 1962 (Simon, 1982b, pp. 56–70) he first attempted to reach out for economicts' attention to the behavioural theory of the firm. That attempt and others that followed met with little success. 'Until I was confronted with these expressions of disinterest and with the radical pragmatism of Friedman's methodological essays I had ingenuously supposed that economists' like other species of empirical scientists, were interested in discovering how the world works – in this case the world of human behavior in economic affairs ... In looking back at the research on economics I have undertaken since 1960, and even some I did during the 1950s, I see that a great deal of it can be interpreted as reaction to this resistance of the profession to novelty it regarded as unnecessary. To what extent I was following a conscious strategy of assault on classical theory, to what extent I was driven by those unconscious fonts of energy about which modern psychology is so eloquent, or to what extent my focus on such topics was coincidence I cannot say with any certainty.' And, in a philosophical vein, he (1982b, p. 5) goes on to say: 'One of the consolations of the vocation of science is that in the long run (though we may all be dead) such issues as the relevance of the behavioral theory of the firm to economics will be settled by empirical facts rather than by the elequence of protagonists of one view or another. In this instance, I am a little less sanguine than I was a quarter-century ago that the facts will render their verdict in my lifetime.'

30. Milton Friedman (1953, p. 34) challenges this and similar criticisms on the grounds of irrelevance and misunderstanding: 'The confusion

between descriptive accuracy and analytical relevance has led not only to criticisms of economic theory on largely irrelevant grounds but also to misunderstanding of economic theory and misdirection of efforts to repair supposed defects. "Ideal types" in the abstract model developed by economic theorists have been regarded as strictly descriptive categories intended to correspond directly and fully to entities in the real world independently of the purpose for which the model is being used. The obvious discrepancies have led to necessarily unsuccessful attempts to construct theories on the basis of categories intended to be fully descriptive.'

31. Radner (1975a and 1975b) has pointed out that mathematical decision theory is increasingly confronted with the limits of rationality, but its models continue to be based on individual optimizing behaviour due primarily to a lack of precise formulation of 'satisficing'. He has attempted to examine the concept of long-run success for the decision-maker (and firm or unit) with respect to two criteria: the probability of survival (i.e. performance in one or more activities never falls below some prescribed levels) and the long-run average growth rate of performance (in one or more goals). In addition, he has attempted to develop a number of related mathematical models of satisficing under uncertainty and to apply them to the analysis of a simple process of cost reduction and technical change.

32. It is interesting to note the somewhat similar attitude of Joan Robinson (1977, pp. 1325–6) who, though she claims that 'the doctrine that firms "maximize profits" collapses as soon as it is taken out of the equilibrium world and set in historical time', stresses that it is a misunderstanding to claim that firms are not governed by the profit motive. 'The specialists who serve a particular corporation depend upon it for their incomes and careers and generally develop a kind of patriotism for it. They have just as much motive to promote its profitability as an old-fashioned capitalist. But the complexity of multidimensional choice in conditions of uncertainty means that maximizing profits, even in the limited sense of preferring more to less profitable policies, is by no means a simple matter.'

33. This should be contrasted with Friedman's (1953, pp. 19–22) famous *as if* 'behavioural' proposition – more about which in the last section of this chapter. He (1953, p. 22) contends that even if we 'let the apparent immediate determinant of business behavior be anything at all – habitual reaction, random choice, or whatnot', only when 'this determinant happens to lead to behavior consistent with rational and informed maximization of returns, the business will prosper and acquire resources with which to expend; whenever it does not, the business will tend to lose resources and can be kept in existence only by the addition of resources from outside'.

34. Williamson (1964) effectively uses a series of case studies to show that

in bad times management cuts down expenses, thus undermining the hypothesis that it had previously been maximizing profits.

35. Marris (1968, p. 45) draws the following conclusion: 'once the classical idealization of capitalism is thus destroyed, there is no *economic* case for its superiority over socialism. Consequently, the attempt to impose capitalism all around the world, in some cases virtually by force, can only be justified on political grounds. The latter, however, seem to get thinner every day. In the miserable developing countries of the "free" world, where we cheerfully give aid to almost any form of dictatorship provided no industries are nationalized ... there is no dearth of greedy *profit* maximizers, many living in considerable luxury. What the nonaffluent majority of the world's population so badly needs is a much greater number of *growth* maximizers.' Solow (1968, p. 52) calls this 'the damndest argument for socialism I ever heard. Who would storm the Winter Palace so that units of production could be "endowed with the social norm of growth maximization (subject to financial constraints)" even if "manipulation of the financial rules to offset various kinds of built-in bias ... would be much easier"?'

36. Though he acknowledges the contribution of Alchian and Demsetz (1972) to the study of technological inseparabilities and hence team organization, Williamson (1981, p. 1565) denies its explanatory value for the existence of such complex hierarchies as the modern corporation.

37. 'The steady equilibrium growth of modern neoclassical theory is, it must be acknowledged, a routine process of replication. It is a dull story compared to the convulsive structural, technological, and social changes described by the historically oriented scholars of development ... The theory conceals, either in aggregation or in the abstract generality of multisector models, all the drama of the events — the rise and fall of products, technologies, and industries, and the accompanying transformations of the spatial and occupational distribution of the population. Many economists agree with the broad outlines of Schumpeter's vision of capitalist development, which is a far cry from growth models made nowadays in either Cambridge, Massachusetts, or Cambridge, England. But visions of that kind have yet to be transformed into a theory that can be applied in everyday analytic and empirical work' (Nordhaus and Tobin, 1972, p. 2).

38. Moreover, Marris and Mueller (1980, p. 58) suggest that Schumpeter (1950) and Galbraith (1967a) are surprisingly close to Baran and Sweezy (1966).

39. On the differences between Nelson and Winter and Schumpeter and their differences with Simon, see Nelson and Winter, 1982, pp. 40 and 36 respectively.

40. In this respect, their model suffers from deficiencies similar to those of neoclassical growth models (see Kalecki, 1970).

41. Marris and Mueller (1980, p. 41) claim that 'although the force of the argument for satisficing is unmistakable, theories of the firm that have so far been developed based directly on the satisficing approach have displayed a tendency to contain too many detailed and specific assumptions to make them easily generalizable for application to broad problems'.

42. Cyert and Hedrick (1972) confirm that despite evidence of unease with the neoclassical theory of the firm it has not been displaced by the non-maximizing theories.

43. Friedman (1977b, pp. 952–3) refers to anecdotes told him by the famous mathematical statistician R. A. Fisher to illustrate how accurately one could infer views in genetics from political views.

44. In the same spirit, but using somewhat different terminology, Myrdal (1972, p. 147) asserts that 'all scientific work has to be based on value premises. There is no view without a viewpoint, no answers except to questions. In the viewpoint applied and the questions raised, valuations are involved.'

45. On the differences in concepts and Koopmans's inductivism versus Friedman's instrumentalism, see Boland, 1979, pp. 516–17.

46. 'The temptation to identify the results of existing economic theory with economic theory as such – and to disqualify both in one breath – is strongest for the experienced economic adviser to government or business, to whom the limitations of existing theory are most painfully apparent. One can hear such feelings reverberate in statements made at professional meetings by outstanding leaders of the economic profession, who in their younger days made important contributions to economic theory' (Koopmans, 1957, p. 147).

47. Shubik (1970, pp. 413–14) also detects this sense of sterility in Samuelson (1947) and in Debreu (1959), though, as he admits, in the latter case 'it is scarcely cricket to criticize a man for doing no more or less than he states that he intends to do'.

48. The stronger version is something of a sophistry. It claims greater merit for a theory whose assumptions are less realistic: 'Truly important and significant hypotheses will be found to have "assumptions" that are widly inaccurate descriptive representations of reality, and, in general, the more significant the theory, the more unrealistic the assumptions' (Friedman, 1953, p. 14). But Friedman (1953) is prompt to add that 'the converse of the proposition does not of course hold: assumptions that are unrealistic (in this sense) do not guarantee a significant theory'.

49. Boland (1979, pp. 511–22) argues that the critics have been unfair to Friedman because they presumed that he was speaking of testing

a theory in the sense of refutation (à la Popper), whereas Friedman only speaks of 'testing for truth (in some sense)'. Furthermore, Friedman's instrumentalism is logically sound; the critics should have addressed themselves to the essence of instrumentalism itself.

50. This contention can be buttressed by Friedman's (1953, p. 15) own words: 'The theory of monopolistic and imperfect competition is one example of the neglect in economic theory of these [good approximation] propositions. The development of this analysis was explicitly motivated, and its wide acceptance and approval largely explained, by the belief that the assumptions of 'perfect competition' or 'perfect monopoly' said to underlie neoclassical economic theory are a false image of reality. And this belief was itself based almost entirely on the directly perceived descriptive inaccuracy of the assumptions rather than on any recognized contradiction of predictions derived from neoclassical economic theory.'

51. Hollis and Nell (1979, pp. 48–9) claim that once we admit that imperfect competition models are superior because they are closer to reality, they are also open to controversy. In particular, 'do supply curves really rise? How are marginal costs to be determined for joint production? Are outputs and costs really continuously variable? Do firms in fact know their marginal revenue curves? And the questions grow more awkward, when we go behind the cost curves to the true basis of supply, the production function . . . Yet, if we cease to assume wide substitution in production, rising supply price, continuous variability, calculation of marginal revenue and so forth, we abandon traditional neo-Classical market behaviour theory . . . So Friedman's neo-Classical critics are well advised to agree with him that the realism of assumptions does not matter' (Hollis and Nell, 1979, p. 49).

52. Leontief (1971, p. 5) views the development of science somewhat similarly to Koopmans: 'True advance can be achieved only through an iterative process in which improved theoretical formulation raises new empirical questions and the answers to these questions, in their turn, lead to new theoretical insights. The "givens" of today become the "unknowns" that will have to be explained tomorrow. This, incidentally, makes untenable the admittedly convenient methodological position according to which a theorist does not need to verify directly the factual assumptions on which he chooses to base his deductive arguments, provided his empirical conclusions seem to be correct. The prevalence of such a point of view is, to a large extent, responsible for the state of splendid isolation in which our discipline nowadays finds itself.' Leontief (1971) offers the example of agricultural economics as a 'healthy balance between theoretical and empirical analysis and of the readiness of professional economists to cooperate wih experts in the neighboring disciplines'.

53. Solow (1967, p. 101), though he is in sympathy with the contemporary mainstream economists – the 'little thinkers' in his words – also warns that 'little-thinking can easily degenerate into mini-thinking or even into hardly thinking at all. Even if it does not, too single-minded a focus on how the parts of the machine work may lead to a careful failure ever to ask whether the machine itself is pointed in the right direction.'

54. Myrdal (1982, p. 311) notes that the modern gradual fading of the term 'political economy' in favour of economics has been 'important as a sign of a change in the pursuit of our work. It pertained to a fundamental difference in approach in studying the economy.'

55. In a jesting mood, Harry Johnson (1971b, p. 6) admitted that though mathematical economics is fascinating, it did not appear to him 'to be a key to the discovery of important truths about the real world, other perhaps than the truth that the world is willing to pay a high price for being dazzled by brilliance'.

56. To those who accuse him of mathematization of economics, Samuelson (1977, p. 868) answers: 'That is one of the mortal sins for which I shall have to do some explaining when I arrive at heaven's pearly gates.' In an unrepentant mood he (1966, p. 1500) speculates: 'What a Daniel-come-to-Judgment I would be, if I, the lamb that strayed fustus' and mustus' from the fold, were to testify before God and this company that mathematics had all been a horrible mistake . . . I wish I could be obliging. Yet even if my lips could be brought to utter the comforting words, like Galileo I would hear myself whispering inside, "But mathematics does indeed help".'

REFERENCES

Alchian, A. (1950) 'Uncertainty, Evolution, and Economic Theory', *Journal of Political Economy*, 58 (June): 211–21.

Alchian, A., and H. Demsetz (1972) 'Production, Information Costs, and Economic Organization', *American Economic Review*, 62 (December): 777–95.

Allais, M. (1943) *A la recherche d'une discipline économique*, Paris: Ateliers Industria.

Arrow, K. J. (1974) 'General Economic Equilibrium', *American Economic Review*, 64 (June): 253–72.

Arrow, K. J. (1975) 'Thornstein Veblen as an Economic Theorist', Project on Efficiency of Decision Making in Economic Systems, *Technical Report no. 16* (February), Harvard University (mimeo).

Arrow, K. J. (1979) 'Jacob Marschak.' in *International Encyclopedia of the Social Sciences*, vol. 18, Biographical Supplement, New York: Free Press, pp. 500–6.

Arrow, K. J. (1981) 'Jacob Marschak's Contributions to the Economics of Decision and Information, *Mathematical Social Sciences*, 1: 335–8.

Arrow, K. J. (1982a) 'Risk Perception in Psychology and Economics', *Economic Inquiry*, 20 (January): 1–9.

Arrow, K. J. (1982b) 'Team Theory and Decentralized Resource Allocation: An Example', *Technical Report no. 371* (February), Center for Research on Organizational Efficiency, Stanford University (mimeo).

Arrow, K. J., and F. H. Hahn (1971) *General Competitive Analysis*, San Francisco: Holden-Day.

Arrow, K. J., and L. Hurwicz (1977) *Studies in Resource Allocation Processes*, Cambridge: Cambridge University Press.

Arrow, K. J., and M. D. Intriligator (eds) (1982) *Handbook of Mathematical Economics*, 3 vols, Amsterdam: North-Holland.

Baran, P., and P. M. Sweezy (1966) *Monopoly Capital*, New York: Monthly Review Press.

Barnard, C. I. (1938) *The Functions of the Executive*, Cambridge, Mass.: Harvard University Press.

Barone, E. (1908) (new edn 1935) 'The Ministry of Production in the Collectivist State', trans. from the Italian (1908), in F. A. von Hayek (ed.), *Collectivist Economic Planning*, London: Routledge, pp. 245–90.

Baumol, W. J. (1959) *Business Behavior, Value and Growth*, New York: Macmillan.

Baumol, W. J. (1970) *Economic Dynamics*, 3rd edn, New York: Macmillan.

Becker, G. S. (1964) *Human Capital*, New York: NBER.

Becker, G. S. (1965) 'A Theory of Allocation of Time', *Economic Journal*, 75 (September): 493–517.

Becker, G. S. (1976) *The Economic Approach to Human Behavior*, Chicago: University of Chicago Press.

Becker, G. S. (1981) *A Treatise on the Family*, Cambridge, Mass.: Harvard University Press.

Ben-Porath, Y. (1982) 'Economics and the Family – Match or Mismatch?' *Journal of Economic Literature*, 20 (March): 52–64.

Bergson, A. (1938) 'A Reformulation of Certain Aspects of Welfare Economics', *Quarterly Journal of Economics*, 52 (February): 310–34.

Blaug, M. (1980) *The Methodology of Economics*, Cambridge: Cambridge University Press.

Boland, L. A. (1979) 'A Critique of Friedman's Critics', *Journal of Economic Literature*, 17 (June): 503–22.

Chipman, J. S. (1982) 'Samuelson and Welfare Economics', in G. R. Feiwel (ed.), *Samuelson and Neoclassical Economics*, Boston: Kluwer-Nijhoff.

Cyert, R. M., and C. L. Hedrick (1972) 'Theory of the Firm: Past, Present, and Future; An Interpretation', *Journal of Economic Literature*, 10 (June): 398–412.

Cyert, R. M., and J. G. March (1963) *A Behavioral Theory of the Firm*, Englewood Cliffs, N.J.: Prentice-Hall.

Dantizig, G. B. (1951) 'The Programming of Interdependent Activities: Mathematical Model', in T. C. Koopmans (ed.), *Activity Analysis of Production and Allocation*, New York: Wiley, pp. 19–32.

Day, R. (1964) 'Review of Cyert and March, *A Behavioral Theory of the Firm*', *Econometrica* 32 (July): 461–5.

Debreu, G. (1959) *Theory of Value*, New York: John Wiley.

Debreu, G. (1982) 'Existence of Competitive Equilibrium', In K. J. Arrow and M. D. Intriligator (eds), *Handbook of Mathematical Economics*, vol. 2, Amsterdam: North-Holland.

Dixit, A. (1982) 'Recent Developments in Oligolpoly Theory', *American Economic Review*, 72 (May): 12–17.

Dobb, M. H. (1973) *Theories of Value and Distribution*, Cambridge: Cambridge University Press.

Dobb, M. H. (1975) 'Revival of Political Economy: An Explanatory Note', *Economic Record*, 51 (September): 357–9.

Dorfman, R., P. A. Samuelson and R. M. Solow (1958) *Linear Programming and Economic Analysis*, New York: McGraw-Hill.

Feiwel, G. R. (1972) *The Soviet Quest for Economic Efficiency*, New York: Praeger.

Fisher, F. M. (1976) 'The Stability of General Equilibrium', in M. J. Artis and A. R. Nobay (eds), *Essays in Economic Analysis*, Cambridge: Cambridge University Press, pp. 3–29.

Friedman, J. (1977) *Oligopoly and the Theory of Games*, Amsterdam: North-Holland.

Friedman, M. (1953) *Essays in Positive Economics*, Chicago: University of Chicago Press.

Friedman, M. (1977a) *Friedman on Galbraith*, Vancouver: Fraser Institute.

Friedman, M. (1977b) 'Nobel Lecture: Inflation and Unemployment', *Journal of Political Economy*, 85(3): 451–72.

Galbraith, J. K. (1967a) *The New Industrial State*, Boston: Houghton Mifflin.

Galbraith, J. K. (1967b) 'A Review of a Review', *Public Interest*, 9 (Fall): 109–18.

Galbraith, J. K. (1973a) 'Power and the Useful Economist', *American Economic Review*, 63 (March): 1–11.

Galbraith, J. K. (1973b) *Economics and the Public Purpose*, Boston: Houghton Mifflin.

Galbraith, J. K. (1976) (original edn 1958) *The Affluent Society*, 3rd edn, Boston: Houghton Mifflin.

Georgescu-Roegen, N. (1970) 'The Economics of Production', *American Economic Review*, 60 (May): 1–17.

Georgescu-Roegen, N. (1971) *The Entropy Law and Economic Process*, Cambridge, Mass.: Harvard University Press.

Hahn, F. H. (1970) 'Some Adjustment Problems', *Econometrica*, 38(1): 1–17.

Hahn, F. H. (1972) *The Share of Wages in National Income*, London: Weidenfeld & Nicolson.

Hahn, F. H. (1973a) *On the Notion of Equilibrium in Economics*, Cambridge: Cambridge University Press.

Hahn, F. H. (1973b) 'The Winter of our Discontent', *Economica*, 40 (August): 322–30.

Hahn, F. H. (1975) 'Revival of Political Economy: The Wrong Issues and the Wrong Argument', *Economic Record*, 51 (September): 360–4.

Hahn, F. H. (1980) 'General Equilibrium Theory', *Public Interest*, Special Edition: 123–38.

Hahn, F. H. (1982a) 'Reflections on the Invisible Hand', *Lloyds Bank Review*, 144 (April): 1–21.

Hahn, F. H. (1982b) 'Stability', in K. J. Arrow and M. D. Intriligator (eds), *Handbook of Mathematical Economics*, vol. 2, Amsterdam: North-Holland, pp. 745–93.

Hahn, F. H., and M. Hollis (eds) *Philosophy and Economic Theory*, Oxford: Oxford University Press.

Hannan, M. T. (1982) 'Families, Markets and Social Structure', *Journal of Economic Literature*, 20 (March): 65–72.

Harcourt, G. C. (1972) *Some Cambridge Controversies in the Theory of Capital*, Cambridge: Cambridge University Press.

Harcourt, G. C. (1975) 'Revival of Political Economy: A Further Comment', *Economic Record*, 51 (September): 368–71.

Hayek, F. A. von (ed.) (1935) *Collectivist Economic Planning*, London: Routledge.

Hayek, F. A. von (1940) 'Socialist Calculation: The Competitive Solution', *Economica*, 7 (May): 125–49.

Heilbroner, R. L. (1973) 'Economics as a "Value-free" Science', *Social Research*, 40: 129–43.

Hicks, J. R. (1939a) 'The Foundations of Welfare Economics', *Economic Journal*, 49 (December): 696–712.

Hicks, J. R. (1939b) (new edn 1946) *Value and Capital*, London: Oxford University Press.

Hicks, J. R. (1975) 'The Scope and Status of Welfare Economics', *Oxford Economic Papers*, 27 (November): 307–26.

Hicks, J. R. (1976) ' "Revolutions" in Economics', in S. J. Latsis (ed.), *Method and Appraisal in Economics*, Cambridge: Cambridge University Press, pp. 207–18.

Hollis, M., and E. J. Nell (1979) 'Two Economists', Appendix to ch. 7 of *Rational Economic Man*, Cambridge: Cambridge University Press, 1975. Reprinted in F. H. Hahn and M. Hollis (eds), *Philosophy and Economic Theory*, Oxford: Oxford University Press, pp. 47–56.

Hotelling, H. (1938) 'The General Welfare in Relation to Problems of Taxation and of Railway and Utility Rates', *Econometrica*, 6 (July): 242–69.

Hurwicz, L. (1972) (1977) 'On Informationally Decentralized Systems', in K. J. Arrow and L. Hurwicz *Studies in Resource Allocation Processes*, Cambridge: Cambridge University Press, pp. 425–59.

Hurwicz, L. (1973) 'The Design of Mechanisms for Resource Allocation', *American Economic Review*, 63 (May): 1–30.

Hurwicz, L. (1979a) 'On the Interaction Between Information and Incentives in Organization', in K. Krippendorff (ed.), *Communications and Control in Society*, New York: Gordon & Breads, pp. 123–47.

Hurwicz, L. (1979b) 'On Allocations Attainable Through Nash Equilibria', *Journal of Economic Theory*, 21(1): 140–65.

Hurwicz, L. (1979c) 'Socialism and Incentives: Developing a Framework', *Journal of Comparative Economics*, 3: 207–16.

Hurwicz, L. (1981) 'On Incentive Problems in the Design of Non-wasteful Resource Allocation Systems', in N. Assorodobraj-Kula *et al.* (eds), *Studies in Economic Theory and Practice: Essays in Honor of Edward Lipinski*, Amsterdam: North-Holland, pp. 93–106.

Johnson, H. (1971a) 'The Keynesian Revolution and the Monetarist Counter-Revolution', *American Economic Review*, 61 (May): 1–14.

Johnson, H. (1971b) 'Reflections on Current Trends in Economics', *Australian Economic Papers*, 10 (June): 1–11.

Kaldor, N. (1939) 'Welfare Propositions of Economics and Interpersonal Comparisons of Utility', *Economic Journal*, 49 (September): 549–52).

Kaldor, N. (1972) 'The Irrelevance of Equilibrium Economics', *Economic Journal*, 82 (December): 1237–55.

Kaldor, N. (1975) 'What is Wrong with Economic Theory', *Quarterly Journal of Economics*, 89 (August): 347–57.

Kalecki, M. (1970) 'Theories of Growth in Different Social Systems', *Scientia*, 105 (May–June): 311–16.

Kantorvich, L., and T. C. Koopmans (1975) *Problems of Application of Optimization Methods in Industry*, Stockholm: Federation of Swedish Industries.

Keynes, J. M. (1973) *The Collected Writings of John Maynard Keynes*, vol. 14, ed. D. Moggridge, London: Macmillan.

Kirzner, I. M. (ed.) (1982) *Method, Process, and Austrian Economics*, Lexington, Mass.: Heath.

Klein, L. R. (1964) 'The Role of Econometrics in Socialist Economics', in *Problems of Economic Dynamics and Planning: Essays in Honour of Michal Kalecki*, Warsaw: Panstwowe Wydawnictwo Naukowe.

Koopmans, T. C. (1957) *Three Essays on the State of Economic Science*, New York: McGraw-Hill.

Koopmans, T. C. (1970) *Scientific Papers of Tjalling C. Koopmans*, ed. M. Beekman, C. F. Christ, and M. Nerlove, Berlin: Springler-Verlag.

Koopmans T. C. (1974) 'Is the Theory of Competitive Equilibrium with Is?' *American Economic Review*, 64 (May): 325–9.

Koopmans, T. C. (1977a) 'Concepts of Optimality and their Uses', *American Economic Review*, 67 (June): 261–74.

Koopmans, T. C. (1977b) 'Some Early Origins of OR/MS', Opening remarks to the ORSA/TIMS meeting, Atlanta, 8 November (mimeo).

Koopmans, T. C. (1979) 'Economics Among the Sciences', *American Economic Review*, 69 (March): 1–13.

Kornai, J. (1971) *Anti-equilibrium*, Amsterdam: North-Holland.

Kurz, M. (1983) 'Review of Shubik, *Game Theory in the Social Sciences*', *Journal of Economic Literature*, 21 (June): 570–2.

Laffont, J.-J., and E. Maskin (1982) 'The Theory of Incentives: An Overview', in W. Hildenbrand (ed.), *Advances in Economic Theory*, Cambridge: Cambridge University Press.

Lange, O. (1938) 'On the Economic Theory of Socialism', in B. F. Lippincott (ed.), *On the Economic Theory of Socialism*, Minneapolis: University of Minnesota Press.

Lange, O. (1942) 'The Foundations of Welfare Economics', *Econometrica*, 10 (July): 215–28.

Lange, O. (1945–6). 'The Scope and Method of Economics', *Review of Economic Studies*, 13: 19–32. Reprinted in D. R. Kamerschen (ed.), *Readings in Microeconomics*, New York: John Wiley, 1969, pp. 3–22.

Lange, O. (1966) *O socjalizmie i gospodarce socjalistycznej*, Warsaw: Państwowe Wydawnictwo Naukowe.

Leibenstein, W. (1974) 'An Interpretation of the Economic Theory of Fertility: Promising Path or Blind Alley?' *Journal of Economic Literature*, 12 (June): 457–79.

Leibenstein, W. (1975) 'The Economic Theory of Fertility Decline', *Quarterly Journal of Economics*, 89 (February): 1–31.

Leibenstein, W. (1976) *Beyond Economic Man*, Cambridge, Mass.: Harvard University Press.

Leontief, W. (1936) 'Quantitative Input and Output Relations in the Economic System of the United States', *Review of Economic Statistics*, 18 (August): 105–25.

Leontief, H. (1941) *The Sturcture of American Economy, 1919–1929*, Cambridge, Mass.: Harvard University Press.

Leontief, H. (1971) 'Theoretical Assumptions and Nonobserved Facts', *American Economic Review*, 61 (March): 1–7.

Leontief, H. (1982) 'Academic Economics', *Science*, 217 (9 July): 104 and 107.

Lerner, A. P. (1944) *The Economics of Control*, London: Macmillan.

Lucas, R. E. Jr (1981) *Studies in Business Cycle Theory*, Cambridge, Mass.: MIT Press.

Mack, R. P., and T. J. Leigland (1982) ' "Optimizing" in Households, Toward a Behavioral Theory', *American Economic Review*, 72 (May): 103–8.

Malinvaud, E. (1972) 'The Scietific Papers of Tjalling C. Koopmans: A Review Article', *Journal of Economic Literature*, 10 (September): 798–802.

Marris, R. (1963) 'A Model of the "Managerial" Enterprise', *Quarterly Journal of Economics*, 77 (May): 185–209.

Marris, R. (1964) *The Economic Theory of Managerial Capitalism*, New York: Free Press.

Marris, R. (1968) 'Galbraith, Solow, and the Truth about Corporations', *Public Interest*, 11 (Spring): 37–45.

Marris R., and D. C. Mueller (1980) 'The Corporation, Competition, and the Invisible Hand', *Journal of Economic Literature*, 18 (March): 32–63.

Marschak, J. (1955) 'Elements for a Theory of Teams', *Management Science*, 1: 127–37.

Marschak, J. (1971) 'Economics of Information Systems', in M. D. Intriligator (ed.), *The Frontiers of Quantitative Economics*, Amsterdam: North-Holland.

Marschak, J. (1975) 'Entropy, Economics, Physics', in N. A. Chigier and E. A. Stern. (eds), *Collective Phenomena and the Applications of*

Physics to other Fields of Science, Fayetteville, N.Y.: Brain Research Publications, pp. 30–7.

Marschak, J., and K. Miyasawa (1968) 'Economic Comparability of Information Systems', *International Economic Review*, 19: 137–74.

Marschak, J., and R. Radner (1972) *Economic Theory of Teams*, New Haven: Yale University Press.

Maskin, E., and J. Tirole (1982) 'A Theory of Dynamic Oligopoly', Working Paper no. 320, Cambridge, Mass.: Economics Department, MIT.

Mises, L. von (1951) *Socialism*, New Haven: Yale University Press.

Mises, L. von (1979) 'The Science of Human Action', Excerpts of ch. 1 of *Epistomological Problems of Economics*, Princeton: Princeton University Press, 1960. Reprinted in F. H. Hahn and M. Hollis (eds), *Philosophy and Economic Theory*, Oxford: Oxford University Press, pp. 56–64.

Morgenstern, O. (1958) 'Obituary: John von Neumann, 1903–57', *Economic Journal*, 68 (March): 170–4.

Morishima, M. (n.d.) 'The Good and Bad Uses of Mathematics: With Special Reference to General Equilibrium Analysis', trans. from the Japanese by Janet Hunter (mimeo).

Mueller, D. C. (1972) 'A Life Cycle Theory of the Firm', *Journal of Industrial Economics*, 20 (July): 199–219.

Myrdal, G. (1962) *Challenge to Affluence*, New York: Vintage Books.

Myrdal, G. (1972) *Against the Stream*, New York: Vintage Books.

Myrdal, G. (1982) 'Political Economy and Institutional Versus Conventional Economics', in G. R. Feiwel (ed.), *Samuelson and Neoclassical Economics*, Boston: Kluwer-Nijhoff, pp. 311–16.

Nelson, R. R., and S. G. Winter (1982) *An Evolutionary Theory of Economic Change*, Cambridge, Mass.: Harvard University Press.

Nordhaus, W., and J. Tobin (1972) 'Is Growth Obsolete?' in *Economic Growth*, New York: NBER, pp. 1–80.

Odagiri, H. (1980) *The Theory of Growth in a Corporate Economy*, Cambridge: Cambridge University Press.

Pasinetti, L. (1962) 'Rate of Profit and Income Distribution in Relation to the Rate of Economic Growth', *Review of Economic Studies*, 29 (October): 267–79.

Posner, R. A. (1973) 'Economic Justice and the Economist', *Public Interest* 33 (Fall): 109–19.

Radner, R. (1972) chs. 1, 9, 10, and 11 in C. B. McGuire and R. Radner (eds) *Decision and Organization: A Volume in Honor of Jacob Marschak*, Amsterdam: North-Holland.

Radner, R. (1975a) 'A Behavioral Model of Cost Reduction', *Bell Journal of Economics*, 6 (Spring): 196–215.

Radner, R. (1975b) 'Satisficing', *Journal of Mathematical Economics*, 2: 253–62.

Radner, R. (1982) 'Equilibrium under Uncertainty', in K. J. Arrow and M. D. Intriligator (eds), *Handbook of Mathematical Economics*, vol. 2, Amsterdam: North-Holland, pp. 921–1006.

Reder, M. W. (1982) 'Chicago Economics: Permanence and Change', *Journal of Economic Literature*, 20 (March): 1–38.

Robbins, L. (1935) *An Essay on the Nature and Significance of Economic Science*, London: Macmillan.

Robbins, L. (1979) 'On Latsis's Method and Appraisal in Economics: A Review Article', *Journal of Economic Literature*, 17 (September): 996–1004.

Roberts, J., and H. Sonnenschein (1977) 'On the Foundations of the Theory of Monopolistic Competition', *Econometrica*, 45 (January): 101–13.

Robinson, J. (1962) *Economic Philosophy*, Chicago: Aldine.

Robinson, J. (1977) 'What are the Questions?', *Journal of Economic Literature*, 15 (December): 1318–39.

Robinson, J. (1980) 'Introduction' to V. Walsh and H. Gram, *Classical and Neoclassical Theories of General Equilibrium*, New York: Oxford University Press, pp. xi–xvi.

Rosenberg, N. (1982) *Inside the Black Box: Technology and Economics*, Cambridge: Cambridge University Press.

Samuelson, P. A. (1947) *Foundations of Economic Analysis*, Cambridge, Mass.: Harvard University Press.

Samuelson, P. A. (1966) *The Collected Scientific Papers of Paul A. Samuelson*, ed. J. E. Stiglitz, 2 vols, Cambridge, Mass.: MIT Press.

Samuelson, P. A. (1972) *The Collected Scientific Papers of Paul A. Samuelson*, vol. 3, ed. R. C. Merton, Cambridge, Mass.: MIT Press.

Samuelson, P. A. (1976) 'An Economist's Non-linear Model of Self-generated Fertility Waves', *Population Studies*, 30 (July): 243–7.

Samuelson, P. A. (1977) *The Collected Scientific Papers of Paul A. Samuelson*, vol. 4., ed. H. Nagatani and K. Crowley, Cambridge, Mass.: MIT Press.

Samuelson, P. A. (1978) 'Maximizing and Biology', *Economic Inquiry*, 16 (April): 171–83.

Schultz, T. W. (1981) 'Policies Affecting Human Resources', in *Colloquium on Alternatives for Economic Policy*, New York: The Conference Board.

Schumpeter, J. A. (1934) *The Theory of Economic Development*, trans. from the German second (1926) edn, Cambridge, Mass.: Harvard University Press.

Schumpeter, J. A. (1949) 'Science and Ideology', *American Economic Review*, 39 (March): 345–59.

Schumpeter, J. A. (1950) *Capitalism, Socialism and Democracy*, New York: Harper & Row.

Schumpeter, J. A. (1954) *History of Economic Analysis*, New York: Oxford University Press.

Sen, A. K. (1976–7). 'Rational Fools', *Philosophy and Public Affairs*, 6: 317–44.

Sen, A. K. (1982) *Choice, Welfare and Measurement*, Oxford: Blackwell.

Sen, A. K. (1983) 'The Profit Motive', *Lloyds Bank Review*, 147 (January): 1–20.

Shackle, G. L. S. (1967) *The Years of High Theory*, Cambridge: Cambridge University Press.

Shapley, L. (1979) 'Game Theory', Rand Paper Series P-6230 (March) (mimeo).

Shubik, M. (1970) 'A Curmudgeon's Guide to Microeconomics', *Journal of Economic Literature*, 8 (June): 405–34.

Shubik, M. (1982) *Game Theory in the Social Sciences*, Cambridge, Mass.: MIT Press.

Simon, H. A. (1947) *Administrative Behavior*, New York: Macmillan.

Simon, H. A. (1982a) *Models of Bounded Rationality*, vol. 1: *Economic Analysis and Public Policy*, Cambridge, Mass.: MIT Press.

Simon, H. A. (1982b) *Models of Bounded Rationality*, vol. 2: *Behavioral Economics and Business Organization*, Cambridge, Mass.: MIT Press.

Smith, V. (1974) 'Economic Theory and its Discontents', *American Economic Review*, 64 (May): 320–2.

Solow, R. M., (1967) 'The New Industrial State or Son of Affluence', and 'A Rejoinder', *Public Interest*, 9 (Fall): 100–8 and 118–19.

Solow, R. M., (1968) 'The Truth Further Refined: A Comment on Marris', *Public Interest*, 11 (Spring): 47–52.

Solow, R. M. (1971) 'Some Implications of Alternative Criteria for the Firm', in R. Marris and A. Wood (eds), *The Corporate Economy*, Cambridge, Mass.: Harvard University Press, pp. 318–42.

Solow, R. M. (1975) 'Cambridge and the Real World', *Times Literary Supplement*, 14 March: 277–8.

Solow, R. M. (1980) 'On Theories of Unemployment', *American Economic Review*, 70 (March): 1–11.

Spadaro, L. M. (ed.) (1978) *New Directions in Austrian Economics*, Kansas City: Sheed, Andrews, & McMeel.

Stigler, G. J. (1961) 'The Economics of Information', *Journal of Political Economy*, 69 (June): 213–15.

Stigler, G. J. (1962) 'Information in the Labor Market', *Journal of Political Economy*, 70 (October): 94–105.

Stigler, G. J. (1968) *The Organization of Industry*, Homewood, Ill.: Irwin.

Stigler, G. J. (1974) 'Free Riders and Collective Action: An Appendix to Theories of Economic Regulation', *Bell Journal of Economics*, 5 (Autumn): 359–65.

Stigler, G. J. (1975) *The Citizen and the State; Essays on Regulation*, Chicago: University of Chicago Press.

Stigler, G. J. (1982) 'The Economists and the Problem of Monopoly', *American Economic Review*, 72 (May): 1–11.

Stiglitz, J. E. (1974) 'The Cambridge–Cambridge Controversy in the Theory of Capital: A View from New Haven', *Journal of Political Economy*, 82(4): 893–903.

Stiglitz, J. E. (1980) *Information and Economic Analysis*, Oxford: Oxford University Press.

Tobin, J. (1982) *Essays in Economics: Theory and Policy*, vol. 3, Cambridge, Mass.: MIT Press.

Wald, A. (1951) 'On Some Systems of Equations of Mathematical Economics', trans from the German, *Econometrica*, 19 (October): 368–403.

Walsh, V., and H. Gram (1980) *Classical and Neoclassical Theories of*

General Equilibrium, New York: Oxford University Press.

Weintraub, E. R. (1983) 'On the Existence of a Competitive Equilibrium: 1930–1954', *Journal of Economic Literature*, 21 (March). 1–39.

Williamson, O. E. (1964) *The Economics of Discretionary Behavior*, Englewood Cliffs, N.J.: Prentice-Hali.

Williamson, O. E. (1970) *Corporate Control and Business Behavior*, Englewood Cliffs, N.J.: Prentice-Hall.

Williamson, O. E. (1975) *Markets and Hierarchies: Analysis and Antitrust Implications*, New York: Free Press.

Williamson, O. E. (1979) 'Transaction-Cost Economics: The Goverance of Contractual Relations', *Journal of Law and Economics*, 22 (October): 233–61.

Williamson, O. E. (1981) 'The Modern Corporation: Origins, Evolution, Attributes', *Journal of Economc Literature*, 19 (December): 1537–68.

Wood, M. K., and G. B. Dantzig (1951) 'The Programming of Interdependent Activities', in T. C. Koopmans (ed.), *Activity Analysis of Production and Allocation*, New York: John Wiley, pp. 15–18.

Part I
Approaches to Resource
Allocation Processes

2 The Potentials and Limits of the Market in Resource Allocation

KENNETH J. ARROW

USEFULNESS OF NEOCLASSICAL THEORY

The prestige status of the purest of pure economic theory has never been higher; and yet there is now, as there has always been, a pervasive scepticism about the descriptive power and normative utility of Walrasian or other varieties of the theory of general competitive equilibrium.[1] The mutual adjustment of prices and quantities represented by the neoclassical model is an important aspect of economic reality worthy of the serious analysis that has been bestowed on it; and certain dramatic historical episodes suggest that an economic mechanism exists that is capable of adaptation to radical shifts in demand and supply conditions.

The interest in the competitive model stems partly from its presumed descriptive power and partly from its implications for economic efficiency. Enormous gains in efficiency can be achieved through the price system, as compared with most conceivable alternatives.

The twin pillars of neoclassical doctrine are the principle of optimization by economic agents, and the co-ordination of their activities through the market. In the market the aggregate of individual decisions is acknowledged, and the terms of trade adjusted until the decisions of the individuals are mutually consistent in the aggregate, that is, supply equals demand. The outcome of the competitive process is then to be evaluated in terms of Pareto efficiency and additional conditions on the resulting distribution of goods.

An allocation of resources through the workings of the economic system is said to be Pareto efficient if there is no other feasible allocation that would make every individual in the economy better off (or, as frequently stated, make every individual as well off and at least one better off). This, however, is a necessary but not sufficient condition for social optimality, for a manifestly unjust allocation, with vast wealth for a few and poverty for many, will nevertheless be Pareto optimal if there is no way of improving the lot of the many without injuring the few in some measure.

The notion of the inner coherence of the economy – the way markets and the pursuit of self-interest could in principle achieve a major degree of co-ordination without any explicit exchange of information, but where the results may diverge significantly from those intended by the individual actors – is surely the most important intellectual contribution that economic thought has made to the general understanding of social processes.

The apparent modesty of the information needed is one of the most appealing aspects of the neoclassical model. In this model, an individual, whether consumer or producer, is the locus both of interests or tastes and of information. Each individual has his own desires, which he is expected to pursue within the constraints imposed by the economic mechanism; but in addition he is supposed to have more information about himself or at least about a particular sphere of productive and consumptive activity than other individuals. However, the utility functions of different individuals cannot easily be known to each other. Indeed, since they have meaning only in terms of observable behaviour, there may be no way of transmitting utility functions from one agent to another. There is in general no way of forcing an individual to reveal his utility function; if he knows that this knowledge will be used in some allocation process, what he will transmit will or at least can be designed to affect that allocation favourably to him.

Contrary to some beliefs, in this model social choice does not completely disappear. Market-clearing prices serve as the communication links that bring into coherence the widely dispersed knowledge about the needs and production possibilities of the members of the economy. Each individual's property is disposed of as he or she will. But the terms on which the exchange takes place, the prices, are in fact the joint result of the supply and demand pressures of all the participants in the economy. The prices are not any sets of numbers but just those causing supply and demand to balance. Hence, they are, if through indirect means, jointly determined by all individuals in the market. The information or messages sent by the participants are the amounts that they are willing to pay and receive at each of various prices for each commodity; the competitive equilibrium in effect aggregates this information and yields a resultant allocation of goods.

Summing up, the modern general competitive equilibrium theory teaches the extent to which a social allocation of resources can be achieved by independent private decisions co-ordinated through the market. We are assured indeed that not only can an allocation be achieved, but the result will be Pareto efficient. But there is nothing in the process that guarantees that the distribution be just. Indeed, the theory teaches us that the final allocation will dpend on the distribution of initial supplies and of ownership of firms. If we want to rely on the virtues of the market but also to achieve a more just distribution, the theory suggests the strategy of changing the initial distribution rather than interfering with the allocation process at some later stage.

While the price system has many virtues, it also has serious limitations. In fact, the price system does not always work and valuable though it is in certain realms, it cannot be made the complete arbiter of social life. In fact, there is a great number of situations where it is necessary or at least desirable to replace the market by social decision-making.

Modern economic theory has gradually refined the conditions under which the price system might not achieve efficient or optimal resource allocation. Many of the discussions have revolved around three classical reasons: indivisibilities, inappropriability, and uncertainty, and around such concepts as increasing returns, externalities, public goods, transaction costs, and market failures, pointing, *inter alia*, to the incompleteness or the limits on the theoretical validity of the price system whereby certain actions though they may lead to private good may result in social ill.

The problem of increasing returns to scale has been much studied in the literature under the heading of marginal-cost pricing and the problem of inappropriability under that of divergence between social and private benefit (or cost), but the theory of optimal allocation of resources under uncertainty has had much less attention. Recent developments have been concerned with the extension of neoclassical analysis to questions of intertemporal transactions under conditions of uncertainty: how uncertainty can tend to destroy markets and the absence of some markets for future goods may cause others to fail; the significance of the relative absence or incompleteness of future markets for a full neoclassical theory; and the critical notion of information that arises only in the context of uncertainty.

Of course, the conclusions of the neoclassical model are valid only under some specific and possibly overly simple hypotheses about the economic world and social and private preferences. After all, the descriptive propositions of neoclassical price theory are only hypothetical propositions (of the form, 'if . . . , then . . . '). As in virtually all scientific generalizations, it is impossible to confine oneself to actual phenomena; it is necessary also to make counterfactual statements about what would happen if some conditions were to prevail, even if they do not.

In many respects the neoclassical theory is highly manipulable and flexible; when faced with a specific issue, it can yield meaningful implications relatively easily. Yet the realities of the Great Depression and of developing countries remind us dramatically that something beyond, but including, neoclassical theory is needed. The existence of idle resources is a prime example of co-ordination failure. Neoclassical microeconomic equilibrium with fully flexible prices presents a beautiful picture of the mutual articulations of a complex structure, full employment being one of its major elements. What is the ralation between this world and either the real world with its recurrent tendencies to unemployment of labour, and indeed of capital goods, or the Keynesian world of an underemployment equilibrium? Not only can the neoclassical theory not explain unemployment, but neither does it do much with the patent fact that competition is limited in intensity.

Indeed, some of the unsolved major problems of modern neoclassical general equilibrium theory include: (i) the relations between microeconomics and macroeconomics, (ii) the failures to incorporate imperfect competition, and (iii) the failures to account for costs of transactions (essential to the theory of money and asset holding generally). Moreover the integration of the demand and supply of money with general competitive equilibrium theory remains incomplete despite attempts beginning with Walras himself. And neoclassical theory has been criticized for ignoring other arguments in the utility function, power, status, social approval, etc. that also motivate individuals, as well as for ignoring some constraints, capacity for calculation and social controls.

RELATIONS BETWEEN COMPETITIVE EQUILIBRIUM AND PARETO EFFICIENCY

Though the view that competitive equilibria have some special optimality properties is at least as old as Adam Smith's invisible hand, a definitive clarification and rigorous statement of the relation is fairly recent. The theoretical notion of Pareto efficiency has been an important clarifying concept in comparing alternative resource allocations, both in theory and in the formation of economic policy. In particular, the close link between Pareto efficiency and competitive equilibrium is the central result for both analysis and policy. The equivalence of the two concepts is stated in the form of two Fundamental Theorems:

> *First Theorem of Welfare Economics*: Every competitive equilibrium is Pareto efficient.

Second Theorem of Welfare Economics: For every Pareto efficient allocation of resources, there is a redistribution of the endowments such that the given Pareto efficient allocation is a competitive equilibrium for the new endowment distribution.

Perfectly competitive equilibrium has its usual meaning: households, possessed of initial resources, including possibly claims to the profits of firms, choose consumption bundles to maximize utility at a given set of prices; firms choose production bundles so as to maximize profits at the same set of prices; the chosen production and consumption bundles must be consistent with one another in the sense that aggregate production plus initial resources must equal aggregate consumption. The key points in the definition are the parametric role of the prices for each individual and the identity of prices for all individuals. Implicit are the assumptions that all prices can be known by all individuals and that the act of charging prices is not itself a consumer of resources.

A number of additional assumptions are made at different points in the theory of equilibrium, but most are clearly factually valid in the usual contexts and need not be mentioned.

The validity of the two Fundamental Theorems rests on the following restrictive hypotheses which are often violated: the existence of all relevant markets (including those for externalities), that is, the hypothesis of completeness or universality of markets, and the convexity of household indifference maps and firm production possibility sets. (Non-convex production possibility sets could be expected to arise from indivisibilities in production processes.) For the First Theorem to be valid the condition of complete markets has to be satisfied, but not that of any convexity. Both conditions have to be satisfied for the Second Theorem to be valid and then the case for the market is strongest. In such a case the problems of equity can be separated from those of efficiency; if the existing distribution of welfare is judged inequitable, rectification should proceed by redistributing endowments ('lump-sum transfers') and then allowing the market to work unimpeded rather than by direct interference with the market in the form say, of price controls of rationing.

If the actual market differs significantly from the competitive model, or if the hypotheses of the two Fundamental Theorems are violated, the separation of allocative and distributional procedures becomes, in most cases, impossible. Moreover, even if feasible, such a separation glosses over problems in the execution of any desired redistribution policy. There are no effective means of transferring endowments from one individual to another without some loss owing to incentives. Recognition of the costs of redistributive transfers entails modification of the concept of Pareto efficiency to take account of losses during the redistributive process.

If either or both of the aforementioned hypotheses are violated, the theory of economic policy suggests certain remedies. Even if these hypotheses are not violated, the final allocation could be achieved in practice in some different way, for example, by a computer that has been provided with all the relevant facts, the preferences and production possibilities for all individuals and productive units and the initial endowments of all factors.

The central role of competitive equilibrium both as a normative guide and as at least partially descriptive of the real world raises an analytically difficult question: does a competitive equilibrium necessarily exist? If convexity holds, then there exists a competitive equilibrium even if markets are incomplete.

Convexity is only a sufficient but not necessary condition for the existence of competitive equilibrium. As long as markets are complete, according to the First Theorem it is possible to have an equilibrium and thus efficient allocation without convexity. However, in view of the central role of convexity in the two Fundamental Theorems, the implications of relaxing this hypothesis have been the subject of intensive examination. The conclusions may be summarized as follows: the Second Theorem and the existence of competitive equilibrium remain approximately true if convexity is replaced by weakened convexity (i.e. there are no indivisibilities large relative to the economy).

Thus the only non-convexities that are important for the present purposes are increasing returns over a range large relative to the economy. In those circumstances, a competitive equilibrium cannot exist.

The price system, for all its virtues, is only one conceivable form of arranging trade, even in a system of private property. Bargaining can assume extremely general forms. Under the assumptions of weakened convexity and complete markets, we are assured that not everyone can be made better off by a bargain not derived from the price system; but the question arises whether some members of the economy will not find it in their interest and within their power to depart from the perfectly competitive price system. It has been noted in literature that it would pay all the firms in a given industry to form a monopoly. But in fact it can be argued that unrestricted bargaining can only settle down to a resource allocation that could also be achieved as a perfectly competitive equilibrium, at least if the bargaining itself is costless and each agent is small compared to the entire economy.

Hence it can be shown that if markets are complete and competitive equilibrium prevails, then no set of economic agents will find any resource allocation that they can accomplish by themselves (without trade with the other agents) and that they will all prefer to that prevailing under the equilibrium. This holds for any number of agents. The implications of the following converse are more profound: if weakened convexity and market completeness hold, and if the resources of any economic agent are small compared with the total of the economy, then, given any allocation not approximately achievable as a competitive equilibrium, there will be some set of agents and some resource allocation they can achieve without any trade with others which each one will prefer to the given allocation.

The above statement and its converse, taken together, strongly suggest that when all the relevant hypotheses hold, (i) a competitive equilibrium, if achieved, will not be upset by bargaining even if permitted, and (ii) for any bargain not achievable by a competitive equilibrium there is a set of agents who would benefit by change to another bargain that they have the full power to enforce.

The argument that a set of firms can form a monopoly overlooks the possibility that the consumers can also form a coalition, threaten not to buy, and seek mutually advantageous deals with a sub-set of the firms; such deals are possible since the monopoly allocation violates some marginal equivalences.

In real life monopolizing cartels are possible for reasons not so far introduced into the analysis: bargaining costs between producers and consumers are high, those among producers low. It is not the presence of bargaining costs *per se* but their bias that is relevant. If all bargaining costs are high, but competitive pricing and the markets are cheap, then we expect the perfectly competitive equilibrium to obtain, yielding an allocation identical with that under costless bargaining. But if bargaining costs are biased, then some bargains other than the competitive equilibrium can be arrived at which will not be upset by still other bargains if the latter but not the former are costly.

⌈A well-operating market system leads to efficiency only under the assumption of perfect competition, but the propensity to monopolize is an intrinsic feature of the profit system and inhibits efficiency. The full set of conditions for a competitive equilibrium is, of course, never met in the real world. The departures therefrom are particularly conspicuous in the case of imperfect competition.⌉ The theory of imperfectly competitive equilibrium is in its infancy, but such a theory is badly needed in the presence of increasing returns on a scale large relative to the economy and is superfluous in their absence.

However significant monopoly power and increasing returns are, departures from the full set of competitive conditions that violate the basic assumption of the universality of markets pervade the real world where time and uncertainty prevail and this has far-reaching implications for the theory. In the real world, characterized by a paucity of future markets, the argument for the allocative function of market prices is seriously weakened.

TIME AND UNCERTAINTY

A major part of economic activities has a future orientation. The intertemporal nature of the economy implies the importance of anticipations of the future in determining the present. A rational production plan includes, very importantly, decisions or at least plans about the future; and similarly with consumption plans.

The opportunities available to a firm might be all the technologically feasible combinations of inputs and outputs, in the present and in the future. The opportunities available to an investor are basically returns over the future from alternative present portfolios. Investment and savings are not only integral parts of our current decisions but in the long run shape the possibilities for further development.

Certainly a most salient characteristic of the future is that we do not know it perfectly. Our forecasts, whether of future prices, future sales, or even the qualities of goods that will be available to us for use in production or consumption, are surely not known with certainty, and they are known with diminishing confidence as the future extends. Hence, it is intrinsic in the decision-making process, whether in the economic world or in any other, that the opportunities available, the consequences of our decisions, are not completely known to us.

Virtually all economic decisions have implications for supplies and demands on future markets. Goods to be produced in the future are effectively economic commodities today. For efficient resource allocation, the prices of future goods should be known today. But they are not. Markets for current goods exist and enable a certain coherence between supply and demand there. But very few such markets exist for delivery of goods in the future. Hence, plans made by different agents may be excessive or inadequate to meet future demands or to employ the future labour force.

The implication first of all is that the information needed by the optimizer is not provided by an existing market. It will be provided by a market that will exist in the future, but that is a bit too late to help in decisions made today. Hence, the optimizer must replace the market commitment to buy or sell at given terms by expectations: expectations of prices and expectations of quantities to be bought or sold. But he cannot know the future. Hence, unless he deludes himself, he must know that both sets of expectations may be wrong. In short, the absence of the market implies that the optimizer faces a world of uncertainty.

If it were possible to have current markets for future as well as present delivery of commodities, then the general equilibrium theory can be extended into the future. Would-be savers can sell their claims today and purchase commodities for delivery in the future. Investors can purchase inputs and finance the purchases by selling today the outputs for future delivery. But very few such forward markets exist in fact. It is an interesting and illuminating question why they do not exist.

Though such markets would serve a social purpose, there are good reasons why they do not exist. To recapitulate: (i) uncertainty about the future, particularly about the specification and technological production conditions of future commodities in a changing world, (ii) differences in information about these uncertainties among the agents in the economy, and (iii) the costs of operating markets in narrowly defined commodities relative to their benefits.

EXTENSION OF GENERAL EQUILIBRIUM THEORY UNDER UNCERTAINTY

When we are concerned with time and uncertainty, the set of possible goods becomes very large indeed, at least as viewed in the modern theory of general economic equilibrium, and the failure of markets to exist in all of them or even in many of them becomes more and more obvious. The question now becomes whether competitive assumptions can be retained and reinterpreted in terms of uncertain outcomes.

The existence of uncertainty need not, in and of itself, destroy the primary role of prices in resource allocation, if markets exist not only for goods but for insurance against alternative possible outcomes. The basic contract to which a price attaches becomes one for delivery of a good contingent on the occurrence of some state of affairs.

If an economic agent is uncertain as to which of several different states of the world will obtain, he can make contracts contingent on the occurrence of possible states. With these markets for contingent contracts, a competitive equilibrium will arise under the same general hypotheses as in the absence of uncertainty. It is not even necessary that the economic agents agree on the probability distribution for the unknown state of the world; each may have his own subjective probabilities. Further, the resulting allocation is Pareto efficient if the utility of each individual is identified as his expected utility according to his own subjective probability distribution.

First consider extension of general equilibrium theory over time. Then, as Hicks argued long ago, the same commodity in the physical sense at different points of time are properly different commodities. We could, therefore, have different markets for them. Using Hicks's device of dating commodities, Arrow and Debreu, in their proof of existence of competitive equilibrium, actually proved the existence of present and future prices which jointly equilibrated supply and demand on all markets present and future. This was presented in greater richness by Debreu in his *Theory of Value*. Taken literally, this procedure implied the existence at the initial moment of markets for all future as well as present transactions, that is, a set of futures markets for all commodities for all future dates.

A futures contract is made now for a future exchange of money against goods. In the intertemporal competitive equilibrium model, money now is exchanged against dated goods. It is easy to see that a complete set of markets for dated goods is equivalent to a complete set of futures markets plus one bond market for each maturity, in which money now is exchanged for money later. The bond market permits each agent to transfer income over time by buying and selling bonds of different maturities. Of course, this model, in either form, resembles the real world very little.

We must be careful that all the assumptions implicit in the competitive equilibrium of the complete set of futures markets are met. One of these, taken almost for granted in our usual textbook presentations, is that the economic agents, the households and the firms, know their tastes and their own opportunities for all the marketed commodities. These opportunities might be related in complex ways. In particular, the producers of the future commodities must know their supply conditions. In the case of agricultural commodities, this means knowing the conditions of the harvest and also the technological opportunities for production (existence of different kinds of fertilizers and machinery, for example). In the case of minerals, it means knowing of new discoveries and of availability of existing mines in areas not yet drilled. It is also true that demanders must know the conditions under which they will use the goods. This requirement may be especially onerous for consumers that are not yet born.

In short, the possibility of a complete set of futures markets, the ideal intertemporal competitive equilibrium, is vitiated by uncertainty, a topic to which I shall come shortly. Before doing so, I would like to make some remarks about the possibility of spot markets when there is not or little uncertainty. Suppose we stick to the strict assumption of certainty for all agents.

Start with a complete set of futures markets and then open spot markets. Clearly, they can exist, but they will be trivial. That is, the price that will prevail must be the futures price for that date. More generally, the futures market can be opened at all points of time between the beginning and the date of execution with trivial effect. The price at each moment will be the original futures price. No transaction will in fact take place.

The set of all futures markets together with bond markets has been shown to be sufficient for achieving efficiency; is it necessary? There is another possible institutional arrangement. Have only spot markets and the bond markets, and assume that individual economic agents can forecast correctly at the beginning all the spot prices. Then, if the forecasts are all correct, each individual agent is faced with exactly the same constraints and opportunities as if there were a complete set of futures markets. The allocation would, therefore, also be efficient.

It will be said that the hypothesis of perfect foresight of future spot prices is so absurd that it need not be considered. But the matter is not so clear, particularly when we think of the theoretical models as parables capable of giving insight rather than literal descriptions.

If there is no uncertainty, why should not the economic agents be able to forecast the future? This question actually points up a need for greater clarity in the meaning of certainty and, more generally, of information. Individuals are in fact uncertain about most relevant matters, but in a competitive price system, this uncertainty does not matter. Each individual agent has his own information, and no two have the same information. We may speak of social certainty if the information of all individuals would, when pooled, imply complete knowledge.

At the moment, I simply reinterpret the classical propositions of welfare economics as follows: Suppose that the information possessed by each economic agent includes its personal characteristics, now and in the future, and possibly more, but need not include all the information available in the economy. Suppose further that there is social certainty. Then the competitive equilibrium of a complete set of present and futures markets is Pareto efficient.

Since each agent may know relatively little about the economy as a whole, there is no logical necessity that forecasts may be so accurate as to replace futures markets. On the other hand, there are more specific reasons why forecasts may have some validity. This dialogue of competing arguments does suggest that the cost—benefit analysis of a futures market must compare it with allocations based on expectations. It also suggests three additional questions:

(1) What determines which futures markets form and which do not?
(2) To what extent is the allocation of goods determined by the futures markets that do exist?
(3) What are the consequences of the incompleteness of the futures markets?

(1) The value of a futures market increases when forecasting on the basis of general information and past behaviour is difficult, but there is enough information in the aggregate to make the futures price a better forecast. For most actual goods, as opposed to claims to goods or money, the economists' abstraction of the market is imperfect. The actual goods delivered have infinite variations in detail, including both specifications and time of delivery. A futures contract requires a careful specification. Even in agricultural markets, the number of futures markets is much less than the number of varieties with economic significance to one side or another. The situation with regard to manufactured goods is usually very different. In detail, they are changing over time. If this account is accurate, it is disturbing; it implies that significant changes in the structure of markets are due to factors not easily encompassed in the usual models of the market.

(2) Even when futures markets exist, then, there is need for a spot market that accommodates details and complexities of exact delivery date and other specifications with which the futures market cannot deal. This means that waiting to trade on the spot market is always an alternative possible strategy for any agent. If, however, enough agents stay out of the futures market and if those who stay out are not representative of the entire set, then the futures market might come to equilibrium at a different price, which will no longer be a good forecast of the spot price. For this reason or possibly others, those not in the futures market may fail to use the futures price as a guide to conduct. I have not seen any study that shows the extent to which the production and allocation of a commodity are in fact influenced by the futures price.

(3) The implication of the incompletness of futures markets has been noted before. Any investment decision, including a commitment on a futures contract, takes into consideration complementary markets. A miller's purchase of wheat futures must take into account expectations as to the price of flour, the wage level, and the cost of milling equipment; for none of these do futures markets exist. The resource allocation may be inefficient to the extent that the anticipations of other prices are incorrect.

Let us suppose now that there are uncertainties, even social uncertainties, but that at each point of time all individuals have the same information. An extension of standard competitive equilibrium is then possible as soon as we recognize that the economic meaning of a commodity given in the physical sense differs according to the actual course of events. We know now that wheat will have a different significance when the state of the world is a bad harvest than when it is a good harvest. Just as we treat the same physical commodity as differing according to date, so we should treat the same physical commodity as differing according to the state of the world in which it is to be delivered.

In a more general sense, there is one ultra-neoclassical approach to the market treatment of uncertainties, in which I take some pride. That is the notion of a contingent market. Instead of letting uncertainty ruin existing markets, we can take it explicitly into account by buying and selling commitments to be carried out only if some uncertain event occurs. We could in principle imagine agreements to transact that will hold if, and only if, a given conceivable technological innovation does not take place, with a second market for transactions valid if the innovation does take place. Then we can restore the possibility of markets. In other words, commodities in the ordinary sense are replaced by contingent commodities; promises to buy or sell a given commodity if, and only if, a certain state of the world occurs. The market will then determine contingent prices. Clearing of the markets means clearing of the contingent markets; the commitments made are sufficiently flexible so that they can always be satisfied.

Futures markets are relatively rare. But contingent markets are virtually non-existent. It is not a mere empirical accident that not all the contingent markets needed for efficiency exist, but a necessary fact with deep implications for the workings and structure of economic institutions. Roughly speaking, information about particular events, even after they have occurred, is not spread evenly throughout the population. Two people cannot enter into a contract contingent on the occurrence of a certain event or state if only one of them in fact knows that the event has occurred. Hence the range of possible contingent contracts becomes limited to those for whom the events are easily verifiable for both parties. The implications of these limits are known in the insurance literature as adverse selection and moral hazard, and they are of immediate practical significance in such matters as health insurance.

Nothing is more obvious than the universality of risks in the economic system. The owner of a business typically is supposed to assume all the risks of uncertainty. Risk aversion is instrumental in the evolution of a series of institutions for shifting risks, but always with some limits. There are no other major institutions in which the shifting of risks through a market appears in such an explicit form as in insurance and common stock. The possibility of shifting risks, of insurance in the broadest sense, permits individuals to engage in risky activities that they would not otherwise undertake. The shifting of risks through the stock market permits an adventurous industrialist to engage in productive activities, even though he is individually unable to bear the accompaning risks of failure.

Common stocks also have some of the elements of risk sharing that characterize a portfolio of contingent contracts and we can think of a common stock as a bundle of contingent contracts. Actually, all securities and, more to the present point, all futures contracts are similarly bundles of contingent securities. By buying or selling a combination of these instruments, an economic agent may try to realize a suitable trade-off between stability and expected return. It is desirable to acquire a portfolio that is negatively correlated with one's own income. It is this observation that is basic to the conventional explanation of hedging. A futures contract as a bundle of elementary contingent commodities provides only an inefficient sharing of risk.

The failures of the market to achieve adequate risk shifting lead to compensatory alterations in social institutions, licensing, bankruptcy and limited liability, and large business organizations. But all of these institutions are steps away from the free working of the price system. Especially, we expect all these institutions to decrease the flexibility and responsiveness of the system to change and innovation. What we observe is that the failure of the price system to handle riskbearing adequately leads to a diminished use of prices even in contexts where they would be most useful in bringing about a careful and flexible confrontation of needs and resources.

EXTERNALITIES, MARKET FAILURES, AND TRANSACTION COSTS

It has been a staple argument that optimal resource allocation will not be achieved by a competitive market system if there are technological externalities. These are goods (or bads) for which no market can be formed. Certain costs are imposed on us by the destructive side effects of our production and consumption. For example, a polluter, an emitter of polluting substances whether it be a car driver or a factory owner, is imposing costs on others, possibly money costs but in any case costs in the sense of making other people worse off. He is not required to incur these costs, therefore he is not required to balance properly the goods that he is achieving, the production of goods in the case of the factory owner or just driving somewhere in the case of the car driver, against the costs that he is imposing upon others. Congestion is a somewhat similar phenomenon; when too many people, again car drivers, for example, come into the same area, each person delays everybody else in the queue and yet is not charged for this cost in any appropriate way.

⌠Other individual decisions have beneficial social consequences that also are not properly priced or costed. Trust and similar values, loyalty or truthfulness, are examples of what the economist would call externalities. They are goods, they are commodities; they have real, practical, economic value; they increase the efficiency of the system, enable you to produce more goods or more of whatever values you hold in high esteem. But they are not commodities for which trade on the open market is technically possible or even meaningful.⌡

Similarly to externalities, because of inappropriability or increasing returns, public goods cannot be left to the market. While externality is a more general concept than public goods, in both cases benefits and costs are not confined to those realizable on the market but should encompass the full social range. The difficulties in understanding and measuring the full range of social consequences are indeed considerable, not to say overwhelming; while progress has been made, no one working in the field will deny that much remains to be understood and to be measured and indeed that there will always remain unmeasurable elements in the economic calculus of any significant policy decision.

⌐The problem of externalities is thus a special case of a more general phenomenon, the failure of markets to exist. Not all examples of market failure can fruitfully be described as externalities. Two very important examples have already been noted; markets for many forms of riskbearing and for most future transactions do not exist and their absence is surely suggestive of inefficiency.⌐

The failure of futures markets cannot be directly explained by inability to exclude and lack of necessary information to permit market transactions to be concluded. Exclusion is no more a problem in the future than in the present. Any contract to be executed in the future is necessarily contingent on some events (for example, that the two agents are still both in business), but there must be many cases where no informational difficulty is presented. The absence of futures markets may be ascribed to a third possibility: supply and demand are equated at zero; the highest price at which anyone would buy is below the lowest price at which anyone would sell. Unlike the first two, the latter case is by itself in no way presumptive of inefficiency. However, it may usually be assumed that its occurrence is the result of failures of the first two types of complementary markets.

Market failure is a more general category than externality; and both differ from increasing returns in a basic sense, since market failures in general and externalities in particular are relative to the mode of economic organization, while increasing returns are essentially a technological phenomenon.

Market failure is not absolute; it is better to consider a broader category, that of transaction costs, which in general impede and in particular cases completely block the formation of markets. It is usually, though not always emphasized, that transaction costs are the costs of running the economic system. An incentive for vertical integration is replacement of the costs of buying and selling on the market by the costs of intra-firm transfers; the existence of vertical integration may suggest that the costs of operating competitive markets are not zero, as is usually assumed in our theoretical analysis.

Monetary theory, unlike value theory, is heavily dependent on the assumption of positive transaction costs; the recurrent complaint about the difficulty of integrating these two branches of theory is certainly governed by the contradictory assumptions made about transaction costs. The creation of money is in many respects an example of a public good.

The sources of transaction costs include: (i) exclusion costs, (ii) costs of communication and information, including both the supplying and the learning of the terms on which transactions can be carried out, and (iii) the costs of disequilibrium; in any complex system, the market or authoritative allocation, even under perfect information, takes time to compute the optimal allocation, and either transactions take place that are inconsistent with the final equilibrium or they are delayed until the computations are completed.

These costs vary from system to system; thus, one of the advantages of a price system over either bargaining or some form of authoritative allocation is usually stated to be the economy in costs of information and communication. But the costs of transmitting and especially of receiving a large number of signals may be high; thus there is a tendency not to differentiate prices as much as would be desirable from the efficiency viewpoint; for example, the same price is charged for peak and off-peak usage of transportation or electricity.

In a price system, transaction costs drive a wedge between buyers' and sellers' prices and thereby give rise to welfare losses as in the usual analysis. Removal of these welfare losses by changing to another system (for example, governmental allocation or cost—benefit criteria) must be weighed against any possible increase in transaction costs (for example, the need for elaborate and perhaps impossible studies to determine demand functions without the benefit of observing a market). [The welfare implications of transaction costs would exist even if they were proportional to the size of transaction, but in fact they typically exhibit increasing returns.]

The identification of transaction costs in different contexts and under different systems of resource allocation should be a major item on the research agenda of the theory of public goods and indeed of the theory of resource allocation in general. Futhermore, it is of fundamental import-ance in evaluating the relative merit of the varieties of capitalist and socialist economies.

It bears noting that the social measures to compensate for market failures or limitations, in turn, involve transaction costs of their own. In the true neoclassical spirit we really postulate that when a market could be created, it will be. I sometimes think that welfare economics ought to be considered an empirical discipline. Implicitly, if an opportunity for a Pareto improvement exists, then there will be an effort to achieve it through some social device or another. In our theories and to a considerable extent in practice, the cheapest way in many cases is the creation of a market; and markets do emerge. If a market is impractical for one or another market failure, then very likely some other social device will at least be tried: government intervention; codes of professional ethics; or economic organizations with some power intermediate between the competitive firm and the government.

NOTE

1. This chapter focuses on and synthesizes arguments that are elaborated at length, *inter alia*, in Arrow, 1969, 1971, 1974a, 1974b, 1978, 1981a and 1981b where the reader will also find references to the literature. For comprehensive references to the most recent literature, see Arrow and Intriligator, 1982.

REFERENCES

Arrow, K. J. (1951) (new edn 1963) *Social Choice and Individual Values*, New York; John Wiley.

Arrow, K. J. (1969) 'The Organization of Economic Activity: Issues Pertinent to the Choice of Market Versus Nonmarket Allocation', in US Congress, Joint Economic Committee, *The Analysis and Evaluation of Public Expenditures: The PPB System*, vol. 1, Washington: GPO, pp. 47–66.

Arrow, K. J. (1971) *Essays in the Theory of Risk-Bearing*, Amsterdam: North-Holland.

Arrow, K. J. (1974a) 'Limited Knowledge and Economic Analysis', *American Economic Review*, 64 (March): 1–10.

Arrow, K. J. (1974b) 'General Economic Equilibrium: Purpose, Analytic Techniques, Collective Choice', *American Economic Review*, 64 (June): 253–72.

Arrow, K. J. (1978) 'The Future and the Present in Economic Life', *Economic Inquiry*, 16 (April): 157–69.

Arrow, K. J. (1981a) 'Introduction: The Social Choice Perspective', in 'Symposium: The Implications of Social Choice Theory for Legal Decisionmaking', *Hofstra Law Review*, 9 (Summer): 1373–80.

Arrow, K. J. (1981b) 'Futures Markets: Some Theoretical Perspectives', *Journal of Futures Markets*, 1 (2): 107–15.

Arrow, K. J., and L. Hurwicz (eds) (1977) *Studies in Resource Allocation Processes*, Cambridge: Cambridge University Press.

Arrow, K. J., and M. D. Intriligator (eds) (1982) *Handbook of Mathematical Economics*, 3 vols, Amsterdam: North-Holland.

3 Information and Incentives in Designing Non-wasteful Resource Allocation Systems

LEONID HURWICZ*

INTRODUCTION[1]

Economists are not always willing to confine themselves to the analysis of what exists, because they regard the economic structure as subject to conscious modification, by legislation as well as other techniques. If one is willing to consider such modifications, one must study their feasibility, and it becomes natural to develop a set of criteria by which to judge their desirability.

On the one hand, one may take the organizational structure as given while considering alternative policies admissible within such a structure. In economics, the problem of choosing income tax rates might be an example of such policy choice within the existing structure. On the other hand, the choice between a free market and one subject to price controls and quantity allocations would exemplify a situation in which the economic structure itself becomes the variable of the problem. It is the latter type of choice that involves 'the designer's point of view', in the sense that in making the choice one is in the position of someone designing the economic organizational structure.

As we proceed to develop suitable categories for analysing organizational structure, it is well to note that such analysis is based on a fundamental, and yet subjective, distinction. The underlying distinction is based on what the designer considers as given (this is, in general, called environment) and what he regards as something he can tinker with (this is what, in general, we call the mechanism). Whether a specific feature of reality

* Research for this chapter was carried out with the aid of NSF grant, NSF–Soc71–3780 AO4 (GS–31276X). An earlier version was presented at a US–USSR seminar in Moscow, June 1976.

(e.g. a set of laws) is to be considered in the category of givens or subject to modification by the designer is, of course, subjective. Depending on where the line is drawn, different normative theories of organizational structure will result.

What would qualify as a mechanism and which mechanisms would be considered 'superior', or even feasible? One could, of course, get by without formalizing what one means by a resource allocation mechanism. But it is then impossible to determine to what extent the various desiderata implicit in the past debates are compatible with one another, or what the 'trade-offs' are among them. Also, in searching for alternatives to known mechanisms for non-classical situations (indivisibilities, increasing returns, externalities, public goods), it helps to have a rigorous formulation of what a resource allocation mechanism is and which of its features are desirable.

It is the function of a resource allocation mechanism to guide the economic agents (producers, consumers, bankers, and others) in decisions that determine the flow of resources. It is natural to demand that the mechanism should guide the agents towards actions that are at least feasible, and even that requirement may be difficult to satisfy. Yet in classical welfare economics we require more than feasilbity, namely, such attributes as efficiency or optimality. After decades of meanderings, we are fairly clear on our options – from efficiency in production (as defined by Koopmans), through optimality (introduced by Pareto under the label of maximum ophelimity), to the maximization of a social welfare function (as defined by Bergson, Samuelson, and Arrow). From our point of view, these different attributes have an important feature in common: they are defined independently of the mechanism. An optimality criterion that presupposes a particular mechanism cannot serve as a legitimate criterion for comparison with other mechanisms.

Specifically, whether an allocation is or is not optimal depends on its feasibility and on the individual preferences, with feasibility determined by the individual endowments and the technology. The individual endowments, the technology, and preferences, taken together, are referred to as the *environment*.[2] More generally, the environment is defined as the set of circumstances that cannot be changed either by the designer of the mechanism or by the agents (participants).

The basic set of performance requirements for processes to be considered are that they be non-wasteful, unbiased, and 'essentially single-valued'. Whether the requirements are or are not met by a given process depends on the environments in which it is asked to operate. The environments that have the properties stated in the classical welfare economics theorems are, naturally, called 'classical'. Thus 'classical environments' are free from externalities or indivisibilities, their sets are convex, etc. In particular, increasing returns are not 'classical'!

Incentives and information are related so as to create a dilemma for systems designers. On the one hand, decentralization seems desirable because, *inter alia*, much information resides in the individual economic units and is not available to the centre. (Or it may be available but only partially or at high cost.) On the other hand, decentralized behaviour rules — which, if obeyed, would yield optimal resource allocation — may be in conflict with the interests of the individual units, and so there is temptation to violate the rules. Furthermore, to the extent that the centre lacks information concerning those units, it will not be able to determine (or prove) that the rules are being violated. Thus the questions arise whether, or under what circumstances, it is possible to design the behaviour rules so that, even in the absence of auditing or inspection, the economic agents could be expected to abide by the prescribed rules, and that the resulting resource allocation would turn out to be optimal.

The issue of incentive compatibility became prominent in connection with the search for an allocation mechanism that would generate optimal resource allocation of public as well as private goods, since the competitive process was clearly inadequate for the task. An alternative mechanism proposed by Lindahl satisfied the requirements of informational decentralization and would yield optimal allocations provided that the participants would act on the basis of truthful information about their respective preferences. The difficulty, stressed by Samuelson, was that in an informationally decentralized system one could not enforce truthful behaviour and, unfortunately, participants could profit by departing from truth. Samuelson's conjecture (formulated in the mid-1950s) was that we were facing a fundamental difficulty — that one could not design an incentive-compatible mechanism guaranteeing optimality for economies with public goods. It is only recently that his conjecture has been shown correct. Indeed it has also been shown that a similar difficulty arises in classical environment economies lacking public goods unless we are in the atomistic case.

We must, however, remind ourselves that these negative results are obtained subject to the requirement of informational decentralization. When this requirement is abandoned, we can imagine inspection systems that, by violating the privacy postulate, might make departures from prescribed behaviour impossible. Again, we seem to run into the dilemma of having to sacrifice either optimality or the self-enforcement feature of informational decentralization.

The above discussion concerned situations in which the participants could manipulate the preference components of their characteristics, that is 'misrepresent' their preferences through strategic behaviour. However, one could imagine an economy in which preferences are centrally known with sufficient accuracy, but there is no central knowledge as to productivity. The problem then arises as to whether such partial central knowledge is sufficient to install a self-enforcing mechanism with optimal equilibria. It turns out, for a change, that the answer is in the affirmative.

Thus the situation changes drastically when preferences are assumed known to the centre, even though production sets are still unknown: here we do have a self-enforcing mechanism guaranteeing optimality as the Nash equilibrium. Suppose, however, that preferences, instead of being centrally known, can become known with a certain expenditure of resources on inspection, etc. Would it be worth acquiring such information? The answer depends on a comparison of the loss of efficiency in the absence of such information (a loss to be expected from our general theorems) with the cost of acquiring the information.

In this chapter, we study certain problems that arise in designing efficient resource allocation systems when information concerning the economy is dispersed among participants in the economic process. We shall focus on the minimal amount of communication required in such systems, taking into account the incentives guiding the behaviour of participants. A measure of 'channel capacity' required for communication is the dimension of the message space (defined in note 6, p. 163) of the process.

In the first section (following the introduction), we construct a model adequate to describe a broad class of resource allocation systems and to illustrate concepts on two versions (A and B) of the well-known Walrasian system against the background of classical (convex, etc.) economies. In particular, we show that the required message space dimensions for the two versions differ.

In the second section, we provide certain basic tools (the Uniqueness Property and the Single-Valuedness Lemma) to be used in finding lower bounds for the dimension of message spaces required by non-wasteful systems.

In the third section, those tools are applied in classical economies. It is shown that, for certain categories of cases, a non-wasteful system (satisfying certain additional requirements) must use a message space of dimension not lower than that used by the Walrasian (B-version) system.

In the fourth section, the same tools are applied in non-classical (non-convex) economies, for example, those exhibiting increasing returns to scale. It is seen that, in contrast to the classical case, even when the numbers of participants and goods are fixed, no finite-dimensional space will, in general, be sufficient.

In the fifth section, we show how the dimensional requirements are affected by the consideration of incentives (analytically represented by Nash Equilibria). It is seen, for instance, that there are cases where a message space is 'too small' to guarantee efficient Nash Equilibria, although it is 'big enough' to yield efficient 'stationary solution' equilibria. That is, incentive aspects increase the required 'channel capacity'.

Also, we show in the fifth section how the study of necessary conditions for the efficiency of Nash equilibria can serve as a point of departure for designing new 'synthetic' systems without any obvious price interpretation. This procedure brings us closer to dealing with the problem of resource allocation as one in which the *system* is an *unknown* to be solved for— given postulates as to its desired operating features.

But it should be emphasized that the systems we have so far obtained by such procedures for simplified situations are to be regarded as merely illustrative. We are still a long way off from designing systems for real economies.

ECONOMIES AND RESOURCE ALLOCATION SYSTEMS[3]

The term *economy* (symbol: e) is used to describe the basic data that are to be taken as given by the designer of an allocation system: the initial resource endowment (land, manpower, capital equipment), the existing technology, and the participants' preferences. A participant can be an individual, a group of individuals, or an organization.

With a given participant i, we can associate his set of economic characteristics (for short, his *characteristic*, denoted by e^i), that is, his initial resource endowment ω^i, his technology T^i and his preference relation R^i.[4] Thus the i-th characteristic is given by:

$$e^i = (\omega^i, T^i, R^i) \qquad i = 1, 2, \ldots, n$$

where n denotes the number of participants.

We shall assume that the whole economy e can be completely described in terms of the characteristics $e^1, e^2, \ldots, e^n$ of the participants,[5] and we shall regard the economy as the n-tuple of characteristics:

$$e = (e^1, e^2, \ldots, e^n)$$

It is also convenient to have symbols for the n-tuples (*profiles*) of resource endowments, technologies and preferences. Thus we shall write:

$$\omega = (\omega^1, \omega^2, \ldots, \omega^n)$$

$$T = (T^1, T^2, \ldots, T^n)$$

$$R = (R^1, R^2, \ldots, R^n)$$

Hence an alternative way of denoting the economy would be by $e = (\omega, T, R)$.

The resource endowment and technology profiles (ω, T) determine which resource allocations are feasible. An *allocation* (denoted by a) is a complete description of the movements and physical transformations of goods and services. Thus it includes a specification of input—output vectors for all producing units, consumption vectors for all households, and covers services rendered by public (collective) goods. The set of *allocations feasible* given the profiles (ω, T) will be denoted by $A(\omega, T)$ or $A(e)$.

The term *efficient allocation* is given different meanings in different parts of the literature although it always presupposes *feasibility*. In *Koopmans's* usage, an allocation is *efficient* if it is feasible and if no other feasible allocation provides more of some aggregate output without calling for less of another aggregate output, inputs being regarded as negative outputs. The set of allocations efficient in Koopmans's sense is completely determined by feasibility data; we shall denote it by $K(\omega, T)$ or $K(e)$.

An allocation is *efficient* in *Pareto's* sense if it is feasible and if no other feasible allocation places any participant higher on his preference scale without placing someone else lower on his preference scale. Clearly, efficiency in Pareto's sense depends on preferences, as well as on resource endowment and technology. The set of Pareto-efficient allocations is denoted by $P(\omega, T, R)$ or $P(e)$.

Since, by definition, efficiency in either sense requires feasibility, we have:

$$K(e) \subseteqq A(e)$$

and

$$P(e) \subseteqq A(e)$$

Under usual assumptions every Pareto-efficient allocation is Koopmans-efficient, but not vice versa. Furthermore, not every feasible allocation is

Koopmans-efficient, so that:

$$P(e) \subset K(e) \subset A(e)$$

(We use the symbol $\subset$ to denote strict inclusion.)

Finally, a social choice function S may be used to select a particular subset $S(e)$ of feasible allocations considered as socially most desirable given the economy e. It is often postulated that this selection would be made from among the Pareto-efficient allocations, that is, that $S(e) \subseteqq P(e)$.

The present chapter does not go beyond the consideration of the above efficiency criteria and so avoids the well-known difficulties in the theory of social-choice functions. However, the nature of the problems discussed here would not be greatly different if social-choice functions or alternative efficiency criteria were introduced.

A *resource allocation system* is viewed here as a communication process among participants leading up to a decision concerning resource allocation. To simplify exposition, we shall only describe a very simple case of an allocation system, consisting of *two* phases: message exchange phase and outcome decision phase.

Message exchanges occur at discrete time points $t = 0,1,2, \ldots$ At each time point t, the i-th participant sends out a message denoted by $m^i(t)$. (Our model is constructed as if this message went to all other participants, but there is no difficult in considering 'addressed messages' that would go to some participants only.)

The content of a message need not at present be specified. It could be a number or set of numbers, a description of a function or of a set. In general, we consider messages to be drawn from some set L, called the *language* of the resource allocation system. A major issue, to be studied below, is that of the 'size' of the language.

The totality of messages exchanged during the first phase of the process could be represented in tabular form as:

$$m^1(0), m^2(0), \ldots, m^n(0)$$
$$m^1(1), m^2(1), \ldots, m^n(1)$$
$$m^1(2), m^2(2), \ldots, m^n(2)$$

. . . .

. . . .

where the t-th row corresponds to the t-th time point and the i-th column to the i-th participant.

We shall now assume that the message exchange process is governed by a system of temporally homogeneous first-order difference equations which could be written as:

$$m^i(t+1) = F^i(m(t)) \qquad i = 1,2,\ldots,n$$
$$t = 0,1,\ldots$$

where:[6]

$$m(t) = (m^1(t),\ldots,m^n(t))$$

Here it is possible to define a *stationary message* (*n*-tuple) $\overline{m} = (\overline{m}^1, \overline{m}^2, \ldots, \overline{m}^n)$ by:

$$\overline{m}^i = F^i(\overline{m}) \qquad i = 1,2,\ldots,n$$

We shall usually assume that the functions F^i guarantee the existence of a stationary message and that the message exchange phase ends by producing such a message.

The second phase of the process translates the stationary message obtained in the first phase into an allocative decision. This is accomplished through a function h (the *outcome function*) which associates a specific allocation a with any given stationary message $\overline{m}$, so that:

$$a = h(\overline{m})$$

We see that to specify a system of the type described one must make a choice of the following entities: a language L, an outcome function h, and the n functions F^i appearing in the difference equations governing the process. These latter functions represent the behaviour of the participant, since they specify messages to be emitted, given the messages previously received. It is clear, however, that the participants' behaviour would, in general, depend on their information concerning the economy in which they are operating. That is, F^i would be different in different economies. To express this dependence we shall replace $F^i(m(t))$ by $f^i(m(t);e)$. Hence the difference equations governing the process will now be written as:

$$m^i(t+1) = f^i(m(t);e) \qquad i = 1,\ldots,n; t = 0,1,2,\ldots,$$

and a stationary message (*n*-tuple) is defined by:

$$\overline{m}^i = f^i(\overline{m};e) \qquad i = 1,\ldots,n$$

$\overline{m} = (\overline{m}^1, \overline{m}^2, \ldots, \overline{m}^n)$. The function f^i is called the i-th *response function*.

For the sake of brevity we shall refer to an n-tuple $f = (f^1, \ldots, f^n)$ of response functions as a *response function*. A *resource allocation system* can now be defined as specified by a language, an outcome function, and a response function, that is, as an ordered triple. (L, h, f).[7] We call such a system *non-wasteful* if it yields efficient (in some specified sense) resource allocations. Formally, a resource allocation system (L, h, f) is *non-wasteful over a class E of economies* if every allocation $a = h(\overline{m})$ is efficient whenever $\overline{m}^i = f^i(\overline{m}; e)$, for m^i in L, $i = 1, \ldots, n$ and e belongs to the class E.

We are now in a position to explain what was meant in the opening paragraph by *information* being *dispersed* among participants. We imagine that, at the beginning of the message exchange phase ($t = 0$), each participant knows his own characteristic but is completely ignorant of the characteristics of other participants. That is, the i-th participant knows e^i but is completely ignorant of e^j for every j different from i. Furthermore, we assume that the only way in which any participant can acquire additional information concerning the characteristics of others is through messages received from them during the exchange phase. Under such circumstances we say that there is a *dispersion of information* concerning the economy. Hence the only basis for choosing a message $m^i(t + 1)$ can be the previous messages $m(t)$, $m(t - 1)$, $\ldots$, $m(1)$, $m(0)$, and the i-th participant's own characteristics e^i. But since we are confining ourselves to first-order processes, the earlier messages $m(t - 1)$, $\ldots$, $m(1)$, $m(0)$ cannot be used. So the difference equation system must be written as:

$$m^i(t + 1) = f^i(m(t); e^i) \qquad i = 1, \ldots, n$$

$$t = 0, 1, 2, \ldots$$

and a stationary message is defined by:

$$\overline{m}^i = f^i(\overline{m}; e^i) \qquad i = 1, \ldots, n$$

This notation indicates that the i-th response function f^i is independent of e^j for every j different from i. That is, the i-th participant determines his response $m^i(t + 1)$ to the message n-tuple $m(t)$ on the basis of his own characteristic e^i but without in any way taking into account the characteristics of others. Such response functions (as well as resource allocation systems using such functions) are called *privacy-preserving*. It is clear that the use of privacy-preserving response functions is unavoidable when dispersion of information prevails.

Formally, nothing prevents the use of messages so complex and detailed that they contain complete descriptions of the participants' characteristics. Thus one could imagine that at the very beginning of the message exchange phase $(t = 0)$, each participant makes up a message $m^i(0)$ containing a complete description of his characteristic e^i. Suppose that one of the participants, say the first one, receives all these messages. Then at time $t = 1$ he has complete knowledge of the economy $e = (e^1, \ldots, e^n)$ and hence could, in principle, calculate the feasible set $A(e)$, as well as the efficient sets $K(e)$ and $P(e)$; indeed, given a social choice function S, he could also calculate the socially desirable allocations $S(e)$.

However, there is a widespread opinion that it would be extremely difficult, if not impossible, for each participant to transmit his characteristic with complete accuracy. Furthermore, the burden of calculations imposed on the first participant would be extremely heavy. Therefore, it is natural to investigate the possibilities of decentralizing the processing of information, thus diminishing the need for transmitting detailed information about characteristics, and also distributing the burden of calculations.

But the question arises whether, or to what extent, such decentralization of information processing is compatible with the achievement of efficient resource allocations. In particular, given a class E of economies, what is the minimum 'size' of the language L such that efficiency of outcomes can be guaranteed for a suitable choice of an outcome function h and of a response function f?

As is to be expected, the answer depends on the class of economies for which we are designing an allocation system, in particular on its convexity properties. But before we can present what is known about the minimum 'size' of the language required for the attainment of efficiency in any class of economies, we shall comment on the relevance of a language 'size' concept and provide a rigorous definition.

Consider an economy in which each participant is a producer or a resource holder and let the Koopmans-efficiency criterion be used, so that preferences may be disregarded. Here the i-th characteristic can be abbreviated $e^i = (\omega^i, T^i)$ where ω^i is a point of the commodity space X and T^i a subset of X. (T^i is the production possibility set. The production function ϕ^i corresponds to a part of its boundary.) Let X be ℓ-dimensional, so that $\omega^i = (\omega_1^i, \ldots, \omega_\ell^i)$, and suppose that the production function is of the Cobb–Douglas type, say:

$$x_1 = x_2^{\alpha_2}, \ldots, x_\ell^{\alpha_\ell}$$

with x_1 the output and x_k, $k = 2, \ldots, \ell$, the inputs. We see that in this case the characteristic e^i can be expressed by the $2\ell - 1$ parameters $\omega_1^i, \ldots, \omega_\ell^i, \alpha_2, \ldots, \alpha_\ell$. Hence the i-th participant could transmit complete information concerning his characteristic e^i if he had at his disposal a 'channel' with the capacity of $2\ell - 1$ numbers. Such a 'channel' would be available if a message could consist of $2\ell - 1$ numbers, that is if the language L were a Euclidean space of at least $2\ell - 1$ dimensions.

This example suggests that when messages are finite numerical sequences, the 'size' of the language may be defined as the *dimension* of the Euclidean space L. The larger this dimension, the more information concerning the characteristics can be transmitted.

Suppose that there is a positive integer K such that, for the given class E of economies, there exists a 'smooth'[8] one-to-one correspondence between every characteristic e^i of any economy e in E and points of the K-dimensional Euclidean space $R^{(K)}$. Then clearly, $L = R^{(K)}$ would be sufficient to transmit a complete description of every characteristic. But there are important situations where language is much smaller than the sufficient number of parameters required to characterize the economy. In particular, a finite-dimensional language may suffice even though the class of economies E over which the system is to be efficient cannot be characterized by a finite number of parameters. Such indeed is the most studied case of the *Walrasian* (perfectly competitive) *system* when applied to the class E^c of what we call *classical economies*, characterized by certain convexity, monotonity, and continuity properties of technologies and preferences.

We shall illustrate this on an example of a class (denoted by E') of pure exchange[9] economies with s economic agents called households, satisfying the following seven conditions. Formally, the absence of production means that (*1*) $T^i = \{0\}$ and so we may use the simplifed notation $e^i = (\omega^i, R^i)$, $\omega^i = (\omega_1^i, \ldots, \omega_\ell^i)$, where ω_j^i is the initial endowment in j-th good held by the i-th household, $1 \leqslant i \leqslant s$, $1 \leqslant j \leqslant \ell$. We shall assume $\omega_j^i > 0$ for all $1 \leqslant i \leqslant s$, and all $1 \leqslant j \leqslant \ell$.

In this economy, an allocation may be written as an s-tuple $x = (x^1, \ldots, x^s)$ of ℓ-vectors $x^k = (x_1^k, \ldots, x_\ell^k)$ where x_j^k is the amount of good j allocated to participant k. We shall assume that (2) an allocation x is feasible if and only if (*2'*)$x_j^k \geqslant 0$ for all k and j, and (*2''*) the total allocated equals the total initial endowment, that is:

$$\sum_{k=1}^{s} x_j^k = \sum_{k=1}^{s} \omega_j^k \text{ for all } 1 \leqslant j \leqslant \ell$$

We shall further restrict the class E' of economies under consideration by assuming that (3) for each i the preference relation R^i is selfish. (R^i is selfish if i cares only about his component x^i of an allocation x. That is, for any four allocations x^*, x^{**}, $x^{\#}$, $x^{\#\#}$, the following condition holds: $x^*R^ix^{**}$ if and only if $x^{\#}R^ix^{\#\#}$, provided that $x^{*i} = x^{\#i}$ and $x^{**i} = x^{\#\#i}$ (in which case the respective i-th components are the same).) Hence in what follows we regard R^i as an ordering between commodity space points (commodity bundles) x^i rather than between allocations x.

(4) R^i is assumed *strictly monotone* in every good; that is,[10] if $x^{*i} \geq x^{**i}$ then x^{*i} is strictly preferred to x^{**i}. Also, (5) R^i is assumed *strictly convex*, that is, such that if a household i is indifferent between commodity bundles x^{*i} and x^{**i}, then it prefers any non-trivial convex mixture $x^{***i} = \alpha x^{*i} + (1 - \alpha)x^{**i}$, $0 < \alpha < 1$, to both x^{*i} and x^{**i}.

We further assume that (6) the preference relation R^i can be represented by a real-valued function u^i whose domain is the non-negative orthant $R_+^{(\ell)}$ of the ℓ-dimensional (Euclidean) commodity space and which has the following properties:

(6') u^i is continuously differentiable; (6'') for every strictly positive commodity space point x^i in $R_{++}^{(\ell)}$, the partial derivative of u^i with respect to the j-th component evaluated at x^i is positive; we write $u_j^i(x^i) \equiv \partial u^i/\partial x_j^i > 0$ for all $1 \leq i \leq s$, and all $1 \leq j \leq \ell$, $e = (e^1, \ldots, e^s)$ in E'.

Before stating our final assumption we now define the *Walrasian* (prefectly competitive) *resource allocation system*.[11] In this system, price vectors are proposed and each participant attempts to maximize his satisfaction subject to the budget constraint — with the proposed prices treated as fixed parameters. One way of formalizing this process is by the difference equation system:

$$\xi^i(t + 1) = \xi^i(t) + g^i[\xi^i(t), p(t); e^i], \quad 1 \leq i \leq s$$

$$p(t + 1) = p(t) + \sum_{i=1}^{s} \xi^i(t) \qquad t = 0,1 \ldots$$

where, for each $1 \leq i \leq s$, every $\omega^i + \xi^i$ is in $R^{(\ell)}$, every p in $R_{++}^{(\ell)}$ and each $e = (e^1, \ldots, e^s)$ in $E', e^i = (\omega^i, u^i(\cdot))$.

It is assumed that:

$$g^i(\eta, p; e^i) \neq 0$$

unless η satisfies the budget (equality) constraint[12] and maximizes i-th satisfaction given the budget. (η is said to maximize i-th satisfaction if:

$$u^i(\omega^i + \eta) \geqslant u^i(\omega^i + \tilde{\eta})$$

for every $\tilde{\eta}$ in $R_+^{(\ell)}$ satisfying the budget (equality) constraint.) We note that ξ_j^i should be interpreted as the *net increment* of holdings by household i of good j, that is, $\xi_j^i = x_j^i - \omega_j^i$.

A *stationary* (perfectly competitive equilibrium) *solution* $(\bar{\xi}, \bar{p})$ of the above difference equation system is obtained if and only if:

$$\left. \begin{array}{l} \bar{\xi} = (\bar{\xi}^1, \ldots, \bar{\xi}^s) \\[4pt] \omega^i + \bar{\xi}^i \geqslant 0 \\[4pt] g^i(\bar{\xi}^i, \bar{p}; e^i) = 0 \end{array} \right\} \quad 1 \leqslant i \leqslant s$$

and

$$\sum_{i=1}^{s} \bar{\xi}^i = 0$$

These are, of course, the well-known conditions of Walrasian (perfectly competitive) equilibrium. The equations $g^i = 0$ express individual satisfaction maximization given the budget, and the last equality requires that aggregate excess demand be zero.

Under the assumed conditions of differentiability, for $i = 1, \ldots, s$, $g^i \equiv (g_1^i, \ldots, g_{\ell-1}^i)$ can be expressed by:

$$g_j^i(\eta, p; e^i) = \frac{u_j^i(\omega^i + \eta)}{u_\ell^i(\omega^i + \eta)} - \frac{p_j}{p_\ell} \quad j = 1, \ldots, \ell - 1$$

Hence, at a competitive equilibrium:

$$\frac{u_j^i(\omega^i + \bar{\xi}^i)}{u_\ell^i(\omega^i + \bar{\xi}^i)} - \frac{\bar{p}_i}{\bar{p}_\ell} = 0, \quad 1 \leqslant i \leqslant s, \ 1 \leqslant j \leqslant \ell - 1$$

and:

$$\bar{p} \cdot \bar{\xi}^i = 0$$

We now proceed to state our final assumption: (7) for every e in E', every stationary solution $(\bar{\xi}, \bar{p})$ of the above difference equation system has strictly positive final holdings, that is:

$$\omega^i + \bar{\xi}^i \equiv \bar{x}^i \gg 0 \text{ for every } i = 1, \ldots, s$$

We shall present two alternative ways of expressing this in our general terminology.

(A) The Walrasian System with a Price-setter

We shall redefine the process as involving $n = s + 1$ participants: the s households $(i = 1, 2, \ldots, s)$ and the $(s + 1)$-st participant called *price-setter*. The message for each participant is of the form $m^i = (m^i_1, \ldots, m^i_{\ell-1})$, $m^i_j \epsilon R$; hence $L = R^{(\ell-1)}$ for every participant and the message space is $M = R^{(s+1)(\ell-1)}$

For each household $i = 1, \ldots, s$, the response function f^i_A is given by:

$$f^i_A(m^1, m^2, \ldots, m^s, m^{s+1}; e^i) \equiv m^i + g^i(m^1, \ldots, m^s, m^{s+1}; e^i)$$

where: $i = 1, \ldots, s$

$$e^i = (\omega^i, u^i(\cdot))$$

$$g^i = (g^i_1, \ldots, g^i_{\ell-1})$$

and:

$$g^i_j(m^1, \ldots, m^s, m^{s+1}; \omega^i, u^i(\cdot))$$

$$\equiv \frac{u^i_j(\omega^i_1 + m^i_1, \ldots, \omega^i_{\ell-1} + m^i_{\ell-1}, \omega^i_\ell - \sum_{r=1}^{\ell-1} m^{s+1}_r m^i_r)}{u^i_\ell(\omega^i_1 + m^i_1, \ldots, \omega^i_{\ell-1} + m^i_{\ell-1}, \omega^i_\ell - \sum_{r=1}^{\ell-1} m^{s+1}_r m^i_r)} - m^{s+1}_r$$

$$j = 1, \ldots, \ell - 1$$

For the price-setter $(i = s + 1)$, we postulate:

$$e^{s+1} = (\omega^{s+1}, u^{s+1}(\cdot))$$

with $\omega^{s+1} = 0$ and:

$$u^{s+1}(x^{s+1}) = 0 \text{ for all } x^{s+1}$$

The price-setter's response function is defined by:

$$f_A^{s+1}(m^1, \dots, m^s, m^{s+1}; e^{s+1}) \equiv m^{s+1} + \sum_{i=1}^{s} m^i$$

The difference equations for the households can be written as:

$$m^i(t + 1) = m^i(t) + g^i[m(t); e^i], \quad i = 1, \dots, s$$

while the price-setter's difference equation is:

$$m_j^{s+1}(t + 1) - m_j^{s+1}(t + 1) - m_j^{s+1}(t) = \sum_{i=1}^{s} m_j^i(t), \quad j = 1, \dots, \ell - 1$$

Hence a stationary solution $\overline{m} = (\overline{m}^1, \dots, \overline{m}^s, \overline{m}^{s+1})$ satisfies the equations:

$$\frac{\overline{u}_j^i}{\overline{u}_\ell^i} - \overline{m}^{s+1} = 0 \qquad \begin{array}{l} i = 1, \dots, s \\ j = 1, \dots, \ell \end{array}$$

(where the $\overline{u}_j^i$ are evaluated at $m = \overline{m}$), and:

$$\sum_{i=1}^{s} \overline{m}_j^i = 0 \qquad j = 1, \dots, \ell$$

The outcome function h_A is given by:

$$\left. \begin{array}{l} \overline{\xi}_j^i = \overline{m}_j^i \qquad j = 1, \dots, \ell - 1 \\[2mm] \overline{\xi}_\ell^i = \sum_{r=1}^{\ell-1} m_r^{s+1} m_r^i \end{array} \right\} \quad i = 1, \dots, s_r$$

and:

$$\overline{\xi}_j^{s+1} = 0 \qquad j = 1, \dots, \ell$$

where ξ_j^k denotes the net increment at equilibrium in holdings of good j by participant k.

Writing:

$$\bar{x}_j^k = \omega^k + \bar{\xi}_j^k, \bar{x}^k = (\bar{x}_1^k, \ldots, \bar{x}_\ell^k) \text{ and } \bar{m}^{s+1} = \bar{p}$$

we may restate the stationarity conditions in the familiar form of tangency conditions:

$$\frac{u_j^i(\bar{x}^i)}{u_\ell^i(\bar{x}^i)} - \frac{\bar{p}_j}{p_\ell} = 0 \qquad \begin{matrix} i = 1, \ldots, s \\ \\ j = 1, \ldots, \ell - 1 \end{matrix}$$

and zero aggregate excess demand condition:

$$\sum_{i=1}^{s} (\bar{x}_j^i - \omega_j^i) = 0$$

(B) The Walrasian System without a Price-setter

There are different ways of formalizing the Walrasian system without introducing a price-setter. For our present purposes we select the following one.

There are now only s participants — the households. The message of each participant $i = 1, \ldots, s$, is of the form $m^i = (m_1^i, \ldots, m_{\ell-1}^i), m_j^i \in R$, so that the language $L = R^{(\ell-1)}$ and the message space $M = R^{s(\ell-1)}$.[13]

$$f_B^k = (f_{B1}^k, \ldots, f_{B\ell}^k)$$

and:

$$f_B^k(m^1, \ldots, m^s; e^k)$$

$$= \frac{u_j^k(\omega_1^k + m_1^k, \ldots, \omega_{\ell-1}^k + m_{\ell-1}^k, \omega_\ell^k - \sum_{r=1}^{\ell-1} m_r^s m_r^k)}{u_\ell^k(\omega_1^k + m_1^k, \ldots, \omega_{\ell-1}^k + m_{\ell-1}^k, \omega_\ell^k - \sum_{r=1}^{\ell-1} m_r^s m_r^k)} - m_j^s$$

$$j = 1, \ldots, \ell - 1$$

We see that the message vector m^s corresponds to the normalized price vector $(p_1/p_\ell, \ldots, p_{\ell-1}/p_\ell)$. Hence it is natural that the last household's response function should be similar to that of the price-setter in the preceding system. We have here, for $j = 1, \ldots, \ell - 1$:

$$f_{B_j}^s(m^1, \ldots, m^s; e^s)$$

$$= \frac{u_j^s(\omega_1^s - \sum_{k=1}^{s-1} m_1^k, \ldots, \omega_{\ell-1}^s - \sum_{k=1}^{s-1} m_{\ell-1}^k, \omega_\ell^s + \sum_{k=1}^{s-1}\sum_{r=1}^{\ell-1} m_r^s m_r^k)}{u_\ell^s(\omega_1^s - \sum_{k=1}^{s-1} m_1^k, \ldots, \omega_{\ell-1}^s - \sum_{k=1}^{s-1} m_{\ell-1}^k, \omega_\ell^s + \sum_{k=1}^{s-1}\sum_{r=1}^{\ell-1} m_r^s m_r^k)} - m_j^s$$

For the first $s - 1$ households, the difference equations of the system can be written as:

$$m_j^k(t + 1) - m_j^k(t)$$

$$= \frac{u_j^s[\omega_1^k + m_1^k(t), \ldots, \omega_{\ell-1}^k + m_{\ell-1}^k(t), \omega_\ell^k - \sum_{r=1}^{s-1} m_r^s(t) m_r^k(t)]}{u_\ell^k[\omega_1^k + m_1^k(t), \ldots, \omega_{\ell-1}^k + m_{\ell-1}^k(t), \omega_\ell^k - \sum_{r=1}^{s-1} m_r^s(t) m_r^k(t)]} - m_j^s(t)$$

$$k = 1, \ldots, s - 1$$

$$j = 1, \ldots, \ell - 1$$

For the last household, the difference equations have the form:

$$m_j^s(t + 1) - m_j^s(t)$$

$$= \frac{u_j^s[\omega_1^s - \sum_{k=1}^{s-1} m_1^k(t), \ldots, \omega_{\ell-1}^s - \sum_{k=1}^{s-1} m_{\ell-1}^1(t), \omega_\ell^s + \sum_{k=1}^{s-1}\sum_{r=1}^{\ell-1} m_r^s(t) m_r^k(t)]}{u_\ell^s[\omega_1^s - \sum_{k=1}^{s-1} m_1^k(t), \ldots, \omega_{\ell-1}^s - \sum_{k=1}^{s-1} m_{\ell-1}^1(t), \omega_\ell^s + \sum_{k=1}^{s-1}\sum_{r=1}^{\ell-1} m_r^s(t) m_r^k(t)]}$$

$$- m_j^s(t), \qquad\qquad j = 1, \ldots, \ell - 1$$

At a stationary solution $m = (\overline{m}^1, \ldots, \overline{m}^{s-1}, \overline{m}^s)$, we have:

$$\frac{u_j^k[\omega_1^k + \overline{m}_1^k, \ldots, \omega_{\ell-1}^k + \overline{m}_{\ell-1}^k, \omega_\ell^k - \sum_{r=1}^{s-1} \overline{m}_r^s \overline{m}_r^k]}{u_\ell^k[\omega_1^k + \overline{m}_1^k, \ldots, \omega_{\ell-1}^k + \overline{m}_{\ell-1}^k, \omega_\ell^k - \sum_{r=1}^{s-1} \overline{m}_r^s \overline{m}_r^k]} - \overline{m}_j^s = 0,$$

$$k = 1, \ldots, s - 1$$

$$j = 1, \ldots, \ell - 1$$

and:

$$\frac{u_j^s[\omega_1^s - \sum_{k=1}^{s-1} \overline{m}_1^k, \ldots, \omega_{\ell-1}^s - \sum_{k=1}^{s-1} \overline{m}_{\ell-1}^k, \omega_\ell^s + \sum_{k=1}^{s-1} \sum_{r=1}^{\ell-1} \overline{m}_r^s \overline{m}_r^k]}{u_\ell^s[\omega_1^s - \sum_{k=1}^{s-1} \overline{m}_1^k, \ldots, \omega_{\ell-1}^s - \sum_{k=1}^{s-1} \overline{m}_{\ell-1}^k, \omega_\ell^s + \sum_{k=1}^{s-1} \sum_{r-1}^{\ell-1} \overline{m}_r^s \overline{m}_r^k]}$$

$$- \overline{m}_j^s = 0, \qquad\qquad\qquad j = 1, \ldots, \ell - 1$$

Denoting the equilibrium net increment vectors by $\overline{\xi}^i = (\overline{\xi}_1^i, \ldots, \overline{\xi}_\ell^i)$ as before, we can write the outcome function h_B as $(\overline{\xi}^1, \ldots, \overline{\xi}^s) = h_B$ $(\overline{m}^1, \ldots, \overline{m}^s)$ where:

$$\overline{\xi}_j^k = \overline{m}_j^k \qquad\qquad k = 1, \ldots, s-1; \quad j = 1, \ldots, \ell-1$$

$$\overline{\xi}_\ell^k = -\sum_{r=1}^{s-1} \overline{m}_r^s \overline{m}_r^k$$

$$\overline{\xi}_j^s = -\sum_{k=1}^{s-1} \overline{m}_j^k, \qquad j = 1, \ldots, \ell-1$$

and:

$$\overline{\xi}_\ell^s = \sum_{k=1}^{s-1} \sum_{r=1}^{\ell-1} \overline{m}_r^s \overline{m}_r^k$$

hence, again:

$$\sum_{i=1}^s \overline{\xi}_j^i = 0 \qquad\qquad j = 1, \ldots, \ell$$

Writing $m^s = p$, where $m_j^s = p_j$ for $j = 1, \ldots, \ell - 1$, and $p_\ell = 1$, we find that the budget constraint is satisfied for all households, that is:

$$\overline{p} \cdot \overline{\xi}^i = 0 \qquad\qquad i = 1, \ldots, s$$

Finally, with appropriate substitutions, the stationary conditions are seen to be equivalent to:

$$\frac{u_j^i(\omega^i + \overline{\xi}^i)}{u_\ell^i(\omega^i + \overline{\xi}^i)} - p_j = 0 \qquad\qquad \begin{matrix} i = 1, \ldots, s \\ j = 1, \ldots, \ell \end{matrix}$$

Thus they are again equivalent to the usual tangency conditions.

Hence the B-version of the Walrasian system, which in classical environments is known to possess Pareto-efficient equilibria, can get by with a message space of dimension $s(\ell - 1)$.

The question arises whether it is possible to devise a system – however different from Walrasian – using a message space of dimension lower than that of the B-version and still guarantee, in classical environments, the existence of Pareto efficiency of the allocations it generates. We shall see below that if the system is required to use privacy-preserving and 'smooth' response and outcome functions, the answer is in the negative.

As was seen above, the requirement that the response functions should be privacy-preserving can be justified on the grounds of information dispersion, that is, on the assumption that information concerning other participants can only be acquired through messages received from them rather than through other channels (e.g. surveys, technological studies).

The requirement of 'smoothness' is justified because without it the concept of dimension of the message space, which is our measure of the channel capacity for information transmitted, becomes meaningless.[14]

As for the A-version, it requires a message space of higher dimension, with a generic element of the form:

$$(m^1, m^2, \ldots, m^s, m^{s+1})$$

where:

$$m^i = (m^i_1, \ldots, m^i_{\ell-1})$$

Hence the message space dimension of the A-version is $(s + 1)(\ell - 1)$, greater by $\ell - 1$ than that of the B-version. We shall see, however, that it has incentive properties absent from the B-version. When incentive conditions (Nash equilibrium) are added, the message space has to be increased in some cases to that of the A-version (e.g. when $s = 2$, $\ell = 2$) but not in others (e.g. when $s = 3$, $\ell = 2$).

TECHNIQUES FOR DETERMINING MINIMAL MESSAGE SPACE REQUIREMENTS

In the preceding sections we saw that, at least for a certain category of classical economies with ℓ goods and s households, there exists an efficient allocation system (Walrasian, version B) using a message space of dimension $s(\ell - 1)$. We then posed the question whether it might be possible to design an alternative non-wasteful privacy-preserving system utilizing a message space of lower dimension and promised to show that the answer is in the negative. This result and its proof are given in the third section. The proof uses certain auxiliary results that are applicable under more general circumstances and that we shall present in this section, proceeding within a framework somewhat more general than that of the preceding section.

Let a be the set of all conceivable outcomes, with generic element a; let $A(e) \subset a$ be the set of outcomes *feasible* in the economy e; and let $D(e)$ be the set of desirable outcomes in e, that is, outcomes feasible in e and possessing a specified property D regarded as desirable, for example efficiency in the sense of Pareto or Koopmans. We wish to find a lower bound on the dimension of a message space M needed in a system guaranteeing that its stationary outcomes would be desirable in the sense of belonging to the set $D(e)$ for every economy e within a given class E of economies.

The resource allocation system is now specified by the languages L_i (not necessarily the same) of the participants, their response functions f^i and the outcome correspondence H.[15] When there are n participants, the message space is defined as the Cartesian product $M = L_1 \times L_2 \times \ldots \times L_n$. Assuming the response functions f^i to be privacy-preserving, we again write the system's difference equation as:

$$m^i(t+1) = f^i(m(t); e^i) \qquad\qquad i = 1, \ldots, n$$

$$t = 0, 1 \ldots$$

where $m(t) = (m^1(t), \ldots, m^n(t))$ and $m^i(t)$ is an element of L_i. The stationarity conditions are:

$$\overline{m}^i = f^i(\overline{m}; e^i) \qquad\qquad i = 1, \ldots, n$$

$\overline{m} = (\overline{m}^1, \ldots, \overline{m}^n)$. The outcome correspondence is written as:

$$\overline{a} \in H(\overline{m})$$

where $H(\overline{m})$ is the set of outcomes generated by a stationary $\overline{m}$. (In the first section, we assumed $H(\overline{m})$ to be a one-element set and so, using the functional notation, we wrote $\overline{a} = h(\overline{m})$.)

Now, under circumstances to be explained below, it can be shown that there exists a (single-valued) function φ defined in M and taking values on a certain sub-set E^* of E. When φ is 'smooth' and E^* is Euclidean, the dimension of M cannot be less than that of E^*. In this way, we shall obtain a lower bound on the dimension of M, namely the dimension of E^*.

Such a function φ turns out to exist in virtue of the so-called Single-Valuedness Lemma below. The crucial property required in this Lemma is that the *desirability correspondence* D,[16] associating with each e in E the set $D(e)$,[17] possess the following *uniqueness property* with respect to E^*.

To simplify exposition, we shall only state the definition of uniqueness and the Lemma for the case of two participants.

Definition Let E^i denote the class of possible values of e^i, $i = 1, 2$, and let $E = E^1 \times E^2$. For a sub-set E^* of E, let:[18]

$$Pr_1 E^* = \{ e^1 \in E^1 : (e^1, e^2) \in E^* \text{ for some } e^2 \in E^2 \}$$

and:

$$Pr_2 E^* = \{ e^2 \in E^2 : (e^1, e^2) \in E^* \text{ for some } e^1 \in E^1 \}$$

The desirability correspondence:

$$D : E \to A(e)$$

is said to have the *uniqueness property on E with respect to E^**, $E^* \subseteq E$, if and only if:

(1) $(Pr_1 E^*) \times (Pr_2 E^*) \subseteq E$

and:

(2) For every $\bar{e} = (\bar{e}^1, \bar{e}^2)$, $\bar{\bar{e}} = (\bar{\bar{e}}^1, \bar{\bar{e}}^2)$, $\bar{e} \in E^*$, $\bar{\bar{e}} \in E^*$

and every conceivable outcome $a \in a$

if $a \in D(\bar{e}^1, \bar{e}^2)$

$a \in D(\bar{e}^1, \bar{\bar{e}}^2)$

$a \in D(\bar{\bar{e}}^1, \bar{e}^2)$

$a \in D(\bar{\bar{e}}^1, \bar{\bar{e}}^2)$

then

$$\overline{e} = \overline{\overline{e}}$$

The Single-valuedness Lemma

Let D have the uniqueness property on E with respect to E^*, $E^* \subseteq E$. Further, let the privacy-preserving system (M, H, f), $M = L_1 \times L_2$, $f = (f^1, f^2)$ be such that:

(1) equilibria exist on $(Pr_1 E^*) \times (Pr_2 E^*)$; that is, the stationarity conditions:

$$m^i = f^i(m; e^i) \qquad i = 1, 2$$

possess a solution $m = (m^1, m^2) \in M$ for every:

$$e \in (Pr_1 E^*) \times (Pr_2 E^*)$$

(2) the system is non-wasteful on $(Pr_1 E^*) \times (Pr_2 E^*)$; that is:

$$H(m) \subseteq D(e)$$

whenever $e \in (Pr_1 E^*) \times (Pr_2 E^*)$ and $\overline{m}$ satisfies the stationarity conditions

$$m^i = f^i(m; e^i), i = 1, 2$$

The, for $\widetilde{e} \in E^*$, $\widetilde{\widetilde{e}} \in E^*$, $\overline{m} \in M$, the relations:

$$\overline{m}^i = f^i(\overline{m}; \widetilde{e}^i) \qquad\qquad i = 1, 2$$

and:

$$\overline{m}^i = f^i(\overline{m}; \widetilde{\widetilde{e}}^i), \qquad\qquad i = 1, 2$$

imply:

$$\widetilde{e} = \widetilde{\widetilde{e}}$$

This means that, under the assumptions of the Lemma, for a given m in M, there can be only one element e of E^* such that $m = f(m; e)$. Hence we may define the (single-valued function) φ with a domain, say, $M^* \subseteq M$ and range containing E^* by the following:

$\varphi(m)$ = the unique element $e \in E^*$ satisfying the stationarity

condition $m = f(m; e)$

Now it is known (see, for instance, Theorem 10-8, p. 257, in Apostol, 1957) that a Lipschitzian function defined on a 'cube' in Euclidean space dimension p into a Euclidean space of dimension q, has a range of at most dimension p. This implies that, when both M^* and E^* are Euclidean and φ is Lipschitzian, the dimension of M^* (and hence of M) cannot be less than that of E^*. The same conclusion follows if φ instead of being Lipschitzian has certain other 'smoothness' properties.[19]

In applications, as seen in the next two sections, the problem consists in finding a set E^* with respect to which the uniqueness property holds. Then the dimension of E^*, say d^*, provides a lower bound for the required dimension of M. If, as sometimes happens, a system is known where $dim\ M = d^*$, then it follows that d^* is the greatest lower bound; that is, d^* is the minimal required dimension. As shown in the next section, this is the case for classical environments.

MINIMAL DIMENSION FOR CLASSICAL ECONOMIES

For the sake of simplicity, we confine ourselves to the particular case of a pure exchange economy (E' of the first section), with $s = 2$, $\ell = 3$, and quadratic utility functions parametrized in the following particular manner. It should be noted that any lower bound for[20] $dim\ M$ obtained for this sub-class of E' with $s = 2$, $\ell = 3$, is also a lower bound for the full class E' with $s = 2$, $\ell = 3$.

Let the i-th utility function be of the form:

$$u_i = -\tfrac{1}{2}x_{i1}^2 + b_{i1}x_{i1} - \tfrac{1}{2}x_{i2}^2 + b_{i2}x_{i2} + x_{i3}, (i = 1, 2)$$

with efficiency in Pareto's sense used as the desirability property. It is known that at a Pareto-efficient interior allocation there must exist

Lagrange multipliers μ_1, μ_2 such that:

$$-\xi_{ij} + (b_{ij} - \omega_{ij}) = \mu_j \qquad\qquad (i = 1, 2; j = 1, 2)$$

$$\xi_{1j} + \xi_{2j} = 0 \qquad\qquad (j = 1, 2, 3)$$

where ω_{ij} denotes the initial endowment and ξ_{ij} the net increment in the j-th good for the i-th household, so that:

$$\xi_{ij} = x_{ij} + \omega_{ij} \qquad\qquad \text{for all } i, j$$

Now the above Pareto-efficiency relations are equivalent to:

$$-\xi + \theta^1 = \xi + \theta^2$$

where:

$$\xi = \begin{pmatrix} \xi_{11} \\ \xi_{12} \end{pmatrix} ; \quad \theta^i = \begin{pmatrix} \theta_1^i \\ \theta_2^i \end{pmatrix} = \begin{pmatrix} b_{i1} - \omega_{i1} \\ b_{i2} - \omega_{i2} \end{pmatrix} \quad i = 1, 2$$

Now suppose that, for a fixed $\xi \in R^{(2)}$:

$$-\xi + \bar{\theta}^1 = \xi + \bar{\theta}^2$$

$$-\xi + \bar{\theta}^1 = \xi + \bar{\bar{\theta}}^2$$

$$-\xi + \bar{\bar{\theta}}^1 = \xi + \bar{\theta}^2$$

$$-\xi + \bar{\bar{\theta}}^1 = \xi + \bar{\bar{\theta}}^2$$

Then, clearly $\theta = \theta^2$ follows. Hence the uniqueness property holds with respect to the set E^* of E defined below. E is the space of dimension 10 defined by, say, all positive values of the parameters b_{ij}, ω_{ij}, and:

$$E^* = \left\{ e \in E : \omega_{ij} = \omega_{ij}^*, \text{ all } i, j \right\}$$

the ω_{ij}^* being arbitrarily chosen constants. Thus:

$$dim\ E^* = 4 = s(\ell - 1)$$

when $s = 2, \ell = 3$. Hence $dim\ M \geqslant 4$.

But, as we saw in the first section, the Walrasian process, version B, uses M of dimension $s(\ell - 1) = 4$ in this case.

Hence $d* = 4$ is the greatest lower bound, that is, the minimal dimension of the message space for this case.

A similar proof shows that, in general, $d* = s(\ell - 1)$ is the minimal dimension of the message space for classical environments of class E'' defined below.

Formally, we may state the following:

Theorem Let a resource allocation system (M, h, f) be 'smooth'[21] and non-wasteful over any class of economies including the quadratic classical economies E'' (defined above). Assume furthermore that (M, H, f) possesses stationary solutions for all economies in E''. Then (a) the dimension of M cannot be lower than $s(\ell - 1)$ where s is the number of households and ℓ the number of goods; (b) there exists a resource allocation system (M, h, f) for which $dim\ M = s(\ell - 1)$, namely the B-version of the Walrasian system.

MINIMAL DIMENSION IN NON-CLASSICAL ECONOMIES

It is not surprising that the situation is very different in non-classical economies, in particular those in which the classical convexity assumptions are violated, since it is known that in the absence of convexity Walrasian equilibria may not exist. For such non-convex economies, especially those *with* production subject to increasing returns, various alternative resource allocation systems have been proposed, including marginal cost pricing (see Lerner, 1937; Hotelling, 1938; Guesnerie, 1975), price schedules varying with quantities purchased (see Arrow and Hurwicz, 1960), and others. However, all proposed systems suffer from serious defects or limitations. It is therefore natural to ask whether one can expect better success with some as yet undiscovered system, or whether the limitations are inherent in the situation with which these systems are expected to cope. In what follows we shall report on two results, which — although very special — throw some light on the issue.

A Non-convex Non-monotone Economy with Production

Consider a class of E_T of economies with two participants (producers) and two goods: a primary good, denoted by t, and a consumer good denoted by y. The total initial supply of good t is T. We shall suppose (although this assumption can be removed) that t is indivisible, that is, that it can only assume integer values: $0, 1, \ldots, T$. If the total initial supply is so distributed that participant 1 has t and participant 2 has $T - t$ units of the primary good, then their respective outputs of y will be denoted by a_t^1 and a_t^2, $0 \leq t \leq T$, so that the total output is $a_t^1 + a_t^2$. We assume that a_t^i range over all non-negative reals.

We are interested in resource allocations that are efficient in Koopmans's sense. In this case, such efficiency is equivalent to the maximization of total output. That is, a resource allocation $\overline{t}$ is efficient if and only if $a_{\overline{t}}^1 + a_{\overline{t}}^2 \geqslant a_t^1 + a_t^2$ for all $t \in \{0, 1, \ldots, T\}$. Now, using the Single-Valued-ness Lemma of the second section of this chapter it has been shown[22] that E_T has the uniqueness property with respect to a sub-set E_T^* of dimension T.[23] Hence the message space M_T required for a non-wasteful 'smooth' resource allocation system must be at least of dimension T. Consider now the class of economies E defined as the union of E_T for $T = 1, 2, \ldots$, ad inf., that is:

$$E = \bigcup_{T=1}^{\infty} E_T$$

It is clear that no message space of finite dimension can be sufficient for 'smooth' systems that would be non-wasteful (in the sense of Koopmans's efficiency) over this class E of economies. This contrasts sharply with the situation in classical production economies where, given the number of goods and participants, there is a finite upper bound on the required dimension of the message space.

It must be admitted that the preceding example is very far removed from classical economies since it lacks not only convexity but also mono-tonicity and divisibility. But it has been shown in Calsamiglia (1975) that a similar difficulty would arise in economies with differentiable and monotone — but non-convex — production functions. It follows that non-convexity be itself calls for infinite-dimensional message spaces if non-wasteful equilibria are to be guaranteed.[24]

So much for negative aspects of the problem. Fortunately, there are also positive findings. In fact, privacy-preserving systems that are non-wasteful in non-classical economies have been designed. The 'greed process' (see Hurwicz, 1960) is privacy-preserving[25] and the resource allocations generated by its stationary solutions are Pareto optimal for all economies that are 'decomposable',[26] even when discontinuities or indivisibilities are present. However, it does not converge to an equilibrium position. This defect has been remedied for continuous (and perfectly divisible) economies, whether convex or not, by systems due to Kanemitsu (1970,

1975) and Osana (1976a). A stochastic system applicable in both (divisible) continous and discrete economies is described in Hurwicz, Radner, and Reiter (1975); this system is privacy-preserving and converges (in probability) to Pareto-optimal allocations.

As is inevitable in the light of the results discussed in the earlier part of this section, such non-wasteful privacy-preserving systems use infinite-dimensional message spaces. The languages employed are families of subsets of the commodity space.

INCENTIVES AND INFORMATION REQUIREMENTS

Except for the mathematical requirement of smoothness, we have so far imposed only an *informational* restriction on the nature of the resource allocation system, namely that it should be privacy-preserving. But it is of interest to ask whether one can design the system so as to provide each participant with *incentives* to follow the rules of the system.

One way of formalizing the notion of incentives is through the concept of (non-co-operative) Nash equilibrium of a game in so-called normal form. When there are n players, such a game is defined by n strategic domain sets S_i and n pay-off functions:

$$v^i : S \to R, S = S_1 \times S_2 \times \ldots \times S_n, R = \text{rules}, i = 1, \ldots, n$$

A point $s = (s_1, \ldots, s_n)$ in S is said to be a *Nash Equilibrium* if and only if, for each $i = 1, \ldots, n$:

$$v^i(\bar{s}) \geqslant v^i(\bar{s}_1, \ldots, \bar{s}_{i-1}, s_i, \bar{s}_{i+1}, \ldots, \bar{s}_n) \text{ for all } s_i \text{ in } S_i.$$

That is, at a Nash equilibrium each player maximizes the value of his pay-off function given the strategies of the other players.

In the context of resource allocation models, the game is defined as follows. Let h be the outcome function (assumed single-valued), $h : M \to A$, $M = L_1 \times L_2 \times \ldots \times L_n$, where M is the message space, L_i the language used by the i-th participant, and the set of conceivable resource allocations. Assume further that each participant has a utility function $u^i : A \to R$. Then a game in normal form is obtained if, for every $i = 1, \ldots, n$, we set:

$$S_i = L_i$$

so that:

$$S = M$$

and define the i-th pay-off function v^i by:[27]

$$v^i(m) = u^i(h(m)) \qquad \text{for all } m \text{ in } M$$

[Note that the domain of u^i is not restricted to feasible outcomes. For instance, if preferences are selfish (see the first section of this chapter), and $a = (x^1, x^2, \ldots, x^n)$ is an allocation with the commodity bundle x^i going to participant i, we may define $u^i(a) \equiv \tilde{u}^i(x^i)$ where $\tilde{u}^i$ is a utility function of the type introduced in the first section.]

We have thus used the languages, the outcome functions and the utility functions to define a game in normal form, and so can speak of the Nash equilibria. What we want to do is to be able to identify such a Nash equilibrium with the stationary position of a resource allocation system. For this, we must introduce an appropriate set of response functions f^i. This can be done most easily if we assume both the outcome function h to be continuously differentiable (C^1) and the n utility functions u^i to be twice continuously differentiable (C^2) in their respective arguments, with L_i an open sub-set of $R^{(k_i)}$, $1 \leqslant k_i < \infty$, for each $i = 1, \ldots, n$.

In this case the outcome function $v^i = u^i o h$ is also continuously differentiable.

We now define the i-th response function by:

$$f^i(m; e^i) = \frac{\partial v^i}{\partial m^i} + m^i$$

where $\dfrac{\partial v^i}{\partial m^i} = \left(\dfrac{\partial v^i}{\partial m^i_1}, \ldots, \dfrac{\partial v^i}{\partial m_{k_i}} \right)$

Such a response function f^i will be called the *utility gradient* response function. Clearly, f^i is privacy-preserving since it only involves the knowledge of u^i and ω^i.

For $\overline{m}$ to be stationary, we must have:

$$\overline{m}^i = \frac{\partial v^i}{\partial m^i} \bigg|_{m = \overline{m}} + \overline{m}^i$$

that is

$$\left. \frac{\partial v^i}{\partial m^i} \right|_{m = \overline{m}} = 0 \qquad\qquad i = 1, \ldots, n$$

But we note that under our assumptions, the i-th of the last set of equalities also constitutes a necessary condition for m^i to be a maximizer of $v^i(m^1, \ldots, m^{i-1}, m^i, m^{i+1}, \ldots, m^n)$ with respect to m^i in L_i, which is in the defining property of a Nash equilibrium in the above game.

Hence, using the utility gradient response functions f^i, we obtain a privacy-preserving resource allocation system (M, h, f) whose stationary positions satisfy the first-order conditions for a Nash equilibrium of the above game. If we were to assume v^i to be concave in m^i, every stationary position would be a Nash equilibrium and vice versa. Note further that, with $h \in C^1$ and $u^i \in C^2$, each response function f^i is continuously differentiable, as are the pay-off functions v^i. Thus the 'smoothness' conditions mentioned in the second section are satisfied.

Given this framework, we now pose the following question whether for a given set of pure exchange classical economies E'' defined below, with s households and ℓ goods, we can find languages $L_1, L_2, \ldots, L_s$ and an outcome function h such that:

(1) the game defined above possesses Nash equilibria for all $e \in E''$

and:

(2) every Nash equilibrium of this game is efficient in the Pareto sense

Where the answer is in the affirmative, we shall raise the question of finding an outcome function h and languages $L_1, L_2, \ldots, L_s$ such that $M = L_1 \times L_2 \times \ldots \times L_s$ is of the lowest dimensions possible.

Note that under the assumed conditions every Nash equilibrium of the game is also a stationary position of the resource allocation system. Therefore, for the cases considered in the first two sections we cannot hope to find M of dimension lower than $s(\ell - 1)$. However, can we find systems with h and L_i such that $dim\ M = s(\ell - 1)$? Since we have now imposed the Nash equilibrium condition over and above the stationarity conditions of the first two sections, this cannot be taken for granted, and indeed is not in general true.

The Case of Two Goods and Two Households

To see this we consider the simplest non-trivial case of a pure exchange economy, with $s = 2$, $\ell = 2$. Further let the utility functions be of the form:

$$\tilde{u}^i(x_1^i, x_2^i) = x_1^i + \theta_i \ell n x_2^i$$

where θ_i is a positive real number. The class E'' is defined as that of all such economies belonging to E' with arbitrary positive initial endowments ω_j^i of the two commodities and each θ_i ranging over all positive reals. The proof of the following result is sketched in Appendix 3.1.

Theorem: Let $L_1 = L_2 = R$, and let $h : L_1 \times L_2 \to R^{(4)}$, h twice continously differentiable (C^2). Then either there exists some $e \in E''$ such that the corresponding (interior) Nash equilibrium is not Pareto efficient or there exists some $e \in E''$ such that there is no Nash equilibrium.

That is, the two requirements (1) and (2) above cannot be reconciled for one-dimensional languages, that is, a two-dimensional message space.[28]

The conclusion of this theorem may seem to be in conflict with the result of the first section, since for $s = \ell = 2$, the B-version Walrasian resource allocation system only requires a message space of dimension $s(\ell - 1) = 2$. But there is no conflict because, as can be rigorously demonstrated, the stationary solutions of the B-version Walrasian system are not Nash Equilibria for any game of the type here under consideration.

This does not mean that, for $s = \ell = 2$, the Walrasian system cannot be interpreted as a game whose stationary positions are Nash equilibria, but only that the B-version is not susceptible of such interpretation. In particular, it is possible to define a game for which stationary solutions of the A-version of the Walrasian system are Nash equilibria. Not surprisingly, we define a three-player game, with the two households and the price-setter as players, and $L_i = R$ for $i = 1, 2, 3$. The outcome function is easily defined: for $i = 1. 2. \; \xi_1^i = m^i$, $\xi_2^i = -m^3 m^i$; for $i = 3$, $\xi_1^3 = -m^1 - m^2$, $\xi_2^3 = (m^1 + m^2)m^3$. (Here superscripts indicate participants.)

We must also introduce a (fictitious) utility function for the price-setter, which can be done by setting:

$$\tilde{u}^3(\xi_1^3, \xi_2^3) = \xi^3$$

It can easily be verified that a Nash equilibrium of the game so defined is the same as Walrasian stationary solution. But, of course, in this version of the Walrasian system we have *dim M* = 3, not 2.

A further question[29] may be raised: for $s = \ell = 2$, it is possible to design a system with [30] *dim M* = 3, possessing the desired properties (existence and Pareto efficiency of the Nash equilibria) without introducing a fictitious third player? It can be shown that, subject to the *qualification* stated below, the answer is in the affirmative. That is, let $L_1 = R^{(2)}$, $L_2 = R^1$, so that $M = R^{(2)} \times R$ and *dim M* = 3. It turns out (see Appendix 3.2) that there exists a C^1 function[31] $h : M \to R^4$ such that the resulting interior Nash equilibria are Pareto efficient. Thus, we have gotten rid of the price-setter, but the dimension of the message space is the same as that of version A. By the above Theorem, nothing better could have been accomplished.

Now the *qualification*: the existence of the Nash equilibria has only been demonstrated for the sub-set of E'' corresponding to some neighbourhood of a point (θ_1, θ_2), not for all (θ_1, θ_2) in $R_{++} \times R_{++}$; also, this game is not normal out of equilibrium.

Of course, the case $s = \ell = 2$ is very special. We do not as yet have a complete theory for arbitrary values of s and ℓ. However, certain special results are of considerable interest. In particular, it is worthwhile to look at the case $s = 3$, $\ell = 2$.

The Case of Two Goods and Three Households

As in the preceding case, it is also true here that the stationary positions of the B-version Walrasian system are not Nash equilibria, while the A-version has a Nash interpretation but with *dim M* = $(s + 1)(\ell - 1)$ = 4. It is therefore natural to ask whether a system yielding Pareto-efficient Nash equilibria exists with *dim M* = $s(\ell - 1)$ = 3. (We know, of course, that one cannot go below $s(\ell - 1)$.) By contrast with the case $s = \ell = 2$ (where the best one could do was to get rid of the price-maker but with *dim M* the same as for the A-version Walrasian system), we can do better than the A-version Walrasian system does for $s = 3$, $\ell = 2$. Again there is a qualification as to the domain of existence of Nash Equilibria.

Specifically, let $L_i = R$ for i = 1, 2, 3. Then there exists a C^1 (in fact, quadratic) outcome function guaranteeing the Pareto efficiency of the (interior) Nash equilibria.[32] The qualification again is that the existence of such equilibria has only been demonstrated for neighbourhoods in the space of $(\theta_1, \theta_2, \theta_3)$. The outcome function is of somewhat complex appearance, but it seems instructive to exhibit it explicitly (we write here m_i instead of m^i):

$$
\begin{cases}
\xi_1^i = -(\tfrac{1}{2}m_i^2 + m_i m_j + m_i m_k) + \tfrac{1}{4}m_j^2 + \tfrac{1}{4}m_k^2 + 2m_j m_k \\
\qquad\qquad\qquad\qquad\qquad\qquad i \neq j \neq k \neq i, \qquad (3.1) \\
\qquad\qquad\qquad\qquad\qquad\qquad i = 1, 2, 3 \\
\xi_2^i = m_i - \tfrac{1}{2}(m_j + m_k)
\end{cases}
$$

(That (3.1) satisfies the first-order necessary conditions for Pareto-efficiency property is shown below. Second-order conditions are easy to verify.)

Thus we have designed a 'synthetic' allocation system,[33] without any obvious price mechanism interpretation, which has a message space M with *dim M* = 3 whose Nash equilibria are Pareto efficient. Since the corresponding A-version of the Walrasian system requires a message space of higher dimension (*dim M* = 4), our 'synthetic' system is, in this respect at least, informationally superior to the Walrasian process (and, in fact, best in view of the theorem of the third section). However, the 'synthetic' system has certain problematic properties: its domain of existence is probably narrower and it may place the participants at utility levels below initial ones. It also has informational disadvantages. It is not presented here as a system to be adopted but rather for didactic purposes. In particular, it shows, in our opinion, that the customary focus on the Walrasian price mechanism provides too narrow a perspective. We may either be overlooking more attractive alternatives or we may have to investigate more deeply the desirable properties of resource allocation systems.

Perhaps a particularly interesting aspect of this analysis is the manner by which we arrive at the above 'synthetic process'. We did this by formulating certain necessary conditions for systems to have Pareto-efficient interior Nash equilibria.

Consider again the case $s = 3$, $\ell = 2$, and require that $L_i = R$ for $i = 1, 2, 3$, that is, that everyone's message m_i be one-dimensional. Change notation so that $\xi_1^i(m), \equiv x^i(m)$ $\xi_2^i(m) \equiv Y^i(m)$, $m = (m_1, m_s, m_3)$. Assume X^i and Y^i to be continuously differentiable (C^1). Then, at an interior Nash equilibrium.

$$u_X^i X_i^i + u_Y^i Y_i^i = 0 \qquad\qquad i = 1, 2, 3 \qquad\qquad (3.2)$$

where subscripts denote derivatives.[34]

The Pareto-efficiency condition is:

$$\frac{u_X^1}{u_Y^1} = \frac{u_X^2}{u_Y^2} = \frac{u_X^3}{u_Y^3} \qquad\qquad (3.3)$$

It follows that:

$$\frac{X_1^1}{Y_1^1} = \frac{X_2^2}{Y_2^2} = \frac{X_3^3}{Y_3^3} \qquad\qquad (3.4)$$

at a Nash equilibrium.

It can be shown, however, that for *dim M* = 3 assumed here, equations (3.4) must hold identically in *m*. Thus (3.4) is an identity constituting a necessary condition on any C^1 outcome function. Of course, there are additional conditions too (rank conditions in particular, as well as second-order conditions). But equations (3.4) provide a point of departure for a systematic search for outcome functions.

In fact, the formulae of our 'synthetic' system given by equation (3.1) were obtained through such a search. Here is a sketch of our search procedure.

First, we wanted outcome functions that would guarantee feasibility throughout – unlike the Walrasian system that only guarantees feasibility at a stationary (equilibrium) solution. That is, we require:

$$\sum_{i=1}^{3} X^i(m) = \sum_{i=1}^{3} Y^i(m) = 0 \qquad \text{for all } m \qquad (3.5)$$

Second, we required that, for each *i*, X^i and Y^i be symmetric with respect to the other two participants *j*, *k* ($j \neq i \neq k$) and that they be (mutatis mutandis) the same for each *i*. Third, we wanted the simplest algebraic forms. Since X^i, Y^i cannot both be linear, we decided to try a linear Y^i and a quadratic X^i. Under these conditions we have:

$$Y^i = am_i - b(m_j + m_k)$$

and:

$$\Sigma Y^i = a\Sigma m_i - 2b\Sigma m_i = 0 \qquad \text{for all } m$$

hence:

$$b = \tfrac{1}{2}a$$

Without loss of generality we then set *a* = 1 (since *a* = 0) would obviously be impossible) and so obtained:

$$i = 1, 2, 3$$
$$Y^i = m_i - \tfrac{1}{2}(m_j + m_k)$$
$$j \neq i \neq k \neq j$$

which is the second formula in equation (3.1).

Now:

$$Y_i^i = 1 \qquad \text{for all } m$$

and so equation (3.6) reduces to:

$$X_t^i(m) = X_2^2(m) = X_3^3(m) \qquad \text{for all } m \qquad (3.6)$$

Assuming X^i to be quadratic, the simplest solution of (3.4) with appropriate sign is such that, for each $i = 1, 2, 3$:

$$X_i^i(m) = -\sum_{j=1}^{3} m_j \qquad (3.7)$$

Thus, for instance:

$$X^1(m) = -(\tfrac{1}{2}m_1^2 + m_1 m_2 + m_1 m_3) + \psi_1(m_2, m_3) \qquad (3.8)$$

and similarly for X^2 and X^3.

The residual terms such as $\psi_1(m_2, m_3)$ must be so selected that $\Sigma X^i(m) = 0$ for all m. A solution symmetric with respect to participants 2 and 3 is obtained by setting[35]:

$$\psi_1(m_2, m_3) = \tfrac{1}{4}m_2^2 + \tfrac{1}{4}m_3^2 + 2m_2 m_3 \qquad (3.9)$$

It will be seen that equations (3.8) and (3.9) correspond to the first formula in equations (3.1) for $i = 1$, $j = 2$, $k = 3$. The formulae for the other two participants ($i = 2, 3$) are obtained by permuting the indices.

This sketch of our procedure for finding an outcome function and thus designing a new resource allocation system shows why we call such systems 'synthetic'.

It is impossible to generalize from the fragmentary results so far obtained. Obviously, the addition of the Nash equilibrium postulate to that of privacy-preservation cannot lower the dimensional requirements on the message space. In fact, in one case ($s = \ell = 2$) the additional Nash equilibrium postulate does raise the required dimension of M from 2 to 3; in another case ($s = 3$, $\ell = 2$), it does not, since here our 'synthetic' process has *dim M* $= 3 = s(\ell - 1)$. Note, however, that when the Walrasian (price) mechanism is used, the Nash equilibrium postulate forces us to go from version B to version A and so raised the dimension of the message space.

Although we have only been able to consider very special cases and may have adopted controversial postulates, it seems that the procedure of 'synthesizing' resource allocation systems given a set of postulates, deserves further study.

APPENDIX 3.1

Denote the outcome functions by $X^i(m)$, $Y^i(m)$, $i = 1, 2$.[36] At an (interior) Nash equilibirum:

$$u_X^i X_i^i + u_Y^i Y_i^i = 0 \qquad\qquad i = 1, 2 \qquad\qquad (3.10)$$

At a Pareto-efficient point:

$$\frac{u_X^1}{u_Y^1} = \frac{u_X^2}{u_Y^2} \qquad\qquad\qquad (3.11)$$

and, for feasibility:

$$\sum_{i=1}^{2} X^i = \sum_{i=1}^{2} Y^i = 0 \qquad\qquad j = 1, 2 \qquad\qquad (3.12)$$

From (3.10) and (3.11) we infer that:

$$\frac{X_1^1}{X_2^2} = \frac{Y_1^1}{Y_2^2} \qquad\qquad\qquad (3.13)$$

at every Nash equilibrium.

Now it can be shown[37] that if equilibrium exists for some economy in E'' (i.e. for some $(\theta_1, \theta_2) \gg 0$), there is an open set M' in the message space M such that every point of M' is a Nash equilibrium fo some $e \in E''$. Hence (3.12) and (3.13) can be regarded as identities in m. Thus (3.12) can be differentiated, so that:

$$\sum_{i=1}^{2} X_j^i = \sum_{i=1}^{2} Y_j^i = 0 \qquad\qquad j = 1, 2 \qquad\qquad (3.14)$$

Substituting (3.14) into (3.13), we get the identities:

$$\begin{cases} X_1^1/X_2^1 = Y_1^1/Y_2^1 \\ X_1^2/X_2^2 = Y_1^2/Y_2^2 \end{cases} \qquad\qquad (3.15)$$

That is:

$$
\begin{vmatrix} X_1^1 & X_2^1 \\ Y_1^1 & Y_2^1 \end{vmatrix} = \begin{vmatrix} X_1^2 & X_2^2 \\ Y_1^2 & Y_2^2 \end{vmatrix} = 0 \qquad \text{for all } m \qquad (3.16)
$$

and so there is functional dependence, say:

$$
X^i(m) = \rho_i(Y^i(m)) \qquad\qquad i = 1, 2
$$

for all m in some neighbourhood.
  Hence:

$$
x_i^i = \rho_i' \cdot Y_i^i \qquad\qquad\qquad (3.17)
$$

For $u^i = \omega_X^i + X^i + \theta_i ln(\omega_Y^i + Y^i)$

using (3.17) in (3.10) yields:

$$
\rho_i' \cdot Y_i^i + \frac{\theta_i}{\omega_Y^i + Y^i} \cdot Y_i^i = 0 \qquad\qquad (3.18)
$$

One can show that $Y_i^i \neq 0$;[38] hence:

$$
\rho_i'(Y^i) + \frac{\theta_i}{\omega_Y^i + Y^i} = 0 \qquad\qquad i = 1, 2 \qquad (3.19)
$$

Now suppose (3.19) holds for some $\overline{Y} = (\overline{Y}^1, \overline{Y}^2)$ and $\overline{\theta} = (\overline{\theta}_1, \overline{\theta}_2), i = 1, 2$. Then, by Pareto efficiency:

$$
(\omega_Y^1 + \overline{Y}^1)/(\omega_Y^2 + \overline{Y}^2) = \overline{\theta}_1/\overline{\theta}_2 \qquad\qquad (3.20)
$$

Consider some $\overline{\overline{\theta}} = (\overline{\overline{\theta}}_1, \overline{\overline{\theta}}_2) \neq (\overline{\theta}_1, \overline{\theta}_2)$ but such that $\overline{\overline{\theta}}_1/\overline{\overline{\theta}}_2 = \overline{\theta}_1/\overline{\theta}_2$. Then Y is Pareto efficient for $\overline{\overline{\theta}}$, as seen from equation (3.20). However, $\overline{Y}, \overline{\overline{\theta}}$ do not satisfy equation (3.19), since (3.19) determines $\overline{\overline{\theta}}_i$ as a (single-valued) function of $\overline{\overline{Y}}^i$. Hence either Pareto efficiency or existence of equilibrium fails for $\overline{\overline{\theta}}$.

APPENDIX 3.2

The following outcome function guarantees Pareto efficiency of Nash equilibria for the case of two households and two goods, here denoted by x and y.

Since it follows from the Theorem of the fifth section for $s = \ell = 2$ that $dim\ M \geqslant 3$, we set $m^1 = (m_0, m_1)$, $m^2 = m_2$, with $m_r \in R$, $r = 0, 1, 2$. That is, the first participant has a two-dimensional language, $dim\ L_1 = 2$, while $dim\ L_2 = 1$. Denoting the outcome functions by $X^i(m)$ and $Y^i(m)$, $m = (m_0, m_1, m_2)$.[39] At a Nash equilibria:

$$u_X^1 X_0^1 + u_Y^1 Y_0^1 = 0$$

$$u_X^1 X_1^1 + u_Y^1 Y_1^1 = 0 \tag{3.21}$$

$$u_X^2 X_2^2 + u_Y^2 Y_2^2 = 0$$

so that, at a Nash equilibrium:

$$\frac{X_0^1}{X_1^1} = \frac{Y_0^1}{Y_1^1} \tag{3.22}$$

Since we require Pareto efficiency (hence feasibility) at a Nash equilibrium, it follows that, whenever (3.22) holds, we must also have:

$$u_X^1 / u_Y^1 = u_X^2 / u_Y^2 \tag{3.23}$$

and:

$$\Sigma X^i = \Sigma Y^i = 0 \tag{3.24}$$

But, by (3.22), equation (3.23) implies:

$$X_1^1 / X_2^2 = Y_1^1 / Y_2^2 \tag{3.25}$$

Thus we have deduced the following *necessary condition* on the outcome functions:[40]

for every $m \in M$;

$$X_0^1(m)/X_1^1(m) = Y_0^1(m)/Y_1^1(m) \tag{3.22a}$$

implies:

$$\sum_{i=1}^{2} X^i(m) = \sum_{i=1}^{2} Y^i(m) = 0 \tag{3.24a}$$

and:

$$X_1^1 / X_2^2 = Y_1^1 / Y_2^2 \tag{3.25a}$$

For sufficiency there are, of course, additional rank and second-order conditions.

It turns out that, at least for small classes of economies, these conditions are easily satisfied by low-degree polynomial outcome functions. The following is an example (in vector and matrix notation):

$$X^i(m) = c^i + a^i m + \tfrac{1}{2} m' B^i m$$

$$i = 1, 2$$

$$Y^i(m) = e^i + d^i m$$

where m' is a row vector while $m = (m_0, m_1, m_2)$ a column vector. a^i and d^i are also row vectors. c^i and e^i are scalars (reals). B is a 3 x 3 symmetric matrix.

A numerical example satisfying the above necessary condition is obtained by setting:

$$c^1 = -3, c^2 = 0, e^1 = -3, e^2 = 0$$

$$a^1 = (3, 2, -5), a^2 = (2, -1, 1), d^1 = (3, 1, -6), d^2 = (2, 0, 2)$$

$$B^1 = -B^2 = \begin{pmatrix} -1 & -2 & -1 \\ -2 & -1 & 1 \\ -1 & 1 & 2 \end{pmatrix}.$$

Consider now the class of economies where $u^i = \omega_X^i + X^i + \theta_i ln(\omega_Y^i + Y^i)$ $\theta_i > 0, i = 1, 2$.

Then it can be shown that sufficient conditions are also satisfied, and equilibria exist in the neighbourhood of the following parameter point:

$$\theta_1 = 5, \theta_2 = 50$$

$$\omega_Y^1 = 10, \omega_Y^2 = 1$$

$$\omega_X^1, \omega_X^2 \text{ any large positive numbers.}$$

For this particular parameter point, the equilibirum message vector is $m = (1, 2, 6)$.[41]

NOTES

1. In order to introduce the main body of this chapter it seems helpful to partly draw in this introductory section on Hurwicz, 1972c, 1973,

1979, and 1981.

2. The term 'economy' is used by many writers as a synonym for our 'environment', but others use it as a synonym for our 'mechanism'. Our choice of terms is designed to avoid this ambiguity.

3. The models and terminology introduced here are close to, but not identical with those in Hurwicz, 1960.

4. The symbol R^i represents the preference map of the i-th participant. Also, $x*R^i x**$ is read as: the i-th participant either (strictly) prefers $x*$ to $x**$ or is indifferent between $x*$ and $x**$.

   In other contexts, the letter R denotes the set of all real numbers, and $R^{(n)}$ is the n-fold Cartesian product of R, that is, the set of all ordered n-tuples of real numbers.

5. This assumption does not rule out externalities.

6. In general, participants may use different languages L_i, so that $m_i \in L_i$, $i = 1, \ldots, n$. The *message space* M is defined as the space of n-tuples $(m^1, \ldots, m^n)$; that is, $M = L_1 \times \ldots \times L_n$.

7. In more general contexts, we define a resource allocation system as the ordered triple (M, h, f) where M is the message space.

8. For example, continuously differentiable. The need for this type of restriction is discussed in Hurwicz, 1972a. See also pp. 132 and 148 this chapter.

9. That is, without production. Note, however, that analogous results are obtained for economies *with* production. Production is eliminated from this model merely to simplify exposition.

10. We use the following notation for vector inequalities: given two vectors $a = (a_1, \ldots, a_r)$ and $b = (b_1, \ldots, b_r)$ with the same number of components r, we write $a \geqq b$ to mean $a_j \geqq b_j$ for every $j = 1, \ldots, r$; $a \geq b$ to mean $a \geqq b$ but not $b \geqq a$ (i.e. $a_j \geqq b_j$ for all j and $a_s > b_s$ for some s); $a \gg b$ to mean $a_j > b_j$ for every $j = 1, \ldots, r$. The set of strictly positive r-dimensional vectors $(a \gg 0)$ is denoted by $R_{++}^{(r)}$. The set of non-negative vectors $(a \geqq 0)$ is denoted by $R_+^{(r)}$.

11. To simplify matters, the definition is given in the context of the E' class of economies.

12. Given the initial endowment ω^i, η satisfies the budget (equality) constraint relative to p if $p \cdot \eta = 0$.

13. See Hurwicz, 1972b, for the special case $s = 3$, $\ell = 2$ and Mount and Reiter, 1974, for the general formula.

14. See Hurwicz, 1972a.

15. A correspondence is a set-valued (multi-valued) function.

16. D represents the property regarded as desirable in a given context, for example, efficiency in a specified sense.

17. For example, in our applications, the desirable property is efficiency in Pareto or Koopmans sense, so to the set $D(e)$ corresponds the set $P(e)$ or $K(e)$.

18. $Pr_i E^*$ is the projection of E^* into E_i.

19. See Hurwicz, 1972a; Mount and Reiter, 1974; Osana, 1976b.
20. *dim M* means the dimension of the set of M, that is, the lowest dimension of any of Euclidean space containing M.
21. The precise meaning of 'smooth' in this context is as follows. Write the stationarity relations in the vectorial form:

    (1) $m = f(m; e)$

    Equation (1) defines a correspondence ρ (i.e. a multi-valued function) from a sub-set of M^* of the space M of messages into the space E of economies, which can be written as:

    $$\rho : M^* \to E$$

    and is defined by;

    $$e \in \rho(m) \quad \text{if and only if } m = f(m; e)$$

    The correspondence ρ is called *quasi-Lipschitzian* if it has a Lipschitzian selection, that is, if there exists a *single-valued* Lipschitz-continuous function:

    (2) $r : M^* \to E$

    such that:

    $$r(m) \in \rho(m) \quad \text{for all } m \in M^*$$

    We call the resource allocation system 'smooth' if the correspondence ρ is quasi-Lipschitzian.
    Note that the above correspondence ρ is the so-called lower inverse of the equilibrium correspondence μ introduced by Mount and Reiter (1974). Following the latter authors, Osana (1976b) has formulated certain conditions on μ which could be used in this theorem instead of our quasi-Lipschitzian condition of smoothness.
22. See Hurwicz, 1972b.
23. E_T^* is defined as follows. Write:

$$\theta^{iT} = (a_0^i, a_1^i, \dots, a_T^i)$$

$$\Theta_T^i = \left\{ \theta^{iT} : a_t^i \geqslant 0 \quad \text{for all } t = 0, 1, \dots, T \right\} \qquad i = 1, 2$$

$$\theta_T = (\theta_T^1, \theta_T^2)$$

$$\Theta_T = \Theta_T^1 \times \Theta_T^2,$$

and

$$\Theta_T^* = \{\theta_T \in \Theta_T : \sum_{t=0}^{T} a_t^1 = \alpha_1, \ \Sigma a_t^2 = \alpha_2, \text{ for some fixed}$$

$$\alpha_1 \geqslant 0, \alpha_2 \geqslant 0; a_t^1 + a_t^2 = a_0^1 + a_0^2 \quad \text{for all } t = 0, 1, \ldots, T\}.$$

Then E_T^* is the subset of E_T in which $\theta_T \in \Theta_T^*$.

24. In this case the system is required by Calsamiglia merely to be continuous rather than 'smooth'.

25. Actually, it is not merely privacy-preserving but also 'informationally decentralized', and not only non-wasteful but also 'unbiased'. (The terms in quotation marks are defined in Hurwicz, 1960.)

26. That is, free of externalities.

27. The Nash equilibrium of the game with this pay-off function is sometimes called 'naive' or 'non-manipulative'.

28. A parallel theorem has also been established for the analogous case with $s = \ell = 2$ where one of the two goods is public.

29. Suggested by Professor S. Reiter, Northwestern University.

30. In the light of the preceding theorem of this section, *dim M* = 3 is the best (lowest) one can hope to do in terms of the dimension of the message space.

31. In fact, a quadratic *h*. See Appendix 3.2 for detail.

32. In the light of the theorem of the third section, *dim M* = 3 is the best (lowest) one can hope to do in terms of the dimension of the message space.

33. The idea of constructing such systems is due to the public goods allocation system in Groves and Ledyard, 1974.

34. We write: $v^i(m) \equiv u^i(\omega_X^i + X^i(m), \ \omega_Y^i + Y^i(m), \ u_X^i = \partial u^i/\partial x^i, \ u_Y^i = \partial u^i/\partial y^i, \ X_i^i = \partial X^i/\partial m_i, \ Y_i^i = \partial Y^i/\partial m_i$.

35. That $\Sigma X^i = 0$ for all m can be seen more easily if we write the outcome formulae as follows:

$$X^1(m) = -(\tfrac{1}{2} m_1^2 + m_1 m_2 + m_1 m_3)$$

$$+ (\tfrac{1}{4} m_2^2 + m_2 m_3) + (\tfrac{1}{4} m_3^2 + m_2 m_3)$$

$$(1') \qquad X^2(m) = (\tfrac{1}{4} m_1^2 + m_1 m_3)$$

$$- (\tfrac{1}{2} m_2^2 + m_2 m_1 + m_2 m_3) + (\tfrac{1}{4} m_3^2 + m_1 m_3)$$

$$X^3(m) = (\tfrac{1}{4} m_1^2 + m_1 m_2) + (\tfrac{1}{4} m_2^2 + m_1 m_2)$$

$$- (\tfrac{1}{2} m_3^2 + m_3 m_1 + m_3 m_2)$$

Now calculate $\Sigma X^i(m)$ by adding the terms in parentheses in the same vertical column. We see, for example, that:

$$-(\tfrac{1}{2}m_1^2 + m_1 m_2 + m_1 m_3) + (\tfrac{1}{4}m_1^2 + m_1 m_3) + (\tfrac{1}{4}m_1^2 + m_1 m_2) = 0$$

for all m. The same is true for the other two columns. The symmetry of the above formulae is also evident.

36. For notation, see note 34.
37. Let θ be such that equilibrium m exists for θ (in E''), so that:

$$\omega_Y^i + Y^i > 0$$

Then, at (θ, m):

$$X_i^i + \theta_i \frac{1}{\omega_Y^i + Y^i} Y_i^i = 0$$

and, therefore:

$$\theta_i = -(\omega_Y^i + Y^i) \frac{X_i^i}{Y_i^i} > 0$$

Hence:

$$\frac{X_i^i(m)}{Y_i^i(m)} < 0 \tag{1}$$

But then the same is true for $\tilde{m}$ sufficiently near m (by the C^2 assumption). Hence $\tilde{m}$ near m are equilibrium values for θ_i, calculated from equation (1^*). (See next note for proof that $Y_i^i \neq 0$.)

38. Suppose $Y_1^1(\overline{m}) = 0$ for some $\overline{m} \in NE$ for $\overline{\theta}$. Then (since $u_X^1 > 0$, $u_Y^1 > 0$), we have $X_1^1(\overline{m}) = 0$.

   Let $\overline{\overline{\theta}} = (\overline{\overline{\theta}}_1, \overline{\overline{\theta}}_2)$ such that $\overline{\overline{\theta}}_1 \neq \overline{\theta}_1$ but $\overline{\overline{\theta}}_2 = \overline{\theta}_2$. Thus $\overline{m}$ is NE for $\overline{\overline{\theta}}$ and so $(\overline{X}, \overline{Y})$ is equilibrium outcome for $\overline{\overline{\theta}}$ if it was for $\overline{\theta}$. But $\overline{Y}$ is not P.O. for $\overline{\overline{\theta}}$. Contradiction.

39. See note 34 for notation.
40. This involves an argument like than in note 37. That is, every m in M satisfying (3.24) is a Nash equilibrium for some $(\theta_1, \theta_2) \gg 0$, and there is a neighbourhood M' in M consisting of such $m's$.
41. Mr Shamlall Gupta, graduate student in economics at the University of Minnesota, assisted in these calculations.

REFERENCES

Apostol, T. M. (1957) *Mathematical Analysis*, Reading, Mass.: Addison-Wesley.

Arrow, K., and L. Hurwicz (1960) 'Decentralization and Computation in Resource Allocation', in Pfouts (ed.) *Essays in Economics and Econometrics*, Chapel Hill University of North Carolina Press, pp. 34–104.

Calsamiglia, X. (1975) 'On the Possibility of Informational Decentralization in Non-Convex Environments', University of Minnesota Ph.D. thesis.

Groves, T., and J. Ledyard (1974) 'An Incentive Mechanism for Efficient Resource Allocation in General Equilibrium with Public Goods', Discussion Paper no. 119, Northwestern University: Center for Mathematical Studies in Economics and Management Science.

Guesnerie, R. (1975) 'Pareto Optimality in Non-Convex Economies', *Econometrica*, 43 (1) 1–29.

Hotelling, H. (1938) 'The General Welfare in Relation to Problems of Taxation and of Railway and Utility Rates', *Econometrica*, 6: 242–69.

Hurwicz, L. (1960) 'Optimality and Informational Efficiency in Resource Allocation Processes', in K. Arrow, S. Karlin, P. Suppes (eds), *Mathematical Methods in the Social Sciences 1959*, pp. 27–46.

Hurwicz, L. (1972a) 'On Informationally Decentralized Systems', in C. B. McGuire and R. Radner (eds), *Decision and Organization*, Amsterdam: North-Holland, Ch. 14, pp. 1–29.

Hurwicz, L. (1972b) 'On the Dimensional Requirements of Informationally Decentralized Pareto-Satisfactory Processes', in the process of publication. Presented at the Conference Seminar in Decentralization, Northwestern University, February 1972.

Hurwicz, L. (1972c) 'Organizational Structures for Joint Decision Making: A Designer's Point of View', in M. Tuite, R. Chisholm, and M. Radnor (eds), *Interorganizational Decision Making*, Chicago: Aldine, pp. 37–44.

Hurwicz, L. (1973) 'The Design of Mechanisms for Resource Allocation', *American Economic Review*, 63 (May): 1–30.

Hurwicz, L. (1979) 'On the Interaction between Information and Incentives in Organizations', in K. Krippendorff (ed.), *Communications and Control in Society*, New York: Gordon and Breads, pp. 123–47.

Hurwicz, L. (1981) 'On Incentive Problems in the Design of Non-wasteful Resource Allocation Systems', in N. Assorodobraj-Kula *et al.* (eds), *Studies in Economic Theory and Practice: Essays in Honor of Edward Lipinski*, Amsterdam: North-Holland, pp. 93–106.

Hurwicz, L., R. Radner and S. Reiter (1975) 'A Stochastic Decentralized Resource Allocation Process', Part I, *Econometrica*, 43 (2): 187–221; Part II, *Econometrica*, 43 (3): 363–93.

Kanemitsu, (1970) 'On the Stability of an Adjustment Process in Non-Convex Environments', presented at the Second World Congress of the Econometric Society, England, September 1970, unpublished.

Kanemitsu, H. (1975) 'A Non-tâtonnement Adjustment Process with Production and Consumption', presented at the Third World Congress of the Econometric Society, Toronto, August 1975, unpublished.

Lerner, A. P. (1937) 'Statics and Dynamics in Socialist Economics', *Economic Journal* 47 (June): 253–70.

Mount, K., and S. Reiter (1974) 'The Informational Size of Message Spaces', *Journal of Economic Theory*, 8(2): 161–92.

Osana, H. (1976a) 'Convergent Non-tâtonnement Resource Allocation Processes for Non-Classical Environments', Discussion Paper no. 76–64, February 1976, Center for Economic Research, Department of Economics, University of Minnesota, Minneapolis.

Osana, H. (1976b) 'On the Informational Size of Message Spaces for Resource Allocation Processes', presented April 1976 at the NBER Conference Seminar on Decentralization, Northwestern University, Evanston, Illinois.

4 Efficient Trading

ROBERT WILSON*

INTRODUCTION

A main concern of economic theory is to explain how markets work. This task has been pursued recently with attention to details neglected in earlier studies. In addition, the scope of the investigation has been widened to address issues about the efficient organization of trade. The purpose of this exposition is to describe some of these developments.

The motivation for the studies is suggested by two queries. First, how do markets work when there are few traders, and each trader takes advantage of opportunities to affect the terms of trade? Second, how does a trader take advantage of private information, and cope with ignorance about information known privately by others? These questions raise basic issues about how best to organize trading when the traders have market power and private information. That is, they pose the problem of how to design trading rules that promote efficient transactions, recognizing the effects of strategic behaviour.

Of these two motivations the role of private information takes precedence. In part this is because private information itself can create market power (we will not be considering such circumstances here). Another reason, however, is that in the absence of private information the trading process can be designed to eliminate market power.[1] The studies assume, therefore, that each trader has some private information. Emphasis is placed on the most obvious candidate: a trader's preferences constitute his private information. Besides the analytical simplicity it allows, an advantage of this focus is the comparison with the Walrasian model that it affords. The Walrasian construction suggests that there exists a price

* The author is grateful for a Guggenheim Fellowship and for research support from the Office of Naval Research (ONR-N00014-79-C-0685) and the National Science Foundation (SES-81-08226). Thanks are due to John Roberts for help with Theorem 2.

169

that will clear the market. If the traders' preferences are common knowledge (among the traders) then this price is also common knowledge, and if the trading rules eliminate market power (as do Schmeidler's, 1980), then the Walrasian outcome is plausibly predictable.[2] In this view the terms of trade and the resulting transactions are nearly a logical consequence of the commonly known facts: the traders' preferences, the lack of market power, and the necessity that markets clear.

If the traders have private information then the terms of trade are not predictable. In this case, the trading rules induce a game of incomplete information among the traders and (as will be seen) market power is inevitable among a finite number of traders. Predictions of prices and transactions in this case depend on a detailed analysis of the traders' optimal strategies. A task of the theory is to compare these predictions with the corresponding Walrasian predictions. For example, in some models one can show that if there are many traders then the Nash equilibrium of the trading game with incomplete information produces outcomes that approximate the Walrasian outcomes. And at a deeper level, one can verify that an efficient trading rule has features *assumed* in the Walrasian construction (e.g. all trades are made at a single price) and can not have other features (such as an absence of market power).

The Walrasian construction can be construed as an axiomatic system stating what transactions must occur if there is no market power, all traders make preferred trades at the same price, and the market must clear. It does not, however, justify these axioms if preferences are not common knowledge, and in particular it provides no description of the key ingredient: how it is that the information about preferences dispersed among the traders is reflected in the price. This poses an issue first enunciated by Friedrich von Hayek.

The motivation for detailed game-theoretic studies of particular trading rules is to elaborate precisely how it is that the trading rules, and each trader's strategic behaviour utilizing his private information, combine to determine terms of trade that reflect substantially all of the dispersed information.[3] Similarly, the derivation of efficient trading rules aims to verify significant structural features, such as the rule of one price for all transactions.

Methodology

The studies employ formulations and methods with common features. The main theme is to interpret the traders' common knowledge as the rules of a game of incomplete information played by the traders.[4] The trading rule is part of this common knowledge. It specifies each trader's set of feasible actions, and for each combination of actions they might choose it specifies the resulting transactions (or a probability distribution over transactions if the outcome of the trading rule depends on an uncertain event). A trader's strategy specifies his action (or possibly a random action) as a function of what he knows, including any private information he may have. Thus, the traders' information and strategies determine their actions, and these together with the trading rule determine their transactions.

For each trading rule particular strategies are assigned to the traders, subject to the requirement that these strategies constitute a Nash equilibrium. That is, a trader's strategy must assign to each state of his private information a feasible action that is among his best responses to the other traders' strategies. Two trading rules are then compared by comparing the transactions they generate in each configuration of the possible states of the traders' private information. The efficiency criteria used to evaluate trading rules are described in the fourth section.

This formulation is applied to exchange economies with a finite number of traders. Various assumptions are imposed to simplify the analysis. There are two goods, one of which is divisible and interpreted as money, and the other is demanded or supplied inelastically by each trader at any money price bounded by a reservation price. In the absence of risk aversion, each trader's utility is linear in money. These features are common knowledge, of course, and it is also assumed that the common knowledge includes all other data of the formulation: the number of traders, each trader's probability assessment of others' private information, etc. A trader's private information comprises only his preferences, namely his reservation price. In the simplest formulations the traders' probability assessments are supposed to derive from a model of reservation prices that are independently and identically distributed. In turn, this symmetry among the traders is reflected in the choice of a Nash equilibrium that treats symmetric traders symmetrically. The Nash equilibrium may be further restricted to be strong or perfect.[5]

Reader's Guide

The main ideas are first illustrated in the next section with the special case of the trading rule for a double auction. One can skip over the mathematical details about the computation of equilibrium strategies on a first reading. The third and fourth sections then develop the technical apparatus needed to characterize efficient trading rules: the third section presents the elements of the theory of incentive compatibility and the fourth section explains the efficiency criteria that are used to compare trading rules in situations with incomplete information. The fifth section derives sufficient conditions for a trading rule to be efficient. These are then applied in the sixth section to establish sufficient conditions that the trading rule for a double auction is efficient in the sense of the criterion of incentive efficiency defined in the fourth section. In order to keep the exposition uncluttered, rèferences to the literature are collected together in the seventh section. Concluding remarks are made in the eighth section.

DOUBLE AUCTIONS

The technical apparatus introduced in the next few sections is rather complicated. To illustrate the ideas we rely on an example of a trading game that has most of the key features and that occupies a central role in the theory. It has also been an important subject of experimental studies.

A double auction has the following trading rule. Each trader submits either a bid or an offer. These are limits on the money prices at which the trader proposes to buy or sell one unit of the good being traded. To determine the resulting transactions the bids are arrayed in descending order to obtain an aggregate demand schedule, and similarly the offers are arrayed in ascending order to obtain an aggregate supply schedule. Intersecting these two schedules determines an interval of prices that clear the market. All traders submitting higher bids receive one unit, and all submitting lower offers relinquish one unit. Selecting one price from this interval determines the money transfers: successful buyers pay this price to the successful sellers. The unsuccessful traders make no transaction.

The precise formulation of this trading rule runs as follows. The traders submitting bids (the *buyers*) are indexed by i in the set $M = \{1, \ldots, m\}$ and those submitting offers (the *sellers*) are indexed by j in the set $N = \{m + 1, \ldots, m + n\}$. Their bids and offers are denoted by r_i and s_j, respectively. The k-th largest of the bids is denoted by r^k, and the k-th smallest of the offers by s^k. Let $r^k = \infty$ if $k = 0$, $r^k = -\infty$ if $k > m$, $s^k = -\infty$ if $k = 0$, and $s^k = \infty$ if $k > n$. The set of prices that will clear the market is then the interval $[p_2, p_1]$ with endpoints:

$$p_1 = \min\{r^k, s^{k+1}\} \qquad \text{and} \qquad p_2 = \max\{s^k, r^{k+1}\} \qquad (4.1)$$

where the number of items traded is:

$$\kappa = \max \{k \mid r^k \geqslant s^k\} \tag{4.2}$$

Selecting a particular price p° from this interval completes the specification. One fairly general specification selects the clearing price p° as an increasing function of the endpoints p_1 and p_2, but here it will suffice to take the convex combination:

$$p^\circ = \mu_1 \cdot p_1 + \mu_2 \cdot p_2 \tag{4.3}$$

with fixed non-negative weights μ_1 and μ_2 summing to one.

If the selected clearing price $p^\circ \epsilon (p_2, p_1)$ then the resulting allocation assigns to each buyer i with a bid $r_i > p^\circ$ one unit of the good in exchange for p° units of money; the other buyers get zero of each. Similarly, each seller j with an offer $s_j < p^\circ$ gets p° units of money in exchange for one unit of the good and the others get zero of each. More generally, let $i(k)$ and $j(k)$ be the assignments that yield $r_{i(k)} = r^k$ and $s_{j(k)} = s^k$; then the buyers $\{i(k) \mid k \leqslant \kappa\}$ trade with the sellers $\{j(k) \mid k \leq \kappa\}$ at the clearing price p°.

One can interpret this trading rule as an algorithm that computes the transactions that maximize the gains from trade (summed over all traders) as measured from the submitted bids and offers. That is, if one represents the reallocation of the good by the sub-set A of $M \cup N$ indicating those buyers and sellers who trade, then the trading rule solves the problem of finding that choice of A that maximizes the gains from trade:

$$\sum_{i \epsilon A} r_i - \sum_{j \epsilon A} s_j \tag{4.4}$$

measured from the bids and offers, subject to the feasibility requirement that the sets $A \cap M$ and $A \cap N$ of buyers and sellers who trade have the same cardinality. It will be important later than this algorithm also solves the problem of maximizing the gains from trade according to any transformed scale of measurement, say:

$$\sum_{i \epsilon A} \phi(r_i) - \sum_{j \epsilon A} \phi(s_j) \tag{4.5}$$

for any strictly increasing function ϕ, since only ordinal comparisons are involved. The further feasibility condition that the money transfers balance is also assured by the construction. The criterion that the gains from trade calculated from the submitted bids and offers are maximized does not imply, however, that all transactions need to be at the same price, and that unsuccessful traders receive no money transfers: these are more specialized features of the trading rule.

An important aspect of this trading rule is that each trader need not lose by participating. For example, a buyer who submits a bid less than his reservation price might break even (if he fails to trade) and he might profit. This property of the trading rule is called *individual rationality*.

An auction is the special case of a double auction in which there is only one buyer ($m = 1$) or only one seller ($n = 1$). In the case of one seller, for instance, the seller offers a single unit of the good at a price no less than his offer s^1. The unit is sold to the buyer submitting the highest bid r^1, provided $r^1 \geqslant s^1$ so that the number of units traded is $\kappa = 1$. In a first-price auction, namely $\mu_1 = 1$, the clearing price $p^\circ = p_1$ is the winning buyer's bid; whereas in a second-price auction ($\mu_2 = 1$) the clearing price $p^\circ = p_2$ is the larger of the second-highest bid r^2 and the seller's offer s^1.

The Trading Game

The trading rule induces a game of incomplete information among the traders that we now formulate.

The trading rule's inputs are bids and offers, and the outputs are transactions. The buyers' available actions, therefore, are bids, and the sellers' are offers, which may be any real numbers. A trader's private information consists of his reservation price, or *valuation*: say buyer i's is u_i and seller j's is v_j. A strategy for buyer i is therefore a function ρ_i that specifies his bid as $r_i = \rho_i(u_i)$ when his valuation is u_i. Similarly, seller j's strategy σ_j specifies an offer $s_j = \sigma_j(v_j)$. The outcome for a buyer i is a pair (x_i, t_i) indicating whether he buys a unit at the market price p°, in which case $(x_i, t_i) = (1, -p^\circ)$, or does not, in which case $(x_i, t_i) = (0, 0)$. In either case, his gain is $x_i \cdot u_i + t_i$. Similarly the outcome for the seller j is a pair (x_j, t_j) that is either $(-1, p^\circ)$ or $(0, 0)$, and his gain is $x_j \cdot v_j + t_j$. The trading rule ensures that the feasibility conditions:

$$\sum_{i \in M} x_i + \sum_{j \in N} x_j = 0 \quad \text{and} \quad \sum_{i \in M} t_i + \sum_{j \in N} t_j = 0 \tag{4.6}$$

for the good and the money transfers are satisfied.

The traders' strategies and the trading rule combine to determine the set A of successful traders and the market price p° as functions of their valuations. Since a trader knows only his own valuation, he regards A and p° as random variables, and he evaluates the expected gain from his strategy using a probability assessment of the others' valuations — supposing, of course, that he can predict their strategies from the Nash equilibrium. We assume here that it is common knowledge that the traders' valuations are independently distributed, and that the buyers' valuations are identically distributed according to the distribution function F with positive and differentiable density f on the unit interval; similarly, the sellers' valuations have the distribution function G and density g.

The probability of the event $\{i \in A\}$ that a buyer i trades is the probability that the clearing price is no greater than his bid, $p^\circ \leqslant r_i$, and analogously for a seller. A trader's main concern, therefore is the probability distribution of the market price p° contingent on his bid or offer. To see how such calculations are done, consider the case that the buyers' strategies are all the same increasing function ρ and the sellers' strategies are all the same increasing function σ. Then the probability that p is a clearing price (not necessarily the selected price p°) is:

$$Pr\{p_2 \leqslant p \leqslant p_1\} = \sum_{\kappa=0}^{m \sqcap n} \binom{m}{\kappa} \binom{n}{\kappa} \cdot \hat{F}^{m-\kappa} \cdot [1 - \hat{F}]^\kappa \cdot \hat{G}^\kappa$$

$$\cdot [1 - \hat{G}]^{n-\kappa} \tag{4.7}$$

Here κ indicates the number of units traded, which cannot exceed the lesser of m and n (denoted by $m \sqcap n$). The probability that a buyer's valuation is too low to yield a bid above p is $\hat{F} = F(\rho^{-1}(p))$, and that a seller's is low enough to yield an offer below p is $\hat{G} = G(\sigma^{-1}(p))$. It is convenient to write this formula as:

$$Pr\{p_2 \leqslant p \leqslant p_1\} = \hat{F}^m \cdot [1 - \hat{G}]^n \cdot \psi_0(J) \tag{4.8}$$

using:

$$J = \frac{[1 - \hat{F}] \cdot \hat{G}}{\hat{F} \cdot [1 - \hat{G}]} \tag{4.9}$$

in the function:

$$\psi_\nu(J) = \sum_{\kappa=0}^{m \sqcap n} \binom{m}{\kappa} \binom{n}{\kappa} \cdot \kappa^\nu J^\kappa \tag{4.10}$$

for $v = 0$. The functions ψ_v have many uses; for example, the expected number of units traded conditional on p being a clearing price is:

$$E\{\kappa \,|\, p_2 \leqslant p \leqslant p_1\} = \psi_1(J)/\psi_0(J) \tag{4.11}$$

and the probability density of, say, p_2 is:

$$Pr\{p_2 = p\} = \hat{F}^m \cdot [1 - \hat{G}]^n \cdot \left([m\psi_0(J) - \psi_1(J)] \cdot \frac{\partial \ln\hat{F}}{\partial p} \right.$$
$$\left. + \psi_1(J) \cdot \frac{\partial \ln\hat{G}}{\partial p} \right) \tag{4.12}$$

Some of the other relevant probability calculations are shown below.

Equilibrium Strategies

The traders' equilibrium strategies can, in the simplest cases, be characterized via differential equations. One such characterization is derived here using the restriction that the equilibrium is symmetric and perfect, and the hypothesis that each trader's strategy is an increasing differentiable function of his valuation.

The derivation can be abbreviated by appealing to an intuitive argument.[6] Consider the situation of a buyer with the valuation u who is bidding against other buyers using the strategy ρ and sellers using the strategy σ. Contemplating the bid p, he considers whether it would be advantageous to lower it to $p - dp$, where dp is a small decrement in the bid. He stands to gain if this would reduce the clearing price should he succeed in trading, and he stands to lose if this would prevent his trading when otherwise he would have succeeded. If his bid p is optimal then the marginal expected gain should equal the marginal expected loss. The former is $H \cdot \mu_1 \cdot dp$, where H is the probability that he trades and that $p = p_1$. The latter is $[u - p] \cdot h \cdot dp$, where $h \cdot dp$ is approximately the probability that the decrement excludes him from trading if h is the probability density that $p_2 = p = p_1$. Hence the requisite condition is that:

$$[u - p] \cdot \frac{h}{H} = \mu_1 \tag{4.13}$$

and if ρ is an optimal strategy for the buyer then this condition must be satisfied when his bid $p = \rho(u)$.

The formula for the probability H is:

$$H = \sum_{\kappa=1}^{m \sqcap n} \binom{m-1}{\kappa-1}\binom{n}{\kappa} \cdot \hat{F}^{m-\kappa}[1-\hat{F}]^{\kappa-1}\hat{G}^{\kappa}[1-\hat{G}]^{n-\kappa} \quad (4.14)$$

Each term in the summation is the probability that κ units are traded given that his bid p must be the κ-th largest bid and between the κ-th and the $(\kappa + 1)$-th smallest offers. The formula for the density h is constructed similarly using the additional requirement that his bid p is also equal to the maximum of the κ-th smallest offer and the $(\kappa + 1)$-th largest bid. Hence, the formula for h has each term in the summation (4.14) multiplied by the extra factor:

$$[m - \kappa] \cdot \frac{\partial \ln \hat{F}}{\partial p} + \kappa \cdot \frac{\partial \ln \hat{G}}{\partial p} \quad (4.15)$$

Combining these formulae yields the ratio:

$$\frac{h}{H} = [m - \bar{k}] \cdot \frac{\partial \ln \hat{F}}{\partial p} + \bar{k} \cdot \frac{\partial \ln \hat{G}}{\partial p} \quad (4.16)$$

where:

$$\bar{k} = \psi_2(J)/\psi_1(J) \quad (4.17)$$

It can be shown that $1 \leqslant \bar{k} \leqslant m \sqcap n$, since $\bar{k}$ is a conditional expectation of κ. A similar construction for a seller with the valuation v yields the analogous optimality condition:

$$[v - p] \cdot \left(\bar{k} \cdot \frac{\partial \ln[1 - \hat{F}]}{\partial p} + [n - \bar{k}] \cdot \frac{\partial \ln[1 - \hat{G}]}{\partial p} \right) = \mu_2 \cdot \quad (4.18)$$

It is easily seen from these optimality conditions that if the price p is both the bid by a buyer with the valuation u and the offer by a seller with the valuation v then p is a convex combination of u and v.

Several special cases are worth pointing out. If $\mu_2 = 1$ as in a second price auction then it suffices to take $\rho(u) = u$; and similarly if $\mu_1 = 1$ as in a first price auction then take $\sigma(v) = v$. In the latter case, for instance, one substitutes $\rho(u)$ for p in the buyers' optimality condition to get the differential equation:

$$[u - \rho(u)] \cdot \left([m - \bar{k}] \cdot \frac{f(u)}{F(u)} \cdot \frac{1}{\rho'(u)} + \bar{k} \cdot \frac{g(\rho(u))}{G(\rho(u))} \right) = 1 \qquad (4.19)$$

In general, the conditional expected number of trades, $\bar{k}$, depends on the buyer's valuation u. Auctions present another special case in which either $m = -1$ or $n = 1$, and $\bar{k} = 1$ identically.

If neither μ_1 nor μ_2 is zero then the traders' optimality conditions are best interpreted as differential equations for the inverse functions $u(p) = \rho^{-1}(p)$ and $v(p) = \sigma^{-1}(p)$. Thus, solving the linear equations derived from (4.13), (4.16), and (4.18):

$$\begin{bmatrix} [m - \bar{k}] \cdot \dfrac{f}{F} & \bar{k} \cdot \dfrac{g}{G} \\[2mm] \bar{k} \cdot \dfrac{f}{1 - F} & [n - \bar{k}] \cdot \dfrac{g}{1 - G} \end{bmatrix} \cdot \begin{bmatrix} u' \\[2mm] v' \end{bmatrix} = \begin{bmatrix} \dfrac{\mu_1}{u - p} \\[2mm] \dfrac{\mu_2}{p - v} \end{bmatrix} \qquad (4.20)$$

for u' and v' yields:

$$\begin{bmatrix} u' \\[2mm] v' \end{bmatrix} = \frac{1}{D} \cdot \begin{bmatrix} -\dfrac{F}{f} \cdot J \cdot [n - \bar{k}] & \dfrac{1 - F}{f} \cdot \bar{k} \\[2mm] \dfrac{G}{g} \cdot \bar{k} & -\dfrac{1 - G}{g} \cdot J \cdot [m - \bar{k}] \end{bmatrix}$$

$$\cdot \begin{bmatrix} \dfrac{\mu_1}{u - p} \\[2mm] \dfrac{\mu_2}{p - v} \end{bmatrix} \qquad (4.21)$$

where $D = \bar{k}^2 - J \cdot [m - \bar{k}] \cdot [n - \bar{k}]$. In these equations one evaluates f and F at $u(p)$, and g and G at $v(p)$, and these are used to compute J and then $\bar{k}$ as before. A somewhat simpler system results if one uses instead the functions $R(p) = F(u(p))$ and $S(p) = G(v(p))$:

$$\begin{bmatrix} R' \\[2mm] S' \end{bmatrix} = \frac{1}{D} \cdot \begin{bmatrix} -(n - \bar{k}) \dfrac{1 - R}{1 - S} & \bar{k} \\[2mm] \bar{k} & -(m - \bar{k}) \dfrac{S}{R} \end{bmatrix} \cdot \begin{bmatrix} \mu_1 \dfrac{S}{u - p} \\[2mm] \mu_2 \dfrac{1 - R}{p - v} \end{bmatrix} \qquad (4.22)$$

where $u = F^{-1}(R)$ and $v = G^{-1}(S)$, and $\bar{k}$ and D are computed using $J = [1 - R]S/R[1 - S]$.

The boundary conditions need to be specified to complete the characterization. The lowest offer that a seller might submit is that price p^* such that $G(v(p^*)) = 0$, namely $p^* = \sigma(0)$. A buyer bidding slightly above that price has a negligible chance of succeeding compared to the prospect that a lower bid will leave him with no trade; hence, invoking continuity, it must be that at p^* he is bidding his full valuation: $u(p^*) = p^*$ or equivalently $R(p^*) = F(p^*)$. Perfectness also requires that $u(p) = p$ for any $p \leqslant p^*$, since if $u(p) < p$ the buyer would be susceptible to errors by the sellers. Symmetrically, at $p \geqslant p^{**} = \rho(1)$ the sellers' strategy must yield $v(p) = p$.

The boundary conditions have a further implication. Taking the limit as $S \to 0$, one gets $J \to 0$, $\bar{k} \to 1$, $D \to 1$, and (using l'Hôpital's Rule):

$$S' \to \mu_1 \frac{S}{u - p} \to \mu_1 \frac{S'}{u' \cdot R' - 1} \tag{4.23}$$

Consequently, it must be that:

$$R'(p^*) = \frac{1 + \mu_1}{u'(F(p^*))} \tag{4.24}$$

or in the original notation: $u'(p^*) = 1 + \mu_1$. A similar procedure produces the equation:

$$S'(p^*) = \frac{1}{n - 1} \left[\frac{\mu_2}{p^*} - \frac{1 + \mu_1}{u'(F(p^*)(1 - F(p^*)))} \right] \tag{4.25}$$

that S' must satisfy at p^* if $n > 1$. If $n = 1$ then $p^* = ([1 - F(p^*)]/f(p^*) \times (\mu_2/[1 + \mu_1])$. A repetition of these methods determines analogous conditions on the derivatives of R and S at p^{**}.

The results of this construction can be summarized in the representation of an equilibrium depicted in Figure 4.1. Below the 45° line is shown the locus of pairs (u, v) such that the bid of a buyer with the valuation u is equal to the offer of a seller with the valuation v. Shown on the locus are gradations indicating the amount of the bid or offer at each point. In the special case, say, that $\mu_1 = 1$ as in a first price auction the offer is the same as the seller's valuation v. In general, buyers' bids understate their valuations and sellers' offers overstate; thus, strategic behaviour ordinarily precludes complete exhaustion of the gains from trade.

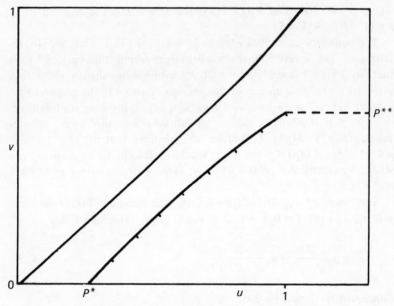

FIGURE 4.1   *Representation of a symmetric equilibrium*

A Class of Symmetric Examples

A special case that enables easy computations is the one in which the
numbers of buyers and sellers are equal $[m = n]$, their probability assessments are uniform $[F(u) = u$ and $G(v) = v]$, and the trading rule treats
them symmetrically $[\mu_1 = \mu_2 = .5]$. In this case it suffices to construct
the traders' strategies in terms of positive number δ and a function ψ
having the symmetry property that:

$$\psi(x) + \psi(1 - x) = 1 \tag{4.26}$$

The construction involves setting:

$$\rho(u) = \psi(u - \delta) \qquad \text{and} \qquad \sigma(v) = \psi(v + \delta) \tag{4.27}$$

and observing that with this specification the differential equations representing the buyers' and sellers' optimality conditions reduce to a single
differential equation for the unknown function ψ depending on a single
variable x. It can be shown that this single differential equation admits a

solution having the symmetry property (4.26) required of the function ψ. In particular, this is consistent with the boundary conditions $\rho(p^*)$ $= p^*$ and $\sigma(p^{**}) = p^{**}$, which take the form:

$$p^* = 2\delta \qquad \text{and} \qquad p^{**} = 1 - 2\delta \qquad (4.28)$$

so that:

$$\psi(\delta) = 2\delta \qquad \text{and} \qquad \psi(1 - \delta) = 1 - 2\delta \qquad (4.29)$$

That is, 2δ is the sellers' minimal possible offer and $1 - 2\delta$ is the buyers' maximal possible bid. Since the differential equation for ψ has only one constant of integration, these two conditions suffice to determine both δ and ψ.

Note that for this class of examples the locus in Figure 4.1 takes the form of a line parallel to the $45°$ line, and each point on the locus is a distance (either vertically or horizontally) of 2δ from the $45°$ line. In the simplest case of one buyer and one seller $[m = n = 1]$ it is possible to obtain the explicit solution $\delta = \frac{1}{8}$ and $\psi = \frac{2}{3}x + \frac{1}{6}$, which yields $\rho(u)$ $= \min\{u, \frac{2}{3}(u + \frac{1}{8})\}$ and $\sigma(v) = \max\{v, \frac{2}{3}(v + \frac{3}{8})\}$. Note that in this case the buyer and seller trade only if the difference in their valuations is not less than the critical value $2\delta = \frac{1}{4}$. Table 4.1 shows how this difference varies as the number of buyers and sellers increases from one to twelve.[7]

Table 4.1

m, n:	1	2	4	8	12
2δ:	.25	.18	.11	.06	.04

As the number of traders increases δ converges to zero and ψ converges to the identity function. An easy way to see this is to observe from (4.16) that:

$$\frac{h}{H} = \left[\frac{m - \bar{k}}{x + \delta} + \frac{\bar{k}}{x - \delta} \right] \frac{1}{\psi'(x)} \geqslant \frac{m}{\psi'(x)} \qquad (4.30)$$

If $\psi'(x)$ is bounded above as $m \to \infty$ then (4.13) implies that $u - p$ $\equiv (x + \delta) - \psi(x) \to 0$, and similarly (4.18) implies that $p - v \equiv \psi(x)$ $- (x - \delta) \to 0$. In view of (4.29) and the fact that $\psi(x)$ is a convex combination of $x + \delta$ and $x - \delta$ (the valuations of a buyer and a seller who bid and offer $\psi(x)$), it follows that $\psi(x) \to x$ and $\delta \to 0$ as m, $n \to \infty$.[8] Thus when there are many traders each trader bids nearly his valuation, and the clearing price is approximately the Walrasian price.

INCENTIVE COMPATABILITY

The trading rule for a double auction studied in the second section is one among the many that can be devised, and indeed, a wide variety of trading rules are found in practice. A purpose of the theory is to sift through these many alternatives to identify those trading rules that promote efficient trades. The task requires a general description of the class of admissible trading rules, a characterization of the expected gains from trade they yield, and a criterion of efficiency that can be used to select among them. The theory of incentive compatibility developed in recent years addresses these requirements to obtain partial answers from a minimum of structural assumptions. The main results of the theory are reviewed in this section for the special case of the economic environment used to study double auctions. All of the assumptions made in the second section are imposed here, except for the possibility that some trading rule other than a double auction might be used.

Direct Revelation Games

In general, a trading rule specifies a set of feasible actions R_i or S_j for each buyer $i \in M$ or seller $j \in N$, together with a function:

$$r : (X_{i \in M} R_i) X (X_{j \in N} S_j) \to A \qquad (4.31)$$

that assigns to each combination of the traders' actions a feasible allocation, or possibly a random allocation. An allocation $\langle (x_i, t_i)_{i \in M}, (x_j, t_j)_{j \in N} \rangle$ indicates whether each trader trades and the transfer he receives. Feasibility requires that the allocation satisfies:

$$\sum_{i \in M} (x_i, t_i) + \sum_{j \in N} (x_j, t_j) = (0, 0) \qquad (4.32)$$

so that the market clears. With such a trading rule a (pure) strategy for a buyer i or a seller j is a function $\rho_i : U_i \to R_i$ or $\sigma_j : V_j \to S_j$ that specifies his action contingent on his private information. In the present context a buyer's private information consists of his valuation $u_i \in U_i$; and a seller's, his valuation $v_j \in V_j$. In the second section each domain U_i and V_j was taken to be the unit interval $[0, 1]$, and for practical purposes one could take the action sets R_i and S_j of bids and offers to be this same interval. Thus a double auction is an instance of a *revelation game* in which a trader is, in effect, asked to report something from his domain of private information that the trading rule treats like a valuation.

Formally, a revelation game has each trader's sets of information states and actions the same: $U_i = R_i$ and $V_j = S_j$. A direct revelation game has the further property that there is a Nash equilibrium in which each trader's strategy is the identity function. That is, each trader finds it optimal to report accurately his private information if he expects each other trader to do the same.

A simple but important fact is that from an arbitrary rule r, and the traders' equilibrium strategies ρ_i and σ_j in the induced trading game, one can construct the trading rule $\hat{r}$ for a direct revelation game via the composition $\hat{r} = r \left[(\rho_i)_{i \in M}, (\sigma_j)_{j \in N} \right]$. The trading rule $\hat{r}$ accepts reports of their valuations from the traders, uses these to compute what they would have bid or offered with the original trading rule r, and then determines the allocation from these in the same fashion that r does. To see that this yields a direct revelation game, observe that if a trader preferred to distort his report of his private information then in the original game he would have preferred to change his strategy — contradicting the Nash equilibrium that was supposed. For example, if a buyer i with the valuation u_i preferred to report the false valuation $\tilde{u}_i$ in the direct revelation game, then he would have preferred to bid $\rho_i(\tilde{u}_i)$ rather than $\rho_i(u_i)$ in the original game when his valuation was u_i.

The salient conclusion from this result is that it suffices in principle to study direct revelation games in order to find efficient trading rules. There often remains a motive, of course, to translate an efficient direct revelation game back into a form of the sort more usually found in practice. Alternatively, given a particular trading rule of practical interest, such as a double auction, the objective is to show whether it is efficient by ascertaining whether the direct revelation game that it induces is efficient.

Characterization of the Expected Gains from Trade

A second result of interest is that the efficiency properties of a direct revelation game (and therefore an arbitrary trading rule) are fully characterized by each trader's chances of trading contingent on his private information. This result is derived below using the assumed features of the economic environment, but it has a much wider range of application. The derivation is for a typical buyer, but it is similar for a seller.

Let $\breve{U}_i(u, \hat{u})$ be the expected gain from trade for a buyer i whose valuation is $\bar{u}$ and he reports $\hat{u}$. The expectation is calculated using the assumption that all other traders report their true valuations. This can be written as:

$$\overset{\circ}{U}_i(u, \hat{u}) = E\{u \cdot x_i + t_i \mid u, \hat{u}\}$$

$$= u \cdot P_i(\hat{u}) - R_i(\hat{u}) \tag{4.33}$$

using the fact that the traders' valuations are independent. Here, $P_i(\hat{u})$ is his probability of trading, and $R_i(\hat{u})$ is his expected payment, if he reports $\hat{u}$. Let $U_i(u) = \overset{\circ}{U}_i(u, u)$ be his expected gain if he reports accurately.

Lemma 1: In a direct revelation game, U_i is convex and non-decreasing, its derivative is P_i almost everywhere, P_i is non-decreasing, and

$$U_i(u) = U_i(0) + \int_0^u P_i(t)dt \tag{4.34}$$

$$R_i(u) = R_i(0) + \int_0^u t dP_i(t)$$

where $R_i(0) = -U_i(0)$.

Proof: A buyer in a direct revelation game must be satisfied to report his valuation accurately, namely, it is required that $U_i(u) \geqslant \overset{\circ}{U}_i(u, \hat{u})$ for any two possible valuations u and $\hat{u}$. This inequality can be written as:

$$U_i(u) \geqslant U_i(\hat{u}) + [u - \hat{u}] \cdot P_i(\hat{u}) \tag{4.35}$$

which implies that U_i has a supporting hyperplane at $\hat{u}$ with slope $P_i(\hat{u}) \geqslant 0$. Consequently, U_i is convex and non-decreasing with the derivative $U_i'(\hat{u}) = P_i(\hat{u})$ for almost all values of $\hat{u}$. The convexity of U_i implies that its derivative P_i is non-decreasing. This implies the first formula in (4.34), and the second is then obtained by integrating by parts. ∎

It is useful to record a convenient formula implied by these results. Let $\alpha_i(\cdot)$ be some function of a buyer's valuation u and define:

$$\bar{\alpha}_i(\hat{u}) = \int_{\hat{u}}^1 \alpha_i(u)dF(u)/[1 - F(\hat{u})] \tag{4.36}$$

namely $\bar{\alpha}_i(\hat{u})$ is the conditional expectation of α_i given that $u \geq \hat{u}$. Then:

$$E\{\alpha_i(u)U_i(u)\} = \int_0^1 \alpha_i(u)U_i(u)dF(u)$$

$$= \bar{\alpha}_i(0)U_i(0) + \int_0^1 \bar{\alpha}_i(u)[1 - F(u)]dU_i(u) \tag{4.37}$$

$$= \bar{\alpha}_i(0)U_i(0) + \int_0^1 \bar{\alpha}_i(u)[1 - F(u)]P_i(u)du$$

$$= \bar{\alpha}_i(0)U_i(0) + E\left\{\bar{\alpha}_i(u)\frac{1 - F(u)}{f(u)}P_i(u)\right\}$$

where the first and last equalities are definitional, the second uses integration by parts, and the third invokes Lemma 1.

Similarly, represent the expected gain from trade for a seller j with the valuation v as:

$$V_j(v) = S_j(v) - v \cdot Q_j(v) \tag{4.38}$$

where $S_j(v)$ is his expected payment and $Q_j(v)$ is his probability of trading. Then V_j is convex and non-increasing, Q_j is non-increasing, and

$$V_j(v) = V_j(1) + \int_v^1 Q_j(t)dt$$

$$S_j(v) = S_j(1) + \int_v^1 t d[1 - Q_j(t)] \tag{4.39}$$

Also, if β_j is a function of v and

$$\bar{\beta}_j(\hat{v}) = \int_0^{\hat{v}} \beta_j(v)dG(v)/G(\hat{v}) \tag{4.40}$$

is its conditional expectation given $v \leq \hat{v}$, then:

$$\epsilon\{\beta_j(v)V_j(v)\} = \bar{\beta}_j(1)V_j(1) + E\left\{\bar{\beta}_j(v)\frac{G(v)}{g(v)}Q_j(v)\right\} \tag{4.41}$$

As mentioned above, a conclusion from these results is that the efficiency properties of a trading rule are completely described by the two functions $P_i(u)$ and $Q_j(v)$ indicating a buyer's and a seller's chances of trading contingent on their respective valuations.

Individual Rationality

As mentioned in the second section, a trading rule is said to have the property of individual rationality if a trader need not lose by participating in the trading process. This property can be formulated in various ways that differ in terms of how strictly one interprets the requirements for participation. For a buyer i with the valuation u_i, the strictest interpretation requires that the allocation ensure non-negative gains from trade in every circumstance, namely, $u_i x_i + t_i \geqslant 0$. Somewhat weaker are formulations that presume some degree of rational behaviour by the buyer. One such formulation requires that a buyer has available an action (non-participation) that will ensure the assignment $(x_i, t_i) = (0, 0)$; a second requires an action that will ensure that $u_i x_i + t_i \geqslant 0$. The latter is the case in a double auction, since a buyer can bid less than his valuation, needs to pay only if he succeeds in trading, and if he trades the price cannot exceed his bid. Each of these formulations implies that a buyer's expected gain from trade using an optimal strategy is non-negative, namely $U_i(u_i) \geqslant 0$. In particular, this formulation is described completely by the requirement that $U_i(0) \geqslant 0$, since it was shown in Lemma 1 that U_i is a non-decreasing function of the buyer's valuation. Lastly, the weakest formulation would only require that $E\{U_i(u_i)\} \geqslant 0$; that is, before knowing his valuation the buyer would assess non-negative expected gains from trade.

Each of these several formulations of the property of individual rationality could be appropriate, depending on the perspective adopted in the design of efficient trading rules and on the institutional features that constrain the implementation of a trading rule. Here we concentrate on the situation in which the traders already know their valuations, and adopt the weakest form of individual rationality consistent with this perspective. Thus, we adopt the convention that a trading rule is individually rational if, in the induced direct revelation game:

$$U_i(0) \geqslant 0 \qquad \text{and} \qquad V_j(1) \geqslant 0 \tag{4.42}$$

That is, each buyer or seller, and in particular one with the least favourable valuation ($u_i = 0$ or $v_j = 1$), must have a non-negative expected gain from participation in the trading process if optimal strategies are used.

The following result shows that the property of individual rationality imposes a constraint on the set of admissible trading rules. As in the second section, we use $A \subset M \cup N$ to indicate the set of buyers and sellers who trade; thus A is a random variable depending on all of the buyers' and sellers' valuations.

Lemma 2: In a direct revelation game:

$$E \left\{ \sum_{i \in A \cap M} \left[u_i - \frac{1 - F(u_i)}{f(u_i)} \right] - \sum_{j \in A \cap N} \left[v_j + \frac{G(v_j)}{g(v_j)} \right] \right\}$$

$$- \sum_{i \in M} U_i(0) - \sum_{j \in N} V_j(1) = 0 \tag{4.43}$$

Proof: Observe that due to the feasibility condition (4.32):

$$E \left\{ \sum_{i \in A \cap M} u_i - \sum_{j \in A \cap N} v_j \right\} = \sum_{i \in M} E\{U_i(u_i)\} + \sum_{j \in N} E\{V_j(v_j)\} \tag{4.44}$$

Using (4.37) with $\alpha_i(u) = \bar{\alpha}_i(u) = 1$, the buyers' terms are:

$$\sum_{i \in M} E\{U_i(u_i)\} = \sum_{i \in M} U_i(0) + \sum_{i \in M} E \left\{ \frac{1 - F(u_i)}{f(u_i)} \cdot P_i(u_i) \right\}$$

$$= \sum_{i \in M} U_i(0) + E \left\{ \sum_{i \in A \cap M} \frac{1 - F(u_i)}{f(u_i)} \right\} \tag{4.45}$$

The sellers' terms are constructed similarly. ∎

Thus, an implication of individual rationality is that the expectation in (4.43) must be non-negative, which constitutes a restriction on how the set A of buyers and sellers who trade can be chosen by the trading rule.

EFFICIENCY CRITERIA

The development of new criteria to decide the efficiency of a trading rule is an accomplishment with subtle but far-reaching ramifications. To be useful such a criterion must take account of the effects of the traders' private information. A welfare comparison that ignores traders' opportunities for strategic behaviour is likely to be inaccurate. And, a comparison that requires information unavailable to the participants is likely to be irrelevant. These considerations pose two basic issues. The first issue concerns the objects compared, and it is resolved by adopting the premise that the comparison must be between the outcomes resulting from Nash equilibria of the games of incomplete information induced by the two candidate trading rules. The second issue concerns the informational basis of the comparison, and it is resolved by adopting the standard that the measures invoked in the comparison must be common knowledge among the traders. The rationale for adopting criteria that meet these requirements is reviewed in this section. In addition, a weak and a strong form of the efficiency criterion are presented. The role of feasibility constraints, such as the individual rationality condition, is explained as well.

Outcomes

Presumably each trader has private information, including at least some information affecting his preferences. The output of a trading rule is an allocation. If it is to ensure gains from trade the allocation must depend upon actions taken by the traders that reveal their preferences. Realizing this, each trader has an incentive to choose his action to maximize his expected gains from trade. Thus, strategic behaviour is endemic and welfare comparisons must be between the games of incomplete information induced by trading rules. A prediction of the outcomes of such games is required. If the prediction itself is to be common knowledge among the traders, which is adopted here as a postulate, then it is necessary that the outcomes result from a Nash equilibrium. That is, if the traders' strategies are common knowledge then each trader's incentive is to adopt his best response to the others' strategies – which is precisely the definition of a Nash equilibrium. (One may, of course, impose stronger requirements, such as that the equilibrium is strong or perfect, or that the traders have dominant strategies.)

As seen in the third section, a technical consequence of this construction is that attention can be confined initially to comparisons among direct revelation games, since a Nash equilibrium of any game generates a direct revelation game with the same predicted outcomes.

Feasibility

The trading rules admitted for comparison must, of course, be technologically feasible. This requirement is summarized in the constraint that the market clear. (The present treatment excludes other technological features, such as the traders' consumption sets, resources used in the trading process, etc.) A further requirement, however, stems from behavioural considerations. The domain of admissible trading rules is confined to those that ensure individual rationality. That is, it is required that no trader stands to lose by participating. We adopt this as a postulate because it is an intrinsic feature of the trading rules found in practice: the efficiency properties of prevalent institutionalized trading rules are explicable only if restrictions are imposed on the design to exclude exploitation of participants, such as the confiscation of endowments. The functioning of markets depends fundamentally on the institution of private property, and the concommitant role of voluntary exchange: to abbrogate these features would present problems of a different character.

In sum, the objects of choice are the various possible direct revelation games that satisfy the feasibility condition that the market clears, and that satisfy individual rationality.

The Informational Basis of Comparison

Welfare comparisons depend sensitively on the information available to measure the traders' gains from trade. After the trading is over it may indeed be apparent that another trading rule would have benefited some buyers or sellers, or that strategic behaviour has left some gains from trade unrealized. Ordinarily, however, the design of a trading rule must be undertaken with no more information than the traders bring to the market, and often with less information. Initially the traders' valuations are known privately and any procedure to elicit their valuations amounts to a *de facto* direct revelation game. Welfare comparisons, therefore, are limited at least to the information available to the traders collectively; that is, to the common knowledge.

The efficiency of a trading rule, moreover, is judged by the criterion of unanimity without regard to distributional criteria: to verify that a trading rule is efficient it is sufficient to establish that no other trading rule would improve each trader's expected gain from trade.

Combining these two desiderata yields a well-defined criterion for efficiency. A trading rule is judged efficient if it is common knowledge that no other trading rule would improve each participant's expected gain from trade. In the following paragraphs this criterion is made operational in two forms, the second stronger than the first due to the temporal perspective adopted for the welfare comparison.

The Interim Perspective: Incentive Efficiency

The *interim* perspective on welfare comparisons presumes that the buyers and sellers already know their valuations. Consequently, a trader's expected gain from trade is evaluated conditionally, contingent on his valuation. A trading rule is efficient in this case, and said to be *incentive* efficient, if it is false that it is common knowledge among the buyers and sellers that some other trading rule would yield greater expected gains for each one of them contingent on their valuations. In the economic environment studied here, this criterion for efficiency takes a special form: incentive efficiency requires that no other trading rule would increase the expected gain from trade for each trader *whatever his valuation might be*. To see this, recall that a trader's valuation is privately known and statistically independent of the other traders' valuations; consequently, for it to be common knowledge among the other traders that his expected gain from trade could be increased requires that it would be increased regardless of what his valuation happens to be — otherwise it could not be known for sure that an improvement is possible.

This criterion can be made operational as follows. Let $\alpha_i(u_i)$ be a positive welfare weighting for buyer i contingent on his valuation u_i, and similarly let $\beta_j(v_j)$ be a positive welfare weighting for seller j contingent on his valuation v_j. With these weighting functions, each trading rule r yields a welfare measure:

$$W[r] = \sum_{i \in M} E\{\alpha_i(u_i(U_i)\} + \sum_{j \in N} E\{\beta_j(v_j)V_j(v_j)\} \qquad (4.46)$$

constructed from the weighted expectations of the traders' expected gains from trade contingent on their valuations. It is straightforward to establish the following operational criterion. Suppose that among all trading rules, or equivalently among all induced direct revelation games, satisfying the feasibility and individual rationality constraints, the trading rule r maximizes the welfare measure $W[r]$ defined in (4.46); then the rule r is incentive efficient.

In practical applications where a given trading rule (e.g. a double auction) is to be tested for efficiency, this criterion is implemented by constructing imputed welfare weights with respect to which the trading rule is optimal.

It is useful to record here the following implication of Lemma 1.

Lemma 3: The welfare measure $W[r]$ in (4.46) can be expressed as:

$$W[r] = \sum_{i \in M} \bar{\alpha}_i(0)U_i(0) + E\left\{\sum_{i \in A} \bar{\alpha}_i(u_i)\frac{1 - F(u_i)}{f(u_i)}\right\}$$

$$\tag{4.47}$$

$$+ \sum_{j \in N} \bar{\beta}_j(1)V_j(1) + E\left\{\sum_{j \in A} \bar{\beta}_j(v_j)\frac{G(v_j)}{g(v_j)}\right\}$$

Proof: This formula is obtained by substituting (4.36) and (4.37), and (4.40) and (4.41), into (4.46), and using the fact that, for example $P_i(u_i)$ is the probability of the event that $i \in A$, namely that i gets to trade, conditional on buyer i's valuation being u_i. ∎

The advantage of this representation of the welfare measure is its explicit recognition of how it depends on the rule by which the set A of buyers and sellers who trade is selected. It should be noted that the non-negativitity of the welfare weights translates into the requirements that $\bar{\alpha}_i(u)[1 - F(u)]$ and $\bar{\beta}_j(v)G(v)$ are non-negative functions of u and v that are non-increasing and non-decreasing respectively.

Ex Ante *Efficiency*

An alternative perspective for welfare comparisons is that the trading rule is designed before the traders know their valuations. It is presumed, of course, that the traders will learn their valuations before the trading rule is implemented, but at the time of the design decision a buyer i, for example, knows only that the valuation he will have later will be drawn according to the probability distribution F, which is all that the other traders will ever know. In this case a buyer i assesses his expected gain from trade as $E\{U_i(u_i)\}$, and a seller j as $E\{V_j(v_j)\}$. The appropriate welfare weightings α_i and β_j in this situation are necessarily constants, not contingent on the traders' valuations, and the corresponding welfare measure has the form:

$$W[r] = \sum_{i \in M} \alpha_i E\{U_i(u_i)\} + \sum_{j \in N} \beta_j E\{V_j(v_j)\} \tag{4.48}$$

The substantive difference between incentive and *ex ante* efficiency thus reduces to whether or not the welfare weightings may be contingent on the traders' types. In particular, an *ex ante* efficient trading rule is also incentive efficient, but the converse is false in general.

Uniform Efficiency

In principle it is possible that the specification of a trading rule utilizes some of the information that is common knowledge among the traders. The rule could, for example, take different forms depending on the numbers m and n of buyers and sellers, or depending on their assessed probability distributions F and G about each other's valuations. There are obvious practical advantages, however, from trading rules that do not depend on these features of the economic environment, and it is certainly true that the familiar forms of market organization do not rely on such ephemeral data as the participants' probability assessments. A double auction, for example, is a well-defined trading rule for any numbers of buyers and sellers, and it operates without any information about the traders' assessed probability distributions. This is true of most popular forms of exchange.

We say that a trading rule is *uniformly* incentive or *ex ante* efficient if its specification does not depend on the numbers of traders, nor on their probability assessments, and it is efficient for a wide class (suitably specified) of economic environments. (The imputed welfare weights may, however, vary across the environments within the class.) For the application we study here, namely the double auction, it suffices to take the class to be those environments obtained by varying the numbers of buyers and sellers, and by varying their probability assessments within certain restrictions that will be specified later.

EFFICIENT TRADING RULES

The concepts and methods developed in the previous two sections provide the tools that enable a study of the efficiency properties of a double auction. The plan of this section and the next is, first, to derive a sufficient condition that a trading rule is efficient (either incentive efficient or *ex ante* efficient), and then to verify circumstances in which this property is satisfied by a double auction. Since incentive and *ex ante* efficiency differ only in whether the imputed welfare weights may be contingent on the traders' valuations, it will suffice initially to obtain a condition sufficient for incentive efficiency. As we have seen in the third section, the key step is to establish which buyers and sellers get to trade depending on all of their valuations; that is, to determine the set A of successful traders for each configuration $\langle (u_i)_{i \in M}, (v_j)_{j \in N} \rangle$ of valuations. And for this it suffices to study direct revelation games, since each trading rule induces a corresponding direct revelation game. The property of a trading rule specified in Definition 2 below turns out to be the one we seek.

Definition 1: A function $\varphi_i : U_i \to \Re$ is a *virtual valuation* for buyer i if it is non-decreasing, $\varphi_i(u) \leqslant u$, and the function:

$$\Phi_i(u) = \int_u^1 [u - \varphi_i(t)] dF(t) \tag{4.49}$$

is non-decreasing and concave. Similarly, a function $\vartheta_j : V_j \to \Re$ is a virtual valuation for seller j if it is non-decreasing, $\vartheta_j(v) \geqslant v$, and the function:

$$\Theta_j(v) = \int_0^v [\vartheta_j(t) - v] dG(t) \tag{4.50}$$

is non-increasing and concave.

Note that (4.49) and (4.50) attain maxima at valuations u and v satisfying:

$$\varphi_i(u) = u - \frac{1 - F(u)}{f(u)} \quad \text{and} \quad \vartheta_j(v) = v + \frac{G(v)}{g(v)} \tag{4.51}$$

if such valuations exist. We will ordinarily write virtual valuations in the form:

$$\varphi_i(u) = u - [1 - a_i(u)] \frac{1 - F(u)}{f(u)} \quad \text{and}$$

$$\vartheta(v) = v + [1 - b_j(v)] \frac{G(v)}{g(v)} \tag{4.52}$$

in which case the requisite properties are that $a_i(u)$ and $b_j(v)$ are in the unit interval, and that $\Phi'_i(u) = a_i(u)[1 - F(u)]$ and $\Theta'_j(v) = -b_j(v)G(v)$ are non-increasing (e.g. it suffices that a_i and b_j are constants). If the functions a_i and b_j satisfy these properties then we will say that they are *satisfactory*.

Definition 2: A trading rule is a *double auction in virtual valuations* (DAVV) if the set A of buyers and sellers who trade maximizes the gains from trade measured in some virtual valuations for the traders; that is:

$$A \in \underset{A'}{Arg\ Max} \sum_{i \in A'} \varphi_i(u_i) - \sum_{j \in A'} \vartheta_j(v_j) \tag{4.53}$$

subject to the feasibility constraint that the cardinalities of $A' \cap M$ and $A' \cap N$ are the same. In applying this definition we adopt the proviso that the functions Φ_i and Θ_j are not all constant.

The motivation for this terminology is apparent from the fact noted in the second section that a double auction maximizes the gains from trade measured in terms of the submitted bids and offers; here, the virtual valuations play the same role.

Theorem 1: A DAVV trading rule for which the minimal expected gains from trade are nil, namely $U_i(0) = V_j(1) = 0$ for each buyer i and seller j, is incentive efficient.

Proof: It suffices to suppose the DAVV trading rule is for a direct revelation game. The hypothesis assures that it is feasible and individually rational. All direct revelation games satisfy Lemmas 1, 2, and 3. We shall argue, therefore, that a DAVV trading rule maximizes a welfare measure of the form (4.47) in Lemma 3 subject to the constraint (4.43) in Lemma 2 and the individual rationality constraints (4.42). First we determine sufficient conditions for a solution to this constrained maximization. Consider the Lagrangian formed from the welfare measure plus a multiplier λ times the left side of constraint (4.43):

$$L[r; \lambda] = E\left\{ \sum_{i \in A} \left[\lambda u_i - [\lambda - \bar{\alpha}_i(u_i)] \frac{1 - F(u_i)}{f(u_i)} \right] \right\}$$

$$- E\left\{ \sum_{j \in A} \left[\lambda v_j + [\lambda - \bar{\beta}_j(v_j)] \frac{G(v_j)}{g(v_j)} \right] \right\} \tag{4.54}$$

$$- \sum_{i \in M} [\lambda - \bar{\alpha}_i(0)] U_i(0) - \sum_{j \in N} [\lambda - \bar{\beta}_j(1)] V_j(1)$$

This Lagrangian is maximized by choosing the minimal values $U_i(0) = V_j(1) = 0$ for the least advantaged traders, provided $\lambda \geq \bar{\alpha}_i(0)$ and $\lambda \geq \bar{\beta}_j(1)$, and by choosing the set A of buyers and sellers who trade contingent on the valuations $\langle (u_i)_{i \in M}, (v_j)_{j \in N} \rangle$ to maximize:

$$\sum_{i \in A} \left[u_i - (1 - \bar{\alpha}_i(u_i)/\lambda) \frac{1 - F(u_i)}{f(u_i)} \right] - \sum_{j \in A} \left[v_j + (1 - \bar{\beta}_j(v_j)/\lambda) \frac{G(v_j)}{g(v_j)} \right]$$

(4.55)

pointwise within the expectation, provided $\lambda > 0$. If λ is positive then it can be normalized to unity by scaling the welfare weights; it is easy to see that λ must be positive since otherwise the individual rationality constraints would not be binding, which is evidently contradictory. The DAVV trading rule accomplishes precisely this maximization if the relationships $a_i(u) = \bar{\alpha}_i(u)/\lambda$ and $b_j(v) = \bar{\beta}_j(v)/\lambda$ hold. Consequently, a DAVV trading rule using virtual valuations as in (4.52), specified by $a_i(u)$ and $b_i(v)$, is optimal with respect to the welfare weights $\alpha_i(u)$ and $\beta_j(v)$ imputed by the specifications:

$$a_i(u) = \int_u^1 \alpha_i(t) dF(t) / [1 - F(u)]$$

$$b_j(v) = \int_0^v \beta_j(t) dG(t) / G(v)$$

(4.56)

corresponding to the scaling $\lambda = 1$. Equivalently:

$$\alpha_i(u) = -\frac{1}{f(u)} \frac{d}{du} \{ a_i(u)[1 - F(u)] \}$$

$$\beta_j(v) = \frac{1}{g(v)} \frac{d}{dv} \{ b_j(v) G(v) \}$$

(4.57)

Since a_i and b_j are satisfactory, these imputed welfare weights are non-negative as required. They cannot all be zero, since a_i and b_j lie in the unit interval, unless a_i and b_j are identically zero, which would contradict the proviso in Definition 2. Thus, the trading rule is incentive efficient. ∎

Theorem 1 does not address the question of whether, given virtual valuations φ_i and ϑ_j for the buyers and sellers, there exists a DAVV trading rule with the requisite properties. That is, it is required that the rule (4.53) for selecting the buyers and sellers who trade in the direct revelation game is supplemented by a rule for determining the money transfers among the traders so that it is a Nash equilibrium for each trader to report accurately his valuation if he expects each other trader to do the same, and that traders with the least advantageous valuations expect zero gains from trade $(U_i(0) = V_j(1) = 0)$. In fact this question can be answered affirmatively.[9]

Hereafter we will refer to a_i and b_j as the buyers' and sellers' *conditional weights* due to their interpretation derived from (4.56) as conditional expectations of the welfare weights.

Ex Ante Efficiency

It is an immediate corollary of Theorem 1 and (4.57) that if the conditional weights have the further property that they are constants independent of the traders' valuations then the incentive efficiency can be strengthened to *ex ante* efficiency.

This is the case, for example, for the class of symmetric examples studied on pp. 180–2 for which the numbers of buyers and sellers are equal $[m = n]$, the probability distributions are uniform $[F(u) = u$ and $G(v) = v]$, and $\mu_1 = \mu_2 = .5$. Recall that in those examples the buyers' and and sellers' strategies are:

$$\rho_i(u) = \psi(u - \delta) \qquad \text{and} \qquad \vartheta_j(v) = \psi(v + \delta) \tag{4.58}$$

for some increasing function ψ and a constant $\delta \in (0, \frac{1}{4})$. Let the welfare weights be constants with $a_i = b_j = (1 - 4\delta)/(1 - 2\delta) \in (0, 1)$; then:

$$\rho_i(u) = \psi([1 - 2\delta]\vartheta_j(v) + \delta) \qquad \text{and}$$

$$\sigma_j(v) = \psi([1 - 2\delta]\varphi_j(v) + \delta) \tag{4.59}$$

This corresponds to the choice $\phi(p) = [\psi^{-1}(p) - \delta]/[1 - 2\delta]$ in (4.5). One sees, therefore, that the set A of buyers and sellers who trade satisfies (4.53), and the hypothesis of Theorem 1 is satisfied. Since the conditional weights are constants in these symmetric examples, it follows that a double auction is *ex ante* efficient, and uniformly so for any numbers of buyers and sellers provided they are equal.

Moreover, as the numbers of traders increase, $m, n \to \infty$ and $\delta \to 0$, so $a_i, b_j \to 1$ and the virtual valuations converge to the actual valuations: $\varphi_i(u) \to u$ and $\vartheta_j(v) \to v$. Thus in these symmetric examples if there are many traders then a double auction fits the Walrasian model in that trades are based on the traders' true valuations.

Although it is not known whether a double auction is *ex ante* efficient in the general case, we shall see in the next section that a double auction is uniformly incentive efficient under fairly general assumptions.

INCENTIVE EFFICIENCY OF DOUBLE AUCTIONS

In order to illustrate how the methods developed in the third and fifth sections are applied, we return to the study of double auctions begun in the second section. Our aim in this section is to establish that a double auction is an incentive efficient trading rule for any probability distributions satisfying the following assumption, provided the numbers of buyers and sellers are large enough.[10]

Assumption: The probability distributions of the buyers' and sellers' valuations have decreasing hazard rates as the valuations become less advantageous; that is, $-f(u)/[1 - F(u)]$ and $g(v)/G(v)$ are decreasing functions of u and v respectively.

This assumption is too strong to be necessary but it permits an easy proof of the main result. We shall also adopt the expedient (as in connection with (4.30)) of assuming that the magnitudes of the derivatives of the buyers' and sellers' strategies are uniformly bounded.

Theorem 2: A double auction is an incentive efficient trading rule if the numbers of buyers and sellers are sufficiently large.

Before proving this result it is worth discussing its significance. In Theorem 1 we saw that a DAVV trading rule is incentive efficient; one might surmise, therefore, that the task of organizing efficient trade is 'solved' by adopting a DAVV trading rule. However, such a trading rule involves using a direct revelation game in which the set of buyers and sellers who trade is selected by maximizing the gains from trade measured by virtual valuations assigned to the traders. In order to specify the virtual valuations one apparently needs to know the probability distributions F and G of the traders' valuations. Even if these are known to the designers of the trading rule (e.g. the traders themselves), this approach presents the unpalatable prospect that the trading rule must be custom designed to fit the probability assessments entertained by the traders. The matter is actually complicated further by the fact that the money transfers needed to implement the direct revelation game depend on both the probability assessments *and* the numbers of buyers and sellers. As a practical matter this way of organizing efficient trade is cumbersome, and in any case it hardly explains the operation of the sort of trading rules found in practice — which are specified quite independently of the numbers of buyers and sellers and their probability assessments, and which employ very simple payment rules.

The significance of Theorem 2, therefore, is its verification that there is a single trading rule, the double auction, that is incentive efficient in a wide variety of economic environments. Moreover, it highlights the practical advantages of the payment mechanism that characterizes the double auction; namely, only those buyers and sellers who trade pay or receive money and all trades are made at the same price. It is this feature that makes the double auction such a robust trading rule for achieving incentive efficiency.

Against these advantages, nevertheless, must be recorded the disadvantages. Whereas the direct revelation game employs a complicated trading rule, it allows the traders the simplest strategies (i.e. direct revelation); in contrast, the double auction employs a simple trading rule and puts the burden on the traders to calculate their strategies (taking into account the numbers of buyers and sellers and the probability distributions of their valuations) as described in the second section. In general, it need not be clear that one or the other of these approaches is necessarily better, but it seems to be true empirically that most trade is organized so as to put the burden on the traders to construct optimal strategies.[11] In addition, we shall see that a double auction imputes particular welfare weights to the traders, whereas the direct revelation game can be designed to implement prescribed welfare weights. If one were to employ stronger distributional criteria about how the gains from trade should be divided among the traders then it is possible that the double auction would be found inadequate.

Proof of Theorem 2: The construction of the symmetric strategies ρ and σ in the second section establishes that the least advantageous valuations yield zero expected gains from trade: $U_i(0) = V_j(1) = 0$. In view of Theorem 1, therefore, it suffices to establish that a double auction is a DAVV trading rule. A double auction maximizes the gains from trade measured according to the traders' bids and offers, or according to any increasing function of the bids and offers, as in (4.5). It suffices, therefore, to find an increasing function ϕ such that $\phi(\rho(u)) \equiv \varphi_i(u)$ and $\phi(\sigma(v)) \equiv \vartheta_j(v)$ are virtual valuations for the buyers and sellers. Recall from the second section that those buyers with valuations $u < p^* = \sigma(0)$ and those sellers with valuations

$v > p^{**} = \rho(1)$ have no chance of trading. It suffices, therefore, to construct $\phi(p)$ for $p^* \leqslant p \leqslant p^{**}$. In order to construct such a function ϕ we define:

$$w(u, v) = \frac{u \dfrac{f(u)}{1 - F(u)} + v \dfrac{g(v)}{G(v)}}{\dfrac{f(u)}{1 - F(u)} + \dfrac{g(v)}{G(v)}} \qquad (4.60)$$

The Assumption assures that w is an increasing function of u and v separately if $u > v$. Note that $w(u, 0) = 0$ and $w(1, v) = 1$. We then use:

$$\phi(p) = \omega(\rho^{-1}(p), \sigma^{-1}(p)) \qquad (4.61)$$

to construct the virtual valuations. Note that $\phi : [p^*, p^{**}] \to [0, 1]$ is well defined since ρ and σ are increasing functions, and as required ϕ is increasing. Also, the virtual valuations so constructed are increasing. With this choice the imputed conditional weights are:

$$a_i(u) = 1 - \frac{u - v}{\dfrac{1 - F(u)}{f(u)} + \dfrac{G(v)}{g(v)}} = b_j(v) \qquad (4.62)$$

for matched pairs (u, v) such that $\rho(u) = \sigma(v) = p$. Since $w(u, v)$ is a convex combination of u and v, and $u > v$, it follows that $a_i(u) \leqslant 1$ and $b_j(v) \leqslant 1$, or equivalently $\varphi_i(u) \leqslant u$ and $\vartheta_j(v) \geqslant v$. Taken together these properties assure that the double auction solves the welfare maximization problem used in the proof of Theorem 1 except that it remains to show that the imputed welfare weights (4.57) are non-negative: this is done by invoking Lemma 4 below, which is proved separately because it has only technical interest. ∎

Lemma 4: A double auction imputes non-negative welfare weights if the numbers of buyers and sellers are sufficiently large.

Proof: It will suffice to show that the buyers' imputed welfare weights in (4.57) are non-negative, since the argument is analogous for the sellers. Suppose to the contrary, therefore, that for some buyer i, and therefore for any buyer, the imputed welfare weighting function $\alpha_i(u)$ is negative over some interval $(u_0, u_1) \subseteq (p^*, 1)$. The argument divides into three parts:

(1) We first show that α_i cannot be non-positive for all valuations u. If it were then in (4.56) a_i would be uniformly non-positive and (4.62) would imply that:

$$\left[u - \frac{1 - F(u)}{f(u)} \right] - \left[v + \frac{G(v)}{g(v)} \right] \geqslant 0 \qquad (4.63)$$

if $\rho(u) = \sigma(v)$. Since ρ and σ are increasing, the Assumption implies that (4.63) would hold more generally if $\rho(u) \geqslant \sigma(v)$, and in particular for any pair of valuations of a buyer and a seller who trade. Since the inequality is strict for some valuation u, it follows that the expectation in (4.43) of Lemma 2 would be positive, contradicting the property of a double auction that $U_i(0) = V_j(1) = 0$. Thus α_i must be positive over some interval of the buyers' valuations, so we can assume that either $u_0 > p^*$ or $u_1 < 1$.

(2) We next show that over any interval (u_0, u_1) with $u_0 > p^*$ for m and n sufficiently large, α_i must be positive if the numbers of buyers and sellers are large enough. From (4.20) one gets the inequalities:

$$\frac{\mu_i/m}{u - p} \geqslant \min \left\{ u' \frac{f}{F}, v' \frac{g}{G} \right\}$$

$$\frac{\mu_2/n}{p - v} \geqslant \min \left\{ u' \frac{f}{1 - F}, v' \frac{g}{1 - G} \right\}$$

satisfied by the equilibrium strategies. Recall that f and g are uniformly positive, say $f, g \geqslant \epsilon > 0$, and we have assumed that ρ', $\sigma' \leqslant B$ uniformly for some bound B independent of m, n so that $u', v' \geqslant 1/B$. Consequently, $\mu_1/m \geqslant [u - p]\,\epsilon/B$ and $\mu_2/n \geqslant [p - v]\epsilon/B$. As $m \sqcap n \to \infty$, therefore, it must be that $u(p) \to p$ and $v(p) \to p$. Moreover, from (4.62) we see that also $a_i(u(p)) = b_j(v(p)) \to 1$. The imputed welfare weights $\alpha_i(u)$ and $\beta_j(v)$ of which the conditional weights (4.56) are the conditional expectations must, therefore, also converge to one. In particular, if the numbers of buyers and sellers are sufficiently large then the imputed welfare weights are positive.

(3) Lastly, consider the case that $u_0 = p^*$ and $u_1 < 1$. That is, a segment of negative welfare weights is an initial segment (p^*, u_1). We will show that this yields a contradiction if n is large enough. The negativity of the welfare weights on the initial segment is equivalent to $a(u)[1 - F(u)]$ being increasing there. It will suffice, therefore, to show that the derivative of $a(u)[1 - F(u)]$ at $u = p^*$ is negative if n is large. Using the Assumption, a direct calculation shows that this derivative is negative if:

$$\frac{v'(p^*)}{u'(p^*)} < \frac{3}{1 + p^* \dfrac{f(p^*)}{1 - F(p^*)}} - 1 \tag{4.64}$$

The second equation in (4.20) takes the following form at $u = p^*$:

$$p^* \frac{f(p^*)}{1 - F(p^*)} \left\{ 1 + [n - 1]g(0) \frac{1 - F(p^*)}{f(p^*)} \frac{v'(p^*)}{u'(p^*)} \right\} = \frac{\mu_2}{1 + \mu_1} \tag{4.65}$$

Consequently:

$$p^* \frac{f(p^*)}{1 - F(p^*)} \leqslant \frac{\mu_2}{1 + \mu_1} \leqslant 1 \tag{4.66}$$

and the right side of (4.64) is no less than ½. Recall from the second section that $u'(p^*) = 1 + \mu_1$; hence, the inequality (4.64) is surely satisfied for n large enough if $v'(p^*) \to 0$ as $n \to \infty$. Assume, therefore that $v'(p^*)$ is bounded above zero. Then (4.65) indicates that $p^* \to 0$ as $n \to \infty$. Since $a(p^*) = 1 - p^* f(p^*)/1 - F(p^*)$ this in turn implies that $a(p^*) \to 1$, and also that $a'(p^*) \to 0$ since $a(u) \leqslant 1$ uniformly as shown in the proof of Theorem 2. Also, $f(p^*) \to f(0) > 0$ and $F(p^*) \to F(0) = 0$. Combining these results yields the desired conclusion:

$$\lim_{n \to \infty} (a(u)[1 - F(u)])' |_{u = p^*} = \lim_{n \to \infty} a'(p^*)[1 - F(p^*)]$$

$$- a(p^*)f(p^*) \tag{4.67}$$

$$= -f(0) < 0$$

Thus, the original supposition is contradicted and we conclude that if the number of sellers is large enough then all of the buyers' welfare weights are positive.

A similar argument verifies that if the number of buyers is large enough then all of the sellers' welfare weights are positive.

In those cases in which the welfare weights imputed by a double auction are constants independent of the buyers' and sellers' valuations one obtains *ex ante* efficiency without the qualifier 'if the numbers of buyers and sellers are sufficiently large'; see part (1) of the proof of Lemma 4. This occurs for the symmetric case examined on pp. 180–2 and 196–7.

BIBLIOGRAPHIC REFERENCES

The results presented here[12] have their origins in the work of Roger Myerson, who developed the main ideas and methods used to study efficient trading processes, and with his co-authors has pursued several applications. A recent summary of the formulation and techniques is in Myerson (1983), including the role of virtual valuations. The first application of the approach was apparently his study (Myerson, 1981) of auctions that are optimal from the viewpoint of a single seller (or buyer) whose valuation is common knowledge, and independently the paper by Harris and Raviv (1981b). Subsequent work along this line is represented by Harris and Raviv (1981a), Matthews (1983), Riley and Samuelson (1981), and Maskin and Riley (1983). The theory of strategic behaviour in auctions is well developed; for example, Milgrom and Weber (1982).

Double auctions between a single buyer and a single seller with privately known valuations were studied initially by Chatterjee and Samuelson (1979) and then from an efficiency viewpoint by Myerson and Satterthwaite (1981) who established *ex ante* efficiency for the case of uniform distributions. Wilson (1982) generalized this result to any equal numbers of buyer and sellers, as described here on pp. 180–2 and 196–7, and Gresik and Satterthwaite (1983) studied numerically the efficiency properties for $m = n \leqslant 12$. The results in the sixth section on incentive efficiency in more general cases were obtained by Wilson (1983). Trading processes for the economic environment assumed here for double auctions have been studied experimentally by Smith *et al.* (1982). Plott and Smith (1978) and others have conducted experimental studies of sequential oral double auctions in which trading takes place over time as bids and offers are proposed and accepted at the discretion of the traders; some analysis of this form has been done by Easley and Ledyard (1982) and indirectly in the studies of sequential bargaining by Fudenberg and Tirole (1983), Sobel and Takahashi (1980), and Cramton (1983a, 1983b).

The theory of incentive compatibility presented in the third section appears in various forms in Myerson (1981), Myerson and Sattherthwaite (1981), Baron and Myerson (1982), Wilson (1982, 1983), and Gresik and Satterthwaite (1983), among several others. Its application to the construction of sufficient conditions for *ex ante* efficiency appears in Myerson and Satterthwaite (1981), Wilson (1982), and Gresik and Satterthwaite (1983), and to incentive efficiency as in the fifth section in Wilson (1983). Applications have also been developed for other economic contexts by, for example, Harris and Raviv (1981b) who address the case of a single seller and multiple units of the good.

Presentations of the ideas underlying *ex ante* and incentive efficiency appear in Harris and Townsend (1981), Holmström (1977), Myerson (1979), and Wilson (1978b), culminating in the formal definitions by Holmström and Myerson (1981). Uniform efficiency is used in Wilson (1983).

An efficient trading rule has been derived by d'Aspremont and Gerard-Varet (1979) without the requirement of individual rationality. Similarly, the trading rule proposed by Groves (1973) would be efficient except for the resources consumed in the operation of the incentive mechanism that induces revelation of preferences.

For economic environments in which the traders' preferences are common knowledge efficient trading rules have been studied by Wilson (1978a), Hurwicz (1979), Schmeidler (1980, 1982), and Dubey (1982). The first of these yields a core allocation and the latter yield a Walrasian allocation. Roberts and Postlewaite (1976) establish that when there are many traders any one trader's gain from strategic behaviour in the Walrasian mechanism is small.

The original proponent of the study of the implementation of efficient trading via well-defined rules for the game played by the traders was, of course, Leonid Hurwicz and no review of current work would be complete without an acknowledgement of his early and many subsequent influential contributions.

CONCLUDING REMARKS

The study of efficient trading processes encompasses much more than we have studied here. As mentioned in the seventh section, for example, much work has been done on trading with complete information, on the design of optimal auctions for a single seller or buyer, including situations where one trader trades multiple units, and on sequential bargaining mechanisms between a single buyer and a single seller. In addition, there is a rich collection of experimental studies.

Here, however, we have confined attention to the case of incomplete information and focused on multilateral trade in a static environment. Even so, the economic environment considered is severely restricted by the absence of multiple goods, elastic demands, risk aversion, and correlation among the traders' preferences.[13] It will be desirable in future research to include these additional features, partly for realism and partly for the sake of completing the theoretical construction. In addition, casual observation suggests that trading processes that take place over time have an important role (e.g. sequential bid and ask markets), and a goal of the theory is to elucidate how it is that sequential processes enable an unfolding of the traders' private information so that eventually nearly all the potential gains from trade are exhausted.

The main point of the present exposition has been to pose the problem of efficient trade and to illustrate the methods that have been developed recently to solve it. The methods are relatively new in the literature of economic theory and it is encouraging that they suffice to illuminate the role of institutionalized trading rules, here represented by the double auction, in promoting gains from trade. One can rejoice as well that a single trading rule suffices to attain incentive efficiency *uniformly* over a fairly wide class of economic environments: the usefulness of market processes to allocate resources and their persistence as institutionalized forms depend ultimately on their robustness in coping with a variety of circumstances.

Posing the problem of efficient trade is, of course, the premier accomplishment of the recent research. It reflects a new perspective on economic phenomena and takes the first step in a reconstruction of the theory to address the realistic features of markets — finite numbers of traders, privately known preferences, and explicit trading rules — requiring new concepts of efficiency and new characterizations of the workings of markets affected by strategic behaviour.

NOTES

1. To argue this point, take the Walrasian model of markets as a standard. Although it is an incomplete model (e.g. it does not specify the

mechanism of price determination, and it offers no prediction of dis-equilibrium outcomes), it does offer a prediction about traders' passive responses to prices calculated to clear markets. The Walrasian theory establishes with impressive generality the existence of prices such that the traders' preferred trades at those prices will clear the market, and exhaust the gains from trade. Perfect competition is one explanation of the traders' inability to affect prices. This explanation is developed elegantly by Roberts and Postlewaite (1976), who show that a trader's gain from manipulating prices by altering his offered trades is small if the number of traders is large. Nevertheless, Schmeidler (1980) has shown that there is a way to specify the trading rule, and thus the game that the traders play, so that the Walrasian outcome results from a strong Nash equilibrium — even if the number of traders is small. Related work in this vein is by Dubey (1982), Hurwicz (1979), Hurwicz and Schmeidler (1978), and Wilson (1978a). The conclusion, then, is that in the absence of private information market power is due to the choice of 'inefficient' trading rules.

2. Some of the experimental results justify this prediction. There have been attempts to justify the Walrasian model on other grounds: a disinterested auctioneer has sufficient information (i.e. the actual empirical distribution of preferences among the traders) to know the market clearing price; the traders learn the market clearing price from their experience in repetitions of the market in a stationary environment (many of the experimental results address this case); prices are adjusted (e.g. in proportion to excess demand) via a tâtonnement process until the market clears; as well as various non-tâtonnement dynamic processes.

3. A trading rule provides an explicit mechanism of price formation, and therefore it induces a well-specified game among the traders. In contrast, an interpretation of the Walrasian set-up as a 'game' in which traders respond to a clearing price with preferred trades at that price is not well specified when preferences are not common knowledge since it leaves unspecified how this price is known to the traders, and what happens if they respond with trades other than the preferred ones.

4. A fact is common knowledge if each trader knows it, knows that each trader knows it, knows that each trader knows that each trader knows it, *ad infinitum*.

5. An equilibrium is strong if no coalition of traders could adopt correlated strategies that would improve the expected gains from trade for each member of the coalition. An equilibrium is perfect if each trader's strategy is a best response to each member of a sequence of the others' strategies, assigning positive probability to every possible action, that converges to the others' equilibrium strategies — that is, the equilibrium strategy is a robust best response against small chances of errors by the others.

6. A complete derivation is in Wilson, 1982 and 1983.

7. Table 4.1 is reproduced from Gresik and Satterthwaite, 1983.

8. A complete proof is given in Wilson, 1982.

9. Money transfers that do the job are constructed by Gresik and Satterthwaite, 1983.
10. We do not prove here that this assumption is consistent with the properties of the traders' strategies assumed in the second section, namely that $\rho(u)$ and $\sigma(v)$ are increasing functions. It is clearly true, however, for a class of distributions that includes the uniform distribution.
11. An obvious counter-example to this general statement is the second-price auction, which enables buyers to submit bids equal to their valuations.
12. Of course the authors cited below do not share responsibility for any errors in the present exposition.
13. There is one case of correlated valuations that is easy to resolve. If it is common knowledge that all traders have the same valuation, even if this valuation is unknown (e.g. each trader has only sample information about the valuation), then it is efficient to have no trade. This observation is due to Sushil Bikhchandani.

REFERENCES

Baron, D. P., and R. B. Myerson (1982) 'Regulating a Monopolist with Unknown Costs', *Econometrica*, 50 (July): 911–30.

Chatterjee, K. (1982) 'Incentive Compatability in Bargaining under Uncertainty', *Quarterly Journal of Economics*, 96 (November): 717–26.

Chatterjee, K., and W. F. Samuelson (1979) 'The Simple Economics of Bargaining', Working Paper, Pennsylvania State University.

Cramton, P. C. (1983a) 'Bargaining with Incomplete Information: A Two Period Model with Continuous Uncertainty', Technical Report 652, Graduate School of Business, Stanford University.

Cramton, P. C. (1983b) 'Bargaining with Incomplete Information: An Infinite Horizon Model with Continuous Uncertainty', Technical Report 680, Graduate School of Business, Stanford University.

D'Aspremont, C., and L. A. Gerard-Varet (1979) 'Incentives and Incomplete Information', *Journal of Public Economics*, 11: 25–45.

Dubey, P. (1982) 'Price–Quantity Strategic Market Games', *Econometrica*, 50 (January): 111–26.

Easley, D., and J. Ledyard (1982) 'A Theory of Price Formation and Exchange in Oral Auctions', Technical Report 461, Kellogg Graduate School of Management, Northwestern University (March, revised July).

Fudenberg, D., and J. Tirole (1983) 'Sequential Bargaining with Incomplete Information', *Review of Economic Studies*, 50: 221–47.

Gresik, T. A., and M. A. Satterthwaite (1983) 'The Number of Traders Required to Make a Market Competitive: The Beginnings of a Theory', Technical Report 551, Kellogg Graduate School of Management, Northwestern University (February).

Groves, T. (1973) 'Incentives in Teams', *Econometrica*, 41: 617–63.

Harris, M., and A. Raviv (1981) 'A Theory of Monopoly Pricing Schemes with Demand Uncertainty', *American Economic Review*, 71 (June) 347–65.

Harris, M., and A. Raviv (1981) 'Allocation Mechanisms and the Design of Auctions', *Econometrica*, 49 (November) 1477–99.

Harris, M., and R. M. Townsend (1981) 'Resource Allocation under Asymmetric Information', *Econometrica*, 49 (January) 33–64.

Holmström, B. (1977) 'On Incentives and Control in Organizations', PhD thesis, Graduate School of Business, Stanford University.

Holmström, B., and R. B. Myerson (1981) 'Efficient and Durable Decision Rules with Incomplete Information', Technical Report 495, Kellogg Graduate School of Management, Northwestern University.

Holt, C. (1980) 'Competitive Bidding for Contracts under Alternative Auction Procedures', *Journal of Political Economy*, 88: 433–45.

Hurwicz, L. (1979) 'Outcome Functions Yielding Walrasian and Lindahl Allocations at Nash Equilibrium Points', *Review of Economic Studies*, 46: 217–25.

Hurwicz, L., and D. Schmeidler (1978) 'Construction of Outcome Functions Guaranteeing Existence and Pareto Optimality of Nash Equilibria', *Econometrica*, 46: 1447–1174.

Maskin, E., and J. G. Riley (1981) 'Optimal Auctions with Risk Averse Bidders', Technical Report 311, Department of Economics, MIT.

Matthews, S. (1983) 'Selling to Risk Averse Buyers with Unobservable Tastes', *Journal of Economic Theory*, 3092): 370–400.

Milgrom, P. R., and R. J. Weber (1982) 'A Theory of Auctions and Competitive Bidding', *Econometrica*, 50 (September) 1089–1122.

Myerson, R. B. (1979) 'Incentive Compatibility and the Bargaining Problem', *Econometrica*, 47 (January) 61–73.

Myerson, R. B. (1981) 'Optimal Auction Design', *Mathematics of Operations Research*, 6 (February) 58–73.

Myerson, R. B. (1982) 'Two-Person Bargaining Problems with Incomplete Information', Technical Report 527, Kellogg Graduate School of Management, Northwestern University.

Myerson, R. B., (1983) 'Bayesian Equilibrium and Incentive Compatibility: An Introduction', Technical Report 548, Kellogg Graduate School of Management, Northwestern University (February).

Myerson, R. B., and M. Satterthwaite (1981) 'Efficient Mechanisms for Bilateral Trading', Technical Report 469S, Kellogg Graduate School of Management, Northwestern University.

Plott, C. R., and V. L. Smith (1978) 'An Experimental Examination of Two Exchange Institutions', *Review of Economic Studies*, 45: 133–53.

Riley, J. G., and W. F. Samuelson (1981) 'Optimal Auctions', *American Economic Review*, 71 (June) 381–92.

Riley, J. G., and R. Zeckhauser (1983) 'Optimal Selling Strategies: When to Haggle, When to Hold Firm', *Quarterly Journal of Economics*, 98(2): 267–89.

Roberts, D. J., and A. Postlewaite (1976) 'The Incentives for Price–Taking Behaviour in Large Exchange Economies', *Econometrica*, 44 (January) 115–28.

Schmeidler, D. (1980) 'Walrasian Analysis via Strategic Outcome Functions', *Econometrica*, 48 (November) 1585–93.

Schmeidler, D. (1982) 'A Condition Guaranteeing that the Nash Allocation is Walrasian', *Journal of Economic Theory*, 28 (December) 376–8.

Smith, V. L., (1976) 'Experimental Economics: Induced Value Theory', *American Economic Review*, 66 (May) 274–9.

Smith, V. L., (1982) 'Microeconomic Systems as an Experimental Science', *American Economic Review*, 72 (December) 923–55.

Smith, V. L., A. Williams, W. K. Bratton and M. G. Vannoni (1982) 'Competitive Market Institutions: Double Auctions *vs* Sealed Bid-Offer Auctions', *American Economic Review*, 72 (March) 58–77.

Sobel, J., and O. Takahashi (1980) 'A Multi-stage Model of Bargaining', Technical Report 80–25, Department of Economics, University of California at San Diego.

Wilson, R. B. (1978a) 'Competitive Exchange', *Econometrica*, 46 (May) 577–85.

Wilson, R. B. (1978b) 'Information, Efficiency, and the Core of an Economy', *Econometrica*, 46 (July) 807–16.

Wilson, R. B. (1982) 'Double Auctions', Technical Report 391, IMSSS, Stanford University (June, revised December) to appear in *Essays in Honor of Leonid Hurwicz*, Minneapolis: University of Minnesota Press (forthcoming).

Wilson, R. B. (1983) 'Incentive Efficiency of Double Auctions', Technical Report, 431, IMSSS, Stanford University (October).

5 Repeated Games

ROBERT J. AUMANN*

Work on repeated games may be broadly divided into two categories: repeated games with complete information, and repeated games with incomplete information. While there are important interrelationships between these two categories, each one represents a coherent and more or less separate body of work with its own set of basic ideas and problems. A closely related area is that of stochastic games, but this will not be surveyed here.

REPEATED GAMES OF COMPLETE INFORMATION

The theory of repeated games of complete information is concerned with the evolution of fundamental patterns of interaction between people (or for that matter, animals; the problems it attacks are similar to those of social biology). Its aim is to account for phenomena such as co-operation, altruism, revenge, threats (self-destructive or otherwise), etc. – phenomena that may at first seem irrational – in terms of the usual 'selfish' utility-maximizing paradigm of game theory and neoclassical economics.

Let G be an n-person game in strategic (i.e. 'normal') form. We will denote by G^* the 'supergame' of G, i.e. the game each play of which consists of an infinite sequence of plays of G. Unless we indicate otherwise,

* This work was supported by National Science Foundation Grant SOC75-21820-AO1 at the Institute for Mathematical Studies in the Social Sciences, Stanford University (IMSSS). It was originally presented as background material for a one-day workshop on repeated games that took place at the IMSSS summer seminar on mathematical economics on 10 August 1978. A slightly revised and updated version was published in 1981 in *Essays in Game Theory and Mathematical Economics in Honor of Oskar Morgenstern* (Wissenschaftsverlag. Bibliographisches Institut, Mannheim). In the current version we have again done a little revising and updating, but the bulk of the material represents the state of the art in 1978.

we will assume that at the end of each 'stage' (i.e. a particular play of G in the sequence), each player is informed of the strategy chosen by all other players at that stage. Thus the information available to a player when choosing his strategy for a particular stage consists of the strategies used by all players at all previous stages. The *pay-off* in G^* is some kind of average of the pay-offs in the various stages; more precisely it may be defined as the Cesaro limit of these averages (the limit, as $k \to \infty$, of the average of the pay-offs $h_i, \ldots, h_k$ to the first k stages), or as the Abel limit (the limit, as the interest rate r tends to 0, of the normalized current value of the pay-off

$$r \sum_{j=1}^{\infty} \frac{h_j}{(1+r)^i}).$$

There are technical difficulties with these definitions, because the limits involved need not always exist; however, for the purposes of this brief survey let us ignore these technical difficulties and proceed with the statement of the theorems.

Theorem 1: The pay-off vectors to Nash equilibrium points in the supergame G^* are the feasible individually rational pay-offs in the game G.

Here a pay-off vector h is called *feasible* in G, if it is a convex combination of pay-off vectors to pure strategy n-tuples in G; i.e. if it is a possible pay-off to a *correlated* strategy n-tuple in G. It is called *individually rational* if for each player i,

$$h^i \geqslant \min_{\tau} \max_{\sigma} H^i(\sigma, \tau),$$

where H is the pay-off function in G, σ ranges over the strategies of i in G, and τ over the strategies of the players in $N \setminus \{i\}$. It should be noted that the min max is not necessarily equal to the max min; in general, it is greater. This is because the set of strategies available to $N \setminus \{i\}$ is not necessarily convex. For example, if the players are confined to using mixed strategies, then we would not in general have min max = max min. The min max is the level of pay-off below which i cannot be forced by the remaining players, but he cannot necessarily guarantee himself this pay-off. If, however, the players in $N \setminus \{i\}$ can correlate their strategies independently of i — for example if they can spin a roulette wheel that i cannot see — then the max min and the min max are equal.

Theorem 1 has been generally known in the profession for at least

fifteen or twenty years, but has not been published; its authorship is ob-
scure. The proof, which rests on the idea of threats of punishment, is in
principle quite simple; it is outlined in Appendix 5.2. We shall call it the
'Folk Theorem'. More or less, it may be considered the starting point or
touchstone for the further developments that will be described below.

The significance of the Folk Theorem is that it relates co-operative
behaviour in the game G to non-co-operative behaviour in its supergame
G^*. This is the fundamental message of the theory of repeated games of
complete information; that co-operation may be explained by the fact that
the 'games people play' — that is, the multiperson decision situations in
which they are involved — are not one-time affairs, but are repeated over
and over. In game-theoretic terms, an outcome is co-operative if it requires
an outside enforcement mechanism to make it 'stick'. Equilibrium points
are self-enforcing: once an equilibrium point is agreed upon, it is not
worthwhile for any player to deviate from it. Thus it does not require any
outside enforcement mechanism, and so represents non-cooperative behaviour. On the other hand, the general feasible outcome does require an
enforcement mechanism, and so represents the co-operative approach. In
a sense, the repetition itself, with its possibilities for retaliation, becomes
the enforcement mechanism.

Branching out from the Folk Theorem there are developments in several
directions, which we will take up in roughly historical order. The first
arose from an attempt to refine somewhat the notion of 'co-operative
outcome' on the co-operative side of the Folk Theorem. Specifically, while
the set of all feasible individually rational outcomes does represent a solution notion of sorts for a co-operative game, it is relatively vague and
uninformative. One would like a characterization, in terms of the supergame G^*, of more specific kinds of co-operative behaviour in the single-
shot game G, for example, of the core. This is achieved by replacing the
notion of equilibrium by *strong equilibrium*, defined[1] as an n-tuple of
strategies for which no *coalition* of players can simultaneously all do
better for themselves by moving to different strategies, while the players
outside of the coalition maintain their original strategies. We then have:

Theorem 2: The pay-off vectors to strong equilibrium points in the
supergame G^* are the elements of the β-core of the game G.

Here the β-core of G is the set of feasible pay-off vectors x such that each
coalition S can be prevented by its complement from achieving for each of
its members i a pay-off larger than x_i. It may be contrasted with the larger
and somewhat more transparent *α-core*, defined as the set of feasible pay-

off vectors x such that no coalition S can guarantee to each of its members i a pay-off larger than x_i. Vis-à-vis the α-core, the β-core plays a role similar to that played by the min max vis-à-vis the max min (compare the discussion of Theorem 1 above).

Theorem 2 was proved in 1959 by the writer of these lines (in *Contributions to the Theory of Games* IV, Princeton University Press, pp. 287–324). The original paper is poorly written and difficult to read. We must, however, not be too harsh in our judgements; bitter experience shows that while the basic ideas in this subject may be quite transparent, it is by no means easy to formulate the proofs in a manner that is at once rigorous, elegant, and brief. A rigorous statement of Theorem 2 may be found on page 551 of the *Transactions of the American Mathematical Society*, vol. 98 (1961). An intuitive outline of the proof may be found on page 23 (Theorem 13) of the 1967 Morgenstern Festschrift[2].

A sort of footnote to Theorem 2 was published in the *Pacific Journal of Mathematics* in 1961 (vol. 98, 539–52). It asserts that in games of perfect information, the strong equilibrium points of G^* are achievable in *pure* supergame strategies. In spite of the classical connection between pure strategies and perfect information, this is not quite obvious. Suppose x is in the β-core and S is a coalition. The complement of S will certainly have a pure strategy τ in G that prevents S from achieving more than x_i for each of its members i. That is, for each strategy σ of S, there will be a member i of S whose pay-off from the pair (σ, τ) will be $\leq x_i$. But it is conceivable that by jumping around from one σ to another, S could, against τ, get more *on the average* than x_i for each of its members i.

To put it differently, mixing really has two functions: secrecy and convexification. It is fairly clear that the first of these two functions is obviated by perfect information, but not so clear that the second one is.

The proof uses the convexity of $v_\beta(S)$ (the set of S-vectors that the complement of S cannot prevent S from achieving). Since x is in the β-core, it is not in the interior of $v_\beta(S)$, and so can be (weakly) separated from $v_\beta(S)$ by a hyperplane with non-negative coefficients. These coefficients are used to combine the pay-offs of S's members into a single number, which is taken as the pay-off to a two-person zero-sum game of perfect information between S and its complement. In case S defects, the complement uses a pure optimal strategy in this two-person zero-sum game.

Soon after John Harsanyi's landmark work in the mid-1960s on the general theory of games of incomplete information[3], attention in the theory of repeated games shifted to the incomplete information case. This extensive work will be surveyed separately in the second section of this chapter.

In the mid 1970s interest in the complete information case started reviving. We mention first the sociologically and biologically oriented applications, such as the papers of Hammond[4] and Kurz[5] on Altruism, and J. Maynard Smith's[6] work on evolution. However, we prefer to postpone discussing these provocative works until after we have described the more recent theoretical developments.

The first of these centres on Reinhard Selten's concept of *perfect equilibrium point*[7]. Experience with Nash equilibrium points in games played over time leads to the conclusion that they can embody elements not usually associated with a purely non-co-operative theory. Specifically, a Nash equilibrium point may dictate a choice that is irrational in a given situation, which makes sense only in terms of deterring the other players from making moves leading to that situation. In other words, it permits empty threats, threats that could never rationally be carried out when the chips are down; and this even when the other players know it to be so. A simple but revealing example is the extensive game with the tree in Figure 5.1, in which (L,L) is a Nash equilibrium point; Player 1 goes left because of 2's rather unconvincing threat spitefully to go left if 1 goes right.

To deal with this problem, Selten introduced his concept of perfect equilibrium point. It is based on what might be called the 'trembling hand principle'. Assume that whenever a player makes a choice, the outcome will be as he intended with a probability that is almost, but not quite, one; each of the other possibilities — those that he did not intend — will occur with an infinitesimal probability. This infinitesimal probability, while it is not large enough to affect the pay-off significantly, does make every situtation (i.e every vertex in the game tree) a possibility that must be reckoned with; it thus eliminates empty threats and thereby drastically reduces the set of equilibrium points.

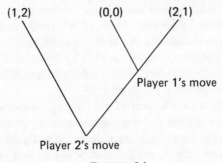

FIGURE 5.1

Two quick applications:

1 A perfect equilibrium point cannot assign positive probability to any 'weakly dominated' strategy[8].
2 In a game of perfect information, the perfect equilibrium points are precisely those obtained by the usual 'dynamic programming' procedure, that is, the one in Zermelo's classic paper on chess. (In non-zero sum games there *are* others — many others!)

In a sense, much of the theory of repeated games is an attempt to cut down, in one way or another, the bewildering wealth of equilibrium payoffs provided by Theorem 1. Thus Theorem 2 obtained a drastic reduction by going to strong equilibria — a reduction that may be too drastic, as the core is frequently empty. The proof of Theorem 1 (see Appendix 5.2) indicates that a reduction can also be expected by going to perfect equilibria, since the proof depends heavily on 'punishments' that may well be harmful to the punisher; they thus constitute precisely the kind of irrational threat that is excluded by the perfectness notion. Unfortunately, we have:

Theorem 3:   The pay-off vectors to perfect equilibrium points in the supergame G^* are the same as the pay-off vectors to the Nash equilibrium points.

In other words, no reduction is achieved by going to perfect equilibria. But while the result itself is certainly disappointing, the proof is actually quite revealing. The equilibrium is held together by an infinite regress of threatened punishments, in which a player who does not punish a defector as he should is in turn punished by the defector for not punishing him. Thus a motorist stopped by the highway patrol may refrain from offering the patrolman a bribe for frear of being turned in by him; and the patrolman would probably indeed turn him in, for fear of being himself turned in by the motorist otherwise. Much of whatever stability society may possess is perhaps traceable to this kind of perfect equilibrium.

This theorem was demonstrated in 1976 by Rubinstein[9] and by Aumann and Shapley[10] independently, with relatively minor differences in formulation. It has not yet been published.

We come next to the subject of discounting. Research in undiscounted supergames has a slightly disconcerting never-never quality. What a person actually does at any particular stage doesn't directly affect his pay-off *at all.* In certain evolutionary applications, where all that seems to matter is long-term survival, such a model is perhaps just what is called for. In the more usual applications, though, it seems rather extreme. There literally is all the time in the world to do anything you might want to do (in the nature of signalling, punishing, repenting and all the other activities that the denizens of this stylized world engage in). Time, far from being money, is for all intents and purposes free.

One good example is the treatment of randomized punishments. Punishing a defector may involve holding him to his min max or close to it, and this in turn will in general involve the use of randomized strategies. This leads to no particular problems when done in connection with Theorem 1. In Theorem 3, though, a punisher who fails to punish must himself be punished, if necessary by the defector. But if the punisher is using randomized strategies and the defector can only observe the pure realizations, how can he tell whether the punisher is doing what he should? In real time this certainly leads to statistical decision problems that are far from trivial. Here, though, it doesn't. Any deviation can be detected with an arbitrarily high probability if one can make as many observations as one likes; and in this case we indeed can, and still have all the time in the world for any subsequent (second-order) punishments that may be called for.

One way to make time 'bite' is to substitute a large but finite number of stages for the infinite number we have been using up to now. But the presence of a last stage which is recognized as such by all players, aside from being unrealistic, creates unnatural terminal effects which propagate themselves backwards and grossly distort the entire analysis. Besides, one cannot have a treatment that is in any sense stationary when the number of stages is fixed and finite.

A more natural way to take account of the value of time is by discounting. A discount factor may be viewed either as a stop probability or a measure of impatience or a combination of the two. It turns out that for small discount factors the set of equilibrium pay-offs is close (in the Hausdorff topology) to that in the zero discount case. As the discount grows, though, the situation changes, and we get some noteworthy effects.

Consider, for example, the prisoners' dilemma in Figure 5.2. In any finite repetition the only equilibrium pay-off is (1,1). This is also an equilibrium pay-off in every discounted version. As the discount rate

3,3	0,4
4,0	1,1

FIGURE 5.2

$\delta = r/1 + r$ grows from 0 to 1, the set of equilibrium pay-offs gradually changes, until only $(1,1)$ remains. However, it does not change continuously. Sylvain Sorin has recently shown that when $\delta = 2/3$, we get the square with vertices $(1,1)$, $(1,3)$, $(3,3)$ $(3,1)$, plus the line segments connecting $(1,3)$ to $(1,3\frac{2}{3})$, and $(3,1)$ to $(3\frac{2}{3},1)$ (see Figure 5.3). As soon as $\delta > \frac{2}{3}$, everything disappears except $(1,1)$ (compare Kurz's second altruism article, in which there is a similar effect).[11]

Also the set of perfect equilibrium pay-offs is continuous near $\delta = 0$, but for $\delta > 0$ it will in general be unequal to the set of equilibrium pay-offs. Lloyd Shapley and I have worked out an example; see Appendix 5.3. As might be expected, the equilibrium nature of a pay-off depends on the available punishments. The perfect equilibrium nature of a pay-off, however, is a more subtle matter; it depends not only on the available punishments, but also on their *costs* to the punisher. Thus there emerges something conceptually akin to the Nash variable threats bargaining model.

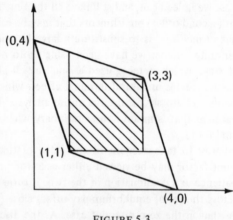

FIGURE 5.3

The next item on our shopping list is a critical examination of Theorem 2, which 'predicts' an outcome in the core. To obtain such a result we had to go from Nash equilibrium points to strong equilibrium points. Now in a sense this is begging the question; strong equilibrium involves group action in its definition, and this already assumes a measure of co-operation. Somehow, one feels that in a sufficiently detailed model, the joint action necessary to achieve a strong equilibrium should *follow* from considerations of individual utility maximization, rather than having to be assumed.

The problem already presents itself in the search for an individualistic justification for Pareto optimality (or efficiency) in terms of repeated games. For a specific example, let us return to the prisoner's dilemma discussed above. In the models we have discussed up to now, whether they are limiting average or discounted with a moderate discount rate, efficient outcomes have always been *possible* as equilibrium outcomes. But invariably, other outcomes — including the highly inefficient $(1,1)$ — have also been possible. Many of us feel strongly that $(1,1)$ is not a rational outcome of a repeated prisoner's dilemma. Can't we somehow narrow down the definition of equilibrium so that it yields efficient outcomes only, while at the same time involving only individualistic concepts?

One approach is that of Kurz's second altruism paper (mentioned in note 11) which considers *stationary* equilibria[12] in repeated games. In the prisoner's dilemma presented above there are actually only two stationary equilibrium outcomes (when $0 \leqslant \delta \leqslant \frac{2}{3}$), namely $(1,1)$ and $(4,4)$. However, if we consider the variant in which the choice of mixed strategies at each stage is observable, then the set of stationary equilibrium outcomes is considerably larger. In fact, we get the shaded corner in figure 5.4 plus the point $(1,1)$. As δ grows the corner shrinks; finally (at $\delta = \frac{2}{3}$) we get only $(3,3)$, plus, unfortunately, $(1,1)$. Thus although discounting appears

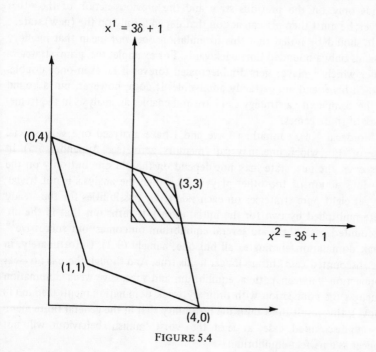

FIGURE 5.4

to eliminate more and more inefficiency, it fails to eliminate the ultimate, 'mulish' inefficiency in which the players just keep playing 'double-cross' no matter what happens.

To try to get around this, let us examine more carefully the concept of stationarity. This is not captured adequately by simply demanding a constant pay-off flow. What we want is stationary *strategies*, not just stationary pay-offs. Now the simplistic definition of stationary strategy in which the players choose the same stage-strategy (or *action*) at each stage is obviously unsatisfactory, since it does not allow for any response to what was done at previous stages. The proper definition would seem to be that a player's action at a given stage depends only on the history, not on the serial number of the stage; but this is also unsatisfactory, since the serial number of the stage can be read off from the history (it is simply its length). To make it work, we would need time stretching infinitely backwards, a concept that has been considered in a game context[13], but is associated with great difficulties.

One way to handle this is to assume that each player has a finite memory. More precisely, his mind has a finite number of 'states'. Before each stage, the player may change the state of his mind in a way that depends only on the previous state and the previous action of the other player; he must then play an action that depends only on the (new) state.

It should be noted that this formulation does *not* mean that memory extends only a bounded time backwards. For example, the 'grim' strategies under which a player gets doublecrossed forever if he even once doublecrossed his friend are certainly admissible. It does, however, put a bound to the complexity a strategy can have and enables an analysis in the framework of finite games.

Mordecai Kurz, Jonathan Cave and I have analysed one very special case of this, which one may call 'memory zero' (see Appendix 5.5). In this case, the new state may not depend on the old one but only on the previous action of the other player. Even then the analysis is not trivial; we get eight pure strategies on each side (four possibilities for the steady state multiplied by two for the initial move). It turns out that in the undiscounted case, there are several equilibrium outcomes; but successive[14] weak domination eliminates all but one, namely (3,3). Unfortunately, in the discounted case this no longer holds true. And though there is no clear connection between perfect equilibrium and successive weak domination (such as the connection with ordinary weak domination mentioned in (1) above), this result does raise the possibility that in the general finite memory undiscounted case, at least the worst 'mulish' behaviour will not appear as a perfect equilibrium.

Finite memory appears also in Smale's work[15] on repeated games; but Smale uses the term in a somewhat different sense. The strategies at each stage are assumed to depend on a fixed finite number of real parameters, each of which sums up some aspect of the history up to that point. Each of these parameters has a continous range, so that in fact the memory can have infinitely many different states. What makes Smale's assumption 'bite' (i.e. gives it substance) is that the function from the parameter space to the strategies must be *continous*.

More distantly related to finite memory is Radner's bounded rationality. This is defined in terms of *ϵ-equilibria*, that is, strategy *n*-tuples such that no player can, by defecting alone, improve his pay-off by more than ϵ. The effect of *ϵ-equilibria* in a large *finite* repetition is much like that of ordinary equilibria in an infinite repetition. Radner has used ϵ-equilibria to analyse the repeated prisoner's dilemma as well as repeated principal-agent problems.[16] The interesting aspect of the principal-agent problem is that the players do *not* get to know, at the end of each stage, just what strategies were used by the other players; the Folk Theorem does not in general apply to such situations (see Appendix 5.1, Problem 2).

We come now to the contributions of Hammond, Kurz, and Maynard-Smith mentioned above. Hammond and Kurz use the theory of repeated games to account for altruism, defined as the act of giving some good to another player without necessarily receiving anything in return. Kurz's 'Altruistic Equilibrium'[17] is essentially an equilibrium in a repeated game in which the players keep giving each other goods, with the punishment strategy ready in the background if they should ever refuse[18].

Finally, we have Maynard-Smith's 'Evolution and the Theory of Games'. Maynard-Smith's 'Evolutionarily Stable Strategy' (ESS) is a special kind of equilibrium point, which is well-suited to the evolutionary application.[19] Formally, however, the ESS is defined directly in terms of the one-shot game, not in terms of the repetition. Evolution seems a 'natural' application of repeated games. Ken Binmore, Drew Fudenberg, Eric Maskin, Edi Karni, David Schmeidler (and perhaps others) have suggested that the EES — or perhaps some other stability concept — might be formally derivable by applying more fundamental concepts (such as survival) to the repeated game, in much the same way that, say, the β-core in the one-shot game may be derived from strong equilibrium points in the supergame.

REPEATED GAMES OF IMCOMPLETE INFORMATION

The stress here is on the strategic use of information — when and how to reveal and when and how to conceal, when to believe revealed information and when not, etc.

The subject has broken itself up naturally into the zero-sum and the non-zero-sum case. That is because problems of revelation and conceal-ment occur already in the zero-sum case, and can be studied there 'under laboratory conditions', without the distractions and complications of co-operation, punishments, incentives, etc. A mathematical theory of con-siderable elegance, depth, and scope has grown up in the last fifteen years, much of which is concerned with the zero-sum case (Appendix 5.6 is a partial bibliography, to which we will refer throughout this part). This theory still has some fascinating open problems, to which I will allude in the sequel. For the purpose of economic applications, though, the non-zero-sum theory is more interesting and challenging; it is also far less complete, so that there is more room for spadework.

One cannot understand the non-zero-sum theory without first reviewing the zero-sum theory, which we now proceed to do. One of two two-person zero-sum games, A and B, is being played repeatedly; Player 1 knows which of the two it is, but Player 2 only knows the probability p that it is A (this probability is common knowledge). This can be viewed as a complete information game G^* in which nature chooses A or B with probabilities p and $1-p$ respectively, and informs Player 1 but not Player 2 of the choice; the game is then played repeatedly.

The central fact of the theory is that the situation cannot be under-stood unless p is allowed to vary. Denote by $u(p)$ the value of $pA + (1-p)B$, that is, the one-shot (or many-shot) game when Player 1 ignores his in-formation. Denote by $v(p)$ the value of G^*. Let Cav u be the least con-cave function that is $\geqslant u$ for each p.

Theorem 4: $v(p) = \text{Cav } u(p)$

To prove this, one starts out with a very simple argument, based on the fact that in a zero-sum situation information can't hurt you, which shows that $v(p)$ must be concave. Next, note that since Player 1 can choose to ignore his information, we must have $v(p) \geqslant u(p)$. Since $v(p)$ is concave, it follows that $v(p) \geqslant \text{Cav } u(p)$.

The opposite inequality is slightly trickier. By the minimax theorem there is a mixed strategy that *guarantees* $v(p)$ to Player 1; therefore he may as well announce it (and use it). Given this strategy, Player 2 can deduce a sequence of posterior probabilities $(p_1, p_2, p_3, \ldots)$ for the contingency that nature originally chose A. The p_k are random variables because they depend on which pure actions were chosen by Player 1 in the various stages; we have $Ep_k = p$ for each k. Now it can be shown that any infinite sequence of probabilities that are conditioned on more and more information converges with probability 1; that is, there is a random variable q such that $p_k \to q$ with probability 1 as $k \to \infty$ (q need not be 0 or 1, and need not be constant). What this means is that after a while, Player 1 will have revealed just about all the information he is ever going to reveal (which is perhaps obvious anyway). From then on he must play the same (or almost the same) whether A or B were chosen – otherwise he would be revealing more. At this point Player 2 thinks that nature has chosen A with probability close to q and Player 1 is essentially ignoring his information. Therefore, Player 1 cannot do better than $u(q)$. On average, therefore, he cannot do better than $Eu(q)$. But since $Ep_i = p$ and $p_i \to q$ almost surely, we have $Eq = p$. Hence by Jensen's inequality

$$Eu(q) \leqslant E \text{ Cav } u(q) \leqslant \text{Cav } u(Eq) = \text{Cav } u(p),$$

and the 'proof' is complete.

The odd thing about the whole procedure is that it is all imaginary; Player 2 cannot *really* assume that Player 1 is using any particular optimal strategy or for that matter an optimal strategy at all. He will *not* be computing any posteriors and must guard his flanks by a completely different procedure, called the *Blackwell strategy*. We do, however, get a guide as to how far Player 1 can go in revealing the true game being played (i.e. in playing differently contingent on A and on B). In fact, what he must do is find two probabilities q_1 and q_2 such that there is an α in $[0,1]$ with $p = \alpha q_1 + (1-\alpha)q_2$ and $u(p) = \alpha u(q_1) + (1-\alpha) u(q_2)$ (see Figure 5.5).

Now let us be given two coins with different parameters r^A and r^B. Suppose Player 1 tosses the coin with parameter r^A if A was chosen by

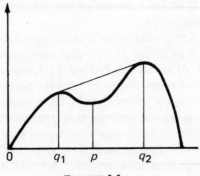

FIGURE 5.5

nature, and the coin with parameter r^B if B was chosen. If Player 2 could observe the outcome of the toss but not which coin was tossed, he could deduce posterior probabilities for A. It can be shown that r^A and r^B can be chosen so that the probability that the coin comes out heads is α, the posterior probability of A given heads is q_1 and the posterior probability of A given tails is q_2. An optimal strategy for Player 1 is then to toss such a coin *once*, and from then on play optimally in $q_1 A + (1 - q_1) B$ or in $q_2 A + (1 - q_2) B$ according as the coin came out heads or tails. Though he is not actually announcing the outcome of the toss, the effect is the same.

(It should be noted that this gives an alternative proof for $v(p) \geqslant \mathrm{Cav}\ u(p)$.)

The zero-sum theory has been developed in much more general situations. Before we describe some of these developments, though, it is necessary to clarify the definition of G^*. Two approaches suggest themselves: *limit of value* means that we consider the value of a k-stage game, divide by k, and then let $k \to \infty$; *value of limit* means that we define the pay-off by some kind of limiting average of the pay-offs and consider the value of the infinite-stage supergame.

Under either approach one could also use the present value of pay-off and let discount tend to zero, but in the context of repeated games this has not been studied much[20].

Intuitively, limit of value is appropriate when we have a large number of stages, and we know how many. Optimal strategies developed under this approach often depend critically on the serial number of the stage. Value of limit is appropriate when there is a large number of stages and we have no clear idea of how many there are. Optimal strategies here are in some sense more stationary than in the limit of value case.

For Theorem 4, all approaches are equivalent. The theorem (and the equivalence between all approaches) still holds when the two games are replaced by any fixed finite number m, but one player still is told exactly which game is being played.

A more significant generalization is to the case when the players are not told, at the end of each stage, exactly what one-stage strategy was used by the opponent (cf. Appendix 5.1, Problem 2). A typical example of this is when the individual stages consist of extensive games, in which case one would know at most the moves made by the opponent, and perhaps not even that; but certainly not the (one-stage) *strategy*. The information the players receive at the end of a stage may depend only on the game being played and on the strategies chosen by the players; that is, in addition to the pay-off matrix there is an 'information matrix' associated with each game.

The central concept here is that of a 'non-revealing strategy', defined as a one-stage mixed strategy which, when used by the informed player, leads to the same distribution of information for the uninformed player no matter which game is actually being played (though the informed player may make use of his information). It can be shown (Aumann and Maschler, 1968) that G^* still has a value in this case; in fact, if $u(p)$ is taken to be the value of the one-stage game in which Player 1 is restricted to using non-revealing strategies, then Theorem 4 applies. The equivalence between all approaches still holds here.

When we abandon the assumption of full information for one player, things get more complicated. First let us consider the value of limit approach. The first, archetypical case (independent types and full revelation of stage strategies) was considered by Stearns (1967), who derived a formula for the sup inf and inf sup pay-offs of these games; from this formula it follows that the value will in general decisively *fail* to exist (i.e. inf sup > sup inf)! Later Mertens and Zamir (1977) greatly generalized Stearns's result by removing the assumption of independent types and, with some restrictions, that of stage-strategy revelation.

The limit of value approach to these games was developed by Mertens and Zamir (1971–2) and Mertens (1971–2, 1973), who showed that in general the limit of the value *does* exist, and gave ways by which it may be calculated. Kohlberg, Mertens and Zamir have relaxed the informational conditions and explored the subject thoroughly in various directions that I will not specify further here.

This recital of results may sound somewhat dry; perhaps the reader is deluded into thinking that what we are discussing here are fairly straight-forward extensions and variations of two or three basic ideas. Nothing could be further from the truth. Many of the works in this area coming after the ACDA (Arms Control and Disarmament Agency) period of 1966–8, far from simply using and embelleshing the earlier ideas, were in fact tremendous *tours de force* of ingenuity, beauty, and depth. The problems attacked were often open for many years in spite of concerted attempts to solve them; the mathematical ideas employed are among the most surprising and original in the theory of games.

Having gotten this off our chest, let us continue with the survey. In our 'proof' of Theorem 4 we described an optimal strategy for the informed player but indicated that the construction of an optimal strategy for the uninformed player was a more complex matter. The construction of such a strategy (called a *Blackwell* strategy because of its reliance on a paper of Blackwell[21] that is fundamental in much of repeated game theory) in a very rudimentary case was done in Aumann and Maschler (1966), and was subsequently extended to much more general situations in Stearns (1967) and in Kohlberg (1975a).

The case of a fixed non-zero discount was considered by Mayberry (1967); his results are rather startling, in that he found that even in the simplest cases, $v(p)$ will be a concave function of p that is not differentiable at any rational value of p (though it must be differentiable a.e. because of its concavity).

The results of Ponssard (1975a, 1975b, 1976), Ponssard and Zamir (1973), and Ponssard and Sorin (1980b) have mainly concerned finite games or games repeated a fixed finite number of stages; some of these results can be considered as complementing the theory surveyed here, which concerns mainly the case of 'many' stages.

I would like to end this survey of the zero-sum situation by mentioning two problem areas that illustrate the subtlety and depth of this research. The first has to do with the speed of convergence (in the 'limit of value' approach). Returning to the situation of Theorem 4, it can be proved that the speed of convergence is always $0(1/\sqrt{k})$; it is often much smaller. Zamir (1971–2) found an example in which the order of magnitude $1/\sqrt{k}$ is actually attained. This order of magnitude is also suggested by the following intuitive considerations: suppose we have $u(p) = \text{Cav } u(p)$, so that aside from 'fine tuning', the informed player must ignore his information. This means that he will play the same mixed stage-strategy at each stage. Now there will always be a natural random variation in the average pay-off. The central limit theorem indicates that this variation will be of the order of $1/\sqrt{k}$. One can think of Zamir's example as one in which the informed player can take advantage of the natural variation, that is, play a strategy that masquerades as a constant mixed stage-strategy, but actually varies slightly from it. The purposeful variation is of exactly the order that the uninformed player might expect as random, but is actually used to the hilt to the advantage of the informed player.

The interesting thing is that the error term is not always of the order $1/\sqrt{k}$, even when $u(p) = \text{Cav } u(p)$. So this kind of 'masquerading' is not always possible.

In a startling piece, Mertens and Zamir (1976a) have shown that *in the particular original example* of Zamir, there is even a much closer connection to the Central Limit Theorem than that outlined above. The normal distribution actually makes an explicit appearance. Obviously there is something behind this that is much more general than this particular example. But what is it?

It's worth stating that Mertens and Zamir's proof has absolutely *nothing* to do with the above intuitive reasoning. Somehow, inexplicably, the normal distribution springs forth from some differential equation. It is all very mysterious and begs for an explanation (in terms of a general theorem).

The second problem area also involves work of Mertens and Zamir. Almost all of the work on this subject uses reasoning that is in some way related to that used in our above 'proof' of Theorem 4; that is, there hovers in the background some imaginary posterior probability of the uninformed player which takes the place, at each stage, of the original exogenuously given *p*. But there is a class of games, called *games without a recursive structure*, in which this reasoning somehow doesn't get off the ground. Mertens and Zamir (1976a) managed to solve *one* such game, and recently Waternaux (1983) extended their methods to a class of 2 x 2 games, but a general theory of such games has not yet been developed.

We come finally to the non-zero sum incomplete information case. In the first instance one simply seeks a characterization of equilibrium pay-offs, in the spirit of the Folk Theorem for the complete information case (Theorem 1). Obviously the incentive-compatibility of revelations is a central issue here, and one could perhaps have hoped for a solution related to the IIC set of Roger Myerson[22]. Unfortunately the issue seems much more complex.

Let us confine ourselves to the two-person case in which there is complete information on one side and the stage strategies become known after each stage. This was attacked in Aumann, Maschler and Stearns (1968), but even in this very simple case only with partial success. Specifically, a sufficient characterization was found, but it was shown not to be necessary. There were even cases in which there are no equilibrium points satisfying the sufficient conditions, though there were *some* equilibrium points.

The basic, inescapable complication in this business is that revelation and signalling get all mixed up and interfere with each other. By *revelation* we mean what happens when the informed player makes use of his information, enabling the uninformed player, at least in principle, to make deductions about the true state of nature. By *signalling* we mean what the informed player actually wants to tell the uninformed player. The desire to signal does not imply an ability to reveal; the signal would have to be incentive compatible, and it will not always be. Though this is well known, a simple example is:

| 4, 4 | 0, 0 | Prob = 0.4 |
| 5, 0 | 4, 4 | Prob = 0.6 |

Player 1 has no strategic choice, but he knows which game is being played; he can try to signal it to Player 2, who must choose a column. *A priori* Player 1 would like to signal the truth, and Player 2 would like to believe him; but obviously he can't, even if in fact Player 1 is telling the truth.

There have been some dramatic recent developments in this area. Sylvain Sorin (1983) has shown that when $m = 2$ (i.e. there are only two possibilities for the game), then an equilibrium point for the repeated game does indeed exist. And Hart (1982) has obtained a complete (necessary *and* sufficient) characterization of the set of all equilibrium pay-offs of the repeated game, when there is complete information on one side, and m may be arbitrary.

Hart's characterization gives an exquisite picture of the slow mutual feeling-out that is characteristic of real-life bargaining for high stakes. It involves periods of time during which the informed player makes partial revelations of information to the uninformed player, alternating with periods during which the two players enter into mutual commitments. The information cannot be revealed all at once, because that might give the uninformed player so much information that he would no longer be interested in entering into appropriate agreements. On the other hand, the agreements cannot come too early and fast, because then the informed player, knowing exactly the consequences of his revelations, might be tempted to lie. The result is a subtle balance between a slow stream of revelations and a slow stream of mutual commitments and agreements, each depending on the other, each incentive-compatible because of the other.

We end by briefly reviewing some of the work that connects *finitely* repeated games of incomplete information with the idea of reputation, yielding an effect much like that of infinitely repeated games. Consider first Selten's 'Chain-Store Paradox' (*Theory and Decision*, 9 (1978): 127–59). Here we have a monopolist who is able to stave off new entrants by predatory pricing. Such pricing causes losses to the monopolist on a short-term basis, but on a long-term basis, staving off the potential entrants more than makes up for this loss. If there are only finitely many stages, the monopolist will not underprice in the last stage, because short-term predatory pricing is unprofitable, and this effect propagates its way backwards, like the double double-cross in the finitely repeated prisoner's dilemma.

In an infinitely repeated game, even with a positive discount (as long as it is not too large), this effect disappears; there is no last stage, so the monopolist is willing to use predatory pricing at any stage to deter entry. Kreps and Wilson (1982) and Milgrom and Roberts (1982) demonstrate a similar effect in a *finitely* repeated chain store game with incomplete information. In their set-up, there is a positive probability – possibly quite small – that the monopolist is vengefully irrational, that is, that he will engage in predatory pricing at the last stage even though it may harm him. The monopolist himself knows whether or not he is of this type, but the potential entrant does not. By engaging in predatory pricing in the early stages of the repetition (and in fact throughout), the monopolist reinforces the potential entrant's feeling that he (the monopolist) may be vengefully irrational, and this will defer the potential entrant from entering. Once there is a distant possibility that the monopolist *may* be irrational, he can establish a useful reputation for actually *being* irrational.

In a similar direction, Kreps, Milgrom, Roberts, and Wilson (1982) have shown that if, in a finitely repeated prisoner's dilemma, there is a small probability that one of the players is an irrational automaton who *always* plays tit-for-tat, then that player is motivated to build up the other player's posterior that this is the case by indeed always playing tit-for-tat, even if in fact he is not such an irrational automaton. Thus with a very little bit of incomplete information, we can get a co-operative effect in a finitely repeated prisoner's dilemma very much like that for the infinitely repeated version.

These approaches are beautifully suggestive, but their slightly *ad hoc* character makes them not entirely satisfactory. In the prisoner's dilemma, it is not sufficient to assume that with some small probability, one of the players will do something unpredictably irrational; we must go further and assume that his irrational type will play precisely tit-for-tat (or some other specified strategy that leads to the friendly outcome). But where did tit-for-tat (or this other specified strategy) come from? We would like it to arise endogenously from the analysis, and not be imposed exogenuously from the outside. Similarly, though predatory pricing seems a logical enough thing to do, it is not an endogenous outcome of the analysis. What this line of research is saying is that certain types of behaviour are self-reinforcing; when put in exogenously with small probability, it becomes rational for the players to try to build up reputations that they behave in this way. This is very beautiful, but we would like more – that certain kinds of behaviour are picked out by the players for reputational build-up, even when they have no preferred status to start with.

All this is closely related to Problem 6 in Appendix 5.1. The idea is that in the right kind of model, an inefficent outcome x is impossible in a repeated game, because all players would be motivated to build up reputations that they would co-operate to reach an outcome y that Pareto dominates x. If you explicitly put in strategies leading to y, even with a small probability, then this would probably work. Without that, we haven't managed to make it work.

This part of our review wouldn't be complete if we didn't mention Rosenthal's seminal work on reputation, 'Sequences of Games with Varying Opponents' (*Econometrica*, 47 (1979): 1353–66).

APPENDIX 5.1

Problems regarding the Complete Information Case

1. Discounting, Perfect Equilibrium, and the Cost of a Threat

I would give first priority to the complete information case with a (fixed) positive discount. For reasons explained in the body of this paper, the positive discount case is in many ways conceptually more attractive than the zero discount case. It is also mathematically more tractable; we have an unambiguously defined pay-off function, and the strategy pairs form a compact space on which the pay-off function is continuous. The preliminary results (see Appendix 5.3) indicate that in this case the perfect equilibrium points involve a close relationship between the effectiveness of a punishment (or threat) and its costs to the threatener. This relationship is certainly worth exploring to the hilt.

2. Imperfect Information at the End of a Stage

I don't mean incomplete information in the sense that we don't know the pay-off, but imperfect information at the end of each stage, in the sense that each player gets only partial information about the strategies used by the other players. Consider, for example, an altruistic equilibrium in Kurz's sense[23] involving three or more people. Suppose that the donor never becomes known; the recipient only gets to know that he received a gift, not from whom. (Maimonides lists eight levels of charity, of which the anonymous donor who lends the recipient money in order to enable him to make his own livelihood is the highest. Aware of human frailties, he admits the lesser levels as well.) It is not difficult to see that the Altruistic Equilibrium survives this change. It's somewhat less clear whether the Altruistic Perfect Equilibrium survives it, and it seems perfectly clear that the Altruistic Strong Equilibrium will *not* survive it.[24] In more general games, even the ordinary equilibrium will not survive: if you do not know who is defecting, whom will you punish? Can one get general characterizations in this case?

3. Intergenerational Equilibrium

The need for intergenerational models was described in note 20 (Jacob & Joseph, etc.) Offhand, I see no reason why it should not be possible to carry this out, but it would certainly be worthwhile to do it explicitly.

4. Extreme Altruism

A more difficult problem is that posed by Kurz's example of the child in the fire ('Altruistic Equilibrium', p. 182). Kurz assumes that the probability is 90 per cent that both the rescuer and the child will die, but this seems extreme; it is unlikely that a model based on rationality at any level could account for a rescue in such a situation. But even if the probability of death is 40 per cent (for rescuer and child), it does not seem easy to account for a rescue on a purely individualistic basis, assuming that the rescuer does not think it likely that *he* will ever have to be similarly rescued.

We may be too hung up on the importance of the individual human being. In fact, groups may be more important. Biologists stress the survival of individual genes; even if we do not wish to assume a biological gene for altruism, there might be a sort of socio-educational 'gene' for it — an idea that is transmitted from generation to generation and survives because the groups who practise and propagate it survive.

5. Finite Memory Models

These were described in the body of the text and certainly bear further investigation. In addition to its intrinsic interest, a finite memory model might make many of the other problems easier to handle.

A particular case of a finite memory model is one in which only actions that are at most a fixed finite number of steps back can be considered ('let bygones be bygones'). This would rule out 'grim' strategies. The zero-memory model is of course of this kind. If the general finite-memory models turn out intractable, perhaps these would be less so.

6. Learning and Efficiency[25]

Kurz's speeder ('Altruistic Equilibrium', p. 184) is signalling other motorists to speed as well; he is teaching them that the true equilibrium in which the world finds itself involves more speeding than they thought. Conversely, his voter is teaching people in general to vote (presumably Pareto superior to not voting). There is a theorem here which Kurz and I have been pursuing for years without success. The 'theorem' says that if an equilibrium point (in the undiscounted game) has several possible pay-offs with positive probability each, then no one can Pareto dominate another; each equilibrium is efficient among those that can actually occur. The idea of the 'proof' is to look at an equilibrium point not as a conscious choice of strategies by n people, but as a sort of probability estimate of what the world really looks like (see Appendix 5.4). In a repeated game, the players will revise this estimate as time progresses. If two outcomes A and B with A Pareto dominating B were possible, then in a state of the world leading to B, each player would try to 'teach' the others that the true state leads to A (even though they may think that this is highly unlikely). Such teaching would be learned with alacrity by the other players.

To make this work one would have to make some kind of assumption under which each of the two equilibrium outcomes in question always retains a positive probability no matter what the players do at each state.

Can this 'theorem' be made into a theorem?

APPENDIX 5.2

Outline of Proof of the Folk Theorem[26]

It is easy to prove that the pay-off vectors to Nash e.p.'s in the supergame G^* are feasible and individually rational in G; the more significant part is the converse. Assume for simplicity that $n = 2$ (there are just two players). Suppose h is a feasible individually rational pay-off vector. Here we may write $h = \sum_{j=1}^{k} \alpha_i h_i$, where the α_i are non-negative weights that sum to 1, and all the h_i are pay-off vectors corresponding to pure strategy pairs in G. Suppose first that the α_i are rational, and express them in the form $\alpha_i = p_i/q$, where p_i are positive integers and q is their sum. The pay-off vector h can then be achieved as a limiting average in G^* by having the players play, for p_1 consecutive periods, an n-tuple that achieves h_1, then for p_2 consecutive periods an n-tuple that achieves h_2, and so on; after q periods, we start again from the beginning.

If the α_i are irrational, the same effect can be attained by approximating to them by rational numbers and playing once through each approximation in turn, to yield the desired limiting average.

This procedure, however, does not yet describe a Nash equilibrium point in G^*, and in fact does not even describe a pair of supergame strategies. A supergame strategy must describe each player's responses to the other player's actions not only when he 'plays along', but also when he 'defects' from a prescribed course of play, such as the one described above. This is where the requirement that h be individually rational comes in.

Since h is individually rational, the pay-off h^i of each player i is at least equal to his min max value (see the discussion following the statement of Theorem 1 in the text). Let τ be a mixed strategy for the other player j that holds i down to his min max value; *a fortiori*, j can, by playing τ, guarantee that i will not receive more than h^i.

We may now describe an e.p. in G^* as follows: the players start by playing to obtain an average pay-off of h, as outlined above. If at any stage a player i 'defects' — that is, does not play the prescribed choice in G for that round — then starting from the next round, the other player j plays the mixed strategy τ. This will hold i down to at most h^i, so that he will have gained nothing by his defection. Thus, h is indeed an e.p.

In this demonstration one can see clearly the role that 'threats' play in enforcing a prescribed 'co-operative' outcome. Repetition of G enables 'endogenous enforcement' of agreements, and thus the basically non-co-operative notion of Nash equilibrium points becomes co-operative in the supergame.

APPENDIX 5.3

Discounted Pay-offs in Repeated Games: Discussion of an Example

by R. J. Aumann and L. S. Shapley

Consider the following pay-off matrix for G (Figure 5.6), the players moving simultaneously:

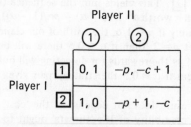

FIGURE 5.6

Here, p and c are positive numbers ('punishment' and 'cost'); we may think of them as being rather large. Thus, II may be in a position to damage I severely, but the cost to himself may possibly be unacceptably large[27].

In the repeated game G^* we shall use the pay-offs $\sum_{t=1}^{\infty} \alpha^t h_t^{\mathrm{I}}$ and $\sum_{t=1}^{\infty} \beta^t h_t^{\mathrm{II}}$ to Players I and II, respectively, where $0 < \alpha < 1$ and $0 < \beta < 1$. Sometimes we shall also assume that $\alpha \leqslant \beta$, that is, that Player I has, if anything, a bigger discount rate (= shorter 'horizon') than Player II.

As is easily seen, G has a unique e.p., namely (②, ①), yielding the outcome $(1, 0)$. This means that the pair of strategies in which I always plays ② and II always ① (regardless of history) is a *perfect* e.p. of G^*, since obviously no defection, even in a subgame, can ever be profitable.

Player II, however, would naturally prefer the outcome $(0, 1)$, corresponding to (①, ①). We shall now investigate under what conditions this outcome can be sustained by an e.p., and by a p.e.p., in the discounted repeated game. Indeed, we shall find that it can be sustained by an e.p. if and only if $p \geqslant 1/\alpha$; and, when $\alpha \leqslant \beta$, that it can be sustained by a p.e.p. if and only if $p \geqslant 1/\alpha$ and $p/c \geqslant (1 - \beta)/\alpha\beta$. Thus, whereas the existence of an e.p. is independent of the cost of the punishment to the punisher, the existence of a p.e.p. is sensitive to this cost.

Let us first consider e.p.'s. We claim that the following 'grim' strategy pair:

$$\begin{cases} \text{I plays } \boxed{1} \text{ always} \\ \text{II plays } ① \text{ so long as I plays } \boxed{1} \text{ , but plays } ② \text{ 'forever' if I ever} \\ \quad \text{plays } \boxed{2} \end{cases}$$

is an e.p. of G^*, provided that $p \geqslant 1/\alpha$, and moreover we claim that if $p < 1/\alpha$ there is no e.p. sustaining (①, ①). To see this, note first that II will certainly not defect, as he cannot possibly improve on the sequence of pay-offs $(1, 1, 1, \ldots)$. On the other hand, if I is to improve on his sequence $(0, 0, 0, \ldots)$, his best chance is to defect to ② at some time t, then keep playing ②. This yields him the sequence $(0, \ldots 0, 1, -p + 1, -p + 1, \ldots)$, which is worth $\alpha^t(1/(1 - \alpha) - p\alpha/(1 - \alpha))$. Since this is profitable to him if and only if $p < 1/\alpha$, the truth of our claims is now evident.

For example, let $p = 2$; then if $\alpha < 0.5$ there will be no e.p. sustaining the $(0,1)$ outcome, as the rewards for defecting will outweigh any possible punishment, whereas if $\alpha \geqslant 0.5$ the strategy pair given above is clearly an e.p.

Note that this result does not depend on the 'cost' c. Yet, intuitively, one feels that the credibility of II's 'threats' ought to be very dependent on the cost. Our next object is to show that a *perfect* e.p. that sustains the $(0,1)$ outcome is not possible for large values of c.

First let us give an example of such a p.e.p. It happens that we can define it in a very simple way, making the instructions to the two players depend only on the immediately preceding round:

(1) In the first round, play (①, ①).
(2) If the choices in round $t - 1$ were (①, ①) or (②, ②), play (①, ①) in round t.
(3) If the choices in round $t - 1$ were (①, ②) or (②, ①), play (②, ②) in round t.

The 'co-operative sequence' resulting from this strategy pair is just a repetition of ($\boxed{1}$, $\textcircled{1}$); this is worth $\beta/(1 - \beta)$ to II and 0 to I. In checking for perfection, it is sufficient to look only at defections in the first round of each subgame G_t^*. If I defects when he is supposed to play $\boxed{1}$, his best sequence from then on is $(1, - p + 1, - p + 1, \ldots)$, which is worth

$$\alpha^t \left(\frac{\alpha}{1 - \alpha} - \frac{\alpha^2 p}{1 - \alpha} \right)$$

to him. So if $p \geqslant 1/\alpha$ he will not have any incentive to defect. II likewise will not defect when he is supposed to play $\textcircled{1}$, as he cannot possibly improve on the pay-off sequence $(1, 1, 1, \ldots)$. When I is supposed to play $\boxed{2}$, a defection could yield him at best the sequence $(-p, -p + 1, 0,0, \ldots)$; this is clearly inferior to the prescribed sequence $(-p + 1, 0,0, \ldots)$. Finally II, when $\textcircled{2}$ is called for at the beginning of G_t^*, will have to compare his prescribed pay-off sequence $(- c,1,1,1, \ldots)$ with sequences like $(0, - c, 1,1,1, \ldots)$, $(0,0, - c, 1,1,1, \ldots)$, etc., or even $(0,0,0, \ldots)$, which he can obtain by defecting for 1,2, etc. rounds, or even forever. In the discounted sum, 'orthodoxy' is worth $\beta^t(- c\beta + \beta^2/(1 - \beta))$, while the various 'heresies' are worth $\beta^k(- c\beta + \beta^2/(1 - \beta))$ for $k \geqslant t + 1$, or 0. So if $c \leqslant \beta/(1 - \beta)$ he cannot gain by defecting. The given strategy pair is therefor a perfect e.p. on the assumptions $p \geqslant 1/\alpha$, $c \leqslant \beta/(1 - \beta)$. (See Figure 5.7).

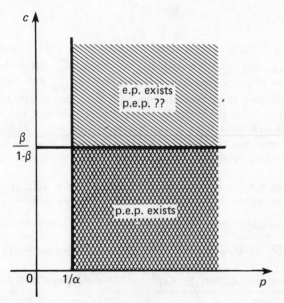

FIGURE 5.7

To wrap up our example, it is necessary to show that there are significant cases, where, because of the positive discount rate, a p.e.p. does *not*
exist. Showing non-existence is a more difficult undertaking, because in
general a p.e.p. can be a very complex thing. In particular, we cannot
ignore the possible use of mixed strategies against a defection. In our
example, if p and c are both large numbers, the threat of a *small probability* of using ② may be enough to keep I in line while keeping the (expected) cost at a level that II can accept.[28] . However, it would be out of
place in this discussion to develop the elaborate technical apparatus of
mixed strategies just for the sake of one example. Instead, we shall adopt
a far simpler expedient, called convexification in pure strategies, which is
essentially equivalent to the introduction of mixed strategies.

In our example, this merely means giving Player II the option of 'scaling
down' his punishment in G, as shown in Figure 5.8.

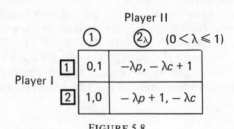

FIGURE 5.8

II now has a continuum of strategies in G, with ②$_1$ corresponding to
the old ② , and ②$_0$ corresponding to the old ① . (However, we still
indicate the latter by a separate column.) Playing ②$_\lambda$ has much the same
effect as playing the mixed strategy { ② with probability λ, ① with
probability $1 - \lambda$}, and it can be shown (though we shall not do it here)
that if the new G^* has no p.e.p. in *pure* strategies that sustains the co-
operative sequence ((1 , ①), (1 , ①),...), then the original G^*
(with the same values of α,β,p,c) has no p.e.p. at all that sustains the
sequence.

Consider now an arbitrary play of the 'new' G^*, with II playing the
sequence of moves $(\lambda_1,\lambda_2,\ldots,\lambda_t,\ldots)$. The total punishment received by
I is then given by $P = \sum\limits_{t=1}^{\infty} \lambda_t \alpha^t p$,   and the total cost incurred by II is C
$= \sum\limits_{t=1}^{\infty} \lambda_t \beta^t c$.   We now bring in the assumption, not used until now, that
$\alpha \leqslant \beta$. This implies that $\sum\limits_{t=1}^{\infty} \lambda_t (\beta^t - \alpha^t) \geqslant 0$, so that $P/C \leqslant p/c$. This inequality shows that it is most 'efficient', in terms of the damage/cost
ratio, for II to punish immediately; he thereby minimizes his cost for a

given level of deterrence. It follows that the game has a p.e.p., of the type described above, whenever there is *any* value of λ such that λp and λc satisfy the inequalities

$$\lambda p \leqslant \frac{1}{\alpha}, \lambda c \leqslant \frac{\beta}{1-\beta} \ .$$

This is illustrated in Figure 5.9.

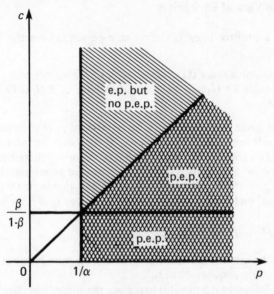

FIGURE 5.9

As we can see, there is a critical ratio of c to p, namely

$$R_0 = \frac{\alpha\beta}{1-\beta} \ ,$$

above which no such λ can be found. For example, if $\alpha = \beta = 0.75$ then $R_0 = 2.25$. If $p = 100$ and $c = 200$ then $c/p < R_0$, and we may, for example, choose $\lambda = 0.014$, giving us $\lambda c = 2.8 < \beta/(1-\beta) = 3$ and $\lambda p = 1.4 > 1/\alpha = 1.33$. A 1.4 per cent chance of II playing strategy ② after a defection by I sustains the perfect equilibrium at $(0,1)$.

We can also make the converse argument. If (c,p) is *not* in the cross-hatched region indicated in Figure 5.9, then there is no way for II to inflict any given amount P of punishment without incurring a cost of more than $R_0 P$. By the foregoing, it is clear that this is above the cost that he can 'afford'; in other words, he would prefer to accept his min max pay-off of zero forever after, rather than carry out the requisite threat. So a perfect e.p. cannot exist.

APPENDIX 5.4

A Bayesian View of Equilibrium

Let n be a positive integer. Define an n-person *information structure* to consist of:

(1) A measurable space (Ω, B) (*the states of the world*), and
(2) An n-tuple $I = (I_1, \ldots, I_n)$ of sub-σ-fields of B (I_i is i's *information σ-field*).

Let G be a game with n players, a finite set S_i of pure strategies for each i, and a pay-off function $H: S_1 \times \ldots \times S_n \to R^n$. Given an information structure (Ω, B, I), a *strategy* of player i is an I_i-measurable function from Ω to S_i. An *equilibrium point* in G is defined to consist of an information structure (Ω, B, I), a probability measure p on (Ω, B), and an n-tuple $s = (s_1, \ldots, s_n)$ of strategies, such that for each j and each strategy t_j of j, we have:

(*) $E H_j(s_{-j}, t_j) \leqslant E H_j(s)$

where E is the expectation operator w.r.t. the measure p, and (s_{-j}, t_j) stands for $(s_1, \ldots, s_{j-1}, t_j, s_{j+1}, \ldots, s_n)$.

In this definition it is possible to replace the single 'objective' probability measure p by n different 'subjective' probability measures p^i. In that case j's expectation operator E would have to be replaced by E_j, but otherwise the definition would not be affected. We refrain from using the more general set-up only for notational simplicity.

There are several ways of viewing an equilibrium point. One is as a self-enforcing agreement. The players agree to use a randomizing device described by (Ω, B, p), to be informed of the outcome in accordance with the I_j, and to act in accordance with the s_i; once having agreed to this, it will be to the advantage of no players to renege. This is the point of view taken in Aumann (1974) (see especially section 9b).

Another point of view is that of 'rational expectations'. Each point ω in Ω is thought of as constituting a complete objective description of a state of the real world. Such a description would of course include the choice $s_j(\omega)$ of each player j in the game G, as well as j's state of information (i.e. the set of all states of the world that j cannot distinguish from ω).

Thus both the information structure and the equilibrium strategies s_i are in a sense tautologically defined. What is not tautological is the probability measure p, which describes how each player views the world, probability-wise. In assuming that this is the same for all players, we are putting ourselves in Harsanyi's 'consistent case'[29]; however, as noted above, this is not an important assumption for us.

This formulation does away with the dichotomy usually perceived between the 'Bayesian' and the 'game-theoretic' view of the world. From the Bayesian viewpoint, subjective probabilities should be assignable to everything, including the prospect of a player choosing a certain strategy in a certain game. The so called 'game-theoretic' viewpoint holds that subjective probabilities can only be assigned to events not governed by rational decision-makers; for the latter, one must substitute an equilibrium (or other game-theoretic) notion. The above formulation synthesizes the two viewpoints: equilibrium is viewed as the *result* of Bayesian rationality, condition (*) appearing as a simple maximization of utility, given player j's subjective probability distribution over the states of the world.

This definition of equilibrium point encompasses the notion of a Nash equilibrium point (i.e. one in mixed strategies) as a special case. But it also encompasses significantly more[30].

APPENDIX 5.5

Repeated Prisoner's Dilemma with Memory Zero

| | | F | | | | D | | | |
		FF	FD	DF	DD	FF	FD	DF	DD
F	FF	3,3	3,3	0,4	0,4	3,3	3,3	0,4	0,4
	FD	3,3	3,3	2,2	1,1	3,3	2,2	2,2	1,1
	DF	4,0	2,2	2,2	0,4	0,4	2,2	0,4	0,4
	DD	4,0	1,1	4,0	1,1	4,0	1,1	4,0	1,1
D	FF	3,3	3,3	0,4	0,4	3,3	3,3	0,4	0,4
	FD	3,3	2,2	2,2	1,1	3,3	1,1	2,2	1,1
	DF	4,0	2,2	4,0	0,4	4,0	2,2	2,2	0,4
	DD	4,0	1,1	4,0	1,1	4,0	1,1	4,0	1,1

FIGURE 5.10

Strategies F and D (Figure 5.10) stand for 'Friendly' and 'Doublecross' respectively. The letter outside the brace indicates the initial move. Inside the brace the two letters indicate the steady-state response to the opponent's playing F and D respectively on the previous move. Each pair of strategies generates a pay-off stream that is periodic in the steady state, and whose average appears in the matrix. For the matrix of the one-shot game and other explanatory material, see the body of the text.

For each player, all strategies except FFD are successively eliminated as follows: First FDF (by DDF) and DFD; then FFF and DFF; then DDF; then DDD; and finally FDD. Five stages are needed in all. Except that of FDF in the first stage, all eliminations are by FFD.

APPENDIX 5.6

A Partial Bibliography of Repeated Games of Incomplete Information

Aumann, R., and M. Maschler (1966) 'Game Theoretic Aspects of Gradual Disarmament', *Report of the US Arms Control and Disarmament Agency/ST-80*, Washington, D.C., ch. 5.

Aumann, R., and M. Maschler (1967) 'Repeated Games with Incomplete Information: A Survey of Recent Results', *Report of the US Arms Control and Disarmament Agency/ST-116*, 287, Washington, D.C., ch. 3.

Aumann, R., and M. Maschler (1968) 'Repeated Games of Incomplete Information: The Zero-Sum Extensive Case', *Report of the U.S. Arms Control and Disarmament Agency/ST-143*, 37, Washington, D.C., ch. 3.

Aumann, R., M. Maschler and R. E. Stearns (1968) 'Repeated Games of Incomplete Information: An Approach to the Non-Zero-Sum Case', *Report of the U.S. Arms Control and Disarmament Agency/ST-143*, 117, Washington, D. C., ch. 4.

Forges, F. (1982a) 'Infinitely Repeated Games of Incomplete Information: Symmetric Case with Random Signals', *International Journal of Game Theory*, 11: 203.

Forges, F. (1982b) 'A First Study of Correlated Equilibria in Repeated Games with Incomplete Information', Université Catholique de Louvain, CORE Discussion Paper 8218.

Forges, F. (1982c) 'A Note on Nash Equilibria in Infinitely Repeated Games with Incomplete Information', Université Catholique de Louvain, CORE Discussion Paper 8220; to appear in *International Journal of Game Theory*.

Forges, F. (1983) 'Correlated Equilibria in Repeated Games with Lack of Information on One Side: A Model with Verifiable Types', Université Catholique de Louvain, CORE Discussion Paper 8302.

Forges, F. (1984) 'Communication Devices in Repeated Games with Incomplete Information', Parts I, II, III, Université Catholique de Louvain, CORE Discussion Papers 8406, 8411, 8412.

Hart, S. (1982) 'Non-Zero-Sum Two-Person Repeated Games with Incomplete Information', Université Catholique de Louvain, CORE Discussion Paper 8203; also Stanford University, IMSSS Technical Report 367; to appear in *Mathematics of Operations Research*.

Kohlberg, E. (1974) 'Repeated Games with Absorbing States', *Annals of Statistics*, 2: 724.

Kohlberg, E. (1975a) 'Optimal Strategies in Repeated Games of Incomplete Information', *International Journal of Game Theory*, 4: 7.

Kohlberg, E. (1975b) 'The Information Revealed in Infinitely-Repeated Games of Incomplete Information', *International Journal of Game Theory*, 4: 57.

Kohlberg, E., and S. Zamir, (1974) 'Repeated Games of Incomplete Information: the Symmetric Case', *Annals of Statistics*, 2: 1040.

Kreps, D. M., D. Milgrom, J. Roberts and R. Wilson, (1982) 'Rational Co-operation in the Finitely Repeated Prisoners' Dilemma', *Journal of Economic Theory*, 27: 245.

Kreps, D. M., and R. Wilson (1982) 'Reputation and Imperfect Information', *Journal of Economic Theory*, 27: 253.

Mayberry, J. (1967) 'Discounted Repeated Games with Incomplete Information', *Report of the U.S. Arms Control and Disarmament Agency/ST-116*, 435, Washington, D.C., ch. 5.

Megiddo, N. (1980) 'On Repeated Games with Incomplete Information Played by Non-Bayesian Players', *International Journal of Game Theory*, 9: 157.

Mertens, J. F. (1971–2) 'The Value of Two-Person Zero-Sum Repeated Games – The Extensive Case', *International Journal of Game Theory*, 1: 217.

Mertens, J. F. (1973) 'A Note on "The Value of Two-Person Zero-Sum Repeated Games – The Extensive Case"', *International Journal of Game Theory*, 2: 231.

Mertens, J. F. (1982) 'Repeated Games: an Overview of the Zero-Sum Case', in W. Hildenbrand, *Advances in Economic Theory*, Cambridge: Cambridge University Press, p. 175.

Mertens, J. F., and S. Zamir, (1971–2) 'The Value of Two-Person Zero-Sum Repeated Games with Lack of Information on Both Sides', *International Journal of Game Theory*, 1: 39.

Mertens, J. F., and S. Zamir (1976a) 'On a Repeated Game Without a Recursive Structure', *International Journal of Game Theory*, 5: 173.

Mertens, J. F., and S. Zamir (1976b) 'The Normal Distribution and Repeated Games', *International Journal of Game Theory*, 5: 187.

Mertens, J. F., and S. Zamir (1977) 'The Maximal Variation of a Bounded Martingale', *Israel Journal of Mathematics*, 27: 252.

Mertens, J. F., and S. Zamir (1980) 'Minmax and Maxmin of Repeated Games with Incomplete Information', *International Journal of Game Theory*, 9: 201.

Mertens, J. F., and S. Zamir (1981) 'Incomplete Information Games with Transcendental Values', *Mathematics of Operations Research*, 6: 313.

Mertens, J. F., and S. Zamir (1982) 'Formalization of Harsanyi's Notions of "Type" and "Consistency" in Games with Incomplete Information', Universite Catholique de Louvain, CORE Discussion Paper 8230; to appear in *International Journal of Game Theory*.

Milgrom, P., and J. Roberts (1982) 'Predation, Reputation, and Entry Deterrence', *Journal of Economic Theory*, 27: 280.

Ponssard, J. P. (1975a) 'Zero-Sum Games with Almost Perfect Information', *Management Science*, 21: 794.

Ponssard, J. P. (1975b) 'A Note on the LP Formulation of Zero-Sum Sequential Games', *International Journal of Game Theory*, 4: 1.

Ponssard, J. P. (1976) 'On the Subject of Nonoptimal Play in Zero-Sum Extensive Games: The Trap Phenomenon', *International Journal of Game Theory*, 5: 107.

Ponssard, J. P., and S. Sorin (1980a) 'The LP Formulation of Finite Zero-Sum Games with Incomplete Information', *International Journal of Game Theory*, 9: 99.

Ponssard, J. P., and S. Sorin (1980b) 'Some Results on Zero-Sum Games with Incomplete Information: the Dependent Case', *International Journal of Game Theory*, 9: 233.

Ponssard, J. P. and S. Sorin (1982) 'Optimal Behavioural Strategies in 0-Sum Games with Almost-Perfect Information', *Mathematics of Operations Research*, 7: 14.

Ponssard, J. P. and S. Zamir (1973) 'Zero-Sum Sequential Games with Incomplete Information', *International Journal of Game Theory*, 2: 99.

Sorin, S. (1979) 'A Note on the Value of Zero-Sum Sequential Repeated Games with Incomplete Infromation', *International Journal of Game Theory*, 8: 217.

Sorin, S. (1980) 'An Introduction to Two-person Zero Sum Repeated Games with Incomplete Information', TR 312, Institute for Mathematical Studies in the Social Sciences — Economics, Stanford.

Sorin, S. (1981b) ' "Big Match" with Lack of Information on One Side', Universite Catholique de Louvain, CORE Discussion Paper 8133; to appear in *International Journal of Game Theory*.

Sorin, S. (1982) ' "Big Match" with Lack of Information on One Side: Part II', Universite Catholique de Louvain, CORE Discussion Paper 8229; to appear in *International Journal of Game Theory*.

Sorin, S. (1983) 'Some Results on the Existence of Nash Equilibria for Non-Zero Sum Games with Incomplete Information', *International Journal of Game Theory*, 12: 193.

Sorin, S. (1984) 'On a Repeated Game with State-Dependent Signalling Matrices', Institut Statistique de l'Université de Paris, Discussion Paper 11.

Sorin, S., and S. Zamir (1984) 'A 2-Person Game with Lack of Information on 1½ Sides' to appear in *Mathematics of Operations Research*.

Stearns, R. E. (1967) 'A Formal Information Concept for Games with Incomplete Information', *Report of the US Arms Control and Disarmament Agency/ST-116*, 405, Washington, D. C., ch. 4.

Waternaux, C. (1983) 'Solution for a Class of Repeated Games without a Recursive Structure', *International Journal of Game Theory* 12: 129.

Waternaux, C. (1983) 'Minmax and Maxmin of Repeated Games without a Recursive Structure', Universite Catholique de Louvain, CORE Discussion Paper 8313.

Zamir, S. (1971–2) 'On the Relation Between Finitely and Infinitely-Repeated Games with Incomplete Information', *International Journal of Game Theory*, 1: 179.

Zamir, S. (1973a) 'On Repeated Games with General Information Function', *International Journal of Game Theory*, 2: 215.

Zamir, S. (1973b) 'On the Notion of Value for Games with Infinitely Many Stages', *Annals of Statistics*, 1; 791.

Stochastic games are not included in this bibliography, although they have important applications to repeated games with incomplete information. The help of Jonathan Dave and Sylvain Sorin in researching this bibliography is gratefully acknowledged.

NOTES

1. In an arbitrary game, not necessarily a supergame.
2. *Essays in Mathematical Economics in Honor of Oskar Morgenstern*, ed. by Martin Shubik, Princeton: Princeton University Press, 1967.
3. As often happens in our business, the work became widely known several years before it was published in 1967–8 (*Management Science*, 14: 159–82, 320–34, 486–502).
4. 'Charity: Altruism or cooperative egotism?' in E. Phelps (ed.), *Altruism, Morality, and Economic Theory*, New York: Russel Sage Foundation, 1975.
5. 'Altruistic Equilibrium', in *Economic Progress, Private Values, and Public Policy* (The Fellner Festschrift), Amsterdam: North-Holland, 1977; see also note 11.
6. *Evolution and the Theory of Games*, Cambridge: Cambridge University Press, 1982.
7. 'Reexamination of the Perfectness Concept for Equilibrium Points in Extensive Games', *International Journal of Game Theory*, 4 (1975): 25–55.
8. σ_1 *weakly dominates* σ_2 if σ_1 yields at least as much as σ_2 to the player using it no matter what the other players do, and more for at least one $(n-1)$-tuple of strategies of the other players.
9. *Equilibrium in Supergames*, Hebrew University of Jerusalem: Center For Research in Mathematical Economics and Game Theory, RM 25, May 1977.
10. Unpublished manuscript.
11. 'Altruism as an Outcome of Social Interaction', *American Economic Review*, 68 (1978): 216–22.
12. Equilibria yielding a flow of pay-offs not depending on the serial number of the period.
13. G. Schwartz, 'Randomizing when Time is Not Well-Ordered', *Israel Journal of Mathematics* 19 (1974): 241–5.
14. If one eliminates all weakly dominated strategies from a game, one obtains a new game to which one can apply the process of weak domination; this can be iterated arbitrarily often. For a concrete example see Appendix 5.5.
15. 'The Prisoner's Dilemma and Dynamical Systems Associated to Non-Cooperative Games', *Econometrica*, 48 (1980): 1617–34.
16. See 'Monitoring Cooperative Agreements in a Repeated Principal-Agent Relationship', *Econometrica*, 49 (1981): 1127–48, and the papers cited there.

17. B. Balassa and R. Nelson (eds.), *Economic Progress, Private Values, and Public Policy*, Amsterdam: North-Holland, 1977, pp. 177–200.

18. 'Do unto me kindness and *truth*, please do not bury me in Egypt' (Genesis 47, 29): the Patriarch Jacob is speaking to his son Joseph. The eleventh-century commentator Rashi explains that 'kindness to the dead is *true* altruism (Khessed shel emmet), as the doer does not expect any quid pro quo'. Since then, the phrase 'true altruism' has been traditionally used for services connected with burial. Perhaps this too can be accounted for 'rationally', by an intergenerational equilibrium model; but it is certainly a more complex matter. A similar problem, though in an entirely different context, was brought up by Ken Arrow in a recent conversation. When Al Capone was released from jail after serving close to ten years, he was physically and mentally a broken man. Nevertheless he was well and respectfully cared for by the mob. More generally, of course, the whole matter of care for the aged and the infirm comes under this heading.

19. Recently Reinhard Selten has taken up the evolutionary theme. See 'A Note on Evolutionarily Stable Strategies in Asymmetric Animal Conflicts'. *Journal of Theoretical Biology* 84 (1980): 93–101.

20. Though in the context of stochastic games it has been; see Bewley and Kohlberg in *Mathematics of Operations Research* 1 (1976), pp. 197–208 and pp. 321–36. Also repeated games with *fixed* non-zero discount have been studied; more on this below. Some of the limiting average results go through without too much difficulty for the limiting discount case; see, for example. Mertens and Zamir, 1971–2.

21. 'An Analog of the Minimax Theorem for Vector Payoffs', *Pacific Journal of Mathematics*, 6 (1956): 1–8.

22. 'Incentive Compatibility and the Bargaining Problem'. *Econometrica*, 47 (1979), 61–73.

23. See note 17.

24. Another example is the principal-agent problem, discussed in the body of the text. See also A. Rubinstein, 'Offenses that May Have Been Committed by Accident – An Optimal Policy of Retribution', in S. J. Brams, A. Schotter, and G. Schwodiauer (eds.), *Applied Game Theory*, Wurzburg: Physica-Verlag, 1979.

25. In this connection see also Kurz's 'Altruism as an Outcome of Social Interaction'. and Tomioka's 'On the Bayesian Selection of Nash Equilibrium' (Ch. V of his thesis).

26. Adapted from an unpublished manuscript by R. Aumann and L. Shapley.

27. Selten's 'chain store paradox' can be thought of as a repetition of this game.

28. This is a realistic consideration in the international 'balance of terror' game, where the pressure of the nuclear deterrent is felt in every situation that creates any perceptible risk that the situation might escalate out of control.

29. J. Harsanyi, 'Games of Incomplete Information Played by Bayesian Players, Pts I–III, *Management Science*, 14 (1967–8): 159–82; 320–34; 486–502.

30. 'Subjectivity and Correlation in Randomized Strategies', *Journal of Mathematical Economics*, 1 (1974): 67–95.

Part II
Oligopoly and Duopoly Revisited

Part II
Oligopoly and Duopoly Revisited

6 Reconsideration of Duopoly Theory: A Co-operative Perspective

MORDECAI KURZ*

CO-OPERATION AS A NORM IN A DUOPOLY

Ever since Cournot's (1838) celebrated treatment of the duopoly problem, the model of two firms in an industry has provided an important and fertile ground for the examination of the foundations of market behaviour. The duopoly level is the simplest situation that brings up the fundamental issues involved in formulating the market behaviour of firms and these include the nature of the strategies employed, the effects of dynamic considerations, the concept of 'reaction' of one firm to the actions of the other, the importance of information, the influence of entry considerations and others. Such celebrated contributions as Bertrand (1882), Edgeworth (1925), Hotelling (1929), Chamberlin (1933), Stackelberg (1934), Fellner (1949), Mayberry, Shubik and Nash (1953) and Shubik (1955, 1959, 1968, 1974) provide only a small sample of papers that highlight the various aspects of the duopoly problem.

The essence of the duopoly problem arises from the fact that in equilibrium, entry into the industry is either not feasible or non-profitable and because of this the output will be produced only by two active firms. Most contributions to the analysis of duopoly may be interpreted as assuming that entry is either impossible or requires significant irreversible (sunk) cost so that an equilibrium condition will make it costly for a third firm to enter, and shortly thereafter exit. One may think of many realistic examples of situations in which two active firms may be in an advantageous

* This work was supported by National Science Foundation Grant SES80-06654 at the Institute for Mathematical Studies in the Social Sciences, Stanford University. The author thanks Peter Hammond and Yair Tauman for valuable comments.

245

market position relative to inactive firms: patent protection, control over a specialized natural resource, large optimal scale of operations relative to the market, extensive irreversible set-up cost of marketing or production, extensive know-how that develops from experience, specialized labour force that takes time to train, and other factors.

An alternative view may be taken by conducting the analysis of the duopoly problem under much weaker conditions of entry. Some writers examine the duopoly problem under the assumption that both firms can produce the homogeneous commodity costlessly and when entry and exit are costless as well then the Baumol, Panzar and Willig (1982) analysis of 'contestable markets' becomes applicable. It is interesting to remark that the analysis of Bertrand's (1882) price duopoly and the view of duopoly as a contestable market lead to the same conclusions and although no explicit formal game-theoretic model of a contestable market was fomulated by Baumol, Panzar and Willig (1982), it appears that such a model would be close in spirit to Bertrand's treatment under the added assumption of costless entry and exit.

It is not clear in which industries the condition of costless entry and exit holds but it is almost universally agreed that in many industries the efficient scale of firms is large relative to the market and most markets are far from being contestable. In many industries entry costs are large and sunk and most major investments in plant and equipment are not reversible and thus exit costs may be prohibitively large. Moreover, extensive economies of scale make the optimal size of a firm large and, in many cases, growing with modern technology. In many situations incumbent firms are able to use this technology with the protection of a patent, licence or other informational advantages that are gained through the sunk investments. Such technological advantages cannot be removed by copying or replication. One must therefore conclude that although contestable markets may provide some yardstick to industrial structure, the reality of many industries may be so far from 'contestability' that this yardstick may not be useful at all. It is the objective of this chapter to examine an industry that operates in a non-contestable market and in which the efficient plant size is large. We shall also assume that entry into the industry is limited by some combination of factors like technological difficulties, heavy sunk cost, irreversible investments or others. This naturally leads to the immediate traditional observation that the model of perfect competition is not the relevant yardstick for the predicted behaviour. However, in such cases, does the traditional model of Cournot or other models of strategic competition provide a better approximation? We doubt it and will offer a different perspective.

It would be accurate to say that virtually the entire literature on oligopoly theory in general and duopoly theory in particular has been developed with the viewpoint of non-co-operative behaviour. In some instances (see for example, Shubik 1959 and 1968) alternative solution concepts from co-operative game theory are cited as possible outcomes, but this is done without any specific formal motivation or justification. Among the concepts that are frequently mentioned in the economic literature is the 'joint profit maximization' criterion that entails, in most instances, transfer payments between the firms. It should be clear, however, that allowing transfer payments between two duopolists makes the industry equivalent to a monopoly with two plants. In more general terms the difference between a multi-plant monopoly (i.e. a 'cartel') and an 'oligopoly' is defined precisely by the availability of transfer payments. On this basis we don't view 'joint profit maximization' as a viable solution concept for the duopoly problem and will conduct the analysis in this chapter under the strict assumption of no transfer payments.

Going one step further in assessing the current views regarding co-operation in an industry, one finds that whenever a study of co-operation in oliogpoly is undertaken it is always conducted under the heading of 'collusive' behaviour. Apart from the secretive-conspiratorial implications of the term 'collusion' it also carries the more important connotation of constituting an act that is carried out against the 'natural' state of competition. In most writing it also tends to suggest a rather transitory state soon to be 'exposed' and be replaced by the 'natural' forces of the market-place. We suggest that the secretive—conspiratorial description of industrial co-operation is misleading. In our view, direct, explicit and verbal communication is neither a sufficient nor necessary condition for the emergence of co-operation. To illustrate the fact that such communication is not a sufficient condition, consider the classical example of the prisoner's dilemma represented in the pay-off matrix (Figure 6.1).

		Player II	
		L	*R*
Player I	*T*	1,1	10,0
	B	0,10	4,4

FIGURE 6.1

It has traditionally been argued that the players cannot communicate and for this reason they will not choose the strategy pair (B, R). Now assume that the players can communicate as much as they wish except that after they complete the communication they must choose their strategies in a non-co-operative way. One way of achieving this is for the players to submit their chosen strategies in sealed envelopes to a referee. It is clear that since (T, L) is a dominant strategy equilibirum, no matter how much the two players discuss their situation, when left to their own devices they would still elect to play (T, L) and not (B, R). This example shows that the presence of direct communications may have no effect on the outcome of a non-co-operative game. Equally important, however, is the observation that *direct and explicit communication is also not a necessary condition for the emergence of industrial co-operation.* It is now well understood that the dynamic reality of repetition over time provides the machinery for co-operation and its enforcement. We discuss this mechanism in a few places below. In this context communication among the players can be achieved through the play itself and without ever exchanging a single explicit word. Since it is easier to think of co-operation as being associated with direct communication, we shall indeed assume throughout this chapter that communication is possible and regard this as no more than a simplifying technical assumption.

Having disposed of the question of communication, consider now two duopolists who operate in a non-contestable market for a homogenous commodity in which there is relatively limited danger of new entries. Perhaps an initial period of competitive behaviour establishes a non-co-operative equilibrium output pattern $(\bar{x}_1, \bar{x}_2)$ where $\bar{x}_1$ is the output of Firm 1 and $\bar{x}_2$ is the output of Firm 2. Although the law does not permit the merger of the two firms into a single multi-plant monopolist, the managements of the two firms are familiar with each other and communicate freely with each other. It is our view that within a very short period the two firms are likely to establish a stable co-operative duopoly equilibrium. Such an equilibrium will establish the procedures for co-operative changes in outputs and price. Underlying any co-operative equilibrium will be the knowledge of both participants that a deviation by any one of them would lead to an immediate retaliation by the other and a most undesirable non-co-operative outcome. Limited memory of a player, asymmetric information about the state of demand or technology and other such important factors may force the players into an occasional price war and other forms of non-co-operative behaviour. These transitory periods may be needed in order to establish a more general knowledge of

($\bar{x}_1$, $\bar{x}_2$) and provide the foundation for the next period of co-operative behaviour.

We remark that the mechanism of repetition as generating and enforcing co-operative oligopoly behaviour is not new to oligopoly theory. In this context the basic paradigm that is used is the so-called 'Folk Theorem' which we accept and which we shall explain below. Most of the recent papers utilizing this approach in oligoply theory concentrate on the structure of the specific strategies that provide the enforcement mechanism even when a stochastic element enters the picture. Such authors as Radner (1980), Porter (1981) and Green and Porter (1981) concentrate on the general class of 'trigger strategies' that can provide the enforcement mechanism for co-operative behaviour. What these writers fail to do is to provide a theory that will identify *which strategies and which outcomes are likely to be adopted by the co-operating firms*. This emphasizes the need to supplement the growing theory of the enforcement mechanism of co-operative behaviour with some progress in the prediction of the outcome of co-operation. We shall explain below that this lack of identification results from the Folk Theorem itself which holds that any individually rational outcome could be supported as a Nash equilibrium of a repeated play. This crucial issue will receive further attention below.

Our main objective in this chapter is to develop a theory of oligopolistic behaviour in non-contestable markets and where optimal firm size is not negligible. We propose a doctrine that holds that such markets will not act in accordance with a Cournot—Nash non-co-operative behaviour but rather will develop a systematic and stable co-operative behaviour. This co-operative behaviour will take the form of an implicit contract among the firms regarding the procedure by which they alter their output in equilibirum. The characterization of this procedure and the resulting equilibrium is the focus of this chapter.

We mention here the papers of Osborne (1976) and Spence (1978) which are related to our analysis. Although they were mostly concerned with a theory of market shares in cartels we shall return to these papers in the fifth section to compare our results with these early contributions. Our approach is also close to the one adopted by Hurwicz (1979b) and other writings on incentive mechanisms. We review this relationship in the third section.

THE INDUSTRY MODEL

We follow the traditional treatment of the duopoly problem in the context of partial equilibrium analysis. We thus assume that prices of all other commodities are fixed and we abstract from economy-wide income effects of the industry under study. The analysis is carried out first for an industry with a homogeneous commodity where the results are more transparent. In the sixth section we treat the case of differentiated commodities. We thus introduce the following notation:

x_j = output level of firm $j, j = 1, 2$

$\underset{\sim}{x} = (x_1, x_2)$

$x = x_1 + x_2 =$ output level of the industry

$c_j(x_j) =$ cost function of firm $j, j = 1, 2$

$p(x) =$ price function which depends only on aggregate output.

Naturally, $p'(x) < 0$

$\pi_j(x_j, x) =$ profit function of firm $j, j = 1, 2$

$\underset{\sim}{\pi} = (\pi_1, \pi_2)$

We have that $x_j \epsilon R_+, x \epsilon R_+$ and:

$$\pi_j(x_j, x) = x_j p(x) - c_j(x_j), j = 1, 2 \qquad (6.1)$$

For the case of an industry with differentiated products we use the following notation:

$p_j(x_1, x_2) =$ price function for firm $j, j = 1, 2$

and we then have:

$$\pi_j(\underset{\sim}{x}) = x_j p_j(x_1, x_2) - c_j(x_j), j = 1, 2 \qquad (6.2)$$

Since we use in the analysis below only the profit functions the notation $\pi_j(x_j, x)$ refers to the industry with a homogenous commodity while $\pi_j(\underset{\sim}{x})$ refers to the case of differentiated commodities.

Assumption A: $\pi_j(x_j, x)$, $j = 1, 2$ are continuously differentiable, quasi concave functions of (x_j, x) over the set $\{(x_j, x) \mid x_j \geqslant 0, x \geqslant 0\}$. For any x_1 there exists $x_2(x_1)$ such that $\pi_1(x_1, x_1 + x_2(x_1)) = 0$ and for any x_2 there exists $x_1(x_2)$ such that $\pi_2(x_2, x_1(x_2) + x_2) = 0$.

We now visualize the firms as having played a non-co-operative game in which $N = \{1, 2\}$ is the set of players, R_+ is the strategy space of each player and the pay-off is $\pi_j(x_j, x)$. In this game a non-co-operative outcome $(\bar{x}_1, \bar{x}_2)$ has been established in the past and is known to both players. We call it *the Initial Position*.

One may think of $\underset{\sim}{\bar{x}}$ as the Cournot–Nash equilibrium of the static non-co-operative game and this is the way we shall think of it in this chapter (note that such an equilibrium in pure strategies does exist in the model at hand). We stress that the arguments in this chapter do not require the assumption that a Nash equilibrium in pure strategies exists. Equally so, it is not needed to identify any such Nash–Cournot equilibrium with the initial position $\underset{\sim}{\bar{x}}$. One does need, however, to think of the initial position as representing an outcome of the underlying non-co-operative universe and to that extent the vector $\underset{\sim}{\bar{x}}$ represents the 'balance of power' in the industry: any co-operative action will constitute an agreed-upon *deviation* from $\underset{\sim}{\bar{x}}$. To indicate the range of co-operative behaviour we need to define the zone of co-operation. One notes the fact that the case of a homogenous commodity is a special case of substitute commodities. To indicate the difference between the cases of substitute and complementary commodities we draw in Figures 6.2(a) and (b) the iso-profit curves of the two firms where in 6.2(a) we assume the commodities to be substitutes while in 6.2(b) we assume them to be complements. An assumption requiring $\pi_j(x_1, x_2)$ to be quasi-concave states that $\{(x_1, x_2) \mid \pi_j(x_1, x_2) \geqslant \alpha\}$ are convex sets and in Figure 6.2(a) this condition is satisfied. In this figure the initial position is $\underset{\sim}{\bar{x}}$ and the efficiency frontier is AB. From the way we draw the isoprofit curves, Firm 1 prefers point A (its profits are higher on lower curves) while Firm 2 prefers point B.

In Figure 6.2(b) we assume the commodities to be complements and thus $\pi_i(x_1, x_2)$ have the opposite curvature thus $\{(x_1, x_2) \mid \pi_j(x_1, x_2) \leqslant \alpha\}$ are convex sets. In this figure Firm 1's profits are higher on higher iso-profit curves thus 1 prefers point A while 2 prefers point B where AB is part of the efficiency frontier.

From Figure 6.2(a) it is clear that for the case of substitute commodities in general and perfect substitutes in particular, given the initial position $\underset{\sim}{\bar{x}}$ the zone of co-operation for the two firms can be defined by:

$$M = \{(x_1, x_2) \mid 0 \leqslant x_1 < \bar{x}_1, 0 \leqslant x_2 < \bar{x}_2\}$$

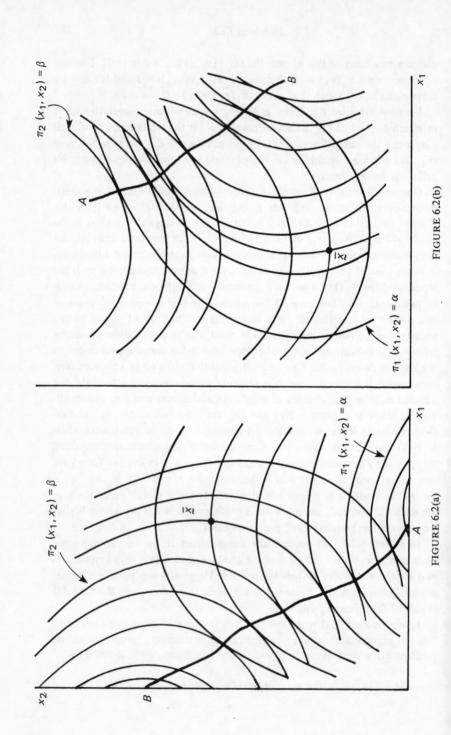

$\pi_2(x_1, x_2) = \beta$

$\pi_1(x_1, x_2) = \alpha$

x_1

x_2

FIGURE 6.2(b)

$\pi_2(x_1, x_2) = \beta$

$\pi_1(x_1, x_2) = \alpha$

x_1

x_2

FIGURE 6.2(a)

This means that co-operative behaviour between the two firms would lead to selection of points (x_1^*, x_2^*) which can be restricted to the set M.

Similarly, in the case of complementary goods the zone of co-operation can be defined by:

$$M^c = \{(x_1 x_2) \mid \bar{x}_1 < x_1, \bar{x}_2 < x_2\}$$

Although in the rest of this chapter we concentrate on the case of substitute commodities it is clear that the case of complements can easily be handled. We can thus introduce the rather natural assumption:

Assumption B: For all $0 \leqslant \underset{\sim}{x} \leqslant \underset{\sim}{\bar{x}}$ we have $\partial \pi_i / \partial x_i > 0$ and $\partial \pi_i / \partial x < 0$, $i = 1, 2$.

Assumption B is really no assumption at all: from (6.1) it is clear that $\partial \pi_i / \partial x_i > 0$ only means that $p(x) + x_i p'(x) > c_i'(x_i)$ which is exactly what co-operation among the firms will achieve. The condition $\partial \pi_i / \partial x < 0$ simply states again that $p'(x) < 0$.

For the case of differentiated commodities we replace Assumption B with Assumption B':

Assumption B': For all $0 \leqslant \underset{\sim}{x} \leqslant \underset{\sim}{\bar{x}}$ we have $\partial \pi_i / \partial x_i > 0$ $i = 1, 2$ and $\partial \pi_i / \partial x_j < 0$ for $i = 1, 2$ $j = 1, 2$.

Examination of the profit function in (6.2) reveals that Assumption B' is really a formalization of the restriction of the analysis to the substitutes case: $\partial \pi_i / \partial x_i > 0$ is an obvious optimality condition and $\partial \pi_i / \partial x_j < 0$ simply means $\partial p_i(x_1, x_2) / \partial x_j < 0$.

THE BASIC PARADIGM OF CO-OPERATION

It was stated earlier that we take the repetition of the game over time to be the fundamental process that enables the formation and enforcement of co-operative behaviour. Both the mechanism as well as the range of possible co-operative outcomes that may result are well known and have appeared in various forms. For example, Luce and Raiffa (1957) discuss it in the context of the supergame and a deeper formal analysis is found in Aumann (1959). An early application in economics was provided by Friedman (1971) followed by many recent writers who exploited this structure (see for example Kurz, 1977; Radner, 1980; Rubinstein, 1979; Green and Porter, 1981, and others). Invoking the mechanism of repetition to generate co-operation is most appropriate in the case of an oligopoly market. Here the game is repeated continuously and within a very short interval of calendar time the players may already have all the verification needed to establish if the implicit co-operative contract is being carried out by all.

The basic theory of co-operation has been formalized as the Folk Theorem which is not associated with any specific author. The theorem itself has two distinct parts: on the one had it states the *fact* that repetition over time, together with the threat strategies which are made available by the repetition, provide the mechanism for co-operation. On the other hand, the theorem contains the rather negative conclusion that in the absence of discounting any individually rational outcome (π_1, π_2) (i.e. an outcome that gives each firm at least what it can assure itself) can be sustained as a Nash equilibrium of the infinitely repeated game. This means that although the Folk Theorem provides the background paradigm for the emergence of co-operation, it cannot provide a basis for predicting any specific co-operative outcome. Some authors hold the view that the existence of multiplicity of potential outcomes in bargaining situations, as predicted by the Folk Theorem, is intrinsic and such ambiguity of the outcome is natural. Our view of this point is that it is not reasonable to expect that a single set of universal principles can be applied to resolve all conflict situations. We further think that much progress can be achieved if we study the problem of co-operation within different families of conflict situations and exploit those features that are unique and natural to each family separately. We approach the problem of co-operation within an oligopolistic industry with the aim of exploiting the important features of market games and this will provide the basis for our modelling below.

In modelling the agreement process we now arrive at the most critical step of the development which is the specification of the criteria for the selection of such an agreement. The standard method for approaching this problem in the social sciences has been to formulate a set of axioms that state what the agreement should be under elementary circumstances in which it is 'self-evident' what the outcome should be. These self-evident situations embody elementary principles of fairness and basic restrictions on the use of power when a compromise is the objective. Although this axiomatic approach has yielded a very rich body of knowledge, a growing number of writers have sought the way to understand co-operative behaviour through the specification of elementary rules according to which the *process* of reaching agreements is conducted. The emphasis on the *process* of reaching agreements and on the *procedure* that defines fairness is well known; apart from such recent writers like Nozick (1974) and

Harsanyi (1977) who employ these principles, the growing literature on incentives and the decentralized implementation of social welfare functions has employed this approach extensively (see, for example, Hurwicz, 1979a and 1979b, and others). In the formulation of the incentive problem it is generally assumed that a planner or a designer has a specific social objective (performance function) that he wants to implement. The problem is how to design a decentralized procedure (i.e. a 'game form') such that its non-co-operative equilibrium yields the same outcome as was desired by the planner.

Turning the incentive problem around, think of the planner's objectives or of the performance function as an 'agreement', or 'implicit contract' among the participants. We then ask the *opposite* question: suppose we restrict ourselves to simple and decentralized procedures (game forms). Do we narrow down the set of agreements that may be implemented as equilibria of the given procedures? As stated, one should have little hope in establishing general principles. However, when restricted to specific classes of conflict situations like oligopolistic markets, one may be more optimistic. In addition, the results will also depend upon the meaning of the requirement that we should restrict ourselves to 'simple' and 'decentralized' procedures. Addressing this particular point, we shall immediately interpret this requirement to mean, here, that the implicit contract among the players must be implemented as a Nash equilibrium of a non-co-operative game where the actions and pay-offs of the players are observable.

In the formulation of an oligopoly problem there is no 'planner' or higher 'authority'. It is thus rather interesting to think of 'an agreement' within the context of our analysis as, in effect, *an agreement to play a non-co-operative game with rules and limitations that constitute the true restrictions that the players accept.* We have already explained that the notion of 'agreement' as a form of agreed-upon 'procedures' or 'rules' rather than outcomes is well known. Yet is appears that this concept may provide a bridge between co-operative game theory and recent work on incentive mechanisms. This important question will be addressed again at the end of the fifth section

IMPLEMENTATION OF IMPLICIT CONTRACTS VIA A GAME FORM

We start by first examining the crucial question of transfers. Since we conduct the analysis under the conditions of no entry an immediate question arises. If the duopolists can agree on any production plan, then the problem of finding a co-operative arrangement among the two firms can be divided into two separate decisions: first the firms maximize joint industry profits, and finding the solution for this problem is straightforward. Then, the duopolists must seek rules of dividing these maximal industry profits between them. A solution to this second problem may require extensive transfer payments and *in our treatment of the duopoly problem such transfers are not feasible*. This means that implicit co-operative agreements between the duopolists must take the form of co-ordination of actions rather than actual integration of operations.

Our view of the issue of transfer payments suggests that to some extent anti-trust policy as practised in many countries has focused on prohibiting oligopolistic industries from turning into cartels via the route of mergers and takeovers. We shall define in this chapter a new concept of 'co-operative duopoly equilibrium' which arises as an implicit contract between the two firms. It thus remains to be investigated whether public policy that permits the formation of cartels could be superior to the policy that prevents transfer payments and results in an equilibrium like the one we analyse in this chapter.

In order to formulate the implicit contract between the duopolists, we shall define a *co-ordination mechanism* that will be implemented via a Nash equilibrium of some non-co-operative game. The essence of this implicit contract is *the agreement between the firms to play the game*. The method of our analysis is to define a general family of such games and then specify an elementary set of desirable properties of the co-ordination mechanism which, in turn, impose restrictions on the generally stated individual strategy spaces. Analysis of the existence and characterization of such equilibria is the ultimate purpose.

Formulation of the Family of Games

We denote by F the family of games $G(\underset{\sim}{\pi}, \underset{\sim}{\bar{x}})$ and this notation is used to indicate that different sets of games are associated with different vectors $\underset{\sim}{\pi}$ of profit functions and vectors $\underset{\sim}{x}$ of initial positions.

We provide here a general definition of the family F by specifying the following characteristics of any game in the family:

(1) The set of players is $N = \{1, 2\}$.
(2) The strategy spaces of the players, $j = 1$, 2, are denoted by $S_j(\underset{\sim}{\pi}, \underset{\sim}{\bar{x}}) \subset R^2$. Each $\sigma_j \epsilon S_j(\underset{\sim}{\pi}, \underset{\sim}{\bar{x}})$ consists of a vector of output changes $\underset{\sim}{z}^j$ such that:

$$\underset{\sim}{z}^j = (z^j_1, z^j_2) \epsilon R^2, \underset{\sim}{z}^j \leqslant \underset{\sim}{\bar{x}}, j = 1, 2 \qquad (6.3)$$

(3) For any 2-tuple of strategies $\underset{\sim}{\sigma} = (\underset{\sim}{z}^1\ \underset{\sim}{z}^2)$ we define the *outcome change* vector $\underset{\sim}{z}$ relative to $\underset{\sim}{x}$ by:

$$\underset{\sim}{z} = \tfrac{1}{2}(\underset{\sim}{z}^1 + \underset{\sim}{z}^2)$$

and the *resulting output* $\underset{\sim}{x}$ by $\underset{\sim}{x} = \bar{x} - \underset{\sim}{z}$. Since $\underset{\sim}{z}^j \leqslant \bar{x}$ it follows that $\underset{\sim}{z} \leqslant \bar{x}$ and $\underset{\sim}{x} \geqslant 0$ thus no additional feasibility conditions are needed.

(4) The *pay-off vector* $H_i(\underset{\sim}{\sigma})$ is then defined by:

$$H_i(\sigma) = \pi_i(\bar{x}_i - z_i, \bar{x} - z) \tag{6.4}$$

where $\underset{\sim}{z} = (z_1, z_2)$ and $z = z_1 + z_2$.

The game is played by each firm proposing a reduction $\underset{\sim}{z}^j$ in the outputs of the two firms (including itself). The actual change in outputs is $\underset{\sim}{z} = \tfrac{1}{2} (\underset{\sim}{z}^1 + \underset{\sim}{z}^2)$ resulting in an outcome vector of $\underset{\sim}{x} = \bar{x} - \underset{\sim}{z}$ and pay-off $H_i(\sigma)$ $i = 1, 2$.

Inspection of conditions (1)–(4) indicates that each pair $(\underset{\sim}{\pi}, \bar{x})$ is associated with a set $G(\underset{\sim}{\pi}, \bar{x})$ of games and each $G(\underset{\sim}{\pi}, \bar{x})$ is a particular member of this set. In the rest of this chapter we shall refer to $G(\underset{\sim}{\pi}, \bar{x})$ as a particular game rather than the entire set $G(\underset{\sim}{\pi}, \underset{\sim}{x})$.

The main object of our analysis is the sets $S_i(\underset{\sim}{\pi}, \bar{x})$ and restrictions on these sets constitute the essence of what we regard as co-ordination. In accepting the restrictions on $S_i(\underset{\sim}{\pi}, \bar{x})$ the duopolists agree to be permitted to act in their best interests so that the desired co-ordinated outcome is implemented by a Nash equilibrium of the game with restricted strategy spaces.

What are reasonable restrictions on the strategy spaces $S_i(\underset{\sim}{\pi}, \bar{x})$? Three properties emerge in a natural way from the description of the game and these are formulated in the following assumptions:

C.1: $S_i(\underset{\sim}{\pi}, \bar{x})$ are closed convex sets.

C.2: $\underset{\sim}{0} \in S_i(\underset{\sim}{\pi}, \bar{x})$ where $\underset{\sim}{0} = (0, 0)$.

C.3: $S_i(\underset{\sim}{\pi}, \bar{x})$ are of full dimension in R^2.

Property C.1 is natural but note that we are not assuming $S_i(\underset{\sim}{\pi}, \bar{x})$ to be compact. Property C.2 permits a player to propose no change at all and property C.3 is essentially a 'free disposal' type of assumption allowing interior strategies which are harmful to i to be feasible.

The 'adding up' condition (3) which defines the outcomes in $G(\underset{\sim}{\pi}, \underset{\sim}{\bar{x}})$ appears rather restrictive since it suggests a strict linear relation among the proposals made by the players. We suggest that this linearity is not essential to the results of this chapter. In order to explain this point suppose first that we replace the condition:

$$\underset{\sim}{z} = \tfrac{1}{2}(\underset{\sim}{z}^1 + \underset{\sim}{z}^2)$$

with a more general condition;

$$\underset{\sim}{z} = F(\underset{\sim}{z}^1, \underset{\sim}{z}^2) \qquad (6.5)$$

where $F(\cdot, \cdot)$ is some function, monotonic in all four variables. Now consider the extreme case where $F(\underset{\sim}{z}^1, \underset{\sim}{z}^2) = \underset{\sim}{0} \in R^2$ for all $\underset{\sim}{z}^1 \in R^2$ $\underset{\sim}{z}^2 \in R^2$. In this case no matter what restrictions are placed on the strategy spaces of the two players the only feasible point is $\underset{\sim}{\bar{x}}$ since for all strategic choices, $\underset{\sim}{z} = \underset{\sim}{0}$. On the other hand, if the outcome function is $\underset{\sim}{z} = \tfrac{1}{2}(\underset{\sim}{z}^1 + \underset{\sim}{z}^2$ then given a strategy $\underset{\sim}{z}^1$ of player 1, any point in R^2 is attainable by the other player provided his strategy space is not restricted and thus *the only restrictions on the outcomes are those imposed on the strategy spaces*. In general, there exists some 'substitution', in terms of outcomes, between restrictions on the strategy spaces and restrictions imposed on the outcome function $F(\underset{\sim}{z}^1, \underset{\sim}{z}^2)$. However, we shall argue that very mild conditions are needed to show that non-linearities in the outcome functions are not relevant. To do this assume that $F(\cdot, \cdot)$ is strictly monotonic and hold $\underset{\sim}{z}^2$ constant at the level $\underset{\sim}{\hat{z}}^2$. Now define the following set:

$$F(R^2, \underset{\sim}{\hat{z}}^2) = \{ \underset{\sim}{z} \mid \underset{\sim}{z} = F(\underset{\sim}{z}^1, \underset{\sim}{\hat{z}}^2), \underset{\sim}{z}^1 \in R^2 \}$$

This set contains all outcomes which are feasible for player 1 if he has an unrestricted strategy space and if player 2 maintains his action at $\underset{\sim}{\hat{z}}^2$. Now define the set:

$$T_1(\underset{\sim}{\hat{z}}^2, \underset{\sim}{\bar{x}}) = \{ \underset{\sim}{y} \mid \underset{\sim}{y} = \underset{\sim}{x} - \underset{\sim}{z}, \underset{\sim}{z} \in F(R^2, \underset{\sim}{\hat{z}}^2) \}$$

Player 1 is said to be *co-operatively effective* if for all $\underset{\sim}{\hat{z}}^2, T_1(\underset{\sim}{\hat{z}}^2, \underset{\sim}{\bar{x}}) \supset M$ This means that if Firm 1 is co-operatively effective then it can, on its own, induce any outcome in the desirable set M provided there is no limitation on the strategies $\underset{\sim}{z}^1$ which it may employ. It should now be clear that if both firms are co-operatively effective the non-linear outcome function $F(\underset{\sim}{z}^1, \underset{\sim}{z}^2)$ places no restrictions on the set of feasible co-operative outcomes in M. Moreover, any limitations on the set of outcomes which can be induced by a player will originate in limitations on the strategy spaces, and in that case the non-linearity of the outcome function plays no role in the analysis.

In seeking agreement the players may agree to restrict their strategy spaces or to impose restrictions on the outcome function. We find it more natural, for the problem at hand, to restrict the strategy spaces and for this reason we adopt the outcome function $\underset{\sim}{z} = \frac{1}{2}(\underset{\sim}{z}^1 + \underset{\sim}{z}^2)$ as a technical simplification.

Co-ordination Mechanism

We turn now to the study of the *co-ordination mechanism* which we denote by the correspondence $\psi(\underset{\sim}{\pi}, \overline{\underset{\sim}{x}})$. This mechanism associates with every pair $(\underset{\sim}{\pi}, \overline{\underset{\sim}{x}})$ a set of allocations $\underset{\sim}{x} \in R^2$ which we can think of as 'coordinated agreement points'. Such points result from the selection of some $\underset{\sim}{z}^j \in S_j(\underset{\sim}{\pi}, \overline{\underset{\sim}{x}})$, $j = 1, 2$ which then yield $\underset{\sim}{x} - \overline{\underset{\sim}{x}} = \frac{1}{2}(z^1 + z^2)$. We study the structure of $\psi(\underset{\sim}{\pi}, \overline{x})$ by specifying a set of elementary properties that the co-ordinated mechanism must satisfy. To state these properties let $\underset{\sim}{x}^* \in \psi(\underset{\sim}{\pi}, \overline{\underset{\sim}{x}})$ then:

P.1: $\underset{\sim}{x}^*$ is individually rational relative to $\overline{\underset{\sim}{x}}$.

P.2: $\underset{\sim}{x}^*$ is Pareto optimal.

P.3: *Nash implementability*: $\underset{\sim}{x}^*$ is implementable by a Nash equilibrium $(\underset{\sim}{z}^{1*}, \underset{\sim}{z}^{2*})$ of some game $G(\underset{\sim}{\pi}, \overline{\underset{\sim}{x}}) \in F$ with $\overline{\underset{\sim}{x}} - \underset{\sim}{x}^* = \frac{1}{2}(\underset{\sim}{z}^{1*} + \underset{\sim}{z}^{2*})$.

P.4: *Stability*: (i) $\underset{\sim}{x}^* \in \psi(\underset{\sim}{\pi}, \underset{\sim}{x}^*)$.
(ii) for any $(\underset{\sim}{\pi}, \overline{x})$ there exists an open neighbourhood $\underset{\sim}{U}$ of $\underset{\sim}{0} \in R^2$ such that for $i = 1, 2$
$$\{S_i(\underset{\sim}{\pi}, \underset{\sim}{x}) \cap U\} \subset S_i(\underset{\sim}{\pi}, \underset{\sim}{x}^*).$$

The properties of individual rationality and Pareto optimality are compelling properties and any concept of 'agreement' under conditions of complete information must necessarily adopt them. It is interesting to note, however, that these two are properties of the *outcome* rather than properties of the *procedure* to reach an outcome. The new properties P.3 and P.4 address the essential ideas of this chapter since they reflect conditions on the process of reaching and monitoring agreements.

The concept of 'Nash implementability' is very common in the incentive literature. It is a well known-decentralization property that reduces drastically the informational requirements of each player. More specifically, apart from knowing the game and the identity of the other players, each player has to know only his own strategy space. The optimal behaviour of the players relative to their own strategy spaces will lead to a unanimously agreed upon outcome. This is one formalization of the idea of 'co-operation' being an 'agreement to play a non-co-operative game' whose solution would be regarded as an agreed-upon outcome. The analytical faults of the notion of Nash implementability may suggest to some that other concepts like dominant strategy equilibrium should be preferable but we shall not examine such alternatives here.

Property P.4 is composed of two parts, both of which attempt to reflect different aspects of the idea that an agreement to an outcome x^* should be stable in the sense that it should not alter the strategic options of the players. We interpret this stability requirement in two ways. First, if we move from $\bar{x}$ to x^* and then treat x^* as a *new initial position* then from that initial position x^* still remains the agreed outcome. A second view of stability relates to the strategic options themselves. In an earlier version of this chapter we simply assumed that $S_i(\pi, \bar{x}) \subset S_i(\pi, x^*)$ thus suggesting that the act of agreement to move from $\bar{x}$ to x^* does not reduce the strategic options of the players. This condition clearly implies P.4 (ii). In P.4 (ii) we weaken this assumption to require that the strategic options of a player are not reduced *only when confined to small deviations*. We formulate this by requiring that for each problem $(\pi, \bar{x})$ there exists a neighbourhood U of the origin of $0 \in R^2$ such that for $i = 1, 2$ $S_i(\pi, \bar{x}) \cap U$ is contained in $S_i(\pi, x^*)$. In Figure 6.3 we show an example in which the condition $S_1(\pi, \bar{x}) \subset S_1(\pi, x^*)$ is not satisfied but P.4 (ii) is satisfied. In this diagram we draw $S_1(\pi, \bar{x}^*)$ as a compact set while $S_i(\pi, x)$ is not. Clearly, there exists a neighbourhood U of 0 such that the 'small' strategies available in $S_i(\pi, \bar{x}) \cap U$ are also available in $S_i(\pi, \bar{x}^*)$. The idea behind this condition is that a player may not be concerned only with the outcome x^* but also with the effect of small deviations from the equilibrium. He may regard it a serious disadvantage if strategic options around the equilibrium were lost owing to an agreement to move the initial position from $\bar{x}$ to x^*. One may also regard P.4 (ii) as a *continuity condition.*

A word about mixed strategies. In the discussion above, such strategies were not allowed as part of the co-ordination mechanism. Thus, if the feasible set of profits is convex, no mixed strategy equilibria are needed, and the problem does not arise. One important reason to exclude mixed strategies is the fact that behind any production level x_i the firm must engage in an investment programme to attain x_i. Since investments are not necessarily reversible, a mixture of x_i with x_i' may not be feasible.

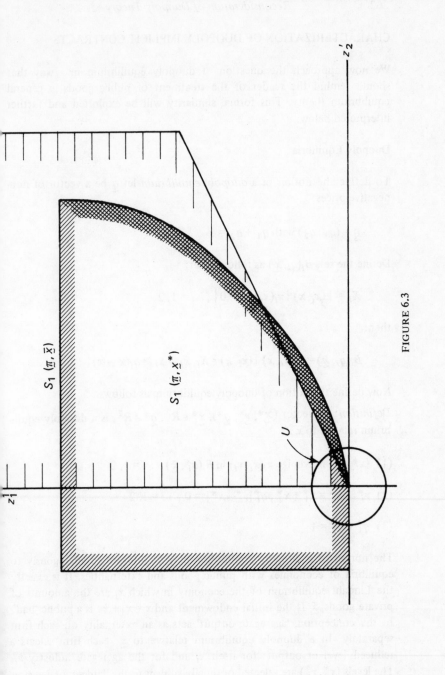

FIGURE 6.3

CHARACTERIZATION OF DUOPOLY IMPLICIT CONTRACTS

We now approach the question of duopoly equilibrium in a way that should remind the reader of the treatment of public goods in general equilibrium theory. This formal similarity will be exploited and further interpreted below.

Duopoly Equilibria

To define the notion of a *duopoly equilibrium* let $\underset{\sim}{q}$ be a vector of non-negative prices:

$$\underset{\sim}{q} = (q_1, q_2) \text{ with } q_1 + q_2 = 1$$

Define the sets $B_i(q_i, \underset{\sim}{x})$ as follows: Let:

$$X_i = \left\{ (x_i, x) \mid \pi_i(x_i, x) \geqslant 0 \right\}, \quad i = 1, 2$$

then:

$$B_i(q_i, \underset{\sim}{\bar{x}}) = \left\{ (x_i, x) \mid (x_i, x) \in X_i, \bar{x}_i - x_i \geqslant q_i(x - x) \right\}$$

Now define the notion of duopoly equilibrium as follows:

Definition: A vector $(\underset{\sim}{x}^*, \underset{\sim}{v}^*, \underset{\sim}{q}^*)$, $\underset{\sim}{x}^* \in R^2$, $\underset{\sim}{q}^* \in R^2$, is a duopoly equilibrium relative to $\bar{x}$ if:

(1) (x_i^*, v_i^*) maximize $\pi_i(x_i, v_i)$ in $B_i(q_i^*, \underset{\sim}{\bar{x}})$, $\quad i = 1, 2$

(2) $v_i^* \geqslant x^* = x_1^* + x_2^*$, $q_i^*[v_i^* - x^*] = 0$, $\quad i = 1, 2$

(3) $q_1^* + q_2^* = 1$

The notion of a duopoly equilibrium may be interpreted analogously to equilibria of economies with public goods and externalities. It is exactly the Lindahl equilibrium of the economy in which x_i are the amounts of private goods, $\underset{\sim}{\bar{x}}$ is the initial endowment and $x = x_1 + x_2$ is a public 'bad'. In this conception, 'aggregate output' acts as an externality on each firm separately. In a duopoly equilibrium relative to $\underset{\sim}{\bar{x}}$, each firm selects a reduced level of output: for itself x_i and for the aggregate industry v_i. The levels (x_i^*, v_i^*) are selected optimally subject to the 'budget. or decision set $\bar{x}_i - x_i \geqslant q_i^*(\bar{x} - v_i)$ and if $q_i^* > 0$ $i = 1, 2$, then we have the unanimity condition:

$$v_i^* = x^* = x_1^* + x_2^*, \quad i = 1, 2 \tag{6.6}$$

The analogy with a Lindahl equilibrium is useful in understanding the notion of duopoly equilibrium as proposed here. In the case of pure congestion externality the *'Lindahl agreement'* leads to a Pareto-optimal allocation by each firm contributing to the reduction of the negative externality at an exchange rate q_i between the aggregate externality x and the private good x_i. In a duopoly equilibrium the reduction in each firm's output is its contribution to the reduction of aggregate output leading to a Pareto-optimal allocation of output where the notion of Pareto optimality is used here only in reference to the profits of the firms.

We finally denote by $D(\underset{\sim}{\pi}, \bar{\underset{\sim}{x}})$ the set:

$$D(\underset{\sim}{\pi}, \bar{\underset{\sim}{x}}) = \left\{ \underset{\sim}{x} \mid (\underset{\sim}{x}, \underset{\sim}{v}, \underset{\sim}{q}) \text{ is a duopoly equilibrium relative to } \bar{\underset{\sim}{x}} \right\} \tag{6.7}$$

To make the analysis interesting we assume in this chapter that $\bar{\underset{\sim}{x}} \notin D(\underset{\sim}{\pi}, \bar{\underset{\sim}{x}})$.

The Basic Theorems

We are now ready to state the two main results of this chapter.

Theorem A: There exists a co-ordination mechanism $\psi(\underset{\sim}{\pi}, \bar{\underset{\sim}{x}})$ satisfying properties P.1–P.4 such that for all $(\underset{\sim}{\pi}, \bar{\underset{\sim}{x}})$, $\psi(\underset{\sim}{\pi}, \bar{\underset{\sim}{x}}) \neq \phi$.

Theorem B: For all $(\underset{\sim}{\pi}, \bar{\underset{\sim}{x}})$, $D(\underset{\sim}{\pi}, \bar{\underset{\sim}{x}}) = \psi(\underset{\sim}{\pi}, \bar{\underset{\sim}{x}})$.

Before proceeding to the formal part of the analysis we briefly discuss the two theorems.

It is important to see the distinction between the process in which the economy reaches points in $D(\underset{\sim}{\pi}, \underset{\sim}{x})$ and points in $\psi(\underset{\sim}{\pi}, \underset{\sim}{x})$. In a duopoly equilibrium the decision sets $B_i(\underset{\sim}{q}_i, \bar{\underset{\sim}{x}})$ are constructed in such a way that *unanimity* is reached between the firms about the final output vector $\underset{\sim}{x}^*$. On the other hand, a Nash equilibrium in $G(\pi, \bar{\underset{\sim}{x}})$ results in *equilibrium change vectors* $\underset{\sim}{z}^j$ which induce an aggregate output vector $\underset{\sim}{x}$ defined by $\bar{\underset{\sim}{x}} - \underset{\sim}{x} = \frac{1}{2}(\underset{\sim}{z}^1 + \underset{\sim}{z}^2)$. These change vectors $\underset{\sim}{z}^j$ are selected from the very general strategy spaces $S_i(\underset{\sim}{\pi}, \bar{\underset{\sim}{x}})$ satisfying a rather elementary set of properties. The conditions P.1–P.4 required of any co-ordination mechanism appear to allow a fairly large set of points in $\psi(\underset{\sim}{\pi}, \bar{\underset{\sim}{x}})$. Yet the equivalence of $D(\underset{\sim}{\pi}, \bar{\underset{\sim}{x}})$ with $\psi(\underset{\sim}{\pi}, \bar{\underset{\sim}{x}})$ leads us to conclude that in the context of oligopolistic co-operation a duopoly equilibrium has such compelling properties that one may view it as a rather comprehensive theory of the outcome of oligopolistic co-ordination.

Theorem B resembles similar results of Hurwicz (1979b) (Theorem 3 and 4) in the context of a production economy with private and public goods where a planner implements a given fixed performance function via a Nash equilibrium of a corresponding game. Since the planner has essentially a fixed game with fixed strategy (message) spaces and a fixed performance function, Hurwicz imposes conditions on the class of admissible economies (in terms of various linearity conditions on utilities) and specifies the behaviour of Nash equilibria of such economies. In contrast we put no restrictions on the class of admissible economies but seek restrictions on the strategy spaces of the players. Hurwicz's main conclusions are that the set of Lindahl equilibria is implementable as Nash equilibria and under additional restrictions the two sets coincide. Although the context of a planned economy is drastically different from ours we still regard our work here as intimately related to Hurwicz's work. Moreover, we seek to establish the basic connection between incentive mechanisms and co-operative game theory and while Hurwicz seeks to identify the Lindahl allocations as implementable in an economy with public goods, we suggest that the structure of the 'Lindahl agreements' has a wider applicability. Here we identify the set of duopoly equilibria relative to $\bar{\underset{\sim}{x}}$ as a reasonable co-operative solution of a wide class of conflict situations. To put it differently, we suggest that any conflict situation that leads to strategic behaviour on the part of the players, has the basic character of interactions among the players. These are similar to externalities, public goods or public bads familiar from the theory of public finance. Thus, our use of the Lindahl construction, which we call duopoly equilibrium, to identify a possible co-operative solution of such situations is not only natural to economic thinking but it also provides a more unified concept of market functioning. We remark that the problem of co-operation is simplified when the object of co-operation is reduced in dimensionality, as is the case in markets with homogeneous products in which the aggregate industry output depresses the profits of all the sellers via the homogeneous effect on price. The allocation problems in such markets have the same structure as models of 'pure congestion' where the common congested atmosphere acts as a 'public bad' on the utility of all the participants. This clearly shows why oligopolistic markets with differentiated commodities will generate a more complex set of co-operative equilibria than the one presented here.

Diagrammatic Representation of Theorem B

Continuing our exposition in Figure 6.2, we use Figure 6.4 to explain Theorem B. In this figure the iso-profit curves $\pi_1(x_1, x_2) = \alpha$ and $\pi_2(x_1, x_2) = \beta$ are drawn and the collection of all tangency points is the set of Pareto-optimal allocations. The initial position is drawn so as to represent the Nash–Cournot equilibrium at which $\partial \pi_i / \partial x_i = 0$, $i = 1, 2$. The point $\underset{\sim}{x}^*$ is a duopoly equilibrium relative to $\underset{\sim}{\bar{x}}$ where the line from $\underset{\sim}{\bar{x}}$ to $\underset{\sim}{x}^*$ represents the price system (q_1^*, q_2^*). In a game $G(\underset{\sim}{\pi}, \underset{\sim}{\bar{x}})$, a Nash equilibrium is attained by one firm selecting $\frac{1}{2}\underset{\sim}{z}^1$ to be equal to the vector

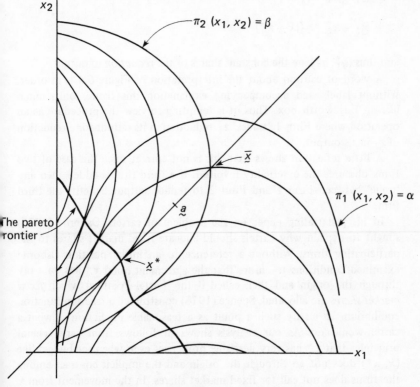

FIGURE 6.4

$(\bar{\underset{\sim}{x}} - \underset{\sim}{a})$ and the second firm selecting $\frac{1}{2}z^2 = (\underset{\sim}{a} - \underset{\sim}{x}^*)$. Since we are drawing Figure 6.4 in the (x_1, x_2) plane the budget sets of the duopolists are defined by the inequalities $(\bar{x}_1 - x_1)q_2^* \geqslant (\bar{x}_2 - x_2)q_1^*$ and $(\bar{x}_2 - x_2)q_1^* \geqslant (\bar{x}_1 - x_1)q_2^*$ and hence the line $(\bar{\underset{\sim}{x}}, \underset{\sim}{x}^*)$ is represented by the equation:

$$(\bar{x}_2 - x_2) = \frac{q_2^*}{q_1^*}(\bar{x}_1 - x_1)$$

It is then clear that as firms move from $\bar{\underset{\sim}{x}}$ to $\underset{\sim}{x}^*$ *they do not, in general, maintain a constant market share.* On the other hand, the aggregate *reduction* in output $(\bar{x} - x^*)$ is shared by the two duopolists at the constant proportions q_1^* and q_2^* since:

$$\bar{\underset{\sim}{x}}_1 - x_1^* = q_1^*(\bar{x} - x^*)$$

$$\bar{\underset{\sim}{x}}_2 - x_2^* = q_2^*(\bar{x} - x^*)$$

and thus (q_1^*, q_2^*) are the constant shares of the *reduction* in output.

A word of caution about the interpretation of Figure 6.4 is in order. Without labels and accompanying explanation this figure looks much like an Edgeworth box. Thus, it is tempting to view the procedure as an operation where Firm 1 'trades' z_1 reduction in its output for a reduction of z_2 in z's output.

A little reflection shows that this is not correct since the case of two firms obscures the externality involved: if a third firm is added then any 'trade' between Firm 1 and Firm 2 to reduce output benefits the third firm.

In his penetrating paper on the problem of cartels, Osborne (1976) sought to explain why cartels should allocate fixed market shares to the participating firms. Without a reference to an initial position Osborne examined conditions to ensure that the agreement point $\underset{\sim}{x}^*$ lies on a ray through the origin and then called it the 'Cartel Point' at which *fixed market shares* are allocated. Spence (1978) constructed a reaction function equilibrium to justify such a point as a reasonable prediction of what a cartel would do. As our analysis shows, it follows from very general principles that $\underset{\sim}{x}^*$ has very desirable properties even when the budget line $(\bar{\underset{\sim}{x}}, \underset{\sim}{x}^*)$ does not go through the origin and the implicit contract among the firms does not call for fixed market shares. In the movement from $\underset{\sim}{x}$ to $\underset{\sim}{x}^*$ firms experience fixed shares of the reduction of output.

Proofs of the Theorems

It is clear that Theorem A follows directly from Theorem B since for any economy that satisfies Assumptions A and B a duopoly equilibrium always exists. (See for example Bergstrom, 1976.) Thus, we need to prove only Theorem B.

A. $D(\underset{\sim}{\pi}, \underset{\sim}{\bar{x}}) \subset \psi(\underset{\sim}{\pi}, \underset{\sim}{\bar{x}})$

If $\underset{\sim}{x}^* \in D(\underset{\sim}{\pi}, \underset{\sim}{x})$ with price q^* then it is well known from the theory of public goods (e.g. see Bergstrom, 1976) that $\underset{\sim}{x}^*$ is an individually rational and a Pareto-optimal allocation. We need to exhibit a co-ordination mechanism $(\psi(\underset{\sim}{\pi}, \underset{\sim}{\bar{x}})$ satisfying properties P.3–P.4 and $\underset{\sim}{x}^* \in \psi(\underset{\sim}{\pi}, \underset{\sim}{\bar{x}})$. We do this constructively by exhibiting a family $G(\underset{\sim}{\pi}, \underset{\sim}{\bar{x}})$ such that $(\underset{\sim}{z}^{1}{}^*, \underset{\sim}{z}^{2}{}^*)$ is a Nash equilibrium in $G(\underset{\sim}{\pi}, \underset{\sim}{\bar{x}})$ and $\underset{\sim}{\bar{x}} - x^* = \frac{1}{2}(\underset{\sim}{z}^{1}{}^* + \underset{\sim}{z}^{2}{}^*) = \underset{\sim}{z}^*$.

Let the set of players be $N = \{1, 2\}$ and the family of strategy spaces defined by:

$$S_i(\underset{\sim}{\pi}, \underset{\sim}{\bar{x}}) = \{\, \underset{\sim}{z}^i \mid \underset{\sim}{z}^i_i \geqslant q_i^*(z_1^i + z_2^i) \ , \underset{\sim}{z}^i \leqslant \underset{\sim}{\bar{x}} \,\} \ i = 1, 2 \tag{6.8}$$

Note that although $(\underset{\sim}{\pi}, \underset{\sim}{x})$ does not appear explicitly on the right of (6.8) it does enter the parametrization of $S_i(\underset{\sim}{\pi}, \underset{\sim}{x})$ via the vector (q_1^*, q_2^*).

Now consider the following set of equations:

$$\begin{cases} z_i^{i*} = q_i^*(z_1^{i*} + z_2^{i*}) & , \quad i = 1, 2 \\ q_i^*(\bar{x} - x^*) = \frac{1}{2}(z_i^{1}{}^* + z_i^{2}{}^*), & i = 1, 2 \end{cases} \tag{6.9}$$

The system (6.9) has four equations and four unknowns z_j^{i*} and a non-negative solution for z_j^{i*} exists. For example:

$$z_j^{i*} = q_j^*(\bar{x} - x^*) \tag{6.10}$$

We now assert that $(\underset{\sim}{z}^{1}{}^*, \underset{\sim}{z}^{2}{}^*)$ is a Nash equilibrium in the game defined by (6.8) above. To demonstrate this assume that $\underset{\sim}{z}^2 = \underset{\sim}{z}^{2}{}^*$ and player 1 will select $z^1 \in S_1(\underset{\sim}{\pi}, \underset{\sim}{\bar{x}})$ so as to solve the following problem:

$$\text{Maximize } \pi_1(\bar{x}_1 - \tfrac{1}{2}z_1^{2}{}^* - \tfrac{1}{2}z_1^1, \bar{x}_2 - \tfrac{1}{2}z_2^{2}{}^* - \tfrac{1}{2}z_2^1) \tag{6.11}$$
$$\underset{\sim}{z}^1 \in S_1(\underset{\sim}{\pi}, \underset{\sim}{\bar{x}})$$

Now consider the following optimization:

$$\text{Maximize } \pi_1(\overline{x}_1 - z_1, x_2 - z_2) \tag{6.12a}$$
$$(z_1, z_2)$$

subject to:

$$z_1 \geqslant q_1^*(z_1 + z_2) \tag{6.12b}$$

By virtue of the fact that $\underset{\sim}{x}^* \in D(\underset{\sim}{\pi}, \overline{\underset{\sim}{x}})$ with prices $\underset{\sim}{q}^*$, the pair (z_1^*, z_2^*) solves the maximization problem (6.12a)–(6.12b). However, it is also feasible in $G(\underset{\sim}{\pi}, \overline{\underset{\sim}{x}})$ since by (6.9) $q_1^* z^* = q_1^*(x - x^*) = z_1^* = \frac{1}{2}(z_1^{1*} + z_1^{2*})$ and $\underset{\sim}{z}^1 = \underset{\sim}{z}^{1*}$ is feasible (and thus optimal) in the more restrictive maximization defined by (6.11) and (6.8). A completely symmetric argument applies to player 2 and it then follows that $\underset{\sim}{z}^{i*}$, $i = 1, 2$ is a Nash equilibrium in $G(\underset{\sim}{\pi}, \overline{\underset{\sim}{x}})$.

To prove property P.4 note first that if $\underset{\sim}{x}^* \in D(\underset{\sim}{\pi}, \overline{\underset{\sim}{x}})$ with prices $\underset{\sim}{q}^*$ it is also true that $\underset{\sim}{x}^* \in D(\underset{\sim}{\pi}, \underset{\sim}{x}^*)$ with prices $\underset{\sim}{q}^*$. This means that we can define $G(\underset{\sim}{\pi}, \overline{\underset{\sim}{x}})$ and $G(\underset{\sim}{\pi}, \underset{\sim}{x}^*)$ with the identical strategy spaces specified in (6.8), that is:

$$S_i(\pi, \overline{\underset{\sim}{x}}) = S_i(\underset{\sim}{\pi}, \underset{\sim}{x}^*) \tag{6.13}$$

and hence $x^* \in \psi(\underset{\sim}{\pi}, \underset{\sim}{x}^*)$.

B. $\psi(\underset{\sim}{\pi}, \overline{\underset{\sim}{x}}) \subset D(\underset{\sim}{\pi}, \overline{\underset{\sim}{x}})$

Let $\underset{\sim}{x}^* \in \psi(\underset{\sim}{\pi}, \overline{\underset{\sim}{x}})$. Hence x^* is a Pareto-optimal allocation that is implemented by a Nash equilibrium of some game $G(\underset{\sim}{\pi}, \overline{\underset{\sim}{x}}) \in F$. This means that there exists $\underset{\sim}{z}^{i*} \in S_i(\underset{\sim}{\pi}, \overline{\underset{\sim}{x}})$ such that $(\underset{\sim}{z}^{1*}, \underset{\sim}{z}^{2*})$ is a Nash equilibrium in $G(\underset{\sim}{\pi}, \overline{\underset{\sim}{x}})$ and $\underset{\sim}{z}^* = \underset{\sim}{z}^{1*} + \underset{\sim}{z}^{2*} = \overline{\underset{\sim}{x}} - \underset{\sim}{x}^*$.

B.1 *Existence of Prices*

Define the following set:

$$T(\underset{\sim}{\pi}, \underset{\sim}{x}^*, \overline{\underset{\sim}{x}}) = \left\{ (z_1^1, z^1, z_2^2, z^2) \,\middle|\, \begin{array}{l} \underset{\sim}{z}^i \in S_i(\underset{\sim}{\pi}, \underset{\sim}{x}) \,, \quad i = 1, 2 \\[6pt] \underset{\sim}{z}^1 = (z_1^1, z_2^1) \,, \ z^1 = z_1^1 + z_2^1 \\[6pt] \underset{\sim}{z}^2 = (z_1^2, z_2^2) \,, \ z^2 = z_1^2 + z_2^2 \end{array} \right\} \tag{6.14}$$

Since the strategy spaces are closed and convex it follows that $T(\underset{\sim}{\pi}, \underset{\sim}{x}^*, \overline{x})$ is closed and convex. Moreover, since $(\underset{\sim}{z}^{1*}, z^{2*})$ is a Nash equilibrium in $G(\underset{\sim}{\pi}, \overline{x})$ the point $(z_1^{1*}, z^{1*}, z_2^{2*}, z^{2*})$ is a boundary point of $T(\underset{\sim}{\pi}, \underset{\sim}{x}^*, \overline{x})$. To prove this point, suppose $(z_1^{1*}, z^{1*}, z_2^{2*}, z^{2*})$ is an interior point of $T(\pi, x^*, \overline{x})$. Since $S_i(\pi, \overline{x}) \subset R^2$ are of full dimension it follows that there exists $(\hat{z}^1, \hat{z}^2)$ in $T(\underset{\sim}{\pi}, \underset{\sim}{x}^*, \overline{x})$ such that $\hat{z}_1^1 < z_1^{1*}, \hat{z}_2^1 > z_2^{1*}$ and $\hat{z}^2 = \underset{\sim}{z}^2*$. But since at $\underset{\sim}{x}^* \partial\pi_1/\partial x_1 > 0$ and $\partial\pi_1/\partial x_2 < 0$ it follows that $\hat{z}^1$ is a more desirable strategy for 1 thus violating the Nash equilibrium property of $(\underset{\sim}{z}^{1*}, \underset{\sim}{z}^{2*})$.

It follows from the supporting hyperplane theorem that there exists a vector of prices:

$$(p_{11}^*, p_{12}^*, p_{21}^*, p_{22}^*) \tag{6.15}$$

such that for all $(z_1^1, z^1, z_2^2, z^2) \in T(\underset{\sim}{\pi}, \underset{\sim}{x}^*, \overline{x})$ we have:

$$p_{11}^* z_1^1 + p_{12}^* z^1 + p_{22}^* z_2^2 + p_{21}^* z^2 \leqslant p_{11}^* z_1^{1*} + p_{12}^* z^{1*} + p_{22}^* z_2^{2*} \\ + p_{21}^* z^{2*} \tag{6.16}$$

and it thus follows that:

$$p_{11}^* z_1^1 + p_{12}^* z^1 \leqslant p_{11}^* z_1^{1*} + p_{12}^* z^{1*} \text{ for all } \underset{\sim}{z}^1 \in S_1(\underset{\sim}{\pi}, \overline{x}) \tag{6.17a}$$

$$p_{22}^* z_2^2 + p_{21}^* z^2 \leqslant p_{22}^* z_2^{2*} + p_{21}^* z^{2*} \text{ for all } \underset{\sim}{z}^2 \in S_2(\underset{\sim}{\pi}, \overline{x}) \tag{6.17b}$$

By Assumption B:

$$\left. \frac{\partial\pi_i}{\partial x_i} \right|_{\underset{\sim}{x}^*} > 0 \quad , \quad i = 1, 2 \tag{6.18}$$

$$\left. \frac{\partial\pi_i}{\partial x} \right|_{\underset{\sim}{x}^*} < 0 \quad , \quad i = 1, 2$$

and hence:

$$p_{11}^* < 0 \quad p_{12}^* > 0 \quad p_{22}^* < 0 \quad p_{21}^* > 0 \tag{6.19}$$

Normalizing both (6.17a) and (6.17b) we can rewrite these conditions as follows:

$$-z_1^1 + q_1^* z^1 \leqslant -z_1^{1*} + q_1^* z^{1*} \text{ for all } \underset{\sim}{z}^1 \in S_1(\underset{\sim}{\pi}, \bar{\underset{\sim}{x}}) \tag{6.20a}$$

$$-z_2^2 + q_2^* z^2 \leqslant -z_2^{2*} + q_2^* z^{2*} \text{ for all } \underset{\sim}{z}^2 \in S_2(\underset{\sim}{\pi}, \bar{\underset{\sim}{x}}) \tag{6.20b}$$

where $q_1^* = -\dfrac{p_{12}^*}{p_{11}^*} \qquad q_2^* = -\dfrac{p_{21}^*}{p_{22}^*}$

Since $(0, 0) \in S_i(\underset{\sim}{\pi}, \bar{\underset{\sim}{x}})$ it follows that:

$$0 \leqslant -z_1^{1*} + q_1^* z^{1*} \tag{6.21a}$$

$$0 \leqslant -z_2^{2*} + q_2^* z^{2*} \tag{6.21b}$$

B.2 *(6.21a) – (6.21b) are Equalities*

$\underset{\sim}{z}^{1*}$ solves the maximization problem:

$$\underset{\underset{\sim}{z}^1 \in S_2(\underset{\sim}{\pi}, \bar{\underset{\sim}{x}})}{\text{Max}} \quad \pi_1(\bar{x}_1 - \tfrac{1}{2}z_1^{2*} - \tfrac{1}{2}z_1^1, \bar{x} - \tfrac{1}{2}z^{2*} - \tfrac{1}{2}z^1) \tag{6.22a}$$

and $\underset{\sim}{z}^{2*}$ solves the maximization problem:

$$\underset{\underset{\sim}{z}^2 \in S_2(\underset{\sim}{\pi}, \bar{\underset{\sim}{x}})}{\text{Max}} \quad \pi_2(\bar{x}_2 - \tfrac{1}{2}z_2^{1*} - \tfrac{1}{2}z_2^2, \bar{x} - \tfrac{1}{2}z^{1*} - \tfrac{1}{2}z^2) \tag{6.22b}$$

From Assumption B and (6.19) it follows that there exist constants ξ_1^* > 0 and $\xi_2^* > 0$ such that:

$$\begin{cases} \left. \dfrac{\partial \pi_1}{\partial x_1} \right|_{\underset{\sim}{x}^*} = \xi_1^* & \left. \dfrac{\partial \pi_2}{\partial x} \right|_{\underset{\sim}{x}^*} = -\xi_2^* q_2^* \\[4mm] \left. \dfrac{\partial \pi_1}{\partial x} \right|_{\underset{\sim}{x}^*} = -\xi_1^* q_1^* & \left. \dfrac{\partial \pi_2}{\partial x_2} \right|_{\underset{\sim}{x}^*} = \xi_2^* \end{cases} \tag{6.23}$$

and hence, at $\underset{\sim}{x}^*$ we can define the functions:

$$\eta_1(\underset{\sim}{x}^*) = -\frac{\dfrac{1}{\partial x_1}\Big|_{\underset{\sim}{x}^*}}{\dfrac{\partial \pi_1}{\partial x}\Big|_{\underset{\sim}{x}^*}} = \frac{1}{q_1^*} \qquad \eta_2(\underset{\sim}{x}^*) = -\frac{\dfrac{2}{\partial x_2}\Big|_{x^*}}{\dfrac{\partial \pi_2}{\partial x}\Big|_{x^*}} = \frac{1}{q_2^*} \qquad (6.24)$$

By P.4 (i) we have $\underset{\sim}{x}^* \in \psi(\underset{\sim}{\pi}, \underset{\sim}{x}^*)$ and hence $(\underset{\sim}{0}, \underset{\sim}{0})$ is a Nash equilibrium in some game $G(\underset{\sim}{\pi}, \underset{\sim}{x}^*)$. Thus, define the set $T(\underset{\sim}{\pi}, \underset{\sim}{x}^*, \underset{\sim}{x})$ in an analogous manner to (6.14) and prove the existence of supporting hyperplane $(p_{11}, p_{12}, p_{22}, p_{21})$ to the set $T(\underset{\sim}{\pi}, \underset{\sim}{x}^*, \underset{\sim}{x})$ at $(\underset{\sim}{0}, \underset{\sim}{0})$. Now define:

$$Q = \left\{ (q_1, q_2) \;\middle|\; \begin{array}{l} q_1 = \dfrac{p_{12}}{p_{11}} \quad q_2 = -\dfrac{p_{21}}{p_{22}} \quad \text{and} \\[2mm] (p_{11}, p_{12}, p_{22}, p_{21}) \text{ is a supporting hyperplane of} \\[2mm] T(\underset{\sim}{\pi}, \underset{\sim}{x}^*, \underset{\sim}{x}) \text{ at } (\underset{\sim}{0}, \underset{\sim}{0}) \end{array} \right\}$$

Using a procedure similar to the one employed in (6.16)–(6.20) above, we note that for any $(\hat{q}_1, \hat{q}_2) \in Q$ we have the following conditions:

$$-z_1^1 + \hat{q}_1 z^1 \leqslant 0 \text{ for all } \underset{\sim}{z}^1 \in S_1(\underset{\sim}{\pi}, \underset{\sim}{x}^*) \qquad (6.25a)$$

$$-z_2^2 + \hat{q}_2 z^2 \leqslant 0 \text{ for all } \underset{\sim}{z}^2 \in S_2(\underset{\sim}{\pi}, \underset{\sim}{x}^*) \qquad (6.25b)$$

On the other hand, using the reasoning of (6.22a)–(6.22b) with respect to $(\underset{\sim}{0}, \underset{\sim}{0})$ being a Nash equilibrium in $G(\underset{\sim}{\pi}, \underset{\sim}{x}^*)$ we conclude that any $(q_1, q_2) \in Q$ is characterized by the two conditions:

$$\frac{1}{q_1} = \eta_1(x^*)$$

$$\frac{1}{q_2} = \eta_2(x^*)$$

It now follows from (6.24) that $(q_1^*, q_2^*) \in Q$. Hence, by (6.25a)–(6.25b) we conclude that:

$$-z_1^1 + q_1^* z^1 \leqslant 0 \text{ for all } \underset{\sim}{z}^1 \in S_1(\underset{\sim}{\pi}, \underset{\sim}{x}^*) \tag{6.26a}$$

$$-z_2^2 + q_2^* z^2 \leqslant 0 \text{ for all } \underset{\sim}{z}^2 \in S_2(\underset{\sim}{\pi}, \underset{\sim}{x}^*) \tag{6.26b}$$

Finally, since $\underset{\sim}{z}^{1*} \in S_1(\underset{\sim}{\pi}, \bar{x})$ and $\underset{\sim}{z}^{2*} \in S_2(\underset{\sim}{\pi}, \bar{x})$ it follows from P.4 (ii) that there exist $\mu_1 > 0$ and $\mu_2 > 0$ such that:

$$\mu_1 \underset{\sim}{z}^{1*} \in S_1(\underset{\sim}{\pi}, \underset{\sim}{x}^*)$$

$$\mu_2 \underset{\sim}{z}^{2*} \in S_2(\underset{\sim}{\pi}, \underset{\sim}{x}^*)$$

and by (6.26a)–(6.26b) we have:

$$-\mu_1 z_1^{1*} + \mu_1 q_1^* z^{1*} \leqslant 0$$

$$-\mu_2 z_2^{2*} + \mu_2 q_2^* z^{2*} \leqslant 0$$

and this implies:

$$-z_1^{1*} + q_1^* z^{1*} \leqslant 0 \tag{6.27a}$$

$$-z_2^{2*} + q_2^* z^{2*} \leqslant 0 \tag{6.27b}$$

Now combine (6.21a)–(6.21b) with (6.27a)–(6.27b) to conclude first that:

$$z_1^{1*} = q_1^* z^{1*} \tag{6.28a}$$

$$z_2^{2*} = q_2^* z^{2*} \tag{6.28b}$$

However, (6.28a)–(6.28b) together with (6.20a)–(6.20b) imply the following 'budget restrictions':

$$z_1^1 \geqslant q_1^* z^1 \text{ for all } \underset{\sim}{z}^1 \in S_1(\underset{\sim}{\pi}, \bar{x}) \tag{6.29a}$$

$$z_2^2 \geqslant q_2^* z^2 \text{ for all } \underset{\sim}{z}^2 \in S_2(\underset{\sim}{\pi}, \bar{x}) \tag{6.29b}$$

B.3 $\underset{\sim}{x}^* \epsilon\ D\ (\underset{\sim}{\pi}, \bar{x})$ *with* $\underset{\sim}{q}^* = (q_1^*, q_2^*)$ *as Supporting Prices*

In order to prove that $\underset{\sim}{x}^* \epsilon\ D(\underset{\sim}{\pi}, \bar{x})$ we need to prove that $\underset{\sim}{x}^*$ is the solution of the following maximization problems:

1. $\underset{(x_1, x)}{\text{Max}}\ \ \pi_1(x_1, x)$

   subject to $\bar{x}_1 - x_1 \geqslant q_1^*(\bar{x} - x)$

2. $\underset{(x_2, x)}{\text{Max}}\ \ \pi_2(x_2, x)$

   subject to $\bar{x}_2 - x_2 \geqslant q_2^*(\bar{x} - x)$

By Assumption B the conditions which then define $\underset{\sim}{x}^*$ can be specified as follows:

$$\eta_1(\underset{\sim}{x}^*) = \frac{1}{q_1^*} \tag{6.30a}$$

$$\bar{x}_1 - x_1^* = q_1^*(\bar{x} - x^*) \tag{6.30b}$$

and:

$$\eta_2(\underset{\sim}{x}^*) = \frac{1}{q_2^*} \tag{6.31a}$$

$$\bar{x}_2 - x_2^* = q_2^*(\bar{x} - x^*) \tag{6.31b}$$

Clearly (6.30a) and (6.31a) are satisfied by (6.24). For $\underset{\sim}{x}^*$ to be a duopoly equilibrium we must also prove (6.30b) and (6.31b) which together require:

$$q_1^* + q_2^* = 1$$

To prove this condition note that since $\underset{\sim}{x}^* \epsilon\ \psi(\underset{\sim}{\pi}, \bar{x})$ it follows that $\underset{\sim}{x}^*$ is Pareto optimal and thus there exist $\lambda_1^* \geqslant 0$ and $\lambda_2^* \geqslant 0$ (with $\lambda_i^* > 0$ for some $i = 1, 2$) such that $\underset{\sim}{x}^*$ maximizes $\lambda_1^* \pi_1(x_1, x) + \lambda_2^* \pi_2(x_2, x)$. Again, using Assumption B we show that $\lambda_1^* > 0$ and $\lambda_2^* \geqslant 0$ and at $\underset{\sim}{x}^*$ we have:

$$\lambda_1^* \frac{\partial \pi_1}{\partial x_1}\bigg|_{\underset{\sim}{x}^*} + \left[\lambda_1^* \frac{\partial \pi_1}{\partial x}\bigg|_{\underset{\sim}{x}^*} + \lambda_2^* \frac{\partial \pi_2}{\partial x}\bigg|_{\underset{\sim}{x}^*} \right] = 0$$

$$\lambda_2^* \frac{\partial \pi_2}{\partial x_2}\bigg|_{\underset{\sim}{x}^*} + \left[\lambda_1^* \frac{\partial \pi_1}{\partial x}\bigg|_{\underset{\sim}{x}^*} + \lambda_2^* \frac{\partial \pi_2}{\partial x}\bigg|_{\underset{\sim}{x}^*} \right] = 0$$

From (6.23) we then have that:

$$\lambda_1^* \xi_1^* - (\lambda_1^* \xi_1^* q_1^* + \lambda_2^* \xi_2^* q_2^*) = 0 \tag{6.32a}$$

$$\lambda_2^* \xi_2^* - (\lambda_2^* \xi_1^* q_1^* + \lambda_2^* \xi_2^* q_2^*) = 0 \tag{6.32b}$$

Now denote the expression:

$$\lambda_1^* \xi_1^* q_1^* + \lambda_2^* \xi_2^* q_2^* = k$$

and using (6.32a)–(6.32b) we have:

$$\lambda_1^* \xi_1^* q_1^* = k q_1^* \tag{6.33a}$$

$$\lambda_2^* \xi_2^* q_2^* = k q_2^* \tag{6.33b}$$

Adding up (6.33a) and (6.33b) we obtain:

$$\lambda_1^* \xi_1^* q_1^* + \lambda_2^* \xi_2^* q_2^* = k(q_1^* + q_2^*)$$

hence, we finally deduce:

$$q_1^* + q_2^* = 1$$

This proves that $\underset{\sim}{x}^* \in D(\underset{\sim}{\pi}, \underset{\sim}{\bar{x}})$.

DIFFERENTIATED COMMODITIES

A duopoly with differentiated commodities can formally be expressed (as in (2)) by the profit functions:

$$(2) \quad \pi_i(x_1, x_2) = x_i p_i(x_1, x_2) - c_i(x_i), \quad i = 1, 2$$

It is clear that the case of a homogeneous commodity is simply the one where for $i = 1, 2, p_i(x_1, x_2) = p(x_1 + x_2)$. The adaptation of the machinery developed earlier to the case of a duopoly with differentiated products is rather simple. A family F^D of games can be defined in exactly the same way as F above except that we replace the pay-off function $H_i(\underset{\sim}{\sigma})$ in condition (4) of the characterization of F by the function:

$$(4')\ H_i^D(\underset{\sim}{g}) = \pi_i(\bar{x}_1 - z_1, \bar{x}_2 - z_2)$$

With the family F^D defined we introduce the co-ordination mechanism $\psi^D(\underset{\sim}{\pi}, \bar{x})$ and properties P.1–P.4 remain unchanged.

A slightly more significant difference exists in the interpretation of the results. Whereas, in the homogeneous case we could write expressions like $z^j = z_1^j + z_2^j$, such a sum has no meaning in the heterogenous case. Since sums like this appear in the definitions of the sets $B_i(q_i, \underset{\sim}{x})$ it may appear that in order to preserve the spirit of Theorem B a major adaptation of the concept of a duopoly equilibrium is called for. We shall now explain that the concept is completely independent of the homogeneity assumption and only a formal adaptation is needed. To see this we recast the inequalities that define $B_i(q_i, \bar{x})$ (p. 262) in the following way: player 1 selects (u_1, u_2) and player 2 selects (v_1, v_2) subject to:

$$(1 - q_1)(\bar{x}_1 - u_1) \geqslant q_1(\bar{x}_2 - u_2) \text{ for player 1} \tag{6.34a}$$

$$(1 - q_2)(\bar{x}_2 - v_2) \geqslant q_2(\bar{x}_1 - v_1) \text{ for player 2} \tag{6.34b}$$

(6.34a)–(6.34b) can be written as:

$$\bar{x}_1 - u \geqslant \frac{q_1}{1 - q_1} (\bar{x}_2 - u_2)$$

$$\bar{x}_2 - v_2 \geqslant \frac{q_2}{1 - q_2} (\bar{x}_1 - v_1)$$

Now define $p = q_1/(1 - q_1)$ (with $p = 0$ if $q_1 = 0$) and $q = q_2/(1 - q_2)$ (with $q = 0$ if $q_2 = 0$) and rewrite (6.34a)–(6.34b) as:

$$\overset{\ast}{x}_1 - u_1 \geqslant p(\bar{x}_2 - u_2) \tag{6.35a}$$

$$\bar{x}_2 - v_2 \geqslant q(\bar{x}_1 - v_1) \tag{6.35b}$$

We elected to use the budget definitions on p. 262 because of the natural intepretation of the prices q_i $i = 1$, 2 as marginal shares which must, in equilibrium, satisfy $q_1^* + q_2^* = 1$. As a share of the total change z the interpretation of q_i is natural in the homogeneous case where we write $z_i \geqslant q_i z$. In the heterogeneous case, there is no natural aggregate and the concept of 'share' is not useful. Instead, in (6.35a)–(6.35b) we obtain a clearer view of how the players 'trade' in the negative effects (externalities) they have on each other. In seeking agreement, (6.35a) suggests that Firm 1 can propose to reduce its output from $\bar{x}_1$ to u_1 in exchange for Firm 2 reducing its output from $\bar{x}_2$ to u_2 which has a total 'value' of $p(\bar{x}_2 - u_2)$ where the numeraire of this valuation is Commodity 1. Similarly, using Commodity 1 as a numeraire, (6.35b) suggests that Firm 2 can propose a reduction of its output valued at $(1/q)(\bar{x}_2 - v_2)$ in exchange for a reduction of $\bar{x}_1 - v_1$ in Firm 1's output. Recalling that this discussion applies to the market with a homogeneous commodity, at a duopoly equilibrium in such a market we have $q_1^* + q_2^* = 1$. However, since:

$$p^* = \frac{q_1^*}{1 - q_1^*} = \frac{q_1^*}{q_2^*} \qquad q^* = \frac{q_2^*}{1 - q_2^*} = \frac{q_2^*}{q_1^*}$$

we conclude that relative to (6.35a)–(6.35b) the equilibrium conditions would include:

$$p^* = \frac{1}{q^*} \text{ if } p^* > 0 \text{ and } q^* > 0 \tag{6.36a}$$

$$p^*[u_2^* - v_2^*] = 0 \tag{6.36b}$$

$$q^*[v_1^* - u_1^*] = 0 \tag{6.36c}$$

It is clear that conditions (6.36a)–(6.36c) do not involve the assumption of product homogeneity and to that extent they highlight the fact that the definition of duopoly equilibrium does not presume product homogeneity. With this in mind we are now ready to return to the analysis of duopoly equilibrium in markets with differentiated commodities.

Let:

$$X_1 = \left\{ (u_1, u_2) \mid \pi_1(u_1, u_2) \geqslant 0 \right\}$$

$$X_2 = \left\{ (v_1, v_2) \mid \pi_2(v_1, v_2) \geqslant 0 \right\}$$

Now define:

$$B_1(p, \underset{\sim}{\bar{x}}) = \left\{ (u_1, u_2) \mid (u_1, u_2) \in X_1, \bar{x}_1 - u_1 \geqslant p(\bar{x}_2 - u_2) \right\}$$

$$B_2(q, \underset{\sim}{\bar{x}}) = \left\{ (v_1, v_2) \mid (v_1, v_2) \in X_2, \bar{x}_2 - v_2 \geqslant q(\bar{x}_1 - v_1) \right\}$$

Definition: A vector $((x_1^*, x_2^*), (u_1^*, u_2^*), (v_1^*, v_2^*), (p^*, q^*)) \in R^8$ is a *duopoly equilibrium* relative to $\underset{\sim}{\bar{x}}$ in a market with differentiated commodities if:

1. (u_1^*, u_2^*) maximizes $\pi_1(u_1, u_2)$ in $B_1(p, \bar{x})$

   (v_1^*, v_2^*) maximizes $\pi_2(v_1, v_2)$ in $B_2(q, \bar{x})$

2. $p^*[u_2^* - v_2^*] = 0 \quad x_2^* = \text{Min}[u_2^*, v_2^*]$

   $q^* = [v_1^* - u_1^*] = 0 \quad x_1^* = \text{Min}[u_1^*, v_1^*]$

3. $p^* = \dfrac{1}{q^*}$ if $p^* > 0$ and $q^* > 0$

Finally, denote by $D^D(\underset{\sim}{\pi}, \bar{x})$ the set:

$$D^D(\underset{\sim}{\pi}, \underset{\sim}{\bar{x}}) = \left\{ (x_1^*, x_2^*) \,\middle|\, \begin{array}{l} ((x_1^*, x_2^*), (u_1^*, u_2^*), (v_1^*, v_2^*), (p^*, q^*)) \text{ is a} \\[4pt] \text{duopoly equilibrium in the market with} \\[4pt] \text{differentiated commodities} \end{array} \right\}$$

Replacing Assumption B with Assumption B′, we now have the following results:

Theorem C: For all $(\underset{\sim}{\pi}, \underset{\sim}{\bar{x}})$, $\psi^D(\underset{\sim}{\pi}, \underset{\sim}{\bar{x}}) \neq \phi$

Theorem D: For all $(\underset{\sim}{\pi}, \underset{\sim}{\bar{x}})$, $\psi^D(\underset{\sim}{\pi}, \underset{\sim}{\bar{x}}) = D^D(\underset{\sim}{\pi}, \underset{\sim}{\bar{x}})$

We conclude that the validity of the results of p. 263 does not depend upon the assumption of homogeneous commodities made on pp. 250–1.

SOME CONCLUDING REMARKS

This chapter proposes a view of duopoly that is in sharp contrast to either the Cournot or the Bertrand view of an oligopolistic industry. It is true that free and costless entry and exit will leave very little room for profitability from duopolistic co-operation. However, we seriously doubt that an oligopoly model of free and costless entry and exit with all investments being reversible is of great interest. This means that if a duopoly enjoys any degree of protection against profitable entry it becomes natural to ask what should we expect the allocation with the duopoly to be.

The co-operative theory that we propose for a duopoly is, in principle, applicable to any oligopolistic industry and the extension of the present model to the case of *n* firms is only nautral. Moreover, the analysis here suggests a general equilibrium theory that integrates the co-operative behaviour of oligopolistic industries with the behaviour of competitive industries. This notion of a general equilibrium is rather novel: it visualizes a state in which firms within oligopolistic industries are acting co-operatively, firms within competitive industries are acting competitively while firms across all industries are acting non-co-operatively. Such a view of economic activity is not entirely new since even the conventional model of a competitive industry visualizes the agents within each firm as acting co-operatively. Yet a theory of a general equilibrium that encompasses co-operative as well as competitive behaviour being formed simultaneously, is yet to be formalized.

REFERENCES

Aumann, R. (1959) 'Acceptable Points in General Cooperative n-person Game', in A. W. Tucker and R. D. Luce (eds) *Contributions to the Theory of Games, Vol. IV* (Annals of Mathematics Studies, no. 40), Princeton: Princeton University Press, pp. 287–324.

Baumol, W. J. (1982) 'Contestable Markets: An Uprising in the Theory of Industry Structure', *American Economic Review*, 72 (1) (March): 1–16.

Baumol, W. J., J. C. Panzar and R. D. Willig (1982) *Contestable Markets and the Theory of Industry Structure*, New York: Harcourt Brace Jovanovich.

Bergstrom, T. C. (1975) 'The Core When Strategies Are Restricted by Law', *Review of Economic Studies*, 42 (130) (April): 249–57.

Bergstrom, T. C. (1976) 'Collective Choice and the Lindahl Allocation Method', in S. A. V. Lin (ed.), *Theory and Measurement of Economic Externalities*, New York: Academic Press, pp. 111–31.

Bertrand, J. (1882) 'Theories mathematique de la richesse sociale', *Journal des Savants*, 68, Paris (September) 499–508.

Binmore, K. G. (1980) 'Nash Bargaining Theory II', ICERD discussion paper 80/14, London School of Economics.

Chamberlin, E. H. (1933) *The Theory of Monopolistic Competition*, Cambridge, Mass.: Harvard University Press.

Cournot, A. A. (1838) *Reserches sur le principes mathematiques de al theorie des richesses*, Paris: M. Riviere.

Dixit, A. (1980a) 'A Model of Duopoly Suggesting a Theory of Entry Barriers', *Bell Journal of Economics*, 10: 20–32.

Dixit, A. (1980b) 'The Roel of Investment in Entry Deterrence', *Economic Journal*, 90: 95–106.

Edgeworth, F. Y. (1925) *Papers Relating to Political Economy*, vol. I, London: Macmillan.

Fellner, W. (1949) *Competition Among the Few*, New York: Alfred A. Knopf.

Friedman, J. W. (1971) 'A Non-Cooperative Equilibrium for Supergames', *Review of Economic Studies*, 28 (113) (January) 1–12.

Green, E. J., and R. H. Porter (1981) 'Non-cooperative Collusion Under Imperfect Price Information', unpublished manuscript, California Institute of Technology (January).

Grossman, S. (1981) 'Nash–Equilibrium and the Industrial Organization of Markets with Large Fixed Costs', *Econometrica*, 49: 1149–72.

Harsanyi, J. C. (1977) 'Rule Utilitarianism and Decision Theory', *Erkenntnis*, 11: 25–33.

Hotelling, H. (1929) 'Stability in Competition', *Economic Journal*, 39 (March) 47–51.

Hurwicz, L. (1979a) 'Outcome Functions Yielding Walrasian and Lindahl Allocations at Nash–Equilibrium Points', *Review of Economic Studies*, 143 (April) 217–26.

Hurwicz, L. (1979b) 'On Allocations Attainable Through Nash Equilibria', *Journal of Economic Theory*, 21 (1) (August) 140–65.

Kurz, M. (1977) 'Altruistic Equilibrium', in B. Balassa and R. Nelson (eds), *Economic Progress, Private Values, and Public Policy*, Amsterdam: North-Holland, pp. 177–200.

Luce, D. R., and H. Raiffa (1957) *Games and Decisions*, New York: John Wiley.

Maskin, E., and J. Tirole (1982) 'Dynamic Oligopoly', private communication.

Mayberry, J. P., M. Shubik and J. Nash (1953) 'A Comparison of Treatments of a Duopoly Situation', *Econometrica*, 31 (January) 141–54.

Novshek, W. (1980) 'Cournot Equilibrium with Free Entry', *Review of Economic Studies*, 148 (April) 473–86.

Novshek, W., and H. Sonnenschein (1980) 'Small Efficient Scale as a Foundation for Walrasian Equilibrium', *Journal of Economic Theory*, 22 (2) (April) 243–55.

Nozick, R. (1974) *Anarchy, State, and Utopia*, New York: Basic Books.

Osborne, D. K. (1976) 'Cartel Problems', *American Economic Review*, 66 (5) (December) 835–44.

Porter, R. H. (1979) 'Detection of Dynamic Cartel Enforcement', unpublished manuscript, Princeton University.

Porter, R. H. (1981) 'Optimal Cartel Trigger Price Strategies', Discussion Paper no. 81–143, University of Minnesota (February).

Radner, R. (1980) 'Collusive Behaviour in Non-Cooperative Epsilon-Equilibria of Oligopolies with Long But Finite Lives, *Journal of Economic Theory*, 22 (2) (April) 136–57.

Rubinstein, A. (1979) 'Strong Perfect Equilibria in Supergames', *International Journal of Game Theory*, 9: 1–12.

Shubik, M. (1955) 'A Comparison of Treatment of a Duopoly Situation (Part II)', *Econometrica*, 33 (October) 417–31.

Shubik, M. (1959) *Strategy and Market Structure*, New York: John Wiley.

Shubik, M. (1968) 'A Further Comparison of Some Models of Duopoly', *Western Economic Journal*, 6 (4) (September) 260–76.

Shubik, M. (1974) 'Information, Duopoly and Competitive Markets: A Sensitivity Analysis', *Kyklos*, 26 (4) 736–60.

Spence, M. (1978) 'Efficient Collusion and Reaction Functions', *Canadian Journal of Economics*, 11 (3) (August) 527–33.

Stackelberg, H. von (1934) *Maktform und gleichgewicht*, Berlin: Julius Springer.

7 The Oligopolistic Industry Under Rivalrous Consonance with Target-Rate-of-Return Objectives

ROBERT E. KUENNE

RIVALROUS CONSONANCE: A THEORY OF OLIGOPOLY[1]

The theory of rivalrous consonance as a tool of analysis of oligopolistic behaviour is grounded upon the premise that every oligopolistic industry is characterized by a *de facto* power structure. Each firm has, within its corporate consciousness, a decision-shaping image of each of its rivals that includes that rival's market threat, leadership or followership status, aggressive or passive bent, objectives, and many other facets of behaviour or attitude relevant to the industry in question. Moreover, each firm may have, over and beyond these one-to-one visions of its relations to its rivals, a sense of obligation to the industry, springing notably from the sector's reputation for dependable products, technological advance, or stable behaviour.

Basically, therefore, each firm views itself as a member of a community in which it possesses neither the anonymity of the pure competitor nor the exclusivity of the pure monopolist. Its behaviour is interpreted as 'communitarian': a mixture of the egoistic and the altruistic, with the latter in large part a reflection of the former, but also containing a genuinely independent component, especially in mature oligopolistic and long-established firms with some pride of ancestry. We mean to capture all of these complicated, interdependent, and industry-unique aspects of the oligopolistic market environment in the concept of 'power structure'. It contains an industry-specific blend of the competitive and the co-operative, reflecting a 'rivalrous consonance of interests' among the firms in their decision-making. Neither 'wars of survival' nor cartel-like joint profit maximization characterize mature oligopolistic functioning, but rather a

281

blend of the two motivations that differs from firm to firm and industry to industry.

The central problem of the theorist of oligopolistic decision-making is to capture this power structure and to develop generalizable rules for so doing. The notion of 'interdependence of decision-making' as the core feature of the market structure is too narrow. It reflects the economist's inability to permit the realistic 'sociological' matrix of the industry to intrude meaningfully upon the conventional, unidimensional 'rationality' approach which enters his modelling in one guise or another: Cournot models, game theory, conjectural variation, joint profit maximization, and the rest. It is difficult to understand how much progress can be registered in the theory of oligopoly without a direct, frontal assault upon the complex task of isolating the firm-to-firm power structure of the industry.

A troublesome implication of this position for the 'one big theory' analyst is the limited generalizability of worthwhile frameworks in oligopoly study. Categories and methodologies may have a unifying function, but the hope that universals can be derived in the form of theorems to yield insights into 'oligopolistic behaviour' must be abandoned. Methods and frameworks must be tailored to specific industry conditions in specific periods, and insights largely confined to those specifics. The 'institutional' dominates the general as the power structure becomes more important in determining the firms' objectives and conditioning their actions, and more diffuse than such simplistic approximations as 'price leadership', 'price followership', or 'dominant firm' structures capture. The oligopoly theorist is not permitted the indulgence of ignoring the rich variety of reality to favour the fascinating abstractions of mathematical methodology. The foible has already reduced the field of general equilibrium theory to a killing ground for potentially insightful theory, but its inherent limitations have fortunately restricted the damage to an overdeveloped purely competitive theory.

Models of oligopoly will have to be numerically specified for the derivation of useful insights, therefore, and displacement analyses will have to be conducted by sensitivity analysis involving finite changes in parameters. A new body of analytical techniques is required to give guidelines to 'simulative theorizing' for the efficient use of such parametric displacements to derive insights into the structure and functioning of the specific industry in a numerically specified environment. Such models will wisely focus upon the efficient derivation of knowledge concerning the structure of the industry and its functional implications rather than the forecasting of prices or outputs into the future.

The derivation of power structures and their usage in a rivalrous consonance framework is but one necessity for operational oligopoly theory. A second is a recognition of the multi-objective nature of the oligopolistic firm's decision-making. A large body of empirical research makes clear[2] that a corporation's policies are shaped by a variety of goals whose implications for optimal prices or quantities may be contradictory. Hence, optimal values for such variables reflect a compromise among the goals and no doubt among the ambitions of the various loci within the firms that champion them. Moreover, different goals tend to receive different emphases among firms within the same industry or between industries, and hence another important constraint upon the generalizability of theory is encountered. Fruitful analysis requires that the goal sets be tailored to each firm during the period under analysis, and that conclusions be generalized with extreme care.

In summary, we desire to formulate frameworks that will permit the derivation of useful structural-functional insights through the incorporation of industry power structures and firms' multiple goals. These methods must permit close tailoring of the models to industry and firm specifics and must also allow 'simulative theorizing' displacements within feasible budget restrictions. Finally, such models must capture the specific blend of the rivalrous and the co-operative that characterizes an oligopolistic community.

In search of such a methodology we have developed the 'crippled optimization' technique within a 'rivalrous consonance' model. Let us assume that m firms i exist in an industry, and each such firm has an objective function $f_i(P; Z_i)$ that encapsulates its *primary* objective in its pricing decisions, where P is the set of industry prices p_i, $i = 1, 2, \ldots, m$, and Z_i is a vector of exogenous factors (national income, prices of imported substitutes, prices of domestic substitutes outside the industry, and so forth) that rival i views as important exogenous factors. The industry is assumed to be price-setting rather than quantity-setting because we believe that decision mode is dominant in the real world. The firm also is associated with a set of goal functions, $g_i(P; Z_i)$, each of which captures a secondary objective in the determination of the firm's prices. For example, the firm's objective function may be to maximize its profits, but subject to goal constraints that specify minimum acceptable market share, upper and/or lower bounds on prices, capacity limitations, maximum sales it will permit a close rival, and so forth.

Each firm then seeks a price, $p_i \in P$, that maximizes or minimizes the sum of its objective function *and its rivals' objective functions* when those rival functions are discounted by 'consonance factors', θ_{ij}, and subject to its own constraint functions. That is, the firm i seeks:

$$\text{Max or Min } V_i = f_i(P;Z_i) + \Sigma_{j \neq i} \theta_{ij} f_j(P;Z_j) \tag{7.1}$$

subject to:

$$g_{i,k}(P;Z_i) \gtrless 0, k = 1, 2, \ldots, n \tag{7.2}$$

$$p_i \geqslant 0$$

In (7.1) firm i seeks to attain a constrained maximum or minimum for its objective function, when that extremum search is crippled by the need to take into account the impact of its pricing decisions upon the objectives of *each* of its rivals. The degree of crippling is proportionate to the importance that firm i attaches to firm j's welfare as revealed by the θ_i vector. Of course, the θ's incorporate the industry's power structure, and are defined in an $m \times m$ matrix, with row vectors θ_i defining the degree of deference shown by firm i to each of its rivals, and with the main diagonal term $\theta_{ii} \equiv 1$.[3]

Each θ_{ij} states, in units of the objective function of firm i, its valuation of a unit of the objective function of firm j. For example, in the case where firms i and j are simply maximizing profits as primary objectives, θ_{ij} states the value in units of its own profit that rival i places upon \$1 of profit or loss for firm j. We shall, in what follows, assume that θ_{ij} ϵ [0, 1], with the lower limit of the interval the Cournot case where the firm pays no heed to its rivals' welfares and the upper limit where it treats the rival's welfare as of co-ordinate importance to its own. Consonance factors within this interval interest us because we are most concerned to analyse 'mature oligopolies' where price wars are eschewed ($\theta_{ij} < 0$) and extreme fear of retribution ($\theta_{ij} > 1$) does not exist. Note, however, that both of these cases can be accommodated in the rivalrous consonance framework.

Each firm solves its relevant systems (7.1) and (7.2) taking its rivals' prices as given, so that in effect m such simultaneous non-linear programming models are solved with the Kuhn–Tucker conditions derived *by differentiating with respect to own-prices only*. Straightforward application of any non-linear programming algorithm may be made to obtain solutions, although we have achieved good results by modifying the Fiacco–McCormick Sequential Unconstrained Minimization Technique (SUMT)[4] either to solve the m programs iteratively and sequentially until a Nash equilibrium is attained or to solve the first-order Kuhn–Tucker conditions simultaneously.[5]

The objective functions that suggest themselves most readily, of course, involve the maximization of 'extended profits', that is, with $f_i(\cdot)$ in (7.1) own-profits and the $f_j(\cdot)$ respective rival profits, subject, of course, to the constraints of (7.2). However, to gain insights into an important realistic oligopolistic motivation and to demonstrate the versatility of rivalrous consonance theory, in this chapter we shall use the model to analyse target-rate-of-return behaviour. Very little seems to have been done in the literature to derive comparative statics insights into the behaviour of firms seeking such an objective, even though the occurrence of the motivation is frequent among large firms.

THE TARGET-RATE-OF-RETURN MODEL: FIRST-ORDER CONDITIONS

We suppose that each firm i in an industry can identify the capital stock K_i dedicated to the production of a good in the commodity group under analysis, and that it aims for a target rate of return $\bar{r}_i$ on such capital. To simplify the analysis, probably at the cost of realism, we shall assume that the firm treats shortfalls and overages of actual rates from target rates as equally undesirable. This is not necessary, as it is possible to build into the objective function any degree of asymmetry desired.

The actual rate of return, r_i, is simply π_i/K_i, where profit is defined as:

$$\pi_i = (p_i - c_i)x_i \tag{7.3}$$

with c_i a constant average (and marginal) cost and x_i sales. The sales function is:

$$x_i = a_i - b_{ii}p_i + \Sigma_{j \neq i}b_{ij}\,p_i + \Sigma_s b_{is}z_{is} \tag{7.4}$$

where $z_{is} \in Z_i$ are exogenous factors. The consonance factors, θ_{ij}, are simply the coefficients that convert *rival target deviations* $(\bar{r}_j - r_j)$ to units of *own target deviations* $(\bar{r}_i - r_i)$.

Firm i's objective function may be written most straightforwardly as:

$$\text{Min } V_i = |s_i| + \Sigma_{j \neq i}\theta_{ij}\,|s_j| \tag{7.5}$$

where firm k's target deviation is symbolized:

$$s_k = \bar{r}_k - r_k \tag{7.6}$$

However, this objective function is difficult to manipulate mathematically and, in addition, 'punishes' departures from target rates only linearly, whereas we anticipate that firms would treat such target deviations as more than linearly undesirable as they grow in size. Both problems could be corrected by the modification:

$$\text{Min } V_i = s_i^2 + \Sigma_{j \neq i} \theta_{ij} s_j^2 \tag{7.7}$$

but it is possible to obtain a function that punishes target deviations more severely by using the exponential form:

$$\text{Min } ETD_i = e^{s_i^2} + \Sigma_{j \neq i} \theta_{ij} e^{s_j^2} \tag{7.8}$$

and we shall use (7.8) as more closely conformant to reality. We will refer to it as firm i's *extended target deviation* (ETD_i) function, and note that it is composed of an *own deviation component* and a *rival deviation component*.

One of the sufficient conditions for each firm's optimization model to yield a global rather than mere local constrained optimum is that (7.8) be convex. To simplify notation, we define firm k's profit margin as:

$$m_k = p_k - c_k \tag{7.9}$$

Then we may write the necessary and sufficient condition for (7.8) to be everywhere (globally) convex in p_i is:

$$\frac{d^2 ETD_i}{dp_i^2} = 2 \left\{ \left[\left(\frac{b_{ii} m_i - x_i}{K_i} \right)^2 (1 + 2s_i^2) + \frac{2b_{ii} s_i}{K_i} \right] e^{s_i^2} \tag{7.10} \right.$$

$$\left. + \Sigma_{j \neq i} \theta_{ij} \left[\left(\frac{-b_{ji} m_j^2}{K_j} \right)^2 (1 + 2s_j^2) \right] e^{s_j^2} \right\} \geqslant 0$$

The summation term is obviously positive if any rival is over- or under-achieving its target rate. As an adverse case, therefore, assume all $\theta_{ij} = 0$. The sign of (7.10) then hinges upon the sign of s_i. If $s_i \geqslant 0$, the condition of (7.10) holds. When $s_i < 0$ it will hold only in neighbourhoods of $s_i = 0$, and hence ETD_i will not be convex outside of these neighbourhoods. In

Figure 7.1(a) we illustrate ETD_i for the case where $\bar{r}_i$ is everywhere greater than or equal to r_i, so that the firm is effectively maximizing profits and convexity rules. On the other hand, Figure 7.1(b) illustrates the non-convexities that occur when r_i lies above $\bar{r}_i$ in domains of p_i. Obviously, in seeking an unconstrained minimum of (7.8) we run the danger of becoming hung up on a local maximum cusp such as exists at p'_i rather than achieving the minimum at one of the points of tangency with the horizontal line at p''_i or p'''_i where $r_i = \bar{r}_i$. Hence, the model will not always be well behaved.

We shall assume that the firms' goal sets are similar in structure and differ only in parameters in order to simplify our presentation. Constraint 1 for firm i is simply a capacity constraint, requiring output to remain within the interval $[0, B_i]$:

1. C_{i1} : $B_i - x_i \geqslant 0$ (7.11a)

Constraint 2 assumes that firm i strives to achieve or surpass a minimum market share, M_i, where M_i is a given level of sales:

2. C_{i2} : $x_i - M_i \geqslant 0$ (7.11b)

The third and fourth constraints assume that the firm has upper and lower limits to admissible prices this period, based upon a benchmark price, $\bar{p}_i$, and an upper bound ratio, T_i^+, and lower bound ratio, T_i^-:

3. C_{i3} : $T_i^+ \bar{p}_i - p_i \geqslant 0$ (7.11c)

4. C_{i4} : $p_i - T_i^- \bar{p}_i \geqslant 0$

Note that C_{i4} replaces the non-negativity restraint upon p_i that would otherwise be necessary.

Systems (7.8) and (7.11) constitute a crippled-optimization non-linear programming model featuring rivalrous consonance, when it is understood that the complete model contains one such set for each of the m firms. It is, of course, a specific version of systems (7.1) and (7.2), and assume that each firm in the industry strives for a target rate of return. Each firm then seeks a constrained crippled minimum by assuming its rivals' prices are given and varying only its price. As rivals' prices do in fact change, along with rival i's, successive iterations re-solve the models until a Nash equilibrium is achieved in which each firm is satisfied with its price given the prices set by all of its rivals.

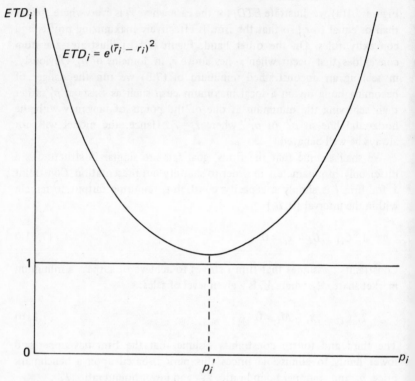

FIGURE 7.1(a)   *Target deviation function for isolated firm i when $r_i < \bar{r}_i$*

On one of these iterations, the Kuhn–Tucker first-order conditions are derived from the Lagrangean form:

$$L_i = ETD_i - \sum_{t=1}^{4} \lambda_{it} C_{it} \qquad (7.12)$$

and are the following:

(a) $\dfrac{\delta L_i}{\delta p_i} \equiv METD_i = s_i((x_i - b_{ii}m_i)/K_i)e^{s_i^2}$

$\qquad + \Sigma_{j\neq i} \vartheta_{ij} s_j (b_{ji} m_j / K_i) e^{s_i^2} - \lambda_{i1} b_{i1}$

$\qquad + \lambda_{i2} b_{ii} + \lambda_{i3} - \lambda_{i4} \geqslant 0$

$\qquad$ where $p_i \, (METD_i) = 0$ $\qquad\qquad (7.13)$

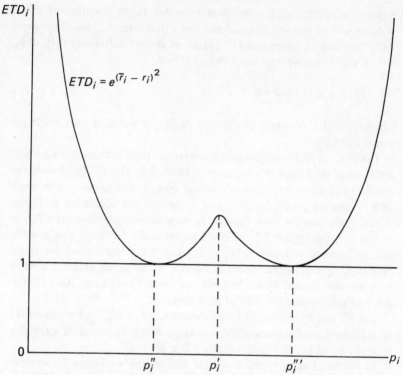

FIGURE 7.1(b)   *Target deviation for isolated firm i when $r_i > \bar{r}_i$*

(b) $\dfrac{\delta L_i}{\delta \lambda_{it}} = C_{it} \geqq 0$

where $\lambda_{it} C_{it} = 0, \quad t = 1, 2, \ldots, 4$

and where $METD_i$ symbolizes the *marginal extended target deviation* for firm i.

If we assume tentatively that none of the constraints binds, then (7.13(a)) may be written, when $e^{s_k^2} \approx 1$:

$$METD_i \equiv s_i((x_i - b_{ii}m_i)/K_i) + \Sigma_{j \neq i}\theta_{ij}s_j(b_{ji}m_j/K_j) = 0 \qquad (7.14)$$

$$\equiv s_i(MRR_{ii}) + \Sigma_{j \neq i}\theta_{ij}s_j(MRR_{ji}) = 0$$

where $MRR_{ki} = \delta r_k/\delta p_i$ is the *marginal rate of return of firm k with respect to* p_i. Hence, the marginal extended target deviation of firm i is composed of an own marginal rate and a rival marginal rate component. As a first step in interpreting (7.14) let us assume tentatively that all θ_{ij} = 0, in which case we may simplify (7.14) to:

$$(\bar{\pi}_i - \pi_i)(d\pi_i/dp_i) = 0 \qquad (7.15)$$

where $\bar{\pi}_i = \bar{r}_i K_i$, or target profit, and $d\pi_i/dp_i$ is *marginal own profit* for firm i, or MOP_i.

Obviously, (7.15) requires that if the target rate of return is not achieved, MOP_i must be 0, but if it is achieved $MOP_i \gtreqless 0$. The ability to state the condition in terms of target and actual own profits permits us to work with a concave profit function and to present the conditions in Figure 7.2 in terms that are more familiar to most economists than the ETD_i in Figure 7.1. On Figure 7.2 we graph actual profit for firm i as a globally strictly concave function of p_i and depict three alternatives for target profit: $\bar{\pi}_i^1$ is everywhere above achievable π_i; $\bar{\pi}_i^2$ is just achievable when π_i is maximized; and $\bar{\pi}_i^3$ can be under- or overachieved by π_i. Also, MOP_i is graphed as the linear function of price that it is.

For $\bar{\pi}_i^1$ and $\bar{\pi}_i^2$ the profit target deviation $s_i K_i = (\bar{\pi}_i - \pi_i)$ is minimized at maximum profit where $MOP_i = 0$ at p_i'. When $\bar{\pi}_i$ intersects $\pi_i(p_i; \bar{p}_j)$, $MOP_i \neq 0$, and (7.15) requires that $s_i = 0$ at p_i'' or p_i'''.

In the latter cases π_i will equal the area $OABp_i''$ on Figure 7.2 whether p_i is p_i'' or p_i''', because, if the latter rules, positive excess profit $Bp_i'p_i''$ must equal the negative excess profit $Cp_i'p_i'''$.[6] The relation between Figures 7.1 and 7.2 should also be made clear at this point. On Figure 7.1(a) the relationship is straightforward for Figure 7.2 when $\bar{\pi}_i^1$ holds, and, of course, for $\bar{\pi}_i^2$ the convex target deviation function 1.a. would merely shift down to tangency with the horizontal line at 1, since $\bar{r}_i$ is attained. The more interesting relationship is with Figure 7.1(b), which is relevant to Figure 7.2 for $\bar{\pi}_i^3$. The target deviation function moves upward from p_i'' to p_i', where it attains a maximum, as is clear from Figure 7.2. The function then falls from p_i' to p_i''', again for reasons that Figure 7.2 reveals.

The danger that we pointed out in the discussion of (7.13) is that an algorithm that searches out a zero-slope point for the target deviation function will find the *maximum* at p_i' rather than the minima at the tangencies with the horizontal line at 1 on Figure 7.1(b). Note that this point on Figure 7.2 meets the first-order condition (7.15), for MOP_i = 0, although it *maximizes* the target deviation. In practice, therefore, we recommend adding a constraint that requires $(\bar{\pi}_i - \pi_i)$ to equal zero,

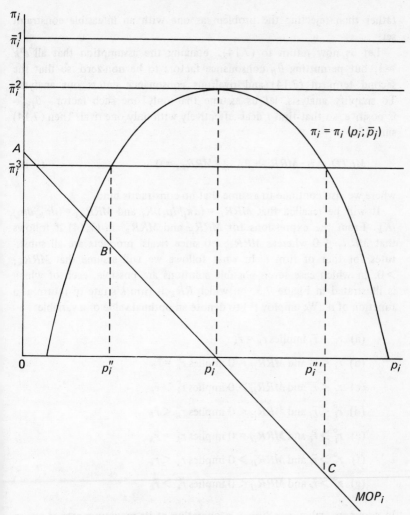

FIGURE 7.2 *The isolated firm i target rate solution possibilities*

which will ensure that p_i'' or p_i''' will be attained, unless one or more other constraints bind. In that case the solution should be recalculated with the profit constraint removed. We have found that the SUMT algorithm works well in this latter instance, permitting the equality constraint to depart from equality to allow inequality constraints to bind, rather than rejecting the problem as one with an infeasible constraint set.

Let us now return to (7.14), retaining the assumption that all $e^{s^2_k} \approx 1$, but permitting θ_{ij} consonance factors to be non-zero, so that the second term of (7.14) and rivalrous consonance enters our analysis. To simplify analysis, let us assume that only one such factor $-\theta_{ik}-$ is positive, so that firm i deals effectively with only one rival. Then (7.14) simplifies to:

$$METD_i = s_i \cdot MRR_{ii} + \theta_{ik}s_k \cdot MRR_{ki} = 0 \tag{7.16}$$

where we also continue to assume that no constraints bind.

It will be recalled that $MRR_{ii} = (d\pi_i/dp_i)/K_i$ and $MRR_{ki} = (d\pi_k/dp_i)/K_k$. From the expressions for MRR_{ii} and MRR_{ki} in (7.14) it follows that $MRR_{ii} \gtrless 0$ whereas $MRR_{ki} \geqslant 0$ since rivals' products are all substitutes for that of firm i. In what follows we will assume that $MRR_{ki} > 0$, in which case seven possible solutions are possible, each of which is illustrated in Figure 7.3, on which RR_k is firm k's rate of return as a function of p_i. We employ ($^\circ$) to denote an optimal value of a variable:

(a)　$r_i^\circ = \bar{r}_i$ implies $r_k^\circ = \bar{r}_k$

(b)　$r_i^\circ < \bar{r}_i$ and $MRR_{ii} = 0$ implies $r_k^\circ = \bar{r}_k$

(c)　$r_i^\circ < \bar{r}_i$ and $MRR_{ii} > 0$ implies $r_k^\circ > \bar{r}_k$

(d)　$r_i^\circ < \bar{r}_i$ and $MRR_{ii} < 0$ implies $r_k^\circ < \bar{r}_k$

(e)　$r_i^\circ > \bar{r}_i$ and $MRR_{ii} = 0$ implies $r_k^\circ = \bar{r}_k$

(f)　$r_i^\circ > \bar{r}_i$ and $MRR_{ii} > 0$ implies $r_k^\circ < \bar{r}_k$

(g)　$r_i^\circ > \bar{r}_i$ and $MRR_{ii} < 0$ implies $r_k^\circ > \bar{r}_k$

In summary, whenever firm i is operating at its maximum-rate-of-return price or is earning its target rate of return, firm k must also be achieving its target rate. When firm i is underachieving its target rate and $MRR_{ii} \neq 0$, then p_i° is at a price where $MRR_{ii} > 0$ or $MRR_{ii} < 0$. In the first case (Figure 7.3(c)) a rise in p_i° to reduce ETD_i should be adopted unless s_k widens, which will happen if $r_k^\circ < \bar{r}_k$, since MRR_{ki} (not shown in Figure 7.3 to reduce clutter) slopes positively with respect to p_i. Hence, r_k° must lie above $\bar{r}_k$. Similarly, when p_i° lies above profit-maximizing price so that $MRR_{ii} < 0$ (Figure 7.3(d)) it would be possible to reduce ETD_i by moving leftward (reducing p_i) if this also reduced s_k. But a reduction in s_k would occur only if $r_k^\circ > \bar{r}_k$, for r_k would fall when p_i falls. Therefore, if p_i° is the optimum it must be true that $r_k^\circ < \bar{r}_k$. Similar interpretations motivate the equilibria when firm i is overachieving (Cases (e), (f), (g) and Figures 7.3(e), (f) and (g)). In all cases, the extents of the deviations of the firms' actual rates from target rates in the equilibrium depend upon the magnitudes of the products of the deviations, the marginal rates of return, and the consonance factors. These magnitudes are not depicted on Figure 7.3.

Cases (b) and (e) in Figures 7.3(b) and (e)) are interesting. If Firm i is at its profit maximizing price in equilibrium and underachieving (Figure 7.3(b)) or overachieving (Figure 7.3(e)) a slight rise or fall in p_i will have no impact upon firm i's own target rate deviation, and hence a movement either up or down if it closed firm k's target rate deviation would improve ETD_i. If $r_k^\circ \neq \bar{r}_k$ then in this situation one of these two movements in p_i would be worthwhile, and p_i° would not have been attained. Therefore, if in fact it has been achieved it must be true that $r_k^\circ = r_k$, for then slight changes in p_i will have no impact on firm k's target deviation. Finally, this motivation also clarifies Case (a) (Figure 7.3(a)), for if $r_i^\circ = \bar{r}_i$ at any p_i° ($MRR_{ii} \gtrless 0$), first-order movements in p_i right or left will not change own target deviation and therefore will be made in the direction that closes firm k's target deviation. Hence, p_i cannot be optimum unless such movements will not impact firm k's target deviation, and this condition implies that firm k is at a price position analogous to p_i'' or p_i''' in Figure 7.1, where $r_k^\circ = \bar{r}_k$.[8]

Consider the realistic implications of these propositions. For example, suppose we have a case where, in some initial price configuration:

(1) $r_i > \bar{r}_k$, so that rival i is a strong rival or, perhaps, is a satisficer willing to settle for approximations to goal achievements;
(2) $r_k < \bar{r}_k$, so firm k is weaker, possibly seeking a larger market share, or perhaps is an overachiever in its goal setting;
(3) θ_{ik} is large, in that firm i worries about firm k's willingness to undercut the price structure of the industry;
(4) $MRR_{ii} > 0$ and large, so that firm i is operating in a highly elastic own-price region of its sales curve;
(5) MRR_{ki} is small, indicating that firm k's sales function has a small cross-elasticity with p_i.

In such a case, as p_i rises past the profit-maximizing price p_i' both firms' target rate deviations close slowly and p_i can be expected to rise into the area where $MRR_{ii} < 0$ and $r_i < \bar{r}_k$, for assumptions (3) and (5) will lead

(a) $r_i^0 = \bar{r}_i$ Implies $r_k^0 = \bar{r}_k$

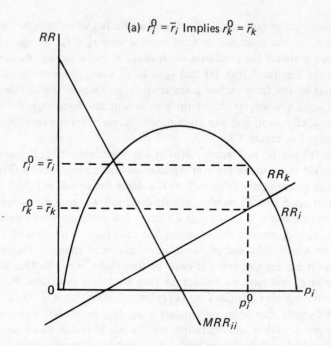

(b) $r_i^0 < \bar{r}_i$, $MRR_{ii} = 0$ Implies $r_k^0 = \bar{r}_k$

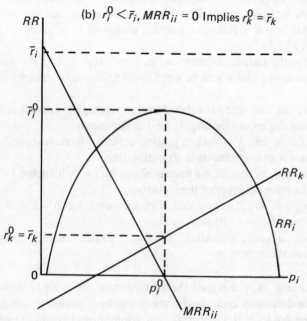

FIGURE 7.3(a)–(g) *Firm i extended target deviation alternative solutions, one rival*

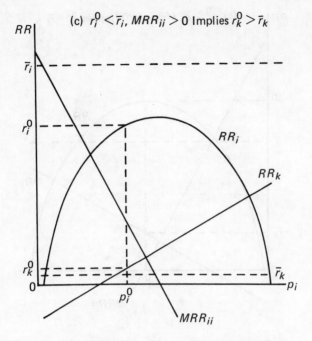

(c) $r_i^0 < \bar{r}_i$, $MRR_{ii} > 0$ Implies $r_k^0 > \bar{r}_k$

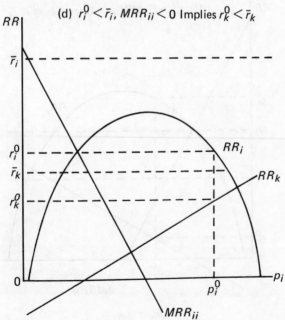

(d) $r_i^0 < \bar{r}_i$, $MRR_{ii} < 0$ Implies $r_k^0 < \bar{r}_k$

Fig 7.3 cont

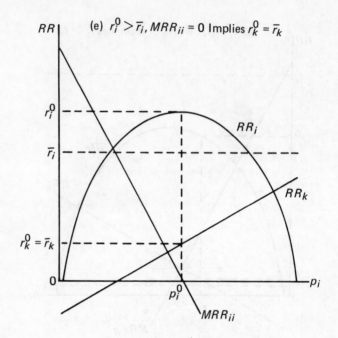

(e) $r_i^0 > \bar{r}_i$, $MRR_{ii} = 0$ Implies $r_k^0 = \bar{r}_k$

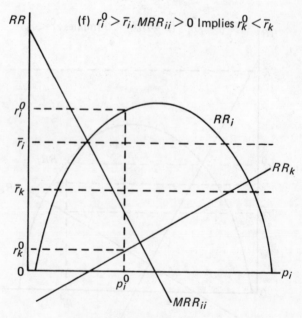

(f) $r_i^0 > \bar{r}_i$, $MRR_{ii} > 0$ Implies $r_k^0 < \bar{r}_k$

Fig 7.3 cont

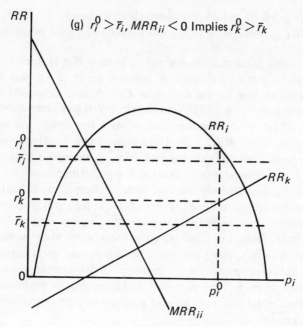

Fig 7.3 cont

firm i to hold a price umbrella above firm k's head and to thereby underachieve rather than overachieve. The type of equilibrium illustrated in Figure 7.3(d) will tend to be approached. A large oligopolist selling a mass-market oriented product, seeking a goal target rate, and worried perhaps about the anti-trust implications of its pricing behaviour as it relates to a smaller rival selling in a somewhat different market segment, may very well hold prices high above what they need be to achieve its target. Target rate pricing behaviour gives its practitioner a low- or high-price option where the target rate is below maximum-profit levels, and its exercise of the high-price option may somewhat paradoxically involve smaller net costs if anti-trust considerations outweigh customer antagonism. 'Preservation of competition' may bear a high social cost in such cases.

Perhaps an even more frequent case in reality is depicted by the following set of assumptions:

(1) $r_i < \bar{r}_i$ and $r_k < \bar{r}_k$, both firms striving towards rates;
(2) $\bar{r}_i \approx \bar{r}_k$, so that both firms share an industry target rate;
(3) θ_{ik} is modestly high;

(4) $MRR_{ii} > 0$ and is high, own-price elasticity large;

(5) MRR_{ki} is moderately high, goods i and k being good substitutes.

Such an initial position cannot continue because if p_i is raised both target rate deviations can be reduced. If, when $r_i = \bar{r}_i$, it is not true that $r_k = \bar{r}_k$, p_i will continue to rise until firm k's extended target rate deviation component in firm i's $METD_i$ counterbalances its own component. If firm k is far below its target in the initial position the equilibrium may occur at a high p_i where $MRR_{ii} < 0$. Once more, rivals' target rate deviations tend to push firms towards the high-price option where target rates are achieved or approached rather than the low-price alternative.

Both of these relatively frequent cases in oligopolistic industries result in prices that are above those that would rule in the absence of consonance, if we assume that firms opt for a low-price option over the high-price option in the latter case. Such a course seems more likely in view of the concerns of firms to avoid customer resentment, avert anti-trust suspicions, and to discourage entry into the industry. Under rivalrous consonance in target rate regimes prices *may well go higher than in profit-maximizing regimes* since the firm pays no goal penalties to do so, as is suggested by the cases above.

In a last consideration of the first-order conditions (7.14) let us drop the assumption that only $\theta_{ik} > 0$ and assume that all $\theta_{ik} > 0$. In this case all that we have based upon the firm k component of firm i's ETD_i and $METD_i$ is simply read as the *sum* in those functions over all rivals j. Some rivals may then be over- or underachieving simultaneously with others which are exactly attaining target rates; however, in rival i's equilibrium their θ_{ij}-weighted target deviation components *summed* must equal $s_i \cdot MRR_{ii}$.

COMPARATIVE STATICS PROPOSITIONS

All of the following comparative statics propositions are valid at what we call the 'first level of analysis', by which we mean that changes in p_i are not assumed to set off reactions in any p_j. Of course, this is highly unlikely in oligopoly analysis – indeed, the hallmark of the industry structure is the non-likelihood of such passivity – and hence whether the tendencies for these reactions persist into the second level of analysis, where we attempt to anticipate such reactions, is a separate question. We may also identify a third level of analysis in which the rivalrous consonance factors are also variable. In this chapter we shall limit our investigations to the first level to identify some deeper tendencies in firm behaviour, recognizing that they may be overridden by higher level reactions.[7]

Suppose now that the marginal cost c_i of firm i rises slightly. Then, by differentiating (7.14) we obtain:

$$\frac{dp_i}{dc_i} =$$

$$\frac{x_i \cdot MRR_{ii}(1 + 2s_i^2) + b_{ii}s_i}{2b_{ii}s_i + K_i \cdot MRR_{ii}^2(1 + 2s_i^2) + K_i[\Sigma_{j \neq i}\theta_{ij} \cdot MRR_{ji}^2(1 + 2s_j^2)]} \quad (7.17)$$

Note that the denominator has all non-negative terms except for the first, which will be negative when $r_i > \bar{r}_i$. Given the magnitudes of its accompanying terms, however, we will assume that the denominator is always positive, so that the sign of dp_i/dc_i will be determined by its numerator, and, further, given the magnitudes of its second term, that the numerator sign hinges upon the sign of MRR_{ii}. Hence, when:

1. $MRR_{ii} > 0$, $dp_i/dc_i > 0$

2. $MRR_{ii} = 0$, dp_i/dc_i $\begin{cases} > 0, \text{ if } s_i > 0 \\ = 0, \text{ if } s_i = 0 \\ < 0, \text{ if } s_i < 0 \end{cases}$

3. $MRR_{ii} < 0$, $dp_i/dc_i < 0$

To motivate these theorems we will demonstrate Case 3 in Figure 7.4 for $MRR_{ii} \lessgtr 0$ and Case 1 for $MRR_{ii} > 0$, with Case 3 of major interest because it is the counterintuitive result. Under rivalrous consonance in a target rate regime, how can a *rise* in own marginal cost induce a *fall* in price? We deal in turn with two subcases that can occur, depending upon the sign of s_i.

In Figure 7.4(a) we present the case where $MRR_{ii} < 0$ and $s_i < 0$. Initial equilibrium for firm i is at p_i°, at which the firm is overachieving $\bar{r}_i$ at r_i° at an $MRR_{ii} < 0$. This implies that $\Sigma_{j \neq i}\theta_{ij}r_i > \Sigma_{j \neq i}\theta_{ij}\bar{r}_j$ at p_i°, as shown. When c_i rises, firm i's rate of return at p_i° falls to r_i'' as the rate of return function shifts downward and to the right. Its MRR_{ii} rises to MRR_{ii}', and, at r_i'', s_i is reduced in absolute amount. Hence, the own target deviation component of $(7.14) - s_i \cdot MRR_{ii}$ — falls in positive

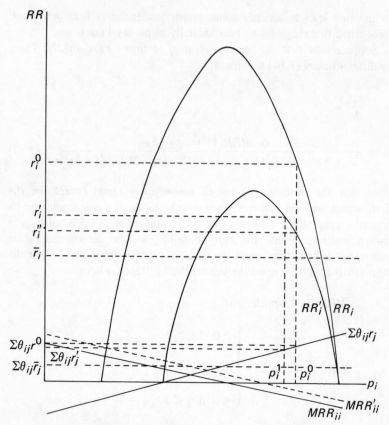

FIGURE 7.4(a)   *Change in p_i with rise in c_i, $MRR_{ii} < 0$*
$s_i < 0$ Implies $\Sigma\theta_{ij}s_j < 0$

value as both terms become less negative, and it no longer equals an unchanged rivals' target deviation component $\Sigma_{j\neq i}\theta_{ij}s_j \cdot MRR_{ji}$. Therefore, p_i must fall to p_i' to induce a simultaneous rise in s_i and fall in the absolute value of the rival target deviation component. Since the rise in s_i is somewhat offset by the fall in MRR_{ii}'s absolute value, the steeper MRR_{ii}' the greater must be the fall in p_i. Equilibrium is reattained at $p_i' < p_i^\circ$, with implied r_i' and r_j', and with r_i' lower. The aggregate rivals' target deviation term will be lower, which implies that most r_j have fallen.

In Figure 7.4(b), $s_i > 0$ at p_i°, implying $\Sigma_{j\neq i}\theta_{ij}s_j \cdot MRR_{ji} > 0$. With the rise in c_i the target deviation s_i widens and a fall in p_i must occur to narrow it as well as balance it by a widening rival target deviation component,

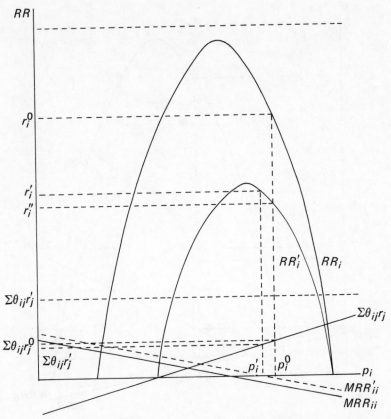

FIGURE 7.4(b)   *Change in p_i with rise in c_i, $MRR_{ii} < 0$*
$s_i > 0$ Implies $\Sigma \theta_{ij} s_j > 0$

until $METD_i$ is brought back to zero level at p_i'. Finally, Figure 7.4(c) presents Case 1 where $s_i > 0$ and $MRR_{ii} > 0$, implying $\Sigma_{j \neq i} \theta_{ij} \cdot MRR_{ji} < 0$. A rise in c_i, therefore, lowers r_i and increases s_i. Since $MRR_{ii} > 0$, p_i must rise to raise r_i, but this in turn induces the rival target deviation component to increase. Price of firm i continues to rise until, at p_i', the rise in s_i and fall in MRR_{ii} are just balanced in the own target deviation component by the rise in the rival target deviation component.

Thus, the interesting theoretical possibility arises that in rivalrous consonance under a target rate of return regime a rise in a firm's marginal cost could lead to cost-induced price *reductions*. When firm i and its rivals are symmetrical in their target rate expectations — underachieving,

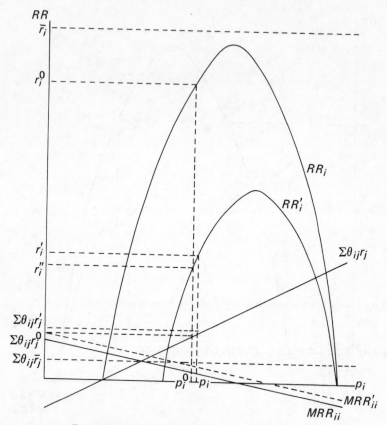

FIGURE 7.4(c)   *Change in p_i with rise in c_i, $MRR_{ii} > 0$*
$s_i > 0$ Implies $\Sigma \theta_{ij} s_j < 0$

overachieving, or exactly achieving – firm i will be led to operate in the region of negative marginal own profit. Price, therefore, will be above the level that maximizes its rate of return. Under these conditions, a rise in its marginal cost and a decline in its profitability will lead firm i to reduce price self-protectively, although rivalrous consonance will temper that price reduction. On the other hand, under conditions that are most likely to occur when firm i and its rivals are asymmetrical in target rate aspirations, p_i will tend to be at less than profit-maximizing levels, and a rise in firms i's cost will lead it to raise p_i, and by less than it would in the absence of rivalrous consonance.

Suppose all $\theta_{ij} = 0$, so that rivalrous consonance is eliminated and the firm operates myopically in a Cournot environment. Then (7.17) yields three results, depending upon the nature of the initial equilibrium. When $s_i > 0$ and $MRR_{ii} = 0$, so that the initial price is at the maximum profit level, $dp_i / dc_i = .5$. When $s_i = 0$ the firm has the choice of selecting p_i below or above the profit-maximizing level. In either case, $dp_i / dc_i = x_i / (K_i \cdot MRR_{ii})$, which is positive in the first case but negative in the second. Whichever the case firm i opts for, the absolute value of $K_i \cdot MRR_{ii}$ will be the same, but because x_i is larger when p_i is smaller, the degree of price rise in the first case will be larger absolutely than the degree of price fall in the second.

Assume, now, that rival k raises its price, p_k, for whatever reason. For purposes of simplifying the expressions to be evaluated, let us define a consonance factor $\theta_{ii} \equiv 1$ which formally depicts the weight firm i assigns to its own target rate deviation. Then, we may write the expression:

$$\frac{dp_i}{dp_k} =$$

$$\frac{K_k b_{ik} s_i + K_i \theta_{ik} b_{ki} s_k - K_i K_k \Sigma_{m=i,j,k} (\theta_{im} \cdot MRR_{mi} \cdot MRR_{mk}(1 + 2s_m^2))}{2K_k b_{ii} s_i + K_i K_k \Sigma_{m=i,j,k} \theta_{im} \cdot MRR_{mi}^2 (1 + 2s_m^2)}$$

$$(7.18)$$

First, assume θ_{ij} and θ_{ik} are zero, so that p_k affects p_i only through firm i's sales function. Then (7.18) reduces to:

$$\frac{dp_i}{dp_k} = \frac{b_{ik} s_i - K_i \cdot MRR_{ii} \cdot MRR_{ik}(1 + 2s_i^2)}{2 b_{ii} s_i + K_i \cdot MRR_{ii}^2 (1 + 2s_i^2)} \qquad (7.19)$$

With regard to (7.14) either $s_i = 0$ and $MRR_{ii} \gtrless 0$ or $s_i > 0$ and $MRR_{ii} = 0$. In the first case:

$$\frac{dp_i}{dp_k} = -\frac{MRR_{ik}}{MRR_{ii}} \qquad (7.20)$$

When $MRR_{ii} > 0$, because $MRR_{ik} > 0$ the expression in (7.20) will be negative; a rise in p_k raises r_i and hence p_i must be reduced to maintain $\bar{r}_i$. In similar fashion, we reason that when $MRR_{ii} < 0$, (7.20) must be positive, so that when r_i rise in p_k it will be necessary to raise p_i to reattain $\bar{r}_i$. In the first case target rate of return motivation leads to what appears to be counterintuitive, but what is indeed explained readily in terms of this unfamilar motivation. To add to the complication, of course, in both instances the firm has the option to leap to the opposite side of the profit-maximizing price unless constrained by price change restraints.

When $s_i > 0$ and $MRR_{ii} = 0$, (7.19) reduces to:

$$\frac{dp_i}{dp_k} = \frac{.5b_{ik}}{b_{ii}} \tag{7.21}$$

Thus p_i will rise with a rise in p_k at a rate that is directly proportional to the marginal rise in sales caused by the rise in p_k and inversely proportional to the fall in sales occurring from the induced rise in p_i.

When we permit the θ-terms to become positive in (7.18) the evaluation of the numerator becomes much more complex; however, the sign of the third term is expected to dominate. More specifically, in the summation it seems likely that the element for $m = i$ will outweigh the others and so give a sign to the numerator that is opposite to the sign of MRR_{ii}. Hence, $dp_i/dp_k > 0$ when $MRR_{ii} < 0$ and vice versa, as we would expect from our discussion of (7.20). However, the other consonance terms in the expression will temper this and may overcompensate, and therefore unambiguous results can be obtained for specific industries only by simulative theorizing.

THE INTRODUCTION OF CONSTRAINTS

The limited capability of classic comparative statics techniques and the recognition of the need for simulative theorizing in oligopoly analysis are even more impressed upon the analyst when the constraint sets (7.11) are reintroduced into the analysis. General results from parametric non-linear programming or postoptimality analysis are derivable only from extensions of classic parametric displacement techniques. Infinitesimal changes in parameters are assumed to move equilibrium with ϵ-neighbourhoods of the original equilibrium, with constraints that are ineffective in the original equilibrium remaining so in the new. Finite parameter changes with potential changes in the pattern of binding and non-binding constraints can only be investigated by simulative theorizing techniques.

In this chapter we will limit the treatment of constraints to an indication of the nature of the changes they introduce into the solutions. For the illustrations we have used to illuminate target-rate-of-return regimes, the constraint set $C_{i1}-C_{i4}$ in (7.11) is simple because in firm i's solutions either none of the constraints will bind or only one will. We illustrate this in Figure 7.5, in which we have introduced the four constraints into firm i's rate of return diagram. Their interpretation is straightforward.

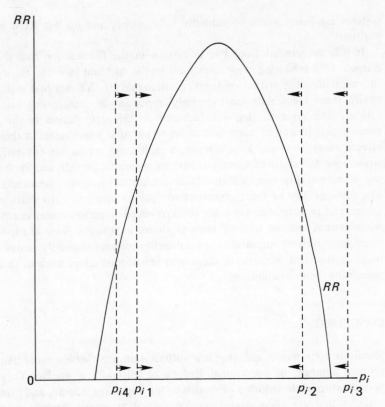

FIGURE 7.5 *The application of the constraint set to firm i's rate of return function*

C_{i1} is a capacity constraint upon output, which translates into a p_i below which price cannot fall without stimulating excessive demand from the standpoint of capacity available to satisfy it. Hence, C_{i1} sets a lower bound on price, p_{i1}. C_{i2} defines a minimum acceptable market share for firm i, and therefore, determines an upper bound on p_i at p_{i2}, broaching which would reduce demand below the acceptable level. C_{i3} imposes a direct constraint upon price, setting an upper bound, p_{i3}, on the basis of acceptable price change, and C_{i4} sets a slower bound on the same basis. Hence, C_{i1} and C_{i4} set lower bounds on price and C_{i2} and C_{i3} set upper bounds. Optimal price may, therefore, either (i) be constrained by the least upper bound (arbitrarily, p_{i2} in Figure 7.5) or greatest lower bound (p_{i1} as drawn), not by both, or (ii) be unconstrained. Also, p_{i1} and p_{i2} will change positions in a full rivalrous consonance model in which rivals' systems are being solved sequentially, whereas p_{i3} and p_{i4} are fixed in position.

It will be recalled from our discussion in the first section that the purpose of introducing these constraint sets is to build into the theory the multi-objective nature of firms' decision-making. We feel that realistically these constraints are extremely important in constraining price actions, and our confining our discussion of those constraints to these remarks should not be construed to depreciate that importance. In their effectiveness, however, we encounter a motivating reason for our early stress upon the study of specific industries in specific periods, and for the use of numerically specified models in simulative theorizing frameworks. The susceptibility of these objectives to changes in priority, to shifts in values, and to adaptations to other firms' revealed objectives makes worthwhile general analysis of their impacts almost impossible. None the less, given their realistic importance, operationally relevant oligopoly analysis must capture and incorporate them, and hence must adopt analysis that reduces its theorem ambitions.

CONCLUSIONS

Rivalrous consonance and crippled optimization are flexible tools that promise a means of operational analysis of oligopolistic pricing. They permit rather close tailoring of models to the important industry and firm specifics that are all-important in that market structure. Among these are the elusive effects of power and authority structures, of goal patterns, and of decision interdependence. They offer the advantage of preserving the relevant identity of each firm in the industry and of detailing the power structure in a pairwise fashion, so that the analysis remains microeconomic. They also permit the design of models that can be solved by non-linear programming techniques in relatively straightforward ways. And, although we have not presented the capability in this chapter, the techniques permit the concerns of suppliers for the welfares of their customers to be included via consonance factors, and the way opened to linking oligopolistic industries in an operational microeconomic general equilibrium framework.

We have shown how some insights are obtainable by applying the methods to the analysis of target-rate-of-return pricing — a motivation that seems to have been largely overlooked by the analytical literature. They reveal that firms may have a lower- and a higher-price option in such industry structure, and that biases may exist towards the higher price option. These insights, of course, must be used as guides to empirical investigation, and in our judgement more informal analysis has indicated the importance of undertaking such formal investigations of industries in which it is a common firm objective.

But these exercises in gaining some general theorems will have been counterproductive if they serve to mask the need for specific industry applications. The use of systematic simulative theorizing methodology upon such specific models may permit us to build a body of insights into realistic oligopolistic decision-making that we lack today. For too long the theorist has pursued the *ignis fatuus* of universal theorems concerning oligopolistic motivation or decisions – false beacons that delude by their promise of global illumination. Theoretically guided, institutionally enriched analysis can never achieve a universal theory of oligopoly, but it can build a body of knowledge that the economic policy-maker and jurist can use effectively as guidelines in their judgements.

NOTES

1. This section contains a brief sketch of the main outlines of the theory of rivalrous consonance of oligopolistic behaviour and of crippled optimization. For a fuller theoretical treatment see Kuenne, 1974a, 1974b, 1978, 1980, and for an application of the framework to OPEC pricing behaviour, see Kuenne, 1978–9, 1979 and 1982.
2. See Kuenne, 1974a, 1978 for a fuller discussion of this empirical work.
3. Of course we do not assert that the firm actually calculates a θ-vector. The consonance factor is a means for the analyst of encapsulating the complex of attitudes in a decision-maker's consciousness that shapes the firm's choices. It is in its function similar to the economist's concept of utility: a meta-thoretical concept, not subject to empirical observation, but useful for designing theories that are capable of yielding operational theorems capable of empirical validation. For an attempt to derive a θ-matrix empirically for application to OPEC, see Kuenne, 1979.
4. See Fiacco and McCormick, 1968.
5. The rivalrous consonance model is static, and by employing a sequential solution technique we do not imply that we are aping the adjustments of rivals to each others' pricing decisions in the real world. In practical applications we have found the use of SUMT to solve the first-order conditions directly to be less time consuming.
6. This follows from the nature of π_i as a parabola with vertex over p' and with p_i'' and p_i''' equidistant from p_i.
7. Both second and third levels are addressed in a book in preparation, *Rivalrous Consonance: A Theory of General Oligopolistic Equilibrium*. Also, a third-level analysis has been published in Kuenne, 1980.

8. This becomes unlikely when the rival deviation component is included in the ETD_i. When such effects are taken into account, there is little likelihood of being misled into believing that p_i' in Figure 7.1, which maximizes ETD_i rather than minimizing it, is the optimum. In the present case this would require the coincidence that at this price it was also true that $r_k = \bar{r}_k$. When more than one rival exists the coincidence becomes even less probable in that all rivals would have to be in this situation for p_i to remain at p_i' when $r_i \geqslant \bar{r}_i$. Hence, the nonconvexity of own target deviation in this circumstance becomes less worrisome in practice.

REFERENCES

Fiacco, A. V., and G. P. McCormick (1968) *Nonlinear Programming: Sequential Unconstrained Minimization Technique*, New York: John Wiley.

Kuenne, R. E. (1974a) 'Towards a Usable General Theory of Oligopoly', *De Economist*, 122: 471–502.

Kuenne, R. E. (1974b) 'Towards an Operational General Equilibrium Theory With Oligopoly: Some Experimental Results and Conjectures', *Kyklos*, XXVII: 792–820.

Kuenne, R. E. (1978) 'General Oligopolistic Equilibrium: A Crippled-Optimization Apporach', in *Pioneering Economics: Essays in Honor of Giovanni Demaria*, Padua: Cedam, pp. 537–77.

Kuenne, R. E. (1978–9) 'A Short-Run Demand Analysis of the OPEC Cartel', *Journal of Business Administration*, 10: 129–64, reprinted in *The Logistics and Transportation Review*, 17: 231–65.

Kuenne, R. E. (1979) 'Rivalrous Consonance and the Power Structure of OPEC', *Kyklos*, XXXII: 695–717.

Kuenne, R. E. (1980) 'Duopoly Reaction Functions Under Cripped Optimization Regimes', *Oxford Economic Papers*, 32: 224–40.

Kuenne, R. E. (1982) 'The GENESYS Model of OPEC, 1974–1980: Structural Insights from a Non-Forecasting Model', *Energy Economics*, 4: 146–58.

Part III
New Developments in the
Theory of Industry Structure

8 Industry Structure Analysis and Public Policy

WILLIAM J. BAUMOL

The structure of industry has long been a concern of public policy, particularly in the arenas of anti-trust and regulation of public utilities. Recently, moves towards deregulation have renewed general concern with the issue, happily just at the moment when economic analysis was producing some major new insights on the subject. This chapter reviews and summarizes some of the new analysis and examines some of its implications for public policy.

An example will bring out the fundamental issue. Industry policy has traditionally focused on such matters as concentration. Markets in which only three or four firms are present have long been considered suspect in terms of possession of monopoly power, misallocation of resources, as havens of inefficiency and exploiters of consumers. Yet when the airlines were recently deregulated, it was widely recognized that many of the routes were actually served by only two or three or even only one airline. One would have thought that under these circumstances deregulation posed a major peril for the public interest. Yet the instincts of those involved in designing the deregulatory policy seemed to reassure them that no particularly serious problem was involved. Indeed, the new analysis confirmed that, for reasons to be made clear in the material that follows, *in cases like the airlines* there may be no need for government intervention and oversight. Rather than too little competition, it is more likely that developments on routes involving only two or three airlines will elicit charges that there is in fact too much competition. In particular, a new type of analysis that has come to be called the theory of *contestable markets* showed why this is so, and its predictions have so far not been inconsistent with observed developments. As we proceed in this chapter the underlying reasoning will become clear.

311

INDUSTRY STRUCTURE: CONCEPT AND SIGNIFICANCE

The term 'industry structure' refers primarily to the division of the industry's activities among the different firms that constitute that industry. But it also includes such characteristics as the number and size distribution of the firms that manufacture and sell the industry's products, the variety and similarity of products that they sell, the nature of the information available to consumers on the prices, qualities, service facilities and other characteristics affecting the desirability of the items they can purchase from the industry, the degree of vertical integration of the firms that constitute the industry (that is, whether the firms characteristically do or not make their own materials, process the raw materials themselves and sell the final products, or whether such tasks are divided up among more or less independent and specialized firms), the spatial characteristics of the market place (that is to say, whether the firms in question are in close geographic proximity or are widely dispersed), the extent to which activities are carried out in a multiplicity of plants or in a small number of factories and the extent to which that industry is subject to foreign competition. In other words, the term industry structure refers to the full range of characterization of the products, enterprises and degree of independence or interdependence of the companies that constitute an industry.

Market structure has generally been considered important by policymakers not for its own sake, but because of its implications for the performance of an industry in terms of the social welfare. And, indeed, such concerns are well-founded because economic analysis has always confirmed that the behaviour of the firms and the industry is inextricably bound up with the nature of the structure of the industry. An industry with one or a very small number of firms has always given rise to suspicion about the prices it will charge to consumers, the quality of the products it will offer, the rate at which technological change will be introduced, the efficiency with which it will use resources and allocate them among various tasks and the diversity of products that it will offer consumers. There is nothing new, then, in the recognition of the connection between industry structure and industry performance. For example, the theory of monopoly has a long and honourable history of effective analysis of the sorts of decision-making that will best serve the profit objectives of the monopolistic firm and the consequences of these decisions in terms of the public interest. What, then, is new and different about the recent analysis?

It is only a slight exaggeration to say that until perhaps a decade ago the economic literature implicitly proceeded as though the number of firms in an industry had somehow been decided by the Fates who revealed at

Delphi that they had arbitrarily condemned one industry to be a monopoly, another to be an oligopoly and a third to be highly competitive. That is, in the standard analysis there was no effort to explain what determines whether any particular industry is monopolistic or oligopolistic or assumes some other form. It was simply taken as a datum that arose out of some mysterious process that had no need of explanation.

In contrast, recent advances in analysis recognize explicitly that market structure is in fact not determined by unidentifiable and indescribable forces, but is the product of the workings of the free market, the technological circumstances of the industry in question, and the economic forces that impinge upon it. Indeed, there is a feedback relationship between the structure of the industry and its behaviour. Business decisions on pricing, advertising, innovation and the like are obviously affected by the structure of the industry in which they are made. But these decisions in turn have their consequences for the structure of the industry, so that both structure and behaviour are mutually dependent. An effective analysis, it is now recognized, must take explicit account of this interdependence and examine its implications for the welfare of consumers and of the public generally.

ENTRY AND CONTESTABILITY

There is nothing novel about the idea that entry barriers are highly relevant for both the structure and performance of an industry, and it transpires that central to the study of the determination of industry structure is the nature of the process by which new competitors enter into a particular industry. The crucial issue, of course, is how easy or difficult it is for entrants to make their way into an industry and to find a secure niche for themselves in it. However, the newer analysis has shown that a second type of entry is also important, that is, not the prospect of entry by a firm seeking to establish a permanent place for itself in a market, but the possibility that entrants can hit and run, taking advantage of a temporary profit opportunity, and then go off to seek similar opportunities in other fields. The most significant consequence of freedom of entry has always been taken to be the constraint it places upon the ability of incumbent firms to take advantage of consumers. That is, if there is sufficient freedom of entry the incumbent firms do not have the power or the freedom to act like prototype monopolists.

The question, then, is what constitutes true freedom of entry or absence of entry barriers, defined so as to assure their ability to constrain incumbent firms sufficiently to prevent them from misbehaving in terms of the requirements of the public interest. Some of the earlier writings on the subject included scale economies among the list of items they classified as entry barriers, arguing that where firms do have scale economies available to them it will be impossible for entrants to coexist with any relatively efficient incumbents. For scale economies provide an advantage to any firm that happens to be larger than its rivals even if the large firm and the small enterprise have equally competent managements. In an industry with scale economies therefore, an incumbent that happens to have grown large because it entered earlier will have an enormous advantage over a potential entrant who can only hope to begin operation on a very small scale initially. Such an industry will tend to end up with only one or a very few large enterprises, and very typically we will find that new firms rarely manage to establish themselves. The newer analysis, however, rejects the notion that scale economies constitute a barrier to entry so long as there are no other entry barriers that supplement the entrance deterring effect of the economies available to larger enterprises. The reason is that in a case in which the only impediment to entry is constituted by scale economies, the incumbent firms will reign supreme only so long as they happen to operate efficiently and earn no excess profits, because if they should prove to be inefficient or to overcharge that will constitute an invitation to hit-and-run entry which will deprive them of profits and perhaps even threaten to take the market away from them permanently. Where hit-and-run entry is possible, the incumbent can indeed protect himself from entry, but he can do so only by behaving as a competitor would and offering consumers all the benefits that competition would otherwise provide.

Of course, that process is not able to restrain the behaviour of incumbents where hit-and-run entry is impractical. This is true if entry requires the new firm to sink large amounts of money into the activity to build huge factories, to lay roadbeds and tracks or to bring in large amounts of capital that can neither be transferred readily to other uses nor sold easily to others. It is for that reason that in contestability analysis the presence of sunk costs is considered to be the prime form of entry barrier and the main type of entry cost that really does impede the workings of the market mechanism and serves as a haven for monopolistic or oligopolistic behaviour using tools such as predation, pre-emption and strategic countermeasures.

PERFECT COMPETITION AS A USEFUL BENCHMARK FOR INDUSTRY STRUCTURE

The preceding discussion suggests that even though the presence of scale economies may cause an industry to be populated by one or a very small number of firms, this in itself need not lead to behaviour whose results are materially different from those associated with competition. It suggests also that the notion of competition that we have inherited from traditional analysis must be reconsidered and broadened substantially. For over a hundred years perfect competition has served as the prototype of ideal industrial behaviour. Whenever the structure of an industry is examined the perfectly competitive ideal is used implicitly or explicitly as a benchmark for the purpose. Nevertheless, it is generally recognized that the use of perfect competition as a criterion of ideal market structure suffers from its very limited range of applicability. There simply are few industries that can be made to resemble the perfectly competitive model.

While a relatively small farm may, nevertheless, be highly efficient, it is hard to imagine tiny automobile manufacturers or tiny steel plants or tiny oil refineries that can produce at reasonable cost and can compete effectively with their giant counterparts in other industrial countries. In any industry in which technology provides economies of scale it is simply undesirable to try to populate the industry with fairly small firms, let alone firms that are tiny. Thus, for such industries the idea of perfect competition is not only a poor ideal but is the very opposite – it is a prescription for inefficiency, high prices and excessive costs. Clearly, for such cases, some other benchmark is required.

CONTESTABILITY AS A STANDARD OF SATISFACTORY MARKET ORGANIZATION

The criterion that has been proposed as a substitute or, rather, as a supplement, is the standard called perfect contestability. A perfectly contestable market is defined formally as one in which equilibrium is impossible if any price charged by an incumbent is such that an entrant who charges a (slightly) lower price for the same item can nevertheless earn a non-negative economic profit. In other words, a contestable market is one in which any such entry-attracting price precludes an equilibrium. Obviously, then, a market with substantial entry barriers is not contestable since such barriers can prevent entrants from taking advantage of the profit-earning opportunity that would otherwise be offered by high prices charged by incumbents, that is, entry barriers permit equilibria with prices that are high relative to their competitive levels. Looked at another way, a market is perfectly contestable if any entrant who changes his mind can exit without sacrificing any of the investment the entry decision required. For then the entrant risks nothing by taking advantage of any earning opportunity presented by the high prices of an incumbent.

Several properties of such markets are implicit in this discussion. A contestable market must always have potential entrants available to it. Those potential entrants must, without restriction, be able to serve the same customers and use the same productive techniques as those available to any and all incumbent firms. Thus, this feature precludes barriers to entry that take the form of availability of productive techniques only to incumbents, or the imposition of costs on entrants that incumbents do not have to bear and have never had to bear in the past.

The curcial feature of a contestable market is its vulnerability to hit-and-run entry. Even a very transient profit opportunity need not be neglected by a potential entrant, for he can go in before prices change, collect his gains, and then depart without cost should the climate grow unattractive to him. The behaviour of firms, industries and markets under perfect contestability follows directly from their definition and their consequent vulnerability to hit-and-run incursions. The main properties of those markets can easily be described.

First, a contestable market never yields excessive profits to anyone. Here excessive profits are defined, as always, as any return exceeding the amount that it is necessary to pay for the capital utilized by the firm. Thus, in a contestable market excess profits must always be zero or negative even if the industry is oligopolistic or monopolistic. The reason is straightforward. Any excess profit means that a transient entrant can set up business, replicate the profit-making incumbent's output at the same cost as his, undercut the incumbent's prices slightly and still earn a profit. That is, the opportunity for costless entry and exit guarantees that an entrant who is content to accept a slightly lower profit can do so by selecting prices a bit lower than the incumbent's. In sum, in a perfectly contestable market the excess profit earned by an incumbent automatically constitutes an earning opportunity for an entrant who will hit and, if necessary, run.

The second characteristic of a contestable market follows from the same analysis as the first. This second attribute of any contestable market is the absence of any sort of inefficiency in production in the industry's operations. For any unnecessary cost, like any excess profit, constitutes an invitation to entry. Of course, in the short run, as is true under perfect competition, both profits and waste may be present. But in the long run they simply cannot withstand the threat brandished by potential entrants who have nothing to lose by grabbing at any opportunity for profit, however transient it may be.

The third pertinent attribute of a contestable industry in the long run is particularly important for the economics of anti-trust and regulation. This attribute asserts that in a perfectly contestable market no cross-subsidy is possible, where this is defined to mean that the price of some product of a multi-product firm is lower than either the corresponding marginal or incremental cost. The reason for this is also straightforward.

Suppose an incumbent, i who earns Profit $\Pi_i \geqslant 0$, sells a vector of outputs, y, at prices P_y and, in addition, sells another output vector x at prices p_x such that $p_x \cdot x$, its revenue from the sale of x, is less than its incremental cost $IR_x \equiv C(x, y) - C(0, y)$. Consider an entrant who opens for business and chooses to sell only y at prices p_y. Then the entrant's profit will be:

$$\Pi_e = \Pi_i - (p_x \cdot x - IR_x) > \Pi_i \geqslant 0$$

In other words, the entrant offering to sell only y can afford to price it at $P_y -\delta$, for some small $\delta > 0$, take over the entire market for y and yet make a profit.

The intuitive explanation is also clear. The sale of any item, x at a price that does not cover incremental cost means that the seller would earn more profit in total if it simply stopped selling x altogether. This necessarily gives an entrant an opening to take advantage of that profit enhancement opportunity.

Finally, the fourth pertinent property of a perfectly contestable market applies where two or more firms sell the same commodity. In that case, the only possible equilibrium price for the item must be one that is precisely equal to its marginal cost. In other words, under perfect contestability even two firms are enough to guarantee that equilibrium prices will satisfy the necessary conditions for (first-best) Pareto optimality — for efficiency in the allocation of resources.[1]

In saying all this it is to be emphasized that contestability theory is not intended as a denial of the possibility or even the likelihood of widespread market failure. No one claims or implies that all the world is contestable or even nearly so. The argument is only that the desirable features just described will emerge in a market in practice *if it should happen* to satisfy the requirements of perfect contestability.

CONTESTABLE MARKETS AND THE DETERMINATION OF INDUSTRY STRUCTURE

So far little has been said about what may be the key contribution of the new theory we are discussing, that is, its analysis of the determinants of the structure of an industry in terms of the workings of the market and the economy. We are now in a position to see just how that works. In a perfectly contestable market the determination of industry structure follows from the conclusion that the industry must, in the long run, operate with absolute efficiency, that is, it must produce its combination of outputs at the lowest cost that is possible. This means not only that each firm in the industry must be efficient, but that the number of firms in the industry must be that which yields the lowest cost of production of the industry's vector of outputs. This must be true not only of the number of firms, but it also must hold for their sizes, for the variety of products that each of them offers and for all the other attributes that constitute the industry's structure. That is to say, in a perfectly contestable market the structure that must emerge in any particular industry in the long run is the structure that produces the industry's output at the lowest possible cost. This conclusion again follows from the ease of entry and exit that is the hallmark of contestability. Suppose, for example, that an industry's output can be produced most cheaply by two firms but that it is currently being supplied, with non-negative profits, by three separate enterprises. In that case, it becomes profitable for two new enterprises or for two of those enterprises that are already in the market to offer that same output at a lower price to consumers in order to capture the market for themselves. Because, by assumption, two firms operate more cheaply than three, these two firms will find that they are able to earn revenues that exceed their costs, including the cost of capital, despite the fact that their prices are lower than those that prevailed when three enterprises were in operation. Similarly, if the number of firms in the industry is below the cost-minimizing level, entry will be profitable. In a perfectly contestable market, therefore, in the long run any efficient organization of industry will always drive out an inefficient organization and the efficient organization will eventually always pervail.

This indicates the economic mechanism that determines the long-run structure of contestable industry. We will see now that it depends on the position of the market's demand relationships and the structure of the industry's costs as determined by its technological arrangements. The nature of market demand determines whether a large or a small volume of the outputs produced by the firms will be absorbed by consumers, and the cost structure determines whether it is most efficient to produce the output quantities consistent with market demand if the industry organized into two or three or one or ten thousand firms. In a contestable market the industry structure that will emerge will always be that one which can provide the volume of output absorbed by the market at the lowest possible cost. In particular, if a market happens to be a natural monopoly over the pertinent range of outputs, efficiency implies that it will, in the long run, be served only by a single firm, and yet even that single firm will never earn any excessive profits. Similarly, if efficiency requires two firms or three, contestability assures us that in the long run this number of firms will ultimately survive.

Thus, the determination of industry structure becomes almost an engineering calculation that determines whether a particular combination of outputs can be produced most cheaply by six or by fifteen or by two enterprises. The calculations, though complicated and technical, are in principle straightforward, because they involve neither more nor less than a comparison of the costs under various different industry structures and recognition that in a perfectly contestable market it will always be the lowest cost industry structure that will emerge and survive in the long run.

Several features of these conclusions are noteworthy. The first is that in a contestable market it is pointless to try to manipulate the number of firms in the market. Even though it may be considered desirable in itself that a market contain a large number of firms, if least-cost production requires that there be only two enterprises, any attempt to break up the two firms into a larger number of entities is an undertaking that is doomed to failure. Even though a larger number of enterprises is somehow established, market forces will dictate that enterprises excessive from the point of view of cost efficiency will not survive. Or rather, they can be made to survive by fiat — by preventing effective competition among the firms. It can be done through a cartel established by government in which each enterprise is assigned its own protected market and kept safe from competitive incursions by others, even if the incursions would reduce prices to consumers and the cost of production to society.

The new analysis also shows, as we have already noted, that in a perfectly contestable market the presence of only a small number of firms need not have the unfortunate consequences for consumer welfare that are usually taken to stem from it. In a perfectly contestable market populated even by only one or two firms we have seen that excessive profits are impossible in the long run because they will attract an influx of hit-and-run entrants, or entrants who may be able to remain permanently. Second, we have seen that in a perfectly contestable market even though the number of firms is as small as cost conditions dictate, no waste is possible and output must always be supplied at minimum cost. In particular, if a single firm is a natural monopoly and operates in a perfectly contestable market it can retain its monopoly and its immunity from entry in the long run. But it is able to achieve this result only by acting as though it were in a heavily competitive industry. It must operate at minimum costs, that is to say, it must indulge in absolutely zero waste and it must price as low as is possible with those costs so that all excess profits must disappear. Consumers will be as well served by such an essentially powerless monopoly as they would be by an industry that is perfectly competitive.

Finally, we may observe that despite its ease of entry and exit such an industry may well have a history characterized by virtual absence of entry and exit. This will be true if (and only if) the incumbents prevent entry not by predatory tactics but by pre-empting it through the commendability of their own performance. Only if the incumbents are efficient, if their prices are correspondingly low and if they earn no excessive profits, will they be rewarded by the absence of entry. But then, of course, it serves the social interest that entry should not take place.

BARRIERS TO ENTRY

Since the behaviour of potential entrants is central to the determination of industry structure and the operation of perfectly contestable markets, it is important to indicate precisely what is meant by a barrier to entry in the new analysis. It is equally important to understand what is not a barrier to entry, for, especially in contestable markets, as we have just seen, the absence of entry does not necessarily imply that there are any barriers to entry, interpreting the term pejoratively. Additional entry may simply have been rendered inefficient by the commendable behaviour of the incumbents. Following earlier writers, an entry barrier is defined in the contestability literature as anything that requires an expenditure by a new entrant into an industry but that imposes no equivalent cost upon an incumbent. Thus, for example, if an incumbent entered an industry before regulation was inaugurated but any entrants now must incur the heavy delay costs and legal fees required to obtain the regulatory agency's permission to enter, then these costs that an entrant must bear but that were never borne by the incumbent constitute a true barrier as it is defined here. Under that definition, however, economies of scale are not a barrier to entry in and of themselves, and in this respect the analysis is in conflict with some traditional views. Economies of scale do, of course, lead to a presumption that the industry is a natural monopoly; but, as we have seen, in the absence of entry barriers in the sense just defined such a natural monopoly can retain its immunity from entry only if its behaviour is essentially competitive. Looked at another way, an entry barrier is defined in the new theory as something that necessarily imposes a cost upon the economy, whereas some of the items traditionally classed as entry barriers in fact exact no such cost.

In the absence of barriers that are created by legal institutions or by deliberate measures taken by incumbents to sabotage entry, there is one form of barrier to entry that seems most common. This type of barrier arises characteristically in industries whose technology requires the firm to sink large amounts of capital before it can carry out its productive and selling activities. Here it is important to recognize that a sunk cost is not the same as a fixed cost. There are many types of fixed outlays that do not constitute sunk costs. A prime example is an expensive airplane in which an airline needs to invest before it can operate along a particular route, say, that between New York and Los Angeles. Even though that airplane costs many millions of dollars, should it transpire after the airline has entered the route that it was not a very profitable opportunity after all, the airline can simply fly out the plane and use it to serve some other route instead. Fixed costs are, then, indeed required for the operation of the airline along that route, but those costs are not sunk, that is, any entry decision can be reversed with little loss to the firm that incurred the outlay. It should be clear that even when entry involves the expenditure of a good deal of money, if the money can be withdrawn quickly and easily, hit-and-run entry is possible virtually by definition. In other words, absence of sunk costs is one of the hallmarks of absence of entry barriers and of contestability of the market.

The converse is also true; where it is necessary to incur substantial sunk costs the entrant is most likely to find the cost of incursions into the market to be high. Sunk costs subject the entrant to two types of risk. The first is the normal sort of risk which, at least at one time, was shared by the incumbent as well; it is the danger that, once the costs have been sunk, it transpires that demands or other market conditions are unconducive to profitable activity, and that the investment therefore turns out to be an expensive mistake. This is not barrier to entry in our sense, because it need not subject the entrant to a risk greater than the incumbent underwent in an earlier period when it first opened for business. However, a sunk cost requirement for entry subjects the entrant to a second risk from which the incumbent may well have been immune; for once the entrant has committed his capital to the new enterprise he becomes vulnerable to damaging countermoves by the incumbent. Suppose, for example, that the incumbent has previously charged non-competitive prices and earned monopoly profits, and an entrant, attracted by this opportunity, incurs the heavy sunk costs required for admission into the market only to find that the incumbent had chosen to revise his price policy. By reducing both prices and profits the incumbent can sap the entry opportunity of its profitability. Had costs not been sunk this would have represented no particular threat to the entrant who, on seeing such a development, could simply have picked up his capital and gone elsewhere. But once costs are sunk he is stuck in his unprofitable position for some considerable period of time. The prospect of such a sequence of events and its recognition by potential entrants constitutes a prime barrier to entry. It is an entry barrier in our sense because it can be a source of heavy losses in consumer welfare. For if such a barrier is effective in precluding entry, it provides the protection the incumbent needs to enable him to charge non-competitive prices, to earn monopoly profits and to make the other sorts of decisions that standard analysis leads us to expect in non-competitive markets.

This observation indicates what the policy-maker should look for in deciding whether a particular market does or does not call for measures to increase economic efficiency and to protect the welfare of consumers. As will be seen next, it also suggests the character of the measures the policy-maker may find it useful to adopt to improve the workings of a market that requires his attention.

ON TRADITIONAL PUBLIC POLICY

It has long been considered proper and appropriate for government to take a hand in the determination of industry structure. This was done in a variety of ways. In many regulated industries there is a long tradition of prohibition or inhibition of entry by new firms. Potential entrants have been required to prove that their entry would serve 'the public convenience or necessity' before a licence was granted to them. Normally this procedure has been lengthy, expensive and by no means a sure thing. Moreover, regulatory agencies have taken it as part of their role to prevent the exit of firms from unprofitable markets. Thus, railroads and airlines were refused permission to close services on unprofitable routes in which they were incurring losses. In regulated industries, then, firms found it difficult to open up for business and, once they opened, found it was difficult to leave — not because of the nature of the industry, but as a consequence of the policies adopted by the regulators.

In the anti-trust arena attempts to influence industry structure were even more blatant and more direct. When anti-rust authorities seek a judicial ruling requiring a large firm to be broken into several smaller enterprises they clearly are attempting to dictate industry structure. Indeed, any of the various types of intervention by the anti-trust agencies designed to increase the number of participants in a market clearly constitutes an attempt to affect the structure of the industry. Anti-trust, regulation and other governmental measures have also had indirect consequences of this sort. This has occurred in a variety of ways. For example, when regulatory agencies have imposed a set of prices upon a utility that involve cross-subsidies favouring certain types of enterprise, or small communities or inner cities, solvency has required those regulated firms' other customer classes to pay prices considerably higher than marginal or average incremental costs to make up for the losses in the subsidized lines of activity. But, then, every market in which prices were well above those costs becomes an invitation to entry, whether or not it serves efficiency or consumer welfare. Thus, such a regulatory pricing policy constitutes an artificial inducement to entry that sometimes has proved irresistible.

Contestability theory provides two observations that are pertinent to all this. First, by emphasizing the fact that market structure is ultimately dictated by market forces, it shows that the attempt by government to change market structure is often likely to be beset by difficulties and is sometimes doomed to failure. Second, the contestability analysis shows that such structural changes, besides being difficult to achieve, may also not be particularly desirable. Where a market is contestable a proliferation in the number of firms is simply unnecessary to achieve the advantages of competition, and is certain to lead to increases in inefficiency and in costs.

Perhaps it is no mere coincidence that the new analysis arose just about the time that the move to deregulation got underway, and that the range and severity of government intervention declined dramatically in a variety of industries such as airlines, banking, railroad transportation and telecommunications. Research often appears to respond to the requirements of the times at which it is carried out.

It should also be noted, incidentally, that 'the other type of regulation' – that of environment, safety in the workplace, etc. (it may perhaps be referred to as social regulation as contrasted with economic regulation of the public utility type) – also has its implications for industry structure. For example, any measures that force firms to reduce their pollution emissions are likely to constitute a relative disadvantage for industries whose emissions are unavoidably heavy. Thus, even this type of regulation is likely to play a significant role in future studies of the consequences of public actions for industry structure. However, such studies are likely to prove less critical of the consequences for industry structure of such social regulation. For while in a highly contestable market it may make little sense to break up a large firm simply as a means to increase the number of enterprises in the market, in contrast, it may very well serve the public interest if a highly polluting firm goes out of business or reduces its scale of operation when it is forced to bear the costs it imposes on society.

POLICY IMPLICATIONS OF CONTESTABILITY ANALYSIS

The implications of contestability analysis for public policy are perhaps best illustrated by returning to the example of airline deregulation. For a long time before it actually occurred economists had argued for deregulation of the airlines, basing their analysis to some extent on lessons derived from the theory of perfect competition. Yet this was at best a shaky basis for their conclusion because it is clear that no airline market can ever approximate the large multiplicity of tiny firms necessary for perfect competition to work. We see now that the advisability of deregulation in the airlines may follow, rather, from the degree to which they approximate perfect contestability. Even though airplanes constitute a heavy investment outlay, the fact that this cost represents highly mobile capital with which it is easy to enter and exit makes the market mechanism effective in the airline industry.

We have seen that contestable markets are characterized by four desirable properties. They must yield no excessive profits, they must operate at minimum cost, that is, at maximal efficiency, they must offer no cross-subsidies, and in a greater variety of cases for which the proposition had previously been accepted, prices must equal marginal costs, so that market forces will impost prices that are consistent with Pareto optimality in resource allocation. This suggests that an appropriate goal of public policy should be to obtain industry performance that is as close to that in a contestable market as is achievable. This ideal should be substituted for the inappropriate and unattainable ideal of approximation to perfect competition.

Contestability analysis also yields a number of more specific conclusions relevant for policy. First, it has brought out the critical importance of freedom of exit. Indeed, it has shown that without freedom of exit freedom of entry becomes impossible. A firm that learns that if it opens for business in some industry it will be prevented by government authorities from reversing its decision, even if its entry proves to have been a mistake, is very likely to judge entry into the industry to be excessively risky and unacceptable. Thus, while programmes designed to prevent exit may have the best of motives – continuation of service to isolated communities, saving of jobs and the preservation of sources of tax revenue to hard-pressed municipalities — contestability analysis shows that in the long run denial of freedom of exit for any of these purposes is likely to exact a heavy cost in terms of economic efficiency and cost to consumers.

A second policy implication of the theory is that a history of absence of entry into an industry is by no means conclusive evidence of the presence of entry barriers. Infrequency of entry in the past may simply have been a response to competitive behaviour by the incumbents, who, by their sheer efficiency, low prices and low profits, made the market unattractive to potential entrants.

Third, the analysis shows that many traditional indicators of unsatisfactory structure or behaviour — concentration, price discrimination, conglomerate mergers, vertical or horizontal integration, etc. — do not automatically call for government intervention, as has traditionally been thought. We have seen that where a market is perfectly contestable even though it contains only a small number of firms, they are required to operate efficiently and to charge reasonable prices. In a perfectly contestable market if the number of firms is small that must be so because it is cheaper for a few large firms to produce the industry's output than for many small ones to do so. And the large firms can retain their markets only if they offer consumers all the advantages of competition. Of course, if a market is not contestable, concentration continues to constitute a significant source of concern and so may the other *per se* indicators.

Finally, the most significant implication of the new analysis is, undoubtedly, the prime importance of reduction of barriers to entry. Certainly all artificial barriers and particularly those that result from government intervention are put into question. But we have seen that the need for a firm to incur heavy sunk costs also constitutes a barrier to entry. If such costs are dictated by technological circumstances it may seem that there is little that can be done about them. Yet there is at least one way in which the resulting problem can be alleviated. Sunk facilities can sometimes be isolated. This occurs in passenger aviation in which, while the airplanes represent capital on wings and therefore do not constitute sunk costs, as we have seen, an airport is very much a sunk investment. If the demand for services at a particular airport declines drastically one cannot just pick up its facilities and move them elsewhere where the need for them is greater. Thus, airports can constitute a barrier to entry that can deter the entry of new firms if their construction and operation is left entirely to free enterprise. Instead, the airports have largely been kept out of the hands of the airlines. They have been isolated from the more contestable portions of aviation markets by keeping them as public property operated by a public agency which can dedicate itself to the encouragement of competition, or at least to avoidance of impediments to contestability. By impartial leasing of airport slots to all comers, airlines can be left free to operate without regulatory constraints while the portion of the industry's capital that constitutes a sunk cost is kept out of their hands.

CONCLUDING COMMENTS

There is much more to the implications of contestability analysis, but space prevents my going into further detail. The theory provides a number of new analytic methods new tasks for empirical research and new results. It offers a standard for public policy that is far broader and more widely applicable than the traditional ideal of perfect competition. It leads to an analysis of industry structure that describes its determinants and the implications for its behaviour. All in all, it constitutes a significant new departure in the analysis of the firm and of the industry in the literature of economics.

NOTE

1. *Proof:* Let a market contain m firms, y_j^k by firm k's output of product j and $Q_j(p)$ be the quantity of j demand by the market at price vector p.

$$\text{Suppose } y_j^k < \sum_{h=1}^{m} y_j^h = Q_j(p) \text{ and } p_j > C_j(y^k).$$

Consider this function of the scalar $t: \psi(t) = p \cdot (y^k + tu^j) - C(Y^k + tu^j)$, where u^j is the vector with zeros for each component except for the jth, which is unity. $\psi(t)$ is the profit earned by an entry plan replicating all of the activities of firm k with the exception of an increase by amount t in the output of good j. Evaluating it at $t = 0, \psi(0) = p \cdot y^k - C(y^k) = 0$, since a firm in a sustainable configuration must earn exactly zero profit. Differentiation yeilds $\psi'(t) = p_j - C_j (y^k + tu^j)$, at $t = 0, \psi'(0) = p_j - C_j(y^k)$ > 0 which is positive by hypothesis.

Thus, the profit earned by the entry plan increases from zero as t is increased from 0. Hence, there exists some $\bar{t} > 0$ such that $\psi(t) > 0$ for $0 < t < \bar{t}$. Moreover, the entry plan is feasible for $0 < t \leqslant Q^j(p)$ $- y_j^k$ so that the entrant's output of good j, $y_j^k + t$, remains no greater than the amount demanded by consumers, $Q^j(p)$. Consequently, for $0 < t \leqslant \min (\bar{t}, Q^j(p) - y_j^k)$, the entry plan is both feasible and profitable, which contradicts the hypothesis that the industry configuration is sustainable. Our result follows – p_j must be equal to $C_j(y^k)$ for firm k's output vector to be part of a sustainable configuration in which firm k is not the sole producer of good j.

REFERENCES

Baumol, W. J. (1977) 'On the Proper Cost Tests for Natural Monopoly in a Mulitproduct Industry', *American Economic Review*, 67 (December): 809–22.

Baumol, W. J. and D. Fischer (1978) 'Cost-Minimizing Number of Firms and Determination of Industry Structure', *Quarterly Journal of Economics*, 92 (August): 439–67.

Baumol, W. J. and R. D. Willig (1981) 'Fixed Costs, Sunk Costs, Entry Barriers, and Sustainability of Monopoly', *Quarterly Journal of Economics*, 96 (August): 405–31.

Baumol, W. J., J. D. Panzar and R. D. Willig (1982) *Contestable Markets and the Theory of Industry Structure*, San Diego: Harcourt Brace Jovanovich.

Panzar, J. C., and R. D. Willig (1981) 'Economies of Scope', *American Economic Review*, 71 (May): 268–72.

Willig, R. D. (1979) 'Multiproduct Technology and Market Structure', *American Economic Review*, 69 (May): 346–51.

9 Monopoly and Sustainable Prices as a Nash Equilibrium in Contestable Markets

LEONARD J. MIRMAN, YAIR TAUMAN, ISRAEL ZANG*

The theory of perfectly contestable markets and sustainable prices, summarized in Baumol, Panzar and Willig (1982) is an extension of the ideas of Bain (1956) in which potential competition, unencumbered by frictions, entry or exit costs, affect an incumbent firm's decisions on prices, outputs and therefore profits. In particular, the theory of perfectly contestable markets studies the effect of the existence of potential entry on market structure, prices and outputs.

The purpose of this chapter is to study properties of an equilibrium in a model with perfectly contestable markets. Namely, given perfectly contestable markets under what conditions, when potential entry is taken into account, would there by only one firm found producing the entire vector of outputs and operating under sustainable prices? It is shown in this chapter that when technology is expressed by a joint sub-additive cost function, the notion of a sustainable monopoly can be derived as a result of a Bertrand–Nash equilibrium of an economy consisting of many potential multi-product firms.

Consider a monopoly producing n infinitely divisible goods and facing a vector $Q(p_1, \ldots, p_n) = Q(p) = (Q_1(p), \ldots, Q_n(p))$ of inverse demand functions. Here $p_j \in E^1_+$ is the market price of good j. Suppose that the monopoly uses the technology expressed by a joint sub-additive cost function $C:E^n_+ \to E^1_+$ (i.e. $C(y + z) \leqslant C(y) + C(z)$ for each $y, z \in E^n_+$) where $C(y)$ is the minumum cost of producing the output vector $y \in E^n_+$.

* We would like to acknowledge the partial support from the NSF through grant SES–81–06207 and the Israel Institute of Business Research at Tel Aviv University.

Denote by $N = \{1, \ldots, n\}$ the set of all goods and let $S \subseteq N$ be a subset of N. Let s denote the number of goods in S (or the cardinality of S) then, for a given $S \subseteq N$, y^S (or similarly $Q^S(p)$) and p^S are vectors in E_+^s denoting quantities and prices, respectively, of goods in S. For $S = N$ the subscript S is omitted. Thus y^S and p^S are the projections of y and p, respectively, on E_+^s. For convenience the notation $z \mid y^s$ with y, $z \in E^n$, will sometimes be used to denote the vector $(y^S, z^{N/S})$ where N/S denotes the complement of S with respect to N, that is, both $z \mid y^S$ and $(y^S, z^{N/S})$ are the vector z except that the co-ordinates in S are replaced by y^S. The convention that $C(y^S) = C(y^S, 0^{N/S}) = C(0 \mid y^S)$ will also be used.

Consider a potential entrant having access to the same technology, expressed by the cost function $C(y)$, as possessed by the monopoly and incurring zero entry and exit costs regardless of the goods and quantities produced. The entrant may produce any vector of quantities y^S of any subset $S \subseteq N$ of the goods at price $\hat{p}^S$. Panzar and Willig (1977) (see also Baumol, Bailey and Willig, 1977) considered two types of entry behaviour and their corresponding sustainability concepts. The first one is partial entry sustainability.

Definition: Sustainability against partial (quantity) entry (PE). The price vector $\bar{p}$ is *PE sustainable* if every triple $(S, \hat{y}^S, \hat{p}^S)$ satisfying:

$$\hat{p}^S \leqslant \bar{p}^S \tag{9.I}$$

and:

$$\hat{y}^S \leqslant Q^S(\hat{p}^S, \bar{p}^{N/S}) \tag{9.II}$$

also satisfies:

$$\hat{p}^S \hat{y}^S - C(\hat{y}^S) \leqslant 0$$

Conditions (9.I) and (9.II) describe the behaviour of a partial (quantity) entrant. For the goods in S, prices are offered that are not greater than those already prevailing in the market (condition 9.I). At these prices *any quantities* up to those determined by the market demand functions evaluated at the new (lower) prices $\hat{p}^S$, for goods in S and the prevailing prices $\bar{p}^{N/S}$, for the rest of the goods (condition 9.II) may be sold. Thus, $\bar{p}$ is *PE* sustainable if a potential entrant *cannot anticipate positive* profits by lowering some or all of the market prices and supplying only a portion of the demand. The second sustainability concept is weaker and specifies that entrants must supply the entire market demand generated by the lower prices they offer.

Definition: Sustainability against full (quantity) entry (FE). The price vector $\bar{p}$ is *FE sustainable* if every triple $(S, \hat{y}^S, \hat{p}^S)$ satisfying (9.I) and:

$$\hat{y}^S = Q^S(\bar{p} \mid \hat{p}^S) \tag{9.III}$$

also satisfies:

$$\hat{p}^S \hat{y}^S - C(\hat{y}^S) \leqslant 0$$

Clearly, *PE* sustainability implies *FE* sustainability. C conditions under which the reverse implication holds are discussed below.

BERTRAND–NASH SUSTAINABILITY

In this section a simple general equilibrium model is studied. Corresponding to this general equilibrium model is a Bertrand–Nash game which is played by many potential producers. Outputs are produced by a joint sub-additive cost function available to all the producers. The equilibrium points of the game are characterized by three properties: outputs are produced by a single firm, monopoly profits are zero, and equilibrium prices are *FE* sustainable. The characterization combined with the discussion of the second section relating *FE* to *PE* sustainability, provides a justification for the above definitions of sustainable prices.

Consider an infinite set M of producers and a finite set $N = \{1, \dots, n\}$ of infinitely divisible outputs. All the producers in M use the same technology. They produce a subset of outputs in N using a single input (labour). The production technology is represented by the cost function:

$$L = C(y_1, \dots, y_n)$$

which measures the minimum amount of input L required to produce the vector $(y_1, \dots, y_n)$ of outputs.

Consumers in this model play a passive role and only their aggregate demands are considered. Behind the scenes it is assumed that consumers are endowed with some positive amount of the input and consume $n + 1$ goods: leisure and the n outputs. The input is used in the model as a numeraire. Thus if $p = (p_1, \dots, p_n)$ is the output price vector (in input units) then $Q_j(p_1, \ldots, p_n)$ is the total amount of the j-th output demanded. Let:

$$Q(p) = (Q_1(p), \ldots, Q_n(p))$$

Let $\bar{E}_+^1 = E_+^1 \cup \{\infty\}$ and $\bar{E}_+^n = \overset{n}{\underset{i=1}{X}} \bar{E}_+^1$. The demand function $Q(\cdot)$ is assumed to be defined on $\bar{E}_+^n$ with the convention that $p_j = \infty$ implies $Q_j(p) = 0$.

The above model is associated with the following game in strategic form. The set of players is the set M of producers. The strategy set of each producer is $\bar{E}_+^n$, that is, the set of output price vectors. This strategy set is consistent with Bertrand's use of prices and not quantities as strategies. An M-tuple of strategies is a function p from M to $\bar{E}_+^n$. The strategy of the i-th producer under p is $p(i) \in \bar{E}_+^n$. Any M-tuple of strategies p determines, as an outcome, the price vector $p = (p_1, \ldots, p_n) \in \bar{E}_+^n$ which is defined by:

$$p_j = \inf \{ p_j(i) \mid i \epsilon M \}, j \in N \tag{9.1}$$

In (9.1) if the *inf* can be replaced by the minimum operation the price p_j is the lowest price offered for the j-th output.

The pay-offs to the producers are defined as their profits. The question is how to define these profits. To answer this question additional notation is needed. For each $j \in N$, let $M_j(p)$ be the set of all 'active producers' of the j-th output under p, that is:

$$M_j(p) = \{ i \epsilon M \mid p_j(i) = p_j \}$$

The set $M_j(p)$ contains all firms willing to produce the aggregate demand $Q_j(p)$ at price p_j. If $M_j(p)$ is not a singleton then $Q_j(p)$ must be allocated in some way among the producers in $M_j(p)$. The main results of this section, however, do not dpeend on the way $Q_j(p)$ is allocated among the firms in $M_j(p)$.

Let $\alpha_j(i, p)$ be a function that determines, for each producer $i \epsilon M_j(p)$ and each M-tuple of strategies p, the part of $Q_j(p)$ to be allocated to the i-th producer. It is required that, for each $j \epsilon N$:

$$i \epsilon M_j(p) \Leftrightarrow \alpha_j(i, p) > 0 \text{ and } \underset{i \epsilon M_j(p)}{\Sigma} \alpha_j(i, p) = 1, \text{ if } M_j(p) \neq \phi$$

The i-th producer, as a result of the M-tuple of strategies $\underset{\sim}{p}$, produces the quantity:

$$y_j^i(\underset{\sim}{p}) = \alpha_j(i, \underset{\sim}{p}) Q_j(\underset{\sim}{p})$$

of the j-th output. Let:

$$y^i(\underset{\sim}{p}) = (y^i_1(\underset{\sim}{p}), \dots, y^i_n(\underset{\sim}{p}))$$

The pay-off $\pi^i(\underset{\sim}{p})$ is the profit under $\underset{\sim}{p}$ to the i-th producer. Namely:

$$\pi^i(\underset{\sim}{p}) = py^i(\underset{\sim}{p}) - C(y^i(\underset{\sim}{p}))$$

where p is defined by (9.1).

Definition: An M-tuple of strategies $\underset{\sim}{p}$ results in a monopoly if for some $i\epsilon M$, $M_j(\underset{\sim}{p}) = \{\, i\,\}$, for all $j\epsilon N$. In particular, if p is the price vector determined by $\underset{\sim}{p}$ then $p = p(i)$ and for each $k\epsilon M$, $k \neq i$, $p(k) \gg p$.

If an $\tilde{M}$-tuple of strategies $\underset{\sim}{p}$ results in a monopoly then its profit under the corresponding price vector p is:

$$\pi(p) = pQ(p) - C(Q(p))$$

Definition: A Bertrand–Nash equilibrium (hereafter *BN* equilibrium) in pure strategies in this model is an M-tuple of strategies $\bar{\underset{\sim}{p}}$ such that for each $p^i \epsilon \bar{E}^n_+$ and for each $i\epsilon M$:

$$\pi^i(\bar{\underset{\sim}{p}}|p^i) \leqslant \pi^i(\bar{\underset{\sim}{p}})$$

where $\bar{\underset{\sim}{p}} \mid p^i$ is the M-tuple $\bar{\underset{\sim}{p}}$ with $\bar{p}(i)$ replaced by p^i. The price vector p determined from $\bar{\underset{\sim}{p}}$ by:

$$p_j = \inf\,\{\,\bar{p}_j(i)\mid i\epsilon M\,\},\ j\epsilon N$$

is called a *BN equilibrium price vector*.

Assumptions

(i) The aggregate demand function $Q(p)$ is continuous on :

$$E^n_{++} = \{\,x\epsilon E^n \mid x_j > 0, j = 1, \dots, n\,\}\,.$$

(ii) The cost function $C(\cdot)$ is strictly subadditive over the set of products N. Namely if $y = y^1 + y^2$ where $y^1, y^2 \in E_+^N$, $y^1 \neq 0$ and $y^2 \neq 0$ then:

$$C(y) < C(y^1) + C(y^2)$$

Theorem 1: Under Assumptions (i) and (ii) any BN equilibrium $\tilde{p}$ yielding a positive level of production results in a monopoly.

Theorem 2: Under Assumptions (i) and (ii), the following two conditions are necessary and sufficient for a price vector $\bar{p}$ to be a BN equilibrium price vector:

 I $\bar{p}$ *is FE sustainable*

 II $\bar{p}$ *is a cost sharing price vector, that is:*

$$\pi(\bar{p}) = \bar{p}Q(\bar{p}) - C(Q(\bar{p})) = 0$$

Remarks

(1) Notice that the pay-off $\pi^i(p \mid p^i)$ is not a continuous function of p^i and thus the existence of a BN equilibrium, in this model, is not guaranteed. The sufficiency part of Theorem 2 implies, however, that any sustainable cost sharing price vector $\bar{p}$ is associated with a BN equilibrium.

(2) PE sustainability cannot, in general, replace FE sustainability in condition I of Theorem 2. First note that PE sustainability is inconsistent with the market mechanism described above. It seems difficult to make PE sustainability consistent with any market equilibrium in the Nash sense since it gives an entrant the opportunity to determine *both* prices and quantities. Corollary 6 below shows, however, that there are wide classes of markets for which PE and FE sustainability are equivalent.

(3) If $\bar{p}$ is a BN equilibrium and if $\pi(\cdot)$ is differentiable then $\partial\bar{\pi}/\partial p_j(\bar{p}) > 0$, for each $j\epsilon N$. This observation follows by the FE sustainability of p and the differentiability of $\pi(\cdot)$.

(4) Notice that in this model the notion of BN equilibrium is equivalent to the notion of strong Nash equilibrium. In a BN equilibrium only deviations by individual producers are considered while in a strong Nash equilibrium the deviations of groups of producers are considered.

(5) The case in which M is finite is very restrictive as is made clear in Pro-

position (3). Hence the set M is assumed to contain infinitely many producers. However, using the notion of $\in$-equilibrium it can be shown that with no restriction on the cardinality of M, conditions I and II of Theorem 2 are necessary and sufficient for p to be an $\in$-BN equilibrium price vector.

Proposition 1: Under Assumptions (i) and (ii) if M *is finite and if* $\bar{p}$ *is a BN equilibrium then the profit function* $\pi(\cdot)$ *has a local maximum at the corresponding BN equilibrium price vector* $\bar{p}$ *and* $\pi(\bar{p}) = 0$

In the one-dimensional case Proposition 3 implies that if M is finite then the price vector $\bar{p}$ is a BN equilibrium price vector if and only if the average cost curve is tangent to the demand curve at $\bar{p}$ and for any price p below $\bar{p}$ the average cost curve is above the demand curve. This is illustrated in Figure 9.1 where $P(y)$ is the inverse demand curve.

Both $\bar{p}_1$ and $\bar{p}_2$ in Figure 9.1 are PE sustainable cost sharing prices. If M is finite then $\bar{p}_1$ is a BN equilibrium price while $\bar{p}_2$ is not. If M is an

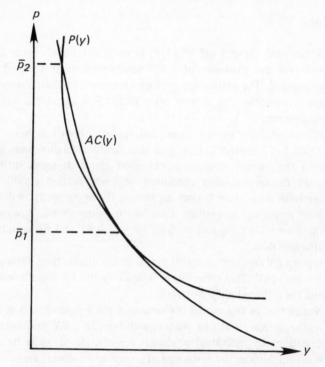

FIGURE 9.1

infinite set then both are *BN* equilibrium prices. This example shows that the finite case ($|M| < \infty$) is considerably more restrictive then the infinite case.

Let $\bar{p}$ be an *M*-tuple of strategies and let $\bar{p}$ be the resulting market price vector, that is for each $j \epsilon N$, $\bar{p}_j = \inf \{ \bar{p}_j(i) \mid i \epsilon M \}$. The following proposition states a necessary conditon as well as a sufficient condition for $\bar{p}$ to be a *BN* equilibrium.

Proposition 2: Under Assumptions (i) *and* (ii):
(a) *A necessary condition for $\bar{p}$ to be a BN equilibrium is that for each $j \epsilon N$ either $\bar{p}_j$ is a local maximum of $\pi(\bar{p} \mid p_j)$ (as a function of p_j) or $\bar{p}_j$ is an accumulation point of $\{ \bar{p}_j(i) \mid i \epsilon M \}$.*
(b) *If $\bar{p}$ results in a monopoly, $\bar{p}$ is FE sustainable and $\bar{p}_j$ is an accumulation point of $\{ \bar{p}_j(i) \mid i \epsilon M \}$, for each $j \epsilon N$, then $\bar{p}$ is a BN equilibrium.*

We now give the proofs of the above results.

Proof of Theorem 1: Let $\bar{p}$ be a *BN* equilibrium. Assume that more than one firm produces positive quantities under $\bar{p}$, that is:

$$y^i(\bar{p}) \neq 0 \quad \text{and} \quad \sum_{k \neq i} y^k(\bar{p}) \neq 0 \tag{9.2}$$

Without loss of generality it may be assumed that $\bar{p}_j > 0$, for each $j \epsilon N$. Let $e = (1, 1, \ldots, 1)$ and let $\in > 0$ be small enough such that $\bar{p} - \in e \, \epsilon \, E^n_+$ Consider the price vector:

$$\hat{p}^i = \bar{p} - \in e$$

Clearly:

$$\pi^i(\bar{p} \mid \hat{p}^i) = \hat{p}^i Q(\hat{p}^i) - C(Q(\hat{p}^i)) \tag{9.3}$$

and:

$$\pi^i(\bar{p}) = \bar{p} y^i(\bar{p}) - C(y^i(\bar{p})) \tag{9.4}$$

Since $\sum_{k \epsilon M} y^k(\bar{p}) = Q(\bar{p})$ we obtain by (9.2), together with Assumption (ii), that:

$$D(\bar{p}) \equiv \sum_{k \epsilon M} C(y^k(\bar{p})) - C(Q(\bar{p})) > 0 \tag{9.5}$$

By the continuity of $Q(\cdot)$ and $C(\cdot)$, for $\in > 0$ sufficiently small there exists an $S(\bar{p}, \in) > 0$ such that:

$$\hat{p}^i Q(\hat{p}^i) - C(Q(\hat{p}^i)) > \bar{p} Q(\bar{p}) - C(Q(\bar{p})) - S(\bar{p}, \in) \qquad (9.6)$$

where $S(\bar{p}, \in) \to 0$, as $\in \to 0$. By (9.3), (9.4), (9.5) and (9.6):

$$
\begin{aligned}
\pi^i(\bar{p} \mid \hat{p}^i) - \pi^i(\bar{p}) &= \hat{p}^i Q(\hat{p}^i) - \bar{p} y^i(\bar{p}) + C(y^i(\bar{p})) - C(Q(\hat{p}^i)) \\
&> \bar{p} Q(\bar{p}) - \bar{p} y^i(\bar{p}) + C(y^i(\bar{p})) - C(Q(p)) - S(\bar{p}, \in) \\
&= \bar{p} Q(\bar{p}) - \bar{p} y^i(\bar{p}) + C(y^i(\bar{p})) - \sum_{k \in M} C(y^k(\bar{p})) \\
&\quad + D(\bar{p}) - S(\bar{p}, \in) \\
&= \sum_{\substack{k \in M \\ k \neq i}} \bar{p} y^k(\bar{p}) - \sum_{\substack{k \in M \\ k \neq i}} C(y^k(\bar{p})) + D(\bar{p}) - S(\bar{p}, \in) \\
&> \sum_{\substack{k \in m \\ k \neq i}} [\bar{p} y^k(\bar{p}) - C(y^k(\bar{p}))]
\end{aligned}
$$

The last inequality follows for sufficiently small $\in > 0$ since $D(\bar{p}) > 0$ and $S(\bar{p}, \in) \to 0$, as $\in \to 0$. Now since each producer makes at least zero profit (the alternative not to produce by selecting $\bar{p}(i) = (\infty, \ldots, \infty)$ is always possible) under the equilibrium $\bar{p}$ the right-hand side of 9.6 is non-negative. Hence:

$$\pi^i(\bar{p} \mid p^i) - \pi^i(\bar{p}) > 0$$

contradicting the fact that $\bar{p}$ is a *BN* equilibrium.

Proof of Theorem 2: First it will be shown that if $\bar{p}$ is a *BN* equilibrium price vector then it satisfies conditions I and II. Indeed let $\bar{p}$ be a *BN* equilibrium that determines the price vector $\bar{p}$. Assume first that a positive profit can be made under $\bar{p}$. *Let $k \in M$*. The k-th firm by offering prices below $\bar{p}$ by a sufficiently small $\in > 0$, becomes the only producer in the market. By the continuity of $Q(\cdot)$ and $C(\cdot)$ the k-th firm makes a positive profit. Consequently it pays the k-th producer to deviate from its equilibrium strategy $\bar{p}(k)$, which is a contradiction. Hence condition II is satisfied. Condition I follows immediately from the definition of a *BN* equilibrium.

Finally let us prove that if M is an infinite set then conditions I and II are sufficient for $\bar{p}$ to be a *BN* equilibrium price vector. Let $\bar{p}$ be an

M-tuple of strategies such that for some $i\epsilon M$, $\bar{p}(i) = \bar{p}$, for each $k \neq i$, $\bar{p}_j(k) > \bar{p}_j$, for all $j\epsilon N$ and $\bar{p}$ is an accumulation point of $\{ \bar{p}(k) \mid k \neq i, k\epsilon M\}$. From condition II profits at $\bar{p}$ for firm i are zero. Hence, using condition I it is now easy to verify that $\bar{p}$ is a *BN* equilibrium. Thus the proof of Theorem 2 is complete.

Proof of Proposition 1: Since M is finite, the *BN* equilibrium price vector $\bar{p}$ cannot be an accumulation point of $\{ \bar{p}(i) \mid i\epsilon M\}$. By Theorem 1, there is a unique producer $i\epsilon M$ such that $\bar{p}(i) = \bar{p}$ and $\bar{p}(k) \gg \bar{p}$ for each $k \neq i$. Thus i remains the only producer even if it changes prices in a small neighbourhood of $\bar{p}$. However such a change cannot yield an increase in i's profit (since $\bar{p}$ is a *BN* equilibrium). Thus $\bar{p}$ is a local maximum of π and by the necessary condition of Theorem 2 (which holds for $|M| < \infty$ as well) $\pi(\bar{p}) = 0$.

Proof of Proposition 2:
(a) Assume that $\bar{p}$ is a *BN* equilibrium resulting in a positive level of prodcution. Let $i\epsilon M$ be the resulting monopoly. By Theorem 2, $\bar{p}$ is *FE* sustainable. Thus:

$$\pi^i(\bar{p}) = \pi(\bar{p}) \geqslant \pi^i(\bar{p} \mid p_j) , \quad \text{whenever } p_j \leqslant \bar{p}_j$$

Now assume that $\bar{p}_j$ is not a local maximum of $\pi(\bar{p} \mid p_j)$. Then in each neighbourhood of $\bar{p}_j$ there exists p_j with $p_j > \bar{p}_j$ such that $\pi^i(\bar{p}) < \pi(\bar{p} \mid p_j)$. Thus, since $\bar{p}$ is a *BN* equilibrium, $\pi(p \mid p_j) \neq \pi^i(\bar{p} \mid p_j)$ which is possible only if for some $k\epsilon M$, $k \neq i$, $\bar{p}_j > \bar{p}_j(k) > p_j$. Consequently, for each neighbourhood U of $\bar{p}_j$ there exists $k\epsilon M$ such that $\bar{p}_j(k) \in U$ and thus p_j is an accumulation point of $\{ \bar{p}_j(k) \mid k\epsilon M \}$.
(b) Let $i\epsilon M$ be the resulting monopoly under $\bar{p}$. Since $\bar{p}$ is *FE* sustainable no other producer in M can make a positive profit. Finally it must be shown that producer i cannot increase its own profit by increasing some of the components of $\bar{P}$. If this could happen then since $\bar{p}$ is an accumulation point of $\bar{p}(k)$, $k \neq i$, the monopoly would lose the market in these components and by the *FE* sustainability of $\bar{p}$ the monopolist cannot increase its profits.

PE, FE SUSTAINABILITY AND BN EQUILIBRIUM

The sustainability notions of Panzar and Willig (1977) or of Baumol, Bailey and Willig (1977) aim to provide conditions that are necessary to deter a potential entrant and to sustain a monopoly through the use of prices. In the first sction a simple general equilibrium model was presented consisting of a number of potential producers and a corresponding game in strategic form played by these producers in which a BN equilibrium of this game results in a monopoly sustained by the equilibrium prices. In the context of this equilibrium *FE* sustainability seems to be the appropriate sustainability concept. However, as is shown in Mirman, Tauman and Zang (1983), if all outputs are weak gross substitutions then any *FE* sustainable price vector is *PE* sustainable. Moreover, since *M* is an infinite set, then a *PE* sustainable cost sharing price vector is a BN equilibrium price vector and vice versa. Namely, if all outputs are weak gross substitutes the two notions, *PE* sustainability and *BN* equilibrium prices, are equivalent. This statement can be made precise as follows. Consider a monopoly operating at a cost sharing vector $\bar{p}$ (i.e. $\bar{p}Q(\bar{p}) = C(Q(\bar{p}))$).

Assumptions

(iii) The cost function C is twice differentiable on $E^n_+ \setminus \{0\}$ and $C_{\ell j} \leqslant 0$, for any $\ell, j \epsilon N$.
(iv) For each $j \epsilon N$, $Q_j(\cdot)$ is differentiable on $E^n_+ \setminus \{0\}$.
(v) The goods in N are weak gross substitutes, namely $\partial Q_j / \partial p_\ell \geqslant 0$, for each $\ell \neq j$.

Proposition 3: Under Assumptions (iii), (iv) *and* (v), *an entrant maximizing profits can select a sub-set* $S \subseteq N$, *prices* $\hat{p}^S$, *such that* $\hat{p}^S \leqslant \bar{p}^S$ *and will produce the entire demand* $Q^S(\hat{p}^S \bar{p}^{N \setminus S})$.

For a proof see Mirman, Tauman and Zang (1983).

Note that a result similar to Proposition 3 was obtained by Panzar and Willig (1977) under a different assumption. Namely, assumption (iii) is replaced by declining average incremental cost (DAIC).

Corollary: Under Assumption (iii), (iv) *and* (v) *any FE sustainable price vector is PE sustainable.*
Proof: This a direct consequence of Proposition 3.

Finally note that the definition of *PE* sustainability in the case in which outputs are not gross substitutes, besides being inconsistent with *BN* equilibrium, suffers from a severe problem. Since the entrant is not required under *PE* sustainability, to supply the entire demand resulting from the new prices, the demand might be manipulated by announcing low prices for goods not produced. For example, consider a market consisting of two complementary goods, for example, petrol and cars. Suppose that the cost of producing these two goods is separable (namely, there is no joint cost) and that the average cost of producing cars is declining. Clearly, if an entrant announces a near zero price for petrol together with a minor reduction in the price of cars a higher demand for cars will result. Thus, the average cost of cars at the new demand will be lower and the entrant will make a positive profit. Hence, as long as sustainable *prices* are considered, it seems necessary to require that an entrant be required to produce the entire demand of the goods offered at reduced prices.

REFERENCES

Bain, J. S. (1956) *Barriers to New Competition*, Cambridge, Mass. Harvard University Press.

Baumol, W. J., E. E. Bailey and R. D. Willig (1977) 'Weak Invisible Hand Theorems on the Sustainability of Multiproduct Natural Monopoly', *American Economic Review*, 67: 350–65.

Baumol, W. J., J. C. Panzar and R. D. Willig (1982) *Contestable Markets and the Theory of Industry Structure*, New York: Harcourt Brace Jovanovich.

Mirman, L. J., Y. Tauman and I. Zang (1983) 'Ramsey Prices, Average Cost Prices and Price Sustainability', mimeo (May).

Panzar, J. C., and R. D. Willig (1977) 'Free Entry and the Sustainability of Natural Monopoly', *Bell Journal of Economics*, 8: 1–22.

10 Modelling the Role of History in Industrial Organization and Competition

DAVID M. KREPS
AND A. MICHAEL SPENCE*

Our objective in this chapter is to describe some recent developments in the area of industrial organization pertaining to the role of history in industrial competition.

To help understand these developments it is useful to begin with a brief review of the traditions of industrial organization. Early work in the subject concentrated on case studies and anti-trust law. But what is usually taught as 'classic' industrial organization is the sort of work associated with the names of Mason and Bain — empirical studies of structure, conduct and performance.

The objective of these studies was to establish the nature of the causal links from basic conditions in the industry and market structure of the industry to conduct of industry members and thence to the performance of the industry. Cribbing heavily from the first chapter of Scherer (1980), basic conditions include things such as the nature of the upstream industry (supply elasticities, nature of competition upstream), characteristics of the product and process (the process technology, durability of the product, extent of unionization), the nature of the demand (price and income elasticity, cross-price elasticity with other products, nature of marketing channels), and other environmental variables (regulation, general business practices, etc.). Market structure encompasses factors such as degree of concentration, product differentiation, and endogenously created barriers to entry. Conduct includes pricing strategies, level of research and development expenditure, investment in new plant and equipment, and so forth. And performance is measured by cost (and rate of cost reduction), allocative efficiency and effects on labour markets, or, more generally, by the

* The authors gratefully acknowledge helpful conversations with Drew Fudenberg. This paper was prepared while the first author was at the Graduate School of Business, Stanford University. We are grateful to the National Science Foundation for financial support.

magnitude of the present value of net benefits to producers and consumers. Of course, there are feedback loops in four categories; for example, conduct clearly affects the level of endogenously created barriers to entry, product strategy (included in conduct) affects the level of product differentiation, and both level of research and development and degree of concentration will affect the technology employed.

Given this basic framework, the idea is to formulate and test empirical propositions about the basic relationships. The usual problems of empirical research in the social sciences impinge. There are many too many variables. It is hard to measure some of them, or even to find good surrogates. It can be hard to find enough 'control groups'. The problem of finding good metrics is especially troublesome in the case of those factors listed under conduct, and so Bain (especially) argued that while the theoretical causal link was from structure to conduct to performance, the sensible thing to do empirically would be to frame and test hypotheses concerning the relationship between structure and performance.

The emphasis in all this work has been on mature and static industries. Indeed, the empirical investigations have almost always been based on static statistical models that purport to characterize equilibria in mature industries. There are, of course, relatively new, immature, and dynamic industries that may be in the sample. These industries create noise in the statistical sense. One might then wish to study the behaviour and performance of immature, dynamic industries, and to include variables pertinent to them. But the growth phase of an industry is more than a statistical inconvenience. The behaviour and performance of a mature industry depend crucially on the history of that industry. Missing from the structure—conduct—performance trichotomy is any explicit consideration of the history of the industry. Every mature industry was once immature, and both its structure and conduct at maturity are influenced by the sort of youth it enjoyed. In the case of structure, this is apparent — extent of concentration, for example, may well be influenced by previous conditions as much as by current conditions. The same is true about the nature of the technology used. For conduct the link is perhaps a bit more tenuous, but we argue that it is there. The extent to which there is any 'implicit collusion' in the industry (and the form of those collusive arrangements) will be a function of the beliefs and expectations of industry participants. And these beliefs and expectations will be influenced by past encounters between participants. Another way to say this is that, when applied to a mature industry, the basic structure, conduct, performance trichotomy omits variables, namely, those variables that would fit under the category of history. Admitting those variables to the model may significantly improve the power of prediction in mature industries. And, of course, to understand properly the role of history, we must first study the process of industry dynamics.

Thus we see a clear demand for the study of immature, dynamic industries and of the effect of industry history on the mature stage of industrial competion. But this demand has been present for a long time. To seek the source of the recent upsurge in such analyses, we must look elsewhere. One source may be a recent shift upwards in the level of 'supply': the dominant methodology in these investigations has been non-co-operative game theory, and there have been recent advances in the 'technology' of this theory and increased diffusion of the technology among economic theorists. A second, demand-side, source, may be recent events in the arena of international competition, especially in global manufacturing industries. The apparent success of Japanese industrial policy is becoming strongly entrenched in popular perceptions. It has therefore become desirable to sort out (i) whether these perceptions have any basis in fact and, if so, (ii) what factors are responsible for that success. As the Japanese industrial policy is reputed to be directed at helping along immature industries, a general study of competition in immature industries is mandated.

We report here on two distinct approaches to the investigation of industry dynamics and the effect of history on industry behaviour and performance. In the first, which we will term the *rational actors* approach, it is maintained that firms are able to anticipate the future consequences of their current actions (up to any dependence on exogenous random factors, which are well understood and anticipated by all concerned). We further subdivide the rational actors analyses into two subgroups.

This sub-division turns on the nature of the linkage between 'immature' and 'mature' stages of industry competition. (Throughout this discussion, we will think of there being only these two stages of competition. Of course, there will typically be a far richer chronological structure than this.) What happens in the immature stage can affect subsequent behaviour and performance through the tangible conditions of the subsequent competition. For example, in the immature stage, firms will accumulate capacity and technical expertise, which in turn will affect their ability to compete. Such things as these will be the basic conditions and industry structure in the Mason—Bain paradigm, the determinates of behaviour and performance. Analysis of the effects of such tangible variables typically proceeds in two distinct stages. First, one analyses the behaviour and performance of the mature industry for various levels of the tangible variables, obtaining 'value functions' for industry participants, functions of the levels of the tangible variables. Implicit in this approach is the assumption that it is the level of these tangible variables and not the way in which those levels were achieved that determines subsequent behaviour and performance. Then one studies the implied behaviour in the immature stage, where the industry participants must weigh current profits and costs against the future values of the tangible variables, as described by the value functions derived in the first step. In other words, dynamic programming in an interactive setting is employed in the usual fashion, with the levels of the tangible variables acting as the state variables that link the stages.

In terms of the study of industry dynamics, two benefits can accrue from such analysis. One learns about the nature of competition in immature industries, given hypotheses about the values of capacity, expertise, and other assets in mature industries. In addition, investment behaviour in the growth phase provides evidence about the value of the tangible variables in mature competition. If the players in the game make reasonably accurate assessments of the value of these assets, then their investment behaviour will reflect those assessments.

This first sub-category of the 'rational actor' analyses is characterized by the simplicity of the linkage between the immature and mature stages, namely, tangible variables such as capacity or (one-dimensional) levels of technical expertise. Clearly, such variables as these give one way in which 'history matters'. But other, less tangible remnants of the past can affect the future: behaviour in mature industries is influenced by participants' expectations as to the actions (and reactions) of their rivals. And these expectations are often influenced by *previous* actions of the participants. In principle, this is no more complex than with tangible variables linking the stages: one analyses mature competition with all the possible 'previous behaviours' as state variables, thereby deriving value functions for 'previous behaviour'. And then the optimal first stage behaviour is computed, using these value functions to weight current profits/costs against the future. But in most cases, the complexity of the set of all possible manifestations of 'previous behaviour' makes analysis of this sort impractical. Instead, analysis proceeds in equilibrium fashion. Hypothesize some immature stage behaviour, derive mature stage expectations from this, and then derive mature stage behaviour and performance. Then (hope to) close the circle by deriving as optimal immature stage behaviour, in consequence of the derived mature stage outcomes, that behaviour that was originally hypothesized. Analyses of this sort add a third benefit to the two listed above. One can examine theoretically hypothesized mature stage behaviour/ expectations by seeing if they can be consistently derived from immature stage behaviour that is optimal in view of the hypothesis.

The rational actors approach, both in the simpler, first sort of sub-category and, even more, in the more complex, equilibrium case, can

require immense levels of rationality on the part of the industry participants. The second general approach to industry dynamics and the role of
history in industry maturity begins with a denial of the ability of firms or
decision-makers to foresee so well the consequences of their actions. Of
course, of one denies 'complete rationality' of industry participants, then
something must be supplied to take its place. Some model of the behaviour
of the firm, however disconnected from rational (or even sentient) decision-
making, must be supplied. In this approach, one begins with hypotheses
about how the firm acts and reacts, and then derives industry-wide consequences of these hypotheses. Thus industrial organization tends to marge
with the 'theory of the firm' especially where that theory is richer than
the neoclassical 'firms-maximize-profits' starting point. Theories of the
firm that involve (somewhat serendipitous) evolution of decision-making
procedures, or adaptation to wholly unanticipated events, or plausible
rules of thumb, are the natural starting points for this approach. In this
chapter, we will widen the scope usually ascribed to industrial organization, in order to discuss some of the recent work in this area and its relation to more traditional industrial organization (hereafter referred to as
IO).

This gives a broad (and somewhat impressionistic) overview of the topics
we will discuss.

The chapter is divided into three parts. The first section concentrates
on the technically simpler, first type of rational actor model, exploring
the nature of competition in immature industries when one 'knows' the
consequences of that competition for the maturity stage. In this section,
we will use as examples the literature on capacity expansion, especially
papers by Dixit (1979, 1980), Fudenberg and Tirole (1982a), and Spence
(1977, 1979). The discussion in this part of the chapter will also provide a
link with the literature on corporate strategy.

The second section will concern the more complex, 'equilibrium'
models. It begins by laying a bit of groundwork. The notion that 'previous
behaviour' impacts future performance through the expectations of industry participants is intuitively appealing. At least, this notion has a long
verbal history in the IO literature. But formal models have been lacking.
Recent advances in non-co-operative game theory give us the hope of
formalizing this sort of 'intangible' linkage, and we begin with a report on
these advances and the preliminary applications that have been made to
topics in IO, such as implicit collusion and entry deterrence. In particular,
to illustrate the idea that past and future must be brought into equilibrium,
we will look at the analysis of entry-deterring limit pricing by Milgrom and
Roberts (1982a).

In the third section, we shift gears and briefly consider the literature on the theory of the firm, with particular emphasis on recent work in 'bounded rationality'. We focus here on the recent book by Nelson and Winter (1982) on the evolutionary theory of the firm.

Two apologies should be tendered at the outset. The reader will note that we have omitted entire topics in IO on which there has been a great deal of work recently. Most notable in this respect is the area of regulation. This is not done because we regard this work as unimportant (quite the reverse), but because it would require many more pages than we have available. More generally, in the topics we do discuss, we have selected illustrations of basic trends (and we have selected those trends) according to our own predilections and interests (more than occasionally coincident with our own work). This chapter is not intended as a complete survey of recent work, but as a statement of opinion on what are some of the interesting directions of recent work.

COMPETITION IN TANGIBLE ASSETS

In the Mason—Bain paradigm, elements of basic conditions and industry structure are identified, and these are examined (in cross-sectional studies) to find their impact on performance measures such as profitability. It is realized conceptually that there is a fundamental feedback loop here — that some elements of basic conditions and industry structure are the results of earlier decisions by industry participants, and the earlier decisions will be influenced by their (projected) impact on subsequent performance — but the static framework adopted does not pursue the implications of identified relations for earlier decisions. (One reasonable justification for this approach is that structure responds relatively slowly to conduct, while conduct and performance are quite immediately influenced by structure.)

The Corporate-Strategy Literature

The implications of the structure—conduct—performance approach have been worked through, at least qualitatively, by researchers in the area of corporate strategy or business policy. The influential book by Porter (1980) contains examples of this sort of analysis. Profits are thought of as rents accruing to scarce factors of production. Thus profitability will be enhanced by (i) the erection of entry barriers (or, if one is speaking of sub-groups within an industry, mobility barriers), and (ii) increases in the bargaining power of firms in the industry *vis-à-vis* suppliers or customers. Entry barriers can be tangible — such as excess capacity, proprietary technological expertise, and economies to scale in advertising, etc. — and intangible, such as the goodwill of industry co-participants for each other, and the badwill they are assumed to hold for interlopers. At this level, this is pretty much classical IO. But where corporate strategists have diverged from standard IO is in their attempts to go on to draw implications for competitive positioning, choice of technology, etc. These normative conclusions are implicit in the usual IO analyses of how structure affects performance; the difference is that they have been made more explicit.

There is a second difference between IO and corporate strategy that arises from the first. IO tends to make the industry the unit of analysis. One will analyse profitability of one industry v. another. In corporate strategy, the unit of analysis is much more the individual firm — the industrial organization helps to describe the external competitive environment of the firm. Specific strategies in the face of various types of existing structure are analysed. Specific strategies are analysed for dealing with specific categories of decisions (capacity expansion, for example). Generally speaking, the greater emphasis on drawing normative implications gives rise to more detailed analysis on the level of the individual firm, which in turn enriches the industry-level analysis.

Another characteristic of the corporate strategy literature serves to distinguish it from the literature that we will discuss below. In the corporate strategy literature, it is typically assumed that rivals will act and react in some hypothesized behavioural fashion. The hypothesized behaviour is generally based on empirical studies of actual industrial behaviour (occasionally fairly casual empiricism). But it is usually not subject to the question: is the hypothesized behaviour rational in any sense? The rational strategies of a single firm are derived — not the equilibrium that ensues if all firms look for rational strategies in response to their environment and to each other.

Equilibrium Models of Dynamic Competition

Some of the recent work in IO has addressed the question of equilibrium in this sort of competition. It is easiest to illustrate with a specific example: the use of irreversible investment in capacity for purposes of pre-emption and entry deterrence, as developed in Dixit (1979, 1980), Fudenberg and Tirole (1982, 1983) and the second paper of Spence here. To take the simplest case, consider a duopoly, with firms indexed by $i = 1, 2$. Profits at any point of time t are assumed to be given by a function of the capacities of the two firms. The reader can think of 'capacity' here as referring to upper bounds on the level of production, or to cost-reducing expertise, or to anything similar. Let $k^i(t)$ denote the capacity of firm i. The rate of profits gross of investment in capacity of firm i at time t is denoted by $\pi^i(k^i(t), k^j(t))$ (where j throughout will mean not i). Whatever interpretation is given to the term 'capacity', it should be such that raising one's own capacity raises one's own profits and lowers the profits of one's rival. Also, these analyses all maintain the hypothesis that the marginal value of one's own capacity falls with increases in one's own capacity and the capacity of one's rival. (In symbols, $\pi^i_i > 0$, $\pi^i_j < 0$, $\pi^i_{ii} < 0$, and $\pi^i_{ij} < 0$, where subscripts denote partial derivatives. (Spence (1977, section 3) and Fudenberg and Tirole (1982a, appendix A) derive such instantaneous profit functions under specific interpretations of the capacity variables.) It is assumed that capacity can be added any rate up to some exogenously imposed upper limit. There are constant returns to scale for the addtion of capital up to this upper limit. Choosing units so that $m^i(t)$ is both the rate of capital accumulation at time t and the dollar investment in capacity at that time, profits net of investment are $\pi^i(s^i(t), s^i(t)) - m^i(t)$, and capacity grows according to $\dot{s}^i(t) = m^i(t)$. In addition to being constrained above, $m^i(t)$ is assumed to be non-negative — capacity investments are irreversible. This, from the standpoint of competitive interaction, is the crucial element of structure. Firms act to maximize the expected discounted present worth of profits, discounting at some given rate r.

Fudenberg and Tirole (1982a) and Spence (1979) analyse this situation, seeking perfect closed-loop Nash equilibria in the strategies of investment in capacity. The modifier closed-loop means that each firm recognizes that the realization of its investment can and will affect the subsequent investments of its rivals. In other words, firms cannot precommit to investment paths — they re-evaluate their investment plans in light of 'new information' concerning the realized investments of their rivals. The modifier perfect takes this a step further: when firms re-evaluate their investment plans, they adopt plans that are optimal for the remainder of the game. This requirement prevents a firm from enforcing a particular outcome by threatening a pattern of investment behaviour that the firm would not subsequently wish to carry out if called upon to do so.

Under appropriate assumptions, capacity 'pre-emption' is possible in equilibrium. By this we mean the following. Suppose that instead of having investment drawn out through time as above, firms simultaneously selected the levels of capacity that they would hold. (With a bit of modification, the reader can also think here of a case where neither side can verify the level of capacity installed by its rival until its own capacity investment programme is completed.) Under the assumptions of these analyses, the outcome would be a 'Cournot' equilibrium in capacities — capacity levels k^1 and k^2 would be such that $\pi^i_i(k^i, k^j) = r$. (This assumes that we begin below these levels.) If the firms are symmetric in terms of the profit functions, this will lead to a symmetric outcome even if one firm starts out ahead of its oppenent in terms of initial capacity. In other words, a lead in terms of capacity investment does not 'deter' the investment of a rival, unless that investment is beyond the Cournot level.

But in the model posed above, a 'head start' in capacity will partially pre-empt the investment of a rival. If one firm has such a head start, then as its rival adds capacity, so can it. And (assuming symmetry) before the firm that is behind reaches the Cournot point, the first firm will be at a level of capacity beyond its point. This will tend to 'cow' the rival firm, since in the perfect closed-loop equilibrium, it must come to terms with this *fait accompli*. If the first firm starts with a large enough lead, it can act something like a von Stackelberg leader in terms of the capacity level — selecting autonomously the level it desires, subject only to the constraint that its rival will do the best it can given the level selected by the firm.

Fudenberg and Tirole (1982a) point out another consequence of this sort of drawn-out investment model. The fact that investment is drawn out allows for some collusion in the final outcome. In general, the game will have multiple equilibria, some of which are better for both firms than are others. To see how this is possible, imagine that the firms start out with the same initial levels of capacity. In the simultaneous investment version of the game, where they do not see capacity investment by rivals until that investment is complete, investment is up to the Cournot point k that is given by $\pi^i_j(k, k) = r$. But at this point $\pi^i_i(k, k) + \pi^i_j(k, k) < r$ — firms have invested beyond the level they would select if they acted collusively. Now consider the drawn-out investment model. When the collusively optimal level of capacity is reached by each (when each has capacity k satisfying $\pi^i_i(k, k) + \pi^i_j(k, k) = r$), each could issue a statement that it has 'enough' capacity as long as its rival goes no further, but that it will be forced to match further investments by its rival. The optimal response by each to this sort of announcement is to cease investment, unless entry is threatened as a result. We will provide more discussion of this sort of implicitly collusive equilibrium in the second part of the chapter, but for now we simply note that it exists in this model because of the continuous-time (drawn-out) nature of investment and the ability of each to monitor the actions of its opponents. (If, say, the investments of a rival were observed with a lag, or if investments were made in discrete chunks or in discrete time, similar sorts of collusive equilibria would emerge, as long as there is an infinite time horizon. See the second section for more detail.)

Having investigated the duopoly model above, Spence (1979) goes on to consider behaviour in a still earlier stage of the industry. Suppose one of the firms is able to invest in capacity before its rival appears. Will it use that opportunity to invest to a level that keeps the rival out altogether? Spence shows that this sort of behaviour can arise — capacity can serve as an effective entry barrier, in the sense of Bain (1956). (Dixit, 1979, 1980, analyses this question in the context of discrete time, two-period models.)

We apologise for the sketchy rendition of these papers that we have given. But we hope that enough detail has been provided for the reader to abstract from this example the following features that make it fairly typical of much of the recent work in this area:

(1) Firms are 'rational', foreseeing the consequences of their actions, and maximizing the discounted present worth of profits. (In models of this genre where there is uncertainty, the typical decision criterion of firms is the maximization of expected net present worth of profits.)

(2) The model focuses on one structural variable to the exclusion of others. In this case, that variable is capacity. (We note again that the term 'capacity' can be interpreted in a number of ways.) What distinguishes this particular analysis from others of this genre is the choice of the variable being studied.

(3) Because of the attention on the variable of interest, other (quite important) parts of the competitive picture are 'black-boxed'. That is, profits (as a function of the levels of capacity) are exogenously given by the function π. Assumptions about the 'profit function' are made, and they are sometimes justified through reference to one of the classic theoretical models of competition in the product market (Bertrand or Cournot). But the exact nature of the competition and how that competition is affected by the strategic investment decisions are typically not explicitly considered. There is a planted axiom here: the level of profits (hence the nature of competition in the product market) is a function of only the current level of the variable of interest (capacity, unit costs, etc.). In the papers cited above, profits at any point in time depend only on the current level of capacities. If one imagined that competition in the product market, hence profits, depended on both the current level of these variables and the manner

in which those levels were attained (for example, if aggressive capacity expansion causes severe and cut-throat competition), then much richer models would be needed.

(4) The analysis is basically dynamic – conditions of competition with regard to the variable of interest are changing. The competitive environment is changing in a non-stationary way as a result of the investment decisions by the firms.

(5) The analysis is equilibrium analysis. Both (or, more generally, all) industry participants understand the competition they are engaged in, and the analysis works out what will happen if they respond optimally to this competition (and to each others' strategies). As noted above, this distinguishes this literature from the bulk of the corporate strategy literature, which is much more concerned with strategic environments that are 'perfectly competitive' in the sense that competitors act in some postulated, behavioural fashion. This literature, therefore, allows us to subject empirical observations about mature industries to the conceptual test: is the purported phenomenon consistent with equilibrium behaviour by industry participants, it those participants are aware of and respond optimally to the phenomenon? Also, as noted earlier, hypotheses about the relationship between performance and the levels of these structural variables in mature industries can be tested by looking at the behaviour of industry participants in the immature stages of the industry, if one adjoins the hypothesis that participants in the immature industry understand this relationship and act optimally accordingly. (See Porter and Spence, 1982, for an analysis of a particular episode of capacity expansion that follows this sort of line.)

(6) Combining (1), (4) and (5), the model of competition is dynamic. As time passes and things happen, firms take cognizance of those things and act accordingly. That is, the equilibria are closed-loop and perfect. This is as opposed to open-loop or imperfect closed-loop equilibria, wherein firms 'precommit' to long-term programmes of investment, etc., commitments that they might subsequently wish to void.

This is not to say that firms might not wish to precommit in certain circumstances, or that, by their actions, they are incapable of precommitment. Precommitment can be a powerful competitive weapon. But if precommitment is a feasible option, it should be modelled as such and then derived as an optimal strategy in an equilibrium. We could do this in the capacity expansion model, for example, as follows: modify the formulation so that either firm can precommit to some level of capacity expansion by, say, signing construction contracts with substantial penalty clauses. If such contracts can be made, the nature of competition is dramatically different: there will be a 'race' to see which firm can sign and credibly announce such a contract first, bearing in mind the possible disastrous outcome where each firm signs such a contract before a credible announcement is made by either. In another context, Maskin and Tirole (1982) exhibit competitive environments where firms willingly precommit in order to foster implicit collusion. And Reingenum and Stokey (1981) consider precommitment in the context of extraction of a non-renewable, common property resource.

Our point is that one should not allow precommitment to enter 'by the back door', through the use of an inappropriate solution concept. If it is possible, it should be explicitly modelled as such. It is this sort of 'back door assumption' that is prevented by the use of perfect, closed-loop equilibria.

The range of papers of this genre is substantial, and to try to cite all of them would be fruitless. Indeed, even to try to cover all the 'variables' upon which studies have focused is dangerous — we are sure to miss some. But we would be remiss not be provide a 'roadmap' to a few of the more prominent examples:

Lumpy Investment, or the Adoption of a New Technology

The issue here can be viewed as a variation on the capacity expansion story, where investment must be made in discrete amounts. Thus the timing of investment by competitors becomes non-trivial. If one firm invests at some time t, the others may be forestalled for a while. Alternatively, one can imagine that firms must decide when to adopt a new and cost-reducing technology. Recent papers include Rao and Rutenberg (1979), Gilbert and Harris (1982), and Fudenberg and Tirole (1983).

Product Differentiation

This is somewhat similar to the lumpy investment/adoption of new technology problem, except that the issue is one of locating products in a product characteristics space. (This includes problems of geographical siting.) See, for example, Prescott and Visscher (1977), Shaked and Sutton (1982), Schmalensee (1982), and Jones (1982).

Learning by Doing and the Experience Curve

If costs fall with accumulated production experience, then production volume becomes (in part) an investment in lower subsequent production costs. A firm temporarily protected from competition (through, for example, a patent) may seek to erect permanent entry barriers by producing in large volume at the expense of current profits. Or competition among firms early on may be very intense, as each tries to maximize volume and so decrease costs sufficiently to shake competitors out of the market. See Spence (1981), Fudenberg and Tirole (1982b), and Lieberman (1982) (who considers the effect of spillovers in the knowledge gained through experience). (Also, Fine, 1983, analyses learning curve investment where the firm can control, at a cost, the rate of learning accrued from cumulative production. But this is done only for a monopoly environment.)

Research and Development

A number of analyses have been done on the problem of a group of firms seeking a single, patentable invention, where all the 'spoils' accrue to the winner. In some cases, the chance of discovery at any time is independent of all previous actions (depending only on the current level of investment in research and development) – Loury (1979), Dasgupta and Stiglitz (1980) and Reingenum (1981, 1982a, 1982b) are representative. In other models, discovery is deterministic, and a small lead in the race is conclusive; see Dasgupta and Stiglitz (1980) and Gilbert and Newbery (1982). Fudenberg, Gilbert, Stiglitz and Tirole (1982) analyse a stochastic model where a small lead is (in any perfect equilibrium) conclusive so long as there is no further revelation of relative positions. It follows that the leader would prefer no further public revelation of positions, while followers would prefer public revelations as often as possible (until some time when they 'leapfrog' ahead and become the leader).

Spence (1982) takes a very different tack on the question of research and development: in his model there is not a single, patentable innovation to be had, but rather (say) a continuum of (increasingly more effective) cost-reducing innovations for all participants. Thus research and development is not 'winner take all'. In a sense, this is precisely like the capacity expansion model above, where one interprets $k^i(t)$ as firm i's level of expertise at time t. The Spence analysis considers the effects of spillovers in research and development – where one firm investing in research and development provides positive externalities for all its competitors. This gives a 'double-edged sword' quality to spillovers: they are informationally efficient, since given levels of expertise for all firms can be achieved more cheaply the higher are the spillovers. But they also dull the incentives of each individual firm to engage in research and development.

And so on. The number of papers of this sort is growing rapidly.

Our chief criticism of this general approach begins with point (2) above and expands from there. Competition in reality is over many variables or in many dimensions at once. These analyses are extremely useful in focusing our attention on the nature of competition in a single variable, but one wonders whether the nature of competition in one variable is not affected by what is happening with regard to a second. In other words, what are the 'general equilibrium' considerations of competition over these variables? We despair of anyone's ability to model adequately the rich structure of realistic competition, and we therefore endorse the idea of studying one variable at a time. But there is a significant potential flaw in this method of analysis that should be kept in mind.

HISTORY AND PREDICTIONS OF FUTURE BEHAVIOUR

We have two aims in this section. We wish to (i) discuss recent advances in the technology of non-co-operative game theory as they apply to some of the classic problems in IO, and (ii) show the sense in which these advances begin to give us a lever with which one can study the impact of historical behaviour on industry participants' expectations of each others' future behaviour.

Game Theory and the Typical Textbook in IO

In most textbooks on IO, game theory is dealt with quickly. This is merciful treatment given the depiction of game theory that is developed. In most cases, game theory is taken to mean the analysis of simultaneous move, bimatrix games. Authors typically will point out that the minimax solution concept has a great deal of force for constant-sum games, but that most examples of industrial competition are not constant sum. As to non-constant-sum games, if these are discussed at all, the typical pattern is to define Nash equilibrium, and then to point out how this notion 'doesn't work' in the case of the prisoners' dilemma. There might also be some discussion of Schelling's (1960) *Strategy and Conflict*, with some wistful remarks about how game theory might be useful if it were capable of dealing formally with the sorts of considerations that Schelling discusses.

Discussions of formal models of implicit collusion are especially prone to this sort of (mis-)treatment. Consider a duopoly, where the two firms have as options (i) conforming to a collusive arrangement, where prices are held 'artificially' high, and (ii) engaging in more competitive pricing, advertising, etc. If both firms collude, each will accrue (let us imagine) one-half the monopoly profits. If each engages in vigorous competition, then each will accrue, say, 'normal' profits. And if one chooses the collusive actions (holding price up, foregoing advertising, etc.) and the second chooses vigorous competition, then the first sustains a loss, while the second captures the entire market, which is worth more than half the monopoly profits. This is typically rendered into a two-by-two bimatrix game, and out pops the prisoners' dilemma – each firm has as dominant strategy vigorous competition. That is, regardless of the strategy chosen by one's rival, one does better with vigorous competition than with collusion. Implicit collusion is not predicted. Since implicit collusion is perceived to be a fact of life, so much for game theory (with, perhaps, some kind words about how hard the theorists are trying, and how the theory does, in other cases, provide some basic qualitative insights into competitive behaviour). It is time for serious (i.e. informal) discussion of the factors that tend to make implicit collusion more or less feasible.

Supergames and Implicit Collusion

This description of the standard textbook account is, of course, something of a caricature. But (our point in all this), recent advances in game theory are beginning (and, we stress, beginning) to allow for serious formal modelling of the sorts of concerns that arise in implicit collusion. The first (and, by far, the better known) technique is supergame (or infinite horizon game) analysis. The reason that one may find implicit collusion in the situation above is that both sides understand that this is not a one-shot game, in which they pick for now and evermore their strategies. Each can elect to act collusively at the start, and then (if the other side colludes) keep it up, for as long as the other side colludes – as soon as the second firm fails to collude, the first can revert to vigorous competition. Faced with this sort of behaviour by an opponent, as long as the 'future rounds' loom large relative to the present, the optimal response is to act collusively, thereby engendering collusion from the first. To act competitively will profit the second firm for as long as it takes the first firm to respond, but after that the second firm will be worse off than if it had colluded throughout.

Let us examine a somewhat more detailed model of this sort. Consider a duopoly where at each date $t = 1, 2, \ldots,$ each firm i $(i = 1, 2)$ chooses a quantity $q_i(t)$ that is brought to the market. The output of the two firms are perfect substitutes, and prices at time t are set according to the total supply $q_1(t) + q_2(t)$, given by the industry demand curve $P(q_1(t) + q_2(t))$. Costs are linear in supply with unit cost c, so firm i at date t nets profits equal to:

$$\pi_i(t) = q_i(t)[P(q_1(t) + q_2(t)) - c]$$

In other words, at each date we have Cournot competition. Assume that P is sufficiently well behaved so that there is unique Cournot equilibrium, where each firm supplies quantity q^C given by:

$$q^C P'(2q^C) + P(2q^C) - c = 0.$$

and that there is a unique monopoly quantity Q^M, the solution of:

$$Q^M P'(Q^M) + P(Q^M) - c = 0$$

Let π^C denote the Cournot equilibrium profits of the two firms, and let π^M denote one-half the monopoly profits.

Imagine that firm 1 uses the following strategy. It will provide $Q^M/2$ in each period, as long as firm 2 does the same. But if at some date t firm 2 provides some different quantity. then at date $t + 1$ and forever after, firm 1 will supply q^C. The optimal response of firm 2 to this strategy is derived as follows. If it supplies $Q^M/2$ in each period, then it will net profits π^M in each period. Assuming it discounts profits at interest rate r, this has net present value π^M/r. Alternatively, firm 2 can supply some other quantity q at some date. At this date, its profits will be $q[P(q + Q^M/2) - c]$. And thereafter, its profits will be no greater than $max_q q[P(q + q^C) - c]$. The latter quantity is maximized at $q = q^C$, for profits π^C. Thus if firm 2 provides quantity $q \neq Q^M/2$ at some date, its net present value of subsequent profits are at most:

$$q[P(q + Q^M/2) - c] + \frac{1}{(1+r)} \frac{\pi^C}{r}$$

As long as $\pi^M > \pi^C$ (which is usually the case) and r is sufficiently small, the strategy of supplying $Q^M/2$ in each period is the optimal response to firm 1's strategy. If firm 2 issues the same 'threat' as has firm 1, then each firm has no incentive to do otherwise, and we get the equal-share collusive outcome as a non-co-operative equilibrium.

This is a fairly old and well-known story. (See Stigler, 1964, and, for the supergame analysis, J. Friedman, 1977.) The crucial idea is that there is always a future, and the one-period gains from defection (from producing other than $Q^M/2$) are outweighted by the discounted losses of getting π^C

forever after instead of getting π^M. This is accomplished here by having infinitely many periods ($t = 1, 2, \ldots$). Alternatively, one could have a finite horizon $[0, T]$ but quantity decisions made continuously and with *instantaneous* (or 'fast enough') response by one firm to defections by the other. In fact, this version of the general story is used by Fudenberg and Tirole (1982a) in producing the implicity collusive equilibria in their analysis of capacity investment described in the first section of this chapter. (But with an infinite horizon model, they could do the same in a discrete time formulation.)

The simple story told above becomes much more complicated when other, more realistic features are added. In the first place, consider what will happen if the demand function is subject to random shocks, so that if $q^1(t)$ and $q^2(t)$ are supplied, the equilibrium price is $p(q_1(t) + q_2(t), \epsilon_t)$, where ϵ_t is the shock. This presents no substantial problem if each firm can observe the amount supplied by its rival. But if all a firm can observe is its own quantity supply and the market equilibrium price, then troubles arise: at any time t, each firm has the incentive to 'chisel', to supply a bit more than is called for in the collusive arrangement, and to blame the resulting lower equilibrium price on the level of the demand shock. After all, one's rival will not be able to tell the difference, and it won't be worth cancelling the collusive arrangement for reasons that could be no one's fault. This sort of problem in implicit collusion (or even in maintaining an explicitly collusive arrangement) is well known in the verbal literature on collusion: the greater is the noise (random shocks) in the market, if that noise is accompanied by inability to monitor the actions of rivals, then the harder it will be to arrive at a collusive scheme. We are seeing here precisely this phenomenon.

Green and Porter (1981) and Radner (1981) investigate this sort of noise and its effect on equilibrium collusion. The conclusions, very roughly summarized, are that this noise does lessen how much collusion can be had in equilibrium. In general, some collusion will still be possible, the more so the smaller is the interest rate, as long as the shocks $\{\epsilon_t\}$ are i.i.d. This is so because small interest rates give one (i) time over which to collect enough data to be (relatively sure) that a rival is chiselling, and (ii) further time in which to punish such behaviour. It is not clear, however, whether one can get 'efficient collusion' in the limit, as the discount rates go to zero – see the discussion in Radner (1981). (An interesting case, not yet investigated to our knowledge, is where the shocks are not i.i.d. but rather exchangeable (that is, i.i.d. with respect to an 'initially unknown' distribution). It seems fairly clear that in this case not even a small interest rate will save one from some non-vanishing amount of chiselling, since a 'shortfall' from one's expectations, no matter how long observed, can never be definitely attributed to one's opponent.)

For a finite (non-zero) rate of interest, Green and Porter (1981) derive equilibria with the following structure (in a special case): a trigger price is set. If ever price falls below this level, then a 'reversionary period' of prespecified duration ensues, in which the firms revert to competitive (Cournot) quantities. Fixing the interest rate, the trigger price, and the length of the reversionary period, one can find (symmetric) quantities that are optimal for the firms to supply during non-reversionary periods. These balance the marginal value of an extra unit of production against the marginal increase in the probability of setting off a reversionary period, which will then yield lesser expected profits for the duration of the reversionary period. Note that the 'loss' relative to efficient collusion is reflected in any lower expected profits in non-reversionary periods and the lower expected profits that acrue in the (inevitable) reversionary periods. (In these equilibria, reversionary periods must be inevitable – otherwise firms are chiselling an insufficient amount.)

Next consider what happens when the firms have different costs of production. Overall profit maximization would call for the lesser-cost firm to produce at its monopoly level. Absent any side payments to the higher-cost firm, this seems unlikely. The higher cost firm ought to get some part of the market. But, lacking symmetry, it is hard to say how much. More generally, asymmetries of any sort complicate the basic story. This idea also appears in the verbal traditions of IO, where it is held that 'differences in objectives' among industry participants, whether due to differences in cost structures, or beliefs about the future, or whatever, will make collusion more difficult to achieve.

This is not to say that there are not implictly collusive equilibria in cases where the firms are asymmetric. Collusive equilibria will typically exist. The problem with asymmetries is that it isn't clear which collusive equilibrium should be picked. As such, the problem of asymmetries is really the tip of a much larger and more pernicious problem: even in symmetric situations, there will typically exist an uncountable infinity of equilibria, with various degrees of collusion and with the 'spoils' of collusion split up in various ways.

For example, consider our simple duopoly above. Suppose that firm 1 adopts the strategy of producing $Q^M \theta$ as long as firm 2 produces $Q^M(1 - \theta)$, for θ between one-half and one. Firm 1 also states that it will revert to producing q^C forever if firm 2 does not comply and produce $Q^M(1 - \theta)$. If firm 2 complies with this, it will have a net present value of $2\pi^M(1-\theta)/r$, which, for θ sufficiently close to one-half, will be better than anything it can get by defecting. Our firm 1 could 'insist' that firm 2 produce even a bit less than $Q^M(1-\theta)$ in response to its own production of $Q^M\theta$ – this may still give an equilibrium, even though it doesn't fully exploit the gains that the two can realize from collusion. It is easy to see that any scheme for quantity outputs that gives each firm more than it gets under Cournot competition will be an equilibrium for all sufficiently small interest rates, as long as this scheme is 'backed' by the threat that any defection will result in subsequent production at Cournot levels. (The range of interest rates for which this is so will depend positively on the difference between the profits accrued by the firms in the scheme and the profits they get from Cournot competition.)

In general, infinitely repeated games come with an embarrassment of riches in terms of the number of possible non-co-operative equilibria. Theorems that characterize the extent of possible equilibria are known (collectively) as the Folk Thereom: Rubinstein (1979) gives a general treatment of the Folk Theorem for undiscounted repeated games (under the additional requirement that the equilibria be perfect). And Abreu (1982) develops the Folk Theorem for perfect equilibria of discounted games, with, as specific application, the Cournot duopoly game above.

This multitude of possible (equilibrium) schemes for implicit collusion is fairly distressing in so far as one would like strong predictions to emerge from the theory. Formal non-co-operative game theory doesn't give the analyst any reason to choose one of these equilibria in preference to another. (It is ironic that the problem isn't that game theory is incapable of producing implicit collusion at all, but that it produces virtually every possible form.) It would seem that the analyst must resort to common-sense prescriptions, for example, symmetric equilibria in symmetric situations. One can also access the ideas of Schelling (1960) concerning a focal point equilibria: when one is confronted with a host of equilibria, look for one that has some particular distinctive character; for example, an equilibrium that partitions markets on qualitative rather than quantitative grounds.

On an intuitive level, it seems fairly clear that in the selection of an equilibrium, history and, in particular, the experiences of the participants will play an important role. This intuition has recently been supported by Roth and Schoumaker (1981). They had pairs of individuals play variations of the following game: the two players would bargain over how to divide 100 'chips', using the following protocol. Each player i ($i = 1, 2$) would simultaneously and independently propose an integer θ_i between zero and one hundred. If $\theta_1 + \theta_2 \leqslant 100$, then each player would get as many chips as he/she named. (The chips are used in a manner that will be explained momentarily.) If, on the other hand, $\theta_1 + \theta_2 > 100$, then a second stage would ensue: the players, simultaneously and independently, would choose whether to repeat their initial proposal or to accede to their opponent's proposal. If the player chose to accede, he/she would get 100 less the number of chips proposed by his/her rival at the first stage. But if the player chose to repeat, his/her prize would depend on what the opponent did. If the opponent also chose to repeat, the player would get nothing. If the opponent chose to accede, the player would get his/her initial offer. Following this ritual of bargaining, each player 'cashes in' his/her chips: if the player has won θ chips, then the player has a $\theta/100$ chance of winning a prespecified prize. To keep things simple, we will assume that player 1 stands to win $40, and player 2, $10.

This simple bargaining game shares many of the characteristics of the implicit collusion problem. If a collusive arrangement can be reached, each side stands to gain. But there are many equilibrium ways to split the potential gain. In the bargaining game as in the case of implicit collusion, there is a wealth of non-co-operative equilibria. In particular, among the equilibria to the bargaining game is where player 1 claims θ of the chips and player 2 claims $100 - \theta$, and neither will accede in the second round. This is an equilibrium for any value of θ between zero and one hundred, inclusive.

In a number of previous experiments, Roth and his associates have studied many variations of this game, attempting to find what variables will do best at explaining the outcomes that are reached. In Roth and Schoumaker (1981), the following is tried. Each player plays this game a number of times (around fifteen). Unbeknowst to some of them, for the first ten or so rounds they are matched against a confederate of the experimenter, who will in some cases insist repeatedly on a 50–50 split and in other cases on, say, an 80–20 split (with the 80 going to whichever player has the $10 prize). (Also, in each round the players are told how their rivals did in previous encounters.) After this conditioning phase, players are matched against each other. As one would expect, those who have been conditioned to 'expect' a 50–50 split continue to play in that fashion. Those who expect the 80–20 split either insist on (if they expect 80 chips) or acquiesce to (if they expect 20) this division. In general, previous experiences explain much more of which outcomes emerge than any other feature of the competition.

In situations that have the potential for implicitly collusive arrangements (where, for example, monitoring the actions of rivals is feasible), it seems almost self-evident that the equilibrium chosen will be powerfully affected by the competitors' expectations as to what they can get, and these in turn will depend on what they and their competitors were able to secure previously. The Roth–Schoumaker experiments give a laboratory demonstration of this hypothesis, and it would be interesting to see an empirical study of it. If it is valid (and, we repeat, it seems to us more a question of how much explanatory power this will have then whether it will have any at all), then competition early on in an immature industry may have profound implications for the subsequent behaviour and performance. This can probably be extended to other historical explanations for behaviour and performance: the reputations and experiences of industry participants gained elsewhere may strongly colour behaviour in a given industry. Thus, for example, an industry that has a structure seemingly conducive to implicit collusion, but that also either (i) had an historical structure that was not condusive to collusion, or (ii) has participants whose experiences elsewhere are largely limited to severe, cut-throat competition, will be unlikely to realize the otherwise feasible collusive outcome.

Can any of this be modelled formally? Does history have a formal role to play in the supergame analysis? It is hard to see how it could. The supergame equilibria hold together because the firms are forward looking: they believe (in a way unspecified by the formal theory) that certain actions will provoke reactions that they would just as soon avoid. In a sense, history matters only because firms threaten to make it matter. (In some cases, such as in Green and Porter, 1981, this threat must be carried out from time to time.) Firms do not look backward to learn from the past. But it is this sort of learning from the past that is intuitively suggested by the Roth and Schoumaker experiments, an intuition that seems impossible to model formally in the sort of supergame formulation above.

To capture formally this intuition, we need another recent innovation from game theory. But before providing this, let us look at one further 'flaw' in the supergame technology. Consider the repeated Cournot duopoly game above, with the following modification. Instead of repeating the game infinitely many times, it is repeated only, say, one hundred times. Will collusion be an equilibrium outcome?

The answer to this is no. To see why, consider what will happen in the last round of the game. With no future rounds, there is no spur to co-operate, no future losses to weigh against current gains. Thus the only possible equilibrium outcome in the final round will be the Cournot outcome, in which each side produces q^C. This is true regardless of anything that happens previously. So now a similar argument can be mounted for the penultimate round: no matter how the two firms act in this round, profits in the future (final round) are fixed. So each will act solely to maximize short-run profits in this round, regardless of what has come before. The only possible equilibrium outcome in the penultimate round, then, is the Cournot outcome. Go back one round more. Since the outcomes of the last two rounds are fixed, in the third-to-last round the firms will consider only their short-run gains and losses, and the Cournot quantities will be supplied, and so forth, with any hope of collusion unravelling from the back. (A precise argument that there is no other equilibrium outcome is a bit more complex than this, but the basic idea is captured above. This argument, in a somewhat different context, can be found in Selten, 1978.)

This is troublesome because the fact that collusion cannot be supported by an equilibrium in the finite horizon version of our repeated game is not supported by experimental evidence. Both in experiments and in carefully staged tournaments, co-operation emerges even though there is a clear and definite limit to the number of rounds that will be played (see Axelrod, 1981).

Reputation and Incomplete Information

We seek, therefore, some way to model the notion that participants really do learn from history (or rather, they can learn from history). The reason that this is difficult in the supergame formulation is that there is nothing for the firms to learn about. If we are to have a formal model in which participants learn from the past (especially from the past behaviour of rivals), then we need to introduce something about which they are initially uncertain. Then we can capture the idea that the flow of events may help resolve this inconsistency. (An axiom planted here is that we are able to model formally the idea of learning only with a Savage-style formulation of a rational economic actor. Unhappily, our arsenal of formal models is bereft of other possibilities.)

This leads us to the second advance in game theory technology that we wish to mention: games of incomplete information. Consider the following variation on the repeated Cournot game, this time with a finite horizon. You think that it is possible that your rival is not so good a game theorist as to be able to work out the precise equilibrium strategy that he/she 'should' employ. Instead, there is a small chance that your opponent will conform to the following mode of behaviour: he/she will output the monopoly quantity $Q^M/2$ for as long as you do likewise, up to some point near to the end of the game. But at the earlier of (i) the next date after you fail to produce $Q^M/2$, or (ii) some random date close to the end, your rival will revert to producing q^C until the end of the game. You are certain, for example, that your rival is sensible enough to realize that outputting q^C

is the 'right' thing to do in the last round. And your rival may produce q^C in the penultimate round as well, regardless of what you do previously. And so on. But you entertain the possibility that your rival will wait for some length of time to begin to produce q^C unless provoked. You also entertain the possibility that your opponent will simply begin to produce q^C in each period, regardless of what you do. And there is a chance that your opponent is a rational individual, who is trying to see what is reasonable behaviour in the face of your uncertainties about him/her. But of one thing you are certain: your opponent will produce q^C in every round subsequent to your production of anything other than $Q^M/2$. (This last hypothesis is the weak link in the suppositions that we make; casual empiricism suggests that 'collusion' can be restored after a reversion to competition. But the argument gets more difficult if we admit this possibility. See Kreps, Milgrom, Roberts and Wilson, 1982, for a model where this sort of thing is possible.)

What should you do in such a circumstance as this? To keep matters simple, assume that there is no discounting of profits between periods. (The notation, but not the story, is a bit more complex when there is a positive interest rate, as long as the interest rate isn't 'too large.') Suppose you assess probability as at least one in one hundred that your opponent will wait until at least round ten from the end to play q^C if you haven't provoked him/her previously. And suppose that there are N rounds left in the game, where N should be thought of as a large number. If you produce $Q^M/2$ in this round, there may be a good chance that you will suffer for it — the chances could be as high as .99 that your rival will take advantage of you. But if this happens you can limit your losses, by producing q^C for the rest of the game. At worst you will lose $Q^M c/2$ in this round, and make Cournot profits, π^C, subsequently. While with probability at least 0.01, you will meet co-operation from your opponent, netting profit π^M in this round. This probability could be higher than 0.01, either because you assess higher probability that your rival is of the 'wait till some later date' variety or because it is optimal for a rational rival to produce $Q^M/2$ — but in any case, you get π^M with probability at least 0.01. In which case, you could try again next round. Again, you might suffer, but there is chance at least 0.01 that again you'll make π^M. And so forth — if you keep this up until your opponent does produce something other than $Q^M/2$ (which will happen eventually), then your losses (relative to obtaining π^C in each period) are bounded, since you'll be taken advantage of at most once. And with probability at least 0.01, you'll make (relative to obtaining π^C in each round) an additional $\pi^M - \pi^C$ for at least $N - 10$ rounds. Your alternative in the current round is to produce other than $Q^M/2$, but then with certainty you'll net π^C in all subsequent rounds. So as long as $\pi^M > \pi^C$ and N is sufficiently large, it is better for you to produce $Q^M/2$ this round than to do otherwise.

Now take this a step further. Put yourself in the position of your opponent, facing a rival who enterains these sorts of thoughts. What will you do with a large number of rounds left to go? If you produce other than $Q^M/2$, you will gain in this round, but your opponent will lapse to producing q^C in subsequent rounds, and the best you'll do will be π^C hereafter. (Again, to keep matters simple we assume that once one side produces other than $Q^M/2$, the two revert to Cournot outcomes for the remaining rounds. If we were being precise about things, we would give conditions under which this is a valid hypothesis, assumptions concerning the initial assessments of the two rivals.) The logic above suggests that, for a while at least, your opponent will produce $Q^M/2$ for as long as you do. So it is clearly better (for large enough N) to 'humour' your opponent and produce $Q^M/2$, at least until (just before) the point where you are no longer certain that this is what he/she will do.

The nature of the loose argument above is as follows. One (or both) of the rivals is initially uncertain about his/her opponent. In this illustration, we have had the first uncertain about the degree of rationality of the opponent – with positive probability the opponent was presumed to play in some behavioural fashion. In such a case as this, it can pay to explore the nature of one's opponent for a bit; one may learn something that can be taken advantage of for a long while. And in the sort of situation above, where the first rival is trying to see whether the second will engage in mutually beneficial co-operation, the optimal behaviour of the second is to encourage the first to persist in this exploration.

This can be modelled formally, using a game with incomplete information. This concept, due to Harsanyi (1967–8), is a means for modelling competitive situations where competitors are initially unsure of things that their rivals initially know. This is not an appropriate forum for detailed definitions, but the basic idea can be given. One imagines that there was once a point in time where the various competitors were on an equal informational footing, where everything known by one was known by the others (and that this is known by all, etc.; technically, all aspects of the situation were common knowledge). From that point in the past, the current situation has evolved because the various participants have received private signals that tell them things not known by their opponents. For example, if one firm is unsure about the cost structure of a second, then one imagines that at some (ideal) point in the distant past, neither knew anything about cost structure; and since then the second firm has learned what is its cost structure. And a non-co-operative equilibrium is sought, where each participant is assumed to condition its actions on the private information that it has received.

This is the key: each participant finds a strategy that is optimal for itself, given the strategies of all others, the basic structure of the game, and the private information that was received prior to the start of competition. If you are uncertain about the cost structure of an opponent, you (i) imagine all the possibile cost structures for that opponent, (ii) come up with a subjective probability assessment over those possibilities, (iii) analyse what strategy your rival will employ as a function of its cost structure, and, thus (iv) arrive at a subject assessment concerning the possible actions of your rival. You can then discover an optimal response for yourself. The thing that makes this *equilibrium* analysis is that your rival is presumed to know of your uncertainties, and it is choosing its strategies knowing that you must 'temporize'. That is, its strategy (as a function of its private information), is an optimal response to your strategy.

This is fairly heady stuff. The story seems to rely heavily on super-rationality of the participants. But by using mathematical tricks, one can analyse with this sort of formulation opponents who are not completely rational, or the possibility that one participant is completely rational and knows that its opponent knows that it is, but is uncertain whether its opponent is certain that it (the first) knows that the second knows that the first is rational. And so forth. One can model, and subsequently analyse, all sorts of situations of initial uncertainty about opponents, the rules of the game, and so on.

And, with this technique, one captures the idea that history matters. At intermediate points in the game, participants use the actions of their rivals to make inferences concerning those things about which they were intially uncertain. For example, in the situation sketched above, if one's rival produced q^C without provocation prior to round ten from the end, then one would know that the rival is not of the sort that will wait this long before acting 'competitively'. Of course, once you know that your rivals will be trying to infer things about you from your actions, you take that into account in formulating your actions. You must weigh against current gains or losses the effect that your actions will have on your reputation, and thus on later results of competition and later profits/losses. Since rivals tomorrow will be looking back to see what you did today, today you should look forward to gauge the consequences of your actions on tomorrow's competition.

Applications of this sort of model to issues in IO have just begun to appear. Kreps, Milgrom, Roberts and Wilson (1982) study a model of 'implicit collusion' a bit different from the formulation outlined above. Also, there have been analyses of predatory behaviour and entry deterrence: here the idea is that a monopolist, in order to forestall entry, will attempt to convince potential rivals that it will engage in predatory practices if faced with entry, even though those practices will hurt the monopoly firm in the short run. Kreps and Wilson (1982) and Milgrom and Roberts (1982b) show that if potential entrants are initially uncertain about whether predation really is costly to the monopolist in the short run, then even if the chances that it is costly are close to one, the monopolist will engage in predation, in an attempt to gain a reputation for being tough. In other words, the monopolist, realizing that potential entrants will look at his/her 'track record' in previous encounters, can effectively threaten to abuse any entrant for demonstration purposes. Even if it costly to abuse entrants in the short run, the long-run gains accruing from forestalling subsequent entry is more than worth it. In Kreps and Wilson (1982), a model is also investigated in which two rivals have a 'reputation war'; each incurs costs in the short run in an attempt to convince the other through its current actions that it is tough, in order to get later gains from this sort of reputation. This sort of equilibrium behaviour is reminiscent of a labour strike or a price war.

An Example – Limit Pricing to Forestall Entry

An excellent application of this sort of analysis is provided by Milgrom and Roberts (1982a). The subject is limit pricing to forestall entry. Bain (1956) and Sylos-Labini (1962) tell the following story: a monopolist is concerned with the possibility that a second firm will enter its market. This monopolist will therefore try to convince the entrant that entry will be unprofitable. One way to do this (goes the story) is to produce at a level sufficiently large so that if this level of production is maintained by the monopolist after entry occurs, then the residual demand curve faced by the entrant will be insufficient to cover fixed costs, etc. The key behavioural hypothesis is that the entrant, in assessing the desirability of entry, believes that the monopolist will maintain its quantity of output in the face of entry.

It is clear that the perceptions of the entrant concerning what will happen in the post-entry market are crucial to the entry decision. Dixit (1980) shows how changing expectations of the post-entry competition (based on current market data) will change the prospects for entry deterrence. To take a particular example, Spence (1977) looks at the prospects for entry deterrence if the entrant assumes that post-entry competition will be very severe price competition, subject only to the limits imposed by output capacities. (That is, post-entry competition will conform to the Edgeworth—Bertrand model.) In this case, the monopolist may be able to deter entry by holding excess capacity 'in reserve', for the price-wars that are expected to follow any entry. On the other hand, if post-entry competition will be Cournot competition, and if variable costs of output are unaffected by the amount of capacity held, then excess capacity is not a barrier to entry.

In this formulation, and in most other formulations in the large litera-ture on this subject, the potential entrant isn't really learning anything of a private nature from the monopolist's pre-entry actions. The monopolist, so to speak, is setting the initial conditions for the post-entry competition. But pre-entry behaviour is not used to communicate to the entrant things about which the entrant is unsure. Milgrom and Roberts (1982a) present models where this sort of 'communication' is present.

Suppose that the entrant is uncertain initially about the costs of produc-tion of the monopolist. In almost any model of post-entry competition that one can think of, this uncertainty would carry over into uncertainty about whether or not the entrant will 'survive' and be profitable if entry occurs. To keep matters simple, imagine that the monopolist has a constant cost technology, characterized by the marginal cost of production c. The entrant would like to enter if this cost c exceeds some critical number c^*, but would prefer to stay out otherwise.

How can the entrant discern the monopolist's costs from pre-entry behaviour? If we suppose that the monopolist makes price-quantity decisions pre-entry in order to maximize short-run profits, then (in most cases) the equilibrium price and quantity (and information about the local elasticity of demand) will reveal the monopolist's marginal costs. Assuming that marginal revenue falls with equilibrium quantities, higher equilibrium quantity leads to lower (inferred) marginal costs. Thus, the entrant who is worried about the monopolist's cost structure and believes that the mon-opolist acts to maximize profits pre-entry will adopt a 'critical number' strategy: if equilibrium quantity pre-entry falls short of some level q^* (that level that gives marginal revenue equal to c^*), then enter. If equilib-rium quantity pre-entry exceeds q^*, then stay out.

If the monopolist understands that the entrant is using this single critical number strategy, then he/she may have some incentive to 'dissemble'. Consider the case where the monopolist's costs are just a bit above c^*. If the monopolist maximizes short-run profits and supplies a bit less than q^*, it will provoke entry. But by producing a bit more than q^* (depressing short-run profits a bit), it can deter entry, because the entrant will (mis)-infer that its costs are below c^*. This short-run sacrifice of current profits will, in some cases, be amply repaid if entry is deterred.

But surely the entrant can work out that this is so. The entrant realizes that since he/she is looking at the monopolist's pre-entry behaviour to infer the monopolist's costs, the monopolist will try to 'bluff' and signal lower costs than it has. There is a delicate, equilibrium interplay to be worked out here. The monopolist chooses a pre-entry quantity to supply as a function of his/her costs. The entrant, anticipating this strategy by the monopolist, can use the pre-entry quantity to make inferences about the monopolist's costs and thus decide whether to enter. Closing the circle, the monopolist will take into account the entrant's use of the pre-entry quantity to determine his/her pre-entry quantity as a function of his/her costs. When we start and finish with the same strategy for the monopolist, having gone through both rounds of optimization, we have an equilibrium in which past behaviour is used as information to predict future behaviour and (hence) performance.

Milgrom and Roberts (1982a) analyse models of this sort, seeking equilibria in expectations and behaviour. They find many different sorts of equilibrium, some in which the monopolist is unable to 'hide' its true cost structure at all, some in which the monopolist can successfully forestall entry that would take place if the entrant knew the monopolist's true costs, and even some where entry takes place that would be be avoided if the entrant knew the monopolist's true costs. The one unambiguous result is that, as long as the entrant is more likely to enter the higher is the pre-entry quantity and the lower the pre-entry equilibrium price, the monopolist will always provide more than (or, in degenerate cases, just as much as) the pre-entry profit-maximizing quantity.

As the authors themselves note, it would be a mistake to take too seriously the precise conclusions of this paper. (Indeed, it would be hard to do so as the conclusions are fairly ambiguous.) They note (and, in Milgrom and Roberts, 1982b, have gone on to show) that multi-period or multi-market 'reputation' considerations can drastically change the analysis. In addition, there are other signals (excess capacity, etc.) that can be sent besides pre-entry quantity. Of particular note are signals about the intentions (as opposed to the capabilities) of incumbents. But this analysis makes the important methodological point that one should look for equilibrium implications when considering models of inference (and subsequent action) based on past behaviour. And it shows that such implications can be formally derived from the analysis of games of incomplete information.

General Comments on Games of Incomplete Information

Games of incomplete information allow the analyst to formulate the idea that industry participants use history to predict future behaviour, intentions, capabilities, etc. With them, one can formalize notions such as reputation. Most importantly, one can subject these notions and ideas to equilibrium analsyis, to see whether hypothesized relationships between past and future can exist if participants are aware of and respond rationally to their existence. But these abilities come at substantial cost, and at the present time the theory is filled with lacunae.

The high cost comes from the level of difficulty in performing the analysis. Computing exact equilibria can be difficult, if not impossible, even in structurally simple models. (Indeed, exact equilibria have not been provided in the applications of these ideas to implicit collusion; see Kreps, Milgrom, Roberts and Wilson, 1982.) Certainly, the current level of technology does not seem to permit analysis of, say, a model of implicit collusion between non-symmetric rivals, where they first engage in some sort of 'sparring' to determine the market shares, etc., that will prevail. Extremely highly stylized models can be analysed, and the analysis of these may give the analyst enough insights with which to proceed. But in so far as these simple models miss important aspects of the problem, this technology may be inadequate to the task.

The chief lacunae that we see is in the design of the 'initial considerations'. The examples that have been analysed suggest that the nature of the equilibrium that arises is extremely sensitive to the initial assessments of participants. Indeed, perhaps the most striking feature of Kreps and Wilson (1982) and Milgrom and Roberts (1982b) is that a very small (one in a thousand) chance that one's rival acts in some particular fashion (regardless of the pecuniary implications) can completely alter the nature of the equilibrium. One complaint we raised against the supergame approach is that there seemed no way to choose formally amongst the multiplicity of equilibria. Using games of incomplete information permits one (to some extent) to 'explain' the equilibrium that arises as a consequence of the formally specified initial beliefs, but it gives no particular guidance (yet) as to the relative power of different initial beliefs.

Moreover, games of incomplete information sometimes suffer as well from a superfluidity of equilibria. In sum, we are encouraged by the concept and the descriptive power it (so far) seems to possess. But a lot of progress in its application remains to be made.

BEYOND RATIONAL ACTORS

A hallmark of the literature that we have surveyed so far is that agents are assumed to have very substantial computational powers, which they use in particular ways. Agents foresee all possible future contingencies; when there is uncertainty, they make (usually unanimous) subjective probability assessments, which they use to make Savage rational choices; they make unerring inferences from past occurrences; and so forth. Moreover, they (and bear in mind that 'they' here means firms) have a clear criterion by which they choose amongst their alternatives: almost invariably, this objective is long-term profit maximization (or, when there is uncertainty, expected profit maximization).

Of course, these are the core assumptions of the analyses in which we are interested. Any sort of study of industry dynamics and the role of history in industrial competition will turn crucially on the assumptions that are made concerning the behaviour of firms. If, for example, one is attempting to model the notion that firms observe the past behaviour of competitors and make inferences about the cost structures of competitors from those past actions, then the part of the model that relates past actions to the (externally unobservable) cost structure will be key, as will be the inferential process used by the first firm. Assumptions such as those above deserve the utmost scrutiny and challenge.

The Evolutionary Theory of Nelson and Winter

Perhaps the most comprehensive attack on the assumptions listed above comes from Nelson and Winter (1982) and their evolutionary theory of economic change. They characterize the traditional theory as having three touchstones:

(1) A firm is characterized by a production possibility set — in mathematical terms, a set of input—output vectors from which it can choose its activity.
(2) The choice of particular activity from the production possibility set is made by maximizing profit (or some close relative of profit).
(3) The various choices of firms are brought into line with one another through an economic (price) equilibrium.

In place of these three, they propose a different triumverate of fundamental concepts:

(1) At any point in time, the 'state of the firm' is described by the rou-

tine(s) of which the firm is capable. This concept of a routine constitutes a blending of two pieces of the traditional theory: the opportunity set and the criterion by which an activity is chosen from that
set. The reason for blending the two is to obtain a better (i.e. more
realistic) depiction of the firm, whose decision-making process is (in
the short run) a feature of the firm as peculiar to the firm as is the
production possibility set. Profit mzximization as the universal
criterion employed by every firm is no more realistic than would be
an assumption of identical opportunity sets.

(2) The firm's collection of routines evolves through time according to
the search behaviour of the firm. Roughly, the firm can change its
routine(s) by searching out others. The formulation of search behaviour consists both of a description of how the firm searches when
it chooses to do so and a description of the decision rule by which the
firm chooses whether to search or not.

(3) The evolution of the economy is guided by a process very much like
biological natural selection. For example (and it is important to regard
this solely as an example), suppose that the prices the firms face are
given exogenuously and fluctuate randomly. (Think of this as an industry that is competitive as an entire entity. An alternative used by
the authors is to imagine that short-run equilibrium prices are determined through something akin to temporary equilibrium, or equilibrium in spot markets.) Thus the current routine(s) of the firms determine their profits in the near term. Imagine that firms reinvest their
profits (or reinvest profits over some level of disbursement) in their
capital stock, according to some part of the routine. Firms that (i)
are relatively more profitable, and (ii) that are relatively better at their
investment 'routine' will grow and prosper. And if we imagine that
firms search for new routines when they find themselves falling
behind in terms of size, then relatively 'unfit' species will change
(mutate), producing stronger stocks.

Nelson and Winter put forward these three 'organizing concepts' as being
more useful for studying dynamics and limited rationality than are the
three aforementioned 'classical' concepts. It should be noted (and they do)
that this does not constitute a system wholly inconsistent with the
classical system (if one allows the classical system to be flexible in regard
to the sorts of computations of which firms are capable); similar ideas can
be (and to some extent, have been) investigated with the classical system.
But Nelson and Winter assert that those attempts have been marked by
tortuous complexity — the classical system isn't as well constructed for the
sorts of questions that they wish to investigate as is their own.

For example, Nelson and Winter argue that theirs is a *disequilibrium* theory, as opposed to the traditional *equilibrium* approach. Their use of these terms is instructive: they do not mean that they do not find equilibria in the sense that conflicting actions/desires are not brought into line by some mechanism. Rather, the system is not in a static or long-run equilibrium – it evolves as time passes, perhaps approaching some stationary regime. In a formal sense, the same could be said for the traditional theory, especially in Radner's (1972) equilibria of plans, prices and price expectations – the spot market equilibria in a Radner economy can (and, in examples, will) exhibit an 'evolutionary' pattern. But, in the traditional theory the emphasis, partially implicit, is on a once-and-for-all equilibrium, where all forces current and future are brought into balance. In the Nelson and Winter system, there is much less 'foresight' present. In the terms of traditional theory, they have a system of temporary equilibria, in which the emphasis is very strongly on the temporal evolution of those temporary equilibria.

Having laid out these three fundamental concepts, they go on (for the most part) to give a few simple parameterizations of the sort of model they have in mind, which they investigate through simulation. To take one example (from ch. 9), they investigate patterns of economic growth and technology development in a model that conforms (roughly) to the description above, where (in addition) the following assumptions are made:

(1) Each firm is characterized at any point in time by a single fixed-coefficients production process.

(2) The set of possible production processes (points in a two-dimensional space of input coefficients, representing inputs of labour and capital required to make one unit of output) is given by 100 points in the space of logs of the two coefficients, generated by random sampling from a uniform distribution over this space (with a bit of fudging).

(3) Firms 'satisfice': they engage in search for better production processes only if their profits fall below some critical level.

(4) Firms that do search for better techniques choose (randomly) between imitation of the techniques of others or search for wholly new techniques. In the latter case, the probability distribution over the 'found' technique is concentrated near the technique that the firm is currently using.

(5) Firms adopt a newly found technique if and only if it outperforms the technique they currently use, where there is a chance of an 'error' in this calculation. (That is, the estimation of the production coefficients is subject to some noise.)

(6) Capital stock depreciates and is replenished internally; any profits

over a required dividend rate (proportional to the physical capital stock) are used to purchase additional capital.

(7) New firms enter randomly if they have production techniques that (in the short run) meet a profitability hurdle.

(8) Wages are set endogenously, through equilibrium in a short-run labour market. (Labour supply is elastic to wages, according to an exogenously given supply curve. Labour demand is inelastic — firms purchase labour sufficiently to utilize fully their capital stock.)

With the model so described, one can (and the authors do) simulate the system, to observe performance. Moreover, one can (and they do) vary some of the important parameters (e.g. probability that a firm will search through imitation, the probability of discovering new techniques distant from currently used technique, the pay-out on capital required before investment can be initiated), in order to perform 'comparative statics'.

The precise results obtained, both in this chapter and in others, are quite interesting. Through simulation, the authors are able to 'replicate' the general macroeconomic results of the traditional theory (e.g. the direction of response to changes in factor supplies or to the 'impatience' of investors), while keeping a microeconomic structure that they find is more true to life. The greater 'realism' of the microeconomic structure becomes especially useful in comparative statics — they can vary paramenters of the economy that have no direct counterparts in the standard theory.

Of course, it is not too difficult to find things to criticize in their precise formulations: behaviour by firms is extremely simple-minded, and while firms may not be the paragons of computation that they are assumed to be in the classical model, they are (perhaps) not so simple-minded as here. In the model outlined above, there are no financial or capital markets. If a firm 'discovers' a new and world-beating technique, it cannot go into the capital markets to raise (suddenly) the funds needed to become a major force in industry. Nor can new techniques be licensed to established firms. This, presumably, gives their results a bias against rapid expansion of new and profitable techniques, although it does maintain a sizeable diversity in the range of techniques employed, thereby fostering faster overall evolution. And so forth. Criticisms against their precise formulation are as rich as is the real world.

But similar criticisms are equally easy to make of more traditional models. What makes such criticisms a bit more nettlesome here is the reliance on simulations as opposed to deductive logic. Simulations of particular models leads one to be unsure which results are the result of particular parameterizations and which the result of 'general tendencies'. It is desirable to complement these simulations with deductively generated results concerning the dynamic behaviour of models of this sort. Nelson and Winter have clearly just begun to develop results along these lines, and we hope (and expect) that further and better results (including deductive results) will be forthcoming.

The more important contribution of this book is in the reorganization of 'fundamental concepts'. There is little doubt that the classical system, applied naively, has some glaring weaknesses. A question we regard as open, however, is whether, as Nelson and Winter assert, attempts to reconcile their concepts with the classical system will prove more tortuous and less enlighting than will simple adoption of their system. We are not so pessimistic as are they on attempts to place their ideas within the classical framework, especially in terms of 'micro-micro-models' of the actions of individuals. (We will report momentarily on two lines of analysis that are moving in precisely this direction.)

It should be noted that their book continues a tradition of argument along 'evolutionary' lines. It gives an eloquent statement of that point of view, but it does not initiate it. M. Friedman (1953), for example, has defended profit maximization along just these lines – if some firms profit maximize and others do not, he argues, then those that do will eventually outpace the others. Also, Simon (in, 1965, for example) has long been working along these lines. Concepts such as 'putting out fires' (see also Radner, 1975), 'standard operating procedures', and so forth, have been studied from the point of view of evolutionary 'fitness'. (Also along these lines, see Axelrod, 1981, for a general treatment of the evolutionary fitness of co-operative behaviour. And see Hannan and Freeman, 1977, for work in the 'population ecology of organizations'.)

Organization Theory

Nelson and Winter give as their chief objection to the classical theory the extent to which that theory assumes 'rationality' on the part of firms. Their concept of a routine is intended precisely to blend the standard ideas of the competences of the firm (usually modelled with a production possibility set) and the choice criterion of the (usually modelled as some variant on profit maximization). They emphasize the inability of firms to carry out the necessary calculations, because the firm will not 'know' all the things of which it is capable, because all future contingencies cannot be foreseen, because mistakes can be made, and so forth. All of these are valid criticisms of the standard model, but there is another set of criticisms that can be levelled that is equally damaging to the classical model.

Theories of rational choice are based on individual decision-making, and not multi-person or organizational decision-making problems. There is no reason, *a priori*, to suppose that an organization such as a firm will have a clear criterion by which 'it' makes choices. At the simplest level, profit maximization as a decision criterion can be justified only when firms are perfectly competitive (that is, when their actions do not change equilibrium price). In any other case (which amounts to most interesting cases in IO), there is no reason to believe that shareholders will unanimously prefer actions that maximize profits. (To take an extreme case, if shareholders consume the output of the firm in proportion to their shareholdings, they will unanimously prefer that firm *not* to exploit any market power that it may have.)

This is not the only problem. Even if shareholders could somehow come to unanimous consent concerning the criterion they wished for the firm to adopt (and assuming that we grant the primacy of their interests in such a case), unless we imagine a world of perfect and complete information, where problems of agency are non-existent, there is no reason to believe that the firm as an entity will adopt that criterion. The firm exists as an entity because it provides, as an organization different from a marketplace, functions that cannot be as well provided by a market. To model, therefore, the firm as a monolithic entity, profit maximizing or otherwise, is a serious oversimplification of reality. (Following M. Friedman, 1953, it might be counter-argued that 'natural selection' will favour profit-maximizing firms. However, before one can take seriously that argument, a demonstration of its validity should be given in a context where there are reasons for firms to exist; that is, where there are real agency problems, etc.)

There has been a good deal of work recently in the theory of organization. This ranges from the more mathematical work in agency theory to more 'verbal' work. Antecedents (over a wide range) would include Coase (1937), Cyert and March (1963) Marshak and Radner (1972), Alchian and Demsetz (1972), Arrow (1974), Williamson (1975), and Jensen and Meckling (1976). Recent papers, representative of the two 'branches' of this line of inquiry, are Holmstrom (1982) and Williamson (1981). We have no desire to launch into a synopsis of this work – that would take another chapter of equal length. But we do wish to point out the relevance of that work for studies of IO and competition: if one wishes to model the behaviour of organizations such as firms, then study of the firm as an organization ought to be high on one's agenda. This study is not, strictly speaking, necessary: one can hope to divine the correct 'reduced form' for the behaviour of the organization without considering the micro-forces within the organization. But study of the organization is likely to help in the design of reduced forms that stress the important variables.

Models of Limited Rationality

And if one can better model and understand the decision-making process of a firm through the study of the microstructure of the firm, then it is possible that similar analytical endeavours may help in understanding the effect on behaviour of limited computational ability/rationality on the part of economic actors. Faced with computational difficulties, or inability to perceive all possible future contingencies, it seems likely that economic agents adopt 'plausible' rules of thumb. Limited rationality does not (necessarily) mean behaviour that is completely random or without any predictable pattern.

There have been a few papers written along these lines. Radner (1975) is one example. Others worthy of citation would be Radner (1980), Smale (1980), and (in the context of learning models where agents 'learn' from equilibrium prices) Bray (1982). A representative of the group (one that fits in well with the subjects discussed in this chapter) is Levine (1981). Roughly speaking, Levine studies strategic investment behaviour (as in Spence, 1979, and Fudenberg and Tirole, 1982a), but where firms in maximizing profits 'estimate' future profits by extrapolating plausibly from current profits. The extrapolation rules range from somewhat less than plausible (the so-called null rule assumes that future profits will be zero regardless of today's actions) to more reasonable linear extrapolation. Levine looks for (and finds) conditions under which the rules studied will perform well, in the sense that they are not grossly outperformed (in equilibrium) by perfect foresight. By doing so, he is finding environments in which such rules of thumb might be expected to 'survive', in the sense that they are not grossly controverted by accumulating evidence.

The efforts that have been made along these lines (at least, in the mathematical branch of theory) are quite preliminary. We are handicapped by the lack of a good axiomatic treatment of limited rationality – the tendency is to model such behaviour as behaviour that is 'rational' according to some incorrect model of the way the world works. (In the area of mathematical psychology, models of choice behaviour have been created that have some basis in experimental work; see, for example, Kahnemann and Tversky, 1970, Tversky, 1972, and Tversky and Kahnemann, 1974.) Such models may or may not be appropriate, and, lacking any theoretical foundation, they are open to the charge of being *ad hoc*. It can only be hoped that further progress along these lines will be forthcoming in the not-too-distant future.

REFERENCES

Abreu, D. (1982) 'Repeated Games with Discounting: A General Theory and an Application to Oligopoly' (mimeo).

Alchian, A., and H. Demsetz (1972) 'Production, Information Costs, and Economic Organization', *American Economic Review*, 62: 777–95.

Arrow, K. (1974) *The Limits of Organization*, New York: Norton.

Axelrod, R. (1981) 'The Emergence of Cooperation Among Egoists', *American Political Science Review*, 75: 306–18.

Bain, J. (1956) *Barriers to New Competition*, Cambridge, Mass.: Harvard University Press.

Bray, M. (1982) 'Learning, Estimation, and the Stability of Rational Expectations Equilibrium', *Journal of Economic Theory*, 26: 318–39.

Coase, R. (1937) 'The Nature of the Firm,' *Econometrica*, 4: 386–405.

Cyert, R., and J. March (1963) *A Behavioral Theory of the Firm*, Englewood Cliffs, N.J.: Prentice-Hall.

Dasgupta, P., and J. Stiglitz (1980) 'Uncertainty, Industrial Structure, and the Speed of R&D', *Bell Journal of Economics*, 11: 1–28.

Dixit, A. (1979) 'A Model of Duopoly Suggesting a Theory of Entry Barriers', *Bell Journal of Economics*, 10: pp. 20–32.

Dixit, A. (1980) 'The Role of Investment in Entry Deterrence', *Economic Journal*, 90: 95–106.

Fine, C. (1983) 'Quality Control and Learning in Productive Systems', PhD dissertation, Stanford University.

Friedman, J. (1977) *Oligopoly and the Theory of Games*, Amsterdam: North-Holland

Frideman, M. (1953) *Essays in Positive Economics*, Chicago: University of Chicago Press.

Fudenberg, D., and J. Tirole (1982a) 'Capital as a Commitment: Strategic Investment to Deter Mobility' (mimeo), *Journal of Economic Theory*, 31: 227–50.

Fudenberg, D., and Tirole (1982b) 'Learning by Doing and Market Performance' (mimeo).

Fudenberg, D., and Tirole (1983) 'Preemption and Rent Equalization in the Adoptation of New Technology' (mimeo).

Fudenberg, D., R. Gilbert, J. Stiglitz and J. Tirole (1982) 'Preemption, Leapfrogging and Competition in Patent Races' (mimeo).

Gilbert, R., and R. Harris (1982) 'Competition and Mergers with Lumpy Investment' (mimeo).

Gilbert, R., and D. Newbery (1982) 'Preemptive Patenting and the Persistence of Monopoly', *American Economic Review*, 72: 514–26.

Green, E., and R. Porter (1981) 'Noncooperative Collusion Under Imperfect Price Information' (mimeo).

Hannan, M., and J. Freeman (1977) 'Population Ecology of Organizations' *American Journal of Sociology*, 82: pp. 929–64.

Harsanyi, J. (1967—8) 'Games with Incomplete Information Played by Bayesian Players', *Management Science*, 14: 159—82, 320—34, 486—502.

Holmstrom, B. (1982) 'Managerial Incentive Problems — A Dynamic Perspective', in *Essays in Economics and Management in Honor of Lars Wahlbeck*, Helsinki: Swedish School of Economics.

Jensen, M., and W. Meckling (1976) 'Theory of the Firm: Managerial Behavior, Agency Costs and Ownership Structure', *Journal of Financial Economics*, 3: 305—60.

Jones, L. (1982) 'A Note on Competitive Foresight and Optimum Product Diversity' (mimeo).

Kahnemann, D., and A. Tversky (1979) 'Prospect Theory: An Analysis of Decision Under Risk', *Econometrica*, 47: 263—92.

Kreps, D., and R. Wilson (1982) 'Reputation and Imperfect Information, *Journal of Economic Theory*, 27: 253—79.

Kreps, D., P. Milgrom, J. Roberts and R. Wilson (1982) 'Rational Cooperation in the Finitely Repeated Prisoners' Dilemma', *Journal of Economic Theory*, 27: 245—52.

Levine, D. (1981) 'Extrapolative Investment Equilibrium', (mimeo).

Lieberman, M. (1982) 'The Learning Curve, Pricing, and Market Structure in the Chemical Processing Industries, PhD dissertation, Harvard University.

Loury, G. (1979) 'Market Structure and Innovation', *Quarterly Journal of Economics*, 93: 395—410.

Marshak, J., and R. Radner (1972) *Economic Theory of Teams*, New Haven: Yale University Press.

Maskin, E., and J. Tirole (1982) 'A Theory of Dynamic Oligopoly, I: Overview and Quantity Competition with Large Fixed Costs' (mimeo).

Milgrom, P., and J. Roberts (1982a) 'Limit Pricing and Entry Under Incomplete Information', *Econometrica*, 50: 443—60.

Milgrom, P., and J. Roberts (1982b) 'Predation, Reputation and Entry Deterrence', *Journal of Economic Theory*, 27: 280—312.

Nelson, R., and S. Winter (1982) *An Evolutionary Theory of Economic Change*, Cambridge, Mass.: Harvard University Press.

Porter, M. (1980) *Competitive Strategy*, New York: Free Press.

Porter, M., and A. Spence (1982) 'The Capacity Expansion Process in a Growing Oligopoly: The Case of Corn Wet Milling', in J. J. McCall (ed.), *The Economics of Information and Uncertainty*, Chicago: University of Chicago Press.

Prescott, E., and M. Visscher (1977) 'Sequential Location Among Firms with Foresight', *Bell Journal of Economics*, 8: 378—94.

Radner, R. (1972) 'Existence of Equilibrium of Plans, Prices and Price Expectations in a Sequence of Markets, *Econometrica*, 40: 289—303.

Radner, R. (1975) 'A Behavioral Model of Cost Reduction', *Bell Journal of Economics*, 8: 196—215.

Radner, R. (1980) 'Collusive Behavior in Noncooperative Epsilon-Equilibria in Oligopolies with Long but Finite Lives', *Journal of Economic Theory*, 22: 136—54.

Radner, R. (1981) 'Optimal Equilibria in Some Repeated Games with Imperfect Monitoring' (mimeo).

Rao, R., and D. Rutenberg (1979) 'Preempting an Alert Rival: Strategic Timing of the First Plant by Analysis of Sophisticated Rivalry', *Bell Journal of Economics*, 10: 412–28.

Reinganum, J. (1981) 'Dynamic Games of Innovation', *Journal of Economic Theory*, 25: 21–41.

Reinganum J. (1982a) 'A Dynamic Game of R&D: Patent Protection and Competitive Behavior' *Econometrica*, 50: 671–88.

Reinganum, J. (1982b) 'Patent Races with a Sequence of Innovations' (mimeo).

Reinganum, J., and N. Stokey (1981) 'Oligopoly Extraction of a Non-renewable, Common Property Resource: The Importance of the Period of Commitment in Dynamic Games' (mimeo).

Roth, A., and F. Schoumaker (1981) 'Expectations and Reputations in Bargaining: An Experimental Study, *American Economic Review*, 73: 362–72.

Rubinstein, A. (1979) 'Strong Perfect Equilibrium in Supergames', *International Journal of Game Theory*, 9: 1–12.

Schelling, T. (1960) *The Strategy of Conflict*, Cambridge, Mass.: Harvard University Press.

Scherer, F. (1980) *Industrial Market Structure and Economic Performance*, 2nd edn, Chicago: Rand McNally College Publishing

Schmalensee, R. (1982) 'Product Differentiation Advantages of Pioneering Brands', *American Economic Review*, 72: 349–65.

Shaked, A., and J. Sutton (1982) Relaxing Price Competition Through Product Differentiation', *Review of Economic Studies*, 49: 3–13.

Simon, H. (1965) *Administrative Behaviour*, New York: Free Press.

Selten, R. (1978) 'The Chain-store Paradox', *Theory and Decision*, 9: 127–59.

Smale, S. (1980) 'The Prisoner's Dilemma and Dynamical Systems Associated to Non-Cooperative Games', *Econometrica*, 48: 1617–34.

Spence, A. (1977) 'Entry, Capacity, Investment and Oligopolistic Pricing', *Bell Journal of Economics*, 8: 534–44.

Spence, A. (1979) 'Investment Strategy and Growth in a New Market', *Bell Journal of Economics*, 10: 1–19.

Spence, A. (1981) 'The Learning Curve and Competition', *Bell Journal of Economics*, 12: 49–70.

Spence, A. (1982) 'Cost Reduction, Competition and Industry Performance' (mimeo), *Econometrica*, 52: 101–22.

Stigler, G. (1964) 'A Theory of Oligopoly', *Journal of Political Economy*, 72: 44–61.

Sylos-Labini, P. (1962) *Oligopoly and Technical Progress*, trans. E. Henderson, Cambridge, Mass.: Harvard University Press.

Tversky, A. (1972) 'Elimination by Aspects: A Theory of Choice', *Psychological Review*, 76: 31–48.

Tversky, A., and D. Kahnemann (1974) 'Judgement Under Uncertainty: Heuristics and Biases', *Science*, 185: 1124–31.

Williamson, O. (1975) *Markets and Hierarchies: Analysis and Anti-trust Implications*, New York: Free Press.

Williamson O. (1981) 'The Modern Corporation: Origins, Evolution, Attributes', *Journal of Economic Literature*, 19 (December): 1537–68.

11 Allocation Mechanisms, Asymmetric Information and the 'Revelation Principle'

MILTON HARRIS
and ROBERT M. TOWNSEND*

INTRODUCTION

The purpose of this chapter is to explain a new approach for predicting both the allocation of resources and the resource allocation mechanism in certain environments in which agents are asymmetrically informed prior to any trading.[1] We illustrate this approach by applying it to a simple pure-exchange environment in which an information asymmetry is present.

The central element of this approach (which is described in more detail below) is to define the concept of an optimal resource allocation mechanism and to characterize such optimal mechanisms and their associated optimal allocations for given economic environments. There are two reasons for approaching the problem in this way, that is, searching for optimal resource allocation mechanisms. The first is simply that one would like to have a theory that *explains* observed mechanisms (or processes or institutional arrangements — we use these terms synonymously). For example, one might wish to explain why auctions are used in certain environments, but not in others.[2] The second is that one would like to have a theory that explains the final allocation of resources in environments with asymmetric information, and to do so, we argue that one must begin with an explicit consideration of mechanisms. To sketch this argument briefly, let us start with the premise that in any economic environment, the observed allocation of resources actually is achieved by some mechanism. We then assert that in some asymmetric information environments *there are allocations consistent with the resource constraints* (i.e. *technologically* feasible) *which, nevertheless, cannot be achieved by any mechanism.*

* This research has benefited from the support of the National Science Foundation.

That is, we assert that the presence of information asymmetries imposes certain incentive constraints on achievable allocations.[3] The point here is that these constraints can only be revealed by an explicit consideration of the processes by which allocations are achieved. Of course, once these constraints are revealed, one can contemplate generating optimal allocations in the usual way as solutions to programming problems that incorporate the constraints. Obviously one way of making sure that information constraints are accounted for in an economic model is simply to analyse the equilibrium of some particular (and explicit) mechanism. This approach is certainly suitable for positive purposes if one believes that the chosen mechanism is a good model of actual arrangements in the environment of interest, and if one is not interested in explaining these arrangements. Yet if one does seek to explain observed arrangements, or if one is interested in normative implications, then one would like to establish that the constraints on allocations of the chosen mechanism cannot be circumvented by some alternative process. This leads us to consider a fairly broad class of available mechanisms.[4]

The approach we describe here uses what has now come to be known as the 'Revelation Principle'.[5] This principle, or results similar to it, has been developed by Harris and Townsend (1978, 1981), Holmstrom (1978), and Myerson (1979). It can be stated simply as:

The Revelation Principle. Any equilibrium allocation of any mechanism can be achieved by a truthful, direct mechanism.

By a *direct mechanism*, we mean a game in which all agents first simultaneously declare values for whatever parameters they have observed, for example, parameters describing their own tastes, etc. After these 'messages' or 'signals' are sent, some allocation is effected as a function of the declarations of all players. This *allocation rule* is specified in advance. Players in a direct mechanism need not tell the truth about their observed parameters. In a *truthful*, direct mechanism, however, there is an equilibrium in which all players do tell the truth: a truthful mechanism, then, is one in which each player is given an incentive (by the allocation rule) not to lie, provided that he expects all other players to tell the truth.

The power of the Revelation Principle is that it enables one to limit his search for optimal mechanisms to direct mechanisms without fear of ignoring a more complicated mechanism that could have produced a better outcome. Specifying a mechanism can, in general, be quite complicated, involving a specification of what strategies are feasible for each agent at each stage, what each agent knows at each stage, and how the final allocation depends on the whole history of signals of the agents. A direct mechanism can, however, be completely specified by its allocation rule. This is simply a function from the set of values of observable parameters to the set of feasible allocations.

The Revelation Principle also implies that we can restrict attention to direct mechanisms in which truth-telling is an equilibrium. This imposes a set of constraints on the allocation rules that guarantee that, for each agent and for each value of his observed parameters, it is optimal to tell the truth given that all other agents are telling the truth. These constraints are generally called 'self-selection' or, following Hurwicz (1972), 'incentive compatibility' conditions. Thus, using the Revelation Principle, an optimal mechanism, and its associated equilibrium allocation, can be found by choosing an *allocation rule* that maximizes some social welfare function (e.g. a weighted average of the utilities of the players) subject to technological feasibility conditions and incentive compatibility conditions. In effect, then, one can search for optimal allocations directly. An example of how this is done is given in the third section.[6]

In the second section, we attempt to motivate the general results, primarily the Revelation Principle. Readers are referred elsewhere for proofs. In the third section, we analyse a specific two-person, two-good, pure exchange environment using the results of the second sections. The fourth section provides a summary and conclusion.

GENERAL RESULTS

First let us specify the general type of economic environment to which the results will apply. Suppose there are a finite number of economic agents, say N, indexed by $i = 1, \ldots, N$. Further suppose that there is a set A of technologically feasible allocations. An element a of A is a vector that specifies each agent's allocation bundle. The set A will incorporate constraints due to the technology of production and exchange and due to resource availability. In order to introduce asymmetric information into the environment, we shall assume that each agent i may *privately* observe the value of a parameter θ_i which affects his tastes.[7] We model agent i's lack of information about the parameters of other agents by assuming that i has a well-defined joint prior distribution over $(\theta_j)_{j \neq i}$. This prior may depend on the observed value of i's parameter, θ_i. Finally, we denote by $U_i(a, \theta_i)$ the utility of agent i for an allocation a if his parameter has value θ_i. When i's parameter value is θ_i, i is said to be of *type* θ_i.

Our next step is to define more carefully the concept of a mechanism. In this chapter we will, as in Myerson (1979), define a mechanism to be what game theorists call a 'game in normal form'. A game in normal form is a particular way of formalizing the intuitive notion of a game. This formalization specifies the set of signals each agent can send and an outcome that depends on the signals sent.[8]

To be somewhat more formal, a normal-form game specifies a set of feasible signals S_i for each agent i and an allocation rule F which associates with each vector of signals $(s_1, \ldots, s_N)$ in $S = S_1 \times \ldots \times S_N$ an allocation $F(s_1, \ldots, s_N)$ in A.[9] We may now define a *mechanism* as any normal-form game, that is, signal sets S_i and allocation rule F.

Our next task is to define what is meant by an equilibrium of a mechanism. This is simply an hypothesis concerning the way we expect players to behave and the outcome that will result. The equilibrium concept we use here is called the Bayesian equilibrium (by Harsanyi, 1967–68) because players' strategies are based on their prior beliefs about the 'types' of the other agents.

The first point to recognize in defining equilibrium is that each player i will choose his signal s_i from his signal set S_i based on the value of his parameter, that is, on his type θ_i. Thus player i's *strategy* is a function that depends on θ_i and whose value is a signal in S_i. Let us denote i's strategy by $\sigma_i(\theta_i)$.

The second point to recognize is that i's optimal strategy, that is, his optimal signal as a function of his type, depends on what signals he believes other players will send. Other players' signals are, in turn, determined by their strategies, σ_j, and their types, θ_j. Therefore, player i's beliefs about player j's signal reflect the strategy that i believes j will use and i's prior on θ_j. In a Bayesian equilibrium, it is assumed that each player i chooses his best strategy *given* the strategies of the other players and *given* i's prior beliefs about their types.

More formally, a vector of strategies $(\sigma_1^*, \ldots, \sigma_N^*)$ is a Bayesian equilibrium of the mechanism defined by the signal sets $S_1, \ldots, S_N$ and the allocation rule F if, for each player i and each possible value of his type θ_i, the signal $s_i^* = \sigma_i^*(\theta_i)$ maximizes i's expected utility given that he believes that each other agent j will be using strategy σ_j^* and given his beliefs about θ_j. In equation form, for each player i and $\theta_i, \sigma_i^*(\theta_i)$ solves:

$$\max E_i \left\{ U_i[F(\sigma_1^*(\theta_1), \ldots, \sigma_{i-1}^*(\theta_{i-1}), s_i, \sigma_{i+1}^*(\theta_{i+1}), \ldots, \right.$$

$$\left. \sigma_N^*(\theta_N)), \theta_i] \mid \theta_i \right\} \quad s_i \text{ in } S_i$$

where $E_i(\ |\theta_i)$ denotes i's expectation over $\theta = (\theta_1, \ldots, \theta_N)$ given that his type is θ_i and using his prior beliefs. Naturally, the equilibrium strategies result in an equilibrium allocation that depends on the actual vector of agent types, θ, that is:

$$a^*(\theta) = F[\sigma^*(\theta)]$$

where $a^*(\theta)$ is the equilibrium allocation and $\sigma^*(\theta) = [\sigma_1^*(\theta_1), \ldots, \sigma_N^*(\theta_N)]$.

We are now in a position to motivate part of the Revelation Principle. In particular, we can show how to derive a *direct* mechanism from any given mechanism. Consider a mechanism represented by signal sets S_i $(i = 1, \ldots, N)$ and allocation rule F. Think of the allocation rule F as being a computer program that uses the signals $s_1, \ldots, s_N$ as inputs and produces an allocation $a = F(s_1, \ldots, s_N)$ as output. Suppose that $\sigma^* = (\sigma_1^*, \ldots, \sigma_N^*)$ is an equilibrium of this mechanism. Instead of having each player compute his optimal signal, based on his type, then feeding this signal into the computer to compute the allocation, suppose we programme the computer to compute signals using σ^* and have each player simply input a value of his parameter. The computer could then use the signals that result from this calculation to compute an allocation using the allocation rule F. This would save the players from computing their optimal signals; the mechanism embodied in the computer program would do it for them. The result is a new mechanism in which players send signals that are interpreted as declared values of their parameters instead of the, possibly much more complicated, signals in the sets S_i. Thus, in the new mechanism, the signal sets are the sets of possible values of the parameters, that is, the new mechanism is a direct mechanism!

Now, what is the relationship between the direct mechanism constructed in the previous paragraph and the original mechanism? In particular, does it yield the same equilibrium outcome $a^*(\theta) = F[\sigma^*(\theta)]$ as the one induced by the equilibrium strategies σ^* of the original mechanism? The answer to this question is, happily yes. To see this, suppose player i believes that, in the new, direct mechanism, all the other players will 'tell the truth', that is, the strategy of agent j is $\psi_j(\theta_j) \equiv \theta_j$ (we use ψ_j to distinguish strategies in the direct mechanism from those of the original mechanism). Now if player i is of type θ_i, *and he reports* θ_i, then he believes the resulting allocation (as a function of θ) will be:

$$a^*(\theta) = F[\sigma^*(\theta)]$$

just as in the original mechanism. On the other hand, reporting some other value of his parameter, say $\hat{\theta}_i$, would result in the outcome:

$$F[\sigma_1^*(\theta_1), \ldots, \sigma_{i-1}^*(\theta_{i-1}), \sigma_i^*(\hat{\theta}_i), \sigma_{i+1}^*(\theta_{i+1}), \ldots, \sigma_N^*(\theta_N)]$$

But the expected utility of this outcome is lower than that of $a^*(\theta)$ by definition of σ_i^*, that is, when player i is of type θ_i, $\sigma_i^*(\theta_i)$, not $\sigma_i^*(\hat{\theta}_i)$, maximizes:

$$E_i\{U_i[F(\sigma_1^*(\theta_1), \ldots, \sigma_{i-1}^*(\theta_{i-1}), s_i, \sigma_{i+1}^*(\theta_{i+1}), \ldots, \sigma_N^*(\theta_N)),$$

$$\theta_i] \mid \theta_i\}$$

over s_i. Reporting $\hat{\theta}_i$ in the direct mechanism would be just like *lying to himself* in the original mechanism, that is, acting as if he were some other type. This shows that player i will report truthfully in the direct mechanism, provided he believes that everyone else will also. In game theory language, telling the truth ($\psi_i^*(\theta_i) \equiv \theta_i$) is a Bayesian equilibrium of the direct mechanism. Moreover, as mentioned above, the equilibrium outcome corresponding to these equilibrium strategies is simply $a^*(\theta)$ when the vector of types is θ. This is exactly as in the original mechanism.

The above argument is the essential idea behind the Revelation Principle which we repeat here for convenient reference;

The Revelation Principle. Any equilibrium allocation of any mechanism can be achieved by a truthful, direct mechanism.

As mentioned above, this result is an extremely useful tool if one is searching for an optimal mechanism or simply an optimal allocation in an asymmetric information environment. This is because the Revelation Principle implies that equilibrium allocations of any mechanism must satisfy certain self-selection (or incentive compatibility) constraints. Suppose that $a^*(\theta)$ is an allocation of some mechanism. We know from the Revelation Principle that $a^*(\theta)$ is also the *truthful* equilibrium of a direct mechanism. What does it mean for $a^*(\theta)$ to be the truthful equilibrium of a direct mechanism? It means first of all that the direct mechanism has an allocation rule G which gives each player an incentive to reveal his type truthfully provided everyone else behaves similarly. Formally, we must have:

$$E_i\{U_i[G(\theta_1,\ldots,\theta_N),\theta_i]\,|\,\vartheta_i\}$$

$$\geqslant E_i\{U_i[G(\theta_1,\ldots,\theta_{i-1},\hat{\theta}_i,\theta_{i+1},\ldots,\theta_N),\theta_i]\,|\,\theta_i\} \quad (11.1)$$

for each i, θ_i, and $\hat{\theta}_i$

Condition (11.1) states that for any player i and any two values of his type θ_i and $\hat{\theta}_i$, if his true type is θ_i, then he prefers the allocation associated with his reporting θ_i to the one associated with his reporting $\hat{\theta}_i$, provided all other players are reporting truthfully. This last caveat is embodied in the fact that the expectations in (11.1) are taken with respect to player i's prior beliefs about the *true* θ_j's. Equation (11.1) is almost the self-selection condition we seek.

The second step in the argument is to recall that if everyone reports truthfully, the direct mechanism represented by G will result in the allocation $a^*(\theta)$, for any vector of types, θ. Thus we must have:

$$G(\theta) \equiv a^*(\theta)$$

Substituting a^* for G in (11.1) gives the self-selection (*SS*) conditions:

$$E_i\{U_i[a^*(\theta_1,\ldots,\theta_N),\theta_i]\,|\,\theta_i\} \geqslant$$

$$E_i\{U_i[a^*(\theta_1,\ldots,\theta_{i-1},\hat{\theta}_i,\theta_{i+1},\ldots\theta_N),\theta_i]\,|\,\theta_i\}$$

for all i, θ_i, and $\hat{\theta}_i$

Thus the (*SS*) conditions are satisfied by the outcome of *any* mechanism. These conditions in effect become constraints on technologically feasible allocations as noted in the introduction to this chapter.

Finally, note that the direct mechanism whose truthful equilibrium allocation implements the original allocation a^* is simply the direct mechanism whose allocation rule $G = a^*$. This makes it trivial to construct a direct mechanism that implements a given allocation a^*, provided, of course, that a^* satisfies the (*SS*) conditions. Moreover, one can search for an *optimal* mechanism by searching for an optimal allocation in the space of allocations that satisfy the (*SS*) conditions using standard mathematical programming techniques.

AN EXAMPLE

In the remainder of the chapter we focus on a simple, pure risk-sharing example consisting of two agents, one consumption good and two states of nature.[10] Agent 1, the informed agent, is presumed to know the true probability that each state will occur, and this is known by the uninformed agent. Agent 2, the uninformed agent, has a prior distribution over these probabilities, and this prior is known by the informed agent. Both agents are assumed to know all other aspects of the environment.

Endowments of the good for each agent for each state are exogenously fixed. Let x_s denote the total endowment of the good in each state s, $s = 1, 2$ with $x = (x_1, x_2) > 0$. These define the Edgeworth box $B = [0, x_1]$ × $[0, x_2]$, (see Figure 11.1). The endowment of agent 2 is represented by $e = (e_1, e_2)$, a point in the interior of the Edgeworth box. The endowment of agent 1 is $x-e$. Similarly, given a point $c = (c_1, c_2)$ in the Edgeworth box, the consumption bundle of agent 2 is c and that of agent 1 is $x-c$.

Each agent i, $i = 1, 2$, has a von Neumann—Morgenstern utility function u_i defined for all non-negative consumption w where u_i is twice continuously differentiable, $u_i'(w) > 0$, $u_i''(w) < 0$ for all $w > 0$ and $u_i'(0) = \infty$. Each agent has as objective the maximization of his expected utility.

Thus if agent i knew the probability of state 1 to be θ, he would evaluate the bundle (w_1, w_2) consisting of w_j units of the good if state j occurs ($j = 1, 2$) by taking the expectation:

$$\theta u_i(w_1) + (1 - \theta)u_i(w_2)$$

Any point c in the Edgeworth box, B, can be evaluated by each agent i in this way given the probability of state 1, θ. Thus, for any point c in B, and any $0 \leqslant \theta \leqslant 1$, let:

$$U_1(c, \theta) = \theta u_1(x_1 - c_1) + (1 - \theta)u_1(x_2 - c_2)$$

$$U_2(c, \theta) = \theta u_2(c_1) + (1 - \theta)u_2(c_2)$$

The functions U_1, U_2 then define the preferences of the two agents over points in the Edgeworth box, B, *given some common value θ for the probability of state 1.*

The curve labelled C in Figure 11.1 is the set of allocations that would be optimal if both agents were informed as to the true value of the parameter θ. Under our assumptions, this curve is independent of the actual

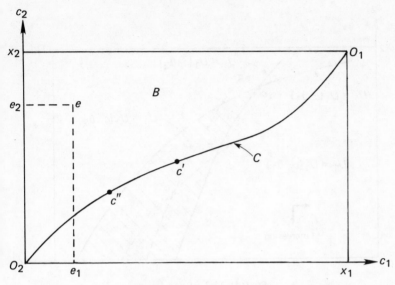

FIGURE 11.1   *Basic concepts*

value of θ so long as both agents agree on its value. Thus C is called the consensus contract curve. Formally:

$$C = \{\, c \in B \,|\, u_2'(c_1)/u_2'(c_2) = u_1'(x_1 - c_1)/u_1'(x_2 - c_2) \,\}$$

It should be emphasized however that preferences do depend on the parameter θ. Geometrically, for each value of θ there corresponds a family of indifference curves for each agent. We assume that both agents believe correctly that this parameter can have only one of two values, θ_1 or θ_2, with $0 < \theta_1 < \theta_2 < 1$. There are then two possible families of indifference curves for each agent, with the 'steeper' curves being associated with $\theta = \theta_2$ (see Figure 11.2). Thus for agent 1, for example, the consumption bundle c in Figure 11.2 is preferred to c' if $\theta = \theta_2$ and conversely if $\theta = \theta_1$.[11]

We assume now that the actual probability of state one, θ, is drawn from a known distribution defined on $\{\theta_1, \theta_2\}$. We denote the probability that $\theta = \theta_1$ by p and the probability that $\theta = \theta_2$ by $1-p$. Agent 2, the uninformed agent, is assumed not to know θ initially but to have the prior distribution given by p. Agent 1, the informed agent, observes the actual realization of θ. Again, both agents are assumed to know all other aspects of the environment.

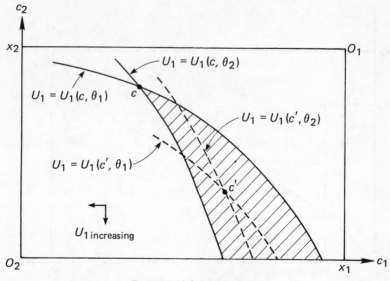

FIGURE 11.2   *Self-selection*

In order to motivate the self-selection result, that certain allocations are not achievable in this environment because of the informational asymmetry, consider the following mechanism. Agent 1 (the informed agent) is asked to name a value of θ, either θ_1 or θ_2. If he names θ_1, then some allocation c' on the contract curve C is effected, and if he names θ_2, then some allocation c'' also on C is effected. This mechanism has some *a priori* appeal since both c' and c'' are full-information Pareto optimal, that is, both are on C. But suppose that $c' \neq c''$, for example as shown in Figure 11.1 In this case, since it is impossible for agent 2 to require agent 1 to name the true value of θ, agent 1 will always claim $\theta = \theta_2$, even if $\theta = \theta_1$ (since $x - c'' > x - c$). Thus the allocation $c = c'$ if $\theta = \theta_1$ and $c = c''$ if $\theta = \theta_2$ is not achievable by this mechanism. (The equilibrium allocation is $c = c''$ for either value of θ.) As shown in the previous section, no matter how complicated we make the mechanism, allocations like:

$$c = \begin{cases} c^1 \text{ if } \theta = \theta_1 \\ \\ c^2 \text{ if } \theta = \theta_2 \end{cases}$$

are *not* achievable in this environment *unless* agent 1 prefers c^1 to c^2 if $\theta = \theta_1$ and vice versa if $\theta = \theta_2$. This condition, which is illustrated in Figure 11.2, is the self-selection condition for this example. Clearly, the allocation $c = c'$ if $\theta = \theta_1$ and $c = c''$ if $\theta = \theta_2$ does not satisfy the self-selection condition and is therefore not achievable.

The remainder of this section is devoted to characterizing an optimal allocation mechanism and its equilibrium allocation for the example.

In searching for an optimal mechanism, we will use the Revelation Principle and consider only direct mechanisms. Thus we will simply search over allocation rules $G(\theta)$. Moreover, we will consider only such rules that result in truth-telling behaviour by agent 1, namely those that satisfy the (SS) constraints of the second section. This procedure will, of course, *not* result in ignoring mechanisms that perform better than the ones in the class we consider. Finally, for purposes of exposition, we will concentrate on finding a mechanism that maximizes the utility of the *uninformed* agent, agent 2, subject to the constraint that the informed agent, agent 1, be willing to participate (i.e. be no worse off than in autarky).[12]

These considerations lead us to characterize an optimal mechanism as an allocation rule $F(\theta) = [c_1(\theta), c_2(\theta)]$ which solves the following maximization problem:

$$\max pU_2[F(\theta_1), \theta_1] + (1-p)U_2[F(\theta_2), \theta_2] \qquad (11.2)$$

subject to:

$$F(\theta_j) \text{ in } B \qquad\qquad j = 1, 2 \qquad (11.3)$$

$$U_1[F(\theta_j), \theta_j] \geqslant U_1(e, \theta_j) \qquad j = 1, 2 \qquad (11.4)$$

$$U_1[F(\theta_1), \theta_1] \geqslant U_1[F(\theta_2), \theta_1] \qquad\qquad (11.5)$$

$$U_1[F(\theta_2), \theta_2] \geqslant U_1[F(\theta_1), \theta_2] \qquad\qquad (11.6)$$

The objective function of this problem is simply the expected utility of the uninformed agent for the allocation F, assuming that the informed agent reveals θ truthfully (i.e. reveals θ_1 with probability p). This assumption is justified by imposing the self-selection constraints, (11.5) and (11.6). Constraint (11.5) guarantees that agent 1 prefers to report $\theta = \theta_1$ when in fact θ is θ_1. Similarly, (11.6) guarantees that agent 1 prefers to report $\theta = \theta_2$ when in fact θ is θ_2. Constraint (11.3) simply imposes technological feasibility, and constraints (11.4) guarantee that agent 1 is no worse off than in autarky for either value of θ (we are assuming that agent 1 can choose whether or not to play after having observed θ). Constraints (11.4) are often called 'individual rationality' constraints.

A solution of the problem (11.2)–(11.6) for a particular value of the endowment e is shown in Figure 11.3 (the proof may be found in Harris and Townsend, 1978). The exact location of $F^*(\theta_1)$ along the consensus contract curve C depends on agent 2's prior beliefs about the probability that $\theta = \theta_1$, namely p. As agent 2 becomes more certain that $\theta = \theta_1$, $F^*(\theta_1)$ moves along C towards point A_1 in Figure 11.3. Point A_1 is, of course, the allocation that gives agent 2 the most utility when $\theta = \theta_1$ subject to the individual rationality constraint (11.4) for $j = 1$. When $p = 1$, $F^*(\theta_1) = A_1$. Note that $F^*(\theta_2)$ is at the intersection of the θ_1–indifference of curve of agent 1 through $F^*(\theta_1)$ (dashed line in Figure 11.3) and the θ_2–indifference curve of agent 1 through the endowment, e. Thus as p approaches 1 (agent 2 is certain that $\theta = \theta_1$), $F^*(\theta_2)$ approaches e (no trade if θ actually turns out to be θ_2). As p approaches 0 (agent 2 is certain that $\theta = \theta_2$), $F^*(\theta_1)$ both converge to point A_2 in Figure 11.3. Point A_2 is the bundle that maximizes agent 2's utility if he

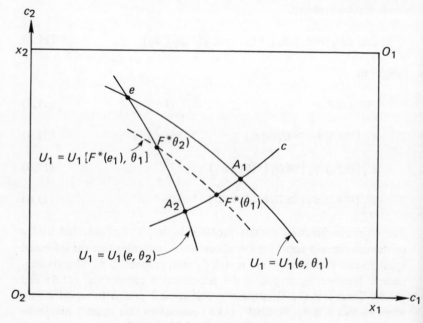

FIGURE 11.3   *Optimal allocation*

knew that $\theta = \theta_2$, subject to individual rationality for agent 1. Thus we see that optimal allocations when information is asymmetric depend on agents' prior beliefs about the vlaues of parameters they cannot observe.

Finally note that the optimal direct mechanism involves agent 1 declaring a value for θ, either θ_1 or θ_2. The allocation is then $F^*(\theta_j)$, as in Figure 11.3, if he declares $\theta = \theta_j$, for $j = 1$, 2. Other mechanisms could, however, also be used to accomplish the same allocation. One such scheme is for agent 2 to start by offering agent 1 any menu of bundles c^1 and c^2, then letting agent 1 choose which one is to be imposed. Obviously, agent 2 would offer $c^j = F^*(\theta_j)$ for $j = 1, 2$, so that this is just the direct mechanism in a thin disguise. One advantage of this version, however, is that the form of the optimal mechanism (signal sets and allocation rule) does *not* depend on the prior beliefs of agent 2. This is not the case for the optimal direct mechanism whose allocation rule F^*, depends on p. Perhaps this is why the alternative scheme has some intuitive appeal.[13]

CONCLUSIONS

In this chapter, we have argued that, to analyse the allocation of resources in certain types of environments with asymmetric information, one must first consider the process by which allocations are achieved. We have presented a methodology for such analyses, and applied this approach to a specific, abstract environment characterized by asymmetry of information between two agents.

In the remainder of these conclusions, we take up several issues not considered previously. In the process, we suggest some directions for further work. First, in our approach, as well as in the signalling literature (see, for example, Spence, 1974; Riley, 1979; Rothschild and Stiglitz, 1976; Wilson, 1977) the prior of the uninformed agent plays a key role in determining the allocation of resources. This is not the case, however, in some other attempts at devising mechanisms to allocate resources under asymmetric information, most notably in the public goods literature (see, for example, Groves and Ledyard, 1977). We explore this difference further in Harris and Townsend (1981).

Second, note that in the example of the previous section, at the end of the optimal direct mechanism, the actual allocation will not be full-information optimal (i.e. on C) if in fact $\theta = \theta_2$. At the time at which this allocation is effected, however, *both* agents are fully informed that $\theta = \theta_2$. Thus, *at that time* there will be gains to further trade (i.e. given *ex post* information). Certainly it is optimal to agree *ex ante* that such *ex post* gains to trade will not be exploited, but in some circumstances such an agreement will be impossible to enforce (since both agents would like to violate it *ex post*). When modelling environments without suitable enforcement possibilities, it may be necessary to impose a constraint that the final allocation be Pareto optimal with respect to the final information structure.

Third, we have not considered the question of from where does an optimal mechanism come; how is it that agents adopt a particular allocation process. In some situations, it may be appropriate to assume that one of the agents has enough 'bargaining power' to impose the mechanism of his choice. If this agent has no private information, one can simply proceed as in the example of the previous section (see also Harris and Raviv, 1981a and 1981b). If the mechanism choice is made by an agent with private information, the choice itself may reveal some of this information. This is a much more difficult problem which has been taken up by Myerson (1982) and Holmstrom and Myerson (1981).

Finally, the approach outlined in this chapter is applicable only when all private information is known at the outset. One would conjecture that some form of the Revelation Principle will apply generally to situations in which private information is revealed over time.[14]

NOTES

1. By asymmetric information, we mean that some agents are *better* informed about some aspects of the environment and this fact is known to other agents.
2. See Harris and Raviv, 1981a, 1981b, and Myerson, 1981, for a start in this direction.
3. This assertion is motivated in the second section; see also Harris and Townsend, 1978, 1981, and Myerson, 1979.
4. The class is broad enough to include most imaginable mechanisms. One of course could restrict attention to a few obvious mechanisms, but that restriction would be counter to the spirit of our chapter — to make as few exogenous restrictions as possible. Our results are 'strong' to the extent that the class we consider is 'large'.
5. We believe the name 'Revelation Principle' was coined by Roger Myerson.
6. See also Harris and Townsend, 1981, and Harris and Raviv, 1981a, 1981b, for additional examples. The literature on contracts, information and incentives is, by now, replete with both implicit and explicit applications of the Revelation Principle. As this is not intended to be a survey chapter, we have made no attempt to provide references to this literature.

7. It is possible to allow one individual to observe several parameters and/or several individuals to observe the same parameter without affecting the results. See Harris and Townsend, 1981.

8. A 'signal' could actually be a whole sequence of functions specifying at each stage what message to send as a function of the history of the game to that stage. In this way sequential games can be modelled as normal-form games. Generally, in using the normal form, one does not spell out the sequential aspects explicitly. This is done in the 'extensive form' version of the game. See Friedman, 1977, for further discussion of normal and exstensive form games. The results presented below can be proved also for extensive-form mechanisms; see Harris and Townsend, 1981.

9. Strictly speaking, we should allow for random allocation rules. For expository purposes, we shall ignore both random strategies and random allocation rules. The results of this section have been proved in this case by Myerson, 1979. In general, optimality may require random allocation rules (but not random strategies), as is argued in Prescott and Townsend, 1982, for example. Random allocation rules are not needed, however, for the example of the the third section, as shown in Harris and Townsend, 1978.

10. This example has been taken from Harris and Townsend, 1978. Several interesting mechanisms for this example are also discussed there.

11. Notice that we are changing slightly our notation here relative to the previous section. Since there is only one parameter in this example, we simply call it θ. Instead of using the subscript to refer to the agent whose type is given by the parameter, agent 1 in this case, we use the subscript to denote a particular value of the parameter θ. We hope that no confusion results.

12. The arguments in Harris and Townsend, 1978, establish that one can generate the entire class of optimal allocations in this way, if one varies the endowment parametrically. Also the particular optimality concept employed here is not critical to the argument. The Revelation Principle can be applied to environments with diverse optimality criteria.

13. The alternative mechanism is sequential, however, thereby falling outside the class of mechanisms considered here. Again, the reader is referred to Harris and Townsend, 1978, for a more general treatment.

14. See Townsend, 1982, for a proof of this conjecture in a particular model.

REFERENCES

Friedman, J. (1977) *Oligopoly and the Theory of Games*, Amsterdam: North-Holland.
Groves, T., and J. Ledyard (1977) 'Optimal Allocation of Public Goods: A Solution to the "Free Rider Problem"', *Econometrica*, 45 (4) (May): 783–810.

Harris, M., and A. Raviv (1981a) 'Allocation Mechanisms and the Design of Auctions', *Econometrica*, 49 (6) (November): 1477–99.

Harris, M., and A. Raviv (1981b) 'A Theory of Monopoly Pricing Schemes with Demand Uncertainty', *American Economic Review*, 71 (3) (June): 347–65.

Harris, M., and R. M. Townsend (1978) 'Allocation Mechanisms for Asymmetrically Informed Agents', working paper no. 35-76-77, GSIA, Carnegie-Mellon University (March 1977, revised September 1978).

Harris, M., and R. M. Townsend (1981) 'Resource Allocation Under Asymmetric Information', *Econometrica*, 49 (1) (January): 33–64.

Harsanyi, J. C. (1967–8) 'Games with Incomplete Information Played by "Bayesian" Players (Parts I–III)', *Management Science*, 14: 159–82, 320–34, 481–502.

Holmstrom, B. (1978) 'On Incentives and Control in Organizations', unpublished PhD dissertation, Graduate School of Business, Stanford University.

Holmstrom, B., and R. Myerson (1981) 'Efficient and Durable Decision Rules with Incomplete Information', Discussion paper no. 495, CMSEMS, Northwestern University (September).

Hurwicz, L. (1972) 'On Informationally Decentralized Systems', in C. B. McGuire and R. Radner (eds), *Decision and Organization* (Amsterdam: North-Holland, ch. 14.

Myerson, R. (1979) 'Incentive Compatibility and the Beginning Problem', *Econometrica*, 47 (January): 61–74.

Myerson, R. (1981) 'Optimal Auction Design', *Mathematics of Operations Research*, 6 (February): 58–73.

Myerson, R. (1982) 'Mechanism Design by an Informed Principle', Discussion paper no. 481, CMSEMS, Northwestern University.

Prescott, E., and R. M. Townsend (1982) 'Pareto Optima and Competitive Equilibria With Adverse Selection and Moral Hazard', working paper, GSIA, Carnegie-Mellon University, forthcoming in *Econometrica*.

Riley, J. (1979) 'Informational Equilibrium', *Econometrica*, 47 (2) (March): 331–60.

Rothschild, M., and J. Stiglitz (1976) 'Equilibrium in Competitive Insurance Markets: An Essay on the Economics of Imperfect Information', *Quarterly Journal of Economics*, 90 (November): 620–49.

Spence, A. M. (1974) 'Competitive and Optimal Responses to Signals: An Analysis of Efficiency and Distribution', *Journal of Economic Theory*, 7 (March): 296–332.

Townsend, R. M. (1982) 'Optimal Multiperiod Contracts and the Gain from Enduring Relationships Under Private Information', *Journal of Political Economy*, 90 (6) (December): 1166–86.

Wilson, C., (1977) 'A Model of Insurance Markets with Incomplete Information', *Jounal of Economic Theory*, 16: 176–207.

12 Production Functions, Transactions Costs and the New Institutionalism

VICTOR P. GOLDBERG*

INTRODUCTION

For most of the postwar period, economic theory has focused on the analysis of impersonal markets. In the past few years, however, there has been a resurgence of interest in the role of institutions in the allocation process: why does some behaviour take place within firms and not within markets? Why are long-term contracts used instead of spot markets? What What determines the structure of long-term contracts? How does the internal organization of a firm affect its performance? Why are some workers compensated by piece-rates, others by hourly wages, and still others by annual salary? What are the effects of seniority provisions or of a legal prohibition of termination of employment contracts at will? Does the structure of employment contracts have an influence on macroeconomic variables? What are the effects of alternative tort liability systems on accident rates? And so forth.

In this chapter I want to consider two concepts – production functions and transactions costs – that have been used and abused in developing the New Institutionalism. If we are to rely on them at all in our exploration of the causes and effects of economic institutions, it will be necessary to subject them to careful scrutiny. My reading is that the transactions cost concept in particular has proved to be misleading and unhelpful and that it would be best if we simply abandoned it. However, the terminology is probably too deeply entrenched for this cold turkey approach

* This author would like to thank the following for comments on an earlier draft: Moshe Adler, Avner Ben-Ner, Ronald Coase, Douglass North, Joseph Ostroy, David Teece, and Oliver Williamson.

to succeed. My more realistic hope is that the following discussion will at least result in the concept being used with greater care then has heretofore been displayed.

THE PRODUCTION FUNCTION

A production function is a technical relationship between inputs and outputs. Mix three units of one input with four of another and out come five units of output. It does not matter who owns the inputs or the outputs. Or does it? The pragmatic answer is that institutional arrangements like ownership do matter, but for the problems under consideration we can assume their effects on the production relationship remain unchanged. That is, the production function implicitly includes the effects of specific institutional arrangements on output. For example, if workers in a firm 'shirk' 20 per cent of the time, a change in the wage-rate would not alter the ratio of their work effort to the amount of work they would provide in the absence of shirking. A second answer is to decompose the production function into a technical production function that translates unobservable inputs (efficiency units) into outputs and has the nice properties of standard theory, and a transformation function that translates observable into unobservable inputs. The former holds regardless of the institutions, but the latter does not. Thus, if workers shirk less in a worker-controlled firm than in a stockholder-owned firm, an hour of worker time would result in more efficiency units of labour in the former. If we assume that a particular institutional change has no systematic effect on this transformation function, then the second line of argument leads to the same results as the first.

If we do assume that both the technical production function and transformation function are independent of institutions, then the effects of alternative institutions are manifested in the relative prices confronting decision-makers and in their objective functions. (The capitalist firm maximizes profits; the worker-controlled firm maximizes profits per worker or some similar concept.) My concern is not with the invariance assumption itself, which can frequently be useful, but with the lack of thought regarding its appropriateness. One need only look at the chapters on welfare economics in virtually all price theory textbooks. Production functions are given. The efficiency conditions are determined in an institutional vacuum. The performance of particular allocation systems is then compared with the efficient one and the conclusion emerges that an impersonal price system or Lange–Lerner central planners could yield the same efficient production. The heroic nature of the assumption that the production relationship is the same across all institutional arrangements is sufficiently obvious that it does not warrant further comment.

I do not want to pursue further the question of the appropriateness of the invariance assumption for comparative general equilibrium analysis or for the comparative statics of the organization of work. Instead, I want to move to a less obvious context. Consider the familiar Coasian example of the railroad sparks and the farmer. (Coase, 1960, pp. 29–34). The amount of damage that occurs depends upon the avoidance behaviour of both the railroad (installing spark arresters, etc.) and the farmers (planting further from the track, etc.). This relationship is summarized in a 'production function for accident avoidance'. To determine the efficient amount of avoidance effort by the two parties we suppose that the railroad and farmer merge so that the 'externality is internalized' – a single decision-maker perceives the benefits and the costs and has the incentive to seek the optimal balance. We then assume that for some reason the merger is not feasible, and ask how incentives could be structured so that the independent parties could be induced to produce the same efficient behaviour as the merged firm.[1] Could taxes, subsidies, or liability rules (tort and nuisance law) produce efficient outcomes? We implicitly assume in such an exercise that there exist some unspecified factors that make the merger solution too costly. We assume further that these unspecified factors have no systematic effect on the cost-effectiveness of the alternatives. In essence, we assume that the technical production function is invariant to institutions but that the transformation function does vary in a systematic, if somewhat peculiar way.

As a variation on this theme, consider the question of the influence of the production technology on whether economic activity is performed within firms or across firm boundaries. For example, does the existence of economies of scale or scope tell us anything about the efficient size of firms or of the efficient firm boundaries (vertical and lateral integration)? The literature is full of answers in the affirmative. 'Natural monopoly' follows from economies of scale;[2] vertical integration is limited by the extent of the market;[3] economies of scope result in multi-product firms.[4] But there is a problem. Why must the economies of scale be achieved within an organization? Why can't they be achieved equally well if the factors of production are owned by independent individuals? In the previous paragraph the implicit assumption was that for unspecified reasons merger was too costly; here we assume, also for unspecified reasons, that anything *but* merger is too costly.

Propositions regarding institutional structure cannot be derived from purely technical production relationships without invoking some other factors. A venerable example of this point is the old problem of efficient firm size in a competitive industry with constant costs. With those cost conditions, the efficient firm size would be indeterminate. Determinacy was achieved only by positing some scarce limiting factor such as entre-preneurial skill. This band-aid solution obscured the more fundamental point. Firm size would be indeterminate with constant costs, decreasing costs, or increasing costs. So long as the costs are independent of the organization form, this must be true. Efficient firm size depends ultimately on organization-specific costs – which are precisely the ones excluded from the technical production function.

This does not mean that there are no predictable relationships between the production technology and institutional outcomes. The statements 'propositions regarding institutional structure cannot be derived from purely technical production functions' and 'a production process ex-hibiting extensive economies of scale will tend to be performed within a single organization' are not logically inconsistent. If the factors that result in scale economies are correlated with those making co-ordination within a single organization desirable, then the statements would be con-sistent. The second proposition can, however, be very misleading if it directs attention away from the elements that determine the relative efficiency of alternative organization structures.

TRANSACTIONS COSTS

My hostility to transactions costs must strike most readers as odd, since the 'new institutional economics' and 'transactions costs economics' are often thought of as synonymous.[5] My concern in this instance is perhaps more semantic than substantive. It does seem to me, however, that 'transaction costs' runs the risk of becoming the 'imperfect capital markets' of the 1980s, the all-purpose answer that tells us nothing.

A bit of history. In his early paper on 'The Nature of the Firm', Coase (1937), in effect, said: if markets work as well as they do in our models, then no alternative system could do better, and most would probably do worse; why then, he asked, would anything but impersonal markets emerge and thrive? Since firms do exist and do thrive, we must ask how such organizations could be superior to the impersonal markets. The answer – or really the first part of the answer – was that impersonal markets weren't so darn perfect anyway; their imperfection he called 'transactions costs'. Two decades later, Coase (1960) conducted the same sort of exercise with externalities. Economists were classifying goods in two categories: for normal goods (with zero transactions costs) markets worked perfectly; for externalities (with infinite transactions costs) markets worked not at all. Coase never bothered to give a precise definition of transactions costs because he didn't take the concept very seriously. It was only the name of whatever it was the economists had been ignoring; the intent in both papers was to move analysis away from a world in which market perfection was an all-or-nothing affair.[6]

Economists have a number of essentially equivalent ways of characterizing the conditions resulting in efficiency. If transactions costs are zero, if all markets exist, if marginal social product equals marginal private product, or if there are no externalities, resources would be allocated efficiently. When there is a shortfall from perfection, as there inevitably must be, there is a tendency to identify its source in terms of the characterization – positive transactions costs, market failure, or whatever. This leap of logic is the source of much of the semantic confusion that has permeated much of the post-Coase discussion of transactions costs.

The phrase 'transactions costs' captures the notion that transacting – engaging in economic activity – requires the use of real resources. It embodies two very different meanings. One focuses on identifiable activities involved in transacting.[7] The concept would presumably include the costs associated with bargaining, negotiating, and monitoring performance – costs usually associated with the activities of purchasing agents, lawyers, accountants, and similar functionaries. It is analogous to the Marxist concept of 'non-productive labour'. What distinguishes these costs from others (or non-productive from productive labour)? Is an accountant's bill for $10 000 less painful than a bill for an equal amount from a steel supplier? Firms incur these costs because it is efficient for them to do so. It is cheaper to pay accountants to perform a task than to bear the additional costs of embezzlement that might occur in their absence. As far as the economic actors are concerned, transactions costs are the same as other costs.

The preceding formulation emphasizes the type of activities that might be included under the transactions cost rubric. An alternative formulation better captures Coase's intent. Transactions costs are those costs most likely to differ under alternative institutional arrangements. They are the cost analogue to the transformation function of the previous section. Thus, if the production function is defined in terms of efficiency units, the transactions costs are the difference between what could have been produced if actual inputs corresponded to efficiency units and what actually happened. The transaction costs are an unobservable residual; they are the opportunity cost of the world not being as nice a place as it otherwise might be. In this formulation, the transactions cost label is a redundancy. If we say that the transactions costs of the worker-controlled gadget-producing firm are higher than its capitalist counterpart we mean no more and no less than that it is less efficient in transforming inputs into outputs.

Propositions regarding relative institutional efficiency, whether normative or positive (e.g. *ceteris paribus*, more efficient institutions tend to survive) should not depend on the level of transaction activity. There is no reason to associate high levels of transaction activity with inefficient outcomes. Some goods are 'transactions-intensive' just as others might be labour- or capital-intensive. The set of activities in the 'transactions sector' could include retailing, wholesaling, advertising, police, and even transportation and education. We can quibble about what the precise boundaries of the sector should be, but the important point is that there is nothing exceptional about the transactions sector. The sector's share can differ over time and across societies, but this tells us nothing about the relative efficiency of the societies in extracting outputs from inputs.[8]

CONCLUDING REMARKS

The production function is ostensibly a relationship between observable inputs and outputs. Economists frequently make the implicit assumption that the production function is invariant to institutions. I am not asserting here that the invariance assumption is inevitably wrong. Rather I am suggesting a behavioural proposition about economists. They exhibit a strong tendency to use the assumption where it doesn't belong. If we were more conscious of what we are doing we would be less likely to make such errors as deriving institutional implications from purely technical production functions.

The transactions costs concept has been particularly misleading because it embodies two very different meanings. On the one hand, it has the natural meaning of costs associated with a set of activities involved in transacting. On the other hand, it can mean a shortfall from what could have been achieved if institutions worked perfectly. There is a strong temptation to join these meanings by attributing the shortfall to a particular set of activities. Much of the confusion involving the transactions cost concept has stemmed from this unfortunate linkage. By explicating this dual meaning, I hope that I have removed one of the barriers to understanding the causes and effects of economic institutions.

NOTES

1. Brown (1973) was the first to utilize this framework to analyse tort law.
2. This error is so ubiquitous that documentation is unnecessary. For a debunking, see Demsetz, 1968; Goldberg, 1976; and Williamson, 1976.
3. See Stigler, 1951. The argument is criticized in Williamson, 1975, pp. 16–19.
4. See Panzar and Willig, 1981; the argument is criticized in Teece, 1980.
5. 'The new institutional economics is preoccupied with the origins, incidence, and ramifications of transaction costs.' (Williamson, 1979, p. 233).
6. In a recent paper, Coase (1981, p. 187) made this point with rather colourful language: 'While consideration of what would happen in a world of zero transaction costs can give us valuable insights, these insights are, in my view, without value except as steps on the way to the analysis of the real world of positive transaction costs. We do not do well to devote ourselves to a detailed study of the world of zero transaction costs, like augurs divining the future by the minute inspection of the entrails of a goose.'
7. Dahlman (1979) discusses critically two characterizations of transactions costs utilized by formal theorists. In one, a fixed proportion of whatever is being traded is assumed to disappear in the transaction itself; they are analytically the same as transportation costs. The second assumes that there are set-up costs for transactions; the cost is fixed independent of the amount exchanged.
8. Thus, it is plausible that the *monetized* transaction sector (or non-productive labour) has increased in the twentieth century, at least in the developed countries. A large amount of the work of the transactions sector is performed outside the monetized sector. Exchange with kinsmen, for example, typically requires less reliance on formal monitoring and enforcement mechanisms than does exchange with strangers. The resources devoted to enhancing mutual trust and co-operative behaviour can be considerable. While there can be considerable cost reductions from trading with insiders, we should note that there also exists an opportunity cost to such autarchy; this cost is exacerbated if maintaining the integrity of the group is accomplished by demeaning the outsiders.

REFERENCES

Brown, J. P. (1973) 'Toward an Economic Theory of Liability', *Journal of Legal Studies*, 2 (June): 323–49.
Coase, R. H. (1937) 'The Nature of the Firm', *Economica* (New Series), 4: 387–405.

Coase, R. H. (1960) 'The Problem of Social Cost', *Journal of Law and Economics*, 3 (October): 1–44.

Coase, R. H. (1981) 'The Coase Theorem and the Empty Core: A Comment', *Journal of Law and Economics*, 24 (April): 183–7.

Dahlman, C. J. (1979) 'The Problem of Externality', *Journal of Law and Economics*, 22 (April): 141–62.

Demsetz, H. (1968) 'Why Regulate Utilities?' *Journal of Law and Economics*, 11 (April): 55–65.

Goldberg, V. P. (1976) 'Regulation and Administered Contracts', *Bell Journal of Economics*, 7 (Autumn): 426–48.

Panzar, J. C., and R. D. Willig (1981) 'Economies of Scope', *American Economic Review*, 71 (May): 268–72.

Stigler, G. J. (1951) 'The Division of Labor is Limited by the Extent of the Market', *Journal of Political Economy*, 59 (June): 185–93.

Teece, D. (1980) 'Economies of Scope and the Scope of the Enterprise', *Journal of Economic Behavior and Organization*, 1 (1980): 223–47.

Williamson, O. E. (1975) *Markets and Hierarchies*. New York: Free Press.

Williamson, O. E. (1976) 'Franchise Bidding for Natural Monopolies — In General and with Respect to CATV', *Bell Journal of Economics*, 7 (Spring): 73–104.

Williamson, O. E. (1979) 'Transaction-Cost Economics: The Governance of Contractual Relations', *Journal of Law and Economics*, 22 (October): 233–61.

Part IV
Welfare Economics and Consumption

Part IV
Welfare Economics and Consumption

13 Welfare Economics

PETER HAMMOND*

INTRODUCTION

After the publication of the two major but rather negative textbooks by
Little (1950) and Graaff (1957), welfare economics seemed to lie mostly
dormant and sterile during the 1960s. Since 1970, however, welfare
economics has undergone a major change. Yet the progress made is not
really fully reflected in any new textbook, even though the second part of
Atkinson and Stiglitz (1980) and the book by Guesnerie (1980) in French
do cover important aspects. Also, the excellent volumes of readings
collected by Arrow and Scitovsky (1969), Farrell (1973) and Phelps
(1973) appeared too soon to reflect more than the very earliest stages of
the new work. Thus the newcomer to welfare economic theory is often
forced to seek his own way through the vast number of articles published
since 1970, and very often will fail to see that the total progress made is
really more than the sum of the new ideas. He will be in very good company too, since most professional economists, including some of those
who helped to bring about the changes, have also failed to appreciate just
how different modern welfare economics has become. Indeed, many
implications of the new work may still remain hidden from all of us, for
all we know, such is the scope of the change.

In this chapter I shall present a relatively non-technical description
of the change and suggest some of the more important works that need to
be consulted for a full appreciation. The chapter commences with a brief
discussion of how welfare economics came to the sorry state it found
itself in by the 1960s.

* This chapter was written while the author was a Fellow at the Institute
  for Advanced Studies of the Hebrew University, whose research support
  is gratefully acknowledged, as is the assistance of Gerard Hamiache.

WELFARE ECONOMICS BEFORE 1970 – OLD, NEW AND PARETO SATISFICING

This is not the place to give a full assessment of developments in welfare economics prior to the progress of the 1970s. Nevertheless, to appreciate fully what happened, some impression of what had gone on before is necessary.

The old welfare economics that was widespread until the 1930s seems now quite crude. It was typified, perhaps, by the work of Edgeworth (1881) who clearly thought that interpersonal comparisons of utility could be made on a more or less firm objective basis. It was also usually believed that the marginal utility of income would definitely decrease as income rose. Assuming then that all individuals have identical marginal utility of income schedules, it follows that income should be distributed equally to achieve a welfare optimum. Much of the work in this style, concerned as it was with describing an ideally functioning economic system, seemed very remote from everyday economic issues. This old welfare economics was really only able to describe a Utopian economy which combined equality with overall efficiency in a full welfare optimum. Practical economists always knew that such a Utopia was most likely unattainable although they were unable to articulate a precise reason why.

Robbins (1932) led a very specific rebellion against this old welfare economics, by insisting that interpersonal comparisons of utility and the presumption in favour of an equal distribution of income were ethical value judgements with no place at all in economic 'science'. Robbins (1938) was, however, very careful not to disallow totally the use of interpersonal comparisons to discuss normative issues in economics. Such issues anyway lie beyond the scope of 'economic science', strictly understood, so introducing unscientific interpersonal comparisons would not after all render unscientific something that was originally scientific.

Many succeeding welfare economists completely misinterpreted Robbins and took a particularly unfortunate step that proved to be a major handicap throughout the ensuing thirty years. In an entirely misguided attempt to be 'scientific', in Robbins's sense, many welfare economists saw fit to exclude even the slightest possibility of making interpersonal comparisons. Following the methodology that Archibald (1959) was later to describe so lucidly, they sought only to identify ways of making all individuals better off simultaneously – or at least of making some individuals better off and none worse off. Such changes are known as 'Pareto improvements'. The concept 'better off' was also intended to be purely factual, relating solely to individuals' preferences, presumably those corresponding to their actual behaviour. This Archibald approach to welfare economics I shall call 'Pareto satisficing', as it is concerned with satisfying the Pareto criterion by finding Pareto-efficient outcomes – that is, those are not susceptible to feasibly Pareto-improving changes.

Long before Archibald, Kaldor (1939) and Hicks (1939, 1940) sought to formulate an entirely 'new' welfare economics that would deal with 'unscientific' interpersonal comparisons of utility by exorcising them altogether. This, of course, is what Pareto satisficing does too. However, pure Pareto satisficing runs into a fundamental difficulty which Harrod (1938) and Hotelling (1938) also noticed. Almost any policy change one considers in practice will not be a Pareto improvement, but will benefit some individuals and harm others. The old wefare economics evaluated such a change by weighing the utility increases of the gainers against the utility decreases of the losers to see which were preponderant. Obviously such a calculation involves 'unscientific' interpersonal comparisons of utility gains and losses. Kaldor and Hicks side-stepped such obvious ethical value judgements by using objective interpersonal comparisons. They proposed that *monetary* rather than utility gains and losses should be weighed against each other, to see whether the gainers could afford to make lump-sum compensation to the losers in a way that left everybody better off. Such a test was called a 'compensation test'. It identified 'potential' Pareto improvements, that is, changes that could potentially be converted into acutal Pareto improvements if they were to be succeeded by suitable lump-sum redistribution of income so that the gainers would compensate the losers.

Scitovsky (1941) soon pointed to the logical difficulties created by such a test. It was all too easy for both the change from policy A to policy B and the reverse change from B to A to be potential Pareto improvements according to the Kaldor–Hicks compensation test. He therefore suggested an ingenious 'reversal' test according to which A would only be judged better than B if not only did the change from B to A pass the Kaldor–Hicks compensation test but also the reverse change from A to B did not pass. Even this Scitovsky test only happens to be logically consistent in a very special case identified by Gorman (1953, 1955) in which, at any set of relative prices for all commodities, all consumers have parallel linear income consumption curves and so parallel linear Engel curves. Moreover, even outside this special case, Chipman and Moore (1980) recently showed how, by fixing a reference price vector once and for all, there is a test somewhat akin to the compensation test which is always logically consistent.

Even if logical consistency can be recovered, however, there is a far more fundamental objection to the Kaldor–Hicks compensation test underlying the 'new' welfare economics. It is true that, in many instances, there is an objective measure of what each individual gains or loses from a change, equal to the individual's net willingness to pay for the change – positive or negative. What remains as an ethical value judgement, however, is the ethical relevance of the interpersonal comparisons between values of this objective measure.

The compensation test compares different individuals' monetary gains and losses by treating all incremental dollars equally, in effect. Yet it hardly requires a very strong sense of moral compassion to regard the dollar a destitute mother needs for medicine to save her dying child as definitely more valuable than the extra dollar an opulent man wants to spend on a better-quality cigar. Even if this is disputed, however, there is no denying that such comparisons are actually very specific interpersonal comparisons of utility, with utility effectively measured in monetary units, and all individuals' incremental dollars being regarded as equally valuable, no matter what the distribution of income may be. Such interpersonal comparisons, of course, are fundamentally ethical value judgements, and treating all incremental dollars equally in this way is no less 'unscientific' than are any other interpersonal comparisons of utility.

Thus denied the use of compensation tests or, indeed, any other method of comparing different individuals' gains and losses, 'scientific' welfare economics appears to be forced back into making purely Pareto comparisons only, as Archibald (1959) suggested. The retreat, however, does not even stop there if welfare economics is to have any ethical relevance at all. And, as Little (1950) argues, if welfare economics is not about ethical recommendations concerning economic policy, it becomes entirely vacuous.

The standard postulate of Pareto-satisficing welfare economics is 'consumer sovereignty', whereby an individual is judged to be 'better off' if he moves to a new outcome that he would himself choose in preference to the old outcome. To give any ethical significance at all to Pareto-satisficing welfare economics, consumer sovereignty must actually claim that it is *ethically* desirable to bring about a change that makes all individuals better off in this sense. Thus interpreted, consumer sovereignty itself becomes an ethical value judgement, without which even Pareto-satisficing welfare economics loses all the ethical force that is its only *raison d'être*. Now, this particular ethical value judgement certainly seems to command support among economists that is widespread, if not almost universal. Nevertheless, where there are young children, where consumers are known to be seriously misinformed, or where tastes are subject to influence by education or by advertising, there are many economists who hold serious reservations about consumer sovereignty. Indeed, when tastes are changing, individuals' choices may well not correspond to any single preference ordering, in which case the whole concept of consumer sovereignty becomes murky. Of course, denying consumer sovereignty and seeking to overturn an individual's own choices amount to paternalism which many find undesirable under any circumstances. Nevertheless, there is no denying that whether to make consumers sovereign or whether to be paternalistic is fundamentally an ethical issue once again. While libertarians especially make consumer sovereignty axiomatic whenever another individual's rights are not infringed, this amounts to an ethical value judgements that not all are willing to accept. So not even Pareto-satisficing welfare economics, based as it is on the *ethical* postulate of consumer sovereignty, is truly 'scientific' or value-free, even though its value judgements may command widespread support in most practical instances. Thus, even the very last refuge of 'scientific' welfare economics cannot be maintained, and the whole attempt to make welfare economics purely scientific has failed utterly.

Once this really rather elementary philosophical point has been understood, the whole point of avoiding interpersonal comparisons of utility is called seriously into question. To the extent that consumer sovereignty and Pareto satisficing may involve much more widely accepted value judgements, it is comforting to rely just on these. But, where further ethical value judgements seem called for, it seems easier now to make them after accepting the need that some must be made. Later on, I shall argue that allowing interpersonal comparisons of utility is in fact essential for welfare economics. That this does not after all involve crossing a border between 'scientific' and 'unscientific' may be a source of comfort to some.

REVOLUTION IN THREE PARTS

The shortcomings of the 'new' welfare economics and of Pareto-satisficing welfare economics were largely exposed by the thorough discussions found in Little's (1950) and Graaff's (1957) admirable textbooks. At the time of Mishan's (1960) survey and for about ten years thereafter, welfare economics seemed submerged in the depths of impracticality. The old welfare economics with its presumption of any optimal income distribution remained an unattainable Utopian dream, despite the worthy efforts of Samuelson's many writings in particular to give it more substance.

Without some such Utopian assumption, even the most basic propositions of applied welfare economics, such as the desirability of free trade or of marginal cost pricing, were laid open to suspicion by the theory of second best alluded to by Little (1950) and developed by Lipsey and Lancaster (1956). Not much was left except a rather difficult search for apparent Pareto improvements, associated with exercises such as measuring the deadweight losses from distortionary taxes, monopoly, etc.

By contrast, the 1970s brought a rich outpouring of many important articles and a few notable books on welfare economics. Together they have achieved a revolutionary break with both the 'old' and the 'new' welfare economics. There were essentially three different parts to the revolution, following each other in quick succession and mutually reinforcing each other. Each part was marked early on by a small number of highly influential works, followed by a flood of later work developing the major new ideas.

In order of appearance, the first part of the revolution was the development of optimal tax theory, most clearly marked by the publication of Diamond and Mirrlees (1971). The second part was the development of the theory of incentives that grew out of widely appreciated work by Hurwicz (1972, 1973), Gibbard (1973) and Groves (1973). The third part was the emergence of a coherent theory of social choice with interpersonal comparisons, securely founded on the principles laid down by Arrow (1951) and suitably extended using ideas originally due to Suppes (1966) and Sen (1970a, 1970b) for incorporating interpersonal comparisons within Arrow's formal framework. This was the third part of the revolution, however, because it was not really until 1976 that Arrow's conditions were completely formulated in a new framework, and in fact the revolution was not really complete until the publication of Roberts (1980a, 1980b). Indeed, the second and third parts of the revolution are so recent that, at the time of writing, there are still a number of important issues that remain unresolved. This is not so true of the first part, however, to which I now turn.

PART ONE: OPTIMAL TAXATION AND MODERN PUBLIC FINANCE

In a setting with just one consumer the problem of optimal taxation and of tax reform had already been addressed by Edgeworth (1897), Ramsey (1927), Little (1951), Corlett and Hague (1953), Harberger (1964a, 1964b) and others. Boiteux (1956, 1971) and Drèze (1964) had discussed the similar problem of public enterprise pricing. Johansen's (1965) book on public finance set up a broad framework, but welfare questions were only addressed rather indirectly. Diamond and Mirrlees (1971) incorporated several very significant new features. The most important, perhaps, was to derive conditions for commodity taxes to be optimal for explicit Bergson social welfare functions. This reintroduced the interpersonal comparisons of the old welfare economics without reverting to the Utopian dream of an optimal distribution of income. The distribution of income might well remain far from optimal, with commodity taxes designed to improve it as far as possible, even if this meant that equity was being bought at the cost of deadweight losses. In fact economists at last had a framework in which they could discuss intelligently the optimal trade-off between the obvious equity gains of well-designed progressive tax systems and the deadweight losses on which so many previous work had concentrated its attention without paying any attention to the rationale for commodity taxes.

A second important feature of Diamond and Mirrlees (1971) was the doubt it cast on some of the negative results of Lipsey and Lancaster's (1956) theory of the second-best. Even if the distribution of income is not optimal because of limitations on redistribution, nevertheless, for suitable commodity taxes, it is still desirable very often to maintain overall production efficiency, as Diamond and Mirrlees (1971) demonstrated. In particular, marginal rates of transformation between the same pair of commodities should be equated between all productive enterprises. While recent work by Diewert (1983) shows that this result depends on there being a wide enough range of tax instruments that are always chosen appropriately, it nevertheless shows that not all conclusions of modern 'second-best' theory need be entirely negative.

As with many other major developments in economics, one can find precursors if one looks hard enough. The problem of optimal taxation had apparently been formulated and partially solved in an unpublished memorandum due to Samuelson (1951). The framework constructed in Meade (1955) was sufficiently general to handle this and many related problems. But it was Diamond and Mirrlees who set off this part of the revolution. Their paper was accompanied by many others, some actually preceding it in their dates of publication, including Little and Mirrlees (1968/1974) and Mirrlees (1969) which considered the implications for shadow pricing rules in cost—benefit analysis, as well as Baumol and Bradford (1970), Dasgupta and Stiglitz (1972) and Mirrlees (1972) on optimal commodity taxation, Mirrlees (1971), Wesson (1972) and Sheshinski (1972) on optimal income taxation, and Stiglitz and Dasgupta

(1971) on providing public goods which have to be financed by commodity taxes. Of these the paper by Mirrlees (1971) which shows how to calculate optimal non-linear income taxes was certainly the most innovative.

By now this particular first part of the revolution has been carried through to an advanced stage. The textbook by Atkinson and Stiglitz (1980) covers most of the important developments during the 1970s, as does Mirrlees' (1983) survey, at a more technical level. I shall not add to these, except to point out how much this first part of the revolution actually depends upon developments in the second part of the revolution that concerns incentives.

Hahn (1973) gave a timely reminder that the whole of optimal taxation theory was essentially built on the assumption that lump-sum taxes and subsidies to bring about an optimal distribution of income are impossible. When lump-sum redistribution is possible there is no reason whatsoever for using distortionary taxes either to redistribute real income or to finance desirable public goods. Nor, indeed, is there any reason to charge prices other than marginal cost for the outputs of productive enterprises, even if such prices fail to cover average costs — for any losses made by such enterprises in charging marginal cost for their outputs can be covered by lump-sum taxes without any distortions. In a footnote, Mirrlees (1971) conceded Hahn's point but he conceded too much, as later work in the theory of incentives was to show (see, especially, Dasgupta and Hammond, 1980). As I shall argue next, the theory of incentives — the second part of the revolution — lent crucial support to the first part by establishing that the lump-sum transfers required to bring about a full optimum were generally not possible. Lerner (1944) and Graaff (1957) had already pointed out that there was a lack of information necessary to carry out such transfers. The theory of incentives went further and showed that there was a very good reason for the lack of such information — if individuals understood the basis on which lump-sum redistribution was to be arranged, they would have every incentive to conceal or distort the information needed to implement optimal lump-sum transfers. Thus only instruments such as commodity taxes are truly feasible, it turns out.

PART TWO: INCENTIVE CONSTRAINTS

This claim that incentives limit the extent to which income redistribution is possible brings me right to the second part of the revolution. In many ways it is the most fundamental of the three parts because it restricts the feasible set from which good economic allocations can be chosen, no matter what the welfare objective may be. Indeed, it even has serious implications for the 'new' welfare economics for precisely this reason. Even if the objectives of the 'new' welfare economics are retained, the presence of incentive constraints still affects many of the old conclusions.

I have already remarked on how it had been recognized that a social welfare maximizing decision-making body was all too likely to lack some of the information it would need to implement a fully optimal policy. In his series of articles on public goods and public expenditure, Samuelson (1954, 1955, 1958, 1969) went further and noticed that procedures for determining what public goods to provide were all too likely to encourage individuals to understate their true willingness to pay for them. This is the 'free-rider' problem – individuals will try not to pay anything at all if they can get away with it and yet can still make use of whatever public goods others contribute to. What gradually became clear in the early 1970s through the fundamental and widely appreciated work of Hurwicz (1972, 1973), Gibbard (1973) and Groves (1973) was just how prevalent this problem of incentive compatibility could be. In particular, Hurwicz showed how, even without any public goods at all, there is still a real problem in devising mechanisms to allocate private goods Pareto efficiently when individuals understand the incentives they have to try to manipulate the mechanism in their own favour.

Once again, quite apart from Samuelson and some related observations by Malinvaud (1972) and by Drèze and de la Vallée Poussin (1971) concerning the 'free-rider' problem, the work on incentives had some precursors. Bowen (1943) and Farquharson (1969) are remarkable early works on the closely related theory of strategic voting which has since been extensively analysed by Pattanaik (1978), Moulin (1982) and Peleg (1983), following the fundamental work of Gibbard (1973), Satterthwaite (1975) and many others. Vickrey (1961) devised what we would now call an incentive-compatible mechanism for auctioning some indivisible object. Two other contributions close to Groves (1973) but less widely noticed were by Clarke (1971) and Smets (1972). Some appreciation of the enormous volume of current work can be gained from the informative survey by Laffont and Maskin (1983) as well as the book by Green and Laffont (1979), but even these represent only a selection of some of the many themes. For welfare economic theory, however, there is a particular rather small part of this large literature which has the most relevance, in my view. This part is concerned with the limitations that incentive constraints impose upon general economic allocation mechanisms, including those that attempt to bring about suitable levels and composition of public expenditure, and those that attempt to redistribute real income.

A general economic allocation mechanism has to specify the entire economic allocation for each possible economic environment. The details of the economic allocation include what amount each consumer has of each commodity, what labour services each worker provides, what production activities are undertaken in the economy, and what public goods are provided. The details of the economic environment include a specification of each consumer's and worker's exogenous characteristics – that is, endowments, needs, (reflected in the feasible set for the consumer), tastes, talents, willingness to pay for public goods, etc. - as well as the production possibilities of the various producers. An allocation mechanism, then, is an immensely complicated function that determines all the details of the economic allocation for every alteration in the complex details of the economic environment. Yet any economic system, be it based on markets, capitalism, communism, or whatever, is essentially such a mechanism, even if nobody knows more than the smallest fraction of all the details.

As explained above, the problem of 'incentive compatibility' is to devise such an allocation mechanism so that it produces desirable economic allocations even when individuals, either as consumers or as workers, attempt to manipulate it to their advantage. The scope for manipulation comes about because each individual is likely to be the person who knows most about his or her own characteristic, so the economic allocation mechanism has to rely to some extent on signals that individuals provide in order to be sensitive to economically relevant changes in personal characteristics. The literature on incentive compatibility models this situation as a 'game' in the mathematical sense of that term due to von Neumann and Morgenstern (1944). For each possible particular allocation mechanism, there is in fact a corresponding game in which individuals play manipulative strategies against one another in order to have the mechanism generate outcomes that are as favourable as possible, given their true preferences. The mechanism is said to be 'incentive compatible' provided that the outcomes it generates in each economic environment really are those that result when players use equilibrium manipulative strategies in the corresponding game.

STRAIGHTFORWARD SYMMETRIC MECHANISMS IN CONTINUUM ECONOMIES

The definition of 'incentive compatibility' that has just been given is still not complete. There are several different senses in which one can speak of 'equilibrium' manipulative strategies. These include Nash equilibrium, dominant strategies, strong Nash equilibrium, maximin, and (since the game really is one of incomplete information) Bayesian–Nash equilibrium in the sense expounded by Harsanyi (1967). As discussed in Dasgupta, Hammond and Maskin (1979) and in Laffont and Maskin (1983), each different kind of equilibrium leads to a rather different notion of incentive compatibility and so to rather different restrictions which have to be satisfied by an incentive-compatible allocation mechanism.

One particularly appealing notion of incentive compatibility stands out from this bewildering crowd. This is the notion of a 'straightforward' mechanism of the kind considered by Gibbard (1973) as well as Vickrey (1961), Clarke (1971), Smets (1972) and Groves (1973). First of all, such a mechanism has the advantage of being 'direct' in the sense that each individual is simply asked to signal a characteristic directly, either in full or perhaps in only a specified part. This avoids a great deal of possible confusion individuals may otherwise experience in trying to understand what exactly they are signalling and what their signal means. Second, straightforwardness requires that each individual's dominant strategy in the game is to announce his or her true characteristic. In no circumstances, then, is any individual encouraged to misrepresent his true characteristic. This has the obviously very desirable feature of not placing at any disadvantage those individuals who are too honest or too unsophisticated to indulge in some possibly rather complicated manipulative strategy that departs from the truth. Only individuals who do not know their own characteristics fully may suffer, and even they should not be beyond help from suitable advisers.

In addition to these practical and ethical advantages, another reason for requiring the economic allocation mechanism to be 'straightforward' in this sense is that other kinds of equilibria present serious problems. Dasgupta, Hammond and Maskin (1979) prove that, if there is a rich enough domain of possible individual preference profiles, any non-dictatorial mechanism that is not straightforward but only incentive compatible in some weaker sense of 'equilibrium' such as Nash, must give rise to multiple equilibrium outcomes in some possible environments. What is worse, moreover, is that, as Sussangkarn (1978) was the first to show, some individuals will definitely do better in some of the equilibria than they do in others, while other individuals will do worse. Thus the eventual outcome of the mechanism could well depend upon an unpredictable power struggle between competing groups. Even if it can be arranged that all the possible equilibrium outcomes happen to be Pareto efficient, as with Maskin's

(1980, 1983) 'profile' mechanisms, for example, not all of them will be judged as equally good when a more sensitive welfare objective is used. Also, with their multiple and non-interchangeable outcomes, the stability of the Nash equilibria becomes a very real issue. Maskin's profile mechanisms meet these objections to some extent because there is a 'focal' equilibrium in which all individuals simultaneously announce the entire profile of all the individuals' respective characteristics. Achieving such an equilibrium, however, effectively throws back on the individuals all the onus of co-ordination that a good allocation mechanism should be carrying. More-over, since even such an equilibrium still cannot always be the unique Nash equilibrium, there remains the difficulty that some individuals may still want to enforce a new equilibrium away from the focal equilibrium which happens to be more favourable for them.

Another plausible restriction upon straightforward economic allocation mechanisms is that they should be 'symmetric' in the sense that each individual's allocation of private goods should depend only on the charac-teristic he claims to have and on the entire frequency distribution of all the individuals' respective characteristics. So, if two individuals' charac-teristics are interchanged, their respective allocations of private goods will also be interchanged, but all the other details of the economic allocation must be completely unaffected. This accords with the usual concept of 'anonymity'. In addition, it implies that any two individuals claiming to have identical characteristics will be treated identically, which is what is often meant by 'horizontal equity'. Stiglitz (1982) shows that this restric-tion leads to nominally Pareto inferior allocations in some cases, because it may be possible to increase all individuals' *ex ante* expected utilities by randomizing so that some identical individuals will be treated better than others *ex post*. The straightforwardness of such a random mechanism is far from robust, however, because those individuals who are less favourably treated *ex post* within a group of individuals sharing the same charac-teristic will be tempted to try to manipulate the mechanism later on if there is ever any scope for revision. In addition, the use by Stiglitz of the *ex ante* Pareto criterion in this context is itself open to question, for reasons discussed in Hammond (1982a, 1983). Thus I find symmetry to be an appealing restriction just as straightforwardness is.

A frequently repeated objection to using straightforward mechanisms is that they are too restrictive. In particular, they often exclude any possibility of reaching Pareto-efficient outcomes in general environments, as was shown early on by Hurwicz (1972) for exchange economies and by Gibbard (1973) for general social-choice mechanisms that are not dic-tatorial. I shall argue later (p. 420) in this chapter that this objection is irrelevant. More troubling, however, is the difficulty there seems to be in constructing any non-trivial straightforward mechanism that works for a broad class of economic environments. This, indeed, is an open problem except in the important special case when the economy is 'large', in the technical sense that there is a continuum of individuals. Such an economy is a mathematical abstraction which is nevertheless useful provided that it approximates well the working of an economy which has a large finite number of individuals. Conditions for such an approximation to be valid still have to be worked out; however, some preliminary results using mechanisms with rationing of private goods suggest that there may well exist such approximate mechanisms in large economies. Nevertheless, most of the positive results to date concerning straightforward mechanisms do concern continuum economies.

If one considers straightforward mechanisms that are also symmetric, as I have argued that one should, then there is another more subtle reason for considering them in continuum economies. The usual kind of welfare criterion, such as a Bergson social welfare function or simply Pareto efficiency, applies separately to each economic environment with its corresponding profile of individual characteristics. Straightforward individual incentive compatibility, however, is really a constraint on the mechanism as a whole which puts interprofile restrictions on the choice of economic allocation. Thus one is often forced into trading off good allocations in some economic environments against good allocations in others, because of these inter-profile incentive constraints. For symmetric mechanisms in continuum economies, however, an economic environment is completely described by the frequency distribution of individual characteristics (as a probability measure). Straightforwardness imposes incentive constraints that only apply when just one individual changes his (announced) characteristic. In a continuum economy, such a change has no effect whatsoever on the frequency distribution of characteristics because each individual by himself is completely insignificant. Then incentive compatibility only constrains allocations within each separate economic environment. In a continuum economy, the choice of allocation in any one environment places no restriction whatsoever on what is possible in different environments even when incentive constraints are allowed for. Thus the trade-off between good allocations in different environments is entirely avoided, and it is possible to look for straightforward symmetric mechanisms in continuum economies which produce good allocations in each and every possible environment separately. This is what some recent work has attempted to do, and I turn to it next.

PRIVATE DECENTRALIZATION AND PUBLIC FINANCE

The analysis of straightforward symmetric economic allocation mechanisms in continuum economies was initiated in Hammond (1979). Some of the results presented there have been elaborated and refined by Champsaur and Laroque (1981, 1982) and by Guesnerie (1981). An application of the analysis to the Mirrlees (1971) model of income taxation can be found in Dasgupta and Hammond (1980).

The main result of this analysis to date is a complete and rather simple characterization of such symmetric straightforward mechanisms. They are precisely the mechanisms which are 'privately decentralizable' by a (possibly non-linear) budget set, common to all individuals, from which each individual chooses his own bundle of private goods. More precisely, in any economic environment there must be such a common budget set with the property that the mechanism allocates to each individual a bundle of private goods that is optimal for him within that budget set, given his true characteristic. It should be observed that individuals do not choose public goods within their budget sets; public goods are simply provided in response to the stated characteristics of individuals, including their willingness to pay for public goods. Also, the common budget set may be affected by all sorts of taxes, non-linear pricing schemes, rationing, etc. Indeed, it is simply an abstract set in private commodity space. Notice too that the common budget set can vary with the economic environment — indeed, in general it must do so to ensure equality of supply and demand or, more generally, that supplies are sufficient to match the demands that individuals make when faced with their common budget set.

If an economic allocation mechanism is privately decentralizable by such a common budget set, then it must in fact be straightforward for the following reason. Because the economy is large, the common budget set will not be affected by any single individual's attempt to manipulate it. Accordingly, any attempt to manipulate simply produces another bundle of private goods within the common budget set, and this new bundle cannot be better than the old precisely because the mechanism is privately decentralizable. Nor can one individual affect the quantities of publicly provided goods either, since again the levels of provision in a large economy will be independent of any one individual's attempts to manipulate the mechanism.

Conversely, to decentralize a symmetric straightforward mechanism, construct a common budget set that is just large enough so that, no matter where an individual's characteristic may lie in the set of possible characteristics, the corresponding private commodity bundle that the mechanism allocates to him lies in that budget set. In more technical language, the set is the range of mapping from the set of individual characteristics to private commodity space which the mechanism induces. To show that this constructed budget set is indeed a private decentralization, notice that it is indeed a budget set common to all individuals and that, by construction, each individual's bundle of private goods lies in it. In addition, an individual who chooses an arbitrary bundle within the set simply chooses a bundle that he could have attained from the mechanism by announcing some suitable characteristics. This also follows from the construction of the common budget set. Then, however, since the mechanism is straightforward, announcing the true characteristic that leads to the arbitrary bundle within the budget set. That is, the bundle allocated by the mechanism is no worse than any other bundle in the budget set for private goods, which exactly meets the definition of 'private decentralization'.

This private decentralization characterization theorem has an immediate and important implication. The optimal taxation approach to public finance – the first part of the revolution – is explicitly concerned with finding an optimal private decentralization. This problem is completely equivalent in large economies to one suggested by the second part of the revolution, namely finding an optimal symmetric straightforward mechanism that respects incentive constraints. Also, it should be noted that these incentive constraints are actually equivalent in a continuum economy to the self-selection constraints that Stiglitz (1982) and others have considered.

To complete this part of the revolution, however, it is really necessary to show that incentive constraints do indeed prevent the attainment of the old kind of full welfare optimum that relies upon lump-sum redistribution of income. For the very special economy considered there, Dasgupta and Hammond (1980) do this and find the full incentive-constrained welfare optimum. More generally, however, Hammond (1979) followed by Champsaur and Laroque (1981, 1982) together show that, for mechanisms in economies where individuals have smooth preferences (Debreu, 1972, 1976) and so differentiable demand functions as well as positive marginal utilities of income, lump-sum redistribution can only take place between individuals in different disconnected components in the space of characteristics. If this space is (topologically) connected, no lump-sum redistribution is possible without violating incentive constraints.

FULL PARETO EFFICIENCY – A COUNTER-REVOLUTION

Back on p. 413 I pointed out that the recognition of incentive constraints has fundamental implications even for the 'new' welfare economics without interpersonal comparisons. The reason is that the set of feasible mechanisms is not only limited by the customary resource constraints, but also by the incentive constraints that result from individuals' characteristics being private information. Thus it becomes of interest to characterize those mechanisms that are Pareto efficient subject to incentive constraints, or 'constrained' Pareto efficient. And of more interest, as I shall argue later, to find mechanisms that are welfare optimal subject to incentive constraints.

Despite these obvious remarks, much of the recent work on incentive-compatible mechanisms ignores the incentive constraints to the extent that it seeks mechanisms producing allocations that are fully Pareto efficient. That is, there can be no Pareto superior allocation, not even one that could only result from a mechanism which violates the incentive constraints. In principle, there are two different Pareto frontiers. One, corresponding to fully Pareto-efficient allocations, ignores incentive constraints. The second does recognize these constraints and so lies within the first. In many cases, however, the two frontiers intersect at points that happen to be fully Pareto efficient despite satisfying incentive constraints. For example, for the continuum economies discussed in the last section, the two frontiers intersect at points corresponding to Walrasian equilibrium allocations with no lump-sum redistribution. Full Pareto efficiency allows only the intersection to be considered even though other incentive-constrained Pareto-efficient allocations may be ethically superior.

This insistence on full Pareto efficiency serves to exclude any redistribution of real income through incentive-compatible commodity or income taxation. Such taxes are 'distortionary' and produce deadweight losses so that the resulting economic allocation can apparently be Pareto dominated. To produce a Pareto superior allocation, however, requires precisely the kind of lump-sum or other redistribution of income that is generally not incentive compatible. Once the incentive constraints are recognized, then the supposed deadweight losses that distortionary taxes introduce are entirely specious. Some authors such as Harris and Townsend (1981) and Stiglitz (1982) have been careful to look only for incentive-constrained Pareto-efficient allocations. Others such as Hurwicz and Schmeidler (1978) have been all too ready to limit themselves to incentive-compatible mechanisms producing only fully Pareto-efficient allocations and, not surprisingly, finding only (undistorted) Walrasian equilibria, with the distribution of income determined from initial endowments without any regard at all for ethical considerations.

The insistence on full Pareto efficiency is surprisingly pervasive. One can understand politicians invoking 'free markets' or 'market forces' as substitutes for thinking about whether perfect competition without any kind of intervention in fact produces a distribution of income so un-acceptable that the efficiency gains do not match the equity losses. It is totally inexcusable, however, for so many professional economists to support such views by claiming that governments should only intervene in those instances where markets fail to achieve fully Pareto-efficient outcomes — for example, because of externalities. Advocates of market forces are wont to emphasize the role of incentives; they should realize that similar incentives make nonsense of the supposed inefficiencies of certain distortionary taxes. Indeed, incentives provide a rationale for many forms of government intervention in order to move the economy around the incentive-constrained Pareto frontier. There may even be scope for quantitative controls on some private goods, as Guesnerie and Roberts (1980) have shown. It is indeed quite possible that the very survival of the poorest individuals in a rural economy depends upon some scheme such as the requisitioning of part of each farmer's produce and the centralized distribution of some essential foodstuffs. In this connection, it is worth remembering that even famine can be fully Pareto efficient unless the poor victims, if they were kept alive, will eventually have enough surplus to enrich the relatively wealthy who will survive anyway (cf. Sen, 1976, 1981). Moreover, even where famine is not fully Pareto efficient because some of its victims do have such a surplus to contribute, the only incentive-compatible way of achieving a Pareto superior allocation may well involve offering bonded servitude as the only alternative to starvation.

However heart-rendering such examples of full Pareto efficiency may be, though, their force depends ultimately on considerations that trans-cend the 'new' welfare economics with its exclusion of interpersonal comparisons and its concentration on Pareto satisficing. This brings us to the third part of the revolution, concerning social choice with inter-personal comparisons, without which the other two parts would be seriously incomplete. For, without interpersonal comparisons, and ethical value judgements regarding the distribution of real income, there is nothing that enables us to compare different points of the incentive-constrained Pareto frontier, and nothing to prevent concentration upon the inter-section of the full Pareto frontier with the incentive-constrained Pareto frontier. Then, the only role of the incentives part of the revolution might be to point out that very few points of the full Pareto frontier are attainable. And the optimal taxation part of the revolution might be totally rebutted on the grounds that the commodity and other taxes it analyses only serve to create inefficient distortions. All three parts of the revolution therefore stand or fall together, with the willingness to make interpersonal comparisons of utility just as important as the other two parts.

PART THREE: BEYOND PARETO SATISFICING

As discussed above in the second section, a lasting legacy of the 'new' welfare economics has been the concentration it enforces upon finding Pareto-efficient or Pareto-superior allocations. Little if any scope is left for ethical concerns regarding the distribution of income, including equality or simple avoidance of extreme poverty. In fact, far too many economists show a preference for the term 'Pareto optimal', with its connotation that an allocation that I call 'Pareto efficient' is indeed 'optimal' or, in other words, one of the best possible. For one who does have ethical views that regard some distributions of the same total income as better than others, many Pareto-efficient allocations may well be very far from 'optimal'. In economic parlance, a state of affairs is 'efficient' when it is impossible to get more of one desirable thing without giving up something else that is also desirable; for example, 'productive efficiency' means that to obtain more of one output or to use less of one input, it is necessary either to give up some (other) output or to use more of some (other) input. And an allocation which is Pareto *efficient* really is 'efficient' in this sense – it is impossible to increase one person's utility without decreasing somebody else's.

Though many economists may be willing to concede this point, there is still a great deal of work that stops short at showing that a particular kind of allocation is Pareto efficient or, even more commonly, that a particular kind of allocation with public intervention such as taxation or regulation of industry is Pareto inefficient. It should be remembered that, if there is any concern at all about income distribution, Pareto efficiency is not a sufficient condition for a true welfare optimum. Also, I pointed out in the previous section, the usual notion of full Pareto efficiency is not even necessary for a true welfare optimum, since full Pareto efficiency disregards incentive constraints.

There is yet another objection to Pareto satisficing, however, which does not even rest upon any particular ethical value judgements. The point is that, for a sequence of social decisions at successive times, Pareto satisficing by itself fails the test of dynamic consistency suggested by Strotz (1956). This can be shown by a very simple example, involving the choice among just three policies A, B and C in a society of two individuals i and j. Suppose that i strictly prefers A to B and B to C, while j strictly prefers C to A and A to B. Then B is Pareto inefficient and Pareto satisficing allows the choice of either A or C, both of which are Pareto efficient. Suppose that plans are made accordingly at an initial date t_0, and that, of the two Pareto-efficient policies, C happens to be selected.

Next, suppose that a little later on, at date t_1, the last chance to choose A has passed by, but that both B and C could still be chosen, because these two policies only diverge from one another after t_1. Because A is no longer feasible, B as well as C is now Pareto efficient. Indeed, B might actually be chosen, because i can argue that j got his way at time t_0 when C was selected over A, so now i should get his way at time t_1 and B should be selected over C. Of course, j will resist this argument by pointing out that the original plan was to select C, and that B is Pareto inefficient. To i, however, both these considerations are irrelevant; he wants the original plan torn up in favour of B, and the opportunity to select A has already passed for ever. The choice between B and C at date t_1 is one that the Pareto criterion on its own cannot decide, and there is a real possibility that B will emerge, even though it was Pareto inferior originally at date t_0. In fact, to avoid such outcomes, it is either necessary to invoke an extreme degree of precommitment to plans drawn up earlier, or else to build into the social decision procedure some way of remembering earlier missed opportunities that were Pareto superior to some of the current options. Neither possibility is appealing. After all, if either is adopted, we need to ask at date t_0 what past commitments were made, or to remember what opportunities were passed over earlier. The whole social decision-making procedure becomes vastly more complex.

It might be objected that this worry could be entirely avoided by choosing A at date t_0, which then rules out policies B and C altogether, since A diverges from this pair before date t_1. However, suppose there is also a fourth policy D which only diverges from A at some date t_2 after t_1. Suppose that, for individual i, D is even worse than C, but individual j ranks D above A but below C. Then D is Pareto inefficient at date t_0 when C is available, but at date t_2, when A is the only alternative, D becomes Pareto efficient. Now it is j's turn to fight for D over A, and the same problem arises as with the choice between B and C at date t_1. So the inconsistency of the Pareto criterion is completely unavoidable in the extended example with four different policies.

In order to avoid such potential dynamic inconsistencies of choice, and to have a good outcomes result no matter what is the sequence in which social decisions are taken, social choice must maximize a (complete) social preference ordering. This is shown in Hammond (1977, 1982b). The Pareto criterion is not a complete preference ordering except in uninteresting societies where all individuals have identical preferences. Moreover, since a *complete* ordering is required, it is not even enough to supplement the Pareto criterion with incomplete distributional criteria such as whether one Lorenz curve lies everywhere above another, as suggested by Blackorby and Donaldson (1977) and by Willig (1981), for example. Thus, we are forced to accept one of the fundamental conditions that Arrow (1951, 1967) imposed upon an 'Arrow' social welfare function or 'constitution', and look for a complete social welfare ordering that reflects individual preferences.

The above example with the three policies *A, B* and *C* can also be used to justify the most contentious of Arrow's conditions, independence of irrelevant alternatives. At date t_0, facing the three options *A, B* and *C*, we think nothing of choosing among them just on 'the basis of their consequences for the individuals in the society, and of ignoring those other options, perhaps long forgotten, that were foregone in the past and so are unavailable at date t_0. But then, at date t_1, when only *B* and *C* remain available, similar reasoning suggests that option *A* is irrelevant to the decision between *B* and *C*, because then *A* has become unavailable. If *A* has to be remembered at date t_1, what did we forget to include at date t_0, in just considering *A, B* and *C*? Such reasoning, as shown in Hammond (1977, 1983), leads directly to Arrow's condition of independence of irrelevant alternatives.

Because of such dynamic considerations, I find the requirements of a social welfare ordering and of Arrow's independence condition both to be extremely appealing. In what follows, I shall consider only social-choice rules that satisfy both these conditions, and also choose only Pareto-efficient outcomes. As will be seen shortly, this virtually forces us to make interpersonal comparisons of utility if a dictatorship is to be avoided.

SOCIAL CHOICE WITH INTERPERSONAL COMPARISONS

An Arrow social welfare function is defined so that the social welfare preference ordering is a function only of the profile of individual preference orderings. In particular, as Arrow (1951) states quite explicitly, interpersonal comparisons of utility are excluded. In the clearest version of the general possibility theorem, Arrow (1967) also imposes three other conditions – there must be an unrestricted domain of individual preference profiles on which the social welfare function is defined, and both independence of irrelevant alternatives and the Pareto condition must be satisfied. I defended the latter two conditions in the previous sections. As for the first, a social welfare function such as majority rule, which is only well defined for restricted preference profiles, is not very useful in many economic environments.

These three conditions by themselves, in the absence of interpersonal comparisons, effectively prevent any trade-off between one person's utility gains and another person's utility losses. Thus, as Arrow proved, there must be a dictator. That is, there must be one individual who decides any issue over which he has a strict preference. This is the 'general possibility theorem'. The only reasonable escape from such a dictatorship is to make interpersonal comparisons of utility.

Without such interpersonal comparisons it is natural to have the social welfare ordering depend only on individuals' preference orderings, as Arrow made it do. With interpersonal comparisons, though, there may be two different societies with corresponding individuals having corresponding preferences, yet in one society individual i is viewed as having a relatively high marginal utility of income whereas in the second society the corresponding individual with the same income is viewed as having a relatively low marginal utility of income. Then if, as in the old welfare economics, marginal utility diminishes as income rises, and if the social choice of income distribution is determined by maximizing total utility, individual i will have a higher income in the first society than will the corresponding individual in the second society. In fact, this small change in interpersonal comparisons of marginal utilities upsets the whole social welfare ordering, even though no change in individuals' preferences has occurred. A similar upset would occur in response to a change in interpersonal comparisons of utility levels assuming that the income distribution were being chosen to equate utility levels between individuals (cf. Sen, 1973). Thus interpersonal comparisons make the social welfare ordering depend on more than just individuals' preferences.

To accommodate various kinds of interpersonal comparisons – of marginal utilities, utility levels, or even more general comparisons – the Arrow framework for social choice was gradually extended. Harsanyi (1955) had already suggested a way of making interpersonal comparisons and of embodying them in a social ordering. Another paper by Suppes (1966) allowed different individuals each to compare one another's utility levels interpersonally, in effect. Sen (1970a, 1970b) first introduced the important concept of a 'social welfare functional'. This allowed the social welfare ordering to be a function(al) of individuals' *utility functions* rather than just of their preference orderings. Because the profile of individual utility functions could be interpersonally comparable, this was a most significant step, as was the related concept of an 'invariance' class of monotonic transformations of individuals' utility functions which would leave the social ordering unaffected. For example, an Arrow social welfare function is then a particular kind of social welfare functional which, because interpersonal comparisons of utility are not allowed to have any effect, must be invariant when any increasing transformation is applied to any one individual's utility function, leaving his preference ordering and others' utility functions unaffected.

These early but important developments cleared the way for the third part of the revolution which allowed interpersonal comparisons of utility to become integrated into the kind of formal social choice theory Arrow had devised. The first steps towards showing how Arrow's axioms could be accommodated within Sen's new framework of social welfare functionals were made by d'Aspremont and Gevers (1977) and by Hammond (1976), summarized by Arrow (1977). In particular it very soon became clear that allowing interpersonal comparisons into the Arrow framework made possible many other and more acceptable rules than Arrow's dictatorship. Later developments are well described by Sen (1977) followed by Roberts (1980a, 1980b), and a recent expository piece is Blackorby, Donaldson and Weymark (1982).

Kelly (1977), Pazner (1979) and Roberts (1980a) have also reverted to Suppes's (1966) original framework in seeing if one might be able to construct a single social welfare ordering that reflects all the different interpersonal comparisons made by different individuals in the society. Clear-cut results have yet to emerge, but it does seem that quite often one particular person's views of what interpersonal comparisons should be will tend to predominate, even if there is not quite a complete dictatorship of interpersonal comparisons. This remains to be explored, however. Nor should dictatorship of interpersonal comparisons be very surprising or objectionable; ethical disagreements are very often matters of personal opinion that are hard to resolve. All that welfare economics can do is to help each individual ethical observer form his personal opinions concerning economic policy; if different individuals hold different opinions because of different ethical value judgements – including, perhaps, different interpersonal comparisons of utility — welfare economics alone cannot be expected to reconcile them.

THE ETHICS OF INCOME DISTRIBUTION

It is important not to lose sight of the basic problem when considering how to make social choices with interpersonal comparisons. This is the central problem of the old welfare economics too — what constitutes a good distribution of income? We have now seen that this question just cannot be answered without making interpersonal comparisons, but how then does one set about making them? What factual information is relevant, and how should it affect interpersonal comparisons? These are extremely difficult ethical questions which a complete welfare economic theory must show how to answer satisfactorily. One of the difficulties is that interpersonal comparisons seem so abstract and removed from day-to-day decisions. There is some hope, however, that such abstraction can be circumvented by confronting directly the question of how income or general commodities ought to be distributed, as in the survey work reported recently by Yaari and Bar-Hillel (1982). There distributional judgements are made explicitly and interpersonal comparisons implicitly, rather than the other way around. In many simple cases, it seems a reasonable degree of consensus can be achieved even among laymen.

This very cursory discussion does not, however, even begin to confront this major unresolved problem for post-revolutionary welfare economics. Nor does it do justice to the large and growing relevant literature on the welfare economics of income distribution and inequality measurement stemming from the important work of Atkinson (1970) and Sen (1973) in particular. In fact, the ethics of income distribution is a large and fundamental enough topic to deserve a discussion of its own, such as Arrow provides in Chapter 3 of the companion volume.

CONCLUSIONS

Since the revolution in welfare economics is continuing, and much important work remains to be done, it is too early to give an overall assessment. One thing is already very clear, however; welfare economics really has emerged from the sterility imposed by the new welfare economics with its refusal to allow interpersonal comparisons. This third and last part of the revolution allows us at last to address the classic issues of public finance, such as how income can be redistributed for economic justice, and how taxes can be raised equitably to finance public goods. Moreover, the explicit Bergson social welfare functions used to answer such questions have been given a sounder theoretical basis that is closely related to Arrow's theory of social choice.

The second part of the revolution, concerning incentives, is no less vital, since that has shown why the Utopian lump-sum redistribution of the old welfare economics really is impracticable. Applied economists always seemed to know that it was without knowing the reasons why, yet those reasons are crucial to our understanding of what redistribution is possible. Now, while there remain some important theoretical issues in analysing the effect of incentive constraints, much progress has been made and their fundamental importance is starting to be understood.

The willingness to make interpersonal comparisons and to discuss economic justice; together with the recognition of incentive constraints, make up the last two parts of the three-part revolution. They also do much to justify the first part, which was the optimal taxation revolution in public finance theory. Indeed, the classic issues of public finance can now be discussed in a much more securely founded welfare theoretical framework than was possible even as recently as the late 1970s. That is the major achievement of the revolution.

Nor is the revolution over. I have already suggested that some of the three existing parts could benefit from further theoretical explorations. Other major developments are also occurring that really go beyond the three parts I have identified. For example, there is the work springing out of Guesnerie's (1977) analysis of tax reforms which seeks to identify directions of welfare improvement subject to incentive constraints rather than to identify incentive-constrained welfare optima. This may rightly be regarded as more practical. Another important topic is the effect of incentive constraints in sequence economies on which very little work at all has yet been done. Such work, moreover, will have to grapple with problems of uncertainty and of incomplete information which have concerned economic theorists greatly in recent years. Nonetheless, rather little work done so far is in the broad 'general equilibrium' setting which is what thorough welfare analysis requires. Also very far from well understood is the welfare economics of private production, as well as all the highly relevant and topical macroeconomic issues such as unemployment, inflation, monetary policy, etc. The hardest work still lies ahead.

REFERENCES

Archibald, G. C. (1959) 'Welfare Economics, Ethics and Essentialism', *Economica*, 26: 316–27.

Arrow, K. J. (1951) (new edn 1963) *Social Choice and Individual Values*, New Haven: Yale University Press.

Arrow, K. J. (1967) 'Values and Collective Decision-Making', in S. Hook, (ed.), *Human Values and Economic Policy*, New York: New York University Press.

Arrow, K. J. (1977) 'Extended Sympathy and the Possibility of Social Change', *American Economic Review*, 67: 219–25.

Arrow, K. J., and T. Scitovsky (eds) (1969) *Readings in Welfare Economics*, Homewood, Ill.: Irwin.

d'Aspremont, C. and L. Gevers (1977) 'Equity and the Information Basis of Collective Choice', *Review of Economic Studies*, 44: 199–209.

Atkinson, A. B. (1970), 'On the Measurement of Inequality', *Journal of Economic Theory*, 2: 244–63.

Atkinson, A. B., and J. E. Stiglitz (1980) *Lectures in Public Economics*, New York and London: McGraw-Hill.

Baumol, W. J., and D. F. Bradford (1971) 'Optimal Departures from Marginal Cost Pricing', *American Economic Review*, 60: 265–83.

Blackorby, C., and D. Donaldson (1977) 'Utility vs. Equity: Some Plausible Quasi-Orderings', *Journal of Public Economics*, 7: 365–81.

Blackorby, C., D. Donaldson and J. Weymark (1982) 'Social Choice with Interpersonal Utility Comparisons: A Diagrammatic Introduction', University of British Columbia, Economics Department Discussion Paper 82–06.

Boiteux, M. (1956, 1971) 'Sur la gestion des monopoles publics astreints à l'équilibre budgétaire', *Econometrica*, 24: 22–40; trans as 'On the Management of Public Monopolies Subject to Budgetary Constraints', *Journal of Economic Theory*, 3: 219–40.

Bowen, H. (1943) 'The Interpretation of Voting in the Allocation of Economic Resources', *Quarterly Journal of Economics*, 57: 27–48.

Champsaur, P., and G. Laroque (1981) 'Fair Allocations in Large Economies', *Journal of Economic Theory*, 25: 269–82.

Champsaur, P., and G. Laroque (1982) 'A Note on Incentives in Large Economies', *Review of Economic Studies*, 49: 627–35.

Chipman, J. S., and J. C. Moore (1980) 'Compensating Variation, Consumer's Surplus, and Welfare', *American Economic Review*, 70: 933–49.

Clarke, E. F. (1971) 'Multipart Pricing of Public Goods, *Public Choice*, 8: 19–33.

Corlett, W. J. and D. C. Hague (1953) 'Complementarity and the Excess Burden of Taxation', *Review of Economic Studies*, 21: 21–30.

Dasgupta, P. S., and P. J. Hammond (1980) 'Fully Progressive Taxation', *Journal of Public Economics*, 13: 141–54.

Dasgupta, P. S., P. J. Hammond and E. S. Maskin (1979) 'The Implementation of Social Choice Rules: Some General Results', *Review of Economic Studies*, 46: 185–216.

Dasgupta, P. S. and J. E. Stiglitz (1972) 'On Optimal Taxation and Public Production', *Review of Economic Studies*, 39: 87–103.

Debreu, G. (1972, 1976) 'Smooth Preferences' and 'A Corrigendum', *Econometrica*, 40: 603–15 and 44: 831–2.

Diamond, P. A., and J. A. Mirrlees (1971) 'Optimum Taxation and Public Production, I and II', *American Economic Review*, 61:8–27 and 261–78.
Diewert, W. E. (1983) 'Cost Benefit Analysis and Project Evaluation: A Comparison of Alternative Approaches', *Journal of Public Economics* (forthcoming).
Drèze, J. H. (1964) 'Some Postwar Contributions of French Economists to Theory and Public Policy, with Special Emphasis on Problems of Resource Allocation', *American Economic Review* (Papers and Proceedings) 54: 1–64.
Drèze, J. H., and D. de la Vallée Poussin (1971) 'A Tâtonnement Process for Public Goods', *Review of Economic Studies*, 38: 133–50.
Edgeworth, F. Y. (1881) *Mathematical Psychics: An Essay on the Application of Mathematics to the Moral Sciences*, London: Kegan Paul.
Edgeworth, F. Y. (1897, 1925) 'The Pure Theory of Taxation', *Economic Journal*, 7, reprinted as pp. 63–125 *of Papers Relating to Political Economy*, vol. II, London: Macmillan.
Farquharson, R. (1969) *Theory of Voting*, New Haven: Yale University Press, and Oxford: Blackwell.
Farrell, M. J., (ed.) (1973) *Readings in Welfare Economics: A Selection from the Review of Economic Studies*, London: Macmillan.
Gibbard, A. S. (1973) 'Manipulation of Voting Schemes: A General Result', *Econometrica*, 41: 587–602.
Gorman, W. M. (1953) 'Community Preference Fields', *Econometrica*, 22: 63–80.
Gorman, W. M. (1955) 'The Intransitivity of Certain Criteria Used in Welfare Economics', *Oxford Economic Papers*, 7: 25–35.
Graff, J. de V. (1957) *Theoretical Welfare Economics*, Cambridge: Cambridge University Press.
Green, J. R., and J.-J. Laffont (1979) *Incentives in Public Decision Making*, Amsterdam: North-Holland.
Groves, T. (1973) 'Incentives in Teams', *Econometrica*, 41: 617–31.
Guesnerie, R. (1977) 'On the Direction of Tax Reform', *Journal of Public Economics*, 7: 179–202.
Guesnerie, R. (1980) *Modèles de l'économie publique*, Paris: Monographies du Séminaire d'Econometrie du C.N.R.S.
Guesnerie, R. (1981) 'On Taxation and Incentives: Further Reflections on the Limits to Distribution', presented to the European meeting of the Econometric Society, Amsterdam.
Guesnerie, R., and K. W. S. Roberts (1980) 'Effective Policy Tools and Quantity Controls', Discussion Paper no. 8014, CEPREMAP, Paris.
Hahn, F. H. (1973) 'On Optimum Taxation', *Journal of Economic Theory*, 6: 96–106.
Hammond, P. J. (1976) 'Equity, Arrow's Conditions and Rawls' Difference Principle', *Econometrica*, 44: 793–804.
Hammond, P. J. (1977) 'Dynamic Restrictions on Metastatic Choice', *Economica*, 44: 337–50.
Hammond, P. J. (1979) 'Straightforward Individual Incentive Compatibility in Large Economies', *Review of Economic Studies*, 46: 263–82.
Hammond, P. J. (1982a) 'Utilitarianism, Uncertainty and Information', in

A. K. Sen and B. Williams (ed), *Utilitarianism and Beyond*, Cambridge: Cambridge University Press, pp. 85–102.

Hammond, P. J. (1982b) 'Consequentialism and Rationality in Dynamic Choice under Uncertainty', Stanford University, Institute for Mathematical Studies in the Social Sciences, Economics Technical Report no. 387.

Hammond, P. J. (1983) 'Ex-Post Optimality as a Dynamically Consistent Objective for Collective Choice under Uncertainty', in P. K. Pattanaik and M. Salles (eds), *Social Choice and Welfare*, Amsterdam: North-Holland, pp. 175–205.

Harberger, A. C. (1964a) 'The Measurement of Waste', *American Economic Review*, 54: 58–76.

Harberger, A. C. (1964b) 'Taxation, Resource Allocation and Welfare', in NBER, *The Role of Direct and Indirect Taxes in the Federal Revenue System*, Princeton: Princeton University Press, pp. 25–70.

Harris, M., and R. M. Townsend (1981) 'Resource Allocation under Asymmetric Information', *Econometrica*, 49: 33–64.

Harrod, R. F. (1938) 'Scope and Method of Economics', *Economic Journal*, 48: 383–412.

Harsanyi, J. C. (1955) 'Cardinal Welfare, Individualistic Ethics and Interpersonal Comparisons of Utility', *Journal of Political Economy*, 63: 309–21.

Harsanyi, J. C. (1967) 'Games with Incomplete Information Played by "Bayesian" Players, I, II and III', *Management Science: Theory*, 14: 159–82, 320–34 and 486–502.

Hicks, J. R. (1939) 'The Foundations of Welfare Economics', *Economic Journal*, 49: 696–712.

Hicks, J. R. (1940) 'The Valuation of the Social Income', *Economica*, 7: 105–24.

Hotelling, H. S. (1938) 'The General Welfare in Relation to Problems of Taxation and of Railway and Utility Rates', *Econometrica*, 6: 242–69.

Hurwicz, L. (1972) 'On Informationally Decentralized Systems', in C. B. McGuire and R. Radner (eds), *Decision and Organization*, Amsterdam: North-Holland, pp. 297–336.

Hurwicz, L. (1973) 'The Design of Mechanisms for Resource Allocation', *American Economic Review*, 63: 1–30.

Hurwicz, L., and D. Schmeidler (1978) 'Outcome Functions which Guarantee the Existence and Pareto Optimality of Nash Equilibria', *Econometrica*, 46: 1447–74.

Johansen, L. (1965) *Public Economics*, Amsterdam: North-Holland.

Kaldor, N. (1939) 'Welfare Propositions in Economics and Interpersonal Comparisons of Utility', *Economic Journal*, 49: 549–52.

Kelly, J. S. (1978) *Arrow Impossibility Theorems*, New York: Academic Press.

Laffont, J.-J., and E. S. Maskin (1983) 'The Theory of Incentives: An Overview', in W. Hildenbrand (ed.), *Advances in Economic Theory*, Cambridge: Cambridge University Press.

Lerner, A. P. (1944), (new edn 1947) *The Economics of Control*, London and New York: Macmillan.

Lipsey, R. G. and K. J. Lancaster (1956) 'The General Theory of Second Best', *Review of Economic Studies*, 24: 11–32.

Little, I. M. D. (1950), (new edn 1957) *A Critique of Welfare Economics*, London: Oxford University Press.

Little, I. M. D., (1951) 'Direct versus Indirect Taxes', *Economic Journal*, 61: 577–84.

Little, I. M. D., and J. A. Mirrlees (1968, 1974) *Manual of Industrial Project Analysis in Developing Countries, Vol. II: Social Cost Benefit Analysis* (Paris: OECD), revised as *Project Appraisal and Planning for Developing Countries*, London: Heinemann.

Malinvaud, E. (1972) 'Prices for Individual Consumption; Quantity Indicators for Collective Consumption', *Review of Economic Studies*, 39: 385–405.

Maskin, E. S. (1980) 'On First Best Taxation', in D. Collard, R. Lecomber and M. Slater (eds), *Income Distribution: the Limits to Redistribution*, Bristol: Scientechnica, pp. 9–22.

Maskin, E. S. (1983) 'Nash Equilibrium and Welfare Optimality', Mimeo.

Meade, J. E. (1955) *Trade and Welfare: Mathematical Supplement*, Oxford: Oxford University Press.

Mirrlees, J. A. (1969) 'The Evaluation of National Income in an Imperfect Economy', *Pakistan Development Review*, 9: 1–13.

Mirrlees, J. A. (1971) 'An Exploration in the Theory of Optimum Income Taxation', *Review of Economic Studies*, 38: 175–208.

Mirrlees, J. A. (1972) 'On Producer Taxation', *Review of Economic Studies*, 39: 105–11.

Mirrlees, J. A. (1983) 'The Theory of Optimal Taxation', in K. J. Arrow and M. D. Intriligator (eds), *Handbook of Mathematical Economics*, Vol. III, Amsterdam: North-Holland, ch. 24.

Mishan, E. J. (1960) 'A Survey of Welfare Economics, 1939–1959', *Economic Journal*, 70: 197–265.

Moulin, H. (1982) *Strategy of Social Choice*, Amsterdam: North-Holland.

Neumann, J. von, and O. Morgenstern (1944, new ed 1953) *The Theory of Games and Economic Behavior*, Princeton: Princeton University Press.

Pattanaik, P. K. (1978) *Strategy and Group Choice*, Amsterdam: North Holland.

Pazner, E. A. (1979) 'Equity, Nonfeasible Alternatives and Social Choice: A Reconsideration of the Concept of Social Welfare', in J.-J. Laffont (ed.), *Aggregation and Revelation of Preferences*, Amsterdam: North-Holland, pp. 161–73.

Peleg, B. (1983) *Game Theoretic Analysis of Voting in Committees*, Cambridge: Cambridge University Press.

Phelps, E. S. (ed.) (1973) *Economic Justice*, Harmondsworth: Penguin.

Ramsey, F. P. (1927) 'A Contribution to the Theory of Taxation', *Economic Journal*, 37: 47–61.

Robbins, L. (1932) *On the Nature and Significance of Economic Science*, London: Macmillan.

Robbins, L. (1938) 'Interpersonal Comparisons of Utility: A Comment', *Economic Journal*, 48: 635–41.

Roberts, K. W. S. (1980a) 'Possibility Theorems with Interpersonally Comparable Welfare Levels', *Review of Economic Studies*, 47: 409–20.

Roberts, K. W. S. (1980b) 'Interpersonal Comparability and Social Choice Theory', *Review of Economic Studies*, 47: 421–39.

Samuelson, P. A. (1950) 'Evaluation of Real National Income', *Oxford Economic Papers*, 2: 1–29.

Samuelson, P. A. (1951) 'Memorandum for US Treasury', unpublished.

Samuelson, P. A. (1954) 'The Pure Theory of Public Expenditure', *Review of Economics and Statistics*, 36: 387–9.

Samuelson, P. A. (1955) 'Diagrammatic Exposition of a Pure Theory of Public Expenditure', *Review of Economics and Statistics*, 37: 350–6.

Samuelson, P. A. (1958) 'Aspects of Public Expenditure Theories', *Review of Economics and Statistics*, 40: 332–8.

Samuelson, P. A. (1969) 'Pure Theory of Public Expenditure and Taxation', in J. Margolis and H. Guitton (eds), *Public Economics*, London: Macmillan, pp. 98–123.

Satterthwaite, M. (1975) 'Strategy-Proofness and Arrow's Conditions: Existence and Correspondence Theorems for Voting Procedures and Social Welfare Functions', *Journal of Economic Theory*, 10: 187–217.

Scitovsky, T. (1941) 'A Note on Welfare Propositions in Economics', *Review of Economic Studies*, 9: 77–88.

Sen, A. K. (1970a) *Collective Choice and Social Welfare*, San Francisco: Holden-Day.

Sen, A. K. (1970b) 'Interpersonal Aggregation and Partial Comparability', *Econometrica*, 38: 393–409.

Sen, A. K. (1973) *On Economic Inequality*, Oxford: Clarendon Press.

Sen, A. K. (1976) 'Starvation and Exchange Entitlements: A General Approach and its Application to the Great Bengal Famine', *Cambridge Journal of Economics*, 1: 33–59.

Sen, A. K. (1977) 'On Weights and Measures: Information Constraints in Social Welfare Analysis', *Econometrica*, 45: 1539–72.

Sen, A. K. (1981) 'Ingredients of Famine Analysis: Availability and Entitlements', *Quarterly Journal of Economics*, 96: 433–64.

Sheshinski, E. (1972) 'The Optimal Linear Income Tax', *Review of Economic Studies*, 39: 297–302.

Smets H. (1972) 'Le principe de la compensation reciproque: un instrument écomomique pour la solution de certains problèmes de pollution trans frontière', Paris: OECD Direction de l'Environment.

Stiglitz, J. E. (1982) 'Self-Selection and Pareto Efficient Taxation', *Journal of Public Economics*, 17: 213–40.

Stiglitz, J. E., and P. S. Dasgupta (1971) 'Differential Taxation, Public Goods, and Economic Efficiency', *Review of Economic Studies, 38:* 151–74.

Strotz, R. H. (1956) 'Myopia and Inconsistency in Dynamic Utility Maximization', *Review of Economic Studies*, 23: 165–80.

Suppes, P. (1966) 'Some Formal Models of Grading Principles', *Synthese*, 6: 284–306.

Sussangkarn, C. (1978) 'A Possibility Theorem for Totally Acceptable Game Forms', University of California, Berkeley (mimeo).

Vickrey, W. S. (1961) 'Counterspeculation, Auctions, and Competitive Sealed Tenders', *Journal of Finance*, 16: 1–17.

Wesson, J. H. (1972) 'On the Distribution of Personal Incomes', *Review of*

Economic Studies, 39: 77–86.

Willig, R. D. (1981) 'Social Welfare Dominance', *American Economic Review* (Papers and Proceedings) 71: 200–4.

Yaari, M. E. and M. Bar-Hillel (1982) 'On Dividing Justly', Hebrew University, Center for Research in Mathematical Economics and Game Theory, Research Memo. no. 51.

14 Some Fundamental Issues in Social Welfare

YEW-KWANG NG*

INTRODUCTION

As noted by Amartya Sen (1979, p. 537), Wassily Leontief has succinctly summarized the normative properties 'on which something like a general consensus of opinion seems to exist' in the formal discussion of public economic policies:

> In the discussion of public economic policies – in contrast to the analysis of individual choice – the normative character of the problem has been clearly and generally recognized. There the mathematical approach has cystallized the analysis around the axiomatic formulation of the (desirable or conventional) properties of the 'social welfare function'. Social utility is usually postulated as a function of the ordinally described personal utility levels attained by each of the individual members for the society in question.
>
> The only other property on which something like a general consensus of opinion seems to exist is that 'the social welfare is increased whenever at least one of the individual utilities on which it depends is raised while none is reduced' (Leontief, 1966, p. 27).

The second property is of course the (strong) *Pareto principle*. The first property is further factorized by Sen into the following three distinct parts:

(1) *Welfarism*
    Social welfare is a function of personal utility levels, so that any two social states must be ranked entirely on the basis of personal utilities in the respective states (irrespective of the non-utility features of the states).

---

* I am grateful to Murray Kemp and David Kelsey for comments.

(2) *Ordinalism.*
Only the ordinal properties of the individual utility functions are to be used in social welfare judgements.
(3) *Non-comparable Utilities.*
The social welfare ranking must be independent of the way the utilities of different individuals compare with each other (Sen, 1979, p. 538).

Sen then launched a vigorous attack on these four conditions. As usually happens between friends, I agree partly with Sen but disagree with him on the other half of his argument. Thus I wish to defend welfarism and the Pareto principle but to question ordinalism and non-comparability.[1] In the next section, an appraisal of Sen's debate with me on welfarism is offered. It is further argued that, even if non-welfarist factors or principles are admitted, ordinalism is still an inadequate basis for social welfare judgements. The necessity of interpersonal comparison of cardinal utilities is stressed in the third section, going beyond Sen's position. The belief in the sufficiency of ordinalism by Samuelson, Mayston, and others is shown to be mistaken and inconsistent with the very Bergson–Samuelson tradition of individualistic social welfare functions. In the fourth section after discussing the ordinalists's fallacy of misplaced abstraction, some methods of measuring cardinal intensities of individual preferences are defended against some criticisms, including: that the Neumann–Morganstern cardinal utility index has nothing to do with individual subjective utility (Baumol), that there is no reason why social choice should depend on individual risk aversion (Samuelson, Hahn), the Allais's paradox, that log-rolling and the market mechanism do not lead to rational social choice (Arrow), and that a just perceivable unit of utility is not an acceptable interpersonally comparable unit (Friedman, Mirrlees).

WELFARISM

Economists in general, and welfare economists in particular, traditionally take social welfare as a function of and only of individual welfares (or utilities).[2] This is called 'welfarism' and was vigorously attacked by Sen (1979). That social welfare should be dependent on individual welfares seems uncontroversial, it is the 'only of' part that may be controversial. I provided a defence of welfarism in Ng (1981a) followed by Sen's (1981) reply. Here, a summary and appraisal of this debate is first offered. Then, it is further argued that the acceptance or rejection of welfarism is not crucial to the inadequacy of ordinalism.

An Appraisal of the Sen–Ng Debate[3]

Welfarism may be criticized on two levels. First, owing to lack of complete information about individual welfares, we may wish to base our social decision on the objective information about the various social states or alternatives. On this point, I am in complete agreement with Sen provided he agrees that this is not an argument against welfarism as such but is rather a consideration of the ways to achieve our objective (even if welfarist) in the absence of perfect information. For example, suppose we agree (for argument's sake) that we should maximize the SWF (social welfare function) of the sum or the production of some other quasi-concave function of individual welfares. If we also have complete information about individual welfares in various social states, what we need to do is just to compare these various sums or products, etc., of individual welfares. However, usually we cannot do just this owing to the lack of information. If we also believe in diminishing marginal welfare of income and similar capacity to enjoy income (or that this capacity is not strongly positively correlated with income and we do not know who has high or low capacity; see Lerner, 1944 and Sen, 1973) then a certain policy may be regarded as desirable if it increases the incomes of the poor and reduces those of the rich without reducing total income. Then, a consideration that affects our social decision appears to be that of income equality or some similar consideration, among others. Our SWF appears to be a function not only of individual welfares but also of some objective indicators such as the equality of income distribution of social states.[4] But it is clear that we use such objective indicators only as indirect measures or estimates of individual welfares. Thus, far from being a rejection of welfarism, the use of such objective indicators serves to achieve our welfarist objective. Such principles as 'giving priority to the interests of the poor over the interests of the rich' need not be non-welfarist if it is derived from a welfarist SWF plus certain other assumptions such as diminishing marginal welfare of income.

Sen's objection to welfarism is, however, much more fundamental since he 'criticises welfarism even when utility information is as complete as it can conceivably be' (Sen, 1979, p. 547), even with completely cardinal, unique and interpersonally comparable individual welfare indices (which we shall be using here). Basically, Sen believes that we may wish to place value on such principles as liberty, non-exploitation, no-torture, etc., over and above or besides their contribution in promoting individual welfares. Thus, even if two social states are exactly the same with respect to individual welfares, we may prefer the one that adheres to these principles to the one that violates them. For illustration, Sen (1979, p. 547) provides the following examples.

Consider a set of three social states, x, y and z, with the following interpersonally comparable cardinal welfare numbers for a two-person community:

	x	y	z
Person 1's welfare	4	7	7
Person 2's welfare	10	8	8

In x, person 2 is eating a great deal of food while person 1 is hungry. In y, person 1 consumes a bit more of the given food supply. While 2 is made worse off (in comparison to x), 1 is made better off by a larger amount and the sum of welfare becomes larger (with diminishing marginal welfare). It is clear that y must be judged to be better than x by utilitarianism, and also by virtually all the criteria that have been proposed using data on individual welfares. Let use take y to be socially better than x.

Consider now z. Here person 1 is still as hungry as in y, and person 2 is also eating just as much. However, person 1, who is a sadist, is now permitted to torture 2, who – alas – is not a masochist. So 2 does suffer, but resilient as he is, his suffering is less than the utility gain of the wild-eyed 1. The utility numbers in z being exactly the same as in y, welfarism requires that if y is preferred to x, then so must be z. But y is socially preferred to x. So z is preferred to x as well, thanks to welfarism (Sen, 1979, pp. 547–8).

In a foonote, Sen adds: 'It is assumed that there are no indirect consequences of torture, e.g. in attitude formation. These indirect effects do not change the nature of the difficulty, even though they can be properly accommodated only in a much more complex analysis.'

The above argument of Sen against welfarism appears very persuasive. However, it seems to me whether one has to reject welfarism on the ground of such moral principles as no-torture depends on whether one believes in these principles as his basic value judgements. 'A value judgement can be called "basic" to a person, if the judgement is supposed to apply under all conceivable circumstances, and it is "non-basic" otherwise' (Sen, 1970, p. 59).[5] Those whose belief in no-torture is more basic than welfarism must withdraw their commitment to welfarism in circumstances like. z. But one, like myself, may also believe in no-torture not as a basic value judgement but as derived from a welfarist SWF because one may believe that in practically all circumstances, torture leads, directly and indirectly, to more harm than good. However, most people believe that it is wrong to inflict harm on others even if the pleasure of doing so exceeds the direct and indirect sufferings caused. Thus, it is very tempting to reject welfarism (and utilitarianism, a specific form of welfarism, in particular) at the immediate intuitive level. But as argued by Hare (1976), the rejection of utilitarianism at the immediate intuitive level is consistent with the support for utilitarianism at a deeper 'critical' level.

One may accept a welfarist SWF as his most basic value judgement. It is, however, difficult to do a precise welfare calculation for every decision made. Thus, it is generally desirable to adopt certain rules such as honesty, liberalism, non-exploitation, no-torture, etc., which generally contribute to the promotion of social welfare as defined by the welfarist SWF. In time, these rules become moral principles and tend to be valued for their own sake even to the extent of persuading people to reject the original welfarist SWF. But in my view, this is confusing the more basic value with less basic values. This is like insisting on telling a cruel, dishonest invading army the truth in order to stick to the principles of honesty. However, I am not advocating giving up these moral principles lightly owing to the enormous long-run implications through attitude formation.

Some people may wish to regard certain principles such as freedom from torture as being based on, say, human rights independent of or over and above welfare considerations. However, if one presses oneself hard enough with the question, 'Why human rights?', I believe that one will most likely come up with a welfarist answer. I enjoy walking. But this enjoyment is based on the violation of the 'rights' of stones, sands, etc., for freedom from being stepped upon. So why don't stones have 'stone rights'? Why do we hear about 'human rights', 'animal rights', etc., but not 'stone rights'? An obvious answer is that stones do not feel pleasure and pain. But this is clearly a welfarist answer. It is possible that certain basic human rights are so definitely conducive to the improvement of welfare and the violation of them on grounds of short-run welfare (or non-welfare) considerations so likely to produce effects very unfavourable to long-run welfare, that the insistence on these human rights on a political or practical level without regard to any welfare consideration becomes defensible. But this does not negate the belief that, on a deeper philosophical level, these rights are ultimately derived from welfare considerations.

Sen believes however that 'any serious theory of human or civil rights will bring in other [than sentient] aspects of people which also differentiate them from stones. The respect and concern that one person owes another can hardly be seen as a function only of the latter's capacity for pleasure. Indeed, even after a person dies and obviously has no further capacity for pleasure or pain, right-based considerations *vis-à-vis* him do not all cease to apply, e.g. they are relevant in disposing of his body, or in defending him against vilification' (Sen, 1981, p. 534). In my view, such post-mortem 'rights' can be explained by the preferences of living individuals and the effects on future behaviour. For example, living persons may want to show respect for people in general and specific individuals in particular by having proper burial in general and national burial for heroes that, in addition, may encourage heroic behaviour. It is true that people differ from stones in many other aspects. For example, stones and even animals cannot exercise such rights as voting in elections. But I am referring to the more elementary rights of freedom from being unnecessarily hurt (which I believe should apply to all sentients). Moreover, if there exist non-sentient objects (super-machines?) that can 'exercise' certain rights (e.g. voting) operationally, I would treat them no more favourably than stones.

While I maintain my basic defence of welfarism given in Ng (1981a), I am happy to make the following three concessions to Sen. First, though I find welfarism a perfectly defensible principle as an ultimate value judgement, it does not mean that those who attack welfarism must thus be wrong in any logical or scientific sense. Since this concern questions of basic value beliefs, perfectly rational and logical persons may differ ultimately. On the other hand, this does not mean that such questions cannot be logically discussed or that the discussion is useless. One may logically show which axioms (including some normative ones) imply certain normative principles or which normative principles imply some desirable or undesirable outcomes. In the process, one may persuade opponents to abandon their initial value judgements which they mistakenly believe to be basic but turn out to be non-basic upon cirtical analysis. (See the appendix of Ng, 1981b, on the use of axiomatic value theories.)

Second, I think Sen is right in believing that the consensus of economists on welfarism is 'based on not examining explicitly the problems of conflict that can and do arise' (Sen, 1981, p. 532). If economists were to seriously consider issues raised by Sen, a significant proportion, if not a majority, of them would probably reject welfarism. This concession is made partly due to the fact that moral philosophers who have pondered over such issues over a long time are notoriously divided in their views with respect to utilitarianism in particular and to consequentialism in general (for example, see Smart and Williams, 1973). 'Ng's own view of the matter should not be confused with a claim that a consensus does exist on this question' (Sen, 1981, p. 532), though I may attempt to persuade economists to stick to welfarism, and for the defectors to re-embrace welfarism after a more 'critical' examination.

The third concession I wish to make is based on practical considerations including the lack of complete information about individual welfares mentioned above. Partly because of this lack of information and partly because of the cost of making a detailed welfarist calculation for each decision, it is sensible to adopt some principles that are generally consistent with the ultimate welfarist objective. In time, these principles are valued for their own sake and these secondary or derived values have to be reckoned with even by a pure welfarist (who may however try at the same time to persuade people not to value non-basic principles over and above their instrumental values so that we can avoid being the slaves of certain 'moral principles' which are no longer conducive to social welfare due to new circumstances). Therefore, while I continue to adhere to a pure welfarist objective at the basic philosophical or 'critical' level, I am quite willing to concede that, at the practical day-to-day (or even year-to-year, decade-to-decade) basis, characteristic of most economic and social decisions, non-welfarist (from the short-term viewpoint) principles have to be reckoned with. At least in this sense, then, Sen's objection to a purely welfarist calculation is important.

After making these concessions to Sen, I am sure I will not jeopardize my friendship with him by adding a caution against his following conclusion: 'Arrow's impossibility theorem can be seen as resulting largely from combining "welfarism" (ruling out the use of non-utility information) with remarkably poor utility information (especially because of the avoidance of interpersonal comparisons)' (Sen, 1979, p. 554). I agree wholeheartedly that the poor utility information (non-cardinalism and non-comparability) is of paramount importance in producing the impossibility result (see the fourth section below). I also agree that the introduction of non-welfarist principles may help social choice in particular instances. However, without richer utility information, the rejection of welfarism itself does not provide a satisfactory solution to the paradox of social choice, as shown below.

The Inadequacy of Non-welfarist Ordinalism

The difficulties of ordinalism, even with the introduction of non-welfarist principles, can be seen by two recent separate (though somewhat related) impossibility results.

First, Ng (1982a) establishes the impossibility of a Non-Cardinalistic Ranking Rule (NCRR), given Anonymity, the Pareto principle, and Universal Domain (or a less demanding condition called Sufficiently Wide Domain). An NCRR 'is a rule which, for any two social states x and y, states the social ranking xOy based on [individual rankings] xO^iy, i

$= 1, \ldots, n$, and/or the values of $x_1, y_1, x_2, \dot{y}_2, \ldots, x_s, y_s$ where $s < m$ and $1, \ldots, s$ need not be the first s variable in $1, \ldots, n'$ (Ng, 1982a, p.), where n is the number of individuals and m is the number of aspects one social state may differ from another. It is called non-cardinalistic because, as far as individual preferences are concerned, it uses only information regarding individual orderings but not regarding individual cardinal utilities (utility differences or levels).[6] Non-preference characteristics of social states are permitted to be used in deciding the social ranking. However, for it to really be a ranking rule (in the sense of a general rule instead of a specific decision), we impose the requirements $s < m$. If $s = m$ all m aspects of the two social states have to be specified (in addition to the n individual rankings) before a social ranking is made. This is hardly a rule. For all ranking rules satisfying neutrality, none of the m objective characteristics is admissible. Thus, by allowing $s < m$ characteristics to be admissible, we are already making a great concession. In other words, we are relaxing $s = 0$ to $s < m$. A ranking rule may thus specify, for example, that if an equal number of individuals prefer x to y and y to x, the social state with a more equal distribution (of some objective factors such as economic goods) is to be socially preferred. Or some other objective specifications (with respect to say public goods, weather, political factors, etc.) may be made.

The essence of Ng's (1982a) proof is sketched with reference to Figure 14.1. For two social states such that the two individuals J and K differ in their strict preferences $(xp^K y, yP^J x)$, suppose the ranking rule dictates yPx (based perhaps on some objective characteristics of the social states). Since social states may differ in aspects not covered by the ranking rule, we can find, given Unrestricted (or Sufficiently Wide) Domain, another two social states z and w such that $zP^J w$ and $wP^K z$, and x is Pareto superior to w and z to y as illustrated in Figure 14.1. This is possible since the ranking rule is non-cardinalistic. Moreover, the movement of z to w satisfies all the non-preference requirements as the movement of x to y. If the ranking rule is anonymous, it must dictate zPw. With the Pareto principles, cyclicity can thus be established.

Two extensions to the above impossibility result may be made. First, with the rejection of welfarism, the Pareto principle need not be acceptable since it is essentially a form of welfarism. Thus, without an extension to free itself of the welfarist aspect, Ng's (1982a) impossibility result as such does not affect the viability of non-welfarist ordinalism. The first extension consists in generalizing the Pareto principle to make it consistent with whatever non-welfarist principles were adopted in the ranking rule. This weaker version of the Pareto principle then says that, provided the non-welfarist principles adopted in the ranking rule are not violated, the usual

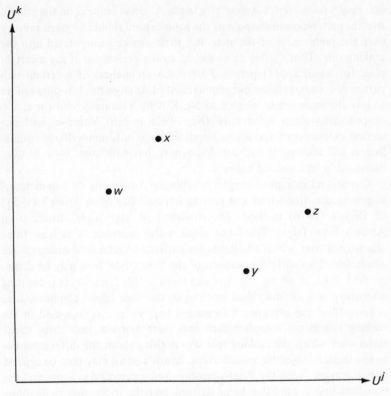

FIGURE 14.1

Pareto principle (weak or strong version as the case may be) applies. This extension does not affect the proof of the above impossibility result. Since $s < m$ is a requirement in the definition of a ranking rule, the example in Figure 14.1 is still possible with all the non-welfarist principles of the ranking rule satisifed or held constant, since the social states in Figure 14.1 may differ from each other in the aspect(s) not covered by the ranking rule. A non-welfarist, non-cardinalistic ranking rule is thus impossible even if we just accept the weakened or extended version of the Pareto principle and Anonymity.

It may be thought that non-welfarist ordinalism may be saved by rejecting Anonymity. But Anonymity is an extremely reasonable condition in the context where non-welfarist principles are admitted. For example, one may wish to reject Anonymity in the Arrovian context on the ground that the preferences of the poor or the handicapped should be given priority over the preferences of the rich. But these can be incorporated into the ranking rule. Thus, 'giving more weight to the preference of say a certain poor (or handicapped) person *J* over the preferences of a certain rich person *K* does not violate our requirement of Anonymity. It is only failure to give the same height weights to Mr. K if he is similarly poor (or handicapped that violates Anonymity' (Ng, 1982a, p. 216). Moreover, with our second extension of the above impossibility result, non-welfarist ordinalism is still impossible without Anonymity but with some form of non-dictatorship, as discussed below.

Our second extension consists of replacing Anonymity by non-dictatorship over the 'free triple' and proving impossibility using Arrow's (1951) or Parks's (1976) method. The condition of 'free triple' differs from Arrow's Free Triple. The latter requires the existence of at least three alternatives over which all alternative patterns of individual orderings are admissible. Two different versions of the 'free triple' here may be distinguished. First, if we use the Arrovian multi-profile frameworks (admitting *alternative* sets of individual orderings), the 'free triple' condition here requires that the objective information $(x_1, y_1, \ldots x_s, y_s)$ used in the ranking rule is not complete such that there exists at least three social states over which the ranking rule says nothing about the differences between them in objective specification. Arrow's proof may then be applied over this triple, with the Pareto principle being extended as above and the non-dictatorship condition being defined over the triple, that is, disallowing a dictator over the triple (cf. Murakami, 1961). Second, if we use a single-profile framework (with a *given* pattern of individual preferences), the 'free triple' condition here requires considerably more than three social states as above but a multitude of social states to allow Parks's (1976) diversity condition to operate and Parks's proof to apply in this non-welfarist framework.

The essential point is that, even if we are prepared to admit non-welfarist principles in our social choices, unless these principles cover virtually all aspects over which social states may differ from one another, there will, in general, exist enough 'free' social states over which the same methods of proving impossibility results may be applied as in cases where welfarism is adhered to. To make the non-welfarist principles cover all aspects of social states does not only make these 'principles' no longer really principles (or rules, or a constitution) but is also quite impracticable, since new aspects will crop up from time to time.

The above rejection of non-welfarist ordinalism consists in operating within the sub-domain where the non-welfarist principles are not violated (or do not differ). An alternative rejection of non-welfarist ordinalism is possible even if all aspects of social states are specified by the ranking rule, provided there is no cardinal measurement of and comparison between the non-welfarist principles and between these principles and individual cardinal preferences (or welfares). Each principle plays the same role as an individual utility. An impossibility theorem or a 'dictatorial principle' can then be established for this expanded framework (Kelsey, 1982). A possible objection to this alternative rejection of non-welfarist ordinalism is that, while individual utilities are subjective and difficult to measure cardinally, many non-welfarist principles or specifications (such as individual income levels) are objective and hence cardinally measurable. However, we can combine the first (Ng's) and the second (Kelsey's) alternatives to form a powerful rejection of non-welfarist ordinalism. Let us allow all aspects of social states to be specified in the ranking rule (as some non-welfarist principles) and agree that many of these specifications can be cardinally measured. But let us agree that there are at least some aspects that cannot be more objectively and cardinally measured than individual utilities, for example, love, keeping of promises, etc. Operating in the sub-domain where the social states differ from each other only in the non-cardinally measurable aspects, one can then establish an impossibility result similar to Kelsey (1982).[7] Thus, the acceptance or rejection of welfarism is not crucial to the impossibility result. Rather, it is the restrictions (non-cardinalism, non-comparability) on the use of utility or non-utility information that produce the impossibility result.

THE NECESSITY OF INTERPERSONAL CARDINAL UTILITIES

I am in complete agreement with Sen with regard to the restrictiveness of non-comparability and ordinalism except that I would go further than Sen in emphasizing the inadequacy of ordinalism, or the necessity of cardinalism. It is true that cardinalism without interpersonal comparability is not sufficient. Thus one can prove impossibility theorems with cardinal utilities but disallowing interpersonal comparison (Sen, 1970, pp. 123–30; DeMeyer and Plott, 1971; Osborne, 1976; d'Aspremont and Gevers, 1977). But comparability without cardinalism is also insufficient. This is so even if we go along with the questionable rejection (Little, 1952, Samuelson, 1967) of Arrow's interprofile framework admitting *alternative* sets of individual preferences. This single-profile impossibility result was established independently at about the same time by Kemp and Ng (1976) and Parks (1976).[8]

While clearly aware of the restrictions of ordinalism, Sen gives some concession to the possibility of social choice without cardinality:

Interpersonal comparability without cardinality is . . . a way out of the impossibility. Ordinal comparisons of different persons' utilities permit the use of such criteria as Rawls's (1971) 'maximin' interpreted in terms of utilities, focusing on the welfare level of the 'worst-off rank' something like a dictator, and though it is not a personal dictatorship, it is possible to argue that it is a rather extreme approach. It appears that with interpersonal comparability without cardinality, the tendency towards such 'rank-dictatorships' is considerable, and it is possible to exclude all *other* possibilities by relatively small extensions of the Arrow condition, *given* the welfarist . . . structure (Sen, 1979, p. 546).

Thus, Sen's concession is a small one. But I would go further in the direction of cardinalism by doubting even the necessity of this mild concession. Apart from the undesirability of 'rank-dictatorship', it can be argued that cardinalism is necessary after all since it can be shown under very general conditions that the general possibility of interpersonal comparability of utility levels implies comparability of utility *differences* (Ng, 1982b).

Samuelson concedes that, 'if utilities are to be added, one would have to catch hold of them ['cardinal indexes of utility'] first, but there is no need to add utilities' (Samuelson, 1947, p. 228; the insertion is from the sentence preceding the quotation). But even if one rejects utilitarianism (which maximizes the sum of utilities) and, say, wishes to go along with the Nash SWF (which maximizes the product) or any other reasonable[9] specific form of SWF, one still has to catch hold of the cardinal indices of utility. If individual utility indices are just ordinal, it would be meaningless to distinguish between, say, the Bentham SWF and the Nash SWF since either one can be transformed into the other by suitable co-ordinal transformation of individual utility indices.

While the Kemp–Ng–Parks impossibility result has been quickly assimilated by welfare economists and social-choice theorists, there remain at least three believers in the adequacy of ordinalism: McManus (1982), Mayston (1980, 1982), and Samuelson (1977, 1981).[10] In particular, it is argued that we can extract more information from individual *orderings* of alternatives than admitted by many frameworks of social choice. If an individual prefers x to y and y to z, the society should count his preference of x over z as more important than this preference of x over y or of y over z.

Consider the example illustrated in Figure 14.2(a) where the arrows indicate the direction of preferences of the only two relevant individuals J and K. If x and y are regarded as socially indifferent, then it is reasonable

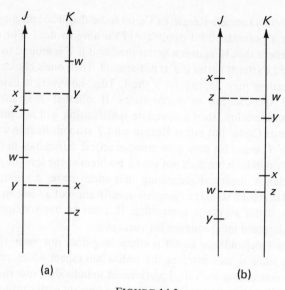

FIGURE 14.2

to argue that *w* should be socially preferred to *z* on the ground of 'secondary Pareto dominance'. (This is so since the difference between *z* and *w* is less than the difference between *x* and *y* for *J* and the reverse is true for *K*.) Thus the social choice between *w* and *z* is not independent of individual preferences with respect to alternatives other than *w* and *z*. The independence of Irrelevant Alternatives (IIA) or some similar condition (such as Kemp and Ng's A3) is thus rejected and with it evaporates the impossibility of ordinalism.

In preparation for our counter-attack, note that there are three distinct aspects of IIA, the preferencism aspect, the ordinalism aspect and the independence (or irrelevance) aspect.[11] The preferencism aspect requires that social choice depends only on individual preferences. If we equate social choice with social welfare maximization and ignore differences between individual preferences and individual welfares, preferencism and welfarism are identical. Given preferencism, the independence aspect requires that the social ordering of any two alternatives (or any sub-set of alternatives) depends only on individual preferences of these alternatives, not on individual preferences for other irrelevant alternatives. Many people find this requirement unacceptable. This is probably due to their neglect of the fact that each social alternative is a complete specification of *all* relevant aspects of a social state. For example, it is often said that whether one (and society) prefers Reagan or Carter to be the president may depend on whether a potential third candidate (T) is alive or dead. For example, one may believe that Reagan is a better president if T is around to do some mischief and Carter is better if T is not around. Then one's choice between two alternatives may depend on a third. This, however, is based on an incomplete specification of social states. If whether T is around is a relevant consideration, then a complete specification will not just involve Reagan versus Carter but rather Reagan with T around, Reagan without T, Carter with T, etc. This may pose some practical difficulties in the actual election of candidates but does not pose a problem at the level of generality of social-choice theory. Recognizing that social states are mutually exclusive and that each state is a complete specification of all relevant factors, the independence aspect is compelling. It is not an overstatement to say that to understand independence is to accept it.

That the independence aspect is compelling does not mean that IIA is acceptable since it also involves the ordinalism aspect which restricts information concerning individual preferences to individual orderings. Those who are willing to go beyond ordinalism and operate with cardinal utilities may thus reject IIA on the ground of its ordinalism aspect. But this alternative is closed to those who believe in the adequacy of ordinalism. What about rejecting IIA on the ground of its preferencism? This is possible but it does not solve the problem. As discussed at the end of the second section, the admittance of non-welfarist (or non-preferencist, for that matter) principles does not remove the inadequacy of ordinalism.

It is true that, owing to lack of perfect information to reveal the intensities of individual preferences, we may wish to use the number of intermediate alternatives (or rather steps of preferences) to give us a rough guide as to the intensity of preference (Goodman and Markowitz, 1952). But the use of intermediate alternatives is reasonable only if it gives us some indication of the intensity of preference. Then independence is not really violated. Rather, the availability of the intermediate alternatives just gives us more information about intensities of individual preferences over the relevant alternatives. Social ranking of any two alternatives is still a function of individual preferences of these two alternatives. In fact, with finite sensibility (that human beings are not infinitely discriminative), we could go all the way to construct fully cardinal utility functions and base our social choice on these cardinal utilities (Ng, 1975a). On the other hand, if the intermediate alternatives do not provide or are not regarded as providing an indication of the intensity of preference, then it is unreasonable to use the number of intermediate alternatives or any other aspects of other alternatives to determine the social ranking of any given two alternatives. For example, suppose xP^JyP^Jz and yP^KzP^Kx. Is it reasonable to say that y should be socially preferred to x since J prefers x to y in one step but K prefers to y to x in two steps? When we introduce more alternatives, we may find that the one step becomes ten steps and the two steps remain at two steps, even if the individual ordinal and cardinal preferences with respect to all the alternatives remain unchanged. Thus, unless intermediate alternatives can give us some indication of preference intensity, they should not alter social ranking. This can be seen even more clearly in the following case.

Consider the divisible case with an uncountable infinity of alternatives and infinite sensibility. Let us also confine attention to the intermediate range (in which no individual is in bliss or in hell) which is usually the only relevant range in practice. (If one believes in the general possibility of ordinalism, then one has to tackle this case.) Then for any individual, and for any relevant social alternative x, there is an uncountable infinity of alternatives preferred to x and an uncountable infinity inferior to x. And for any two relevant alternatives x, y such that not xI^iy, there is an uncountable infinity of alternatives 'in between' x and y. Thus if we eschew information about non-preference information (preferencism) and also eschew information about cardinal utilities (ordinalism) and consider only individual orderings, we see that, for any two pairs of alternatives x and y, z and w, if xP^Jy, zP^Jw, yP^Kx, wP^Kz (no other individuals or all others are indifferent), as illustrated in Figure 14.2, the standing of x against y with respect to individual orderings is exactly the same as that of z against w, even if account is taken of the number of alternatives or steps of preferences in between, above and/or below. Thus, if social choice is dependent only on individual orderings, xRy entails zRw. But this violates secondary Pareto dominance. As shown above, *if xIy* then one should have wPz. This is very compelling (given xIy) since the difference between z and w is less than the difference between x and y for J but the reverse is true for K. If society regards the preference of x over y by J as just overbalanced by the dispreference of K and declares xIy, then it is reasonable to require wPz as argued convincingly by Mayston (1980, 1982) and McManus (1982). However, they fail to see that, unless we rely on information concerning the cardinal intensity of preferences (violating ordinalism) and/or on non-preference information (violating preferencism), we simply cannot to begin with declare xIy without also committing ourselves to wIz, and thus violating secondary Pareto dominance. To see this, consider part (b) of Figure 14.2 which is derived from Part (a) by just compressing the scale of K. Since absolute scale is arbitrary for ordinal preferences, both figures give us exactly the same ordinal information. Then, instead of declaring

xIy, why not declare wIz instead that implies xPy from secondary Pareto dominance? As far as individual orderings are concerned, the standing of x against y is exactly the same as the standing of z against w. Unless we use something other than individual orderings there is just no way of discriminating between the two pairs. The belief in the adequacy of ordinalism, even after being enriched with the reasonable argument of secondary Pareto dominance, is thus mistaken.[12]

Samuelson (1981) has recently clarified his view on the question under discussion. He still insists on the adequacy of ordinalism but has apparently given up what is called preferencism here and weak individualism by Kemp and Ng (1982). Thus he writes, 'Note that my BISWF [Bergsonian individualistic social welfare function] is *not* formulated in terms of "an ethical *ranking*" determined as an output of a function whose input variables are [only] individual *rankings*' (Samuelson, 1981, p. 235). In other words, social choice or social welfare depends on something other than individual rankings (or orderings). Since cardinalism is explicitly rejected, this something extra must be something other than individual preferences, a violation of preferencism or individualism. But Samuelson keeps calling his SWF individualistic. By this he means that individual preferences are to be respected in the sense of accepting the Pareto principle ('honouring people's autonomous tastes when those lead to unanimity'). But in arriving at social orderings over alternatives where individual preferences conflict (such as x v. y and z v. w illustrated in Figure 14.2), the violation of either ordinalism or individualism is inevitable.

It is tempting for a third party to view the debate between Kemp/Ng and Samuelson as a question of semantics or misunderstandings, that both sides are correct in their respective beliefs in the possibility and impossibility of individualistic ordinalism because their definitions of individualism differ. This interpretation however does not square with the following Bergson–Samuelson tradition.

Bergson (1938) and Samuelson (1947, p. 229; 1981, p. 224) first write their economic welfare function as dependent on the amounts of commodities consumed and productive services performed by all individuals. Using Samuelson's (1947) notations:

$$W = W(x_1^1, \ldots, x_n^1; \ldots; x_1^s, \ldots, x_n^s; v_1^1, \ldots, v_m^1; \ldots; v_1^s, \ldots, v_m^s)$$

(14.1)

where n, m, s are the numbers of commodities, productive services, and individuals respectively. Next, Bergson (1938, p. 318) makes the assumption of 'The Fundamental Value Propositions of Individual Preference: if the amounts of the various commodities and types of work were constant for all individuals in the community except any ith individual, and if the ith individual consumed the various commodities and performed the various types of work in combinations which were indifferent to him, economic welfare would be constant.' A factual assumption implicit in this Fundamental *Value* Proposition may be noted: the absence of externalities of consumption. Otherwise, my shifting from cups to cans may leave me indifferent but the empty cans may adversely affect others. But the important point here is not this factual part of the Fundamental Proposition but its value part that allows Bergson and Samuelson to write W as not directly dependent on the objective variables but on the individual utilities:

$$W = W[U^1(x_1^1, \ldots, x_n^1; v_1^1, \ldots, v_m^1), \ldots, U^s(x_1^s, \ldots, x_n^s; v_1^s, \ldots v_m^s)]$$

$$(14.2)$$

If the factual assumption is not made, all we have to do is to allow other individuals' consumption and services into each individual utility function. (The difficulty of universal externality, as analysed in Ng, 1975b, thus created does not concern us here.) In other words, the value part of the Fundamental Proposition is really welfarism (or preferencism; the two being identical where individual welfares and preferences are not distinguished and social welfare maximization and social choice are equated), requiring that social welfare depends only on individual utilities.[13] More formally, rid of its factual part, the Fundamental Value Proposition becomes the Pareto indifference rule which is shown by Sen (1979, p. 540) to imply welfarism if we do not place any domain restriction and accept independence, both of which are implict in the general framework of writing $W = w(x)$, that is, (14.2) above, since $W(x)$ depends only on the social state of x, not on another social state.

Thus, the above Bergson–Samuelson tradition (which, like most economists, I find perfectly reasonable) really implies full individualism in the sense of Kemp and Ng (1982), requiring social welfare (or social choice) to depend only on individual (cardinal or ordinal) preferences and not on objective variables such as x_j^i directly. This tradition is upheld by Samuelson himself (1981) in the latest paper on the subject that I know of. Thus, the interpretation that Samuelson is correct given his concept of individualism is inconsistent with the very Bergson–Samuelson tradition itself.

I would concede to the possibility of 'individualistic' ordinalism if the popular and reasonable Bergson–Samuelson tradition as represented by

(14.2) were revised to:

$$W = W[U^1(x^1_1, \ldots), \ldots, U^s(x^s_1 \ldots), x^1_1, \ldots v^s_m]$$ (14.3)

where the objective variables $x^1_1, \ldots, v^s_m$ also enter the function directly so as to allow social choice or social welfare judgements to be based on, say, the amounts of chocolates consumed by the various individuals. I do not accept though that such a procedure is truly individualistic.

It is true that I conceded in the second section that, due to such practical difficulties as the lack of perfect utility information, we may use certain non-welfarist principles or information in our social choice. But if these non-welfarist principles and information are to serve ultimately the welfarist objective, they must be selected as to avoid the violation of the Pareto principle. To do so, they must be ultimately based on interpersonal comparison of cardinal utilities (Ng, 1982a). To see this point informally, consider the following non-welfarist rule: medical care should be provided equally. Clearly, such a rule will in general conflict with the Pareto principle. For one thing, it would be silly to provide medical care equally to the healthy and to the sick. Suppose it is improved to read: medical care should be provided equally to all sick persons. But what about different kinds and different degrees of sickness; It may be a good practical rule to give priority to a patient with a bee-sting over a patient with an ant-bite. But such rules can be, generally speaking, consistent with the Pareto principle only because they are made on sensible interpersonal comparison of cardinal utilities – a person with a bee-sting is likely to suffer more disutilities than one with an ant-bite. Even here, exceptions are possible. What if a particular person is sensitive to ant-bites such that he suffers enormously without treatment. Should the general rule of the priority of bee-stings be overridden in this case? Yes, or perhaps one wants to include these 'exceptions' into the rule itself. But isn't 'suffering enormously in comparison to a bee-bite for a normal person' an instance of interpersonal comparison of cardinal utility?

Thus, even if we do allow non-welfarist principles or objective variables such as $x^1_1, \ldots, v^s_m$ into our welfare function (14.3) on practical gounds, they are used, to be consistent with the spirit of individualism, as no more than indirect indicators helping us to estimate the individual preferences more accurately. Ultimately, we want something like (14.2), not (14.3). With (14.2), ordinalism is impossible, as has been proved many times now by Kemp and Ng (1976), Parks (1976), Pollak (1979), and Roberts (1980).

THE MEASUREMENT OF CARDINAL UTILITIES

The Ordinalist's Fallacy of Misplaced Abstraction

Ordinalists are of three types. First there are those who accept the concept of cardinal utilities as meaningful and useful but practically difficult to obtain and hence wish to build social-choice theory only on individual orderings. A representative economics is Arrow. Second, there are those who regard the concept of cardinal utilities as meaningful but redundant since ordinalism is sufficient both for individual choice and social choice. A representative economist is Samuelson. Third, there are those who believe that individual utilities *are* ordinal and totally reject cardinalism as old-fashioned and mistaken. I do not think they are represented by any prominent economists but their views are encountered from time to time in conversation and in textbooks.

The confusion with respect to utility measurability is partly the result of the use of the same term 'utility' both as a measure of subjective satisfaction and as an indicator of objective choice or preference. Another source of confusion is the insufficient distinction between measurability in principle and measurability in practice. For utility as a measure of the subjective satisfaction of an individual, it seems clear that it is cardinally measurable in principle, though the practical difficulties of such measurements may be very real. These difficulties include inaccuracies and possible insincerity in preference revelation. Moreover, even the individual himself may have difficulties in giving a precise measure. For example, I prefer a grapefruit to an orange and prefer an orange to an apple. If you ask me, 'Do you prefer a grapefruit to an orange more strongly than an orange to an apple?' (Question A), then I will say, 'It depends on what kind of fruits I had in the immediate past and what sort of meal I am having'. If all these are known, then I will be able to give a definite answer. Thus, subject to practical difficulties, my subjective utility is cardinally measurable. If it was just ordinally measurable, I would not just have some difficulties in answering Question A, I would dismiss it as meaningless. It seems clear that any individual will be able to compare the difference in subjective utility between having an apple and an orange and that between an orange and a house, and able to compare the differences in subjective disutility between a bite of an ant and a sting of a bee and that between a sting of a bee and having his right arm cut off.

It also seems meaningful to say that I was at least twice as happy in 1982 as in 1966. If I have a perfect memory, I may even be able to pin down the ratio of happiness at say, 2.8. It also seems sensible for someone to say, 'Had I known the sufferings I had to undergo, I would have committed suicide long ago', or 'If I had to lead such a miserable life, I would wish not to have been born at all!' Hence, it makes sense to speak of negative or positive utility. Thus, somewhere in the middle, there is something corresponding to zero utility:

> There can be little doubt that an individual, apart from his attitude of preference or indifference to a pair of alternatives, may also desire an alternative not in the sense of preferring it to some other alternatives, or may have an aversion towards it not in the sense of contra-preferring it to some other alternative. There seem to be pleasant situations that are intrinsically desirable and painful situations that are intrinsically repugnant. It does not seem unreasonable to postulate that welfare is +ve in the former case and −ve in the latter (Armstrong, 1951, p. 269).

Hence it seems clear that utility as a subjective feeling is in principle measurable in a full cardinal sense.

On the other hand, we may use a utility function purely as an objective indicator of an individual preference ordering such that $U(x) > U(y)$ if and only if he prefers x to y and $U(x) = U(y)$ if and only if he is indifferent; and we may not be interested in anything in addition to the above ordinal aspect of the utility function. Then any monotonically increasing transformation of a valid utility function is also an acceptable indicator and a utility function possesses only ordinal significance. For some problems (such as the theory of consumer choice), knowledge of the preference orderings is all that is required and hence an analyst can justifiably abstract away the cardinal aspect of the utility function. This, however, does not mean that, for problems (such as social choice) where the intensities of preference are relevant, one cannot preceed to adopt cardinal utility functions, provided due attention is paid to the problem of practical difficulties. To deny the use of cardinal utility is then to commit what may be called the 'fallacy of misplaced abstraction'.

The third type of ordinalists mentioned in the opening paragraph of this section are thus clearly mistaken and can be said to have committed fallacy of misplaced abstraction. The second type are also mistaken if individualism or the Bergson–Samuelson tradition is accepted, as argued in the preceding section. The question remains whether the practical difficulties of discovering intensities of preferences are so great as to make the concept of cardinal utility, though perfectly acceptable in principle, useless in practice. Let us thus consider some methods of revealing preference intensities.

The Expected Utility Hypothesis

An important method of constructing cardinal utility indices is by observing (or interrogating) individual choices involving risk. If the choices of an individual satisfy certain reasonable axioms (Neumann and Morgenstern, 1947; Marschak, 1950), there exists a utility index unique up to a positive or affine transformation such that the individual will choose in accordance with the maximization of expected utility. With such an index, all we need is to agree on is an origin to make the index completely cardinal (unique up to a proportionate transformation), but not necessarily interpersonally comparable.

However, does the utility index constructed by the Neumann–Morgenstern method actually measure the subjective utility of the individual? A firm negative answer has been given: 'what relationship, if any, does the N–M cardinal utility theory have to that of the neoclassical utility theorists? It is generally (though not universally) agreed that there is none – the two utility measures have nothing in common insofar as their cardinality is concerned' (Baumol, 1977, p. 431; see also Baumol, 1951 and 1958). Baumol is right, at least formally. However, the N–M utility index actually approximately measures the neoclassical subjective utility (except that the former leaves the zero point undefined) if the following premise holds approximately (as it no doubt does in my case): faced with choices involving risk, an individual chooses to maximize the expected value of his subjective utility (the Expected Subjective Utility Premise). For example, choosing between the certainty of winning one million dollars and a fifty-fifty chance of winning two million dollars and nothing, I will certainly choose (as will most other individuals) the certainty of winning one million *because* the gain in subjective utility of winning two million is less than twice that of winning one million. Provided I answer truthfully and carefully, one can in fact constrcut my subjective cardinal utility index using the N–M method just by interrogation. And one can *explain* my (as well as most other individuals) risk aversion by diminishing marginal (subjective) utility of income.[14]

In this connection, it may be mentioned that, just as Baumol is right if the Expected Subjective Utility Premise (ESUP) is not at least approximately true, so are Samuelson (1947, p. 228n) and Hahn (1982, p. 195) in their failure to see why social choice might depend on individual risk aversion. This dependence is clear once ESUP is accepted. The degree of risk aversion reveals the degree at which subjective marginal utility of income diminishes. Since social welfare is a function of (not necessarily 'only of') individual utilities, how rapidly marginal utilities diminish has obviously important effects on social choices that affect individual income levels.

Even if all individuals do *attempt* to maximize their respective expected subjective utilities, I do not think that ESUP applies more than approximately. This is so because of the difficulties of estimating the true values of one's subjective utilities in various outcomes and the corresponding probabilities. Also, certain prospects may also have 'first-glance appeal' in their favour not warranted by closer scrutiny. Third, many individuals are affected by possible regrets owing to their choice. These considerations I believe explain much, if not completely, such paradoxes as Allais's (see Allais and Hagen, 1979). To illustrate, consider the following two questions (Allais and Hagen, 1979, p. 89):

(1) Do you prefer Prospect *A* to Prospect *B*?
    A: certainty of receiving 100 million dollars.
    B: a 10 per cent chance of winning 500 million, plus an 89% chance of winning 100 million, plus a 1 per cent chance of winning nothing.
(2) Do you prefer Prospect *C* to Prospect *D*?
    C: an 11 per cent chance of winning 100 million, plus an 89 per cent chance of winning nothing.
    D: a 10 per cent chance of winning 500 million, plus a 90 per cent chance of winning nothing.

Many people prefer *A* to *B* and *D* to *C*, violating the Savage axiom of independence which dictates that the preference *A* to *B* entails the preference *C* to *D*. An explanation of the paradox is the disutility of regret one will have if one chooses *B* over *A* and the 1 per cent chance of not winning the 100 million eventuates. If one is not presented with a choice like this, the utility of winning nothing is just zero. But with such a choice, the utility of not winning the 100 million might be a lifetime full of regret and could be a big negative amount. On the other hand, for the choice of *D* over *C* one probably would not have much regret for not winning because the choice of *C* also entails a high probability of not winning. This is just an instance of the problem that for some cases, the *process* of choice itself may affect utility, not just the outcome as narrowly defined. Another instance is that some individuals may enjoy risk taking (gambling) as such. If we are interested in individual utilities associated with outcomes of, say, income levels as such, such paradoxes may create some practical difficulties in some cases but do not generally invalidate the estimates of subjective utility indices by the N–M method or some other methods (Fisher, 1927;

Frisch, 1932; Vickrey, 1945; Van Praag, 1968; Kapteyn and Wansbeek, 1982; Camacho, 1982).

The Expected Subjective Utility Premise may be questioned on the ground that an individual may not only be risk averse with respect to income but also with respect to utility such that he may not be maximizing the sum of his subjective utilities weighted by probabilities but rather some strictly quasi-concave function in these. Since the various outcomes in a prospect are mutually exclusive and since the subjective utility is by definition what the individual is finally interested in, I regard such behaviour as the commission of the fallacy of the diminishing marginal utility of utility against which I hope to argue elsewhere.

Measures Based on Willingness to Pay (or Allocate Votes)

A method of voting a little more advanced than the ranking method is to allocate a certain (equal or unequal) number(s) of votes to each voter who is then free to distribute his votes among different alternatives. Ignoring complications created by game-strategic behaviour (on which see Pattanaik, 1978), this allows some degree of preference intensities to be revealed. In addition to this, preference intensities may also be revealed even in the simple one-voter-one-vote case provided votes are taken on a number of issues either simultaneously or consecutively allowing, log-rolling (such as vote-trading agreements) to take place between voters (Buchanan and Tullock, 1962, pp. 330–2; Coleman, 1966; Miller, 1977). Though log-rolling cannot, in general, arrive at a stable equilibrium (Park, 1967) and cannot be relied upon to reveal true individual preferences (Mueller, 1967), it may contribute by providing richer information for social choice, and tend to make social decision more transitive.

Arrow rejects the log-rolling argument on the ground that 'a social state is a whole bundle of issues, and I presupposed that all possible combinations of decisions on the separate issues are considered as alternative social states. That this included log-rolling seemed to me so obvious as not worth spelling out' (Arrow, 1963, p. 109). This argument misses the point that, with log-rolling, the relative intensities of preferences are revealed somewhat and hence we may no longer wish to be bound by the ordering aspect of IIA (Independence of Irrelevant Alternatives). However, social decisions with log-rolling or with votes-allocation violates IIA not only in its ordering aspects but also its independence aspect. This can be seen most clearly where the alternatives concerned are small in number. A change in individual preferences with respect to some alternatives or the removal or includsion of some alternatives changes the possibility of log-rolling and the allocation of votes so much that the social ordering of the unaffected alternatives may change.

The potential non-optimality of the above violation of independence can be seen by a simple example. Suppose I strongly prefer x to y but only very marginally prefer y to z which I find indifferent to w. If all four alternatives are on the agenda, I may allocate 99 votes to x and one to y. However, if x is not relevant, I allocate 100 votes to y. But my mild preference of y over z and w has not increased. If that mild preference is counted as one vote (against, say, someone else's moderate preference of z over y of say ten votes), it should not count as 99 votes if x is irrelevant. Ideally, one would like to reallocate the endowment of votes each time the set of alternatives and/or the relative strength of preferences changes. But if we know how to allocate the endowments of votes optimally in accordance to the detailed intensities of preferences, we will know the socially optimal alternative (according to whatever SWF) without the trouble of voting. Nevertheless, the method of vote allocation may be 'acceptable' (though not optimal) and the allocation of endowment may be based on partial knowledge of *likely* preference intensities. For example, a department may adopt the constitution that members of staff will be allocated more votes over issues directly related to their interests or specializations.

The use of market mechanism to allocate resources is essentially similar to the use of vote allocation in that each individual uses his endowment to affect the outcome in the way he desires.[15] Thus, the market solution also violates the independence conditions.[16] Ideally, then, one wants a change in endowment each time there is a change in objective and/or subjective conditions. Since this is not practicable, the market solution may again be regarded as 'acceptable' provided the distribution of endowment or income can be maintained to be 'satisfactory'.

It is true that an individual's influence on resource allocation of private goods in a market economy differs from his influence on social decision through voting since each dollar expenditure 'counts' while each vote usually does not 'count' *ex post* and usually only 'counts' *ex ante* probabilistically. But this difference is reduced by the extension of the use of market-type mechanisms such as the Clarke (1971, 1980)–Groves (1970, 1973) incentive-compatible mechanism or market-based methods such as cost–benefit analysis to allocate resources for public goods.

The Finite Sensibility Approach

Unlike the previously discussed methods, this approach provides a natural unit that may be used for interpersonal comparison. The approach is based on the concept of finite sensibility and has a long tradition. The concept was touched on as far back as 1781 by Borda and in 1881 by Edgeworth.[17] Edgeworth took it as axiomatic or, in his words, 'a first principle incapable of proof', that the 'minimum sensibile' or the just perceivable increments of pleasure, of all pleasures for all persons, are equatable (Edgeworth, 1881, pp. 7ff., 60ff.). Armstrong (1951), Goodman and Markowitz (1952), and Rothenberg (1961) have also discussed the problem. It has also been explored in its more positive aspects in decision theory and psychology, using the term 'just noticeable difference' (see Fishburn, 1970, for a survey).

Assuming finite sensibility, Ng (1975a) derives the Bentham (or utilitarian) SWF based mainly on the following postulate:[18]

> Weak Majority Preference Cirterion (WMP): For any two alternatives (or social states) x and y, if not individual prefers y to x and (1) if n, the number of individuals, is even, at least $n/2$ individuals prefer x to y; (2) if n is odd, at least $(n - 1)/2$ individuals prefer x to y and at least another individual's welfare level is not lower in x than in y, then social welfare is higher in x than in y.

As Mueller observes:

> WMP is obviously a combination of both the Pareto principle and the majority rule principle that is at once significantly weaker [hence more acceptable as a sufficient condition for a social improvement] than both. In contrast to the Pareto criterion it requires a majority to be better off, rather than just one [individual], to justify a move. And, in contrast to majority rule, it allows the majority to be decisive only against an indifferent minority. In spite of this apparent weakness, the postulate nevertheless proves strong enough to support a Benthamite social welfare function (Mueller, 1979, pp. 181–2).

The reason why WMP leads us to the Bentham SWF is not difficult to see. It requires that individual welfare differences sufficient to give rise to preferences of half of the population must be regarded as socially more significant than differences not sufficient to give rise to preferences (or dispreferences) of another half. Since any group of individuals comprising 50 per cent of the population is an acceptable half, this effectively makes a just perceivable increment of welfare of any individual equivalent to that of any other individual (Ng, 1975a; Ng and Singer, 1981).

The main objection to WMP and the resulting Benthamite SWF is that it may lead to a very unequal distribution of income. Apart from incentive effects, it is doubtful that differences in sensibility will lead to a great inequality of income if we apply the Bentham SWF. Psychological studies in pain sensation show that the pain thresholds are very close for different individuals (e.g. averaging 230 ± 10 standard variation), as are the number of just noticeable differences (Hardy, 1952, pp. 88, 157). If there are more differences in the capacity to enjoy income, these are probably due to 'learning by doing' and a long-run SWF will take acount of that.

If we ask ourselves why do we want to give more weight to the poor, we may have a number of answers. The most obvious one is that incomes of the poor meet more urgent needs. But this is taken care of by reckoning in terms of utilities instead of incomes. Second, it may be said that the consumption of the rich is self-defeating owing, for example, to the snob effect, the desire to keep with the Joneses, etc., while the consumption of the poor (if spent on, say, education and health) may have very beneficial long-run effects. This again can be taken care of by allowing for all forms of externalities, etc. If some inequality still persists after taking all ill effects into account, I cannot see why this is not an optimal distribution if it maximizes aggregate welfare. Consider the much-cherished principle, 'From each according to his ability; to each according to his needs' (which I personally approve of, assuming no disincentive effect). Why doesn't it read, 'An equal amount of work from each; an equal amount of income to each?' If a weak man is tired by four hours of work, it is better for a strong man to work longer to relieve him. Similarly, if a less-sensitive man does not enjoy the extra income much, it is better that a more-sensitive man receives more of it. What prevents us from seeing such a simple analogy?

For choices involving risk, there is a problem as to whether we should maximize welfare as a function of expected utilities, that is, $WE = W(E^1,$ $\ldots, E^1) \equiv W(\Sigma_s \overset{S}{=} {}_1 \Theta_s U_s^1, \ldots, \Sigma_s \overset{S}{=} {}_1 \Theta_s U_s^1)$, or expected welfare as a function of *ex post* utilities, that is $EW = \Sigma_s \overset{S}{=} {}_1 \Theta_s W(U_s^1, \ldots, U_2^1)$, where Θ_s is the probability of state s and S is the number of all possible states. There seems to be good grounds for adopting either method. If welfare is a sum (unweighted or weighted with constant individual weights k^i) of utilities, then the two methods are equivalent. Thus $EW = \Sigma_s \Theta_s \Sigma_i k^i U_s^i$ $= \Sigma_i k^i \Sigma_s \Theta_s U_s^i = WE$. Hence the Bentham SWF we obtained frees us from the agonizing choice of maximizing WE or EW, and we may use either one, as convenience dictates. Looking at the matter from the opposite sequence, one may say that the fact that *EW* and *WE* are both appropriate objective functions lends support to WMP and the Bentham SWF. If welfare is not a sum of individual utilities, then the maximization of *EW* or *WE* will not, in general, yield the same result. Therefore, if either one is a reasonable objective function, the other cannot be so unless social welfare is a sum of individual utilities.

Another type of objection to WMP should now be discussed. First, it is argued that a just perceptible improvement may differ across different experiences even for the same individual. 'On many occasions, a just perceptible improvement in musical performance means much more to me than a just perceptible quantity of drink' (Mirrlees, 1982, p. 69). This I think may be due to the difference in time period involved and/or to possible future effects. A just perceptible quantity of drink may last only a fraction of a second while the musical performance probably a couple of hours. Moreover, Mirrlees may also value the recollection of a high-quality musical performance. As it is, WMP is formulated in an atemporal basis and hence does not cover the complication introduced by differences in time period. With time as a dimension, one should then select a just perceptible improvement over a just perceptible length with neither future nor eternal effect as the standard unit, and use indirect measurement (Ng, 1975a, section 9) for experiences difficult to be so measured.

Now consider the following objection raised in a personal discussion by David Friedman (cf. Sen, 1970a, p. 94; Pattanaik, 1971, p. 150). If individual welfare levels are continuous (which is the assumption used in Ng, 1975a), then even an indifference may involve a welfare difference. It is thus clear that a just perceivable increment of welfare should be regarded as interpersonally equatable. For example, a person poor in perception or reporting may fail to notice or report a welfare difference more significant in some subjective sense than one noticed or reported by another more perceptive person. On the other hand, if welfare levels are discontinued so that individual welfare does not change until an increment of pleasure is perceived, then these discontinuous little jumps in welfare may differ across individuals in some sense and hence should not be regarded as equivalent.

My reply to the above objection is several fold. First, it may be noted that the above objection is not against the principle of the Bentham SWF (i.e. W as an unweighted sum of W^i) but just against the way the various W^i should be best measured or interpersonally compared. In other words, if the marginal preference of a person half as perceptive (in terms of reporting a given amount of subjective welfare) as another is counted twice as important, the above objection will presumably no longer apply. Thus, this objection is properly regarded rather as pointing to the difficulty of making interpersonal comparison of welfare than as an objection against the Bentham SWF as such.

Second, if we shy away from making any interpersonal comparison of cardinal individual welfares, then a SWF is impossible. Thus, for the question of which SWF to adopt, we must accept some form of comparison. Most methods of interpesonal welfare comparison are rough estimates (if not guesstimates) perhaps partly influenced by personal value beliefs. It seems to me that the method of measuring the levels of just perceivable increments of pleasure offers to date the most promising objective way of making interpersonal comparison. (On some practical difficulties and ways to overcome them, see Ng, 1975a, section 9.) If we accept the above objection, it just means that even this best available method is not ideal. With finite sensibility (which is an indisputable fact) and without some form of interpersonal comparison, we cannot make a reasonable social choice except in the unlikely cases where every individual strictly prefers x and y. Even the indifference of one individual is sufficient to cloud the issue unless we are prepared to make the interpersonal comparison that any welfare difference associated with his indifference is not strong enough to overshadow the preferences of others. Third, even if it is true that a just perceivable increment of welfare differs across individuals either due to different 'perceptive' powers or due to different 'jumps' in welfare, how are we to know whose just perceivable increment is larger and whose smaller? In the absence of specific knowledge regarding this, it seems best to regard them as equal (cf. Lerner, 1944, pp. 29ff; Sen, 1973). If we adopt the convention of designating an average just perceivable increment of welfare as one, then the just perceivable increment of any particular individual, in the absence of any specific knowledge, may be expected to have a probability distribution such as depicted in Figure 14.3, that is, he is just as likely (if at all) to have a lower as a higher then average value.

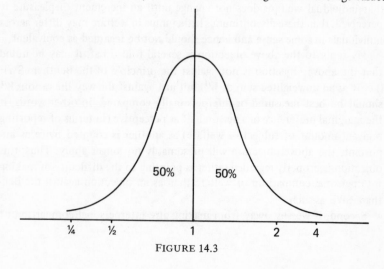

FIGURE 14.3

We can thus minimuze our mistake by taking his increment to be one, the average value (Ng, 1980).

Our arguments for taking a just perceivable increment of welfare as equatable across individuals (at least in the absence of an eudiamonometer) seem to be supported by the following argument of Harsanyi:

> The metaphysical problem would be present even if we tried to compare the utilities enjoyed by different persons with identical preferences and with identical expressive reactions to any situations. Even in this case, it would not be inconceivable that such person should have different susceptibilities to satisfaction and should attack different utilities to identical situations . . . identical expressive reactions may well indicate different mental states with different people. At the same time, under these conditions this logical possibility of different susceptibilities to satisfaction would hardly be more than a metaphysical curiosity. If two objects or human beings show similar behaviour in all their relevant aspects open to observations, the assumption of some unobservable hidden difference between them must be regarded as a completely gratuitous hypothesis and one contrary to sound scientific method. (This principle may be called the 'principle of unwarranted differentiation'.) In the last analysis, it is on the basis of this principle that we ascribe mental states to other human beings at all: the denial of this principle would at once lead us to solipsism. Thus in the case of person with similar preferences and expressive reactions, we are fully entitled to assume that they derive the same utilities from similar situations (Harsanyi, 1955, 317).

CONCLUDING REMARKS

I have defended welfarism and the Pareto principle and argued further that, even if non-welfarist principles are accepted and the Pareto principle correspondingly extended, ordinalism is still an insufficient basis for social welfare judgements, interpersonal comparable cardinal utilities are still essential. Some methods of measuring cardinal utilities (Neumann–Morgenstern index, some voting and market mechanisms, the use of just noticeable differences) are defended against some criticisms. While these methods are not ideal, they can contribute to more informative social welfare judgements.

The shyness of economists in tackling interpersonal comparable cardinal utilities is partly the result of the methodological mistake of regarding interpersonal comparisons of utility as value judgements and hence scientifically meaningless. (Affected by the influential writings of Robbins, 1932, 1938.) I have argued elsewhere (Ng, 1972; 1979, appendix 1 A) that interpersonal comparisons of utility are not value judgements but (possibly subjective) judgements of fact. The interpersonal judgement that *J* will be made much better off than *K* will be made worse off by changing from *x* to *y* does not imply that *y* should be chosen over *x*. This is so only if we accept that utilitarian value judgement that we should maximize the sum of individual utilities. If we accept the amazingly popular (but to me clearly unacceptable) value judgement of maximizing the utility of the worst-off individual. we have the choose *x* over *y* if *K* is the worst-off. Moreover. the measurement of cardinal utilities based on finite sensibility outlined above and in more detail elsewhere (Ng, 1975a) also provides an objective method of making interpersonal comparison of utilities. It is time that more effort be made in this direction, as effectively appealed by Mueller (1979), pp. 181–3).

NOTES

1. Since the Pareto principle is essentially a form of welfarism, our defence of welfarism can also be used to defend the Pareto principle which will thus not be independently defended.
2. I ignore here the differences between individual welfare (happiness) and indivial preference (utility), on which see Ng, 1979, section 1.3.
3. This debate is conducted in a framework where non-human sentients (gods, spirits, animals, and possibly plants, viruses, etc. (on which see Ng, 1983a)) are assumed non-existent or their welfares held constant, and problems like national boundaries, number of individuals, etc. are ignored.
4. A different welfarist reason for including such apparently 'non-welfarist' indicators into the short-run SWF is their effects on welfare in the long run. For example, a less unequal distribution of income may promote social harmony.
5. See also Sen, 1967. I define basicness somewhat differently:' a value judgement [is] basic to a person if it is not derived from some other value judgment and he believes in it for its own ethical appeal' (Ng, 1979, p. 19). Whether this definition differs from Sen's depends on the interpretation of 'all conceivable circumstances' in Sen's definition.
6. It may be thought that NCRR is a misnomer as a ranking rule based on interpersonal comparison of utility levels, such as the Rawlsian maximum rule, need not involve cardinal utilities as interpersonal comparison of utility differences (unit comparability) does. However, Ng (1982b) shows that level comparability implies some unit comparability under very general conditions. It may also be noted that NCRR subsumes an element of independence that is, however, compelling due to the mutually exclusive nature of social states, each of which is an exhaustive specification of all relevant details, see Ng, 1979, p. 144) and the fourth section of this chapter.
7. I leave the formal proofs of the various suggested propositions, ex-

tensions or conjectures to those interested in rigorous logical exercises.

8. After a series of correspondence, Kemp and Ng drafted their paper in 1973. Parks' draft was also completed in 1973. While Parks's result was published a few months later than that of Kemp and Ng, the discoveries were virtually simultaneous. For generalizations of their results, see Pollak, 1979; and Roberts, 1980. For an application to measures of inequality, see Hammond, 1976.

9. Any form that is not lexicographic (which involves some form of dictatorship) and satisfies the Pareto principle.

10. In McManus's (1982, note 5) own words, 'the view that Samuelson attacks is far more common than he states'.

11. The ordinalism and independence aspects are noted by Quirk and Saposnik (1968, p. 110) and analysed by Sen (1970, pp. 89ff.). Osborne (1976) calls the preferencism aspect individualism and the independence aspect localism (in my view, a misnomer, since it suggests a kind of myopia while independence involves nothing of that sort and is quite reasonable). Kemp and Ng (1982) call the preferencism aspect weak individualism and the preferencism and independence aspects combined individualism.

12. It may be noted that the method for aggregating ordinal assessments suggested by Toda, Sugiyama, and Tagawa (1982) violates independence.

13. To be fair to Bergson, it should be noted that this is true only for economic welfare while social welfare may depend on non-economic factors, $r, s, t \ldots$ However, we may either follow Bergson in holding these non-economic factors constant or define our Fundamental Value Proposition as covering changes in these non-economic factors as well. With either alternative, our argument remains valid.

14. While the Expected Subjective Utility Premise is very reasonable, it comes close to assume the result. Ng (1983b) derives the result (that a $N-M$ utility function is subjective in the sense of Edgeworth) from a set of axioms no stronger than that for the $N-M$ hypothesis.

15. I was drawn to note this similarity by my student Eric Ralph who I hope will pursue the issue in more detail.

16. Arrow's (1951, p. 59) assertion that 'the market mechanism does not create a rational social choice' is thus correct though could be misleading since (i) the ordering aspect of IIA need not be met by social choice through the the market which does reveal intensities of preferences, (ii) if the distribution of income can be more or less (continuously) maintained to be 'satisfactory' (optimal), the market solution is acceptable (ideal).

17. Thus, when I was giving a seminar at Nuffield College early in 1974, upon which my 1975a paper is based, a participant interjected, 'Why can't you wait a few more years until 1981?'

18. For other arguments in favour of social welfare as separable in, linear in, and an unweighted sum of individual utilities, see Vickrey, 1945; Fleming, 1952; Harsanyi, 1953, 1955; d'Aspremont and Gevers, 1977; Maskin, 1978; Sugden and Weale, 1979; and a survey by Ng, 1981b.

REFERENCES

Allais, M. and O. Hagen (1979) *Expected Utility Hypothesis and the Allais Paradox*, Dordrecht, Holland: Reidel.

Armstrong, W. E. (1951) 'Utility and the Theory of Welfare', *Oxford Economic Papers*, 3: 257–71.

Arrow, K. J. (1963) *Social Choice and Individual Values*, New York: John Wiley.

Baumol, W. J. (1951) 'The N–M utility Index – An Ordinalist View', *Journal of Political Economy*, 59: 61–6.

Baumol, W. J. (1958) 'The Cardinal Utility Which is Ordinal', *Economic Journal*, 68: 665–72.

Baumol, W. J. (1977) *Economic Theory and Operations Analysis*, 4th edn, London: Prentice-Hall.

Bergson (Burk), A. (1938) 'A Reformulation of Certain Aspects of Welfare Economics', *Quarterly Journal of Economics*, 52: 310–34.

Borda, J. C. de (1781) 'Memoire sur les elections au scrutin', *Memoires de l'Academie Royale des Sciences*, English trans A. de Grazia, Isis, 1953.

Buchanan J. M., and G. Tullock (1962) *The Calculus of Consent*, Ann Arbor: University of Michigan Press.

Camacho, A. (1982) *Societies and Social Decision Functions*, Dordrecht, Holland: Reidel.

Clarke, E. H. (1971) 'Multipart Pricing of Public Goods', *Public Choice*, 11 (Fall): 17–33.

Clarke, E. H. (1980) *Demand Revelation and the Provision of Public Goods*, Cambridge, Mass: Harper & Row Ballinger.

Coleman, J. S. (1966) 'The Possibility of a Social Welfare Function', *American Economic Review*, 56 (December): 1105–22.

D'Aspremont, C., and L. Gevers (1977) 'Equity and the Informational Basis of Collective Choice', *Review of Economic Studies*, 44 (June): 199–209.

DeMeyer, F., and C. R. Plott (1971) 'A Welfare Function Using "Relative Intensity" of Preference', *Quarterly Journal of Economics*, 85: 179–86.

Edgeworth, F. Y. (1881) *Mathematical Psychics*, London: Kegan Paul.

Fishburn, P. C. (1970) 'Intransitive Indifference in Preference Theory: A Survey', *Operations Research*, 18: 207–28.

Fisher, I. (1927) 'A Statistical Method for Measuring "Marginal Utility" and Testing the Justice of a Progressive Income Tax', in *Economic Essays Contributed in Honour of John Bates Clark*, New York: Macmillan.

Fleming, M. (1952) 'A Cardinal Concept of Welfare', *Quarterly Journal of Economics*, 66 (October): 366–84.

Frisch, R. (1932) *New Methods of Measuring Marginal Utility*, Tubingen: Mohr.

Goodman, L. A., and H. Markowitz, (1952) 'Social Welfare Functions Based on Individual Rankings', *American Journal of Sociology*, 58: 257–62.

Groves, T. (1970) 'The Allocation of Resources under Uncertainty: The Informational and Incentive Roles of Prices and Demands in a Team',

PhD dissertation, University of California, Berkeley.

Groves, T. (1973) 'Incentives in Teams', *Econometrica*, 41 (July): 617–33.

Hahn, F. (1982) 'On Some Difficulties of the Utilitarian Economist', in A. Sen and B. Williams, *Utilitarianism and Beyond*, Cambridge: Cambridge University Press.

Hammond, P. (1976) 'Why Ethical Measures of Inequality Need Interpersonal Comparisons', *Theory and Decision*, 7: 262–74.

Hardy, J. D. *et al.* (1952) (new edn 1967) *Pain Sensations and Reactions*, Baltimore, New York: Hafner.

Hare, R. M. (1976) 'Ethical Theory and Utilitarianism', in H. D. Lewis (ed.), *Contemporary British Philosophy*, London: Allen & Unwin.

Harsanyi, J. C. (1953), 'Cardinal Utility in Welfare Economics and in the Theory of Risk-taking', *Journal of Political Economy*, 61 (October): 434–5.

Harsanyi, J. C. (1955) 'Cardinal Welfare, Individualistic Ethics, and Interpersonal Comparison of Utility', *Journal of Political Economy*, 68 (August): 309–21.

Kapteyn, A., and T. J. Wansbeek (1982) *The Individual Welfare Function: Measurement, Explanation and Policy Applications*, The Hague: Staatsnitgeverij.

Kelsey, D. (1982) 'The Role of Information in Social Welfare Judgements', typescript.

Kemp, M. C., and Y-K, Ng. (1976) 'On the Existence of Social Welfare Functions, Social Orderings, and Social Decision Functions', *Economica*, 43 (February): 59–66.

Kemp, M. C., and Y-K, Ng. (1982) 'The Incompatibility of Individualism and Ordinalism', *Mathematical Social Sciences*, 3 (July): 33–8.

Leontief, W. (1966) *Essays in Ecomomics: Theories and Theorizing*, New York: Oxford University Press.

Lerner, A. P. (1944) *The Economics of Control*, New York: Macmillan.

Little, I. M. D. (1952) 'Social Choice and Individual Values', *Journal of Political Economy*, 66 (October): 422–32.

McManus, M. (1982) 'Some Properties of Topological Social Choice Functions', *Review of Economic Studies*, 49: 447–60.

Marschak, J. (1950) 'Rational Behaviour, Uncertain Prospects and Measurable Utility', *Econometrica*, 18: 111–41 and 312.

Maskin, E. (1978) 'A Theorem on Utilitarianism', *Review of Economic Studies*, 45 (February): 93–6.

Mayston, D. (1980) 'Where Did Prescriptive Welfare Economics Go Wrong?', in D. A. Currie and W. Peters (eds), *Contemporary Economic Analysis*, vol. II, Proceedings of 1978 AUTE Conference, London: Croom Helm.

Mayston, D. (1982) 'The Generation of a Social Welfare Function under Ordinal Preferences', *Mathematical Social Sciences*, 3 (September): 109–29.

Miller, N. R. (1977) 'Logrolling, Vote Trading, and the Paradox of Voting', *Public Choice*, 30 (Summer): 51–76.

Mirrlees, J. A. (1982) 'The Economic Uses of Utilitarianism', in A. Sen and B. Williams (eds), *Utilitarianism and Beyond*, Cambridge: Cambridge University Press.

Mueller, D. C. (1967) 'The Possibility of a Social Welfare Function: Comment', *American Economic Review*, 57 (December): 1304–11.

Mueller, D. C. (1979) *Public Choice*, Cambridge: Cambridge University Press.

Murakami, Y. (1961) 'A Note on the General Possibility Theorem of the Social Welfare Function', *Econometrica*, 29 (April): 244–6.

Neumann, J. von, and O. Morgenstern, (1947) *Theory of Games and Economic Behavior*, Princeton: Princeton University Press.

Ng, Y.-K. (1972) 'Value Judgements and Economists' Role in Policy Recommendation', *Economic Journal*, 82 (September): 1014–18. Reprinted in W. Marr and B. Raj, *How Economists Explain: a Reader in Methodology*, Washington: University Press of America, 1983.

Ng, Y.-K. (1975a) 'Bentham or Bergson? Finite Sensibility, Utility Functions, and Social Welfare Functions', *Review of Economic Studies*, 42 (October): 545–70.

Ng, Y.-K. (1975b) 'The Paradox of Universal Externality', *Journal of Economic Theory*, 10 (April): 258–64.

Ng. Y.-K. (1979) (new edn 1983) *Welfare Economics: Introduction and Development of Basic Concepts*, London: Macmillan.

Ng, Y.-K. (1980) 'Toward Eudaimonolgy: Notes on a Quantitive Framework for the Study of Happiness', *Mathematical Social Sciences*, 1 (September): 51–68.

Ng, Y.-K. (1981a) 'Welfarism: A Defence Against Sen's Attack', *Economic Journal*, 91 (June): 527–30.

Ng, Y.-K. (1981b) 'Bentham or Nash? On the Acceptable Form of Social Welfare Functions', *Economic Record*, 57 (September): 238–50.

Ng, Y.-K. (1982a) 'Beyond Pareto Optimality: The Necessity of Interpersonal Cardinal Utilities in Distributional Judgements and Social Choice', *Zeitschrift fur Nationalokomie*, 42 (3): 207–33.

Ng, Y.-K. (1982b) 'Interpersonal Level Comparability Implies Comparability of Utility differences', typescript.

Ng, Y.-K. (1983a) 'Some Broader issues of Social Choice', in P. K. Pattanaik and M. Salles (eds), *Social Choice and Welfare*, Amsterdam: North-Holland.

Ng, Y.-K. (1983b) 'Expected Subjective Utility: Is the Neumann–Morgenstern Utility the Same as the Neoclassical's?', typescript.

Ng, Y.-K. and P. Singer, (1981) 'An Argument for Utilitariansim', *Canadian Journal of Philosophy*, 11 (June): 229–39.

Osborne, D. K. (1976) 'Irrelevant Alternatives and Social Welfare', *Econometrica*, 44 (September): 1001–15.

Park, R. E. (1967) 'The Possibility of a Social Welfare Function: Comment', *American Economic Review*, 57 (December): 1300–4.

Parks, R. P. (1976) 'An Impossibility Theorem for Fixed Preferences: A Dictatorial Bergson–Samuelson Welfare Function', *Review of Economic Studies*, 43 (October): 447–50.

Pattanaik, P. K. (1970) *Voting and Collective Choice*, Cambridge; Cambridge University Press.

Pattanaik, P. K. (1978) *Strategy and Group Choice*, Amsterdam: North-Holland.

Pollak, R. A. (1979) 'Bergson–Samuelson Social Welfare Functions and the Theory of Social Choice', *Quarterly Journal of Economics*, 93 (February): 73–90.

Quirk, J. and R. Saposnik (1968) *Introduction to General Equilibrium Theory and Welfare Economics*, New York: McGraw-Hill.

Rawls, J. (1971) *A Theory of Justice* Oxford: Clarendon.

Robbins, L. (1932) *An Essay on the Nature and Significance of Economic Science*, London: Macmillan.

Robbins, L. (1938) 'Interpersonal Comparison of Utility: A Comment', *Economic Journal*, 48 (December): 635–41.

Roberts, K. W. S. (1980) 'Social Choice Theory: The Single-Profile and Multi-Profile Approaches', *Review of Economic Studies*, 47: 441–50.

Rothenberg, J. (1961) *The Measurement of Social Welfare*, Englewood Cliffs, N.J.: Prentice-Hall.

Samuelson, P. A. (1947) *Foundations of Economic Analysis*, Cambridge, Mass.: Harvard University Press.

Samuelson, P. A. (1967) 'Arrow's Mathematical Politics', in S. Hook (ed.), *Human Values and Economic Policy*, New York: New York University Press.

Samuelson, P. A. (1977) 'Reaffirming the Existence of Reasonable Bergson–Samuelson Social Welfare Functions', *Economica*, 44 (February): 81–8.

Samuelson, P. A. (1981) 'Bergsonian Welfare Economics', in S. Rosefielde (ed.), *Economic Welfare and the Economics of Soviet Socialism: Essays in Honour of Abram Bergson*, Cambridge, Cambridge University Press.

Sen, A. K. (1967) 'The Nature and Classes of Prescriptive Judgements', *Philosophical Quarterly*, 17: 46–62.

Sen, A. K. (1970) *Collective Choice and Social Welfare*, Amsterdam: North-Holland.

Sen, A. K. (1973) 'On Ignorance and Equal Distribution', *American Economic Review*, 63 (December): 1022–4; reprinted in Sen (1982).

Sen, A. K. (1979) 'Personal Utilities and Public Judgements: Or What's Wrong with Welfare Economics?', *Economic Journal*, 89 (September): 537–58; reprinted in Sen (1982).

Sen, A. K. (1981) 'A Reply to "Welfarism: A Defence Against Sen's Attack"', *Economic Journal*, 91 (June): 531–5.

Sen, A. K. (1982) *Choice, Welfare and Measurement*, Oxford: Basil Blackwell.

Smart, J. J. C., and B. A. O. Williams (1973) *Utilitarianism: For and Against*, Cambridge: Cambridge University Press.

Sugden, R., and A. Weale, (1979) 'A Contractual Reformulation of Certain Aspects of Welfare Economics', *Economica*, 46 (May):111–23.

Toda, M., K. Sugiyama and S. Tagawa (1982) 'A Method for Aggregating Ordinal Assessments by a Majority Decision Rule', *Mathematical Social Sciences*, 3 (October): 227–42.

Van Praag, B. M. S. (1968) *Individual Welfare Functions and Consumer Behaviour*, Amsterdam: North-Holland.

Vickrey, W. (1945) 'Measuring Marginal Utilities by Reactions to Risk', *Econometrica*, 13 (October): 319–33.

15 The Welfare Economics of Foreign Aid

MURRAY C. KEMP
AND SHOICHI KOJIMA*

INTRODUCTION[1]

It is part of received doctrine among specialists in the theory of international trade that unilateral transfers harm the donor country and benefit the recipient. In sharp contrast to that doctrine, it has been asserted by specialists in the theory of economic development that, frequently, foreign aid does more harm than good in the recipient country and operates to the advantage of exporters in the donor country.

Some of the more flagrant disparities of conclusion can be traced to equally flagrant disparities of ethical criterion. Thus the act of extending foreign aid is praised as discharging the donor's moral obligations, as possessing virtue in its own right independently of its instrumental properties; and, at the other extreme, it is damned as promoting government intervention in the recipient.

However, the disparity of ethical judgements does not completely account for the disparity of conclusions. There remains a large residue of confusion traceable ultimately to differences of factual assumption, that is, to differences of opinion about how the world economy works. Thus the standard trade-theoretical doctrine, that aid benefits the recipient and harms the donor, is based on the very strict factual assumptions that the recipient and donor trade only with each other, that neither country is hampered by commodity taxes or other distortions, and that the two countries taken as a whole are dynamically stable in the Walrasian sense.[2] And the counter-claim that aid may harm the recipient often is argued from the factual assumption that the amount received in aid is spent on

---

* The views expressed in this chapter are not necessarily those of the United Nations.

projects that are wasteful in a quite literal sense. Thus Peter Bauer has stated that:

> [it] is by no means unusual for projects to absorb domestic inputs of greater value than the net output, especially when the cost of administering the projects and the explicit or implicit obligation to maintain and replace the fixed assets originally donated is also considered. Large losses in activities and projects financed by aid have been reported in many poor countries. In fact they have been a recurrent theme of official reports in India and Ceylon. Though it is difficult to assess in each instance exactly what costs have been taken into consideration in these documents, the losses have often been so huge that it is safe to assume that the country would have been better off without the project (Bauer, 1971, pp. 99–100).

Aid financed projects may be ill-conceived without being blatantly wasteful in the manner indicated by Bauer. Indeed it is likely that only a small proportion of all aid is applied in a grossly wasteful way. On the other hand, donors almost always require that aid be spent in a manner not closely related to private preferences in the recipient countries, indeed not closely related to *any* well-behaved preferences; and they normally finance the aid by means of distorting taxation. Thus it seems that most aid-financed programmes fall in the middle ground between complete efficiency and gross inefficiency. Clearly, one cannot rule out by appeal to standard trade theorems the possibility that such programmes perversely leave the donor better off and/or the recipient worse off. Nor can we be sure without further analysis that perverse outcomes are possible. For aid-financed projects falling in this middle ground we need a new analysis that will yield necessary and sufficient conditions for donor-enrichment and recipient-impoverishment.

Let us say that aid is *tied in the recipient country* if it is spent inefficiently in terms of individual preferences in that country, and that aid is *tied in the donor country* if it is financed inefficiently. Thus whether or not aid is tied is a question of how it is spent and how it is financed. It is not a question of the numeraire in terms of which aid is accounted nor of the form in which it is offered. Evidently this definition of tying is uncommonly broad. For example, aid may be tied in the recipient not because the donor attaches strings but because the government of the recipient is incompetent or unrepresentative. Moreover, the definition is relevant however the aid is applied – whether to private or public goods, whether to consumption or investment goods. In this chapter we shall for the most part follow the conventions of the trade-theoretical literature on 'the transfer problem', assuming that aid is spent on private consumption goods, like hospital services and powdered milk. However, that is a matter of convenience and continuity only and it will be shown that our analysis can be reworked to accommodate public consumption goods, like guns and anti-malaria programmes, as well as investment goods, like highways and dams.

In the present chapter we seek to rework the economics of foreign aid under relaxed assumptions. In particular, allowance will be made for the possibility that aid is tied, in whole or in part, in the donor or in the recipient. It will be verified that the donor may benefit and the recipient suffer and that these outcomes are compatible with market stability. Indeed the formal analysis of later sections culminates in a set of necessary and sufficient conditions for perverse outcomes in stable economies.

We are not the first to have demonstrated that international transfers might have perverse outcomes. Thus David Gale (1974) has shown that if there is a third country, not a party to the transfer but trading with one or both of those parties, then both the donor and the recipient may be left better off.[3] On the other hand, Brecher and Bhagwati (1982) have shown that the recipient may be harmed by a gift if its production is distorted by taxes and if one commodity is inferior in consumption.[4] Brecher and Bhagwati also note that aid may be accompanied by production 'additionality requirements' (as in the administration of the US PL 480) and suggest that such requirements may give rise to the impoverishment of a small recipient. In the light of these findings, we note that our own demonstration of the possibility of perverse outcomes relies not on inferiority nor on the presence of a third country nor on additionality requirements. We note also that we manage with just the standard pair of commodities.

We begin, in the second section, by establishing our notation and demonstrating the possibility of perverse outcomes in a special case, with aid wholly tied in the recipient and wholly untied in the donor and with only private consumption goods recognized. Then, in the third section, we offer a general treatment of the case in which both goods are specialized to private consumption, culminating in a necessary and sufficient condition for perversity combined with market stability. Finally, in the fourth section, we demonstrate that, after some reinterpretation of terms, the analysis and conclusions of the third section apply to economies in which each of the two produced commodities can play any or all of the roles of private consumption good, public consumption good, private intermediate good and public intermediate good.

PRIVATE CONSUMPTION GOODS – A SPECIAL CASE

There are two countries, α and β; and there are two commodities, 1 and 2. Each commodity is a private consumption good. In an initial world trading equilibrium country α exports commodity 1 and country β exports commodity 2. The initial equilibrium is disturbed when α extends aid to β.

The following notation will be employed:

T the amount of aid, in terms of commodity 2, from country α (the donor) to country β (the recipient); initially, $T = 0$;

p the price of commodity 1 in terms of commodity 2;

u^j the utility derived from privately budgeted consumption in country j ($j = \alpha, \beta$);

v^j the utility derived in country j from consumption not privately budgeted ($j = \alpha, \beta$); initially $v^j = 0$;

$w^j \equiv u^j + v^j$ the welfare of country j ($j = \alpha, \beta$);

e^j the expenditure function of country j, expenditure in terms of commodity 2 ($j = \alpha, \beta$);

r^j the revenue function of country j, revenue in terms of commodity 2 ($j = \alpha, \beta$);

$c^{ji}(p, u^i)$ the compensated private demand for commodity i by country j ($i = 1, 2; j = \alpha, \beta$);

$x^{ji}(p)$ the output of commodity i in the country j ($i = 1, 2; j = \alpha, \beta$);

$z^{ji}(p, u^j) \equiv c^{ji}(p, u^j) - x^{ji}(p)$ the excess private demand of country j for commodity i ($i = 1, 2; j = q, \beta$).

The aid is financed in α by means of lump-sum taxes. The private budget constraint of α is therefore:

$$e^{\alpha}(p, u^{\alpha}) = r^{\alpha}(p) - T \tag{15.1}$$

The aid is spent by the government of β; it therefore influences the welfare w^{β} of β but does not enter its private budget constraint:

$$e^{\beta}(p, u^{\beta}) = r^{\beta}(p) \tag{15.2}$$

The description of world equilibrium is completed by the market-clearing condition:[5]

$$z^{\alpha 1}(p, u^{\alpha}) + z^{\beta 1}(p, u^{\beta}) + m^{\beta}T/p = 0 \tag{15.3}$$

where m^β is the proportion of aid spent by the government of β on commodity 1 $(0 \leqslant m^\beta \leqslant 1)$.[6] Equations (15.1)–(15.3) contain the three variables u^α, u^β and p, as well as the parameter T. The system is assumed to possess a unique solution $(p^*, u^{\alpha*}, u^{\beta*})$ with p^* positive and finite.

Differentiating (15.1)–(15.3) with respect to T we find that:

$$
\begin{pmatrix}
e_p^\alpha - r_p^\alpha & e_u^\alpha & 0 \\
e_p^\beta - r_p^\beta & 0 & e_u^\beta \\
z_p^{\alpha 1} + z_p^{\beta 1} - (T/p^2) z_u^{\alpha 1} & z_u^{\beta 1}
\end{pmatrix}
\begin{pmatrix}
dp \\
du^\alpha \\
du^\beta
\end{pmatrix}
=
\begin{pmatrix}
-1 \\
0 \\
-m^\beta/p
\end{pmatrix}
dT
$$

(15.4)

where subscripts indicate differentiation $(e_p^\alpha \equiv \partial e^\alpha / \partial p, r_p^\alpha \equiv dr^\alpha / dp$, etc.). Recalling the envelope result that $e_p^j - r_p^j = z^{j1}$ $(j = \alpha, \beta)$, choosing units of utility so that $e_u^j = 1$, and recalling that $T = 0$, (15.4) reduces to:

$$
\begin{pmatrix}
z^{\alpha 1} & 1 & 0 \\
z^{\beta 1} & 0 & 1 \\
z_p^{\alpha 1} + z_p^{\beta 1} & z_u^{\alpha 1} & z_u^{\beta 1}
\end{pmatrix}
\begin{pmatrix}
dp \\
du^\alpha \\
du^\beta
\end{pmatrix}
=
\begin{pmatrix}
-1 \\
0 \\
-m^\beta/p
\end{pmatrix}
dt
$$

(15.5)

Solving:

$$
\Delta \frac{dp}{dT} = -\frac{m^\beta - pz_u^{\alpha 1}}{p}
$$

$$
\Delta \frac{du^\alpha}{dT} = -(z_p^{\alpha 1} + z_p^{\beta 1}) - \frac{z^{\beta 1}(m^\beta - pz_u^{\beta 1})}{p}
$$

(15.6)

$$
\Delta \frac{du^\beta}{dT} = \frac{z^{\beta 1}(m^\beta - pz_u^{\alpha 1})}{p}
$$

where:

$$
\Delta \equiv z_p^{\alpha 1} + z_p^{\beta 1} + z^{\beta 1} \cdot (z_u^{\alpha 1} - z_u^{\beta 1})
$$

(15.7)

is the determinant of the matrix of coefficients in (15.5).

We seek to attach a sign to Δ. To this end, consider the dynamic system consisting of (15.1), (15.2) and:

$$\dot{p} = z^{\alpha 1}(p, u^{\alpha}) + z^{\beta 1}(p, u^{\beta}) \tag{15.8}$$

Linearizing the system at the equilibrium values of the variables, we obtain:

$$z^{\alpha 1} \cdot (p - p^*) + (u^{\alpha} - u^{\alpha}*) = 0$$

$$z^{\beta 1} \cdot (p - p^*) + (u^{\beta} - u^{\beta}*) = 0$$

$$\dot{p} = z_p^{\alpha 1} \cdot (p - p^*) + z_u^{\alpha 1} \cdot (u^{\alpha} - u^{\alpha}*) + z_p^{\beta 1} \cdot (p - p^*)$$

$$+ z_u^{\beta 1} \cdot (u^{\beta} - u^{\beta}*) \tag{15.9}$$

where the functions z^{ji}, z_p^{ji} and z_u^{ji} are evaluated at $(p^*, u^{\alpha}*, u^{\beta}*)$. Eliminating $(u^{\alpha} - u^{\alpha}*)$ and $(u^{\beta} - u^{\beta}*)$, and defining $\pi \equiv p - p^*$, (15.9) reduces to:

$$\dot{\pi} = \Delta \pi \tag{15.10}$$

Thus for local stability of the system it is necessary and sufficient that:

$$\Delta < 0 \tag{15.7a}$$

Returning to (15.6), we see immediately that if the system (15.9) is stable and if the recipient government has a higher marginal propensity to buy the donor's export good than do individuals in the donor country, that is, if $m^{\beta} > p z_u^{\alpha 1}$, then $dp/dT > 0$, that is, the terms of trade turn in favour of the donor. Can they turn so far in favour of the donor as to cancel the welfare loss directly associated with aid? Bearing in mind that the pure substitution terms $z_p^{\alpha 1}$ and $z_p^{\beta 1}$ are negative and that, by assumption $z^{\beta 1} > 0$, it follows from (15.6) and (15.7) and (15.7a) that for both stability and $du^{\alpha}/dT > 0$ it is necessary and sufficient that:

$$-\frac{z^{\beta 1}}{p}(m^{\beta} - p z_u^{\beta 1}) < z_p^{\alpha 1} + z_p^{\beta 1} < -z^{\beta 1}(z_u^{\alpha 1} - z_u^{\beta 1}) \tag{15.11}$$

Evidently this condition can be satisfied without inferiority. However it does require that the recipient's offer curve be inelastic at the point of initial equilibrium. Consider the first inequality of (15.11). Making use of the well-known relationship between substitution terms:

$$p z_p^{\beta 1} + z_p^{\beta 2} = 0$$

and of the identity between marginal propensities to consume:

$$pz_u^{\beta 1} + z_u^{\beta 2} = 1$$

that inequality can be rewritten as:

$$z_p^{\beta 2} + z^{\beta 1} z_u^{\beta 2} < pz_p^{\alpha 1} - (1 - m^{\beta})z^{\beta 1} < 0 \qquad (15.12)$$

But the left-hand expression in (15.12) is the total derivative $dz^{\beta 2}/dp$; hence $dz^{\beta 2}/d(1/p) < 0$. Thus the recipient's offer of its export commodity decreases when its terms of trade improve, implying that the recipient's offer curve is inelastic.

Consider now the fate of the recipient. We have, from the definition of w^{β}:

$$\frac{dw^{\beta}}{dT} = \frac{du^{\beta}}{dT} + \frac{dv^{\beta}}{dT} \qquad (15.13)$$

But:

$$\frac{dv^{\beta}}{dT} = \frac{\partial v^{\beta}}{\partial \bar{c}^{\beta 1}}\frac{d\bar{c}^{\beta 1}}{dT} + \frac{\partial v^{\beta}}{\partial \bar{c}^{\beta 2}}\frac{d\bar{c}^{\beta 2}}{dT}$$

where $\bar{c}^{\beta i}$ is that part of the consumption of commodity i in country β that is not privately budgeted. Moreover:

$$\frac{\partial v^{\beta}}{\partial \bar{c}^{\beta i}} + \frac{\partial u^{\beta}}{\partial c^{\beta i}} \qquad i = 1, 2$$

$$\frac{\partial u^{\beta}}{\partial c^{\beta 1}} = p \frac{\partial u^{\beta}}{\partial c^{\beta 2}}$$

and:

$$\frac{d\bar{c}^{\beta 1}}{dT} = \frac{m^{\beta}}{p}, \frac{d\bar{c}^{\beta 2}}{dT} = 1 - m^{\beta}$$

Hence:

$$\frac{dv^{\beta}}{dT} = \frac{\partial u^{\beta}}{\partial c^{\beta 2}} = 1 \qquad (15.14)$$

and, recalling (15.6), (15.13) reduces to:

$$\frac{dw^\beta}{dT} = \frac{du^\beta}{dT} + 1 \qquad\qquad (15.15)$$

$$= \frac{1}{p\Delta} \left[p(z_p^{\alpha 1} + z_p^{\beta 1}) + z^{\beta 1}(m^\beta - pz_u^{\beta 1}) \right]$$

$$= \frac{du^\alpha}{dT}$$

(Equation (15.15) can be obtained less formally by observing that, since the initial equilibrium is Pareto optimal, a small change in the real income of α must be accompanied by an opposite change in the real income of β and by applying the normalization $e_u^j = 1$.)

Proposition: Let aid be wholly tied in the recipient, wholly untied in the donor. If and only if condition (15.11) is satisfied, the world economy is stable, the donor benefits from aid and the recipient suffers.

Before passing to the general case, let us pause to consider the common-sense of the proposition. Because the aid is marginal it has the same direct welfare effect however it is spent by the government of β (recall equation (15.14)). But its indirect welfare effects, through prices, do depend on how it is spent. If $m^\beta \neq p z_u^{\beta 1}$, that is, if the government's marginal propensity to spend on the first commodity differs from the corresponding marginal propensity to consume of individuals in β then, in effect, the Engel curves of β contain kinks at the initial equilibrium point. The kinks operate to moderate or magnify the price effects of the transfer. In particular, if $m^\beta > p - z_u^{\beta 1}$, that is, if the marginal propensity of the β-government is larger than that of β-individuals then any aid-induced increase in p (improvement in α's terms of trade) must be exaggerated and it is this exaggeration of the price change that lies behind any perverse welfare outcomes.

Finally, we seek to forestall a possible criticism. We have shown that, even in a stable two-country world, foreign aid may be paradoxical in its effects on national welfare. However, in our model there are not two but three agents — the donor country α, the private sector of the recipient country β, and the government of β — and this might suggest that, formally, ours is merely a special setting of a well-known result. However it is easy to verify that the possibility of donor-enrichment remains even if the private sector of β is suppressed. And by reversing the roles of α and the government of β one can confirm the possibility of recipient-impoverishment with only two agents.

PRIVATE CONSUMPTION GOODS – THE GENERAL CASE

Attention has been focused on an extreme case, in which the whole of aid is tied in the recipient, untied in the donor. We now sketch, briefly, a general analysis in which a proportion $1 - t^j$ of the aid is tied in country j $(j = \alpha, \beta)$, where $0 \leqslant t^j \leqslant 1$. Thus the parameters t^α and t^β indicate the degree of inefficiency in the supply and application of aid. In the case considered in the second section, $t^\alpha = 1$ and $t^\beta = 0$.

Instead of equations (15.1)–(15.3) we now have, respectively:

$$e^\alpha(p, u^\alpha) = r^\alpha(p) - t^\alpha T \tag{15.16}$$

$$e^\beta(p, u^\beta) = r^\beta(p) + t^\beta T \tag{15.17}$$

$$z^{\alpha 1}(p, u^\alpha) + z^{\beta 1}(p, u^\beta) - [m^\alpha(1 - t^\alpha) - m^\beta(1 - t^\beta)] T/p$$

$$= 0 \tag{15.18}$$

and instead of (15.5) we have:

$$\begin{pmatrix} z^{\alpha 1} & 1 & 0 \\ z^{\beta 1} & 0 & 1 \\ z_p^{\alpha 1} + z_p^{\beta 1} & z_p^{\alpha 1} & z_u^{\beta 1} \end{pmatrix} \begin{pmatrix} dp \\ du^\alpha \\ du^\beta \end{pmatrix} = \begin{pmatrix} -t^\alpha \\ t^\beta \\ [m^\alpha(1 - t^\alpha) - m^\beta(1 - t^\beta)]/p \end{pmatrix} dT \tag{15.19}$$

whence, solving:

$$\Delta \frac{dp}{dT} = t^\alpha z_u^{\alpha 1} - t^\beta z_u^{\beta 1} + [m^\alpha(1 - t^\alpha) - m^\beta(1 - t^\beta)]/p$$

$$\Delta \frac{du^\alpha}{dT} = t^\alpha(z^{\beta 1} z_u^{\beta 1} - z_p^{\alpha 1} - z_p^{\beta 1}) + t^\beta z^{\alpha 1} z_u^{\beta 1}$$

$$- z^{\alpha 1} [m^\alpha(1 - t^\alpha) - m^\beta(1 - t^\beta)]/p$$

$$\Delta \frac{du^\beta}{dT} = -t^\alpha z^{\beta 1} z_u^{\alpha 1} - t^\beta (z^{\alpha 1} z_u^{\alpha 1} - z_p^{\alpha 1} - z_p^{\beta 1}) -$$

$$- z^{\beta 1} [m^\alpha (1 - t^\alpha) - m^\beta (1 - t^\beta)]/p \qquad (15.20)$$

From the definition of w^j:

$$\frac{dw^j}{dT} = \frac{du^j}{dT} + \frac{dv^j}{dT} \qquad j = \alpha, \beta \qquad (15.21)$$

and, by a slight extension of earlier reasoning:

$$\frac{dv^\alpha}{dT} = -(1 - t^\alpha) \frac{\partial u^\alpha}{\partial c^{\alpha 2}} = (1 - t^\alpha) \qquad (15.22)$$

$$\frac{dv^\beta}{dT} = (1 - t^\beta) \frac{\partial u^\beta}{\partial c^{\beta 2}} = (1 - t^\beta)$$

It can then be calculated that;

$$\frac{dw^\alpha}{dT} = \frac{du^\alpha}{dT} - (1 - t^\alpha) = - \left[\frac{du^\beta}{dT} + (1 - t^\beta) \right] = -\frac{dw^\beta}{dT}$$

and that for stability and perverse welfare effects ($dw^\alpha/dT > 0$, dw^β/dT < 0) it is necessary and sufficient that:

$$\frac{z^{\beta 1}}{p} [(1 - t^\alpha)(m^\alpha - pz_u^{\alpha 1}) - (1 - t^\beta)(m^\beta - pz_u^{\beta 1})] < z_p^{\alpha 1} + z_p^{\beta 1}$$

$$< - z^{\beta 1} (z_u^{\alpha 1} - z_u^{\beta 1}) \qquad (15.23)$$

it is easy to verify that when $t^\alpha = t^\beta = 1$ (the conventional case) condition (15.23) cannot be satisfied. On the other hand, (15.24) can be satisfied whatever the relative values of t^α and t^β provided only that one of t^α and t^β is less than one. It can be verified also that, when $t^\alpha = 1$ and $t^\beta = 0$, (15.24) reduces to (15.12) and that, when $t^\alpha = 0$ and $t^\beta = 1$, (15.24) reduces to:

$$\frac{z^{\beta 1}}{p} (m^\alpha - pz_u^{\alpha 1}) < z_p^{\alpha 1} + z_p^{\beta 1} < - z^{\beta 1} (z_u^{\alpha 1} - z_u^{\beta 1}) \qquad (15.24)$$

and we obtain a proposition companion to that of the second section. By earlier reasoning, the first inequality of (15.24) can be rewritten as:

$$-(z_p^{\alpha 1} - z^{\alpha 1} z_u^{\alpha 1}) < z_p^{\beta 1} - m^\alpha z^{\beta 1}/p < 0 \qquad (15.25)$$

But the left-hand expression in (15.25) is the total derivative $-dz^{\alpha 1}/dp$. Hence the donor's offer of its export commodity decreases when its terms of trade improve, implying that the donor's offer curve is inelastic.

Theorem: If and only if condition (15.23) is satisfied, the world economy is stable, the donor benefits from aid and the recipient suffers.

PUBLIC CONSUMPTION GOODS, PRIVATE AND PUBLIC INTERMEDIATE GOODS

Throughout the second and third sections we have maintained the assumption that each of the two commodities is a specialized private consumption good. However, most non-private international aid is spent on public goods, either public consumption goods or public intermediate goods. In the present section we therefore vary our earlier assumption and sketch the implications of allowing for the possibility that each commodity is versatile, capable of serving as a private consumption good or as a pure public consumption good, as a private intermediate good or as a public intermediate good. It will be shown that those implications are approximately nil, that subject to straightforward reinterpretation our earlier conclusions (summarized by inequality (15.23) and by the Theorem) carry over.

Of course the achievement of such a striking effect requires careful staging. In particular, it is assumed in the present section, as in the second and third sections, that before the advent of aid each country enjoys an efficient allocation of resources. This means that in country j the marginal utility derived from commodity i is the same whatever the role it plays – as private or public consumption good, as private or public intermediate good. This in turn implies that however the aid is spent – whether by individuals or by government, whether on private consumption goods or on public, whether on private intermediate goods or on public – it will generate the same increment of welfare as when it is spent entirely on one private consumption good or the other. It implies also that formula (15.23) continues to serve provided only that m^j is interpreted as the proportion of aid spent on commodity 1 in all of its roles and that pz_u^{j1}

is interpreted as country *j*'s marginal propensity to consume commodity 1, when the allocation of expenditure over the two commodities and the allocation of each commodity to its several roles are optimally chosen.

Thus the introduction of public consumption goods and of private and public intermediate goods leaves intact our general conclusion that international aid may generate perverse welfare changes, both in the donor and in the recipient country. Indeed, given the special assumptions (staging) of this section, the precise Theorem of the third section carries over after only minor reinterpretation.

FINAL REMARKS

Ours will not be the last word on the welfare implications of tied foreign aid. Indeed, in some respects our discussion has been quite narrow in scope, and it is to be hoped that others will be quick to offer a bolder analysis.

For example, it bears emphasis that the Theorem of the third section is a *local* result; it relates to small changes around a base of zero. But the world economy is non-linear. What is the case locally may be quite otherwise for substantial changes in the amount of aid: sufficiently large aid programmes may have perverse welfare implications, sufficiently small programmes non-perverse implications.

Moreover, our discussion has been unrelentingly static. In a more ambitious analysis one would want to consider economies progressing through time, not necessarily in a steady state and receiving or giving aid at a rate that is itself dependent on time. In the context of such an analysis one could ask questions that make no sense when one is bound to think in static terms. How does a change in aid affect the path of local saving or the path of private foreign investment? Can the inefficient use of aid during one sub-period give rise to perverse welfare changes in another subperiod?[6] But one would not expect an explicit dynamic analysis to overturn the qualitative conclusions of the preceding two sections.

NOTES

1. Some passages in this section, and the analysis of the second section, are borrowed from Kemp and Kojima, 1982.
2. See Samuelson, 1947, p. 29.
3. Gale's example involves pure exchange, two commodities and individual preferences of the fixed proportions type. But perverse out-

comes are possible without those special features. Thus Léonard and Manning (1982) have shown how to construct whole families of two-commodity examples characterized by smooth preferences, market stability and perverse welfare outcomes of Gale's type; and Guesnerie and Laffont (1978) have shown that such 'advantageous reallocations' are possible with any larger number of commodities. The phenomenon of perversity in three-country economies is further discussed by Yano (1982) and by Bhagwati, Brecher and Hatta (1982). Unaware of the earlier work of Gale and of Guesnerie and Laffont, Brecher and Bhagwati (1981) examined the welfare implications of an international transfer in the context of a two-country but three-agent model and reached conclusions of Gale type.

4. The finding of Brecher and Bhagwati was anticipated in part by Ohyama (1972) who suggested that the recipient might be harmed by a gift if its production, consumption or trade is distorted by taxes of given magnitude, and noted that the result is more likely if one good is inferior in consumption. He also observed that the recipient cannot be impoverished if its tariff rate adjusts to hold imports or exports to its pre-aid level.

On the other hand, it an unpublished paper, Hatta (1973) showed that if there is a uniform wedge between consumer and producer prices in a closed economy then a transfer from one agent to another might leave the recipient worse off; and he showed that this outcome is consistent with market stability.

5. Alternatively, we may make use of the market-clearing condition:

$$z^{\alpha 2}(\quad) + z^{\beta 2}(\quad) = 0 \tag{A15.3}$$

However, from (15.1) and (15.2):

$$pz^{\alpha 1} + z^{\alpha 2} + T = 0 \tag{A15.1}$$

$$pz^{\beta 1} + z^{\beta 2} \quad = 0 \tag{A15.2}$$

Substituting from (A15.1) and (A15.2) into (A15.3), we obtain (A15.3).

6. These questions often have been asked at the empirical level. See, for example, Papanek, 1973; and Mosley, 1980.

REFERENCES

Bauer, P. T. (1971) *Dissent on Development Studies and Debates in Developmental Economics*, London: Weidenfeld & Nicolson.

Bhagwati, J. N., R. A. Brecher and T. Hatta (1982) 'The Generalized Theory of Transfers and Welfare' Columbia University, mimeo

Brecher, R. A., and J. N. Bhagwati (1981) 'Foreign Ownership and the Theory of Trade and Welfare', *Journal of Political Economy*, 89: 497–511.

Brecher, R. A., and J. N. Bhagwati (1982) 'Immiserizing Transfers from Abroad'. *Journal of International Economics*, 13: 353–64.

Gale, D. (1974) 'Exchange Equilibrium and Coalitions: An Example, *Journal of Mathematical Economics*, 1: 63–6.

Guesnerie, R., and J. -J. Laffont (1978) 'Advantageous Reallocations of Initial Resources', *Econometrica*, 46: 835–41.

Kemp, M. C., and S. Kojima (1982) 'Tied Aid and the Paradoxes of Donor-enrichment and Recipient-impoverishment', University of New South Wales, mimeo.

Hatta, T. (1973), 'Compensation Rules in Multiple-consumer Economies', Johns Hopkins University, mimeo.

Léonard, D., and R. Manning (1982) 'Advantageous Reallocations: A Constructive Example', University of New South Wales, mimeo.

Mosley, P. (1980) 'Aid, Savings and Growth Revisited', *Oxford Bulletin of Economics and Statistics*, 42: 79–95.

Ohyama, M. (1972) 'Trade and Welfare in General Equilibrium', *Keio Economic Studies*, 9: 37–73.

Papanek, G. F. (1973) 'Aid, Foreign Private Investment, Savings and Growth in Less Developed Countries', *Journal of Political Economy*, 81: 120–30.

Samuelson, P. A. (1947) *Foundations of Economic Analysis*, Cambridge, Mass. Harvard University Press.

Yano, M. (1982) 'Welfare Aspects of the Transfer Problem: on the Validity of the "New-orthodox" Presumptions', Cornell University, mimeo.

16 The Technology of Joint Consumption

LAURENCE J. LAU*

INTRODUCTION

It has frequently been asserted that 'two can live as cheaply as one'; that is, there are economies of scale in joint consumption. Casual empiricism indicates that the existence of such economies may be plausible. For example, a one-bedroom apartment can accommodate a couple as well as a single individual. For another example, a space heater can provide warmth for one or more individuals. For still another example, a television set may be viewed simultaneously by several individuals.

What precisely does it mean, however, to say that 'two can live as cheaply as one'? Clearly two can always live as cheaply as one if the standard of living is allowed to be lowered. Thus, implicit in the statement must be the maintenance of some kind of standard. A reasonable interpretation is therefore that it is *possible* for two individuals living together to *each* achieve the same level of individual satisfaction (as measured by the respective individual utility functions) as that achieved by a single individual living alone under the same total expenditure constraint, other things being equal.[1] Of course, the two individuals living together may also derive satisfaction solely from the company of each other, unrelated to the consumption of any goods and services. Such satisfaction, however, must be excluded from our consideration here. To the extent that such satisfaction is important, we shall have underestimated the individual utilities of

* I am grateful to Kenneth Arrow and George Feiwel for their insightful suggestions. This note was completed while I was a Fellow at the Center for Advanced Study in the Behavioral Sciences. Financial support provided by National Science Foundation Grant no. BNS8206304 at the Center is gratefully acknowledged. This work was also partially supported by National Science Foundation Grant no. SOC77-11105 at the Department of Economics, Stanford University.

the two individuals living together relative to the individual utility of the single individual living alone and thus the economies of joint consumption.[2]

It is important to note that the primary concern here is with the technological possibilities of joint consumption. Whether both of the individuals *actually* achieve the same level of individual satisfaction as the single individual depends not only on the technology of joint consumption but also on the individual utility functions and the rules of allocation of consumption expenditures and distribution of consumption goods and services within the two-individual household.[3] Whether they *can*, however, depends only on the technology of joint consumption and the individual utility functions.

The traditional approach to the modelling of joint consumption consists of specifying the quantity of a commodity consumed by a household as a function of the number of individuals in the household (with adjustments for age and sex as necessary), prices and total expenditure. However, even if all individual utility functions are identical,[4] the rules of allocation and distribution may still vary from household to household. Thus, corresponding to the same technology of joint consumption, given the number of individuals in the household, prices and total household expenditure, the resulting actual pattern of household consumption may still differ across households.[5] In any case, it is not in general possible to relate directly the dependence of the quantities of consumption commodities consumed on the number of individuals in the household to the economies of scale in the technology of joint consumption. In particular, the former is the result of the complex interactions among the technology, the individual tastes, and the household rules of allocation and distribution. In order to identify the technology of joint consumption,[6] it is necessary to specify it explicitly and independently of the individual utility functions and the household rules of allocation and distribution.

The purpose of this chapter is to propose a new approach to modelling the technology of joint consumption within a household, with a view to the potential empirical identification of the nature of the economies of scale if they indeed exist. The technology of joint consumption is specified explicitly and independently of the individual utility functions and household rules of allocation and distribution. The basic new idea consists of distinguishing between the quantity of a consumption commodity purchased and the quantities of the 'services' that this commodity provides to each individual of the household. The quantities of the services provided to each individual are assumed to be produced by the purchased commodity in accordance with a production function, using the purchased commodity as an input.

More specifically, let there be two individuals in the household and m commodities, $X_1, \ldots, X_m$. Each commodity provides a service to each of the two individuals in accordance with a production function which is represented as:

$$f_j(X_{1j}, X_{2j}) = X_j, \qquad j = 1, \ldots m$$

where X_{ij} is the quantity of the service of the jth commodity consumed by the ith individual. It is always non-negative. The $f_j(\cdot)$s may also be referred to as 'purchase requirement functions'. Implicit in this analysis is the assumption that each individual has a utility function $U_i(X_{i1}, \ldots, X_{im})$ which depends only on the quantities of services consumed by the individual himself. The household is assumed to have internal rules of allocation of consumption expenditures and distribution of consumption goods and services. An example of such a rule is the maximization of a welfare function which is a function of the individual utilities subject to the production function and the budget constraints.

It is tempting to interpret the X_{ij}s as either characteristic commodities or outputs of 'household production'. We do not make this interpretation because we want to associate the X_{ij}s directly with actual individual demands that are identifiable under specified circumstances.

PROPERTIES OF THE JOINT CONSUMPTION TECHNOLOGY

We begin by specifying plausible properties for the production functions $f_j(\cdot)$s which are assumed to be defined over the whole non-negative orthant of R^2.

(1) *Origin.* If the quantities of services of the jth commodity provided to each individual are zeroes, the quantity of the jth commodity purchased is zero, that is:

$$f_j(0, 0) = 0, \qquad j = 1, \ldots, m$$

(2) *Positivity.* If the quantities of services of the jth commodity are not identically zeroes, the quantity of the jth commodity purchased is positive, that is:

$$f_j(X_{1j}, X_{2j}) > 0 \quad \text{unless} \quad X_{1j} = X_{2j} = 0; \qquad j = 1, \ldots, m$$

(3) *Single-consumer equivalence.* If there is only a single consuming individual for a commodity, then the quantity of the service is equal to the quantity of the commodity purchased, that is:

$$f_j(X_{1j}, 0) = X_{1j} \qquad j = 1, \ldots, m$$

(4) *Symmetry.* The production function is independent of the final consumer of the service, that is:

$$f_j(X_{1j}, X_{2j}) = f_j(X_{2j}, X_{1j}); \qquad j = 1, \ldots, m$$

(5) *Monotonicity.* If the quantity of the service to an individual is to be increased, holding the quantity of the service to the other individual constant, the quantity of the commodity purchased is not decreased, that is:

$$f_j(X'_{1j}, X_{2j}) \geqslant f_j(X_{1j}, X_{2j}) \quad \text{for all } X'_{1j} \geqslant X_{1j}, \qquad j = 1, \ldots, m$$

(6) *Quasiconvexity.* For a fixed quantity of a commodity purchased, the set of all feasible pairs of services $\{ X_{1j}, X_{2j} \}$ is a convex set, that is the set

$$\left\{ \begin{bmatrix} X_{1j} \\ X_{2j} \end{bmatrix} \mid f_j(X_{1j}, X_{2j}) \leqslant \bar{X}_j, \begin{bmatrix} X_{1j} \\ X_{2j} \end{bmatrix} \geqslant 0 \right\} \text{ is convex; } j = 1, \ldots, m$$

(7) *Homogeneity.* If the quantities of services provided to the individuals are increased in the same proportion, the quantity of the commodity purchased is also increased in the same proportion, that is:

$$f_j(\lambda X_{1j}, \lambda X_{2j}) = \lambda f_j(X_{1j}, X_{2j})$$

(8) *Subadditivity.* The sum of quantities of services *jointly* provided is always greater than or equal to the quantity of the commodity purchased, that is:

$$X_{1j} + X_{2j} \geqslant f_j(X_{1j}, X_{2j}), \qquad j = 1, \ldots, m$$

Property (2) implies that any non-zero quantity of service requires a positive quantity of the commodity to be purchased.

Property (3) implies that if there is only a single individual in the household there can be no economies of joint consumption.

Property (6) implies that the production possibility frontier of the jth commodity takes the form of the curve in Figure 16.1.

Properties (2), (6) and (7) together imply that the production function is convex.[7] But notice that the homogeneity property (7) does not imply that there are no economies in joint consumption. The economies arise from property (8), subadditivity.

Property (8) implies that the sum of quantities of services consumed is at least as great as the quantity of the commodity purchased. It cannot be strictly smaller because then each of the individual consumers will be better off purchasing and consuming separately. In the case in which the commodity is a completely private good, for example, clothing, it is reasonable to suppose that:

$$f_j(X_{1j}, X_{2j}) = X_{1j} + X_{2j}$$

In other words, there are no particular economies of joint consumption. In the case in which the commodity is a public good, for example, housing,

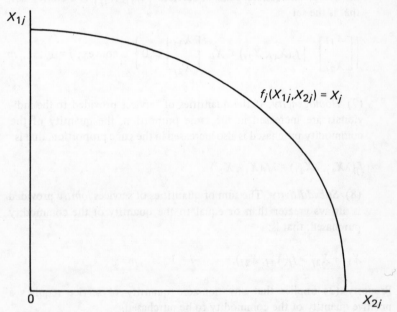

FIGURE 16.1   *A production possibility frontier of the technology of joint consumption*

it is plausible to suppose that:

$$f_j(X_{1j}, X_{2j}) = \max(X_{1j}, X_{2j})$$

$$\leqslant X_{1j} + X_{2j}$$

An example of a production function that has all the above properties is:

$$f_j(X_{1j}, X_{2j}) = \left(X_{1j}^{r_j} + X_{2j}^{r_j}\right)^{\frac{1}{r_j}}, \quad r_j \geqslant 1.\,[8]$$

We now show that properties (2), (3), (6) and (7) imply property (8).

Lemma 1: Properties (2), (3), (6) and (7) imply property (8).

Proof: Properties (2), (6) and (7) together imply that $f_j(\cdot)$ is homogeneous of degree one and convex. Consider:

$$\tfrac{1}{2}(X_{1j} + X_{2j}) = \tfrac{1}{2}f_j(X_{1j}, 0) + \tfrac{1}{2}f_j(0, X_{2j}), \text{ by property (3)}$$

$$\geqslant f_j(\tfrac{1}{2}X_{1j}, \tfrac{1}{2}X_{2j}), \text{ by convexity}$$

$$\geqslant \tfrac{1}{2}f_j(X_{1j}, X_{2j}), \text{ by homogeneity of degree one.}$$

Thus:

$$X_{1j} + X_{2j} \geqslant f_j(X_{1j}, X_{2j})$$

Q.E.D.

Can we characterize the class of production functions that have properties (1) through (7) (hence also property (8))? By homogeneity (assuming $X_{1j} > 0, X_{2j} > 0$):

$$f_j(X_{1j}, X_{2j}) = X_{1j}f_j(1, X_{2j}/X_{1j})$$

By symmetry:

$$X_{1j}f_j(1, X_{2j}/X_{1j}) = X_{2j}f_j(1, X_{1j}/X_{2j}) \qquad (16.1)$$

or:

$$f_j(1, X_{2j}/X_{1j}) = \frac{X_{2j}}{X_{1j}} f_j(1, X_{1j}/X_{2j})$$

or:

$$f_j^*(z) = f_j^*\left(\frac{1}{z}\right) z$$

where $z \equiv X_{2j}/X_{1j}$ and $f_j^*(z) \equiv f_j(1, z)$. We thus obtain the functional equation:

$$f_j^*\left(\frac{1}{z}\right) z = f_j^*(z) \qquad z > 0 \qquad\qquad (16.2)$$

with the condition:

$$f_j^*(0) \equiv \lim_{z \to 0+} f_j^*(z) = \lim_{z \to 0+} f_j(1, z) = f_j(1, 0) = 1, \text{ by property (3). (16.3)}$$

We note that once $f_j^*(z)$ is specified for $0 < z \leqslant 1$, the values of $f_j^*(z)$ for $z > 1$ can be obtained from equation (16.2) as:

$$f_j^*(z) = f_j^*\left(\frac{1}{z}\right) z$$

For $z > 1$, $0 < 1/z < 1$ and for these values $f_j^*(1/z)$ is well defined. Thus, $f_j^*(z)$ can be written as:

$$f_j^*(z) = \begin{cases} h(z), & 0 \leqslant z \leqslant 1 \\[2em] h\left(\dfrac{1}{z}\right) z, & z > 1 \end{cases}$$

where $h(z)$ is a positive, real-valued function of a single variable defined over the interval $[0, 1]$ with $\lim_{z \to 0+} h(z) = h(0) \equiv 1$. Moreover, any $f_j^*(z)$ extended this way over the whole non-negative real line will by construction satisfy the functional equation (16.2) and yield a production function $f_j(X_{1j}, X_{2j})$ with the symmetry property. We note also that $f_j^*(z)$ is continuous at $z = 0$ and 1 by definition.

However, in order for $f_j(X_{1j}, X_{2j}) = X_{1j}f_j^*(X_{2j}/X_{1j})$ and hence $f_j^*(z)$ to have all the properties implied by a joint consumption technology, it is not sufficient for $h(z)$ to have monotonicity and convexity properties on $[0, 1]$. Additional restrictions must be satisfied by $h(z)$ on $[0, 1]$. We proceed to derive these restrictions.

By the origin property:

$$f_j(0, 0) = \lim_{z \to 0} zf_j^*\left(\frac{z}{z}\right)$$

$$= \lim_{z \to 0} zf_j^*(1)$$

$$= \lim_{z \to 0} zh(1)$$

$$= 0$$

Thus, $h(1)$ must be finite. By the positivity property.

$$f_j(X_{1j}, X_{2j}) = X_{1j}f_j^*(X_{2j}/X_{1j})$$

$$= X_{1j}h(z), \text{ if } z \equiv \frac{X_{2j}}{X_{1j}} \leqslant 1$$

$$> 0, \forall z \in [0, 1] \text{ if } X_{1j} \neq 0$$

Thus, $h(z) > 0, \forall z \in [0, 1]$.

By the single-consumer equivalence property:

$$f(X_{1j}, 0) = X_{1j}f_j^*(0)$$

$$= X_{1j}h(0)$$

$$= X_{1j}$$

Thus, $h(0) = 1$.

By monotonicity, if $z_1 \geqslant z_2$, $f_j^*(z_1) \geqslant f_j^*(z_2)$. This implies that $h(z)$ must be non-decreasing over its domain $[0, 1]$. In addition, for $z_1 > 1$,

$z_2 > 1, z_1 \geqslant z_2$ one must have:

$$h\left(\frac{1}{z_1}\right)z_1 \geqslant h\left(\frac{1}{z_2}\right)z_2$$

or:

$$\frac{h(y_1)}{y_1} \geqslant \frac{h(y_2)}{y_2} \qquad\qquad\qquad (16.4)$$

where $y_1 \equiv 1/z_1$; $y_2 \equiv 1/z_2$; $y_1, y_2 \in (0, 1]$, $y_1 \leqslant y_2$. Note that the inequality (16.4) implies that the function $h(z)/z$ is non-increasing over $(0.1]$ and achieves its minimum at $z = 1$. It follows that:

$$h(z) \geqslant h(1)z, \qquad \forall z \in (0, 1] \qquad\qquad (16.5)$$

Moreover, for $z_1 \geqslant 1, z_2 \leqslant 1$, one must have:

$$h\left(\frac{1}{z_1}\right)z_1 \geqslant h(z_2)$$

or:

$$h(y_1) \geqslant h(z_2)y_1 \qquad\qquad\qquad (16.6)$$

where $y_1 \equiv 1/z_1 \leqslant 1$. The inequality (16.6) must hold for all values of $z_2 \leqslant 1$. In particular, it must hold for the maximum $h(z_2)$ for all such values, which turns out to be $h(1)$ because of monotonicity. If $h(y_1) \geqslant h(1)y_1$, $h(y_1) \geqslant h(z_2)y_1$ for all $z_2 \leqslant 1$, given the monotonicity of $h(z)$ on $[0, 1]$. We conclude that equation (16.6) is implied by equation (16.5) which is in turn implied by equation (16.4). Equation (16.4) is clearly an additional restriction independent of the monotonicity and convexity properties of $h(z)$ over $[0, 1]$.

It is worth noting that under the assumption of once differentiability of $h(z)$, the monotonicity of $h(z)/z$ over $(0, 1]$ implies:

$$\left(\frac{d}{dz}\right)\left(\frac{h(z)}{z}\right) = \frac{h'(z)z - h(z)}{z^2} \leqslant 0, \qquad \forall z \in (0, 1]$$

or:

$$\frac{d \ln h(z)}{d \ln z} \leqslant 1$$

In other words, the elasticity of the normalized production function with respect to the normalized quantity of service must be less than or equal to unity over $(0, 1]$.

By convexity, $f_j^*(z)$ must be convex over the non-negative real line. This implies that $h(z)$ must be convex over its domain $[0, 1]$. In addition, for $z_1 \geqslant 1, z_2 \geqslant 1$, one must have:

$$(1 - \lambda)f_j^*(z_1) + \lambda f_j^*(z_2) \geqslant f_j^*((1 - \lambda)z_1 + \lambda z_2), \forall \lambda, 0 \leqslant \lambda \leqslant 1$$

or:

$$(1 - \lambda)h\left(\frac{1}{z_1}\right) z_1 + \lambda h\left(\frac{1}{z_2}\right) z_2 \geqslant h\left(\frac{1}{(1 - \lambda)z_1 + \lambda z_2}\right)$$

$$((1 - \lambda)z_1 + \lambda z_2) \quad (16.7)$$

Let $y_1 \equiv 1/z_1$ and $y_2 \equiv 1/z_2$. Then equation (16.7) may be rewritten as:

$$(1 - \lambda)\frac{h(y_1)}{y_1} + \lambda \frac{h(y_2)}{y_2} \geqslant h\left(\frac{1}{(1 - \lambda)\frac{1}{y_1} + \lambda\frac{1}{y_2}}\right)\left((1 - \lambda)\frac{1}{y_1}\right.$$

$$\left. + \lambda\frac{1}{y_2}\right) \quad (16.8)$$

It is necessary to show that equation (16.8) holds for all $0 < y_1, y_2 \leqslant 1$, and $0 \leqslant \lambda \leqslant 1$. Let:

$$(1 - \mu) \equiv \frac{(1 - \lambda)\frac{1}{y_1}}{(1 - \lambda)\frac{1}{y_1} + \lambda\frac{1}{y_2}} ; \qquad \mu \equiv \frac{\lambda\frac{1}{y_2}}{(1 - \lambda)\frac{1}{y_1} + \lambda\frac{1}{y_2}} \quad (16.9)$$

Note that by definition $0 \leqslant \mu \leqslant 1$ and $\dfrac{1}{(1 - \lambda)\frac{1}{y_1} + \lambda\frac{1}{y_2}} = (1 - \mu)y_1 + \mu y_2$

Substituting equation (16.9) into equation (16.8), we obtain:

$$(1 - \mu)h(y_1) + \mu h(y_2) \geqslant h((1 - \mu)y_1 + \mu y_2) \tag{16.10}$$

However, equation (16.10) is known to hold for all values of μ between zero and unity and for all y_1 and y_2 less than one because of convexity of $h(z)$ over $[0, 1]$. We conclude that it is sufficient for $f_j^*(z)$ to be convex on $[1, \infty)$ if $h(z)$ is convex on $[0, 1]$.

However, $f_j^*(z)$ must be convex on its entire domain $[0, \infty)$, which implies that it must be sub-differentiable (or equivalently have a supporting hyperplane) everywhere on its domain except possibly on the boundary.[9] This implies that for every $z_2 \in (0, \infty)$, there exists a sub-gradient of $f_j^*(z)$ at z_2 denoted $f_j^{*'}(z_2)$ such that:[10]

$$f_j^*(z_1) - f_j^*(z_2) \geqslant f_j^{*'}(z_2)(z_1 - z_2), \forall z_1 \in [0, \infty) \tag{16.11}$$

In particular, this inequality must hold at $z_2 = 1$. If $z_1 < 1$, equation (16.11) becomes:

$$h(z_1) - h(1) \geqslant h'(1)(z_1 - 1), \qquad 0 \leqslant z_1 < 1 \tag{16.12}$$

where $h'(1) \equiv f_j^{*'}(1)$. We note that $(z_1 - 1)$ is always negative. Equation (16.12) may thus be rewritten as:

$$h'(1) \geqslant \frac{h(1) - h(z_1)}{1 - z_1}, \qquad 0 \leqslant z_1 < 1 \tag{16.13}$$

In particular:

$$h'(1) \geqslant \frac{h(1) - h(0)}{1 - 0} \tag{16.14}$$

$$\geqslant h(1) - 1$$

$$\geqslant 0$$

But if $z_1 \neq 0$, $z_1^* \equiv \dfrac{1}{z_1} > 1$. For z_1^*, equation (16.11) becomes:

$$h\left(\frac{1}{z_1^*}\right) z_1^* - h(1) \geqslant h'(1)(z_1^* - 1) \tag{16.15}$$

or:

$$\frac{h(z_1)}{z_1} - h(1) \geqslant h'(1)\left(\frac{1}{z_1} - 1\right), \qquad 0 < z_1 < 1 \qquad (16.16)$$

Equation (16.16) may be rewritten as:

$$h(z_1) - h(1)z_1 \geqslant h'(1)(1 - z_1), \qquad 0 < z_1 < 1 \qquad (16.17)$$

or:

$$\frac{h(z_1) - h(1)z_1}{(1 - z_1)} \geqslant h'(1), \qquad 0 < z_1 < 1 \qquad (16.18)$$

The inequality in equation (16.18) must be true in the limit as z_1 approaches zero because of the continuity of the left-hand side of equation (16.17) at $z = 0$. Thus:

$$h(0) = 1 \geqslant h'(1) \qquad (16.19)$$

Equations (16.14) and (16.19) together imply that:

$$1 \geqslant h'(1) \geqslant h(1) - 1 \qquad (16.20)$$

In other words, any sub-gradient of $f_j^*(z_2)$ at $z_2 = 1$ must be no greater than 1 and no less than $h(1) - 1$. It follows from convexity that any sub-gradient of $h(z_2)$, $z_2 \in (0, 1)$ must also be no greater than 1 and any sub-gradient of $f_j^*(z_2)$ $(\equiv h(1/z_2)z_2)$, $z_2 \in (1, \infty)$, must also be no less than $h(1) - 1$. Equation (16.20) also implies that $2 \geqslant h(1)$.[11]

Equation (16.11) can hold for $z_2 = 1$ for some $h'(1)$ if and only if equations (16.13) and (16.18) hold simultaneously for some $h'(1)$, implying:

$$h(z_1) - h(1)z_1 \geqslant h(1) - h(z_1), \qquad 0 \leqslant z_1 \leqslant 1$$

or:

$$h(z_1) \geqslant \frac{h(1)(z_1 + 1)}{2}, \qquad 0 \leqslant z_1 \leqslant 1 \qquad (16.21)$$

We note, however, that the bound in equation (16.21) is implied by the combined bounds of:

$$h(z) \geqslant h(0) = 1, \qquad z \in [0, 1], \text{ by monotonicity} \tag{16.22}$$

and:

$$h(z) \geqslant h(1)z, \qquad \forall z \in (0, 1] \tag{16.5}$$

For $z \leqslant 1/h(1)$, $1 \geqslant h(1)(z + 1)/2$, and equation (16.22) provides a better bound. For $1 \geqslant z > 1/h(1)$, $h(1)z \geqslant h(1)(z + 1)/2$, and equation (16.5) provides a better bound. The bound in equation (16.21) is automatically satisfied if the other restrictions hold.

We now show that $f_j^*(z)$ is actually sub-differentiable at $z = 0$. For this to be true, there must exist $h'(0)$ such that:

$$f_j^*(z) - f_j^*(0)$$
$$= f_j^*(z) - 1 \geqslant h'(0)z, \qquad \forall z \in [0, \infty) \tag{16.23}$$

Since $f_j^*(z)$ is non-decreasing, the left-hand side is always non-negative. The choice of $h'(0) = 0$ clearly satisfies equation (16.23) as well as monotonicity of $h(z)$. We conclude that $f_j^*(z)$ (and hence $h(z)$) is sub-differentiable at $z = 0$. Of course there may be other sub-gradients $h'(0)$ in addition to 0.

The implications of the sub-differentiability condition in equation (16.11) may thus be summarized as: There exists a sub-gradient $h'(1)$ at $z = 1$ such that:

$$\text{(i)} \quad h(z) - h(1) \geqslant h'(1)(z - 1), \qquad \forall z \in [0, 1) \tag{16.12}$$

and:

$$\text{(ii)} \quad h(z) - h(1)z \geqslant h'(1)(1 - z), \qquad \forall z \in (0, 1) \tag{16.17}$$

Equation (16.20) follows from equations (16.12) and (16.17) and is hence not an independent implication. We note parenthetically that by combining equations (16.12) and (16.20), we obtain:

$$(1 - z) \geqslant h'(1)(1 - z) \geqslant h(1) - h(z)$$

or:

$$h(z) \geqslant z + h(1) - 1, \qquad \forall z \in [0, 1] \tag{16.24}$$

By combining equations (16.17) and (16.20), we obtain the same inequality. The bound in equation (16.24) can be shown to be better than the bound in equation (16.5).

We now show that convexity of $f_j^*(z)$ over both $[0, 1]$ and $[1, \infty)$ and the sub-differentiability of $f_j^*(z)$ at $z = 1$ are sufficient to imply that $f_j^*(z)$ is convex over $[0, \infty)$.

Lemma 2: Let $f_j^*(z)$ be a finite, real-valued function of a single variable defined on the non-negative real line. $f_j^*(z)$ is convex over the intervals $[0, 1]$ and $[1, \infty)$ and is continuous at $z = 1$. If $f_j^*(z)$ is sub-differentiable at $z = 1$, then $f_j^*(z)$ is convex over the whole non-negative line.

Proof: The proof is by contradiction. Suppose $f_j^*(z)$ is not convex over $[0, \infty)$. Then there exists $z_1 < 1, z_2 > 1$ and $\lambda, 0 < \lambda < 1$, such that:

$$(1 - \lambda)f_j^*(z_1) + \lambda f_j^*(z_2) < f_j^*((1 - \lambda)z_1 + \lambda z_2) \tag{16.25}$$

$(1 - \lambda)z_1 + \lambda z_2 \neq 1$. Otherwise $(1 - \lambda)f_j^*(z_1) + \lambda f_j^*(z_2) < f_j^*(1)$, and $f_j^*(1)$ lies strictly above a part of a straight line joining $f_j^*(z_1)$ and $f_j^*(z_2)$ and hence $f_j^*(z)$ does not have a supporting hyperplane (equivalently is not sub-differentiable) at $z = 1$. Thus, either $(1 - \lambda)z_1 + \lambda z_2 > 1$ or $(1 - \lambda)z_1 + \lambda z_2 < 1$. Suppose the former case is true. One can then decrease λ until either:

$$(1 - \lambda^*)z_1 + \lambda^* z_2 = 1 \tag{16.26}$$

or:

$$(1 - \lambda^*)f_j^*(z_1) + \lambda^* f_j^*(z_2) = f_j^*((1 - \lambda^*)z_1 + \lambda^* z_2) \tag{16.27}$$

(or both). If equation (16.26) is true and the strict inequality in equation (16.25) continues to hold, then, as argued above:

$$(1 - \lambda^*)f_j^*(z_1) + \lambda^* f_j^* \qquad (z_2) < f_j^*(1)$$

so that $f_j^*(z)$ is not sub-differentiable at $z = 1$, a contradiction. If equation (16.27) is true, then we find that on the interval $[(1 - \lambda^*)z_1 + \lambda^* z_2, z_2]$ which is contained in $[1, \infty)$, convexity is violated, contradicting the assumption that $f_j^*(z)$ is convex over $[1, \infty)$.

Suppose the latter case is true, an analogous argument applies. We conclude that the lemma is true.   Q.E.D.

By subadditivity:

$$X_{1j} + X_{2j} \geqslant f_j(X_{1j}, X_{2j})$$

or:

$$X_{1j} + X_{2j} \geqslant X_{1j} f_j^*(X_{2j}/X_{1j}), X_{1j} > 0, \text{ by homogeneity or:}$$

$$1 + z \geqslant f_j^*(z), \qquad \forall z \in [0, \infty) \tag{16.28}$$

By combining equation (16.28) with equation (16.11), we obtain:

$$z_1 + 1 \geqslant f_j^*(z_1)$$

$$\geqslant f_j^*(z_2) + f_j^{*\prime}(z_2)(z_1 - z_2), \qquad \forall z_1 \in [0, \infty)$$

For any z_2, if $f_j^{*\prime}(z_2) > 1$, then by the choice of a sufficiently large z_1, the above inequality can be reversed, contradicting the sub-differentiability of $f_j^*(z_2)$ on its domain. We conclude that $f_j^{*\prime}(z_2) \leqslant 1$, $\forall z_2 \in [0, \infty)$. In other words, all sub-gradients of $f_j^*(z_2)$ must be less than unity. If $f_j^*(z_2)$ is differentiable, then its derivative must be less than unity in value.[12]

For $0 \leqslant z \leqslant 1$, equation (16.28) implies that:

$$z + 1 \geqslant h(z) \tag{16.29}$$

In particular:

$$2 \geqslant h(1) \tag{16.30}$$

For $z > 1$, equation (16.28) implies that:

$$z + 1 \geqslant h\left(\frac{1}{z}\right)z$$

or:

$$\frac{1}{y} + 1 \geqslant \frac{h(y)}{y} \tag{16.31}$$

where $y \equiv \dfrac{1}{z} < 1$. However, equation (16.31) implies and is implied by:

$$y + 1 \geqslant h(y), \qquad 0 \leqslant y < 1$$

which is implied by equation (16.29). We conclude that equation (16.29) is the only additional restriction imposed by subadditivity on $h(z)$.

It is worth noting that under the assumption of once continuous differentiability of $f_j(X_{1j}, X_{2j})$ and hence $f_j^*(z)$, the implications of convexity can be stated in a much simpler way. First, once continuous differentiability implies that:

$$f_j^{*'}(z) = \begin{cases} h'(z), & 0 \leqslant z \leqslant 1 \\ -h'\left(\dfrac{1}{z}\right)\dfrac{1}{z} + h\left(\dfrac{1}{z}\right), & z \geqslant 1 \end{cases}$$

However, $f_j^{*'}(z)$ must be the same at $z = 1$. Thus:

$$h'(1) = -h'(1) + h(1)$$

or:

$$h'(1) = \frac{h(1)}{2}$$

In other words, the elasticity of the normalized production function with respect to the normalized quantity of service is exactly equal to $\frac{1}{2}$ at $z = 1$. Second:

$$f_j^{*''}(z) = \begin{cases} h''(z), & 0 \leqslant z \leqslant 1 \\ h''\left(\dfrac{1}{z}\right)\dfrac{1}{z^3}, & z \geqslant 1 \end{cases}$$

It is easily verified that $f_j^{*''}(z)$ has an unique value at $z = 1$. Moreover, if $h(z)$ is convex on $[0, 1]$, so that $h''(z) \geqslant 0$, $f^{*''}(z) \geqslant 0$ on $[0, \infty)$. In other words, $f_j^*(z)$ is convex on $[0, \infty)$.

This, then, completes our characterization of the function $h(z)$ and hence of $f_j^*(z)$ and $f_j(X_{1j}, X_{2j})$.

SUMMARY AND CONCLUSION

The discussions in the second section may be summarized in the following theorem:

Theorem 1: A technology of joint consumption with properties (1) through (8) can be written in the form:

$$f_j(X_{1j}, X_{2j}) = X_{1j}f_j^*(X_{2j}/X_{1j}) \tag{16.32}$$

$$= \begin{cases} X_{1j}h(X_{2j}/X_{1j}), & 0 \leqslant \dfrac{X_{2j}}{X_{1j}} \leqslant 1 \\[3em] X_{2j}h(X_{1j}/X_{2j}), & \dfrac{X_{2j}}{X_{1j}} > 1 \end{cases}$$

where $h(z)$ is a finite, positive, real-valued function of a single variable defined on the closed real interval $[0, 1]$ with the following properties:

(1) *Boundary points.* $h(0) = 1$. $\lim\limits_{z \to 0+} h(z) = h(0) = 1$. $h(1)$ is finite.

(2) *Monotonicity.* $h(z)$ is non-decreasing on its domain. $h(z)/z$ is non-increasing over $(0, 1]$.

(3) *Convexity.* $h(z)$ is convex on its domain.

(4) *Subadditivity.* $z + 1 \geqslant h(z)$.

(5) *Sub-differentiability.* There exists a sub-gradient $h'(1)$ at $z = 1$ such that:

    (i) $h(z) \geqslant h(1) + h'(1)(z - 1)$, $\forall z \in [0, 1)$,   and

    (ii) $h(z) \geqslant h(1)z + h'(1)(1 - z)$, $\forall z \in (0, 1)$

Proof: It has been shown in the second section that any production function with properties (1) through (8) can be written in the form of equation (16.32) where $h(z)$ has the stated properties. It may be verified directly that any production function as defined in equation (16.32) has properties (1) through (8). Q.E.D.

Examples of $h(z)$s satisfying the stated conditions are:

    (1) $h(z) = (1 + z^{r_j})^{\frac{1}{r_j}}$, $r_j \geqslant 1$,[13] $0 \leqslant z \leqslant 1$

For this $h(z)$, $f_j(X_{1j}, X_{2j}) = (X_{1j}^{r_j} + X_{2j}^{r_j})^{\frac{1}{r_j}}$

(2) $h(z) = 1$, $0 \leq z \leq 1$

For this $h(z)$, $f_j(X_{1j}, X_{2j}) = \max(X_{1j}, X_{2j})$

An example of an $h(z)$ that fails to satisfy the sub-differentiability condition at $z = 1$ is:

$h(z) = e^{z-1} + 1 - e^{-1}$

It is readily verified that:

(1) $h(0) = 1$

$\lim_{z \to 0} h(z) = h(0) = 1$

$h(1) = 2 - e^{-1}$

$h(z) > 0$, $\forall z \in [0, 1]$

(2) $h(z)$ is non-decreasing on $[0, 1]$; $\dfrac{h(z)}{z}$ is non-increasing on $(0, 1]$

(3) $h(z)$ is convex on $[0, 1]$

(4) $z + 1 \geq h(z)$, $\forall z \in [0, 1]$.

However, the sub-differentiability condition requires that there exists a $h'(1)$ such that:

$h(z) - h(1) \geq h'(1)(z - 1)$, $\forall z \in [0, 1)$ (16.33)

and:

$h(z) - h(1)z \geq h'(1)(1 - z)$, $\forall z \in (0, 1)$ (16.34)

We note first of all that $h(z)$ is differentiable on $(0, 1)$. By convexity:

$h'(1) \geq h'(z)$, $\forall z \in (0, 1)$

$\lim_{z \to 1-} h'(z) = e^{z-1} = 1$

But $1 \geqslant h'(1) \geqslant h(1) - 1$, by equation (16.20). Thus, $h'(1) = 1$. Equations (16.33) and (16.34) then become, respectively:

$$e^{z-1} + 1 - e^{-1} \geqslant 2 - e^{-1} + z - 1, \qquad \forall z \in [0, 1) \qquad (16.35)$$

and:

$$e^{z-1} + 1 - e^{-1} \geqslant (2 - e^{-1})z + 1 - z, \qquad \forall z \in (0, 1) \qquad (16.36)$$

It may be verified that equation (16.35) is satisfied, whereas equation (16.36) is not.[14]

We have thus characterized the admissible form of the technology of joint consumption under a set of plausible conditions. Once the technology of joint consumption is specified, it can be appended to the individual utility functions and the household rules of allocation and distribution to generate the household demand functions which in turn can be empirically estimated. It is possible to identify the parameters of the techology of joint consumption using consumption data on one- and two-individual households. It is, of course, desirable to extend this research to cover the case of an arbitrary but finite number of individuals in the household. In addition, the obvious relationship between the technology of joint consumption and the form of the so-called commodity-specific household equivalent consumption scale[15] should be explored systematically. Finally, with a knowledge of the technology of joint consumption, it is possible to address the question 'Can two live as cheaply as one?' with reference to hypothetical individual utility functions. These extensions must be left to the future.

NOTES

1. Strictly speaking, in order for this interpretation to make sense, it is necessary to be able to make meaningful interpersonal comparisons of the levels of individual utilities.
2. It may be argued that under our interpretation, if satisfaction derived solely from the company of each other is excluded, it is unlikely that 'two can live as cheaply as one'. However, the economies of joint consumption are still of interest. For example, one may well ask whether two can live as cheaply as one and a half.
3. For example, one rule of allocation and distribution may be the maximization of a household welfare function which is itself a function of the individual utility functions subject to the total household expenditure constraint.
4. Unfortunately the typical two-individual household consists of a man and a woman whose utility functions are unlikely to be identical.

5. The pattern of *individual* consumption in a multiple-individual household is in general not directly observable.
6. The concept of a techology of joint consumption is independent of the possibility of interpersonal comparison of levels of individual utilities.
7. See Berge, 1963, pp. 208–9, Theorem 3.
8. It can be verified that if $r_j < 1$, $f_j(\,.\,)$ fails to have the convexity property.
9. For a discussion of sub-differentiability and sub-gradients of convex functions, see Rockafellar, 1970, pp. 213–26.
10. Note that it is not necessary that $f_j^{*'}(z_2)$ be unique for each z_2 as $f_j^*(z)$ is not necessarily differentiable.
11. This also follows from $z + 1 \geqslant h(z)$, which is shown below.
12. Note that this property follows from the fact $z + 1 \geqslant f_j^*(z)$ and the convexity of $f_j^*(z)$. It is not an independent property.
13. Note that this example includes the special case of $h(z) = 1 + z$, and hence $f_j(X_{1j}, X_{2j}) = X_{1j} + X_{2j}$.
14. For equation (16.36), note that the left-hand and right-hand sides of the inequality are exactly equal for $z = 0$ and $z = 1$. The left-hand side is strictly convex on the closed interval $[0, 1]$ and the right-hand side is a straight line. Thus, the left-hand side must be strictly less than the right-hand side on the interior of the closed interval $[0, 1]$.
15. Let a complete (not necessarily integrable) system of household consumption demand function be given by:

$$X_j = D_j(p, M; n), \qquad j = 1, \ldots, m$$

where X_j is the quantity of the jth commodity demanded, $j = 1, \ldots, m$; p is the vector of the prices of the m commodities, M is total household expenditure, and n is the number of individuals in the household. A set of functions $s_j(n)$, $j = 1, \ldots, m$ is said to be a set of commodity-specific household equivalent consumption scales if:

$$D_j(p, M; n) = s_j(n)D_j(s_1(n)p_1, \ldots, s_m(n)p_m, M; 1),$$

$$j = 1, \ldots, m$$

In other words, the 'per capita' household demand, $D_j(p, M; n)/s_j(n)$, is the same as that of a single-individual household with the same total expenditure but with the prices scaled up by the $s_j(n)$ factors, $j = 1, \ldots, m$. Note that in general one expects $s_j(n) \leqslant n, j = 1, \ldots, m$. If $s_j(n) = n, j = 1, \ldots, m$, then:

$$\frac{D_j(p, M; n)}{n} = D_j(np_1, \ldots, np_m, M; 1)$$

$$= D_j(p_1, \ldots, p_m, \frac{M}{n}; 1), \text{ by homogeneity of degree}$$

zero, $j = 1, \ldots, m$

In this special case, the per capita household demands are precisely equal to those of a single-individual household with income equal to the per capita income.

REFERENCES

Berge, C. (1963), *Topological Spaces, Including a Treatment of Multi-Valued Functions, Vector Spaces and Convexity*, New York: Macmillan.

Rockafellar, R. T. (1970) *Convex Analysis*, Princeton, N. J.: Princeton University Press.

Index*